EAST AFRICA AND ITS INVADERS

FROM THE EARLIEST TIMES TO THE DEATH OF SEYYID SAID IN 1856

BY

R. COUPLAND

C.I.E., M.A., HON. D.LITT. (DURHAM)
FELLOW OF ALL SOULS COLLEGE
BEIT PROFESSOR OF COLONIAL HISTORY IN THE
UNIVERSITY OF OXFORD

OXFORD
AT THE CLARENDON PRESS

Oxford University Press, Ely House, London W.1

GLASGOW NEW YORK TORONTO MELBOURNE WELLINGTON
CAPE TOWN SALISBURY IBADAN NAIROBI LUSAKA ADDIS ABABA
BOMBAY CALCUTTA MADRAS KARACHI LAHORE DACCA
KUALA LUMPUR HONG KONG TOKYO

FIRST EDITION 1938

REPRINTED LITHOGRAPHICALLY IN GREAT BRITAIN
AT THE UNIVERSITY PRESS, OXFORD
FROM SHEETS OF THE FIRST EDITION
1956, 1961, 1965, 1968

PREFACE

SOME years ago I undertook to write a book about the life and work of Sir John Kirk at Zanzibar. That book will, I hope, be published early next year. But it was impossible for me to write it without acquainting myself with the previous history of Mid-East Africa, and this has proved a lengthy task. Except in the period of Portuguese occupation, only the barest outline of it was known: its main substance lay buried in rarely opened files at the Record Office and the India Office. Prolonged research was needed, and this book is the result.

Much of it is concerned with matters of relatively small importance; for East Africa, till very recent times, lay outside the great currents of history. But the story told from Chapter VI onwards has at least the interest of a description, in which no detail of any moment within the author's knowledge has been omitted, of race-contact in that corner of the world a century ago—of the way in which Asiatics dealt with the Africans and of the motives and methods with which Europeans 'invaded' their country.

My warm thanks are due to the Rhodes Trustees for assisting me to pay my first visit to East Africa in 1928, and to Sir Edward Grigg, Sir Claud Hollis, and Sir Donald Cameron for their generous hospitality and for enabling me to see as much as possible in the time available of the territories they then administered. Sir Claud Hollis has also read the whole of this book in proof, and it has benefited beyond measure from his great knowledge of East Africa. I am under similar obligation to Mr. R. H. Crofton, Colonial Secretary at Zanzibar at the time of my visit, who helped me to examine the local archives and has subsequently supplied me with invaluable information, and to Mr. C. H. Ingrams, who not only guided my first steps in the field of East African history, but also, when he was Assistant Colonial Secretary at Mauritius, most kindly consulted the archives at Port Louis on my behalf and provided me with transcripts of important documents. Nor must I omit to thank Mr. W. T. Ottewill, Superintendent of Records at the India Office, for the unfailing readiness with which he has responded to my frequent requests for his assistance, and the authorities of the Essex Institute and the Peabody Museum at Salem, Massachusetts, for their courtesy on the occasion of my visit in 1933. I am also indebted to Mr. J. Simmons for a careful reading and correction of the proofs.

R. C.

WOOTTON HILL,
July, 1938

CONTENTS

I.	East Africa and the East Africans	1
II.	The Arab Colonies	15
III.	The Portuguese Conquest	41
IV.	France and Britain in the Indian Ocean (1740–1805)	73
V.	Seyyid Said at Muscat	108
VI.	British Reconnaissances (1792–1812)	154
VII.	Britain and the Slave Trade	186
VIII.	Owen's Protectorate	217
IX.	The Fate of the Mazrui	271
X.	Seyyid Said at Zanzibar: Economics	295
XI.	Seyyid Said at Zanzibar: Politics	321
XII.	Traders from America and Germany	361
XIII.	The Missionary Invasion	387
XIV.	The French at Zanzibar	421
XV.	The British at Zanzibar	459
XVI.	Second Attack on the Slave Trade	494
XVII.	The Kuria Muria Islands	524
XVIII.	The End of an Epoch	546
	Index	557

Map I. The Western Indian Ocean and its surroundings
II. Mid-East Africa } *at end*

ABBREVIATIONS USED IN THE FOOTNOTES

ADM.	Admiralty Records. Public Record Office.
BENGAL P.C.	Bengal Political Consultations. India Office Records.
B.M. ADD. MSS.	British Museum, Additional Manuscripts.
B.P.C.	Bombay Political Consultations. India Office Records.
B.P.S.C.	Bombay Political and Secret Consultations. India Office Records.
B.R.	Selections from the Records of the Bombay Government. No. xxiv. New Series. Bombay, 1856.
C.O.	Colonial Office Records. Public Record Office.
D. B.	Duarte Barbosa.
F.O.	Foreign Office Records. Public Record Office.
I.O.	India Office Records.
J.A.S.	Journal of the African Society.
J.R.G.S.	Journal of the Royal Geographical Society.
PARL. PAP. or P.P.	Parliamentary Papers.
R.H.D.	Revue d'histoire diplomatique.
R.S.E.A.	Records of South Eastern Africa, ed. G. M. Theal. Capetown, 1898–1903.
S.P.	British and Foreign State Papers. (London, 1841 onwards).
T.B.G.S.	Transactions of the Bombay Geographical Society.

I
EAST AFRICA AND THE EAST AFRICANS

I

THE Old World, with all the manifold differences between its parts, possesses a measure of natural unity. Its three continents compose a single mass of land, and the history of their three peoples, never wholly disconnected, has become more and more closely interwoven in the course of time. Europe and Asia have deeply influenced each other's life, and between them they have gone far to shape the destiny of their more backward, more passive neighbour. All the coasts of Africa have been subject to invasion from one or both of them. The north has been occupied and ruled alternately by Europeans and Asiatics. The south has become the home of a European nation. On the west, nearer to Europe than to Asia, the Europeans have been the dominant invaders. On the east, nearer to Asia than to Europe, the Asiatics were the first in possession, and, save for an interval of some two hundred years, they maintained their hold till very recent times and still surpass the Europeans in numbers.

Geography dictated that the destiny of north and south should be different from that of east and west. The contact of Europe or Asia, as the case may be, with North and South Africa has been far more intimate and decisive than their contact with East and West Africa for the simple reason that, while at the northern and southern ends of the continent the climate is temperate, the vast expanse between them lies within the Tropics. Arabs from South Arabia, parts of which are among the hottest places in the world, might find life more congenial at Mombasa or Zanzibar; but the main stream of their expansion, conquest, and settlement flowed round the Mediterranean littoral from Syria to Spain. And for Portuguese or Dutchmen, Frenchmen or Englishmen, tropical Africa might provide a livelihood, but never, except at certain points and within relatively narrow limits, a home.

But history records another kind of contact between the peoples of different continents. In parts of Asia, pre-eminently in India, where the climate, though not fully tropical, is unsuited for European colonization, Europeans established commercial outposts three or four centuries ago; and economic interest led in due course to political ascendancy, till the whole of India was subjected directly or indirectly to European government and to the influence of European civilization. A similar fate has befallen tropical Africa, but its 'partition' among European Powers, its subjection to European rule, was delayed, with minor exceptions, till about fifty years ago, till a generation after the close of the period covered in this book. Why was that? Geography again supplies in part the answer. The rim of the great inland plateau which constitutes most of Africa falls to sea-level so near the coast, and so steeply, that the valleys of the rivers draining it do not spread out into broad alluvial plains, rich in vegetation, facilitating the growth of large sedentary populations, open to access from without, natural centres for the development of civilization. The present-day backwardness of the tropical African people has not been mainly due to their physical characteristics. The history of tropical Africa would have been other than it has been if it had possessed a St. Lawrence, an Amazon, a Euphrates, a Ganges, a Yangtze, or another Nile south of the Sahara. As it was, when the Arabs in their age of sea-power sailed out in search of trade and wealth, though, as will be seen in the next chapter, a number of them were diverted to East Africa, it was in India, in the East Indian Islands, in China that they set up their principal trading-posts; and when the Europeans followed in their tracks, it was likewise the luxury goods of India and the Far East that they were after, goods which for ages past had found their way to Europe overland, spices which grew nowhere else, and silk and metal-work and china, products of a stable civilization and old-established crafts. Tropical Africa grew no such spices till the nineteenth century.

Tropical Africa had no such civilization. So, though stories were rife of gold to be had in Africa, and the Portuguese, as will appear, attempted to exploit it, European merchant adventurers as a whole hurried past the unattractive coast to get as quickly as might be to the East. Nor, when perforce they landed for water or food, was there anything to tempt them, except the golden legend of Monomotapa, to explore the interior of the continent. There were no gently flowing rivers, no broad fertile valleys to lead them by easy stages to well-peopled and productive lands up-country. They found a narrow maritime plain, often covered with forest and jungle, narrower on the east coast than on the west; and at the back of it the rivers, often obstructed at the mouth by sandbanks or the shallow channels of a delta, came rushing from the plateau in falls and rapids barring navigation. It seemed, therefore, that with one important exception, to be mentioned presently, there was no great business to be done in Africa, no prospect of expanding trade, nothing comparable with the immeasurable opportunities of the East. So, in due course, as the sea-route became more familiar and seamanship more skilful, merchantmen sailing for the Indies struck out across the great gulf formed by the eastward recession of the African coast beyond Cape Verde. Of the many thousand travellers who nowadays cross the Atlantic every year between Europe and Capetown, only a very few have ever seen Nigeria. And East Africa, of course, at any rate northwards of Madagascar, became still more secluded from the current of trade and travel. The Suez Canal was not opened till 1869, and in earlier ages the country now known as Kenya and Tanganyika seemed far remote from Europe and European interest. The voyage from Liverpool to Zanzibar round the Cape is nearly three times longer than the voyage from Liverpool to New York.

There is another reason, not the outcome of geography, for the slow development of alien influence and control in Africa as compared with India. Both on the east and on the west invaders from other continents did establish a trade, a great trade, fed, as time went on, from ever-widening sources in the vast interior. But the Slave Trade did not promote the spread of foreign interest or economic development or political expansion in Africa. Until its ultimate long-delayed reaction on humanitarian opinion, the Slave Trade obstructed, almost indeed prevented, the growth of any relationship between the peoples of the three neighbour continents other than the nexus between the European and Asiatic slave-buyers and slave-hunters, together with the native agents they employed, and the Africans they hunted and bought. The Slave Trade kept the African interior in a chronic state of inter-tribal war; for chief fought chief to get captives to sell for fire-arms and spirits. Thus the Slave Trade, on the one hand, held back the upland peoples at their primitive level, while, on the other hand, it closed the door to all the external aids they needed to stimulate their progress. Tropical Africa became the slavers' preserve. Scientists, missionaries, 'legitimate' traders would trespass in it at their peril. It could not be brought into the normal network of world trade. It could not become acquainted with the ideas, customs, creeds of other peoples. It could not even be explored.

2

A closer view of mid-East Africa—the stretch of country between Somaliland and Mozambique with which this book is mainly concerned—will illustrate the effect of geography in secluding the great bulk of the African continent from the rest of the world. Its reinforcement by the Slave Trade will become increasingly apparent as the narrative proceeds.

Central Africa is barred off from the north by an arid wilderness only penetrated by the Nile. It was not till they reached Senegal that Portuguese explorers on the west coast found the desert giving place to vegetation and so gave Cape Verde its name. On the east coast the wilderness extends a long way farther south. The traveller who approaches it from the Red Sea must sail beyond the latitude of Cape Verde before he sights the rock-strewn slopes of Cape Guardafui glinting in the brazen sun, and he must follow the long low cliffs of Somaliland for some hundreds of miles farther before he sees the landscape of sand and stone changing to the landscape of the tropics. From Kismayu onwards the patches of vegetation begin to spread, and from Lamu right away to Delagoa Bay the coast is as tropical as that of Nigeria. A stretch of flat, moist, teeming soil, covered with a tangle of wild growth, runs inland from the sand-dunes built up by the sea. Rivers traverse it, the Juba, Tana, Sabaki, Pangani, Rufiji, Rovuma, and other lesser streams down to the great Zambesi, some of them spreading into deltas at the mouth. At times the shore is pierced with creeks and inlets, banked with mud and fringed with mangrove, and at times it is broken into islands or groups of islands, often, like Mombasa, only separated from the mainland by a narrow strip of sea. Farther out lie three bigger islands, Pemba, Zanzibar, and Mafia, some thirty, twenty, and ten miles distant from the coast, all of them coral islands and very fertile. There are harbours, too, at intervals along the coast. Lamu, Mombasa-Kilindini, Tanga, Pangani, Dar-es-Salaam, Kilwa,[1] Port Amelia, and Mozambique can all shelter ocean-going ships, and for smaller craft there is plenty of safe anchorage under the lee of an island or up a shielded creek. The climate, finally, of this maritime belt, though too tropical for Europeans to make their homes there, is not unkindly, nor more unhealthy than tropical malarious districts are bound to be. The heat is softened by sea-breezes. The average temperature ranges from 76° to 86°. Life is far pleasanter there than in the fiery furnace of the Red Sea or the Persian Gulf.

A green, productive, not inhospitable coastland, it might seem to invite invasion, and from early times, as will be seen, Asiatics came from north and east and settled there, followed by Europeans pushing up from the south as soon as they had found the way. In due course a string of little towns were built by these invaders all along the coast. But that was all. An inward spread of the invasion such as led in other continents to the occupation of the interior was prohibited by

[1] Kilwa Kisiwani or 'Kilwa on the Island'.

Nature until in very recent days her veto was defied and her defences broken through by modern science. Northwards of the Tana River the maritime belt merges into a waste of sand and scrub, growing drier and drier till, as it slopes up towards the Abyssinian mountains, it becomes virtually a desert. Southwards the belt narrows. It is less than thirty miles broad at Mombasa, less than fifty at Dar-es-Salaam; and behind it lies one of the most formidable barriers imaginable to the movement of man and the transport of his goods—a stretch of rising ground, over 100 miles in breadth, waterless for the most part and clothed with a dense jungle of thorn-trees and thorn-bushes, broken only by the unsightly baobab, the doum palm, and the borassus. In Kenya this horrid country is known as the Nyika—a Swahili word meaning 'forest and thorn country'—and every traveller who had to make his way through it on foot before the railway was built or aeroplanes invented has put on record how he hated it. It prolongs itself southwards across Tanganyika in a broad zone of 'bush', so dry that, save for a short time after rain and for a few scattered evergreen trees, it looks like an endless thicket of dead sticks.

Nor do the rivers offer an easier passage to the interior. In this respect, indeed, East Africa is worse off than West Africa. The Zambesi alone can compare with the Senegal, the Gambia, the Niger, or the Congo; and the Zambesi is not only difficult to enter but, as Livingstone discovered to his bitter disappointment, it is barred by the Kebrabasa Rapids above Tete. The Rovuma, which Livingstone also hoped would give him easy access to the uplands, peters out far sooner into sand-banks, rocks, and rapids. The Rufiji is only navigable for about 100 miles. The Pangani breaks into falls not far inland. The Tana and the Juba are both navigable for about 200 miles in the rainy season; but the Juba only leads to the northern wilderness, and the Tana, though it winds through forests and a wealth of vegetation springing from rich alluvial soil, has never served as a waterway to the Kenya Highlands, mainly, no doubt, because, like the Juba and the Sabaki, it is barred at the mouth by the sand thrown up by the wind-driven sea.[1]

Till barely fifty years ago, therefore, there was no effective invasion, no conquest of East Africa beyond the narrow strip of coastland. Arab merchants penetrated to the interior and here and there established trading settlements: European missionaries followed them a few stages on their inland track: but, till the dawn of the present century, there was no permanent occupation of the land, no attempt at home-making, no inward advance of the coastal invaders' civilization. That process, which has now been operating for a generation, would have begun, one might suppose, in far earlier times but for nature's obstacles. For beyond that dry and thorny barrier there lies the most attractive country, in European eyes at any rate, in all mid-Africa.

There is first the Kenya Highlands, an irregular volcanic plateau, about 300 miles from the coast, its plains and valleys hoisted by seismic energy to heights of 6,000 and 7,000 feet and more above sea-level. It is a wholly different country from the moist luxuriant maritime plain or the dry inhuman Nyika —open, varied, fertile country, grassland and woodland, lakes and streams, downs and mountains. The forest-clad ridge of the Aberdares rises in places to over 12,000 feet. Supreme over all is Mount Kenya, 17,040 feet high, capped with ice and snow. Right through the Highlands cuts the Great Rift Valley, outcome of a gigantic subsidence or 'fault' in the earth's crust, stretching, it appears, from the Red Sea or even, maybe, from the Dead Sea as far as Lake Nyasa. Its floor, as it crosses the Kenya Highlands, is from 20 to 30 miles wide: its walls at times climb steeply for 2,000 or 3,000 feet. But the strangest feature of this strange land is its climate. Here, surely, is the heart of the Tropics. The Equator itself runs within a few miles of Mount Kenya. Yet such is the effect of altitude that the days are never burning hot and the nights are cool and sometimes frosty.

[1] For Livingstone's disappointments, see the author's *Kirk on the Zambesi* (Oxford, 1928), chaps. iv and vii.

Secondly, about 100 miles south of the Kenya Highlands and about 200 miles from the coast, there is a belt of almost alpine country encircling Mount Kilimanjaro, a vast extinct volcano, lifting its snowy dome to 19,321 feet. Its base is about 100 miles round, and on its southern slopes and those of its neighbour, Mount Meru, another volcano, 14,995 feet high, there is fertile soil and bracing air between 4,000 and 6,000 feet. Thrown out north, east, and south at varying distances from the Kilimanjaro massif are a number of lesser bastions—the hill country about Kibwezi and Voi and the Pare, Usambara, and Uluguru Mountains. But their peaks are not above 8,000 feet, and their valleys and uplands, well watered though they are and beautiful, are more tropical in climate than the Kenya Highlands. Thirdly, some 300 miles south of Mount Kilimanjaro and some 250 miles from the sea, there is a stretch of fine, airy, highland country, above the 5,000-foot level, round about Iringa. Its aspect is less striking and varied than the Kenya Highlands: it lacks their rich volcanic soil; and in the cool months the winds are bleaker and the nights chillier. Fourth and last, about 150 miles south-west of Iringa, there are open uplands spreading at an average level of 4,000 feet to the borders of Northern Rhodesia and Portuguese East Africa, walled off from Lake Nyasa by the Livingstone Mountains.

All these highland districts might well have tempted European immigrants to settle long ago if access to them had been easier. Europeans are settled in all of them to-day. Yet even so they could never have given scope for the incessant 'trekking' which made the Union of South Africa, still less for the mass-migration which made the United States. There are no 'great open spaces', no boundless veld or prairies, in East Africa waiting for European homes. Those four areas of potential settlement are relatively small. The Kenya Highlands are about one-half the size of Minnesota and about one-fifth the size of Manitoba. And, if those areas rise above the Tropics, they rise like islands from a tropical sea. Between them and the coast, between one of them and another, stretch the jungle

East Africa and the East Africans

and the drought. Beyond them westwards the land sinks again to the Great Lakes and the hot wild core of Africa.

3

The first invasions of East Africa occurred in the far distant past. Long before history begins it was the scene of one of those primeval race-migrations which determined the character and distribution of historical mankind. Age after age, wave by wave, a pastoral Caucasian people, speaking a Hamitic language, pressed southwards from the Nile Valley and Abyssinia into Negroland, the mid-African home of the black-skinned, fuzzy-haired, thick-lipped Negroes, themselves, it is thought, immigrants of a still earlier epoch from the north. 'Better armed and quicker witted than the dark agricultural Negroes', those eastern Hamites, as they have been called, established an ascendancy spreading slowly farther and farther to the south, till, with the exception of relatively small and isolated groups, the whole population of Central Africa became in blood and culture to a greater or less degree 'hamiticized'. Thus, thousands of years before the Christian era, all East Africa was inhabited by a hybrid people in which Negro and Hamitic strains were variously mingled.[1]

It is unnecessary here to enumerate the tribes among which this people is now divided; and not very much more than enumeration would be possible. At any distance from the coast the mere names and locality of most of the tribes were unknown, as their country was unknown, to the outer world until some fifty or sixty years ago; and for a full scientific description of them the material is not yet to hand. Modern anthropological study of East Africa has only just begun. For the purpose of this introductory chapter it will suffice to sketch the barest outline of the racial or linguistic grouping and to mention those few tribes which now and again on subsequent pages of this book emerge for a moment from the darkness. There has been no large-scale migration, it would seem, for

[1] This section is based on Professor C. G. Seligman's invaluable summary, *Races of Africa* (London, 1930).

many generations past, so that the broad lines of distribution as they stand to-day hold good for the period covered by most, if not all, the history about to be recorded.

In the extreme north, the last waves of the old southward movement can be seen halted, as it were, and stabilized before they penetrated Negroland. The Galla, a group of eastern Hamites, traditionally hailing from Arabia, first appear in history as the occupants of the stony country extending from Abyssinia to the Gulf of Aden. In the fifteenth century they were pressing west and south. Behind them came the Somali, a kindred people, but more nomadic, more purely pastoral and more powerful than the Galla. They pushed the Galla before them and occupied most of their land. Their final subjugation of the coastland north of the River Tana was accomplished as late as 1872. To-day the Galla are scattered across the northern steppe of Kenya from the Tana to Abyssinia, while the Somali possess the long stretch of sandy seaboard country which bears their name.

Next to these Hamites southwards are the 'half-Hamites', the outcome of ancient contact with the Negroes but distinguished from the other hybrids by the marked preponderance of Hamitic strains in their physique and speech and culture. They are located in a wide sweep of country from round about Lake Rudolph, across Kenya and Tanganyika, as far as a line running roughly west from the mouth of the River Pangani. They are negroid folk, predominantly straight-nosed and often straight-haired, and mainly pastoral. Their most famous tribe, of which something will be heard later, is the Masai, a martial, high-handed, formidable people—the Zulus of the North, they might be called—who graze their great herds of cattle over the savannah-land from the Kenya Highlands to Ugogo.

Next come the East African members of that huge congeries of peoples, covering most of Africa south of a line drawn roughly from the Cameroons to Kenya, who all speak what is basically a common language and on that linguistic ground alone are given the common name of Bantu. They constitute the vast majority of the East African people, and it is more with them, necessarily, than with eastern Hamites or half-Hamites that the history of East Africa is concerned. The only Bantu tribes which need be mentioned here are the following—the Nyika, inhabitants of the wilderness described in the preceding section of this chapter; the Kamba, neighbours to north and west of the Nyika; the Taita, neighbours of both the foregoing, occupying the Taita Hills; the Chagga, on the slopes of Kilimanjaro; the Sambaa and Sagara, in and about the Usambara and Usagara Mountains; and the Nyamwezi, the dominant tribe of the central Tanganyika uplands.

There remain the mixed people of the maritime belt, the Swahili, 'a mixture of mixtures', arising (as will be seen in the next chapter) from the impingement of Asiatic immigrants on the Bantu who lived on the coastland or were brought down to it from the interior as slaves. Every degree of Afro-Asiatic combination and wide diversity of physique and culture are to be found in their ranks; but they possess—and have disseminated far inland—a common tongue, a Bantu language freely modified by Arabic and betraying also in its vocabulary the influence of Asiatic and European invasion.

The most significant fact about this African population of East Africa is that it is so small. The area covered by Kenya and Tanganyika is over 500,000 square miles. Its native inhabitants are roughly numbered at 8 millions. That is a density of 16 to the square mile, which is only one-third of the average density of population in the world as a whole, and far less than that of other areas, such as southern India, where the physical conditions are not so different from those of East Africa as to be incomparable. The reasons for this small East African population cannot be determined with scientific certainty. It will be suggested in a later chapter that the major cause has been the Slave Trade and the inter-tribal warfare it provoked.[1] But it may also have been due to the dryness and infertility of some parts of the country and to the very luxuriance of tropical growth in others. Great stretches of the

[1] See p. 35, below.

interior are covered, league after league, by forest or jungle or thick grass, growing head-high or higher. In such country it has never been an easy task for the inhabitants to sustain a rising population. Indeed, one of the most striking aspects of it is the failure of its human occupants so far to subdue its nature to their will. There are many districts in East Africa where men, though they have not yet achieved those wide clearances of wood and wilderness which have long ago opened up most of the cultivable soil of other continents to habitation, have at least asserted their presence and marked the land as visibly their land. But there are other tracts where man seems at a casual glance to be no more important in the scheme of nature than the animals. In Europe and Asia, wrote one of the ablest Englishmen who have taken part in the administration of East Africa, the work of man is to be seen wherever he exists.

Whether he builds temples or factories, whether he makes or mars the landscape, we are conscious that the character and appearance of the country depend on him. Here in [central] Africa man . . . in no way dominates or even sensibly influences nature. His houses produce no more scenic effect than large birds' nests; he cannot lift himself above the scrub and tall grass: if he cuts it down it simply grows up and surrounds him again.

And he went on to argue that this 'dense pall of vegetation' has held the spirit of African man in bondage and deprived him of the inventiveness, energy, and mobility which other races have attained.[1]

Sir Charles Eliot was writing, with a touch of exaggeration perhaps, about the heart of the continent. Nearer the coast, both west and east, Africans have long proved themselves free-spirited, inventive, energetic. But the race as a whole, it is true, is more backward than any other of the major races; and this, like its paucity in numbers, may in part be due to exceptional difficulties in much of their natural environment.

Throughout the period dealt with in this book, therefore, the East Africans must be conceived of as a primitive people.

[1] Sir Charles Eliot, *The East Africa Protectorate* (London, 1905), 286.

Their society, it is safe to say, was simple in character and limited in scope. An articulated state existed some centuries ago in Uganda, but nearer the sea no similar organization is on record, with the single exception of the Kingdom of Usambara, of which some description will be given in due course.[1] Tribes fought and conquered each other, but nothing came of it—no political agglomeration, narrowing the field of war. The Masai, for example, the most famous fighters, only raided and destroyed and carried off the cattle from their weaker neighbours' lands. They did not annex or try to govern them. Again excepting Usambara, there seems to have been nothing in East Africa comparable with the states and 'empires' built up in the west. Even less able, therefore, were the Africans in the east than in the west to resist disciplined invaders, especially if they were armed with guns. It was Nature, more than man, that so long delayed the European occupation of the interior.

If the European occupation could have happened earlier and if —an essential condition—it could have been disassociated from the Slave Trade, the East Africans might likewise have begun earlier to emerge from their primitive life, to combat more effectively their physical environment, to grow in prosperity and population. For while invasion and conquest in backward countries may mean nothing but degradation and destitution for their inhabitants, they can mean, paradoxical though it sounds, a kind of liberation. The present European occupation of East Africa has had its drawbacks for the Africans, but also its advantages. It only began some forty or fifty years ago, yet already inter-tribal warfare and slave raiding have been wholly suppressed; the country has been opened up by road and rail and air; its natural resources have been improved and exploited with the aid of modern science; in many areas new means of access to new markets have meant an increase in production and a rise in the standard of living; and for the country as a whole the framework of a modern state and a nucleus of social services have been built up. More security for life and property, better crops, better health, better education—those

[1] Chapter X.

are the ways in which the subjection of the East Africans has begun to free them from the perilous, cramping, static conditions of a tropical life secluded from all helpful contact with the rest of the world. And the sum of it is that the East Africans are now at last in a position to begin to make East African history themselves.

But the period of East African history to be related in this book breaks off long before that. On nearly all, though not quite all, its pages the history of East Africa is only the history of its invaders. And the stage on which they play their part is only a narrow slice of huge East Africa. Not many miles back from their settlements and ports and market-places a curtain falls, shrouding the vast interior of the continent in impenetrable darkness, 'where ignorant armies clash by night'. But the reader should remember that the East Africans, though invisible, are always there, a great black background to the comings and goings of brown men and white men on the coast. In the foreground, too, on the historical stage itself, the East Africans are always the great majority, dumb actors for the most part, doing nothing that seems important, so eclipsed by the protagonists that they are almost forgotten, and yet quite indispensable. For the life of the invaders, Arab sheikh or Indian trader or European farmer, has been maintained from first to last on a basis of African labour. It is broadly true to say that nothing can be done in tropical Africa unless Africans help to do it.

II
THE ARAB COLONIES[1]

I

THE first invasions of East Africa recorded in history came from Asia, not Europe. Naturally the Asiatics were there first. They were next-door neighbours. From Zanzibar it is only about 1,700 miles to Aden and about 2,200 to Muscat. The straight course over the Indian Ocean from Mombasa to Bombay is 2,500 miles, not much more than the length of the Mediterranean Sea. And there is a peculiar device of nature that has facilitated human intercourse in that part of the world ever since men first went down to the sea in ships. Every December the trade-wind or 'monsoon' begins to blow from the north-north-east, and continues blowing with remarkable steadiness till the end of February. Every April till September the process is reversed: a strong wind blows from the south-south-west. Now the western shore of the Indian Ocean follows a fairly straight line from Zanzibar across the mouth of the Gulf of Aden to the Gulf of Oman, and it runs almost exactly from south-west to north-east. At the Gulf of Oman it bends eastward to the mouth of the Indus and then south-south-east

[1] Authorities for this chapter: (*a*) *Primary*: Salil-ibn-Razik, *History of the Imams and Seyyids of Oman*, trans. and edited by G. P. Badger (Hakluyt Society, London, 1871); 'Chronicles of Kilwa', edited by A. S. Strong (*Journal of the Royal Asiatic Society*, N.S. xxvii, 1895); 'History of Pate', trans. by A. Werner (*Journal of African Society*, 1914–15); *Travels of Ibn Battuta*, trans. by S. Lee (London, 1829); fuller text in M. Guillain, *Documents sur l'histoire, la géographie et le commerce de l'Afrique orientale* (Paris, 1856); and native tradition preserved in C. H. Stigand, *The Land of Zinj* (London, 1913); Albuquerque's *Commentaries*, the *Book of Duarte Barbosa*, and Vasco da Gama's, Linschoten's and Lancaster's *Voyages* in the Hakluyt Society's series. (*b*) *Secondary*: W. H. Ingrams, *Zanzibar* (London, 1931), and section iv of *Zanzibar, an account of its People, Industries and History* (Zanzibar, 1924); J. Strandes, *Die Portugiesenzeit von Deutsch- und Englisch-Ostafrika* (Berlin, 1899); L. W. Hollingsworth, *Short History of the East Coast of Africa* (London, 1929); F. B. Pearce, *Zanzibar* (London, 1920); G. M. Theal, *History and Ethnography of South Africa before 1795* (London, 1904); Sir A. Wilson, *The Persian Gulf* (Oxford, 1928).

down the length of India. Merchant adventurers, therefore, setting out in their little sailing-ships from the coast of Arabia or the Persian Gulf in the winter could be certain that the wind would blow them steadily down the African coast and that in the spring, when they had spent a few months in trading, it would blow them just as steadily home again. This useful phenomenon must have been known to Eastern seafarers at a very early date—certainly long before it was known to Europeans and given the name of 'Hippalus' from its reputed discoverer; and from it arose the seasonal coming and going of Arab traders between their homeland and East Africa which became in time, and still is to-day, a regular annual practice. Nor was it Arabs only or Persians that took advantage of the 'monsoon'. Bombay is more than 20 degrees north of Zanzibar and Karachi more than 30, so that merchants from north-western India, as soon as they learned to trust in the persistence of the wind, could make the voyage to Africa across the ocean almost as safely as the Arabs who hugged the shore. It is probable that Hindus were trading with East Africa and settling on the coast as early as the sixth century B.C. Almost certainly it was they who introduced the coconut-palm.

The antiquity of this contact between Asia and East Africa could be safely inferred from the facts of geography alone, but it is confirmed by historical evidence. Among the useful 'Pilots' or guides for navigation and trade compiled in the great age of Greece and Rome was a *Periplus of the Erythraean Sea*, the Greek name for the Indian Ocean. It was written about A.D. 80 by a Greek merchant-seaman of Berenike, a port on the Red Sea coast of Egypt; and in the manner of such guides it describes the voyage down the Red Sea and the African coast, enumerating in due order the promontories and other landmarks, the river-mouths, harbours, anchorages, and the coastal towns where trade can be done, with occasional notes as to the character of the inhabitants, their forms of government, and the local products they have for sale. The East African section extends from Cape Guardafui to Zanzibar or the Rufiji River, beyond which, says the author, 'the unexplored ocean curves round towards the west, and running along by the regions to the south of Aethiopia and Libya and Africa, it mingles with the western sea'. Most of the natural features and some of the 'market-towns' mentioned in the *Periplus* can be given their modern names; but these questions of identification are of small importance; and the most interesting passages are those which describe, all too briefly, the general political situation. The inhabitants of the coast were apparently of negroid race, since they were 'very great of stature', and living under a tribal system, since there were 'separate chiefs for each place'. But these native chieftainships, it appears, had long been under some form of Arab suzerainty. The name 'Ausanitic', which the author of the *Periplus* gives to the coastland as a whole, betokens its conquest some centuries earlier by the Arab state of Ausan, and for his own day he specifies the sovereignty over it as belonging 'under some ancient right' to 'the Mapharitic chief' who can be identified as one of the Sabaean kings of South Arabia. 'And the people of Muza [Mocha]', the *Periplus* continues, 'now hold it under his authority, and send thither many large ships, using Arab captains and agents who are familiar with the natives and intermarry with them and who know the whole coast and understand the language.' As to trade, there are two or three valuable notes. The merchants of Mocha imported lances, hatchets, daggers, awls, and glass, 'and at some places a little wine and wheat, not for trade, but to serve for getting the goodwill of the savages'. They exported ivory in great quantity, rhinoceros-horn, tortoise-shell, and a little palm-oil. Ships also came from the Indian coast of the Indian Ocean, 'bringing to those far-side market-towns the products of their own places'. One other item of commercial information is still more interesting because it introduces the theme which is to run like a scarlet thread through all the subsequent history of East Africa until our own day. The coast near Ras Hafun produces, says our author, 'slaves of the better sort which are brought to Egypt in increasing numbers'. So those well-armed Arab traders did not always seek to conciliate the natives with wine and wheat. Centuries before the agents of Europe began the same ugly business in the West, the agents of Asia in the East were stealing men and women from Africa and shipping them overseas to slavery.[1]

Thus, like a flash-light, the *Periplus* reveals the salient features of the contact between Asia and East Africa as it was in the first century A.D. and had been evidently for ages past. Then darkness falls again for about five hundred years. The later classical geographers go little beyond the *Periplus*, and presently the outposts of European civilization in the north are retreating before the advance of Asia. When light is thrown again on East Africa it comes from Arab, not from European, sources. And, if it is only an intermittent light, thrown by local chronicles and the narratives of voyages, supplemented by the lessons of ruined monuments and at some points by coins and pottery discovered in the soil, it is enough at least to show the steady continuance and the gradual strengthening of the inter-continental connexion.

About A.D. 600, then, when the Indian Ocean emerges from the darkness, it is seen to be studded with Asiatic merchant ships. Arabs had been accustomed to the direct voyage to southern India and Ceylon and even as far as China long before the new national strength and stimulus they acquired from the rise of Islam carried them so swiftly to the front of history. From the sixth century onwards to the sixteenth they were the masters of the Indian Ocean. Commercial relations between Europe and Asia depended almost wholly on their carrying-trade, bringing the goods of the East to the Persian Gulf and the

[1] *The Periplus of the Erythraean Sea*, ed. W. H. Schoff (London and New York, 1921), 26–9 and notes. For the Sabaean king, see Ingrams, *Zanzibar*, 64–5. Ras Hafun is a striking promontory about 100 miles south of Cape Guardafui. Few slaves were obtained so far north in later times, when the main area of 'production' lay west and south-west of Zanzibar. See p. 300, below. The identity of the two last items on the list is uncertain. 'The island of Menouthias' might be either Zanzibar, or its consort Pemba (as Ingrams argues), or, less probably, Mafia, about 100 miles farther south; and the 'market-town' of Rhapta may have stood where Pangani now stands or at the mouth of the Rufiji.

THE ARAB COLONIES

Red Sea and thence overland to the Mediterranean. Permanent Arab trading settlements, anticipating those of Europe, were established at Calicut on the Malabar coast of India, and later at Malacca on the Malay Peninsula; and thence a network of trade in spice and other oriental luxuries reached out over the East Indies, Siam, the Philippines, and China. And in this far eastern world, also, little Arab settlements grew up here and there. At Canton, for example, there was an important Arab 'colony'. Nor was the sea-trade confined to Arabs or Persians. Their visits to the East were returned. Throughout the dark centuries those Indian ships mentioned in the *Periplus* continued to cross the ocean to the 'far-side market-towns' in East Africa. Malayans, also, and Javanese appear in Madagascar, but this is probably a case of earlier race-migration rather than of trade. Of the Chinese coins of various periods found along the African coast the earliest, belonging to the eighth century, may have been brought there by Arabs or Indians; and there is apparently no certain evidence of Chinamen actually visiting East Africa before the fifteenth century. There was an Arab tradition in the twelfth century that at some time the Chinese, owing to great troubles at home, transferred their trade to the islands that lie off the Zinj (Negro) coast;[1] and Marco Polo relates that Kubla Khan sent messengers to Madagascar 'on the pretext of demanding the release of one of his servants who had been detained there but in reality to examine into the circumstances of the country'.[2] But, whether from first-hand knowledge or from Arab sources, the early Chinese books make frequent allusions to East Africa. A treatise on geography and trade in the twelfth and thirteenth centuries mentions the Ta'shi (Arab) people of the Ts'ong-pa (Zanzibar) country who follow the Ta'shi religion and wear blue cotton garments and red leather shoes. 'The climate is warm and there is no cold season. The products of the country consist of elephants' tusks, native gold, ambergris, and yellow sandal-wood. Every year Hu-ch'u-la [Gujerat] and the Ta'shi localities along the

[1] Al-Idrisi (*c.* A.D. 1150), Ingrams, *Zanzibar*, 89.
[2] *Travels*, book iii, ch. 26 (London, 1818), 707.

sea-coast send ships to this country with white cotton cloths, porcelain, copper, and red pepper to trade.'[1] Another passage refers to an island near the K'un lun country, probably Madagascar, where 'there are many savages with bodies as black as lacquer and with frizzled hair. They are enticed by food, then caught and carried off for slaves to the Ta'shi countries where they fetch a high price. They are used as gate-keepers. It is said they do not long for their kinsfolk.'[2] But those and other similar references to East Africa leave the question of direct contact from the Chinese side unsettled.

Thus East Africa had its place in the network of trade that chequered the Indian Ocean. Goods from the Zinj country found their way over Asia and into Europe. The chief of them was still ivory, always so plentiful in East Africa where elephants were only hunted for their tusks and never, as in North Africa and Asia, tamed for the service of men in peace or war.[3] Some gold was also exported, probably from the mines of Rhodesia, and a tenth-century chronicle describes the houses of Siraf on the Persian Gulf as built of wood from Zanzibar[4]— the name, meaning Negro coast, which was first given by the Arabs to the mid-African coast in general and afterwards in particular to the island which still bears it. And there was that other article of export which was one day to take the lead of ivory and all the rest in volume and value—slaves.

[1] Chan ju k'ua, cited by Ingrams, *Zanzibar*, chap. viii, on which the above text is mainly based. Of the Ts'ang-pa country, the passage quoted also says: 'To the west it reaches to a great mountain'—which is possibly the earliest known reference to Kilimanjaro.
[2] Ingrams, *Zanzibar*, 94. Another reference, probably to Pemba: 'They are black-bodied wild men: if you entice them with food, you barter as many as you like to do work for the foreign trader.' For a seventeenth-century reference, see p. 34, note, below.
[3] Masudi noted in A.D. 915: 'Elephants are extremely common in the Land of Zinj; but they are wild and none are kept in captivity. The natives do not employ them in warfare nor for any other purpose, but they hunt them merely in order to kill them. It is from this country that large elephant-tusks are obtained. Most of the ivory is carried to Oman, whence it is sent to India and China.' Cited by Hollingsworth, 44.
[4] Istakhri, cited by Wilson, op. cit. 94.

Meantime the Arab hold on the Zinj coast was being strengthened by colonization: and, as it happened, the first Arabs to settle there came from the district of Arabia, whose rulers were destined in later times to establish all along that seaboard a kind of colonial empire and to set on a sultan's throne at Zanzibar a dynasty whose latest representative is sitting there to-day.

2

The district of Oman occupies the south-east corner of Arabia. With the Indian Ocean on two sides of it and the great Arabian desert on the third, it lies, like an island, aloof from all its neighbours. As long as its own people were united, it could defy the two great powers in the north and east, the Turks and the Persians, even in their most aggressive and expansive moods; and the sovereignty of the Arabian Caliph himself was never long maintained, except as a formality, in Oman. In the middle of the eighth century a ruler of the country was elected with the title of Imam, and for the next ten centuries, with a break between 1150 and 1300, a succession of elected Imams was maintained. The people of Oman were of mingled Arab stock; the dominant strain was derived from a section of the Azd tribe which had drifted along the coast from Yemen; others had come down across the desert from Nejd. Most of them lived inland, and their only important seaboard town was Muscat. But Muscat, with its steep-set citadel and rock-girt harbour, looking out across the sea-way to the Persian Gulf, was a tempting doorway to the life and wealth of the sea. Men of Oman, therefore, played their part in the growth of Arab trade in the Indian Ocean. In the eleventh century they were known for their excellence in ship-building. They used to sail, says a Persian writer, to 'the islands that produce the coco-nut'—Zanzibar and its satellites, perhaps—where they felled the trees, shaped ship's timber from the trunks, spun cordage from the bark to sew the planks together and make rigging, wove the leaves into sails, and, loading the finished ship with coco-nuts, returned home to market them.[1] But the doorway of Muscat opened outwards and not inwards. It had no prosperous or well-peopled hinterland like the great ports of Siraf or Hormuz: it did not command, like Basra, the overland route to Europe: and its mariners were tempted to seek quicker means of wealth than peaceful trade. In course of time the pirates of Oman became the terror of the Persian Gulf and its approaches.

These were the people, self-contained and independent, an island-people as it were, fierce and daring, at home on the sea as in the desert, who began—so far as recorded knowledge goes—the process of permanent Arab settlement and organized dominion in East Africa. During the twenty years that followed the Prophet's death in A.D. 630, the main body of the Arabs were carrying the sword of Islam through Persia, Syria, and Egypt and setting out on the westward path of conquest that led them along the whole length of northern Africa and finally across the narrow straits to the Pyrenees. But in this great national movement the isolated Omani took no share. They were quarrelling indeed, as often before and after, with their Arab kindred. About A.D. 695, under their chiefs Suleiman and Said, of the house of Azd, they rose in rebellion against the overlordship of Abdul Malik, the Caliph (684–705). This time, however, their bid for independence failed. Invaded and outnumbered, they fought bravely till hope was gone, and then Suleiman and Said, with their families and others of their tribe, fled oversea to the land of Zinj. At what points in it they settled is unknown.[2]

The other three settlements on record were likewise settlements of refugees, but not from Oman. It is related that about A.D. 740, as a result of a schism among the Shiites, a body of Arab schismatics known as Zaidiyah sought refuge in East Africa and settled in the neighbourhood of Shungwaya.[3] Then, about 920, according to tradition, the 'seven brothers of El

---

[1] Abu Zaid Hassan of Siraf, quoted by Wilson, op. cit. 59.
[2] For a tradition as to the sites, preserved at Pate, see Ingrams, op. cit. 74. Another tradition of Arab settlement in the seventh century, ibid. 76. [3] Port Durnford.

Hasa', probably Arabs and possibly of the El-Harth tribe, flying from persecution, founded Mogadishu and Barawa. To the same century belongs the similar tradition of 'Hassan-bin-Ali and his Six Sons'. It tells of a son begotten by the Sultan of Shiraz of an Abyssinian slave-woman, who was out-rivalled by his better-born brothers and so departed with his six sons for Africa. They sailed in seven ships, and one ship stopped and one son founded a settlement at each of six separate places. Three of these are named—Mombasa, Pemba, and Johanna in the Comoro Isles. Hassan himself founded Kilwa. A story in the vein of the *Arabian Nights*; but it was repeated with minor variations by several court-chroniclers of Shiraz and by the author of the ancient Arab *Chronicles of Kilwa*, and it contains a solid core of history within its wrappings of romance. That the Persians who shared with the Arabs in the trade of the Indian Ocean shared also in the settlement of East Africa is certain. They have left unmistakable traces in its architecture and pottery and language. And there are many natives now living along the coast who retain the tradition of ships from Shiraz landing parties of settlers at different points and sometimes claim themselves to be descended from them.[1]

Too much importance, however, should not be ascribed to

[1] The so-called *Chronicles of Kilwa* are an abstract in Arabic of a lost history of the Kilwa colony, called *Sinet el Kilawia*, which was probably used by de Barros in his *Asia* (Lisbon, 1552-3). This abstract belonged some sixty years ago to an Arab sheikh of Zanzibar, and, having been stolen, fell into the hands of the British consular court. The judge was Kirk, who at once detected the historical value of the abstract; and the Sultan Barghash had a copy made for him before it was returned to its lawful owner. Kirk presented this copy to the British Museum. The Arabic text, which covers in bald summary the whole period from the foundation of Kilwa to the coming of the Portuguese, is printed in the *Journal of the Royal Asiatic Society* (N.S. xxvii, 1895) with a commentary by A. S. Strong. The original *Sinet el Kilawia* seems to have existed in 1812, when the 'Sultan' of Kilwa talked proudly to the captain of a British frigate 'of his kingdom having been established for a period of nearly 1,200 years ... and that written testimonies remain of the crown during that time having descended without interruption in his family'. J. Prior, *Voyage along the Eastern Coast of Africa* (London, 1819), 78. For coins struck by Sultans of Kilwa and their historical significance, see J. Walker, *Numismatic Chronicle*, series v, vol. xvi (1936), 43-81.

these traditions of particular settlements at particular times. Already at the date of the *Periplus* Arabs were making at least temporary homes in East Africa and intermarrying with natives; and it is more than probable that the Arab and Persian colonization of the coast was a long and gradual process which began in remote antiquity and continued more or less steadily for centuries, speeded up, doubtless, on occasion by bands of fugitives not only from local feuds along the Arabian and Persian littoral but also from the waves of war and conquest that swept from time to time through the backlands in the north, and sometimes also by zealots of some persecuted sect who, like the Puritan founders of New England, sought in the colonial field the religious freedom denied to them at home.

3

Of the manner in which this Asiatic fringe of Africa lived and grew through the Middle Ages little detailed knowledge has survived. The Arabic *Chronicles of Kilwa*, the Swahili *History of Pate*, and other similar local compilations are bleak annals, mainly concerned with the names and succession of the ruling sheikhs or sultans.[1] More helpful is the occasional light thrown by the work of Arabs who did not themselves reside in East Africa—by the map, for instance, compiled and annotated by the Arab al-Idrisi at the court of Count Robert of Sicily in the twelfth century, and by the books of such Arab travellers as Masudi of Bagdad (tenth century), Yaqut, the Greek freedman (thirteenth century), and especially Ibn Battuta of Tangier (fourteenth century). Inferences also can be drawn from the accounts of the Portuguese at the end of the fifteenth century as to the conditions that prevailed before they came. These are scanty sources; but an outline sketch, sufficient for the present purpose, can be drawn from them.

It is clear, to begin with, that the Persian element in the

[1] The text of the Swahili *History of Pate* is published with translation and notes by A. Werner in *Journal of the African Society*, 1914–15, 148, 278, 392. For other local 'histories', see list in Ingrams, *Zanzibar, an account of its People, Industries and History*, Appendix III, xvi.

The Arab Colonies

colonial population, higher though it was in culture and author of all the most beautiful remains of local art, was gradually merged and absorbed in the Arab element; and it will be simpler henceforward to speak of the chain of coastal colonies and their civilization in general as Arab. The chief points of settlement, running from north to south, were Mogadishu, Barawa, Siu, Pate, Lamu, Malindi, Kilifi, Mombasa, Vumba, Pemba, Zanzibar, Mafia, Kilwa, Mozambique, and Sofala, which last was in Masudi's day and apparently remained 'the limit of navigation of the vessels of Oman and Siraf in the Sea of Zinj', for the reason, no doubt, that southwards of Cape Corrientes the 'monsoon' ceases to blow, irregular gales are more frequent, currents stronger, and the climate colder. Settlements were also made in course of time on the Comoro Islands, half-way between Cape Delgado and the northern end of Madagascar, and down the west coast of huge Madagascar itself.[1] Most of these sites were on islands; some of them, like Zanzibar, lay a fair distance from the coast; others, like Kilwa or Mombasa, were only separated from the land by a narrow inlet of the sea, just as Tumbatu, the first and for long the principal town of Zanzibar, was separated from its mother-island. Therein the Arab settlers were doing what other sea-faring and colonizing peoples in other lands had done before and did after. Mombasa and Zanzibar and the rest stand in the same class as Tyre and Tarshish or Singapore and Hong Kong—'jumping-off places', secured by sea-power, for the exploitation or occupation of the mainland. Each point, whether insular or not, was strongly fortified, and within the ramparts substantial towns grew up. It is recorded of Kilwa, Mombasa, and Mozambique and is probably true of most of the other towns that they were laid out in regular streets and that the houses of the Arabs were usually of stone and mortar, with large windows and terraces not unlike those of southern Europe, doors and frames of wood often beautifully carved

[1] Prior's journal contains interesting notes on the Arabs settled in Madagascar and the Comoro Islands 'from time immemorial'. Prior, op. cit. 47–59.

and embossed with metal, and spacious courts and gardens. And since the whole coast was converted to Islam in the ninth or tenth century, every town had its mosques, decorated sometimes with exquisite Persian art.

Here, in a softer air and more perennial warmth than their ancestors had known on the hard Arabian coast or the highlands behind the Persian Gulf, the colonists maintained their traditional ways of life. And of all their Arab customs none was more tenaciously kept up than the custom of internal strife—strife in the family or the tribe over the succession to the rulership of each little 'city-state' and strife between state and state for political and commercial supremacy. Those local 'histories' have little to tell of the dynasties of rulers they enumerate save how they made war on other towns along the coast and subjected or failed to subject them. Any political unity, therefore, anything like a single Arab 'empire' in East Africa, was never in those days achieved. The nearest approach to it was the overlordship exercised for varying periods over a varying number of other towns by the one which happened at the time to be the strongest or the most aggressive. Pate, for example, is recorded, with a touch of exaggeration perhaps on the part of the local chronicler, to have conquered about 1335 the whole coast from Malindi to Kilwa excepting Zanzibar.[1] Mombasa, similarly, dominated part at least of the coast in the twelfth century;[2] and Mogadishu, Pemba, and Zanzibar at one time or another lorded it over other towns. But the most famous and lasting of those hegemonies seems to have been that of Kilwa. Mistress of Sofala and its gold trade from the beginning of the twelfth century, Kilwa had once brought all the coast and islands, including the Comoros, under her control; and when the Portuguese first came to East Africa at the end of the fifteenth century, Kilwa was still the ruling city along the southern section of the coast. At Mozambique, where he first put in, da Gama found that 'the captain of the

[1] *History of Pate* (*J.A.S.*, 1914–15), 159.
[2] For the dominion of Mombasa under the Mazrui in the eighteenth and nineteenth centuries, see pp. 217–21, below.

country' was a representative of the Sultan of Kilwa, on whose behalf he collected heavy dues on all the merchant shipping of the neighbourhood; and Sofala, Quilimane, and Angoche were similarly subject.[1] Northwards, also, Kilwa was influential, if no longer dominant: the Sultan's daughter, it appears, was married to the Sultan of Mombasa.[2] Thus, through the centuries, now this little state and now that achieved predominance by force or diplomacy or dynastic alliance—predominance, but never complete or permanent control. And in the course of the unending conflict bitter feuds grew up and became traditional. The fatal hatred between Mombasa and Malindi was an old story before the advent of the Portuguese.

In their love of strife and lack of unity then, as in most other things, the Arab colonists in East Africa were true to their stock. But the society which grew up round them was not a purely Arab society. Like other colonists in that and other continents, the Arabs in Africa were an aristocracy of race. Closely associated with them, but not of the ruling class, were the Indian residents whose connexion with the coast was as old as theirs. Much of the ocean-shipping was Indian-owned and Indian-manned; and since Arabs in general seem never to have shown much aptitude for the technique of business, it is probable that the Indians were from the earliest days what they still are in East Africa—the masters of finance, the bankers and money-changers and money-lenders. Probably, too, much of the actual trade was either directly in their hands or managed by them for wealthy land-owning Arab proprietors, and probably, then as now, they monopolized the lesser retail trade. But if the Indians thus rendered an essential service to the community as a whole, the Arabs had to pay in the long run for not doing it themselves. Dependence on Indian industry and skill might help them to get rich, but it was bound, slowly but surely, to weaken their economic independence and

---

[1] E. Correa, *The Three Voyages of Vasco da Gama*, trans. H. E. J. Stanley (Hakluyt Society, London, 1869), 84; *The Book of Duarte Barbosa* (Hakluyt Society, London, 1918), 18. Prior, op. cit. 78. Strandes, 99. Angoche lay 100 miles south of Mozambique. [2] Correa, 95, note 1.

initiative.[1] Besides the Indians there was a growing half-caste population of varied hue and varied status—the more Asiatic clinging to the skirts of Arab society, the more African swelling the numbers of a new mixed race of the maritime belt, of Moslem faith and hybrid speech, now known as Swahili.[2] Thus the retinue of the Sheikh of Mozambique in 1498—the first East Africans to meet the first European voyagers up the coast—were described by one of the chroniclers of the voyage as 'fair men, and dark men, and others swarthy, because they were sons of Cafre women of the country and white Moorish merchants who since a long time have so established their commerce throughout all the Indian countries that they have remained as natives thereof'.[3] Last but not least in numbers came the African slaves whom the Arabs reserved from their slave-trade to work in their houses and gardens and plantations and to serve as caravan-porters and soldiers.

So much for the internal composition of the Arab colonies. It remains to consider the setting in which they stood, to paint in, so to speak, round those bright spots of colour on the coast a broad belt of black, stretching away unbroken from the Indian Ocean to the Great Lakes and beyond, and to examine briefly the mutual relations and reactions between the immigrant Asiatics and that overwhelming mass of native Africans.

4

The life of the tribes along the coast was, of course, profoundly affected by the plantation of a chain of Arab colonies in their midst. But it was a gradual and probably not a very violent process. First, the traders came and went: then, at long intervals, here and there a settlement was made. There is no native tradition of a dark age of conquest; and, though more or less force was probably needed at times for the acquisition of land, the unwarlike coastal natives must have

[1] See pp. 84–5, below.
[2] Swahili means 'Coast People', from the Arabic *sahil*, 'coast'.
[3] Correa, op. cit. 86.

been easily subjected by the Arabs. Before long, no doubt, they realized that the masterful and well-armed strangers from the sea had come to stay and acquiesced in the inevitable. Abou-Zaid-Hassan observed in the tenth century that the people of Zinj were fond of fighting, but 'the Arabs', he added, 'exercise a great ascendency over them. When a man of this nation sees an Arab, he prostrates himself before him.'[1] And, whether such submissiveness was general along the coast or not, the intercourse of the immigrants with the natives seems as a rule to have been close and friendly. Intermarriage, as has been seen, began early, and produced the Swahili people, sharing the faith and, at varying social levels, the general life of the Arabs. Away from the towns a tribe might maintain its old ways unchanged, but the coast-population as a whole acquired in course of time a more or less common Afro-Asiatic character.

But this infusion of Arab blood and civilization never extended far from the sea. One obstacle, especially in the northern area, was the more martial and independent character of the upland tribes. If the Arabs had ever wished to conquer them and occupy their land, they might well have found the task beyond their strength. At times, indeed, those formidable fighters came raiding to the coast. The *Chronicles of Kilwa* record repeated attacks by natives in the early years of the settlement. The third sultan, grandson of the founder, was forced to fly for refuge to Zanzibar.[2] And centuries later, when Ibn Battuta came to Kilwa, he heard of the constant fighting that went on with the natives of the mainland. 'The inhabitants of Kilwa', he says, ' are addicted to the *jehad*, for they occupy a country contiguous to that of the infidel Zinj.'[3] Again, at the end of the period, Barbosa in his description of Mombasa states that 'the men thereof are oft-times at war and but seldom at peace with those of the mainland, and they carry on trade with them, bringing thence great store of honey, wax,

[1] Guillain, i. 189.
[2] *Journal of the Royal Asiatic Society*, N.S. xxvii, 1915, 388.
[3] Guillain, i. 294.

and ivory'.[1] That seeming paradox contains the key to the relations of the Arabs as a whole with the upland tribes. Trade was the sole motive of their contact with them. The other motives, scientific, religious, economic, which prompted their European successors in a later age to be more enterprising and interfering, did not appeal to them. Sea-shore merchants, they did not want, it seems, to know much about the great unknown continent at their backs. They attempted no systematic exploration of it. They never produced a local al-Idrisi or a map. Nor did they feel any call to confront the hardships and dangers of the interior simply in order to propagate their faith.[2] Nor, again, did they desire, like the immigrants of our own day, to occupy and cultivate for themselves large areas of land. All they wanted was to exchange their Asiatic textiles and metal-work and beads for native produce—ivory and Rhodesian gold, ambergris and slaves. For that they were ready to take risks and, if it was necessary, to fight. But only, it may be assumed, if it was necessary—only, for instance, to keep the trade-routes open or to prevent interference with friendly customers, never for the sake of mere conquest or dominion.

The contact between the races, in fact, was no more than the limited, sporadic, and intermittent contact of commerce. From the days when they first came to East Africa the Arab traders must have begun to push farther and farther inland in quest of the goods they wanted. And since their caravans moved slowly and could not move at all in the rainy season, the traders must soon have got used to being away from the coast for many months, and they presently acquired the habit of staying for a year or so up-country at convenient places for doing business and storing goods. At one or two such places, in course of time, they established permanent inland settlements.[3] That and no

[1] *The Book of Duarte Barbosa*, 21.
[2] It is unlikely that Ibn Battuta's *jehads* at Kilwa were inspired by religious zeal. He mentions only one specific war, of which he writes that the Sultan Hasan attacked the Zinj and 'obtained much booty from them'. Guillain, i. 294.
[3] There is no evidence of any such settlement before that at Sena which is first mentioned in the sixteenth century, see p. 50, below.

more was the extent of their intercourse with the tribes of the hinterland—little else than the coming and going in the dry seasons of itinerant traders, no close or widespread contact, no social fusion, nothing in the least resembling the relations with the tribes along the coast. Yet, slight as it seems at first sight, this intercourse had a deep and lasting effect on the Africans. It was not so much what they got from the Arabs—the sight of strange men and things, new notions, a breath of outside air entering the closed circle of their life, the fascinating luxuries of cloth and brass-wire bangles and beads. It was rather what they gave the Arabs besides their ivory—themselves.

5

Not all the slaves obtained from the interior were exported. Many of them were retained by the Arabs for service in their coast towns and neighbouring plantations. Others were enrolled in the substantial bodies of native troops which were maintained in some of the Arab colonies.[1] But the great majority were shipped overseas. Some of them were taken to Egypt[2] and may have passed thence to the cities of Greece and Rome in the classical age; but most of the 'Aethiopian' slaves which figure in Greco-Roman literature had probably been brought down the Nile from 'Nubia' or the Sudan. In any case it was to Asia that the mass of slaves from East Africa were consigned. In Turkey and Arabia and Persia they became a large and permanent element in the population. No figures are available till relatively recent times, but in 1835 the slaves in Oman constituted no less than a third of the population, and there is no reason to suppose that some such proportion had not been established long before. The Negro slave is a familiar figure in Arabic literature; and the eunuch observed by Ibn Battuta in the Sheikh's palace at

---

[1] When Tristão da Cunha and Albuquerque attacked Barawa in 1506 most of the 6,000 men paraded for its defence were Africans armed with spears and bows and arrows (Theal, op. cit. i. 253). In this and other cases most of the Africans were presumably slaves, not mercenaries. For slaves in the army in Iraq, see next page.

[2] See p. 17, above.

Mogadishu[1] has a hundred counterparts in the Bagdad of the *Arabian Nights*.

Their lot, it is often said, was not unbearable, since kindness to slaves is one of the duties inculcated by the Koran; and, no doubt, these East Africans, as a general rule, were as docile and dutiful in the gardens and harems of their Moslem masters as the West Africans were in a later age on the estates of Christian planters in the West Indies and America. But they did not always show that mute submission to their fate which, in view of their strong physique, has always seemed so strange a feature of African slavery; and once or twice, when a chance was given them, they took it. Thus in Iraq in A.D. 850, just a century after Abu'l Abbas, ruler of Bagdad, had set a dangerous precedent by enrolling 400 Zinj slaves in his army, they rose in revolt with a Negro called 'Lord of the Blacks' at their head. Again, in 869, when the rebel Persian adventurer, Al Kabith, summoned the slaves to freedom, they flocked in tens of thousands to his side. In 871 he led them to the capture and sack of Basra, and for fourteen years he dominated the Euphrates delta.[2] So deep a mark was left by his reign of terror that, when only forty years later Masudi visited the country, he was told by every one that 'the chief of the black slaves' had caused the death, by famine or the sword, of at least a million people.[3]

Into India, also, Africans were being imported, cargo by cargo, throughout this period; and a still more striking example of their capacity for self-assertion comes from the old Moslem kingdom of Bengal. It is written that King Rukn-ud-din Barbak, who ruled at Gaur from 1459 to 1474, possessed 8,000 African slaves and was the first king in India to promote them in large numbers to high rank in his service. Again it was a dangerous precedent. The slaves at court became insolent and licentious; and when in 1486 the 'wise and beneficent' Fath Shah attempted to restrain and punish them, they murdered him and set the eunuch they had chosen as their leader on the

---

[1] Guillain, i. 282.   [2] Ingrams, *Zanzibar*, 78–9.
[3] Maçoudi, *Le Livre de l'avertissement et de la révision* (trans. B. C. de Vaux, Paris, 1897), 471–2.

throne with the title of Barbak Shah. There he might have remained, it seems, but for the energy of another African, Indil Khan, who had risen to high military command and was loyal to Fath Shah. Returning to Gaur from a distant expedition he killed Barbak, and, since Fath's son and heir was only two years old, at his widow's urgent bidding he accepted the crown with the title of Saif-ud-din-Firuz. 'Firuz had already distinguished himself as a soldier and administrator, and during his short reign of three years he healed the disorders of the kingdom and restored the discipline of the army. His fault was prodigality, and despite the warnings and protests of his counsellors he wasted the public treasure by lavishing it on beggars.' He was succeeded in 1489 by Fath Shah's young son under a regency exercised by another African; but before a year was out yet another African, Sidi Badr, murdered both child-king and regent and usurped the throne. 'This bloodthirsty monster, in the course of a reign of three years, put most of the leading men in the kingdom to death.' In 1493 he was killed at the head of a sortie against rebel forces that were besieging Gaur, and with his death this remarkable Negro régime in Bengal came to an end. An Asiatic from the Oxus country was elected to the throne, and one of his first acts was to expel all the Africans from the kingdom. It is recorded that the exiles, many thousands in number, were turned back from Delhi and Jaunpur and finally drifted to Gujarat and the Deccan, where also the Slave Trade had created a considerable Negro population. Had they been suffered to stay in Bengal, it is conceivable that they might have mastered the kingdom as the Mamelukes, three centuries later, mastered Egypt.[1]

There is no evidence that the Arab slave-traders found large markets for their wares farther east than India; but a number of Africans were probably shipped to China. In 976 a great sensation was produced at the court of the Tang emperor by the arrival of an Arab envoy with a 'negro slave' in his suite; and after that date Chinese books repeatedly refer to 'negro slaves'

[1] Sir W. Haig, *Cambridge History of India* (Cambridge, 1928), iii. 268–71.

and, as has already been noticed, to the Arab Slave Trade which produced them. But it seems probable that China absorbed only a small fraction of the vast host of slaves which Asia, century after century, was steadily filching away from Africa.[1]

Nor was there any change—the process of depopulation was, if anything, intensified—when, at the outset of the sixteenth century, the control of the east coast passed for a period from Asiatic into European, from Moslem into Christian, hands. The Portuguese were the first to trade in slaves in West Africa: they were second in East Africa only because the Arabs were before them. Like the Arabs, they not only stole or purchased Africans for their own service, but also exported them oversea. But this European export of slaves from East Africa was not comparable in volume or duration with the Arab; it was indeed an adjunct of the latter, for it was mainly from Arab or Afro-Arab slave-hunters that the Portuguese dealers obtained their supplies. Asia, not Europe, bears the chief responsibility for the damage done by the Slave Trade to East Africa.

The extent of that damage can never be computed. Enslavement was practised, no doubt, from the earliest days among the Africans themselves; but when, with the coming of the strangers from Asia, they found that slaves were at least as useful an article of barter as ivory wherewith to purchase those attractive luxuries from the outer world, a new and constant incentive was provided for intestinal war. Tribe attacked tribe for the sole purpose of obtaining slaves. To that extent the Arab invasion of inner Africa intensified its barbarism. But it did more harm than that. Unlike the old local enslavement, the new Slave Trade depopulated the country. Exact calculation is impossible;

[1] E. Bretschneider, *On the Knowledge possessed by the Ancient Chinese of the Arabs and Arabian Colonies, etc.* (London, 1871), 13–22; Ingrams, *Zanzibar*, 88–95. Ingrams's location of 'K'un lun' in East African waters rather than in Malaya, as previously suggested, seems certainly right. For the continuance of the Slave Trade in the seventeenth century in Portuguese hands or by Arab smugglers, see Bretschneider, 15, note, quoting a Chinese book of 1607: 'The body of the inhabitants of K'un lun is black as if covered with black varnish. They make slaves from amidst their own people and sell them to foreign merchants, receiving in exchange dresses and other articles.'

but it has been estimated on the basis of trustworthy statistics available for certain years that the European Slave Trade in the Atlantic was responsible for the removal from Africa of at least twelve million Africans; and certainly a great many more, perhaps an equal or even higher number, perished in the process. Now the European Slave Trade did not begin till the sixteenth century, it did not reach its full volume till the eighteenth, and in the course of the nineteenth it was suppressed. But the Arab Slave Trade began, as has been seen, before the Christian Era, and it did not stop till some fifty years ago; and though its output in any single year can never have reached the highest figures of the European trade, the total number of Africans it exported from first to last through all those centuries must have been prodigious. The small population of East Africa in proportion to its area has already been remarked; and several minor reasons for the singular scantiness of human beings in East Africa compared with other tropical or sub-tropical parts of the world can be adduced. But the major reason, if all its effects, direct and indirect, are coolly appraised, would seem to be the steadily continued abduction and destruction of the people, men, women and children, by the operation of the Slave Trade over a period of at least two thousand years.[1]

6

Slaves, then, ranked high among the raw materials of Africa which the Arabs were busy exchanging for the manufactured goods, the cloth and metal-work and beads, of India, Persia, and

[1] The explorer Speke, for example, wrote as follows of the east side of Lake Tanganyika as he first saw it in 1858: 'How the shores should be so desolate strikes one with much surprise. Unless in former times this beautiful country has been harassed by neighbouring tribes and despoiled of its men and cattle to satisfy the spoilers and be sold to distant markets, its present state appears quite incomprehensible. In hazarding this conjecture it might be thought that I am taking an extreme view of this case; but when we see everywhere in Africa what one slave-hunt or cattle-lifting party can effect, it is not unreasonable to imagine that this was most probably the cause of such utter desolation here. These war-parties lay waste the tracts they visit for endless time.' *What Led to the Discovery of the Source of the Nile* (London, 1864), 218. See also p. 175, below.

Arabia. And it was from first to last on this 'middleman's' trade that their little urban societies on the coast supported themselves. The economic basis of their life, indeed, was almost wholly mercantile. They manufactured little themselves. Ibn Battuta records that a fine cloth was woven at Mogadishu and exported to Egypt;[1] and al-Idrisi had heard of iron-mines being worked at Malindi and Sofala;[2] but those are the only allusions made by any of the Arab travellers to the existence of local industries for overseas markets.[3] Nor did the Arabs attempt through all those centuries to exploit the agricultural resources of the country. They introduced oranges and other fruits from the East, they cultivated plantations of palms and grew sorghum, millet, beans and rice along the rivers near their towns, but mainly for local consumption. No crops, no cereals or cotton, were grown on a commercial scale. It was the same with live stock. Cattle, goats, sheep and poultry were bred for their own use and comfort, not for sale abroad. The old familiar indigenous commodities of Africa—ivory and slaves and Sofala gold, coco-nuts and coco-nut oil and ambergris—sufficed for their export trade, and their export trade sufficed to make them prosperous.[4]

Prosperous they certainly were. Ibn Battuta, who was acquainted with the standards of Arab life on the Mediterranean coast and at Mecca in the fourteenth century, was surprised by the wealth and civilization of East Africa. Kilwa he describes as 'one of the most beautiful and best-built towns'. Mombasa is a 'large' and Mogadishu an 'exceedingly large city'. Mogadishu appears, indeed, when Ibn Battuta visited it about 1332, to have been the most important place on the coast. At certain seasons

[1] Guillain, i. 280. [2] Idem, i. 205, 224.
[3] Duarte Barbosa, visiting the coast at the beginning of the sixteenth century, noted that at Sofala 'the Moors have now recently begun to produce much fine cotton in this country, and they weave it into white cloth, and because they do not know how to dye it or have not got the needful dyes, they take the blue or coloured cloths of Cambay and unravel them, and weave this thread with their own white thread, and in this manner they make much coloured cloth by means of which they get much gold'. *Book of D. B.* 9.
[4] For cultivation and stock see Strandes, 92–3. Pine-apple, maize, and manioc were introduced from America by the Portuguese.

of the year pilgrims came in crowds to its 'great mosque' from all the neighbouring towns. And Ibn Battuta was deeply impressed by the piety and civility of its people. 'The custom here', he says, 'is that, whenever any ships approach, the young men of the city come out and each one addressing himself to a merchant becomes his host. If there be a theologian or noble on board, he takes up his residence with the Kadi.' Ibn Battuta himself was met on the beach by the Kadi and his pupils and lodged for some days in 'the students' house' as the guest of the Sultan 'whom they style *Sheikh*'. He was very well fed. The usual meal consisted of a large dish of flesh, fish, fowl, and vegetables laid over rice roasted in oil, plantains boiled in new milk and served with curdled milk, preserved lemons, pickled pepper-pods, and a strange fruit like an apple with a stone in it. 'One of these people', observes their guest at last, 'eats as much as several of us. It is their custom. They are extremely corpulent.'[1]

Mogadishu figures also in the Chinese records of the Ming dynasty. The chronicler speaks slightingly of its barren, mountainous, and dry surroundings—'it sometimes does not rain for years'—but 'the houses', he says, 'are built of stone'.[2] And it was Mogadishu that took the lead in the trade between East Africa and China which, to judge from the fragments of Ming ware found in the ruins of the coast towns, reached its zenith in the fourteenth or fifteenth century. In 1427 an envoy from Mogadishu was sent to China, and in 1430 a fleet of Chinese junks visited Mogadishu.[3]

Europeans, similarly, when they first came to this unknown, out-of-the-way part of barbarous Africa, were astonished to find a civilized society implanted there, comparable at any rate in all the signs of material well-being with what they were accustomed to in Europe. The first East Africans whom Vasco da Gama set eyes on were the Sheikh of Mozambique and his retinue. They wore robes of velvet and silk and gold thread,

[1] *Travels of Ibn Battuta*, trans. by S. Lee (London, 1829), 56–7; and French translation of a fuller text in Guillain, i. 280–6.
[2] Bretschneider, 21.
[3] Ingrams, *Zanzibar*, 90; Strandes, 87. This is the first certain evidence of the presence of Chinamen in East Africa, but see p. 19, above.

their turbans were of silk and gold, and their swords and daggers were mounted in silver. Da Gama did not stop at Mogadishu, but it was observed in passing to be 'a large town with houses of several stories, big palaces in its centre, and four towers around it'.[1] At Malindi, a 'noble city', da Gama's envoy was received by the 'king' in a palace strewn with carpets and rugs and furnished with stools inlaid with ivory and gold; and the 'king' gave him 'two coloured silk cloths with gold fringes and a ring with a blue stone very pretty to look at'.[2] Duarte Barbosa, visiting the coast some ten years later, tells the same story. He speaks of Kilwa as 'a Moorish town with many fair houses of stone and mortar, with many windows after our fashion, very well laid out in streets, with many flat roofs. The doors are of wood, well-carved, with excellent joinery. Around it are streams and orchards and fruit-gardens with many channels of sweet water. . . . And in this town was great plenty of gold, as no ships passed to or from Sofala without coming to this island'. 'Of the Moors', he continues, 'there are some fair and some black: they are finely clad in many rich garments of gold and silk and cotton, and the women as well; also with much gold and silver in chains and bracelets . . . and many jewelled ear-rings in their ears.' Mombasa, again, is 'a very fair place, with lofty stone and mortar houses, well alined in streets. . . . Their women go very bravely attired. . . . It is a place of great traffic and has a good harbour in which are always moored small craft of many kinds and also great ships, both of those which are bound to and from Sofala and others which come from Cambay and Malindi and others which sail to the islands of Zanzibar'. The 'fair town' of Malindi, the 'great town' of Barawa, the 'very great town' of Mogadishu, are all described by Barbosa in similar terms—prosperity and abundance, great profits from trade, great wealth.[3] In

[1] *Da Gama's First Voyage*, 88.
[2] Correa's *Voyages of Da Gama*, 86, 120–1.
[3] Of Mogadishu Barbosa wrote: 'Many ships come hither from the great kingdom of Cambaya, bringing great plenty of cloths of many sorts and divers other wares, also spices: and in the same way they come from Aden. And they carry away much gold, ivory, wax, and many other things.' *Book of D. B.* 31.

The Arab Colonies

the islands, likewise, in Mafia, Pemba, and Zanzibar, they 'live in great luxury, clad in very good fine silk and cotton garments which they purchase at Mombasa from the merchants from Cambay who reside there. The women of these Moors go bravely decked with many jewels of fine Sofala gold, silver too in plenty, ear-rings, necklaces, bracelets and ankle-rings, and they are dressed in good silk clothes'.[1]

Evidently, then, by the end of the fifteenth century the Arab colonists in East Africa, unknown to the western world, had attained a high level of material civilization. They were as well fed, well clad, and well housed as Europeans. They lived a civilized life. But it was not, it seems, a cultured life. In other countries the Arabs not only preserved and passed on to their Christian enemies the legacy of Hellenism; they made their own contribution to the literature, art, and science of the world. In the tenth and eleventh centuries the centres of Arab learning at Cordova, Toledo, and Seville illumined the darkness of medieval Europe. As late as the thirteenth century the academic schools of Bagdad were still superior to those of Oxford, and there was more education and enlightenment to be found at Cairo or Tunis or Fez than in any Christian city. But in East Africa no trace of this higher life appears. The Arab travellers say nothing of such things. Fragments of architecture, some fine carving, some bits of pottery have survived, but nothing else—no other works of art nor any writing that deserves the name of literature or science. It is difficult, indeed, to understand how the great age of the Arabs in East Africa could have been so rich in wealth and comfort and yet so poor in culture.

And now, at the end of the fifteenth century, their great age was over. Those unexpected visitors from Europe had seen

[1] *The Book of D. B.* i. 19–31. See also the description of Kilwa in da Gama's second voyage. 'The city comes down to the shore and is entirely surrounded by a wall and towers within which there may be 12,000 inhabitants. The country all round is very luxuriant with many trees and gardens of all sorts of vegetables, citrons, lemons, and the best sweet oranges that were ever seen, sugar-canes, figs, pomegranates, and a great abundance of flocks, especially sheep. . . . And in the port there were many ships.' Correa, 291–2.

them in their glory—their lofty houses, the rich colour of their life, the gold and silver and bright silk dresses, the packed warehouses on the quays, the harbours thronged with shipping: the Portuguese had seen all those signs of wealth to be got in East Africa, and they were covetous.

III

THE PORTUGUESE CONQUEST[1]

I

BETWEEN A.D. 1450 and 1550 the political expansion of Asia, sustained for seven centuries by the conquering force of Islam, reached and passed its climax. At the close of that period Moslem Arabs and Moslem Turks still ruled and were long to continue ruling the African as well as the Asiatic coasts of the Mediterranean. But the Christian recovery of western Europe, beginning with the capture of Toledo in 1085 and of Sicily in 1091, was completed by the capture of Granada in 1492; and if, by way of balance, in eastern Europe the tide of Turkish conquest was still advancing up to the battle of Mohacs and the sieges of Vienna, after 1583 it began slowly but steadily to recede towards that south-eastern corner where to-day the Turks still keep their 'bridge-head' on European soil. Christian Europe, in fact, as one of the first moves in a new age of energy and enterprise, was opening a counter-attack on Moslem Asia. And not on land alone. Barred by the Turkish and Arab dominions from the land-route to the sources of oriental trade, she applied her new discoveries in the art of navigation to the search for an alternative route by sea; and it was in pursuit of that quest that Columbus collided with the island outposts of America in 1492 and Diaz rounded the southern end of Africa in 1486. The latter event was not by much, if at all, the less important of the two. It marked the beginning of a new and a long chapter in the relations between Europe and her two neighbour-continents—a chapter in which she was destined to attain the mastery of the Indian Ocean and to secure by degrees and in varying measure the economic and political control of its Asiatic and African coastlands.

The first part of that chapter was written quickly and firmly

---

[1] The chief authority for this chapter is Strandes's invaluable work. Theal's volume, though old-fashioned and undocumented, is also useful, but confines itself mainly to the coast south of Cape Delgado.

by the Portuguese. Within a single generation that little maritime state not only explored and appropriated the new sea-route to India and beyond but seized and monopolized the whole system of Eastern trade. Nor was that achievement a matter of accident or good luck. It was long designed and carefully prepared. While Diaz was sent to find a new way to the promised land, other servants of Dom João II were commissioned to spy out the land itself by the old ways. One of these latter was João Pires de Covilhão, who left Lisbon in 1487, proceeded by way of Egypt to Aden, thence to Calicut and Goa and back to Hormuz, and thence down the African coast to Sofala and back to Cairo, whence he dispatched to his master a full report on the trade of the Indian Ocean. Meantime the slow business of building and equipping ocean-going ships was put in hand at Lisbon. Before it could be completed João II died; but under his successor, Manuel, who had also felt the call of the East, the work was pressed on, and in 1497 Vasco da Gama with three[1] ships, following in Diaz's track, rounded the Cape, and in the course of the next year visited, one after another, the chief Arab settlements from Mozambique to Malindi. Thence he struck across the open sea to Calicut. In 1499 he returned to Lisbon by the same route.

The object of this historic voyage was only exploratory, not acquisitive. It was a reconnaissance in force. And da Gama, though prepared to fight his way at need, played the part of a friendly stranger in pursuit of peaceful trade. At Mozambique, the first of the four African ports he touched at on his outward voyage, the Arabs on their side were, outwardly and to begin with, no less friendly. All the courtesies were observed. The Sheikh paid a ceremonial visit to da Gama's flagship. But when they realized that these unexpected visitors were not only infidels but interlopers in the Indian trade, their attitude changed; and it was probably only by weighing anchor that the Portuguese evaded a surprise attack. At Kilwa, suzerain

[1] Barros adds a fourth store-ship to Correa's three: it was wrecked off Pangani.

The Portuguese Conquest

of Mozambique, and at Mombasa, Kilwa's ally,[1] whither news of the strangers and their intentions had arrived ahead of them, there was the same uneasy tension. At Malindi, on the other hand, bitter rival of Mombasa and always ready to treat her enemies as friends, there was no sign of suspicion or hostility, and after long and amicable intercourse da Gama and the 'King' entered on a pact of peace and friendship. It was to serve Malindi well in days to come: but her friendliness was no more due to any fears of the future than was the antagonism of her sister-colonies. Lords of their own seas and the trade thereof, the Arabs of East Africa never imagined that those few ships from Europe, well armed though they were, portended any serious danger to their monopoly and the wealth and power it had so long assured them.

They were soon to learn. Da Gama's reconnaissance was quickly followed by a general assault. Francisco d'Almeida and Affonso d'Albuquerque, who were in charge of it, were both great men. Of the two Almeida was the more cautious and perhaps, in the light of after-history, the wiser statesman, content to hold command of the sea, averse to spending the limited strength of Portugal on territorial dominion, while Albuquerque, more sanguine and ambitious, was bent on creating an empire of the East. Footholds on dry land, trading-posts and forts and garrisons, seemed to him no less essential than sea-power, and not in India only. He was convinced, like other empire-builders after him, that the approaches to India, the routes to Europe and the Far East, ought also to be safeguarded; and, as he scanned the map, he fixed on three places outside India itself as the 'principal keys' to the eastern world and its wealth—Malacca, Aden, and Hormuz, commanding the gateways to the Spice Islands, the Red Sea, and the Persian Gulf. There remained the sea-route to Europe by East Africa along which lay no such narrow entrances and exits or such

---

[1] According to a contemporary Portuguese account the 'King' of Mombasa at the time of da Gama's first voyage was married to the daughter of the 'King' of Kilwa. Correa, 95, note 1. See p. 27, above.

commanding key-points. The reduction of the whole of that coast, therefore, and the appropriation of its trade were an essential part of the Portuguese plan.

It was quickly and effectively carried out. On his second voyage to India in 1502 da Gama touched at Kilwa, and under threat of burning the town compelled the Sultan to acknowledge the supremacy of the King of Portugal and to pay him an annual tribute of 1,500 metikals of gold (about £900). Zanzibar came next. The green island—its harbour full of dhows engaged in the coastal trade, its gardens and orchards thick with vegetables and oranges—had favourably impressed the Portuguese when da Gama put in there on his first return voyage from India. In 1503 Ruy Lourenço Ravasco, after some sharp fighting on the beach, obtained the submission of the Arab townsmen and levied an annual tribute of 100 metikals of gold (about £60). The next attack was part of a comprehensive plan for establishing Portuguese supremacy on all the coasts of the Indian ocean. In 1505 a fleet of over twenty ships with 1,500 men aboard left Lisbon with Almeida in command under orders to plant military settlements at some six commercial and strategic points on a great arc from South-East Africa to South-West India. For the African sector there were three objectives. The first, the occupation of Sofala, the immediate key to the gold-supply, was quickly achieved by a subsidiary force under Petro d'Anaya. Torn by the usual factions, the local Arabs made no open resistance to the invaders, and by the end of the year a Portuguese colony had been founded and a fort built and garrisoned. Meantime Almeida had made for the second objective, Kilwa, once Sofala's overlord and master of the gold trade. The 'King', aware that for two years past the tribute promised to da Gama had not been paid, evaded a meeting with Almeida and fled inland. When the Portuguese landed, most of his subjects followed his example, leaving the ancient city to be occupied and looted without a fight. A massive fort was built at the edge of the sea, and 150 Portuguese officials and soldiers were stationed in it. Almeida then sailed north to his third objective, Mombasa. No settlement was intended there

The Portuguese Conquest

at this time; but, if the colony at Kilwa was to prosper, if a monopoly of East African trade was to be acquired, then the power of Mombasa—a greater town now than Kilwa, inheritor of Kilwa's dominion north of the Pangani River, boasting a population of 10,000 to Kilwa's 4,000[1]—must be subordinated to Portuguese policy or broken up. Neither task was to prove easy, and, when Almeida sent one of his ships to take soundings at the entrance to the harbour, the cannon-ball from a shore-battery which pierced its hull was the forerunner of many challenges to come. An envoy, offering friendship and protection if the ruler of Mombasa would become the tributary vassal of the Portuguese Crown, was greeted with defiant cries and not allowed to land. And when Almeida attacked in force, the Arab and Swahili townsmen, backed by 1,500 African bowmen from the mainland, fought long and fiercely in the narrow streets. In the end they were driven out with heavy loss; and for the rest of that day and most of the next the town was given up to looting. A vast store of booty was collected—gold, silver, ivory, amber, not to mention cattle and provisions—so vast that some of it was left behind because there was no room for it in the ships. Eight hundred, similarly, of the thousand prisoners, mostly women and children, were set free. Finally the town was set on fire at several points and, a strong wind aiding, was thoroughly burnt out. When the Portuguese had gone and the people of Mombasa crept back to their gutted and blackened town, they found, wrote the Sheikh to his fellow ruler at Malindi, 'no living thing in it, neither man nor woman, young or old, nor child, however little: all who failed to make their escape had been killed and burnt'.[2]

'Be on your guard', the letter ended: but Malindi hated Mombasa more than she feared the Portuguese; and, as Almeida passed on his way to execute the rest of his commission in India and to assume the Viceroyalty of the East,[3] he rewarded the

---

[1] Strandes, 91–2.   [2] Translation in Strandes, 73–4.
[3] Almeida was killed in a skirmish with Hottentots near Table Bay in 1510, and was succeeded in control of the Portuguese Indies by Albuquerque.

loyalty of Portugal's only friend in East Africa by the gift of a share in the plunder from Mombasa.

In 1506 another fleet of fourteen ships was sent out to East Africa under Tristão da Cunha and Albuquerque. Starting from Mozambique they first reconnoitred the west coast of Madagascar. They found the customary little Arab colonies there, trading with Kilwa, Mombasa and Malindi; but, disappointed, it seems, at their lack of precious metals, they left them alone and sailed on to Kilwa and Malindi. Three coast-towns in the northern area were then dealt with—Lamu, Oja, and Barawa. Lamu at once submitted and agreed to pay a tribute of 600 metikals (about £360). Oja, at the mouth of the Ozi river, refused allegiance to any one but the Caliph in Egypt, and was stormed, sacked, and burnt. Barawa likewise was defiant, parading an army of 6,000 African spearmen and bowmen from the warlike tribes of that Somali coast; and so stubborn was their resistance that over forty Portuguese were killed and over sixty wounded before the town was won. The invaders left it, like Mombasa, a stripped and smouldering ruin.

They made next for Mogadishu, reputed to be one of the richest and strongest towns on all the coast. The beach, as they anchored, was thronged with soldiers, many of them horsemen; and their envoy, a prisoner from Barawa, was cut to pieces as soon as he landed. Had time permitted, Mogadishu would doubtless have suffered the fate of Barawa; but the sailing-season was near its end, and the Portuguese pressed on to the island of Socotra, where, after overcoming the desperate resistance of its colony of Arabs from the South Arabian mainland, they built and garrisoned a fort with a view to creating a permanent base for naval operations in the Red Sea. The island, however, proved too barren even to support the garrison, and in a few years' time it was withdrawn and the fort demolished.

One step remained to complete the Portuguese design. In 1507 Mozambique, which had been regularly used as a port-of-call by shipping bound for and from India, was 'colonized'. A fort, a hospital, a church, and quarters for the garrison and

The Portuguese Conquest 47

official staff were built. The settlement was meant at the outset to be dependent on Sofala; but it soon took the lead in population and in volume of trade, and the rapid decline of Kilwa made it the most important town on the coast. After 1550 Mozambique became what it remains to-day, the head-quarters of Portuguese administration in East Africa.

The conquest of East Africa was thus achieved in less than ten years from its discovery. By 1509, when a separate Governor-General was appointed for the Portuguese possessions in Africa and Arabia, the work of subjection and occupation was complete. Except Malindi, which enjoyed a privileged status as an independent ally, all the chief Arab colonies on the coast from Barawa to Sofala, together with the islands of Zanzibar, Pemba, and Mafia, had either accepted tributary vassaldom to the Portuguese crown or were so broken in power and wealth as to be unable to resist the same subjection whenever the Portuguese should choose to impose it. Apart from Mogadishu, only Madagascar and the neighbouring island-groups to west and east, the Comoros and the Mascarenes, had escaped conquest: they had been looked at, but left alone.

Meanwhile the Portuguese had been similarly engaged on the Arabian and Persian coast. Muscat had been sacked and Hormuz occupied. Any doubt as to who were the masters of the Indian Ocean was finally set at rest by the destruction of a great Moslem fleet of Egyptian, Arab, and Persian ships at the battle of Diu in 1509. Only Aden defied attack. The rest of the great design, including an outpost at Malacca, had been achieved when in 1515 Albuquerque died at Goa, the central point of his imperial system. 'I leave the chief place in India in Your Majesty's power,' ran his last letter to his sovereign, 'the only thing left to be done being the closing of the gates of the Straits.'[1]

2

Thus, in a few short years, the whole of the long-established Arab control of the coasts and waters of the Indian Ocean

[1] Wilson, op. cit. 121.

passed into European hands. The Arabs had fought, of course, and often fiercely; but the soldiers and sailors of Portugal's heroic age had been more than a match for them. Nor, when the issue had been decided, was any concession granted to the vanquished. The Portuguese in the East, it has often been remarked, were relentlessly aggressive and exclusive: and in East Africa as elsewhere there was no question of peace or co-operation with other occupants of the field. They meant to obtain for themselves as much of the trade of the Indian Ocean as their superior force could secure. On sea they maintained a rigid monopoly. From the earliest phase of their conquest Arab ships were attacked as a matter of course and driven from their own waters. The ancient Arab connexion with India was severed. Even the coastal shipping had to steal furtively from creek to creek. And on land commercial intercourse with the inland tribes was restricted and in certain areas forbidden. Gold, for example, was to be bought by the Government direct from the natives and not through Arab or Swahili middlemen.

The effect of this ruthless policy on the Arab colonies was inevitably ruinous. The roots of their old prosperity had been cut, and they entered on a period of withering decline. But the process was unequal. The three official Portuguese settlements —Kilwa, Mozambique, Sofala—with their forts, garrisons, and gunboats were all on the southern section of the coast. Northward of them little groups of Portuguese colonists established themselves at various points, in Zanzibar and Pemba and as far away as Pate; but these were, so to speak, unofficial colonies, unfortified and ungarrisoned, and along that northern section Portuguese authority in government or trade was not effectively or consistently enforced. Not only Malindi but subject towns like Mombasa, Zanzibar, or Lamu were allowed to keep their own sultans or sheikhs and their own forms of local government. The only regular intrusion of Portuguese authority was the exaction of the annual tribute. In trade, similarly, the northern towns were freer than the southern. Portuguese patrols might make the sea-routes dangerous, but land restrictions could not be enforced without Portuguese soldiers on the spot. Thus, though all the Arab colonies were far poorer and weaker than they once had been, some of those in the north retained at least a semblance of their former selves. It was their sister-towns in the south that felt the full weight of the conquest. There lay the field of systematic Portuguese occupation, of direct Portuguese rule. There the Portuguese monopoly of trade could be rigidly enforced. And for the Arabs and Indians the result was devastating. Deprived of their livelihood, many of them 'closed down' and sought a new life in Madagascar or the freer north. At Kilwa the population fell so fast that the prohibition of inland trade was for a time suspended, when at once the exiled business-men began returning to their old homes. But orders soon came from Lisbon for the strict maintenance of the monopoly; again the population dwindled; and, when in 1509 the Portuguese fort was abandoned and its garrison removed to Mozambique, the town had already sunk beyond hope of recovery. Historic Kilwa's history was ended. She will figure again in this book. She was to become a great centre for the sale and export of slaves. Her natural advantages, her harbour, her connexion with the interior were to attract, more than once, the acquisitive attention of European strategists and merchants. But she never again played a leading part in the Arab politics of East Africa. And if Sofala and Mozambique fared better, particularly the latter, it was not as the Arab colonies they once had been. They were Portuguese colonies now; and their Arab population, kept in rigorous subjection and denied their old commercial opportunities, wilted away. It may be said, in fact, that the Arab character which its first colonizers had given to this southern part of the coast was virtually deleted by the Portuguese conquest. It became the Portuguese East Africa we know to-day.

But the change was little more than a change of dominion. The Portuguese had taken the place of the Arabs as middlemen-traders, importing calico and beads from India and exchanging them for gold and ivory and presently for slaves, and that was all. The main difference was that the new-comers were less successful at the business. Whereas the Arabs had not traded only in their sea-towns but had sent out caravans to buy and sell far and wide in the interior, the Portuguese neither employed the Arabs to do this itinerant trading on their behalf nor attempted it themselves. They seem to have imagined that, if they kept up a supply of Indian goods in their warehouses at Sofala and Mozambique, the Africans would come crowding to their doors with gold and ivory for sale. But this did not happen. It was officially estimated that before the conquest the annual export of gold from Sofala had exceeded one million metikals (about £600,000). No doubt this was an exaggerated figure, but the output in the early years of Portuguese control was the merest fraction of it. For a period of eight months in 1513, for instance, it was only between six and seven thousand metikals (about £4,000), of which less than one-twelfth had been obtained from African traders from the interior.[1]

It was the disappointment felt at Lisbon at the meagre yield of the new African 'Eldorado' that prompted the only efforts made to penetrate inland. At Sena, about 100 miles up the Zambesi, the site (as has been noticed) of a little Arab colony, a trading-post was established in 1531, and another at Tete, higher up the river, a few years later. This advance towards the Manika goldfield substantially increased the amount of gold obtained, and it was followed by a bold attempt to reach the field itself. But Francisco Barreto's ascent of the Zambesi Valley with a force of 1,000 men in 1572 ended in disaster. His troops were decimated by fever, and, when he himself succumbed to it, his only achievements, if so they can be termed, had been an easy victory over a local Bantu tribe and the destruction of the Arab colony at Sena.[2] Barreto's successor, Homem, was only a little more successful. He did reach

[1] Strandes, 99-100. Theal, 284-6. A century later the annual output had risen as high as 200,000 metikals (about £120,000). For the valuation in sterling, see Strandes, 47, and Theal, 259, note.

[2] Informed by a Swahili resident of a plot to poison a well, Barreto ordered a sudden attack on the Arab settlement. All the Arabs and Swahili were killed except the informer and 17 prisoners. The latter were put to death, some with torture. Theal, 321-4.

Manika, by way of the Revue, and made an agreement with a tribe of the locality, the Tshikanga, to permit the entry of Portuguese traders or their agents in return for an annual gift of cloth, but he could do no more. A permanent occupation of the interior was impracticable and never contemplated.

The exploration, similarly, of Delagoa Bay in 1544 was not followed up. No settlement, no 'factory', was established here, nor any attempt made to open up another route to the goldfields. The Portuguese occupation of East Africa in fact extended very little farther than the Arab occupation. The Portuguese conquest was only a conquest of the Arab colonies. Like the Arabs, the Portuguese absorbed the local Africans of the coast as a lower caste of their colonial society. Since Portuguese women rarely emigrated, there was a similar, perhaps more frequent, mingling of blood; and a similar half-breed population rapidly grew up. But the tribes of the interior remained just as little affected by the coming of the Portuguese as they had been by the coming of the Arabs. The new invaders left them undisturbed and independent. Only their trade was wanted, and the pursuit of that was permitted readily enough by the leading chiefs in return for regular gifts of cloth and beads and bangles. There were quarrels, of course, at times, and occasionally fighting. The fort at Sofala was unsuccessfully attacked in 1506. A small Portuguese force was cut up near Mozambique about 1580. But peaceful, if not friendly, relations seem to have been the rule, mainly, no doubt, because there was so little contact. Portuguese explorers or prospectors did not venture far inland. No organized attempt was made to penetrate the continent till the end of the eighteenth century. Only, indeed, in the cause of their faith were the Portuguese more enterprising than the Arabs. The first Christian mission to the people of East Africa was undertaken by the Jesuits in 1560. They made their way to the court of the paramount chief of the Makalanga inland beyond Manika, but in 1561 their leader, Gonzalo da Silveira, was murdered, and in 1562 the mission was abandoned. The Dominicans followed, planting stations on the coast and up the Zambesi Valley. But with all their patience and courage—and there were Dominican as well as Jesuit martyrs—the missionaries made scarcely more impression on East Africa than the soldiers and the merchants.

Thus the Portuguese invasion of East Africa, though the time of it was Portugal's golden age, had little positive results, political or economic. Its chief historical importance lies in the bare fact that it gave the Portuguese a hold upon a section of the coast which they have never since lost. Of the rest of Albuquerque's empire, all or almost all was soon to pass into other hands. The decline of Portugal after its annexation by Philip II of Spain in 1580 coincided with the invasion of the East by rival European peoples along the sea-way Portugal had opened; and in the course of the next century the Portuguese were robbed of all their eastern realm except one or two ports in the Indies and that fever-ridden stretch of African coastland between Cape Delgado and Delagoa Bay.

3

The first French ship rounded the Cape of Good Hope in 1529, forty-three years later than Diaz; the first English ship in 1580, homeward bound on Drake's world-voyage; the first Dutch ship in 1595. French overseas enterprise was engaged for a time elsewhere, but the Dutch and the English, like the Portuguese before them, proceeded from discovery to reconnaissance and from reconnaissance to organized attack. Covilhão's work was done again and far more thoroughly by Linschoten, and the publication of his survey of Eastern lands and seas in 1596 was followed by a series of small Dutch expeditions and in 1602 by the foundation of the Dutch East India Company. Englishmen, similarly, like Stephens and Fitch, revealed to London merchants the golden prospects of eastern trade: in 1591 Lancaster, with 'three tall ships', was sent to India by da Gama's East African route: and in 1600 the English East India Company was founded. Thereafter, both from England and from the Netherlands, armed trading-fleets were regularly sailing east and spreading out over the whole com-

The Portuguese Conquest

mercial sphere from the Red Sea to the Philippines. Under this double impact the Portuguese collapsed. One or two important footholds, such as Goa and Malacca, they retained; but they were driven from Hormuz by the Persians with English aid in 1622, and by 1650 they had ceased to be serious competitors in any field of eastern trade. The only real rivals thenceforward were the Dutch and the English and presently the French, and for a century a long three-sided contest for supremacy went on. At first the Dutch had easily headed the English in all areas. They had planted colonial settlements at Mauritius[1] in 1644 and at Table Bay in 1652; they had finally wrested Ceylon from the Portuguese in 1658; and by the end of the century their 'factories' and forts were dotted all over the East—in the Persian Gulf, on the coasts of India, in the Malayan archipelago. But by 1750 they were withdrawing from the Gulf and from most of their positions in India in order to concentrate their resources on their virtual monopoly of the East Indies. They retained Ceylon and their colony at the Cape, but over the centre of the field—continental India and its approaches by the 'overland' route—the French and the British became in the second half of the eighteenth century the principal claimants to the heritage of the Portuguese.

Late-comers—their East India Company was not founded till 1664—the French entered the field mainly by the sea-route. Bourbon, an island outpost in the Indian Ocean, was occupied in 1642. From 1665 onwards repeated but ineffective efforts were made to colonize Madagascar. Mauritius, which had been abandoned by the Dutch in 1712, was reoccupied and renamed 'Île de France' in 1715. Meantime, centres for the Indian trade had been established southwards at Pondicherry in 1674 and northwards at Chandanagore in 1676. But it was not till the middle of the eighteenth century that the French interested themselves closely in the approach by the land-route. In 1755 a French residency was established at Basra and in 1765 a consulate. The English, on the other hand, who

[1] Mauritius was first visited by a Dutch ship in 1598 and named after the Stadtholder, Maurice of Nassau.

were likewise established on Indian soil at Surat (1612), Bombay (1665), Madras (1639), and Calcutta (1650), had no outposts at all on the sea-route in 1750; their attempt to plant a settlement at St. Augustine Bay in Madagascar in 1645 had tragically failed; but, after a long contest with the Dutch, they had secured a firm hold on the trade of the Persian Gulf with head-quarters at Basra and Bushire. Of the next sixty-five years, only seventeen were years of peace. Of the three Franco-British wars, the first two, the Seven Years War and the War of American Independence, left the British, thanks to Clive and Warren Hastings, the paramount European Power on Indian soil; the third, the Revolutionary and Napoleonic War, was the most protracted and at times the most evenly contested, but it was also in the end the most decisive, and nowhere more so than in the Indian Ocean. After 1815 the British were masters of its waters and able, when and where they chose, to dominate its coasts.

The East African seaboard (it will have been observed) figures scarcely at all in this story of European rivalry in the Indian Ocean. There, and there only, the new-comers, racing for the East, left the 'Portingales' in possession. Why? It was not because they knew nothing about it. Linschoten gave a fairly full description of the coast—the fine harbour at Mozambique, frequented by the Portuguese ships in the Indian trade, its richness and abundance 'in all kinds of things'; Sofala with its fort, 'where the rich mine of gold lyeth'; Kilwa, Mombasa, Malindi, Barawa, and the rest; the Portuguese export-trade to India, 'gold, ambergris, ebon wood and ivory, and many slaves, both men and women, which are carried thither because they are the strongest in all the East countries to do their filthiest and hardest labour wherein they only use them'.[1] And Lancaster, like Linschoten before him, put in at several points along the coast to obtain sweet water, fresh meat, and oranges and lemons. At one of the Comoro Islands, apparently Great Comoro, he entertained the 'king' together with other

[1] Linschoten's *Voyage*, i. 24–33.

The Portuguese Conquest

members of the 'Moorish' colony on board the *Edward Bonaventure*, and 'had some conference with him of the state of the place and merchandises'; but, though they seemed friendly and at first allowed water to be taken from the shore, they finally set upon Mr. Mace, the master, and thirty seamen and murdered them. 'They be very treacherous', Lancaster quietly observes, 'and diligently to be taken heed of.' At Zanzibar he lay at anchor for three months awaiting the change of wind to carry him to India. He found a small Portuguese 'factory' established there, but no officials or garrison. Already, it seems, the Portuguese had taken alarm at English penetration of the Indian Ocean; for the local 'Moors' told Lancaster of 'the false and spiteful dealings of the Portugals towards us which made them believe that we were cruel people and man-eaters, and willed them if they loved their safety in no case to come near us'. The death of the ship's surgeon, Arnold, 'negligently catching a great heat in the head, being on land with the master to seek oxen', does not seem to have suggested to Lancaster that the island was as peculiarly unhealthy as English visitors of a later day supposed. Indeed, he gave Zanzibar a very good character. 'This place', he wrote, 'for the goodness of the harbour and watering and plentiful refreshing with fish, whereof we took great store with our nets, and for sundry sorts of fruits of the country as cocos and others which were brought us by the Moors, as also for oxen and hens, is carefully to be sought for by such of our ships as shall hereafter pass that way.' Pass, not stop; the idea of developing any trade with Zanzibar did not occur to Lancaster—except for 'some thousand weight of a kind of grey and white gum', presumably gum-copal, Lancaster found nothing worth taking aboard.[1] In 1608, again, Captain Sharpeigh in the *Ascension* saw something of the East African coast or at least of the islands off it. Following Lancaster's route to India, he touched at Comoro, finding 'the natives faithful and courteous', but getting no water. For some unstated reason he did not call at Zanzibar, but went on for the

[1] *Voyages of Sir James Lancaster to the East Indies* (Hakluyt Society, London, 1877), 6–8, 26.

water he needed to Pemba. 'At first', he records, 'the people seemed friendly, but afterwards they made a treacherous attack on a party engaged in filling the water-casks when one man was killed, another wounded, and a third was missing.'[1]

Thus both the Dutch and the English and in due course the French became acquainted with the coast—they were all of them bound, indeed, to break their long Indian voyage there— yet it was only the Dutch who attempted there as elsewhere to oust the Portuguese and take their place. In 1604 they made a vigorous attack on Mozambique. They repeated it in 1607 and again in 1608. Each time they were repelled by the strength of the fortifications and the obstinate resistance of the garrison; and thereafter they contented themselves with their port of call at Table Bay. The French, for their part, concentrated on the Mascarene islands and shunned the mainland. The English touched and took in water and passed on, seeking no permanent foothold, until, at the end of the contest, the best of the outposts their rivals had established—Table Bay, Mauritius, Ceylon—fell into their hands.

The reason for this neglect of the coast was almost certainly its bad hygienic reputation. Nearly all the early travellers speak of the heat and unwholesomeness of Mozambique and its neighbourhood. All of them lost several members of their crews, at one point on the coast or another, from 'flux' or fever. It was only the lure of 'Sofala gold', no doubt, that tempted the shrewd Dutch to make those costly and repeated attacks. And indeed the successors of the Portuguese were wise not to follow their example in that particular field. Its occupation, still more its permanent settlement or colonization, would have drained their strength without giving them any reward comparable with what they could and did win in other fields. There was not enough to be made from the gold and ivory and ambergris or even, in those days, from the Slave Trade. The economic exploitation of the East African coast at a substantial profit has proved difficult enough with the aid of modern science.

[1] Two accounts of this voyage in the India Office archives are printed in *Lancaster's Voyages*, 120–30.

In the seventeenth and eighteenth and early nineteenth centuries it was impossible.

4

If the stronger European nations had not left East Africa alone, if they had expelled the Portuguese and taken their place, the status of the Arab colonies, though they might have received more liberal treatment, would not have been radically changed. As it was, the old masters of the coast were given a chance of coming back into their own. In the northward towns, remote from the centre of the Portuguese administration at Mozambique, unfettered by resident officials or permanent garrisons, each, as Linschoten observed in 1583, 'a kingdom in itself', the Arab oligarchies, high-spirited, mindful of their past, fiercely hating the Portuguese and their restrictions and exactions, had never despaired of winning their freedom. For some eighty years, indeed, they bowed to a tyranny they dared not try to break. Only Mombasa gave trouble in the earlier years. The lesson taught its inhabitants in 1505 was soon forgotten. Their houses rebuilt, their courage and pride restored, they made no pretence of submissiveness to Portuguese authority. When Nuno da Cunha anchored in their harbour in 1522, he was forbidden to send his men ashore except for the purchase of provisions. In 1528, therefore, prompted and assisted by Malindi, Zanzibar, and Pemba, the Portuguese once more attacked Mombasa. This time the defence was less desperate, and the Sheikh agreed to accept the King of Portugal as overlord and pay him a tribute of 500 metikals of gold (about £300). But such promises, it seemed, were of little result without a garrison to see that they were kept; and, since troops could not be spared for that, it was decided to destroy the town again. So again, and even more thoroughly than before, Mombasa was burnt out. But again, as soon as the Portuguese had gone, its rebuilding was begun; and, though this second lesson had left a deeper mark, though for half a century Mombasa gave no trouble, yet neither there nor elsewhere along the coast, except perhaps at Malindi, was Portuguese dominion, however imperfectly enforced, less hated as time went on, nor the old independence forgotten, so that, almost as a matter of course, with the beginning of the decline in Portuguese power and prestige began a series of Arab revolts.[1]

The first of them was aided and abetted by the arrival of an unexpected ally from the north. From 1580 onwards the Portuguese had been troubled by Turkish corsairs in the Red Sea and the Persian Gulf; and in 1585 one of the more adventurous Turkish commanders, Mirale Bey, came cruising down the African coast on the chance of picking up a prize. He had only a single galley with about eighty men aboard, but he told the Arabs that he had been commissioned by the Sultan of Turkey to free them from the Portuguese yoke, and that a great Turkish fleet was following in his track. At town after town he was welcomed with enthusiasm. Mogadishu, Barawa, Kismayu, Faza, Pate, Lamu, and Kilifi all readily exchanged the overlordship of Christian Philip II for that of Moslem Murad III. Mombasa naturally was in the forefront. Her Sheikh not only accepted the new yoke, but wrote to the Sultan asking him to build a fortress at Mombasa and man it with a permanent Turkish garrison. How far Mirale penetrated southwards is not known, but that he attacked and looted some of the Portuguese settlements may be inferred from the recorded fact that in the spring of 1586 he sailed back to the Red Sea with fifty Portuguese prisoners and a store of plunder worth over £50,000.[2]

It was more a triumph for the Turk than for his Arab friends, whom he had tempted to give rein too soon to their hatred of Portuguese rule. It was not the Sultan's armada but a Portuguese force of 18 ships and 650 men, summoned from Goa by loyal Malindi, that appeared on the coast at the beginning of 1587. But the punishment it inflicted was relatively light. Mogadishu, which owing, no doubt, to the strength of its walls and the warlike reputation of its people had never been subjected by the Portuguese, was left alone. Mombasa for once made no resistance, and the Portuguese, as might have been expected, found little left to plunder in the evacuated

---

[1] Strandes, 117–23.   [2] Idem, 144–6.

The Portuguese Conquest

town. The Sheikhs of Pate and Lamu escaped the penalties of rebellion, the one by pleading that it had been forced on him, the other by running away. It was only on Faza that the weight of Portuguese vengeance fell. The town was sacked and fired; the Sheikh and several hundred of the inhabitants, men, women and children, were massacred; the shipping in the harbour was burnt, and all the plantations destroyed.[1]

At the end of the next year (1588) Mirale Bey came south again. The Portuguese demonstration had not deterred the Arab colonies from sending messages to his base in the Red Sea, begging him to fulfil his promise to deliver the coast from the Christian yoke and offering contributions to the cost of the expedition; and when he appeared, with a squadron this time of five ships, his reception was as cordial as before. From Mogadishu southwards every town he touched at acclaimed him as its saviour, except, of course, Malindi, where shots were fired at his anchored ships at night. At Mombasa he landed and entrenched his troops at the harbour-mouth and began to prepare for an attack in alliance with Mombasa on Malindi. Had he sailed farther south, he would have been no less eagerly welcomed. As it was, the people of Pemba, encouraged by his appearance off the coast, rose one night in revolt, drove out their pro-Portuguese ruler, and massacred most of the Portuguese then living on the island.[2]

Meanwhile the news of Mirale's second raid had reached Goa from Malindi, and a strong force of 20 ships and 900 men had been hastily assembled and dispatched. Calling at Barawa, Lamu, and Malindi, where the King and the Portuguese commandant joined it with two ships, the fleet reached Mombasa early in March 1589. A prompt assault was completely successful. The Turkish entrenchments were easily stormed and their defenders driven into the town. The Turkish ships were attacked inside the harbour and as easily captured. On March 7 the town itself was looted and burnt, and its walls breached. The inhabitants, Arabs, Turks and Swahili, fled to the centre

[1] Idem, 147.   [2] Idem, 151-2, 155.

of the island. What happened to them there was not the doing, at any rate directly, of the Portuguese.[1]

About twenty years before the events just recorded, the Zimba, a militant Bantu tribe, akin to the Zulus in race and culture, had broken northwards from their home in the neighbourhood of modern Zululand. Arriving in due course at the Zambesi, one horde of them swept up the valley and overwhelmed the Portuguese and Arab colonies at Sena and Tete. Another horde turned seawards, and in 1585 it began moving up the coast, laying waste the country-side and killing and (it is said) eating its inhabitants. Mozambique itself would have been attacked, no doubt, if it had not lain secure on its chosen island-site; as it was, the city was brought near to famine through the destruction wrought on the food-crops along the seaboard. It was just at this time that the northern Arab towns were rising to the call of Mirale Bey; and the presence of the Zimba in the south may account for the failure of the Portuguese Government at Mozambique to take action against him. But the savages did not settle in the south. They moved slowly, very slowly, northwards. In 1587 they reached Kilwa, and since the narrows there were not enough protection, they stormed it and slaughtered some three thousand of its diminished population. Resuming their slow advance, they appeared, two years later, before Mombasa. They found its natural strength enhanced by the presence of Mirale Bey. Turks as well as Arabs manned its walls. Turkish ships forbade the crossing of the encircling water. So they sat down, several thousand strong, to besiege the place from the mainland; and presently they observed the arrival of the Portuguese, the destruction of the Turkish ships, and the capture of the town. Burning to take a hand in the fighting they begged the Portuguese commander to be permitted to cross to the island; and after a week's delay the permission was granted. The sequel is the ghastliest incident in all the grim history of Mombasa. The Zimba combed out the island with their spears. For the

[1] Strandes, 152–4.

wretched townsfolk and their demoralized Turkish friends the only refuge was the sea. Many were drowned. Over two hundred were rescued by the Portuguese ships—among them Mirale Bey, who was taken in chains to Lisbon.[1]

Soon after this the destructive course of the Zimba was stayed at last. When, still moving northward, they reached Malindi and tried to storm the walls, they were caught in rear by some 3,000 warriors of the Segeju, a warlike tribe from up-country, and driven off with heavy loss. Of the sequel no record has survived; but apparently, after the check at Malindi, this African invasion of East Africa ebbed away and lost itself in the interior.[2]

Mombasa was not the only sufferer from the Portuguese punitive expedition. The old suzerainty was forcibly restored in Pemba. Pate and Siu were heavily fined. Manda was laid in ruins and its palm-groves cut down. The King of Lamu, a brother of the King of Kilifi, and two townsmen of Pate who had rashly gone to the Red Sea to invite Mirale's aid, were beheaded. In 1589 the squadron returned to Portugal. It had done its work; for the moment the Arab coast-towns were cowed and submissive; but the lesson of Mirale Bey's successes, short-lived though they had been, was not overlooked at Lisbon. Portuguese dominion over the coast as exercised from Mozambique was clearly not strong enough; if the Turks should attack again, their advance must be blocked farther north; so in 1591 it was decided to create a new centre of government at Mombasa. In 1593, with labour from Malindi and masons from India, the building of a strong citadel, to be called 'Fort Jesus', was begun on the crest of the low cliff beside the entrance to the harbour. In due course a Portuguese garrison of 100 men was installed there, and at its head a commandant and staff with authority over all the coast from Barawa to Cape Delgado. Nor was the new Mombasa to be only a military and administra-

[1] Strandes (153–5), who points out that compassion for an enemy was not to be expected in those days. Another tradition maintains that the Zimba were invited by Mombasa to help in the defence against the Portuguese, and then turned on their hosts. Theal, 352–8.
[2] Strandes, 158.

tive post: it was to be like Mozambique a Portuguese colony; and orders were sent from Lisbon to encourage settlement and cultivation on the island. There was some response. A few plantations were started with slave-labour. But most of the fifty Portuguese colonists to be found at Mombasa in 1615, living side by side with 'banian' merchants in one long street under the shadow of the fort, were traders, not farmers. There were similar developments elsewhere. By 1635 there was a strong body of Portuguese residents at Zanzibar—which, though in close commercial contact with Mozambique, was no longer tributary to Portugal—and there were some thirty at Pate. And, while the Dominicans and Jesuits were active in and about Mozambique, the Augustines had settled and built churches at Mombasa within the walls of the fort, at Zanzibar, and at Faza. In trade, too, there was more Portuguese activity north of Cape Delgado. There was a steady interchange, mostly in foodstuffs, between Mombasa, Pate, and its neighbours, Pemba and Zanzibar, the latter islands also supplying Mozambique; and, while there was no direct trade with Portugal, gum-copal, ivory, and slaves were regularly exported to India in return for Indian cloth. The reaction, in fact, from the Turkish attack had made the Portuguese position on the northward coast, both politically and economically, stronger than it had ever been. In earlier days it had rested mainly on the unbroken loyalty of Malindi. Its basis now was the new Mombasa with its new Fort Jesus. Malindi, indeed, was quite overshadowed. Its Portuguese garrison had been transferred to Mombasa; the Portuguese traders had quickly followed; and at last, uneasy at losing touch with his powerful friends and exposed to attacks from the Segeju, the King of Malindi himself, Hasan-bin-Ahmed, removed to Mombasa whence he governed his old 'kingdom' from a distance. As a reward for his fidelity the Sultanate of Mombasa was taken from the local Arab family in which it had long been hereditary and conferred on him, together with the gift of an estate and one-third of the customs revenue.[1]

[1] Strandes, 159, 163, 171–4, 187.

The Portuguese Conquest 63

As chance would have it, in this conjunction of Malindi with Mombasa lay the seed of trouble which, in less than a generation, was to overshadow the new Portuguese régime. Wise officials would have maintained as friendly relations with their brother-in-arms at Mombasa as at Malindi. But a breach was opened by one arrogant and grasping commandant, and widened by another. The quarrel persisted, and at last, in 1614, Sultan Hasan was invited to Goà to state his case to the Viceroy. There is no reason to suppose that justice would not have been done by the higher authority; but Hasan, now thoroughly mistrustful of his old friends, believed that, if he went to Goa, he would never return. He fled to the mainland, where he was murdered at Rabai by the Nyika for a bribe of 2,000 pieces of cloth from the Portuguese. This unsavoury incident was taken seriously at Lisbon. An inquiry exonerated Hasan of disloyalty to Portugal, and orders were issued that Hasan's son, Yusuf, then a boy of seven, should be taken to Goa and there educated for the succession to his father's throne, which would be occupied in the meantime by one of his older kinsmen as regent. The plan was carried out. In 1630 Yusuf was duly installed at Mombasa, an educated young man now, well grounded in the Christian faith by the Augustines of Goa, and known by the civilized name of Dom Jeronimo Chingulia. But the sequel was not what the Portuguese had hoped. Back at Mombasa, at home among his own folk, Yusuf soon began to shed the unnatural character imposed on him at Goa. His very familiarity with the Portuguese, his very knowledge of their language and culture, made him feel more bitterly the subjection of his people and, despite the trappings of the sultanate, of himself to their yoke. Islam, too, regained its hold. Faith in Christ gave place to fear of the Inquisition. And on a mind thus unsettled and excited preyed the memory of his father and the thought that his murder had gone all those years unpunished. The outcome was a desperate act of revenge and liberation. On a feast day in August 1631, in the midst of the festivities, Yusuf gave the signal for revolt by responding to the commandant's friendly greeting with a sudden dagger-thrust.

His followers threw themselves on the company, and in a short space of time every Portuguese man, woman, and child in Mombasa, excepting only four priests and one layman who escaped to Pate, were dead. Yusuf-bin-Hasan, no longer Dom Jeronimo, took a leading part in the slaughter—it was he who cut down an Augustine priest as he stood at the altar celebrating mass—in the desecration of the church and the destruction of its contents, and in the forcible reconversion or murder of native converts to Christianity.[1]

Messages were promptly dispatched up and down the coast, calling on all the Arab towns to follow the example of Mombasa. But, since there was no such display of force as Mirale Bey had shown, the response this time was feeble. At one or two of the smaller towns, Tanga, for instance, and Mtangata, there were successful risings; but the Portuguese communities at Zanzibar and Pate, the next largest to that at Mombasa, were left unmolested. And at the end of the year a squadron of six ships from Goa appeared off Mombasa, with 600 Portuguese troops on board, charged to exact a terrible payment for Yusuf's crime. Landings were made on the island; but Fort Jesus, in which Yusuf with some 200 Arabs and Swahili and as many more Nyika stood at bay, soon showed, as it was often to show again, that it was virtually impregnable by direct assault. Three months were wasted and then the Portuguese returned discomfited to Goa. But it was, of course, impossible for the Viceroy to acquiesce in this result. A second expedition was quickly fitted out and dispatched to Mombasa, and this time the Portuguese were surprised to find the fort dismantled and the town in ruins. Whether Yusuf felt unable to resist a second attack or whether there was schism among his followers or whether the Nyika were bribed away is uncertain. At any rate, he left Mombasa, and busied himself in stirring up revolt along the coast. He was not altogether unsuccessful. For several years sporadic fighting continued, mostly in the neighbourhood of Pate. But in 1637 Yusuf, whom the Portuguese had tried in vain to capture, died, according to one report at the hands of

[1] Strandes, 184–200.

The Portuguese Conquest

Red Sea pirates, according to another peaceably at Jedda. And in 1639, Francisco Seixas Cabreira, who had been appointed commandant of Mombasa at the age of 27, could boast that Portuguese honour had been vindicated and Portuguese dominion re-established. From Pate to Pemba the Arab towns had been castigated and humbled, while at Mombasa the old Portuguese community had been re-established—settlers transferred from Pate, Faza, and Zanzibar, women shipped across from Goa— and safeguarded by the restoration of Fort Jesus. Over its gateway may still be read to-day the inscription carved there in 1639 by the vigorous young commandant recording how he rebuilt the fort and commanded it for four years, and how he subdued the rebels on that coast, and 'made the kings of Otondo, Manda, Luzira, and Jaca tributary', and 'personally inflicted on Pate and Siu a punishment hitherto unknown in India, even to the razing of their walls', and 'punished the Nyika and chastised Pemba and its rebellious people, putting to death on his own responsibility the rebel kings and all the principal chiefs'.[1]

5

But the energy of individual soldiers could not avail much longer to support the crumbling structure of Portuguese imperialism. The last stage in its gradual displacement from the system of the Indian Ocean was opening. Supplanted on its eastern side by the Dutch and English, the Portuguese were now driven also from its northern side. The Persians had taken Hormuz from them in 1622, and in 1650 the Omani, recovering their old energy and independence under Imam Sultan-bin-Seif, ejected them from Muscat and the whole Arabian seaboard. Only East Africa remained of their empire in the East, and into that last preserve the victorious Omani speedily pursued them. The news of the Portuguese expulsion from Arabia at once relighted the old fires all down the coast; and Mombasa straightway took the lead in an appeal to Sultan-bin-Seif to rescue his fellow Moslems and fellow Arabs as he had rescued his own people from the tyranny they had so long

[1] Idem, 200-18.

endured together. Sultan-bin-Seif did all he could to answer the call. His sea-power was growing fast, and, though he had not ships enough as yet to attack Mombasa, in 1652 he made a raid with a small squadron on the Portuguese settlements at Pate and Zanzibar and wiped them out. It is evidence of anxiety at Lisbon that Francisco Seixas Cabreira had been sent out again to his old post at Mombasa; but all he could do was to punish the Arabs of Zanzibar and Pemba for invoking or assisting the Omani attack. He was not strong enough to meet the Omani themselves, still less to follow them to Muscat; and the response to appeals from Lisbon to Goa for reinforcements and munitions was so meagre as to be almost useless. By 1660 Sultan-bin-Seif had built up an efficient little navy, and in that year, at the invitation of Pate, he descended on the coast, and attacked and captured Faza and Mombasa town, but not Fort Jesus. Finally, in 1669, just before or just after the end of his victorious reign, the Omani pushed their attack right home to Mozambique and, according to one account, nearly succeeded in storming the fort.[1]

A decade later the Portuguese made a last attempt to recover their grip on the coast. The Viceroy himself, Pedro de Almeida, set sail in 1678 from Goa with a strong force and, having established his base at Mozambique, delivered an attack on Pate, which had now taken the place of Mombasa as the most restless and unruly of the Arab towns. Aided by some thousand men from Faza—for the feud between Pate and Faza was now as bitter as that between Mombasa and Malindi had been—Almeida succeeded in reducing Pate by the end of the year. Siu, Lamu, and Manda, which had also attempted to free themselves from Portuguese control, were then quickly brought to heel. The Portuguese had always dealt severely with rebellion, but the ferocity of the punishment now exacted suggests a new consciousness of failing strength. The Arab rulers of all four towns and 200 other men of standing were beheaded. Heavy indemnities were extorted, and a vast amount of loot,

[1] Strandes, 225–31. S. B. Miles, *Countries and Tribes of the Persian Gulf* (London, 1919), 214.

The Portuguese Conquest

especially gold and ivory, was packed into the ships. A stern lesson, but at the last moment it was robbed of most of its moral effect. An Arab squadron arrived from Muscat; and after a few days' brisk fighting the Portuguese were forced to evacuate Pate and hurry away with their booty to Mozambique (January 1679). It is not surprising, therefore, that Pate was soon giving trouble again. In 1686 it rebelled once more, and in the following year it was once more attacked, captured, looted, and fined. This time the 'king', with twelve of his elders, was sent to Goa, where he purchased his return to Pate by signing a promise to expel all Omani from the town and to build two forts for the permanent occupation of a Portuguese garrison. The sequel was as ignominious as before. The Portuguese squadron had barely arrived at Pate with a hundred men and the returning 'king' when five ships with three or four hundred Omani bore down from the north and drove the Portuguese away.[1]

For the last act in the drama of Portuguese decline the scene shifts back to Mombasa. So far the growing superiority of Oman in the Indian Ocean had only shown itself in isolated engagements with the Portuguese. Thus, besides those minor incidents at Pate, the Portuguese colony at Diu was stormed and sacked in 1670 and that at Bassain in 1674. But it was not till nearly the close of the century that a full-scale effort was made to respond to the persistent appeals of the East African coast-towns north of Cape Delgado for a final deliverance from Portuguese rule. That meant the capture of Mombasa; for Mombasa was now as strong a centre of Portuguese power in the north as Mozambique in the south. Early in 1696, accordingly, Imam Seif-bin-Sultan, son of Sultan-bin-Seif, sent out a fleet of seven warships and ten dhows and about 3,000 men to attack Mombasa. Warned of its approach, the inhabitants had stocked Fort Jesus with provisions—there were two springs of water within its walls—and, as soon as the Omani ships drew in and began to bombard the defences on the water-side, the whole population abandoned the town and crowded into the fort, till at last it contained about 2,500 men, women, and

[1] Strandes, 232–40.

children of whom a little more than 50 were Portuguese soldiers, officials, and settlers. On March 13 began the longest siege that Fort Jesus ever endured. Cut off from the rest of the island by the enemy's trenches, their access to the sea confined to a strip of land exposed to the enemy's gunfire, the defenders were soon short of food and of firewood to cook it. Disease and desertion thinned their ranks, and, when in November the Omani general's offer to spare their lives if they would surrender was proudly rejected, the numbers were down to twenty Portuguese and some 1,500 others. A successful sortie was impossible. Their only hope lay in succour from without; but, when at the end of the year a relief expedition of four ships and 770 men arrived from Goa, it succeeded indeed, after some sharp fighting, in getting supplies of food and munitions and about 100 men into the fort, but then, conceiving his duty done, the commanding officer sailed off to Zanzibar and Mozambique. A few months later a terrible and incurable disease, seemingly not unlike bubonic plague, attacked the garrison. Three or four victims died each day. At the end of January 1697 there were only twenty men under arms. In June only the second commandant—the first had died in the previous year—an Augustine priest, and two soldiers survived of all the Portuguese. A little later these too were dead, and the fort was commanded for three weeks by a prince of the ruling house of Faza, loyal as Malindi of old to the Portuguese cause. In September a Portuguese general arrived with a handful of troops from Mozambique and succeeded in entering the fort. In November he also died, a few weeks before a second attempt at relief was made from Goa. It was no more successful than the first; and for yet one more year the tragic siege dragged on. In the middle of December 1698 a third fleet from Goa found the red flag of Oman flying on the fort. It had fallen only a day or two earlier. The besiegers, it appears, had learned at last by accident how incredibly feeble the garrison now was—eight Portuguese, three Indians, and two women. On December 12 or 13, they easily stormed the walls. The Portuguese died fighting.[1]

[1] Strandes, 246–70; a full and interesting account.

The Portuguese Conquest

The siege had lasted thirty-three months, and the most remarkable feature of it, apart from the heroic endurance of the garrison, was the lack of fighting. The Omani forces, though their numbers varied, probably never fell much below one thousand and could easily have been reinforced from Muscat, but, except in resisting the attempts at relief, very little Arab blood was shed; and it remains a mystery why the besiegers never tried till the very end to carry the fort, strong as it was, by a direct assault, or why indeed Seif-bin-Sultan did not lose patience and send orders to attack. The second significant feature of the siege is easier to understand. Excuses for the failure to relieve the fort were plentiful—lack of money for the outfit of an expedition, difficulties of wind and weather, the unreliability of pressed troops—but nothing could show more clearly the collapse of Portuguese power in the Indian Ocean than its inability to save the key-position on the northern section of the African coast.

A few more years, and the issue was finally decided. The Portuguese made a last effort: successive expeditions for the recapture of Mombasa and the north were dispatched from Lisbon and Goa in 1699, 1703, and 1710, but all were fruitless; and though they seized their chance in 1728—when the Arab governors of Mombasa and Zanzibar were at feud and when Oman itself was temporarily crippled by civil disorder and Persian aggression—and actually recovered Mombasa and with it the control of the north, they were expelled again by the Omani in two years' time.[1]

It was now clear that the Omani, as long as they were undivided and undistracted, were a stronger power in East Africa than the Portuguese. At the outset of the eighteenth century, indeed, their piratic fleets so dominated all the trade-routes of the Indian Ocean that even Dutch and English merchantmen learned to dread the sight of them. And so from 1740 onwards, when the great Ahmed-bin-Said, scion of the Albusaid dynasty and founder of a new line of Omani rulers, had reunited his countrymen and freed them from the Persians,

[1] Idem, 273–98.

the Portuguese abandoned hope of reconquering the north. The Arabs, on their part, were content to let them alone in the south. East Africa, in fact, to use a phrase of later days, was 'partitioned' between colonists from Europe and colonists from Asia. On Mozambique and the little settlements under its control—Quilimane, Ibo, Inhambane, and Sofala on the coast, Sena and Tete up the Zambesi—the Portuguese retained and still retain their hold. North of the Rovuma the Arabs reasserted for a century and a half their old commercial and political dominion.[1] Once more the string of Arab colonies were free from external control except from Arab Oman. But there was now a vital difference in their life. The Portuguese conquest had made no positive mark on the northern part of the coast. If physical conditions, especially the climate, had been different, the Portuguese might have tried to do in East Africa what they succeeded in doing in Brazil. As it was, their rule was purely external; it was never identified with the interests of the country; it was only maintained by force; and that force was only used to obtain immediate profit from a monopoly or restriction of trade. The coast was never occupied, except by little garrisons. It was never settled: the number of Portuguese colonists north of Cape Delgado in the most peaceful and prosperous years cannot have been more than one hundred. It was never developed; manioc, maize, and pineapples were introduced by the Portuguese, but their cultivation of these and other products was on a small scale. Nor was there any expansion of overseas trade with Europe or Asia; on the contrary, the economic life of East Africa became more and more confined to the interchange of goods along the coast. In every way, in fact, Portuguese rule was as profitless to the inhabitants of East Africa, Asiatic and African, as it was to the Portuguese themselves; and the only substantial difference it made to East Africa in the course of

[1] An officer cruising up the coast in a British frigate in 1812 reported that Portuguese authority stopped at Cape Delgado, 'neither fact nor courtesy, notwithstanding any assertions to the contrary, giving them claim to a league farther; for the authority of the Arabs begins at the last-mentioned point'. J. Prior, *Voyage along the Eastern Coast of Africa* (London, 1819), 32.

The Portuguese Conquest

two hundred years was its effect on the Arab colonies. There and there only the change was great indeed. They had passed their prime, it is true, when the Portuguese first came; but they were still a power, political and commercial, in the world of the Indian Ocean; and the wealth and beauty of their towns had taken the new-comers from Europe by surprise. But now that the Portuguese had come and stayed two centuries and gone, those gilded pictures were scarcely recognizable; and what was henceforward to startle European visitors was the evidence they were to find in crumbling walls and ruined mosques and streets long overgrown by the jungle that those towns had once been rich and powerful. Trade they had still after 1740, in all the old exports, and especially in slaves; but the range of it had narrowed to the western sector of the Indian Ocean. Their sea-power was wholly gone. They lay, indeed, in a backwater, aloof from the rest of the world and ignored by it. Their only political link with other lands was the continued submission of Zanzibar to Oman. Even the seismic wave of the Napoleonic War, which swept across and around the Indian Ocean, overrunning India and Egypt, lapping at the shores of Persia and Arabia, engulfing islands so near as Madagascar and the Mascarenes, only rippled once or twice and faintly the stagnant waters of the East African coast.[1]

But, though the Arabs of East Africa played no part in the history that was being made so near to them, it was still in a sense their history. They could not see the French and British warships fighting over the horizon, nor watch the comings and goings of the French and British diplomatists at Muscat, nor know that the outcome of it all would go far to determine their own fate. But in fact those events portended nothing less than the re-entry of Europe into their corner of the world. At the end of that contest, either the French or the British, each now as powerful as once the Portuguese had been, would be masters of the Indian Ocean; and the masters of the Indian Ocean would be able to do what they liked with its coasts. If, then,

[1] Strandes, 315–22. For later descriptions of the coast-towns, see p. 329, below.

the thread of Arab history in East Africa turns away for a time from Mombasa and Malindi, which lay outside the Anglo-French battle-field, to Muscat, which was one of its main strategic points, it is no aimless digression to pursue it, for it leads back to East Africa in the end.

IV
FRANCE AND BRITAIN IN THE INDIAN OCEAN (1740-1805)

I

IN 1740, the date which has been taken as roughly marking the final transference of East Africa north of the Rovuma from Portuguese rule to the partial and intermittent 'overlordship' of Oman, Britain and France were about to enter on a period of conflict which, with intervals of precarious peace, was to last till 1815. And this, of course, meant war not only on European waters and the Atlantic but also in the Indian Ocean. In that area, at the outset, the antagonists were more or less evenly matched. In India itself the British company was more firmly established than the French; but, while the British had no strategic post or naval base on the long sea-route from Europe nearer India than St. Helena—the Cape and Ceylon were Dutch—the French had recently created an invaluable base in the heart of the Indian Ocean at Île de France. La Bourdonnais, who came out as Governor in 1735, might have taken a high place in history if his insight and vigour had not been thwarted by the jealousy of his rivals and the weakness of the government at home. As it was, in the short ten years allowed him, he virtually made Mauritius. Quickly recognizing the strategic value of the island and its excellent natural harbour, he set himself to strengthen the young colony in every way. He built houses, roads, bridges, government offices, hospitals. He created a new capital at Port Louis. He started shipbuilding. And to promote the prosperity of the existing French settlers and to encourage the immigration of new ones, he greatly extended the sugar-planting begun by the Dutch, established cotton and indigo factories, and introduced manioc from Brazil; while to provide labour for the plantations he revived the trade in slaves which the Dutch, when they occupied the island, had opened up with Madagascar and Mozambique. By the end of the century there were over 100,000 slaves in

Île de France and Bourbon as against less than 20,000 whites and half-whites.[1]

But La Bourdonnais's main interest was naval. He strongly fortified Port Louis, and provided it with the same sort of equipment for the maintenance and repair of a fleet as that of the British base which faced him across the water at Bombay. In 1740, after five years' strenuous work, he returned to France and succeeded in persuading the authorities in Paris to take advantage of the opportunity he had made for them. He urged that, since war with Britain was clearly imminent, a naval force should be promptly stationed at Port Louis so that, directly war was declared, it could descend on the British ports in India before they could be reinforced from home. The French Government agreed, and La Bourdonnais sailed for his island boasting 'that he would carry out the greatest *coup* ever achieved upon the sea'.[2] But in 1742 the plan was dropped in Paris and the ships ordered back to France. The war came in 1744. The moment for the *coup* passed. In due course a British fleet arrived in Indian waters. But La Bourdonnais was determined that at least one blow should be struck from Île de France, even if it had only his own local resources behind it. In 1746 he armed seven French merchantmen and, taking the lead in his flagship, sailed for the Bay of Bengal. An indecisive action with a British squadron proved a strategic victory; for the irresolute British commander, Peyton, avoided further fighting, and La Bourdonnais arrived unhindered at Pondicherry. Thence he made for Madras, and in a few days forced its surrender. If his luck had lasted and if he could have made a friend instead of an enemy of Dupleix, the subsequent history of the French in India might have been more glorious than it proved. But the monsoon opened with a gale which wrecked three of La Bourdonnais's ships and drove the rest dismasted back to the shelter of Port Louis. Before the year was ended, he was

---

[1] C. Grant, *History of Mauritius* (London, 1801), 566: rough statistics for 1799. Île de France: 10,000 whites and mulattos, 55,000 slaves; Bourbon: 8,000 whites and mulattos, 48,000 slaves.

[2] P. E. Roberts, *History of India* (Oxford, 1916), i. 99.

recalled, a discredited and ruined man, to Paris, where the Bastille and an early death awaited him.[1]

2

La Bourdonnais's idea of using Île de France as a base for attacking the British in India was to be revived (as will be seen) at later stages of the Franco-British conflict. Meantime the island, together with Bourbon, previously the more important and prosperous colony but now fast losing its lead, and the little French settlements on Rodriguez and the Seychelles, remained the only European foothold on the western waters of the Indian Ocean; and, while La Bourdonnais, with his eyes on the East, had thought only of making it 'the bulwark of our settlement in India', it had its westward aspect also. It lay only 500 miles from Madagascar, 1,150 (as the gull flies) from Mozambique, and 1,700 from Zanzibar as against 2,100 from Colombo and 2,500 from Bombay. And both from Île de France and from Bourbon lines of trade were now radiating westwards to East Africa, a trade which brought in cattle and other foodstuffs but particularly slaves, the indispensable instruments of economic development. Madagascar was the nearest and richest source of supply; but so bad was its climate and so persistent the hostility of its warlike inhabitants that French traders could only maintain a precarious footing on its east coast, and they soon began to look beyond it to the mainland. The whole coast-line was supposed, of course, to be a Portuguese preserve wherein all foreign trade was barred. But south of the Rovuma, where there were Portuguese officials and garrisons to enforce the embargo, French traders found that by judicious bribing they could obtain slaves for Île de France and Bourbon even at Mozambique itself and also at Ibo.[2] North of the Rovuma, despite the fact that there was now no

[1] Grant, 198–208 (work in Île de France); 234–81 (expedition to India with La B.'s reports and other documents). Roubaud, *La Bourdonnais* (Paris, 1932), 45–56. C. P. Lucas, 'The Mediterranean and Eastern Colonies', in *Historical Geography of the British Colonies* (Oxford, 1906), 134–6. G. A. Ballard, *Rulers of the Indian Ocean* (London, 1927), 248–56. [2] See p. 79, below.

Portuguese occupation of the ports at all, the Government still stubbornly maintained its claim to a monopoly. As late as 1739 and 1744, when the French East India Company, backed by its Government, tried to obtain permission to trade at Mombasa and Pate, it was stiffly refused at Lisbon; and the Viceroy at Goa was warned to be on his guard against a French attempt to violate the Portuguese domain by force.[1] But force was not needed to break through a barrier of paper and pretence, and French interlopers from Port Louis were soon nosing their way into the forbidden field. One of them, Morice by name, from about 1770 onwards made several voyages up and down the coast, and for three successive years he obtained from the Arab Governor at Zanzibar and from the Sultan or King (as he calls him) of Kilwa an exclusive right to purchase slaves, which he shipped not only to Île de France but also by the long route round the Cape to the French West Indies. The profits of his trade were so substantial and the possibilities of its expansion seemingly so great that in 1777 Morice boldly submitted to the authorities at Port Louis a detailed scheme for the commercial exploitation of the whole area, of which the two main points were the creation of a new company to finance and control the undertaking and the establishment of a new colony at Kilwa to serve as its focus and head-quarters.[2] He explained, to begin

[1] Strandes, 301.
[2] The scheme is preserved in a manuscript book of 202 pages now in the Bodleian (Rhodes House Library). No reference to it can be found in the Mauritius Archives to-day. It was submitted to a M. de Cossigny at Port Louis, either the soldier of that name who acted as Governor of Île de France from 1790 to 1792 or, more probably, his cousin, an engineer in the government service. The book contains, besides Morice's memorandum and sundry notes, a series of *questionnaires*, some of them dated in June and July 1777, giving Cossigny's questions and Morice's answers in parallel columns. The questions cover not only all conceivable aspects of Morice's project, political, commercial, and financial, but also a multitude of subjects not directly connected with it, e.g. the character and customs of the African natives. Morice was clearly an intelligent observer, and though his knowledge seems to have been confined to the towns and to what he was told of the townspeople, his answers are always interesting and, in the lack of other evidence, valuable. He reports a general ignorance of the interior. The existence, however, of a

with, that the field lay open and so far unoccupied. Portuguese pretensions to control the northward coast had now been given up; and no other Europeans had as yet made a lodgement there. To Cossigny's question, 'Les Anglois fréquentent-ils cette côte?' Morice baldly answers 'Non'. Only a few Arab traders from Surat in British India come bartering salt and cloth for slaves. It is the Dutch he fears, coming up from the Cape. A Dutch ship had been seen at Zanzibar, and its master had written to the King of Kilwa asking permission to trade there. 'If we are not beforehand in taking possession of Kilwa, it's a hundred to one the Dutchmen will be there within three years.' The Arabs, for their part, and those of Kilwa in particular, desired a French connexion, mainly for the commercial profit they would get from it. 'They are vaguely aware of the King's power, of the strength of France, and of our superiority over them; but they want to enjoy the immediate advantage of trading with us, and do not worry much about the future.'[1]

For the choice of Kilwa Island as the base Morice gives several reasons—its healthiness, the fertility of its soil, its present and potential production of cotton, sugar, and indigo, its wealth of timber for ship-building, its fine harbour, 'better than Brest or Toulon', the friendliness of its Arab and Swahili residents who

vast inland sea was widely known, and he was told that 'on the other side is an immense country which has been traversed by the natives who after two months' journey have found the ocean and seen ships manned by Europeans'. Morice rightly suggests that this is the coast of Angola. MS. 45–6.

[1] Morice MS. 1–2, 72, 65, 57–8, 12, 71. Morice calls the Arabs and half-Arabs of the coast-towns 'Moors' and uses 'Arabs' only for residents in Arabia, especially Muscat. He seems to have thought that all the 'colonists' came originally from the Red Sea coast and that their antagonism towards the Omani was due as much to a difference in type and origin as to their love of independence. — Morice's dealings with Kilwa were long remembered there, and the account given to Prior when he visited Kilwa in 1812 bears out Morice's statements. 'About the commencement of the American War an adventurer from the Isle of France touched here on a commercial speculation. The Sultan highly rejoiced at the prospect of a direct intercourse with Europeans, received him well, promoted his views, and he soon returned with a full cargo of slaves and ivory in exchange for arms, ammunition, tobacco, and some dollars.' Prior's *Voyage*, 67.

numbered about 200 out of a total population of some 2,000 (600 'free Africans', 1,200 slaves), the peaceable character of the agricultural tribes which occupied the villages of the mainland and offered a good market for imported wares, and so forth.[1] But Morice's trump-card was the formal treaty which—with the capacity he claimed to possess of understanding and 'managing' the Arabs—he had obtained from the King of Kilwa and three of his elders.

'We give our word [it ran] to M. Morice of the French nation that we will supply him with one thousand slaves a year at 20 piastres apiece; and he will give the King a present of 2 piastres for each head of slaves. Anyone else, be he French, English, Dutch or Portuguese etc., will only be allowed to trade in slaves when M. Morice has obtained his slaves and does not want any more. This contract has been made between him and us for one hundred years. As a guarantee of our promise we will give him the fort in which he can put as many guns as he likes and hoist his flag. The French and the King and people of Kilwa shall henceforth be as one. Those who attack one of us will attack us both. Done, December 14, 1776.'[2]

Morice recommended that this treaty of his—*en bon citoyen*, he would sacrifice his private interests—should be taken over by the French Government, that sufficient land on Kilwa Island for the proposed 'establishment' should be purchased from the Arabs, and that the fort, which had long been dismantled and half-ruined, should be restored with local stone and slave labour and equipped with six guns and a garrison of 150 men from Île de France. A surgeon, a chaplain, three or four pilots, and a number of skilled workmen should be sent, but, at the outset at least, no missionaries. French settlers would soon be attracted and should be encouraged to start plantations on the adjacent mainland. Morice, in fact, was anticipating the growth of a French colony on the lines of Île de France with a French town like Port Louis on Kilwa Island. On the political

[1] Morice MS. 4–5, 43, 46–8, 176, &c.
[2] Ibid. 59; a French translation of the Arabic text, signed by Morice, captain of the *Abyssinie*, and witnessed by three Frenchmen. It is interesting to compare this treaty with that made by Captain Owen at Mombasa in 1824; see pp. 235–6, below.

side the French administration—Cossigny was clear on this—would be responsible for keeping order throughout the district and would control the police. But otherwise the government of Kilwa outside the limits of the French *enclave* would be left to the Arabs as at present. There should be no interference with their religion or customs.[1]

The French East India Company, which had now paid its way, had been dissolved in 1769, and the administration of its settlements, including the Mascerenes, had been taken over by the Crown. To finance and execute his scheme, therefore, the initial cost of which he estimated at about one million livres, Morice proposed that a new company should be created with a monopoly of the whole field of East African trade. It should take over the existing trade with Madagascar; agents should be posted at Tamatave on the east coast and on the west at Bombetoke where the Arabs had a colony and an entrepôt for the distribution of the Indian wares they brought from Surat. The Company should also control the Slave Trade with Mozambique and Ibo which, though forbidden by the Portuguese Government, had been and could be profitably carried on with the connivance of the local officials. Nor should the fertile and beautiful Comoro Isles be overlooked. They were linked by the Arab Slave Trade with Bombetoke; and one of them, Johanna, was often visited by English ships sailing to and from India by the Mozambique channel. Northwards, the extension of the Company's trade would depend on its relations with Zanzibar which, with Pemba attached to it, was the only point on the coast under the effective control of the Imam of Muscat. Beyond it lay opportunities of trade with Muscat itself and with the Red Sea and the Persian Gulf.[2]

The high profit Morice expected from the Company's operations would be derived from just such a triangular system as had long been established between Europe, West Africa, and the West Indies and was in Morice's day making big fortunes for French and British business men. French goods of all sorts—

[1] Morice MS. 9–13, 72, 138, 167.
[2] Ibid. 1–8, 22, 50, 71, 73–4, 195.

fire-arms, powder, bayonets, and brandy figure first on the list for sale to natives, especially in Madagascar, but not for Mozambique, where an embargo on arms and powder was strictly enforced for fear of native risings—would be shipped to Surat, where part of them would be sold and Indian cloth bought. With this and with the remainder of the French goods the ship would cross to Kilwa. Kilwa was to be the central depot, where the goods for sale would be stored for distribution as needed up and down the coast, and the goods purchased would be collected for export. Of the latter, some 500 pounds of ivory a year could be counted on, and there would be a steady growth in the production of live stock and foodstuffs for the Mascarenes. But the mainstay of the Company's operations and the chief source of its profits would be the Slave Trade. Morice was prepared to guarantee an annual output for the first four or five years of over 3,000 slaves from Kilwa and about 2,000 from Mozambique and Ibo. Thereafter the figure would rise to 10,000 a year. Thus not only would the requirements of Île de France and Bourbon be fully satisfied, but a surplus would be available for shipping to the West Indies.[1]

All in all, it was a well-thought-out and a promising scheme. In the Indian Ocean as well as over the Atlantic the European Slave Trade had still, as will be seen, many profitable years of life before it. But, as with other promoters of commercial enterprise in the tropical world, Morice's objective was more than economic. A French colony at Kilwa, or, if not there, at Zanzibar or Mombasa—that is his immediate aim; that, as he says on one of the opening pages of his *mémoire*, is the subject with which it deals. But his patriotic dreams ranged far beyond a single colony. Nothing is said in the *mémoire*, he writes—and there is clearly much he could say—about East Africa in general, a fertile land and well peopled and equipped with safe harbours, nor about the views that could be held of 'the future of an immense country, the ownership of which could be acquired without difficulty or bloodshed or expense'. It was a French empire in East Africa that gilded Morice's horizon.[2]

[1] Morice MS. 14, 19, 35.   [2] Ibid. 4–5.

It will be related in a later chapter of this book how, less than fifty years after this attempt by a French merchant-captain to use a private contract with the Sultan of Kilwa as a lever for bringing about a French occupation of the coast, a British naval captain concluded a similar contract with the Sheikh of Mombasa and similarly pleaded that it should be confirmed and implemented by his Government. There was one great difference. In 1776 a British merchant might well have made it, as Morice made it, his immediate aim to promote the Slave Trade in East Africa; but Owen's immediate aim in 1824 was to abolish it. The primary condition of Morice's treaty was that one thousand slaves should be sold to him every year. The primary condition of Owen's treaty was that no slaves should be sold to any one any more. Otherwise the two documents were not unlike. Each provided for the occupation of the fort by a European garrison, for the hoisting of a European flag, for joint defence against external attack. But it is still more interesting that the main obstacle to an official acceptance of the treaty and all it might involve was in each case the same—the fact that the Imam of Muscat was involved.[1]

Cossigny at Port Louis—it is clear from his notes and questions—approved of Morice's scheme in principle, though he thought a settlement on the mainland would be better than on Kilwa Island, mainly because there would be less risk of trouble between the French and their Arab neighbours; and he recommended that the *mémoire* should be forwarded to Paris. But in his detailed discussion of it he raised and more than once repeated the point that nothing must be done to compromise the relations of Île de France with Muscat. Morice tended to make light of difficulties with the Imam. His one *point d'appui* in East Africa, Zanzibar, was (Morice allowed) important, with its 60,000 inhabitants and its old-established hold on the coastal trade; but there were only some 300 Omani there, and the Omani were hated by all the other Arabs and half-Arabs along the coast. Morice seems even to have contemplated a joint attack with Kilwa on Zanzibar and the expulsion of the

[1] For Captain Owen's operations, see Chapter VIII.

Omani from the island. But Cossigny took a more serious view of trouble with Muscat. The Kilwa project, he notes, seems advantageous; 'but it is essential for our nation to remain at peace with the Arabs [of Oman] so as to obtain from them liberty to trade at Muscat since that town is the only considerable outlet that exists on the African [or Arabian] coast for the sugar and other products of Île de France'. A liaison with Muscat, he says again, 'would facilitate our commercial contact with the Persian Gulf and Surat and would enable us to spread our trade along the Arabian coast'. If the trade in slaves is flourishing at Muscat, might it not be profitable to create a French 'establishment' in its neighbourhood, rather than, or as well as, at Kilwa? To which Morice could only reply that the existing amount of trade between Île de France and Muscat was relatively small, that Muscat was not a source of slave-production but only an entrepôt for the Slave Trade between Africa and Asia, and that the certainty of satisfying the vital need for sufficient slaves in Île de France and Bourbon was the chief merit of a scheme of settlement at an African centre of slave-export such as Kilwa. Cossigny acquiesced in this reasoning, but on one point he would not yield an inch. An attack on Zanzibar must not be thought of. It would bring the Imam of Muscat into play; and 'he has close relations with Surat and might perhaps call to his aid the English who love to shove their oar in (*se fourrer*) everywhere, above all if it is a question of hurting us and of extending their trade and their dominion'. 'Observe', the careful official goes on, 'that peaceful trade is the surest and most profitable thing for us, and do not lightheartedly (*par gaieté de cœur*) discard our opportunities in that respect at Muscat.' 'Very well,' replies the merchant, 'your remarks about the English are very true; but you will see, if the Dutchmen get a chance, they won't be as timid as we are.'[1]

The French 'invasion' of East Africa, thus contemplated by a French slave-trader and, more coolly, by a French official, never took place. The Government was prepared, indeed, to

[1] Morice MS. 50–62, 88–90, 96–7, 102, 120–1, 138, 161, 198, 200–2.

take advantage of Morice's arrangements for a regular supply of slaves, and in due course a French frigate arrived at Kilwa and a treaty of commerce was concluded, fixing the price of slaves at 32 dollars (roughly £8) or about the same as the price fixed by Morice. When a British naval officer called at Kilwa in 1812, he found that the townspeople still vividly remembered the coming of Morice, and the frigate, and the treaty, and the great increase in trade. 'Several large ships', they told him, 'arrived from France to carry slaves to Java and other parts of the East as well as to their own and the Spanish West Indies.'[1] But beyond a treaty, which cost nothing, the Government declined to go. No big new East African Company was founded. There was no French occupation of Kilwa fort and island, no colony. The reason may have been partly the renewal of war with Britain in 1778; but probably the main deterrent was what had troubled Cossigny—the fear of entanglement with Oman. And indeed the event showed that the Imam had his eye on Kilwa. Had the French occupied it, he could have done nothing. As it was, Hamed-bin-Said (1779–92) or his successor Sultan-bin-Ahmed (1792–1804), attracted by the growth of Kilwa's trade, attacked and mastered the town, installed a Governor beside the local Sultan, and exacted a quota of the customs revenue by way of tribute.[2] This was a sharp reversal of Morice's project of driving the Omani from Zanzibar, and it pushed the whole idea of a French colony still farther into the background. There, however, it lingered on. Other officials than Cossigny were to take an interest in East Africa. Other merchants of Port Louis were to dream Morice's dream and seek as he sought to tempt their Government along the path of territorial expansion. But for the next generation French interests in East Africa were regarded as quite a minor issue. At Paris and at Île de France the key-position in the north-western section of the Indian Ocean seemed, as it once had seemed to Albuquerque, to be the town that held the gate of the Persian Gulf.

[1] Prior, 67.
[2] Idem, 67–8. Prior was told that this happened 'shortly after the treaty'. There is no other evidence as to the date.

3

Commercial relations between Île de France and Muscat were easy enough to maintain up to a point. As Cossigny had said, the French could sell their sugar and other products at Muscat and buy there some of the foodstuffs they required—grain, salt fish, dates, and coffee. But any considerable extension of this trade would be difficult. In the first place, successive Imams, more mindful than the Sultan of Kilwa of what Portuguese dominion had meant in the past and what the intrusion of other Europeans might mean in the future, had stubbornly refused permission for the establishment of any permanent European 'factories' on the coast of Oman. Secondly, whereas British traders had not yet entered the East African field except as passers-by on the Indian sea-route, the East India Company was now firmly established in the Persian Gulf with agencies at Basra and Bushire; and for their ships and for others bound to and from the ports of the Red Sea Muscat was a regular port-of-call. British warships, too, on the watch for the Arab pirates who infested those waters, put in from time to time at Muscat. The frigate *Seahorse*, for instance, made Muscat her base for two months in 1775, with Midshipman Horatio Nelson on board.[1]

Nor could a commercial *entente* with Oman remain long unaffected by political issues. The strategic position of Muscat, as important in war as in trade, forbade it. Indeed, the very establishment of a naval base at Île de France made it quite inevitable that Muscat would sooner or later be drawn into the field of Anglo-French conflict. For one of the purposes of the base was to attack the British trade-routes on the flank; and, if the chief of these, the Cape route, lay south of Port Louis, the next most important was the northern route from Bombay dividing at Muscat on its way to the Gulf or the Red Sea. Questions of neutrality, of sheltering and watering and so forth, were bound to arise; and, though the Arabs of Oman might do their best to hold aloof from the conflict and avoid entangle-

[1] Miles, ii. 274.

ment with either party, they had to learn, like other peoples in other parts of the world, that neither interests of trade nor traditions of past friendship nor the rules of international usage could protect them from interference at the hands of warring Europe. It is difficult to live a peaceful life in the middle of a battlefield.

The first impact came quickly. In 1759 three privateers, commanded by the famous Comte d'Estaing, attempted, in defiance of the Imam's neutrality, to cut out a British merchantship sheltering in Muscat cove, and were fired on and driven off by the Muscat forts.[1] A similar incident occurred in 1778 and again in 1781; and on this last occasion injury was added to insult, for the French privateers, having tried and failed to seize a British ship at Muscat, captured off Sohar a fifty-gun frigate of the Omani navy, the *Saleh*, which was carrying a cargo of British goods from India to Basra. Hitherto the rulers of Oman had had no opportunity of sustaining their dignity and independence by retaliation; but this time one of the guilty privateers, *La Philippine*, rashly returned to Muscat for food and water, whereupon Hamed-bin-Said ordered two of his ships to attack her. After a two hours' fight she was forced to surrender and the crew were put under arrest. But there was little desire at Muscat, especially among those who were interested in the trade with Île de France, for a serious quarrel with the French; and Hamed recognized that concession was the best diplomacy. He sent *La Philippine* and the crew to Port Louis with a strong protest to Governor de Souillac against the violation of his neutrality, and wrote also to Louis XVI declaring his wish to maintain the old-established friendship between Oman and France. His case was backed both by de Souillac and by J. F. X. Rousseau, the capable French Consul-General at Bagdad through whom Hamed's letter to the King was forwarded; and the authorities in Paris, though they held that the *Saleh* had been justly seized because

---

[1] A. Auzoux, 'La France et Muscate aux XVIIIe et XIXe siècles', in *Revue d'histoire diplomatique*, xxiii (1909), 522—a valuable study based on the French Archives. Guillain, ii. 202-3. Miles, ii. 268-9.

a search had been refused, decided that restitution should be made. Delays and accidents obstructed the execution of this decision for several years, and in the meantime Hamed gave a new and signal proof of his friendliness. In 1785, when de Rosily, who had been sent out to make a hydrographical survey in the area of the Persian Gulf and to report on the general situation, visited Muscat with three French warships, Hamed conceded the permission, so long desired, for the establishment of a 'factory'. No use, however, was made at the time of this special favour, and when a party of British officers called at Muscat on their way to Persia in 1787 they were told that the old ban against all European 'factories' was still in force.[1] The *entente* was still further strengthened when at last in 1790 the French ship *Escurial*, renamed for the occasion *Saleh*, was escorted to Muscat by a French frigate and ceremoniously handed over. Tardy as it was, and though the new *Saleh*—so Hamed said—was 'very small and not worth a quarter of the old', this act of reparation made a deep impression. Vows of amity were again exchanged, and again a concession was made to France. Not only was the suggestion that a French consul should be appointed for Muscat warmly welcomed, but a promise was given that he should be provided with an official residence free of cost.[2]

The trouble with the privateers was only a minor reaction of Anglo-French rivalry on the affairs of Oman; and soon after 1790 the main current of the conflict was washing up against that jutting corner of Arabia.

It has sometimes been supposed that the French idea of launching an attack on the British in India by way of Egypt and the Middle East sprang new-born from Napoleon's brain. But already in the years that followed the humiliating conclusion of the Seven Years War it had figured among the many plans for recovering what had been lost in Asia and America.

---

[1] Auzoux, xxiii. 529–33. Miles, ii. 282–3.
[2] Auzoux, xxiii. 537–9. H. Prentout, *L'Île de France sous Decaen* (Paris, 1901), 335. Guillain, ii. 205–7. Miles, ii. 277–8.

FRANCE AND BRITAIN IN THE INDIAN OCEAN

After 1763 'French agents in an almost constant stream passed to and fro through Egypt, surveying its strength and resources and estimating its value as a French colony'; and after the resumption of war with Britain in 1778 proposals were discussed for a Franco-Persian alliance pointed against India, for the occupation of Egypt and the control of Arabia, and for cutting a canal through the Isthmus of Suez. Through the decade of peace after 1783 the idea lived on. French officers were commissioned to examine the relative merits of the alternative 'overland' routes to India by Suez and by Basra; and in 1785 a secret treaty of amity and commerce was concluded with the Mameluke Beys at Cairo. The Egyptian line of attack in the next war could be used in peace, it was thought, to undercut British trade pursuing the longer route round the Cape.[1]

But Egypt was only the first stage of an advance on India; and the strategists' eyes, which had already glanced at Persia, were soon sweeping round the Indian Ocean and lighting among other points on Muscat. The importance of Oman in the general scheme of the Indian Ocean was stressed by Souillac and Rousseau in their plans for making good the seizure of the *Saleh*; and it was stressed again by de Rosily, who pointed out the close and constant intercourse between Oman and the native principalities of India and recommended the establishment of a consulate at Muscat as an essential part of a French naval and commercial system radiating through the Indian Ocean from a new centre in the Seychelles.[2]

The scheme, therefore, was already in French minds when the fight with England was resumed in 1793; and it was soon taking concrete shape in the war-plans of the Directory. 'Egypt offers us', said Talleyrand, 'the means of ousting the English from India by sending a body of 15,000 troops from Cairo by way of Suez.'[3] The French consulate at Cairo, which

---

[1] H. L. Hoskins, *British Routes to India* (N.Y. and London, 1928), 27–9.   [2] Auzoux, 529. Prentout, 332.
[3] Hoskins, 55, citing E. Charles-Roux, *L'Angleterre, l'Isthme de Suez et l'Égypte*, 369.

had been suppressed in 1777, was revived in 1793, and in 1795 its occupant, C. Magallon, supplied the Directory with a timetable for the voyage of ten thousand troops to India. If they left Toulon in June, he wrote, they could reach India by way of Suez in September, and the English, taken unawares, would be driven from Bengal in one campaign.[1] Since Muscat was an essential stopping-place on such a voyage, it is significant that in 1795 the project of a consulate, discussed for ten years and more, was finally adopted. By the decree of March 3 the Committee of Public Safety established the consulate, and M. Beauchamp, scientist and traveller, was appointed to the post.[2] In 1796 the first of several French missions of a semi-scientific, semi-diplomatic character arrived at Teheran. And then, in 1797, the great idea took on new life and vigour in Napoleon's mind. 'To ruin England utterly we must seize Egypt', he said. 'Through Egypt we come into touch with India.' It had been said before, but it needed a Napoleon to act on it. On July 2, 1798, he disembarked at Alexandria with his Army of the East.

At Cairo, the first stage of the long march accomplished, he gathered into his hands all the strings of the web that covered the lands and waters between him and his goal. He wrote to Île de France informing M. Malartic, the Governor, of the occupation of Suez and Cosseir by French garrisons;[3] and he wrote to the Sherif of Mecca to declare his friendship and pave the way for an eastward move.[4] Two other threads he picked up had just been spun at Île de France. In the previous January envoys from Tippoo of Mysore had come to Port Louis, proposed a French alliance for the work of driving the British out of India, and obtained Governor Malartic's assurance that a force of volunteers would be raised in the island to go to his aid.[5]

[1] Dispatches of June 17 and Oct. 1, 1795. Hoskins, 52–3, citing Charles-Roux, 342–3.
[2] Auzoux, *R.H.D.* xxiv (1910), 235. Prentout, 332.
[3] *Correspondance inédite officielle et confidentielle de Napoléon Bonaparte avec les cours étrangères* (Paris, 1819), iv. 379.
[4] Ibid. iv. 5.
[5] P. E. Roberts, *India under Wellesley* (London, 1929), 42–3.

About this time also Malartic confirmed the old *entente* with Muscat by sending Sultan-bin-Ahmed, who had succeeded Ahmed-bin-Said on the Omani throne in 1792, a welcome gift of artillery and ammunition.[1] Pursuing these two threads, Napoleon wrote (January 25, 1799) to Sultan-bin-Ahmed in the following terms:

À l'imam de Muscat

Je vous écris cette lettre pour vous faire connaître ce que vous avez déjà appris sans doute, l'arrivée de l'armée française en Égypte. Comme vous avez été de tout temps notre ami, vous devez être convaincu du désir que j'ai de protéger tous les bâtiments de votre nation et que vous engagiez à venir à Suez, où ils trouveront protection pour le commerce. Je vous prie aussi de faire parvenir cette lettre à Tippoo-Saib par la première occasion qui se trouvera pour les Indes.

BONAPARTE.

'Vous avez déjà été instruit', began the letter to Tippoo, 'de mon arrivée sur les bords de la mer Rouge avec une armée innombrable et invincible, remplie du désir de vous délivrer du joug de fer de l'Angleterre'; and it went on to ask Tippoo to send news of the political situation in India and 'a competent person who enjoys your confidence' to confer with Napoleon at Suez.[2] It happened that Beauchamp, who had been delayed by other tasks, was at this time in Egypt on his way to open the new consulate at Muscat; but Napoleon, instead of using him to take those letters to Muscat and to establish a personal link with Sultan, kept him for a while in Egypt and then sent him on a mission to Constantinople, where he was arrested and imprisoned by the Turks.[3] The letters, entrusted to less careful hands, never reached their goal. They were intercepted by a British agent at Mocha[4] and in due course read with interest in Bombay, Calcutta, and London. But the snapping of this particular thread in the diplomatic web proved of small

---

[1] Miles, ii. 270. For date, which Miles vaguely puts earlier, see p. 95, note 1, below.
[2] *Correspondance inédite officielle et confidentielle de Napoléon Bonaparte avec les cours étrangères* (Paris, 1819), iv. 192. English translation in Miles, ii. 240.
[3] Auzoux, xxiv. 236.   [4] Miles, ii. 290.

importance at the moment. Cut off from reinforcements by the Battle of the Nile, blocked in Syria by the defence of Acre, alarmed by the growing weakness of the Directory at home, Napoleon decided in the autumn of 1799 to abandon the Egyptian expedition. Packing the whole plan of campaign in the East away in the back of his mind, he slipped through Nelson's cruisers and landed at Fréjus on October 9. A month later he made himself master of France.

4

Throughout this period the British position in the north-west angle of the Indian Ocean had been inferior to that of France. In commercial relations with Oman (as has been seen) the French had taken the lead. Although no violation of Omani neutrality by British warships is recorded, it was to the French that the privilege of a 'factory' had been at last conceded in 1785, and to them alone. Of a British consulate, likewise, there was no question at that time. And this lack of any close official connexion with Oman and of any permanent establishment on its coast proved a serious weakness to the British side in the recurrent wars with France. For it meant that nothing could be done to prevent the use of Muscat as a base for the destructive attacks of the French privateers on British shipping in the Indian Ocean—nothing, that is, except an attempt by force or otherwise to obtain control of the port. And the British-Indian Governments were far too much preoccupied with their difficulties in India to think of any such adventure on the dangerous ground of Arabian politics. They were content to maintain as best they could such friendly relations with Oman as were essential for the normal use of the trade-routes to the west and north.

It was this question of trade-routes and communications that first brought Egypt into the field of British-Indian policy. In the interlude of peace between 1763 and 1778 the British interest in that country was as innocent of military and political designs as it was in Oman. There were no British agents there. James Bruce was astonished to find in 1768 that not one of his countrymen was established in Egypt even for trade, but at Jedda in the following year he met two British merchantmen who had come trading from Bombay. From that chance meeting sprang the notion of developing trade between India and Egypt. It was quickly taken up in India. A company of business men in Calcutta backed it. Warren Hastings, soon after his appointment as Governor-General in 1772, encouraged it. And Hastings, as might be expected of him, had a second and bigger idea. He was 'induced', he told the Court of Directors in 1773, 'by the prospects which the introduction of this new and untried channel of trade afforded him both of improving the general commerce of those Provinces and *of establishing a new and continual communication of letters with the Honble. Court in England,* to take a concern in it'.[1] With that dispatch the long and romantic story of the overland route began. Between 1777 and 1780, despite the marked coldness for the plan exhibited at first by Lord North's Government, the route by Suez was regularly used by the authorities both in England and in India for the conveyance of their most important or urgent dispatches. It was by this route that the news of the French entry into the American War in 1778 reached British India early enough for Pondicherry to be attacked and captured long before help could arrive from France. At the end of the war, on the other hand, the route was not in use, so that fighting continued in India with the loss of many lives long after it had ceased in Europe.[2]

One of the effects of this war was to swing the balance of the British Empire from West to East. The American colonies being lost, the strength and wealth of Britain seemed now to depend on the maintenance of her hold on Asia.[3] And it was at this time that, largely owing to the representations of George Baldwin, an adventurous and patriotic merchant who had

[1] Hoskins, 6–7. Italics not in the original.
[2] Idem, 10, 18, 33. One of the messages sent in 1778 reached Madras from London in sixty-eight days.
[3] For some suggestions as to the effect of the American Revolution on British ideas about India, see the author's *The American Revolution and the British Empire* (London, 1930), chap. vi.

acquired a special interest in Egypt, British statesmen first began to recognize the danger of French intrigues at Cairo. 'France in possession of Egypt', wrote Baldwin to the India Board of Control in 1785, 'would possess the master-key to all the trading nations of the earth . . . and England would hold her possessions in India at the mercy of France.' In 1786, accordingly, it was decided to establish a permanent official post in Egypt, and Baldwin himself was appointed to fill the double role of Consul-General and Agent of the East India Company. He was instructed *inter alia* 'to protect His Majesty's subjects in their trade and lawful avocations' and 'to watch the motions of the French'; but 'the great aim of Mr. Baldwin's residence at Cairo', as the Court of Directors told the British Minister at Constantinople, 'is the opening of a communication to India through Egypt'. The task was not easy. Baldwin found Egypt in confusion. The Turks were in the country, suppressing the Mamelukes and restoring the Sultan's rule. But Baldwin did what he could. He appointed subordinate agents at Alexandria and Suez and negotiated with the Turkish Pasha. By the end of 1787 plans had been prepared for one regular annual exchange of dispatches with India by way of the Channel ports, Leghorn, Alexandria, and Suez. But they were never put into execution. British statesmen, it appeared, were again in danger of forgetting the strategic importance of Egypt. In 1790 a committee of the Privy Council reported that the prospects of British trade in Egypt were negligible and, while admitting the value of the country as a link between Europe and Asia, coolly contemplated its occupation by some other European Power. In 1792 Grenville at the Foreign Office suggested to Dundas at the Board of Control that Baldwin's post was useless and expensive; and in 1793, when war with France had actually begun and the French consulate at Cairo was about to be re-established, the British consulate was abolished. It is one of the minor ironies of history that, before receiving notice of his dismissal, Baldwin had proved once more the value of the Egyptian link with India. By forwarding through Suez the secret information from London that hostilities with France were imminent he enabled the British to repeat the *coup* of 1778 by a surprise attack on Pondicherry.[1]

It needed, perhaps, a force no less dynamic than Napoleon to open eyes so closely shut, but certainly they opened wide at the startling news of his landing at Alexandria. It gave a new meaning and coherence to reports from other and more distant quarters, to the recent revelations of the dangerous hold established by French military officers on certain native states in India, to the rumours that had trickled in of French intrigues in the Middle East. The interception of Napoleon's letters to Tippoo and Sultan-bin-Ahmed fitted into the picture. The great plot against British power in the East was revealed. It would be difficult, no doubt, to execute, and it was possible to exaggerate its immediate danger; but it was far too grave a matter to justify the taking of any avoidable risk, and the awakened British Governments in England and India set themselves promptly and efficiently to concert and carry out the needed counter-moves.

In India, as it happened, a man of rare ability and courage had just succeeded to the governor-generalship. For the last five years Sir John Shore had acted as the obedient instrument of the pacific Indian policy adopted by the British Government and Parliament after the American War. The new interest in India was coloured by no imperial dreams of wars and annexations. It concentrated on the conservation, consolidation, and better government of the vast areas already under British rule; and Pitt's historic India Act of 1784 gave statutory expression to the doctrine that 'to pursue schemes of conquest and extension of dominion in India are measures repugnant to the wish, the honour, and the policy of the nation'. But these good intentions could only be carried out by abstaining from all intervention in the unceasing conflicts between the Indian States; and when Sir John Shore, the second Governor-General appointed under the Act, strictly applied this policy in obedience to his orders, the results were disastrous. The Company's friend and ally, the Nizam of Hyderabad, was left in the lurch

[1] Hoskins, 33–44.

and not unnaturally antagonized. Its enemies, Tippoo and the Mahrattas, grew more powerful and aggressive. All over India its unintelligible aloofness was ascribed to weakness and fear. A better atmosphere for French intrigues could scarcely be imagined.[1] But Wellesley, who landed at Calcutta in May 1798, two months before Napoleon landed at Alexandria, was determined, with no less good intentions, to reverse the process, and, trusting in the friendship of Pitt and Grenville in the Cabinet and Dundas and his successor, Castlereagh, at the Board of Control, he was ready to neglect and at need to disobey the anxious injunctions of his Directors at the India House. Before the year was out, he had won back the Nizam of Hyderabad to his old allegiance and secured the disbandment of his French-trained army; neutralized for a time the hostility of the Mahrattas; and made careful preparations for an attack on the isolated Tippoo. Early in 1799 the attack was delivered. On May 4 Seringapatam, the capital of Mysore, was stormed and Tippoo himself killed fighting in the breach.

Action, meantime, had been taken to forestall the possible advance of Napoleon into the Middle East. In 1798, while a British delegation under Harford Jones was on its way from England to Bagdad to counteract the work of the French agents in Iraq and to secure the safe passage of Indian dispatches by the Euphrates route, Wellesley was taking similar action in the area of the Persian Gulf. He had seen at once that the first thing to do was to obtain the key to its door or at least to prevent it falling into other hands. Already, it seemed, French influence at Muscat had become dangerously strong. The commercial connexion with Île de France was as close as ever. The privateers were still very much in evidence. And it was thought that Sultan-bin-Ahmed, who employed a confidential French physician, was personally attached to the French 'interest'. Wellesley decided to act firmly and at once. In the autumn

[1] Shore wrote to Dundas, Aug. 26, 1795: 'If the French were to appear in force here, and success should attend their exertions, no dependence could be placed on the alliance or friendship of the Mahrattas, Tippoo, or the Nizam.' H. Furber, *The Private Record of an Indian Governor-Generalship* (Cambridge, Mass., 1933), 78.

of 1798 he instructed Mirza Mehdi Ali Khan, a trusted Persian agent in the Company's political service who was about to take up his duties as Resident at Bushire, to call at Muscat on his way and negotiate a treaty. It was the first political intervention of the British in the affairs of Oman, and it was almost startlingly successful. Had Sultan-bin-Ahmed with the instinct of a sea-going race understood what sea-power meant? Had he read the lesson of the Battle of the Nile? Or, if he still believed in the power of Napoleon, did he think him too powerful—and too near? For whatever reason, he swung abruptly over to the British side. Earlier in 1798, so the Company's native agent at Muscat reported, 'the French had stood much higher in the Imam's favour than the English', but he had now become 'as strong in his expressions of partiality for the English'.[1] And certainly Wellesley's envoy found no difficulty whatever in the discharge of his commission. The terms he had been instructed to propose were accepted without demur, and on October 12 a treaty between 'the Honourable the East India Company and His Highness the Imam of Muscat' was signed and sealed.[2]

This treaty, the first political compact between a British government and a ruling prince of Arabia, was a decisively pro-British document. After formal declarations of fidelity and friendship in the first two of its seven articles, Article III (in its English translation) read as follows:

'Whereas frequent applications have been made, and are still making, by the French and Dutch people for a factory, *i.e.* a place to seat themselves in, either at Muskat or Bunder Abbas, or at the other parts of this Sirkar, it is therefore written that, whilst warfare shall continue between the English Company and them, never shall, from respect to the Company's friendship, be given to them throughout all my territories a place to fix or seat themselves in, nor shall they get even ground to stand upon, within this State.'

[1] J. W. Kaye, *Life of Sir John Malcolm* (London, 1856), i. 106, note. The factor gave as the reason for the Imam's liking for the French 'their paying him more attention and sending him presents of cannon etc.', and for his change of attitude 'that they had lately captured one of his vessels'. For the cannon, see p. 89, above. There is no other evidence that anything similar to the *Saleh* incident had occurred since 1790.

[2] Miles, ii. 291.

In the sharpest possible contrast with this article stood Article VII:

'In the port of Bunder Abbas,[1] wherever the English shall be disposed to establish a factory, making it as a fort, I have no objection to their fortifying the same and mounting guns thereon, as many as they list, and to forty or fifty English gentlemen residing there with seven or eight hundred English sepoys; and for the rest the rate of duties on goods, on buying and selling, will be on the same footing as at Bussora and Abusheher.'

This abandonment of the traditional veto on 'factories' and still more on forts is striking enough, especially in view of the offer made to de Rosily in 1785, but it was not all. In the fifth article Sultan bound himself to admit English vessels coming to water at Muscat into the cove but to keep French vessels outside it, and, furthermore, to take part with the English in any naval engagement with the French in Muscat waters, though not on the high seas. As a final touch, it was provided in Article IV that 'a person of the French nation who has been for these several years in my service' should be dismissed immediately on his return from a voyage he had taken to Île de France. But perhaps the most remarkable feature of the whole document is its one-sidedness. The British representative, it appears, guaranteed that the ports of British India should remain open to Omani ships, but even this simple undertaking, important though it was for Muscat, was not set down in the treaty.[2]

But this triumph of British diplomacy on its first entry into the Arab field was not so complete as it seemed. In a few months' time, reports reached India that Sultan was again on friendly terms with Île de France; and these suspicions were confirmed by the intercepted letter from Napoleon. Was it possible that Sultan had so readily signed the treaty for the

[1] Bunder Abbas, also known as Gombroon, is on the Persian coast due north of the northernmost point of Oman. Sultan had captured it in 1794 and retained it as a dependency of Muscat on payment of an annual 'rent' of 6,000 tomans to the Persian Government (Miles, ii. 287). A British occupation of it was actually contemplated in 1808: see p. 129, below.

[2] English Text of Treaty: B.R. 248–9. For the open ports, see pp. 97–8, 105, below,

simple reason that he did not mean to keep it? The danger from Napoleon might now be less acute, but Wellesley was still determined to take no risks, and at the end of 1799 Captain John Malcolm, setting out on the first of his historic missions to the Persian Court, was instructed to call at Muscat and confirm and stiffen the Treaty of 1798. He took with him a certain Mr. Bogle, a surgeon: for in faithful execution of Article IV at any rate Sultan had dismissed his French physician and asked for an Englishman to be sent from Bombay to take his place. Arrived at Muscat on January 8, 1800, and finding Sultan absent on a naval expedition, Malcolm interviewed the Governor, who was well acquainted, as it chanced, with British India, having paid sixteen visits to Bombay and one to Calcutta. To him and his fellow councillors Malcolm expounded in vigorous terms the strength of the British and the weakness of the French.

'He told them how we had beaten the French in the East; how we had deprived them of all their possessions there except the Mauritius, "an unproductive island and no object of conquest"; and how the Dutch had lost almost everything in Asia, except Batavia, where they were shut up by their apprehensions of the English cruisers. Then he told them how the French "seized upon Egypt, and, making themselves masters of the avenues to the sacred cities of Mecca and Medina, would doubtless have retained possession of them, had not God favoured the exertions of the British arms in that quarter". "By His mercy," added Malcolm, "the French have sustained such signal defeats that the miserable remnants of their army are now anxious only for a safe retreat from Egypt." Then he spoke of the great victories we had achieved in Mysore; told how the intrigues of the French and the aggressive designs of the Sultan had been baffled by the wisdom of our statesmen and the courage of our troops; how the reduction of Tippoo's power had placed us in possession of the whole coast of Malabar, and how, with the exception of the islands of Ceylon, Malacca and Amboyna, there was not a port from Surat to Calcutta in which a vessel could anchor without the consent of the English. What then, he asked, was to become of the famed commerce of Muscat if the harbours of the whole Indian peninsula were to be closed against the merchant-ships of Muscat by the fiat of the paramount power?'[1]

[1] Kaye, op. cit. i. 106–8: based on Malcolm's journal.

A forcible allocution, richly coloured and adroitly pointed to suit a Moslem audience: and as to the final question, what answer indeed could be returned to it, to quote Malcolm's biographer, 'except an avowal of the fact that the prosperity of Muscat was dependent on the favour of the English'? That, at any rate in effect, was the Governor's answer. Of more practical importance, it was Sultan's answer too. For Malcolm pursued him to the Persian Gulf, caught him near Kishm Island on January 18, boarded his flagship, and treated him to a similar oration with the same result. The biography again deserves quotation:

'Then Malcolm spoke of the regret with which the Governor-General had perceived the recent disposition of the Imam to league himself with the French, and expressed a hope that he was now convinced that it was his true policy to enter into and observe such covenants with the English Government as would tend not only to the political security but to the commercial prosperity of the country under his rule. And to this end he proposed to establish at Muscat an English gentleman of respectability as the agent of the East India Company. Malcolm paused, and the Imam asked if he had anything else to request. Receiving an answer in the negative, the Arab placed his hand upon his head, then on his breast, and said that he consented to the proposal from his head and his heart; that he was willing to sign and seal the agreement at once, and would be equally willing if it stipulated the establishment of a thousand English gentlemen instead of one at Muscat.'[1]

And so, in cold prose, a short treaty was drawn up, and promptly signed. The first of its two articles renewed the Treaty of 1798. The second provided for the permanent residence at Muscat of 'an English gentleman of respectability' to act as intermediary in all intercourse between the Imam and the Company.[2] It was no accident that the requisite gentleman was immediately available. When Malcolm sailed off to attack the bigger and harder task awaiting him at Teheran, Mr. Bogle stayed behind, charged with the care of the Company's interests as well as the Imam's health.[3]

[1] Kaye, i. 109–10.   [2] Text: B.R. 249–50.
[3] Kaye, i. 106.

At every other vital point, meantime, action was being taken to reduce the danger of a French advance. In 1799 a naval force under Admiral Popham had been sent from Bombay to block the exit from the Red Sea. A military post was established on Perim Island, but, the climate proving deadly, the troops were temporarily transferred to Aden, whose ruler, the Sultan of Lahej, warmly welcomed their arrival and offered to conclude forthwith a treaty of alliance. True to the Company's tradition of avoiding any unnecessary interference in Arabia, Popham was only prepared to promise the Sultan help against the French if and when he should need it; but in 1802 a Treaty of Amity and Commerce was concluded, giving British trade a regular and permanent footing at Aden on favourable terms.[1] Other moves were made in the north. Harford Jones had remained at Bagdad as the Company's Political Agent and in 1802 was admitted to consular status by the Porte.[2] In 1800 Malcolm obtained his treaty from the Shah providing for mutual aid against a French attack and for the expulsion of all Frenchmen from Persia. Nor were the island bases of French sea-power overlooked. In 1801 Wellesley collected a force of Indian troops in Ceylon for an attack on Île de France under Arthur Wellesley's command, and the bold project only failed of execution through Admiral Rainier's arrogant refusal to take orders from the Governor-General. Wellesley's next idea was to use the troops for an assault on Java,[3] but, before this second plan matured, they were directed to the other side of the Indian Ocean. The British Government had decided that the 'Army of the East', however disabled by its leader's desertion, should not remain in undisputed mastery of Egypt. In 1801 a British force landed at Aboukir, defeated the French at Alexandria, and advanced on Cairo, while the Indian regiments under General Baird sailed from Bombay by way of Mocha and Jedda to Kosseir and thence marched across

---

[1] Hoskins, 60, 65. Treaty in Aitchison's *Treaties, Engagements and Sannads*, vii, No. lii. The total dues to be paid were only 2 per cent. for ten years and 3 per cent. thereafter. [2] Hoskins, 64.
[3] P. E. Roberts, *India under Wellesley* (London, 1929), 147–8.

the desert to the Nile. In September the capitulation of Alexandria prescribed the complete evacuation of Egypt by the French. Under the Peace of Amiens, signed on March 27, 1802, the British army was also withdrawn, and Egypt was restored to Turkish sovereignty.

Thus, at the close of the first round in Napoleon's fight with England, his scheme for crippling her by striking at British India had been frustrated. Nor was that negative result the only outcome of the British countermoves. British statesmen had been awakened to the strategic importance of the lands and waters of the Middle East and the routes that approached and traversed it. They had realized that the capture of Capetown and Ceylon was not enough to safeguard their position in far-off India. Mainly to that end, they had quickly wrested the naval control of the Mediterranean from the French. Solely to that end, they had invaded Egypt, they had intervened in Persia and Iraq, and—what was largely to determine the course of events to be recorded in later chapters of this book—they had entered for the first time into the field of Arab politics. The Arabs of the Red Sea coast, at Jedda and at Mocha, had watched the unprecedented spectacle of a British fleet conveying a British-Indian army through waters which twenty years earlier had been virtually unknown to British warships. At Aden, likewise, British-Indian soldiers had been seen, and a beginning had been made there of what was one day to become a permanent political connexion with the British. And, last but not least, at Muscat the British-Indian authorities, breaking their long tradition of aloofness and acquiescence, had so firmly impressed their will as to convert it, to all appearance, from an instrument of French to one of British policy. Taken as a whole, the effect of these countermoves was impressive. But, be it said again, they were countermoves. Nothing but the menace of the French attack had prompted them. As at other times and other places in the history of the British Empire, British interests had been both strengthened and enlarged not by any deliberate design of aggression or aggrandizement but by a tardy recognition of the needs of self-defence.

5

The French danger in the East had been weakened by the British countermoves but not eliminated. Napoleon had remembered—he never forgot—his oriental dream, and he seized on the breathing-space provided by the Peace of Amiens to pick up again the threads he had dropped in 1799. He dispatched Colonel Sebastiani on a secret mission to Egypt and virtually challenged Britain to renew the war by publishing his report, which declared that Egypt could easily be reoccupied with a French army of six thousand men. But that was only one thread. The master-strategist was looking, as he had looked before, beyond Egypt to the Indian Ocean; and this time he began to construct a naval side to his scheme for the invasion of India. The early triumph of the Revolution in the Low Countries had put the Dutch colonies at the service of French policy, so that India was encircled by a ring of hostile *points d'appui* from Table Bay to the Moluccas. Three links in the chain had been promptly snapped by the British seizure of the Cape, Ceylon, and Malacca in 1795; but Île de France and her satellites on the west and Java and her satellites on the east still lay at Napoleon's disposal. Might he not evade in those distant seas the British fleets that thwarted him in Europe, and from those invaluable naval bases contrive to launch surprise attacks across the water on Bombay, Madras, Calcutta? In 1801, before the peace was concluded, he sent Marshal Daendals to Batavia to rally and reorganize the Dutch colonial forces in Java; and in 1802 he nominated General Decaen as 'Captain-General of the East', to take charge of the projected operations in the Indian Ocean. On March 6, 1803, Decaen sailed from Brest with seven ships and some 2,000 men. At the Cape he found the British preparing to evacuate in favour of the Dutch, according to the Amiens agreement. At Pondicherry, on the other hand, he found that Wellesley, warned of the imminence of renewed war, had refused to carry out his orders to restore the French possessions in India. But Île de France rather than Pondicherry had been recommended by the Minister of Marine, Decrès, as the more defensible base of operations, and in August Decaen arrived at Port Louis and took over the government from Malartic's successor, Magallon. He was soon convinced that Decrès's choice had been right, and his dispatches spoke in ardent terms of the felicitous strategic situation of the island and the prospects of the great design. It seemed as if La Bourdonnais's 'greatest *coup*' was after all to be achieved.[1]

Nor, of course, was Muscat omitted from this second edition of the scheme. 'Mascate est une place importante', wrote Talleyrand in a report to Napoleon in 1802. 'L'Imam qui y gouverne, et dont la domination s'étend fort avant dans l'intérieur des terres et même sur quelques districts de la côte de Mozambique est un prince indépendant sous tous rapports.'[2] Apart from the loose use of 'Mozambique' for East Africa, this account of the position was as true as it was concise; and, though Talleyrand was presumably unaware of the terms of the treaties with Malcolm, Magallon's dispatches had suggested that Sultan-bin-Ahmed was by no means a British pawn and was anxious, indeed, to maintain the best relations with the French. In 1801 Magallon had wisely restored three Muscat ships taken by the privateers, and he had boldly taken this opportunity to send a small body of French troops to assist Sultan in an expedition against Bahrein Island. In the following year—so Magallon reported—Sultan had written to complain of 'the vexatious conduct of the English Government' and to ask for 'the special friendship and protection of the Republic' and for the appointment of a French agent at Muscat. This appeal was accompanied by a gift of Arab horses, to which Magallon responded with the gift of his own favourite rifle and, still more useful, some more cannon and munitions.[3] But

---

[1] Prentout, 330. For a close study of Napoleon's designs on India by land and sea, see pp. 371-90 and 468-74 of this scholarly work. For Decrès and Decaen on the strategic situation of Île de France, see pp. 122-3, below.   [2] Auzoux, *R.H.D.* xxiv. 244.

[3] Ibid. 242-3. Magallon failed to prevent the seizure of another Muscat ship in 1803, as to which Sultan sent his usual protest to Port Louis. Prentout, 331.

before news of these courtesies had reached Paris Talleyrand had made up his mind that a new move on Muscat was an essential part of the greater scheme, and in October 1802 he recommended the dispatch of an official mission headed by M. de Cavaignac. Napoleon agreed, and Cavaignac sailed with Decaen's expedition, commissioned to re-establish contact with Sultan-bin-Ahmed, and, if circumstances were favourable, to remain as French Resident at Muscat.

An able and ambitious man and as ardent a disciple of his master as Decaen, Cavaignac started on his mission determined to play a substantial part in establishing French naval power in the Indian Ocean. At the Cape he heard from a passing merchantman of the recent mission from Muscat to Port Louis and the request for a French agent,[1] and he wrote from there to Magallon asking a number of pertinent questions. What were the precise terms of the agreement of 1790? What was the volume of trade between Muscat and Île de France? Could Muscat be made an entrepôt of French commerce with Arabia, Turkey, Persia, and Sind? And lastly—a proof that the possibilities of that particular part of the world had not been forgotten since Morice's day—what openings were there at Kilwa, Mombasa, Zanzibar? Could the Imam be induced to grant a French concession on that East African coast?[2] . . . Cavaignac was delayed at Pondicherry, but when he arrived at Muscat on October 3, 1803, his hopes at once rose high. Sultan-bin-Ahmed was away, engaged in fighting the Wahabi; so also was Captain Seton, who had succeeded Mr. Bogle as British Resident in 1801. Those of the Muscat Arabs, therefore, who were interested in the trade with Île de France, and on that account had always favoured the French connexion, were for the moment in the ascendant; and Cavaignac found himself warmly welcomed in that quarter, and the objects of his mission strongly approved. But this initial success was all he got. Sultan returned to Muscat on October 12 and gave audience to the officers sent to ask him to receive the representative of the French Government and to provide him with a residence

[1] Auzoux, 246. [2] Prentout, 335.

in accordance with the promise made in 1790. A few hours later Sultan sent his reply. He could not receive a French agent and consul, he said in effect, on account of the engagements recently entered into with the English, and he declined an interview to discuss the subject; but, as he wished to remain on friendly terms with the French, his harbours would always be open, as before, to their vessels, and he would be happy to listen to any proposal they had to make on commercial matters.[1]

It was at once apparent that Sultan in his recent dealings with Magallon had been merely 'hedging', or, to use the loftier language of diplomacy, engaging in a policy of 'reassurance'. It was only natural. Britain and France, it was clear, had not yet finished their fight in the East, and the French, though worsted at the moment, might win in the end. It was wise, therefore, to keep up the old friendship with them behind the backs of the British. It was wise to complain to Magallon of British interference and to suggest that the presence of British residents at Muscat was unwelcome. And, since for the moment a truce had been declared in Europe, it was even feasible, though rather risky, to offer secretly the same privilege to the French. But it may well be doubted whether Sultan desired the offer to be so promptly accepted, and when it came to a straight and public issue, when he was asked to install Cavaignac under Seton's nose, he took no time to make up his mind. In Europe men might still tremble at Napoleon's name, but in the world that Sultan knew British fortunes had risen in the last few years and French had sunk. He had observed the collapse—or so it seemed—of the plan for invading India. He had heard of Napoleon's disappearance from Egypt and of the subsequent ejection of the army he had left behind. He had marked Baird's demonstration of amphibious power on the other side of Arabia. He had learned, no doubt, that the British were on good terms with the Turks and welcome at Bagdad. He was probably aware—since few secrets can be kept from the bazaars of the East—that Malcolm had got his way with the Shah of Persia as he had with himself. And, to cap it all, the news was now

[1] Miles, ii. 301.

arriving of the opening victories of Lake and Arthur Wellesley against the vastly larger forces of the Mahratta league.[1] The British, clearly, were masters of most of India, whatever the French might say, and the threat to close its ports to Omani trade had lost nothing of its force.

There was yet another argument, nearer home, and stronger perhaps than any other. Sultan, it will be remembered, was away from Muscat, when Cavaignac arrived, on a campaign against the Wahabi. Those militant Puritans of Islam are well enough known to-day as the masters of Arabia; but it was not till 1800 that, moving eastward from their desert-centre in Nejd, they began to threaten the peace and independence of Oman. In that year they crossed the north-west frontier and built a fort at Baraimi, about 200 miles from Muscat. Sultan, unable to dislodge them, had to be content with a precarious truce. In 1803 they declared open war, and Sultan, deserted by the Shah of Persia and the Pasha of Bagdad, who had helped him at the outset in the hope of keeping the Wahabi from the Persian Gulf, was forced to obtain a three years' peace by paying a large indemnity, promising an annual tribute of 12,000 dollars, and admitting a Wahabi representative to Muscat. But the Wahabi soon broke their bargain and, pouring down from Baraimi, laid waste the coastland belt of the Batineh with fire and sword. Sultan met them and was routed near Sowaik, and he was gathering another and larger force for the defence of Muscat when the Wahabi commander learned that his master, Amir Abdul Aziz, had been assassinated, and determined to withdraw.[2] It was in the breathing-space thus suddenly conceded him that Sultan returned to Muscat to deal with Cavaignac's demands, and it can scarcely be doubted that his mind was full of the Wahabi danger. It was bound to recur. It would probably be more than he could meet alone. Persians and Turks had already failed him once. Was it possible these Christian strangers, who seemed so closely interested in Muscat,

[1] Fall of Aligarh in August and battle and occupation of Delhi in September 1803. Battle of Assaye, Sept. 23.
[2] Miles, ii. 293-8.

might help him? If so, he had no doubt which to choose. He might not like the British, their manners might be 'vexatious', but, at that moment at any rate, they seemed clearly stronger than the French. He would offend, he might alienate them, by admitting Cavaignac. He decided not to risk it.[1]

Cavaignac was bitterly disappointed. He waited another day in the faint hope that his Arab partisans, though their leader told him that 'most of the Muscat merchants and the Governor himself were now devoted to the English', might yet secure a more favourable response from Sultan, and then slipped away from Muscat in the middle of the night.[2] He left a letter for Sultan explaining that it was useless for him to stay, since 'le parti anglais domine dans le divan'; and, as he sailed south, he began to convince himself that, even if he had succeeded in his mission, it would still have been right for him to come away. A French Resident, he finally reported to Talleyrand, was not wanted at Muscat. 'Ce pays et ses habitants sont tout à fait misérables. Le souverain n'est qu'un chef de Bédouins.' French relations with such a country could be adequately handled by 'un agent commercial de la dernière classe'.[3] Napoleon would never have made that mistake; but his disciple had allowed his disappointment to drive many things from his mind. He had forgotten, for instance, about that base for trade and sea-power in East Africa.

So British 'influence' remained entrenched in Oman. The privateers from Île de France continued, despite the treaties, to avail themselves of Muscat's shelter and supplies, and their attacks on British shipping were as damaging as ever. It was estimated that the loss they inflicted from the beginning of the war in 1793 up to 1804 amounted to about three millions sterling; and it was a provoking, if piquant, feature of the business that Sultan and the Muscat merchants kept 'agents at Port Louis specially to purchase English goods and prizes', and that ships so purchased were sent brazenly to the ports of the

[1] Auzoux (op. cit. 251) definitely ascribes Sultan's choice to the Wahabi danger.   [2] Auzoux, 251.
[3] Prentout, 339. Miles, ii. 301.

Persian Gulf and even to Calcutta for resale.[1] Writing in 1819 of his residence at Muscat in 1809, an Italian physician declared that of the forty square-rigged ships of between 300 and 700 tons belonging to that port 'almost all' were 'English prizes purchased at the Isle of France during the late war'.[2] But nothing short of a military and naval occupation of Muscat could cure that evil; and on all other counts the advantages obtained in 1800 seemed sufficient. Captain Seton remained at Sultan's ear. No rival agent disputed his authority. If the key to the gate of the Persian Gulf was not exactly in his pocket, it was at any rate beyond the reach of any Frenchman.

And then in 1804 this tranquil and, from a British viewpoint, satisfactory position was suddenly disturbed. Sultan-bin-Ahmed was killed in a fight with Jawasmi pirates. The succession was hotly disputed between the leading members of the Albusaid family; and Oman seemed to be drifting fast into another of those long periods of schism, disorder, and debility which had so often followed the deaths of its rulers in the past. In that case anything might happen. Other forces in the Middle East—in Arabia, in Iraq, in Persia—might be drawn like vultures to the decaying kingdom. British diplomacy would have to build again on those shifting sands. But in fact the death of Sultan was not the prelude to Oman's dissolution but to her renascence. In 1806 a young Arab of the princely house broke with traditional violence on to the stage of history. When, fifty years later, he died, he had made Oman a greater, wealthier, stronger state than it had been since the Dark Ages; he had given it a new place in international relations; and—a final achievement which makes him the central figure of the story told in this book—he had recovered, unified, and extended the Arab dominion in East Africa and brought it back into close touch with the life of the outer world.

[1] Miles, ii. 302. For details of the privateering, see Prentout, 504–9. For Shore's complaints of the losses to shipping, see Furber, op. cit. 32, 50. In 1794 he authorized a half-hearted and ill-organized attack on Île de France which was easily repulsed. Ibid. 53–5.
[2] V. Maurizi (see next footnote), *History of Seyd Said* (London, 1819, translated from Italian), 30.

V

SEYYID SAID AT MUSCAT

I

By the end of 1805 Bedr-bin-Seif, one of Ahmed-bin-Said's nine grandsons, had proved the most successful of the claimants to Sultan-bin-Ahmed's throne. If he did not yet rule Oman, at least he reigned at Muscat. But he had only achieved this measure of success by inviting and accepting the support of the Wahabi, who had by no means abandoned their purpose of dominating Oman and rooting out its infidelities. It was an unnatural and unpopular alliance, and bought at a humiliating price. Tribute was paid to the Wahabi, a body of their cavalry was stationed within the Omani frontier to overawe the country, and their Puritan code was sternly enforced. Bedr's authority was contested, therefore, by a 'patriot' party which favoured the claims of another of Ahmed's grandsons, Said-bin-Sultan; and early in 1806, though he was but a youth of fifteen, Said was induced by the pressure of his supporters or by personal ambition or by fear for his own life to make a bid for power. Accordingly he invited his cousin to a conference, and in the course of a seemingly friendly conversation drew his knife and stabbed him. Bedr escaped, desperately wounded, through the window, but was overtaken and dispatched by Said's followers. Murder was one of the orthodox paths to an Arab throne, and the young assassin was at once acclaimed by the 'patriots' as the saviour of his country. Thenceforward, though he nominally shared his authority for the first few years with his elder brother Salim, 'Seyyid' Said, as he styled himself—for since about 1795 the Imamate had become a purely religious office distinct from the secular power—was the actual, though not always undisputed, ruler of Oman till his death in 1856.[1]

[1] Miles, ii. 308–9, followed more or less closely by Guillain and Said-Ruete (the latter wrongly prefers Burton's authority to Miles's and dates the murder in 1807). V. Maurizi, an Italian physician (known as Sheikh Mansour) who practised in Constantinople, Anatolia, Egypt, and Bagdad, and, after acting as a French Government agent at Mocha, entered Seyyid

2

It was no safe or restful throne that young Said had usurped. Enemies encompassed him within and without his realm. There were turbulent tribes in the outer parts of Oman. There were more insidious foes about his person. Any of his blood-relations might conceivably treat him as he had treated his cousin. Intrigues were incessant: one of them in later years centred round his own eldest son. More than once in the course of his long reign he had to deal with open revolt. And this internal insecurity was intensified by external danger. The Wahabi were determined to maintain their domination. The Jawasmi, fierce freebooting sea-folk who lived on the south-west side of the Persian Gulf and gave it its old name of 'Pirate Coast', had been growing in strength and audacity, destroying the trade and menacing the liberty of Oman. And in the background stood the French and British, engaged in a seemingly endless conflict in which at any moment Oman might be fatally embroiled.

Said's first task was to come to terms with the Wahabi, or rather to accept their terms. He could not fight them unaided, and, 'patriot' though he was, he submitted to the murdered Bedr's yoke—the payment of tribute, the adoption of Wahabi doctrines, the presence of a Wahabi garrison at Burka. On those conditions he obtained a truce and bided his time. With the Jawasmi no such agreement was possible. They continued to prey on Omani trade. Said's attacks on their ports were beaten off. Again it was clear that he needed allies. Only with help from outside could the Jawasmi power be broken.

Said seems quickly to have realized that the most effective help would be British help. But the Bombay Government had no quarrel with the Wahabi, and, though its trade had suffered from the Jawasmi pirates almost as much as Said's, it had just

Said's service in 1809, adopts a version of the story more favourable to Said in which Bedr is represented as coming uninvited and in a threatening mood to meet Said. But neither this nor any other version acquits Said of the actual murder. V. Maurizi, op. cit. 10. For the Imamate, see Badger, op. cit., appendix A. Europeans, as will be seen, still called the ruler of Muscat 'Imam'.

succeeded (February 6, 1806), through Seton's agency, in securing an undertaking from their chiefs that British shipping should not be molested if Jawasmi traders were admitted to British-Indian ports.[1] There would be difficulties, therefore, in getting British help, and difficulties also in receiving it. British friendship meant French hostility. Already, indeed, relations with Île de France had been strained by Sultan's rejection of Cavaignac and the tenderness for British feelings it had implied. When, early in 1804, a cruiser was sent to Muscat with dispatches for Cavaignac, whom Decaen supposed to have been duly installed as Resident, her captain reported that, while the leading Arabs were full of apologies and protested that Cavaignac's departure had been due to a misunderstanding, their leaning towards the British side was unmistakable.[2] Nor had Decaen been deceived when at the end of 1805 Bedr, having established himself in Sultan's place, wrote to assure him that he was as much a friend of France as Sultan and to express the hope that ships from Île de France would continue to resort to Muscat.[3] And when, a few months later, Said had taken Bedr's place, French coldness had been further chilled by a recurrence of the old trouble with the privateers. This time it was significantly the French who had a grievance, not the British. In the course of July a privateer from Île de France, the *Vigilant*, put in at Muscat for shelter and repairs. There she was detected by the captain of a British frigate who promptly requested Said to order her out of Muscat. To refuse would have been a violation of ordinary neutrality, still more of the Malcolm Treaty. The *Vigilant* was compelled to leave and was promptly captured by the frigate.[4] Some months later, another French privateer fell in with eight Muscat merchant-ships near Ceylon. They were stopped and boarded and all the money and some of the cargo they contained removed. When the Arabs protested that it was a novelty for the French to steal the property of Muscat folk, the captain replied that the old friendship had been ended by the rejection of Cavaignac and the treatment of the *Vigilant*.[5]

[1] Miles, ii. 307.   [2] Prentout, 447.   [3] Idem, 448, note 3.
[4] For Said's account see letters cited p. 112, note 1. For the French captain's report, Prentout, 448.   [5] See letters cited p. 112, note 1.

This quarrel with the French was the more awkward for the young usurper because he did not know quite where he stood with the British. Seton was away. After his negotiations with the Jawasmi he had accompanied a small naval expedition sent from Bombay to Mocha in search of the pirates who had recently seized an American ship and massacred its crew.[1] And, though Said had written to the Governor of Bombay, Mr. Jonathan Duncan, announcing his accession and asking that the old 'habits of amity and alliance' might be maintained, he had received no answer. Said waited till September, and then he wrote to Decaen. 'I am anxious', he said, 'to cultivate the ancient amity which has always reigned between my ancestors and the French nation, and hope that Your Excellency will consider my country as belonging to France and count on my willingness to obey any commands with which she may honour me.' He was hoping, he added, to recover the *Vigilant* from Bombay; but 'Your Excellency is doubtless aware of the effrontery and pride of the English nation as well as of their power in India'.[2] Decaen took those flowing sentences for what they were worth and penned a stiff reply, demanding the restoration of the *Vigilant* and inviting Said to send an envoy to discuss the matter.[3] Thereupon Said wrote again to Duncan, repeating the gist of his first letter and complaining that it still remained unanswered. 'It has been rumoured', he added, 'that several men of war have been dispatched towards Mocha and Arabia Felix under the orders of Captain Seton, and I was expecting that they would touch here on their return voyage and that I should have an opportunity of meeting Captain Seton. But they have returned, it would seem, to Bombay.'[4] Another month passed and still no answer. At the beginning of December Said determined to break the silence by sending his confidential minister or Vakil to seek an audience of the Governor. The way was prepared by a letter written, doubtless at Said's instance,

[1] For the tragedy of the *Essex*, see Miles, ii. 512.
[2] Said to Decaen, 17.ix.1806; French translation in Prentout, 448, and Auzoux, *R.H.D.* xxiv. 257.
[3] Decaen to Said, 21.x.06. Prentout, 449. Auzoux, 258.
[4] Said to Duncan, 31.x.06 (B.P.C., Nov.–Dec. 1806).

by the Company's Indian broker at Muscat, declaring that Said wished 'with all his heart and soul' for the Company's friendship; and before the end of the month the Vakil arrived at Bombay. The letter he presented from his master referred to his previous letters to which 'to my surprise, good and kind Sir, you have not yet favoured me, your true friend, with a reply: may the course, however, tend to good'. It also dealt with the *Vigilant* episode and the attack on the Muscat ships off Ceylon.[1] But Said's most urgent communication was not committed to writing. It was a verbal message, delivered by the Vakil, asking outright for British protection against the French.[2]

The silence of the Bombay Government had been due, as Said had probably guessed, to the irregularity of his own position.[3] In Seton's absence from Muscat and the consequent lack of trustworthy information as to what Said had actually done and what his real authority in Oman was, an immediate recognition of his accession had seemed unwise. But already, as it happened, before the Vakil's arrival forced Duncan's hand, news had reached Bombay which made it difficult to ignore any longer what was happening at Muscat. The shores of the Indian Ocean were one vast whispering-gallery: rumours of Said's dealings with Decaen had soon reached Surat; and, anxious to please the British, the Chief of Surat informed Duncan that Said had agreed to receive a French Resident at Muscat and was about to send a mission to Port Louis. Said in league with France? It was certainly time for the British to take a hand: and Duncan wrote to Said in courteous terms, explaining that his silence had been due to 'the daily expectation of the return of Captain

---

[1] Broker to Duncan, 3.xii.06; Said to Duncan, received 18.xii.06 (B.P.C., Nov.–Dec. 1806).

[2] For the 'verbal messages' see the broker's letter cited in the preceding note.

[3] Miles says (ii. 310): 'The dynastic change and the conduct of Said appear to have been viewed with disfavour by the British authorities', which Said-Ruete (p. 21) construes as 'The tender consciences of the Bombay Government were affronted.' But there seems to be no evidence that the moral factor entered into the question.

Seton from his voyage to Mocha, upon which it was meant to depute him to your presence'. As to the *Vigilant*, she had already been sold as a prize and gone from Bombay: otherwise the Government would have bought her in and sent her to Muscat, despite the fact that she had been permitted, while sheltering there, to be completely refitted and equipped for further depredations on British trade. The question of protection against the French had been referred to Calcutta, and Said would at once be informed of the Governor-General's decision. This friendly letter was followed by another from the Vakil which Duncan 'caused him to write as from himself to the Imam', informing Said of the rumour from Surat—an evidently false rumour (so he was caused to write), since Said must be aware that, if he linked himself with France, he 'could not expect that the Arabian trade and shipping from Muscat would experience the welcome it receives at present in the ports of India'. If indeed there was any colour at all for the rumour, it must be taken for granted that the sole purpose of the alleged mission would be the recovery of the property seized by the French off Ceylon.[1]

Copies of this correspondence were submitted to Calcutta and approved, and the suggestion that Said's request for protection might be met in part and for the time being by sending one of the Company's cruisers to Muscat was also approved. But that, of course, was no final solution of the problem, and the Supreme Government took occasion to lay down the principles which should govern British policy in Oman, in a long and reasoned dispatch to Bombay.

Its tone could not be Wellesley's tone, for Wellesley's 'forward policy' was now out of fashion. After some years of increasing friction—the controversy between the Court of Directors and their insubordinate Governor-General becoming steadily more acute: public opinion in England, especially when the danger of a French attack on India seemed to have passed

[1] Duncan to Said, 22.xii.06; Aka Mohammed Bhebanny to Said, 24.i.07 (B.P.C., Nov.–Dec. 1806, Jan.–Feb. 1807). For the privileges accorded to Omani shipping at British-Indian ports, see pp. 212, 216, below.

over, swinging nervously against a policy of constant wars and falling dividends: even Wellesley's friends in the Government faltering at last and drawing away—the great proconsul had resigned in 1805, and the aged and infirm Cornwallis had been persuaded to return to India and revive the pacific policy of his previous administration. On his death before the year was up, his office had devolved, pending the appointment of his successor, on Sir George Barlow, the senior Member of Council, who had served Shore and Wellesley with equal loyalty and competence and was now instructed to reverse the latter's policy and reproduce the former's. Once more the statutory injunction of 1784 was to be obeyed. Once more commitments with any native prince were to be avoided unless the express consent of the authorities in London had been obtained. So history was repeated. Barlow could not undo all Wellesley had done; but he obediently withdrew the protection promised to the Rajput princes and left them, as Shore had left the Nizam, to face Mahratta enmity alone. It was not to be expected, therefore, that Seyyid Said's plea for protection would be well received by the Government at Fort William or that it would seize the opportunity—as indeed for good or ill it was—of binding Muscat to the British side by a regular alliance. In his case, indeed, the virtues of 'non-intervention' would have the unusual merit of involving no breach of faith.

The dispatch to Bombay began, accordingly, by setting a limited interpretation on Said's appeal. It could only be for the protection of his trade from privateers, since the French were too weak to attack Muscat, and Said strong enough to repel them if they did; and this protection would be afforded as hitherto by Admiral Pellew's fleet. 'But we shall be happy to learn that the necessity of it has been obviated as speedily as practicable by an accommodation between the Government of Muscat and the Isle of France which shall place them relatively in the condition of neutrality which existed antecedently to the late illicit depredations of the French upon the trade of Muscat.' To serve that end it might be advisable to try to recover the *Vigilant* and enable Said to restore it to the French. The treaties of 1798 and 1800, it was true, had pledged Muscat to active alliance with the British Government against the French; but that pledge had never been operative, and Muscat had always acted as a neutral. It was Muscat's interest that it should 'resume its neutral character and conduct', and the British interest, too, provided that neutrality was understood to preclude any permanent French 'establishment' within the territories of Oman. No further commitment on the British side was desirable except in one contingency. A French attempt to force Said out of his neutrality into an alliance would have to be forestalled by a British alliance. But it ought not to be conceded for any less urgent cause. The British Government 'could not derive any material advantage from the active co-operation of the State of Muscat', while the obligation 'to afford permanent protection' to its shipping would lay an additional burden on the navy. An alliance, moreover, might commit the British Government to guaranteeing Muscat against French resentment at the conclusion of the war, 'an obligation which might embarrass the negotiations for peace and which perhaps we are not authorised to contract without the previous sanction of the Government at home'.[1]

This dispatch and its sequel afford one of many illustrations of the difficulty inherent in the policy of aloofness towards native rulers, whether inside or outside India, once pursued by Shore and now again by Barlow. Said, to whom the substance of the dispatch was communicated by Seton on his return from Mocha, could not mistake its meaning. It was a plain refusal of a British alliance. It was an equally plain recommendation to keep on good terms with the French. And thereby it offered Said an opening which, whether with an inborn and precocious talent for diplomacy or on the shrewd advice of his Arab elders, he was quick to seize. He bowed to the refusal and accepted the recommendation—more wholeheartedly, perhaps, than Barlow had intended. He sent Majid-bin-Khalfan, one of his most trusted confidants, straightway to Port Louis with full power

[1] Supreme Government to Government of Bengal, 23.iv.07 (Bengal P.C., vol. xvi, April 1807). The dispatch has been condensed in the above text and the sequence of its argument modified for the sake of clarity.

not merely to settle the business of the privateers but to conclude a treaty of 'amity and commerce'. On June 16, 1807, it was signed by him and Decaen.[1]

The first treaty between Oman and a European Power—the Treaty of 1798, confirmed and extended in 1800—had been virtually unilateral. This second treaty took the normal bilateral form. Seyyid Said and the Emperor of the French bound themselves to extend to each other's subjects 'the privileges of the most favoured nation' in all matters of commerce and navigation. Their merchant-ships and their privateers with their prizes were to be free to use respectively all French ports and all the 'ports, harbours, beaches, countries, islands, towns and places dependent on the sovereignty of His Highness the Imam of Muscat', enjoying the same privileges and immunities, and paying no higher customs-duties than those paid by the subjects of the most favoured European nation.[2] The French were to be entitled to confiscate (1) contraband of war (from which horses, sulphur, and saltpetre were excepted as being products of the Imam's territories and constituting one of the chief branches of his subjects' trade) if found in Muscat ships destined for the port of an enemy of France, and (2) any property of Muscat subjects if found in enemy ships.[3] Two further articles were of special importance. On the one hand, French 'commercial agents' were to be permitted, if 'it suited France', to reside at Muscat or any other places dependent on the Imam, with the same rights and prerogatives as those enjoyed by the similar agents of most-favoured nations.[4] On the other hand, in view of Muscat's trade with British India, its ships were to be allowed to visit enemy ports without breaking their neutrality but not to trade between two such ports.[5] This last provision, as Decaen was aware, conflicted with Napoleon's policy in Europe; and, when its text arrived in Paris, ratification was

[1] Prentout, 449; cf. Auzoux, *R.H.D.* xxiv. 260.
[2] Copy of the treaty in the Mauritius Archives, Articles II and XI. The treaty is summarized by Prentout (449–50) from copies in the Paris Archives. See also Auzoux, 270.
[3] Article V.   [4] Article X.   [5] Article VI.

indefinitely postponed mainly on the ground that it was at variance with the Decrees of 1806 and 1807 instituting the 'Continental Blockade'. But Decaen in his distant island could dispense with diplomatic pedantry. Without waiting for confirmation from Paris he declared the treaty to be provisionally in force. Rules made for Europe might surely be broken in Asia if the balance of local interests could thereby be swung over from the British side to the French.

Decaen, indeed, was hoping by means of the treaty to wipe out the fiasco of Cavaignac's mission and resume the forward policy thereby interrupted. And, like Cavaignac, he was not thinking only of the economic and political importance of Muscat: he was thinking also of East Africa. The maintenance of French trade and of the Slave Trade in particular along the coast was as vital as ever to the economic life of Île de France. The Omani subjection of Kilwa may have terminated the Sultan's formal treaty of commerce with the French, but there is no reason to suppose that there had been any interruption in the supply of slaves. With Zanzibar, too, a steady trade had been maintained, mainly in slaves, but also in ivory and gold-dust; and, as at Muscat itself, trade had engendered there a friendly feeling for the French. 'The people are partial to that nation', reported a British officer in 1812, 'and lately were little less than hostile to the English.'[1] It so happened, moreover, that Decaen's attention had been drawn to the Arab section of the coast by the increasing difficulty of trading with the Portuguese section. During the Peace of Amiens, French traders had been outrivalled at Mozambique by American, Dutch, and British; and in 1804, after the resumption of the war, Decaen had written to Governor d'Almeida protesting that, though Portugal was neutral, British merchants were unfairly favoured. Little response save smooth words was obtained or indeed to be expected in view of the situation in Europe; and the business men of Port Louis began to ask whether it would not pay them to abandon the unequal contest in Mozambique and concentrate on an expansion of trade and influence northwards where, as yet,

[1] Prior, 81.

no European Power had intruded. If they could get the backing of the Government, so much the better; and in 1804 the attempt made in 1777 to persuade the authorities to take action on the coast was repeated.[1] Morice's part was played this time by a merchant named Dallons, who had been trading with Muscat and the chief East African ports for five years past, and now submitted to Decaen the fruits of his personal experience in the form of 'some reflections on our commerce with the various Arab establishments on the coast of Africa'. It was a rich field, he pointed out, for French trade. Many and various were the local products suitable for export, especially slaves and especially at Zanzibar. But trade was handicapped by the excessive duties imposed by the local governors, whose rapacity was little checked by the orders of their titular overlord at Muscat. Fair treatment, he urged, could only be secured by the intervention of the French Government 'in an imposing manner'. The Sultan of Muscat should be informed of the 'bad faith and ill will' displayed by the local officials in their dealings with French traders, and a firm agreement made with him as to the duties to be paid. But the execution of any such agreement would depend on French official pressure at the dominant point, Zanzibar. The actual occupation of that island, 'advantageous though it would otherwise be to our Government, would only injure us because it would awaken the vigilance of our enemies'. But a French Resident should be established there, with privileges of free trade and the right to communicate directly with the Sultan of Muscat. 'It has been proved by constant experience'—the point was repeated—'that our commerce will only prosper with Government protection.' Another merchant of Île de France, Ducombez by name, submitted a similar document, entitled 'Notes and Observations on the Commerce of Mozambique'. He went farther than Dallons. He went as far as Morice. He recommended an act of territorial expansion—the 'acquisition', as he put it, of a point on the coast, such as Kilwa or Zanzibar. These documents illuminate the East African aspect of Decaen's treaty. It is significant that it permitted the installation of

[1] For Morice and the Kilwa project of 1777, see pp. 76–82, above.

French representatives at other places than Muscat. It is significant, too, that the first French consul accredited to Said's dominions was M. Dallons.[1]

Directly and prospectively the Treaty of 1807 was a success for Decaen. And so also it might have seemed for Said. He had restored the old friendly relationship with Île de France—to the special satisfaction, doubtless, of those of his subjects who lived on the trade with the island—and he had obtained 'protection' for his shipping from French privateers. He had done, in fact, what Sultan had failed to do without provoking what Sultan had dreaded, a rupture with the British. Had he not acted on their advice? But Said, none the less, was dissatisfied. His good relations with the French were of far less moment than his bad relations with the Wahabi. At any time they might throw off the truce and pursue their confessed ambition of conquering all Oman, establishing their own government at Muscat, and enforcing the observance of their tenets by fire and sword and torture.[2] Said's diplomacy, therefore, had only achieved a 'second best'. As Barlow, of course, had realized, he wanted 'protection' for more than his ships, he wanted it for his whole country and for his own throne. And he knew, like Sultan, that only the British could give it him.

A glimpse of Said's mind is afforded by the memoirs of Maurizi, the Italian physician who was living at Muscat and attending Said at this time. Decaen, it appears, was well informed of the Wahabi danger and realized how the fear of it was always pushing Said towards the British camp. Since France, pending the realization of Napoleon's schemes, could not supply him with the requisite protection, he instructed Consul Dallons to urge Said to submit to his fate and embrace the Wahabi faith. Thus only could he save his people and himself; for it was useless to hope for or to trust in British aid. This last point was driven home by Maurizi himself. With an eye, perhaps, to past

[1] Decaen and d'Almeida: Prentout, 445. Dallons's 'Reflections': Mauritius Archives, *Gouvernement Decaen*, vol. ii, No. 119. Ducombez: Prentout, 445.   [2] Miles, ii. 312.

events in India he declared an alliance of Said with the Company would only lead to his subjection to its power. But Said was unmoved. After all, subjection to the Company might well be more endurable than subjection to the Wahabi. He still clung to his dream of an alliance. And with a curious glimmer of understanding—almost as if he knew that the Company's conduct in India was, or at least could be, controlled in the last resort by public opinion in England—he observed that 'a treaty with the Government of Bombay would render him more respectable in the eyes of the whole English nation'.[1]

3

It happened that at this very time, when the British authorities in India were holding Said at arm's length, encouraging him to keep on friendly terms with Decaen, and shrinking from any commitments that might embarrass British diplomacy in making peace with France, Napoleon had once more taken up his plan of Asiatic conquest and was giving it its final and most grandiose form. In the year of Trafalgar and Austerlitz he had not forgotten Persia, the half-way house to India. In 1805 a French mission had arrived at Teheran, and another in 1806. Their arrival was opportune because Persia, deeply and rightly afraid of aggression on the part of Russia, her immediate neighbour on the north, was in desperate need of help from any quarter. She had already appealed to the British Government in India, but with no success, since Russia was Britain's ally against Napoleon. Naturally, therefore, the French missions were well received, and in 1807 a return mission from the Shah was sent in quest of Napoleon in Europe. It found him in the plains of Poland on the morrow of Eylau and the eve of Friedland. On May 4, in his camp at Finkenstein, Napoleon and the Persian envoy signed a treaty by which, in return for a promise of help against Russian aggrandizement, the Shah was bound to reverse his earlier relations with England, to expel all Englishmen from Persia and their ships from its ports, and to urge the Afghans and the tribes of

[1] Maurizi, 74–5. Decaen's knowledge of the Wahabi: Prentout, 450, note 4.

Kandahar to join their forces with his for an attack on British India. It was provided, further, in Article XII that, if the French themselves should move on India, their army should have free passage across the soil of Persia and their fleet free access to the harbours of its Gulf. Armed with this treaty, General Gardane was dispatched to Teheran with instructions to investigate the landing-places and the roads, the enlistment of auxiliaries, and the provision of live-stock and water, by way of preparation for the march of a French army of 20,000 men on India, starting either across Syria from Aleppo or, after a sea-voyage round the Cape, from a base in the Persian Gulf. In Gardane's train went twenty-four French officers and three hundred men, the vanguard, as they told the Persians, of the coming army. When Friedland followed and then Tilsit, the design expanded. Russia, converted from enemy to ally, was now to take a hand. 'All Europe having combined against England,' wrote Napoleon in November, 'we can think about an expedition to India. The more chimerical it appears, the more it will alarm England when it is actually undertaken, and what could not France and Russia accomplish! Forty thousand Frenchmen, to whom the Porte would allow passage through Constantinople, in co-operation with forty thousand Russians advancing over the Caucasus would be sufficient to spread terror through Asia and to conquer it.' A few months later he was contemplating a subsidiary expedition of six thousand men to Aboukir. Nor was India itself forgotten and the part which Tippoo had been meant to play. 'The French are smoothing their way', reported Governor-General Minto in the spring of 1808, 'by swarms of agents of all ranks, qualities and countries all over the East; and they are beginning to be heard of at the courts of our Indian princes.'[1]

[1] A. de Gardane, *Mission du Général Gardane en Perse* (Paris, 1865), 16–25. Fournier, op. cit. i. 449, ii. 39. In February 1808 Napoleon pressed the plan on the Tsar. 'An army of 50,000 troops, French, Russian, and perhaps also Austrian, could be thrown into Asia by way of Constantinople; once they reached the Euphrates, England would sink prostrate at the feet of Europe.' Ibid. ii. 37. Gardane in Persia: Hoskins, 69–73. Intrigues in India: *Lord Minto in India*, 106.

In this third edition of the plan the emphasis was on the land-march, but naval co-operation was essential, especially if the alternative of beginning the march on the coast of the Persian Gulf was to be adopted; so Île de France was again a cardinal point in the design. Gardane was bidden to establish regular communications with Decaen from Teheran, and Decaen, in a dispatch written a few weeks after Finkenstein, was informed of the terms of the treaty and of Gardane's mission and instructed to make contact from his end.[1]

The dispatch was welcome, no doubt, to Decaen. Four years had passed since he had come to Port Louis, sharing in Napoleon's dream and burning to play his part in its fulfilment, and there he had stayed, isolated in his island, starved of soldiers and stores and money, while great things happened in Europe and nothing in the Indian Ocean. Apart from the anti-British activities of his agents in India and the harrying of British shipping by his cruisers and privateers, there was little he could have done. Away on the eastern flank he had established a liaison with the Spanish Philippines and the Dutch East Indies; but only strong garrisons could make them safe or formidable bases for attacks on British trade or the Indian coast. Westwards and nearer to hand he had done something, but not much, to maintain and extend the French footing in Madagascar. As early as 1800 Napoleon had interested himself in that huge island. He had called for reports on it, and some of their authors, playing up to his mood, had drawn a pleasing, if premature, picture of Madagascar under the French flag. Settled with French colonists, it would more than make up for the loss of St. Domingue. It would become a centre of trade with Mozambique, Muscat, Surat. Its timber would provide the ships, its warlike natives the army, for an assault on India. A fleet based on its ports would cut British communication with the East. Meantime, immediate use could be made of it as a source of supplies, a *magasin général*, for Île de France and Bourbon. Thus Madagascar had not been overlooked in the framing of Napoleon's Eastern plans. It had indeed gone far to

[1] Prentout, 459–60.

determine the choice of Île de France as Decaen's head-quarters. 'Sa situation', Decrès had written in 1802, 'la rend de la plus haute importance tant pour réaliser les vues qu'on doit avoir de Madagascar que pour menacer Hindoustan'; and Decaen, reporting from Port Louis to Napoleon himself in 1804, had dwelt in similar terms on the two-faced strategic outlook of his island-base. 'De l'Île de France on porte des regards sur l'Inde ou sur l'Île de Java et ses dépendances ou plus modérés sur la vaste et fertile contrée de Madagascar.' In the same year he had sent a small naval expedition to Fort Dauphin, the southernmost of the three or four old French settlements on the east coast of the island which maintained a precarious existence on the proceeds of the Slave Trade and of furnishing the Mascarenes and passing ships with fresh provisions. But the results had been discouraging. The climate, it was clear, remained the obstacle it had always been to the settlement of permanent French colonists; and the suspicious attitude of the natives towards all European intrusion and their constant wars among themselves were obvious obstacles to the growth of a flourishing trade. Decaen, accordingly, had abandoned the idea of colonization, but he had done what he could to keep the French flag flying and French trading active at Fort Dauphin, Foulpointe, and Tamatave. Early in 1807 he had appointed M. Mariette, an officer of the merchant marine, as 'commercial agent' to reside at Tamatave with authority to supervise the operations of the traders and to regulate their dealings with the natives; and on his death within two months M. Sylvain Roux had been sent to take his place. Thus by 1808, when all the plans and hopes of 1802 for the Indian Ocean were revived, Decaen could not claim to have made much progress in Madagascar in the interval. The French connexion had been maintained; but no closer relations had been established with the Malagasis, no concessions obtained, no permanent settlement attempted. The supply of provisions to the Mascarenes, especially rice and beef, had been increased: in 1807, indeed, they had saved the impoverished colonies from famine. And the flow of slaves had been kept up. For six or seven years past, reported Roux in 1808, about 2,000 slaves, obtained by Arab traders from the African mainland and marched across the island, had been sold each year to the French merchants.[1]

It was unfavourable conditions in the country itself rather than his lack of naval and military forces which had denied Decaen any substantial achievement in Madagascar. Beyond it, on the other hand, on the African mainland, a chance had been offered him which with ships and soldiers at his disposal he might well have seized. French influence and trade in Mozambique, as has been seen, had declined; and Napoleon's attack on Portugal in the autumn of 1807 had thrust the colony clean over to the enemy's side. To secure it for France was obviously desirable if only to forestall its occupation by the British; and in the course of 1808—not long after Decaen's hopes of the great design had been renewed—two opportunities for intervention in Mozambique presented themselves. One was a report that the Arab population wanted to invite Seyyid Said, as they had once (it was said) invited his father, to aid them in a rising against the Portuguese. The other was more promising. Two Portuguese officers at Mozambique secretly proposed, if sufficient support were forthcoming from Île de France, to attempt a *coup d'état* to set up a pro-French administration. But Decaen had no troops to spare, and, though the idea of sending a couple of warships tempted him, it seemed safer to await the coming of the expedition.[2]

It appears, then, that in all the wide field entrusted to Decaen as 'Captain-General of the East' his re-establishment of French influence at Muscat had been his most useful achievement; and, soon after the great news reached him that Napoleon was looking East again, he was offered a means of strengthening the *entente*. Said had found that the Treaty of 1807 was not quite satisfactory. It put out of business those thirty or forty of his ships which had been accustomed every year to make a round voyage to Bombay, the coast of Coromandel, and Bengal. In April 1808, therefore, he sent an envoy to Port Louis asking that Muscat ships might be permitted to trade between as well as

[1] Prentout, 15, 301–30, 475–90.   [2] Idem, 445–7.

with the ports of British India. This concession would involve, of course, a still more glaring breach of Napoleon's blockade decrees, but Decaen did not hesitate to grant it. On June 17 he signed a subsidiary agreement to that effect, and wrote to Paris pleading that the importance of securing Said's genuine friendship should be recognized, especially in view of the projected expedition. Muscat, he pointed out once more, commanded the entrance to the Persian Gulf: and Said's fleet—some 50 ships of from 250 to 800 tons, and over 500 dhows—could help the French to close its waters to the British.[1]

Meantime Decaen had sent his brother home to urge that the naval side of the plan should not be confined to co-operation in the land-march from the Persian Gulf and that the schemes of 1801 for a direct attack on India from the sea should be revived. His mission was successful. René Decaen had a long interview with Napoleon in Paris on January 27, 1808; and when he enthusiastically combated and minimized the difficulties of effecting a landing on the Indian coast, the Emperor was quite excited. 'Two or three times in the course of our conversation', reported René, 'he took my cheeks between his hands, his whole face sparkling with delight.' In the following May, Napoleon ordered Decrès to make preparations to dispatch nine warships and eleven smaller vessels with 4,600 men to Île de France in October, to be followed by another fleet including three warships and carrying 12,000 men. About the same time 20,000 men should be sent to Egypt. Then, while the British Government was distracted by a feigned attack on Ireland launched from Flushing and Boulogne, the army gathered at Port Louis would suddenly descend on India.[2]

4

Rumours of this revival of Napoleon's designs in the East soon spread in England and in India, and provoked the inevitable reaction. The difficult policy of aloofness and quiescence was dropped as it had been dropped before. The countermoves began again. And again it fell to a new Governor-

[1] Idem, 451. Auzoux, 261–2.   [2] Prentout, 465–7, 470.

General to make them. Lord Minto, who arrived at Calcutta and relieved Barlow of his temporary duties in July 1807, was not another Wellesley. He was a Whig. He had almost worshipped Burke. He had figured, though reluctantly, as a manager of Warren Hastings's impeachment. He had not the temper nor perhaps the capacity to play the autocrat as played by Wellesley in a warring India. But he was not required to deal with internal trouble on that scale: throughout his six years of office the Mahrattas, the Nizam, and the Rajput princes maintained an uneasy balance of power; and in his policy outside India, in his countermoves against the French, Minto not only showed a vigour, an efficiency, and a breadth of vision comparable with Wellesley's but secured the approval and support both of the Directors and the Tory Government at home and even of Wellesley himself. Diplomatic commitments and military operations were no longer dreaded and censured in those stirring years. The whole atmosphere was changing. Soon after Minto left England, events in Spain were ushering in the last phase of the long war, and Minto's work in India, begun in self-defence, became part of the general counter-attack which was not merely to check Napoleon's power but to destroy it.

Historians have sometimes doubted whether the march of a French army through the Middle East was ever really practicable, and Napoleon, as has been noticed, hoped that British statesmen would regard it as chimerical. But Napoleon did not understand British statesmen as well as they understood him.

'If the French armies [wrote Minto in February 1808] have been liberated by a pacification of Russia and by the continued submission of the Powers of Europe, the advance of a considerable force of French troops into Persia under the acquiescence of the Turkish, Russian and Persian powers, cannot be deemed an undertaking beyond the scope of that energy and perseverance which distinguish the present ruler of France.... From that centre of local power they may be enabled gradually to extend their influence by conciliation or by conquest towards the region of Hindustan and ultimately open a passage for their troops into the dominion of the Company. Arduous as such an undertaking must necessarily be, we are not warranted in deeming it in the present situation of affairs to be altogether chimerical

Seyyid Said at Muscat

and impracticable under the guidance of a man whose energy and success appear almost commensurate with his ambition, but deem it our duty to act under a supposition of its practicability and to adopt whatever measures are in our judgment calculated to counteract it.'[1]

Minto's plan of campaign, being framed to meet the same danger, followed the same lines as Wellesley's—a diplomatic counter-attack on land and an assault by sea on the French naval bases in the Indian Ocean. The latter part of it, which Wellesley had never been able to put in operation, was still delayed for a few years, but the former was set on foot without delay. In the course of 1808 three missions were dispatched to the States which lay immediately to the north and west of the Company's territories in northern India—one to the King of Cabul, as the Afghan sovereign was then called, one to Ranjit Sing, ruler of the Sikhs, and one (for which Seton was summoned from Muscat) to the Emirs of Sind. All three missions were more or less successful in forestalling French advances, but those territories were only what Minto called his 'second line of defence'. 'If this great conflict is to be maintained,' he said, 'we ought to meet it as early and as far beyond our own frontiers as possible. We ought to contest Persia itself with the enemy and dispute every step of their progress.' The sooner, therefore, the position and prestige of Gardane and his formidable staff at Teheran could be undermined the better; and more momentous than the other three missions was the fourth, which left Bombay for Persia on April 17 with Malcolm, as in Wellesley's day, but now high in the Company's service and a general, at its head. 'Opposition to France in Persia', Minto had written, 'is the anchor on which our hopes must rest'; and he had instructed Malcolm to sound the Persian Government as to the possibility of a large British-Indian force, 20,000 or 25,000 men, being sent to oppose a French invasion at or beyond the Persian frontier.[2]

---

[1] *Lord Minto in India*, 101–2.
[2] Minto, 107. Minto to Malcolm, 9.iii.08. Kaye, *Life of Malcolm*, i. 410. Malcolm's primary instructions were 'To detach the Court of Persia from the French alliance; and to prevail on that Court to refuse the passage of French troops through the territories subject to Persia, or the admission of French troops into the country. If that cannot be

Nor was Minto concerned only with the prospect of a land-march through Persia and the Afghan passes. Something was also known at Calcutta of the naval side of Napoleon's scheme. And, while it seemed doubtful if he would ever be able to obtain control of the Indian Ocean, he was credited with the intention of seizing a port near the mouth of the Persian Gulf. A force, collected at Île de France, would descend without warning on the chosen spot—probably Gombroon (Bunder Abbas), it was reported—and 'endeavour to take root there' as a prelude to the 'grand design'. The danger of such a move was clear enough to Minto. The French once at Gombroon, he wrote, could easily make contact with 'our professed enemies in India'. The passage to the west coast and the outskirts of the Mahratta realm would be short. The Arab shipping in the Gulf would provide all the transport needed. Indeed, if the French succeeded in establishing such a base, 'I should feel the occasion to be so important and so urgent as to require an immediate and powerful effort to dislodge the enemy.' 'We shall be prepared', he told Malcolm, who was instructed to raise this question also at Teheran, 'to push off 4,000 or 5,000 men on the first summons'; and, as it was, a force of 450 men and two six-pounders accompanied Malcolm's mission, enough, as he said, 'to defeat any small detachment which may be landed from the Mauritius—an event, however improbable, it seems prudent to guard against'.[1]

In Minto's mind, as in Decaen's, this part of Napoleon's scheme pointed straight at Muscat. Gombroon, indeed, was actually under Said's rule.[2] And, as soon as the rumour of the French designs reached Calcutta, Seton was instructed to ascertain its effect on Said. His report was reassuring. Said, like Sultan, wanted friendship and trade with Île de France, but, if it came to taking sides in the Franco-British conflict, Said, like Sultan, knew which side to choose. If Napoleon should come

obtained, to admit English troops with a view to opposing the French army in its progress to India, to prevent the cession of any maritime port and the establishment of French factories on the Coast of Persia.' Minto, 110. [1] Idem, 54–7. Kaye, 410–12. [2] See p. 96, note 1, above.

and conquer, his choice might have to be revised; but that danger seemed far less near at hand and far less terrible than the ever-present, ever-menacing Wahabi, from whom the British alone could save him if only they would. Said was 'disinclined', therefore, wrote Seton, 'to admit the establishment of the French at the port of Gombroon'. Then Minto took a further step. By the Treaty of 1798 Said's father had explicitly agreed to the occupation of Gombroon by seven or eight hundred of the Company's sepoys; but that clause had never been acted on, and it was Sultan's treaty, not Said's. Nor, of course, in the event of a real emergency, could any limit be set to the number of troops that might be required. Minto therefore instructed the Resident to obtain Said's agreement to the use of British forces for the defence of Gombroon if the French should attack it.

'It would be desirable to obtain the Imam's specific and written consent to the introduction into that port of any number of British ships of war with permission to land troops if deemed necessary for the defence of it. . . . It would, of course, be proper to afford to the Imam every assurance that the British Government has no design to establish its authority at Gombroon, that its sole object is to secure the possession of that port against the attempts of the French, and that the port will be evacuated if such should be the desire of the Imam when all immediate apprehension for its safety shall have ceased.'

The Resident, the dispatch continued, would probably find it easy to obtain what was wanted, since the local garrison at Gombroon was evidently inadequate to resist unaided a French attack; but in case of emergency 'His Majesty's naval officers would not of course hesitate to enter the port of Gombroon without the previous declared consent of the Imam'.[1]

Said made no difficulties. He was determined, indeed, to establish the strongest claim he could on British friendship and gratitude. On the arrival of a reconnoitring squadron from Bombay in March 1808, he saw to it that a full supply of fuel, water, and other requirements was forthcoming; and he wrote

[1] Supreme Government to Government of Bombay, 22.ii.08 (I.O., *Bengal Secret and Separate Consultations,* Jan.–March 1808, No. 5).

to Duncan asking him 'to allow of no interruption in our correspondence or hesitation in commanding my services, as was only consistent with a state of amity and close alliance'. A month later (April 30) Malcolm arrived off Muscat on the first stage of his journey to Teheran. He was armed with a general authority not only in Persia but for the furtherance of British interests in all the neighbouring Arab States; and additional instructions suggested that he should put in at Muscat 'for the express purpose of communicating with the Imam and of observing the actual situation of affairs at that place'.

'By a personal communication with the Imam your influence, ability and address might enable you to replace British interests in that quarter on an advantageous footing, and lay the foundation of arrangements calculated to defeat the views of the French as far as the success of those views depends upon the Imam.'

These instructions reached Bombay after Malcolm had sailed. When, therefore, he arrived off Muscat, he only 'lay to for a few hours' and had no such talk with Said as he had had with his father in 1800.

'The young Imam [he noted in his journal] sent me a thousand civil messages with a quantity of fruit, and expressed great regret that I could not land as he would, he said, have been delighted to see his father's friend and one who had taken great notice of him as a boy. I had seen him about eight years ago, and given him the model of a 74-gun ship as a present. He was then about ten or eleven years of age, and gave promise of good temper and intelligence; but this promise has not, I understand, been fulfilled.'

If Malcolm had seen Said, he might have questioned this opinion at least of his intelligence; and, indeed, it seems curious that the importance of a personal interview was not so obvious to him as it had been to Minto when he drafted those additional instructions. Perhaps he underrated the capacity of this upstart princeling of seventeen and thought he could do all the business that was needed with the confidential adviser whom Said sent on board with his compliments and gifts, one Mahomed Gholam, 'a very old acquaintance' of Malcolm's. To him Malcolm frankly explained the measures which the Government of India contemplated to forestall the danger of a French invasion. He told him that he would not 'insist' on obtaining what the Government of India in fact desired, namely a 'written engagement' from the Imam,

'because I did not wish by so public an act to precipitate a rupture between him and the French and because I was satisfied that a sense of his own interest and indeed preservation would, after I had stated to him the intentions of the British Government, secure his acting in every particular as was wished; and that I certainly must expect that the Imam would issue orders to his officers to give possession of any of his positions in the Gulf that the English might require for the purpose of opposing the French, and, should he do so, he might depend upon their being restored the moment that the emergency was past.'[1]

High-handed treatment of this kind might or might not succeed at Muscat: it completely failed at Teheran. Underestimating the strength of the French position in Persia, Malcolm sent on a member of his staff from Bushire with instructions to deliver a letter of formal greetings to the Shah and to negotiate himself with the Shah's ministers—or, rather, to deliver an ultimatum. Gardane and the whole of the French mission, he was to say, must be immediately expelled from Persia: otherwise Malcolm would at once return to India and the Persian Government must expect, without delay, to suffer the consequences of incurring British enmity. . . . Unhappy Persia! She only wanted to maintain her national integrity. The only European Power that directly threatened it was Russia. Finkenstein had given her the promise of French protection: but now Tilsit had made Russia France's friend. It had also, however, made Russia Britain's enemy, and so given the Government of India an opportunity of quietly convincing the Shah that French protection was now less assured and persuading him to give Britain at least an equal footing with France at Teheran. But to expect him to make a sudden break was unreasonable.

[1] Said to Duncan, 22.iii.08 (B.P.C., April 1808, p. 3609). Malcolm's general instructions: I.O., *Bengal Secret and Separate Cons.*, 1808; Kaye, i. 409. Additional instructions: 25.iv.08 (ibid., No. 15). Malcolm at Muscat: Malcolm to Minto, 1.v.08 (I.O., *Bengal Secret and Separate Cons.*, Aug. 1–20, 1808; Kaye, i. 414–16).

Gardane and his imposing mission were at his door. A Russian embassy was on its way from Georgia. Was Persia to face the united hostility of both the allied Powers with no certainty of help from Britain? . . . Inevitably Malcolm's demand was rejected. His envoy was forbidden to proceed beyond Shiraz, and he was himself directed to communicate with the Viceroy of Fars. Malcolm did the only thing he could do. He immediately embarked and left Bushire for Bombay. In a firm, yet generous, minute Minto ascribed the failure of the mission to the initial blunder of attempting to secure its object by intimidation rather than persuasion.[1]

Minto passed the same judgement on the minor matter of Malcolm's dealings with Said. 'Malcolm's proceedings at Muscat', he wrote, 'have been affected with the original sin of his whole system.' But no such proof of failure could be forthcoming in this case as in that of Persia. The young Imam, after all, was not the Shah. Muscat was more exposed to British men-of-war than Teheran to a British army. Nor had the demand for the admission of British troops to Omani ports been so immediate as the demand for the expulsion of the French from Persia. Opinion, indeed, at Calcutta, backed by Malcolm, was now inclined to prefer the seizure of the Persian island of Karrack to the occupation of Gombroon or any other of Said's ports. Muscat tended, therefore, to fall again into the background; and, when Seton was recalled to India in order to conduct the mission to Sind, British interests were left in the hands of the Company's Hindu broker.

[1] Kaye, 419-22, gives Malcolm's defence. Minto, 113-20. The following passage from Minto's draft minute deserves quotation: 'The dignity of our Sovereign and of our national character will not be impaired by forbearance, which is due from the strong towards the weak. In my opinion the most dignified basis on which we can treat with Persia is that of *common interest*. The measures we have to propose to Persia are those which I sincerely think can alone afford her any prospect of escaping from the pressing danger of being involved in the general scheme of French conquest. I would avow at the same time, without scruple or disguise, that we also have an interest in securing Persia against its occupation by French armies and that the defence of Persia will be an additional means of security to ourselves.'

This neglect was by no means pleasing to Said. Whatever he may have thought of Malcolm's manners, he wanted to keep in the closest possible touch with British India. At this very time, it is true, he had concluded his second treaty with Decaen; but Decaen was no more able than before to help him against the Wahabi or the Jawasmi, and the advent of Napoleon seemed no nearer. Twice Said wrote to Duncan at Bombay and got no answer. He wrote a third time in February 1809, to express his satisfaction that Seton had at last returned to his post, and took occasion to complain of Duncan's silence in unusually stiff terms. 'Some time ago I addressed a communication to you . . . and have been in expectation of receiving your answer; but I have failed to experience any token of your regards in this instance. For the rest you are master of your acts. I may observe, however, that this is very far removed from personal kindness.' This time Duncan replied at once, explaining that his silence had not been due to 'inattention' but to the lengthy inquiries he had been obliged to make in order to answer the questions raised by Said as to the purchase by neutrals of British ships captured by the French—a practice, it may be remembered, in which the Imams and their subjects had long indulged. Duncan made no apology for omitting even to acknowledge Said's previous letters, and his closing expressions of friendship were not warm. 'For all further particulars I refer you to Captain Seton', whose kind reception by the Imam accorded with 'the intimate connexion and harmony between the two States'.[1]

Seton, indeed, was Said's best friend. For some time past he had been urging his superiors to recognize the dangers threatening Oman, and in 1808 he had put it to Malcolm—and Malcolm had agreed—that nothing but British intervention could save it from subjection to the combined forces of the Wahabi and Jawasmi. But, though the control of Muscat by Arab fanatics or pirates would inflict a disastrous blow on British influence and trade in the whole area of the Persian Gulf, the authorities at Calcutta and Bombay were still unwilling to move: and Said

[1] Said to Duncan, 9.ii.09; Duncan to Said, 15.iii.09 (*Bombay Political and Secret Cons.*, March 24–April 7, 1809, pp. 2575–9).

could do nothing but take any chance that offered itself of renewing his old appeal at least for co-operation, at most for a regular alliance. An incident in the spring of 1809 reveals this persistent diplomacy at work on a relatively trivial matter. A letter from a Hindu secret agent of the French addressed to his employers in Gardane's mission was intercepted on its way to Teheran. It contained nothing of interest, nothing except such sanguine reports of public opinion as, no doubt, their author thought were wanted. 'The French are expected in India as the Messiah by the Hebrews.' 'The Arabs of the Persian Gulf do not at all like the English, but eagerly long for the French.' And so forth. But Seton also had his agents, and from them he learned that the 'Frenchman' carried about with him on his person something that might contain more valuable information—a packet the contents of which could be seen through a tear in the cover to be written in cipher. Money was offered for it, but with no result. Then Seton tried another line. In conversation with Mahomed Gholam he casually observed 'how advantageous it must be even to his Government to obtain a knowledge of the views and intentions of the French in Persia which might be attained from their packets'. 'The packet could only be taken from the "Frenchman",' replied Mahomed, 'by taking the skin with it; and we could not break with the French Government till we are assured of an offensive and defensive alliance with the British Government. On *that* I will send you both the agent and the packet immediately.'[1]

A British alliance Said could not have, and, at the time this incident was reported to Bombay, even British co-operation against the Jawasmi, still more against the Wahabi, seemed as unobtainable as ever. Seton was informed that the Governor-General in Council deemed it 'inexpedient to adopt any decisive line of conduct at present with respect to the Jawasmi pirates'. For the protection of trade naval officers were instructed to

[1] Malcolm and Seton on Muscat: B.P.S.C. April 14–May 6, p. 3554. Miles, ii. 315. French Agent to the Interpreter of the Legation at Teheran, 28.iii.09 (B.P.S.C., as above, pp. 3549–50). Seton to G. of B., 16.v.09 (ibid., May 9–24, 1809, pp. 4421–4).

attack and destroy any pirate ships they might meet, but not to go off their course in quest of them. A few months later, however, for reasons to be explained presently, this half-and-half policy was at last abandoned; and it must have been a satisfaction to Seton to be able to inform Said that an expedition against the Jawasmi was being fitted out at Bombay and that his co-operation therein was invited. It was one of his last official acts. He died at Muscat on August 2. And, for all its conventional effusiveness, the letter of regret Said wrote to Duncan may well have been sincere. 'Alas! a hundred thousand times I say Alas! at the loss of so kind and valuable a friend.' Perhaps in those early and anxious years of his reign, as at its safe and prosperous close, perhaps in Seton's day as in Hamerton's, Said had detected in the British officer stationed at his court a friendliness, a frankness, and a sense of honour as useful to him as they were rare in the world in which he moved.[1]

5

It so happened that Said's fortunes were linked at last with those of British India by common action against a common enemy at a time when their greater common danger was fast receding and soon to disappear. By the summer of 1809 the shadow of Napoleon no longer reached as far as the Persian Gulf. In the spring of 1808, when he was impatiently pressing Decrès to hurry on the preparations for the naval surprise attack on India by way of Île de France, the first demonstration had just been given of the rise of a new force in Europe which was presently to undermine the whole structure of his power. One of the measures decided on by Napoleon at Tilsit was the complete subjugation of the Iberian peninsula with a view to tightening the 'continental system' for the strangling of British trade, obtaining the free use of the Spanish fleet, and guaranteeing the security of his western flank before turning to the East. By the end of 1807 Portugal had been forced to declare war on England;

[1] Supreme Govt.'s decision (13.iii.09), reaffirmed by Bom. Govt. (21.iv.09): B.P.S.C. April 14–May 6, pp. 3554–5. Said to Duncan, 8.viii.09 (B.P.S.C. Aug. 5–Sept. 1, pp. 8002–4). Hamerton, p. 471, below.

and not only Lisbon but the chief towns of Spain, France's uncomfortable ally for twelve years past, had been occupied by French troops. By the middle of 1808 one of Napoleon's most cynical diplomatic games had been played to its end, the wretched puppets of the Spanish royal house had been tricked and discarded, Murat and a French army were in Madrid, and Joseph Buonaparte was King of Spain. But the gamester had overreached himself at last. On May 2 a popular rising at Madrid, not easily suppressed, proclaimed the awakening of Spanish nationalism. In a few weeks all Spain was in revolt. In July General Dupont was surrounded at Baylen and forced to surrender with 17,000 men—the first break in the tradition of French invincibility—and King Joseph, after only nine days in his capital, withdrew with all the French troops behind the Ebro. In August, in response to the Spanish patriots' appeal, Sir Arthur Wellesley landed with 12,000 British troops near Lisbon, defeated Junot at Vimiero, and secured the French evacuation of Portugal. The Peninsular War had begun.

The military importance of this diversion in the West might seem relatively slight: but its continuance would both prevent the success of Napoleon's 'continental system' and weaken his strategic position in central Europe. He determined to eliminate it once for all. Part of the 'Grande Armée' was rapidly transferred from Germany. Fresh troops were raised in France. In December over 250,000 French soldiers were in Spain with Napoleon himself at their head, the Spanish armies were scattered and broken, and the British driven back to Corunna and the sea. But, though Napoleon might seem to have mastered Spain, Spanish nationalism was not crushed; and away on his other flank the earlier events of 1808, the check to his diplomacy, the blow to his prestige, had intensified the new nationalist ferment in Prussia; and Austria, the natural leader of a pan-German war of liberation, was arming. In January 1809 Napoleon suddenly left Madrid for Paris. In April he was at war with Austria. In July he fought one of his most brilliant battles at Wagram. In October he imposed the Treaty of Schönbrunn on the humiliated Habsburg. And amid the pomp and lustre of his marriage with an Austrian archduchess in the following spring he might seem to have not merely recovered but strengthened his dominion over Europe. In fact the process of its downfall had begun. Wellington, as Talavera had made him, was entrenched in Portugal. Stein and the Prussian soldiers were waiting for the chance of a revolt. The Tsar was swinging back from distrustful friendship towards open enmity. It was only two years now to 1812. And, if Europe had still to endure the last bloody act of the long drama, Asia was to be left beyond its scope. Napoleon's dream of oriental conquest had been dissipated by the Spanish mob at Madrid on May 2, 1808. Thereafter he was never to get farther east than Moscow.

Napoleon was slow to acquiesce in the abandonment of his designs on India. Throughout that eventful May of 1808 he was constantly thinking of the expedition. As late as June 10 he finally determined its composition—56 ships, 10,600 seamen, and 19,600 soldiers with rations for the voyage, for storage at Île de France, and for the subsequent descent on India. But by June 28 he had begun to ask himself 'si je dois détacher du continent d'Europe des forces considérables'; and on July 7 he tells Decrès that, unless the Spanish insurrection could be quickly suppressed, an expedition on the projected scale must be postponed. That was the last of it. On August 19 Napoleon directed that twenty frigates should be sent out in pairs to prey on British trade 'dans tous les coins de l'univers'. One pair was to make for Île de France. Not a word now of an 'Army of India'.[1]

Thus the turn of the tide in Europe left Decaen stranded again on Île de France. More than a pair of frigates was needed to revive his fast-fading vision of French Empire in the East. The Spanish revolt had thrown the Philippines into the arms of Britain. Communications with Java were no longer safe or regular. His own islands were now exposed to an intermittent blockade. If the British felt strong enough to take the offensive, the French flag might soon cease to fly anywhere in the Indian Ocean.

[1] Prentout, 472–4.

Decaen's fears were Minto's hopes. 'A ship has just arrived from England', he wrote in February 1809, 'which left on September 17. She has brought us the triumphs of Sir A. Wellesley in Portugal. What a sunshine has broken upon the world!' News of Talavera followed; and, though the sky was soon clouded again by Napoleon's prompt recovery of the Peninsula, the menace of his designs on India grew less and less as the year advanced. Not only was Napoleon tied, for the moment at any rate, to Europe: but the prospect of his march through Asia now seemed somewhat more 'chimerical' than before.

'If Europe is entirely subdued, the King of Men may carry his views to the eastward, but I am strongly inclined to believe that they would be limited to disturbing us by inciting some of the Asiatic States to make incursions into Hindustan supported and directed by partial aid in small bodies of French and perhaps Russian troops and good European officers. The difficulties in the way of an advance by a large European army are scarcely surmountable. However, we should always have ample notice; for rapidity is practicable in the invasion of Spain or Italy, but is simply impossible in transporting a French army to the Indus with all its artillery, stores and apparatus the whole of which must attend it; for the most indispensable equipments of a great European force do not exist on this side of Vienna, and can neither be kept up nor, if lost or wasted, can be renewed in Asia, except only in our own provinces where all the resources of war abound and are to us at hand.'

For a time Minto was preoccupied by the 'Madras Mutiny'; but, as soon as that deplorable incident had been firmly closed, he began to revive the plans, cherished by Wellesley eight years earlier, for a counter-attack on the chain of French positions encircling India which, if successful, would finally destroy the possibility of an invasion from Europe by depriving it of all the advance-bases it would need.[1]

The land-route had already been secured by yet another change of front by Persia. The Shah had found French promises illusory. Gardane and his 'advance-guard' had remained at Teheran, but no main army came marching eastward. Persia

[1] Minto, 180–3.

had been left, moreover, to deal with Russia single-handed: the French would not even mediate as a friend of both parties. And so the Shah had begun to turn once more to the British. In 1809 the issue came to a head. Gardane and his mission withdrew: in their place came a British envoy, Harford Jones: and instead of the Franco-Persian treaty an Anglo-Persian treaty was concluded under which 'every treaty or agreement' between Persia and 'any one of the Powers of Europe' became 'null and void' and the Persian frontiers were closed to any European force advancing towards India. These negotiations were controlled from London, for the Foreign Office had decided to take relations with Persia into its own hands. When, therefore, in January 1810, Minto dispatched Malcolm on his third mission to Persia, it was not so much to do business as to maintain the prestige of the Government of India as a great Asiatic Power. Nothing showed more clearly the reaction of events in Europe on the politics of the Middle East than the contrast between Malcolm's reception on this occasion and the last. The Shah made all the amends he could. He pointedly put Malcolm at least on an equal formal footing with Harford Jones, and personally on an even higher footing. Among other marks of his esteem he created a new order of the Lion and the Sun, of which Malcolm was the first recipient: he could not give him, he said, the same decoration he had given Gardane. Clearly the Persian swing-over to the British side had been quite wholehearted. There could be little danger now of the Shah acquiescing in any French designs on the Persian Gulf. None the less, it still seems odd that, when Malcolm stopped off Muscat on his journey, he again did not trouble to go ashore and visit Said.[1]

There remained the sea-route with its two French strongholds in the Dutch East Indies and the Mascarenes, which had so long troubled British India as bases not only for the projected expedition from Europe but immediately and continuously for the destruction of British merchant-shipping.

[1] Kaye, vol. ii, chap. i. Mr. Hankey Smith was left at Muscat as a temporary liaison officer. Treaty of 1809: Aitcheson, *Treaties*, &c., vi. 384.

French cruisers and privateers had been more active in these last few years than ever before. They infested all the waters of the Indian Ocean from the Moluccas to Natal, making famous in the records of French naval history the names of such ships as *Sémillante* and *Revenant* and such sailors as Bouvet and Robert Surcout. In six months from October 1808 they captured eighteen British ships with cargoes worth over £300,000. In the course of 1809 they took no less than six of the East India Company's 'Indiamen'. The total loss they inflicted ran into millions. No wonder Minto had longed from the outset of his administration to strike at the source of so much injury, and had chafed at the delay imposed on him by financial stringency in India and prohibitive orders from home. But early in 1810 he felt free to move, even in anticipation of permission from London. Already in the spring of 1809 he had sent out two small expeditions, one east to seize Amboyna, the other west to occupy Rodriguez, the little eastward outpost of the Mascarenes, then inhabited by three French settlers with some seventy slaves. The latter acquisition enabled the blockade of Île de France and Bourbon, which had hitherto been broken at intervals by the ships' having to go to the Cape for revictualling, to be maintained more closely and continuously. It was at Rodriguez, also, that a force of 4,000 men was assembled early in the summer of 1810 for the attack on Bourbon. On July 7 a landing was effected, and on July 10 the island capitulated. By the first week of the following November reinforcements from India had brought up the strength of the assailants to about 10,000. At the end of the month they were put ashore on Île de France, and Decaen, his garrison so reduced that it could not fully man the walls of Port Louis, was compelled to capitulate on December 2. A few weeks later (February 20, 1811) Sylvain Roux surrendered the fort at Tamatave and the other French posts in Madagascar to a British squadron.

In the East, meantime, two more Molucca islands had been occupied, and in the summer of 1811 a force of over 10,000 men was gathered at Malacca for the conquest of Java. Minto himself accompanied the expedition with Stamford Raffles on his

Seyyid Said at Muscat

staff. Early in August the invaders landed and occupied Batavia without fighting. On the 26th the entrenchments at Cornelis, to which the enemy—French, Dutch, and native troops—had withdrawn, were stormed under heavy fire. There was little further resistance, and on September 16 General Jannsens, who had succeeded Marshal Daendals in charge of the administration, signed the capitulation.

Thus swiftly all Napoleon's footholds in the East, both French and Dutch, passed out of his possession, and for the few remaining years of the war Britain's control over the waters and coasts and islands of the Indian Ocean was undisputed. But, when peace came at last, Britain did not retain all her conquests. For the stability of Europe and for the security and reputation of their own country British statesmen desired that the restored monarchy of France and the new kingdom of the United Netherlands should not be unduly weakened. In the Treaty of 1814, accordingly, together with other concessions in other parts of the world, the East Indies were restored to the Netherlands and Bourbon to France. Mauritius 'and its dependencies' were retained, and at first it was supposed that the 'dependencies' included not only Rodriguez and the Seychelles, which had been named in the treaty, but also the French posts in Madagascar. When, however, the French Government claimed that those posts, not having been mentioned in the treaty, should be regarded as having been restored to France like Bourbon, the British Government acquiesced and instructed the Governor of Mauritius, Sir Robert Farquhar, to hand over 'to the French authorities at Bourbon such establishments as the Government of France possessed on the coasts of the island of Madagascar' on January 1, 1792. By 1818 Agent-General Roux was back at Tamatave; French traders were again at work at their other depots on the coast; and some of the native tribes in that vicinity, notably the warlike Sakalava, had been induced to accept the protection or suzerainty of France.[1]

---

[1] The case for British retention of the Madagascar posts, advanced by Farquhar, rested on the English translation of Article VIII of the treaty. After declaring that French colonial possessions captured in the war

So the end of the long Franco-British conflict in the western Indian Ocean, while it left Britain the stronger Power, did not eliminate France: and those acts of retrocession meant that French policy as well as British was to play a part in shaping the future of East Africa.

6

The end of the long war must have been welcome to Said. From the beginning of his reign his fortunes had been at the mercy of the great belligerents. The integrity of his territories, his own independence, had never been secure. A French landing on his soil had been threatened, a British occupation of it projected. And if indeed Napoleon had come East, Said's little kingdom might have been caught between the combatants and trampled underfoot. But now those dangers were over: and he had emerged from them on the right side. Up to 1809 he had managed to keep on friendly terms with Port Louis without antagonizing Bombay. In 1810, just when the balance of the war was taking its last swing, he had become definitely linked with the British by a brotherhood-in-arms. There had been some luck in it, no doubt, and Seton had played his part, but the main credit for the diplomacy of those ten war-years must go to Said—and in 1814 he was only twenty-three.

It was not only Said's diplomacy, however, that brought about that decisive co-operation between British and Omani troops; nor was it only Seton's warning—though it had weight, no doubt, and was backed by Malcolm—that, if Oman were overwhelmed by its enemies, the Persian Gulf could be virtually closed to British trade and influence. The main reason which stirred the Government of India at last from its aloofness was that the Jawasmi had proved themselves incorrigibly and unforgivably its enemies as well as Said's. In 1806 their leading

were to be restored, the French text ran 'à l'exception . . . de l'Île de France et de ses dépendances, nommément Rodrigue et les Séchelles', and the English 'with the exception . . . of the Isle of France and its dependencies, especially Rodriguez and the Seychelles'. Acceptance of French claim: Bathurst to Farquhar, 18.x.16 (C.O. 168. 3).

chief, Sultan-bin-Suggur, had signed with Seton at Bunder Abbas a treaty which bound him and all his dependants to 'respect the flag and property of the Honourable East India Company'; but, though the Bombay Government had shown in the ensuing years a patience which seemed to some of its own officers inexhaustible, the pirates' promise had not been kept for long. In 1808, their fleet enlarged by captures to over 60 big dhows and over 800 other vessels, capable all told of carrying 19,000 men, the Jawasmi resumed their assault on British shipping. In that year they attacked five of the Company's cruisers and gunboats, four of them unsuccessfully, but the fifth, the *Sylph*, of only 78 tons, was surrounded by a swarm of pirate boats, boarded and captured, and her crew massacred. Worse than that was the case of the *Minerva*, a British merchant-ship hailing from Bombay. The pirates got aboard her after a running fight of several days, hewed the captain in pieces, slaughtered most of the crew, and kept the lady passenger captive till a heavy ransom had been paid. It was these and other similar attacks which convinced Minto that the policy of patience had been played out. In the summer of 1809 he directed the Bombay Government to prepare a punitive expedition for the 'Pirate Coast' and to invite the Imam of Muscat to co-operate.[1]

Thus Said had realized at last the primary object of his external policy—an actual, if only temporary, alliance with the British. And at first the results were all he could have hoped. Seton's place was quickly filled. In his reply to Said's announcement of Seton's death, Duncan informed him that Mr. W. C. Bunce, who had previously been posted at Bussora, had already been instructed to proceed to Muscat and that his first task would be to discuss the forthcoming measures against the Jaswami. 'I confidently rely on your Highness extending every assistance to the objects of this expedition, which has indeed been primarily undertaken at your Highness' instance'—Duncan also could be diplomatic—'as so earnestly expressed through the late Resident.' The chief requirements would be pilots, provisions, and fresh water, for which due payment would be made.

[1] B.R. 303–5. Miles, ii. 313–16. Treaty, B.R. 75.

All this, of course, Said was ready to provide when in due course two frigates, nine cruisers, and several transports carrying over 1,000 British regulars and some thousand Indian troops arrived at Muscat. On November 11 an attack was delivered on Ras al Khyma, one of the most formidable of the Jawasmi strongholds, at the northern end of the 'Pirate Coast' just inside the Gulf. It was captured and burnt and the ships lurking in its backwater destroyed. Next, the British force took and burnt Linjah; then it seized Luft and restored it to one of Said's dependants; and then, on January 4, 1810, this time accompanied by Omani ships and troops under Said's command, it attacked Shinas, on the seaward side of the peninsula, outside the Gulf, and after fierce fighting carried it by storm. And then, when it seemed as if the power of one of Said's two implacable enemies was at last to be broken, the other intervened. A Wahabi army was at this time at Baraimi led by the Emir's ablest general, Mutlak al-Mutairi; and, since the Jawasmi had recently submitted to the Emir's overlordship—their leader, indeed, Husain-bin-Ali, was nominally Ibn Saud's viceregent on the 'Pirate Coast'—Mutlak marched at once to the rescue, but arrived at Ras al Khyma too late to save it. At Shinas he was also late, but the place had only just fallen, and the British and Omani forces were still there. His arrival put Colonel Lionel Smith, the British commanding officer, and Seton, his political agent, in a difficult position. They were well aware that the avoidance of a quarrel with the Wahabi was a fixed point of policy at Bombay and Calcutta: the possibility, indeed, of being involved with the Wahabi had been the dominant reason for not attacking the Jawasmi before; and on this very expedition they had been instructed to let the Wahabi know that the British desired to remain at peace with them, and to avoid 'all operations on land otherwise than might be momentarily necessary for the more effectual destruction of the pirate vessels in their harbours'. And now the Wahabi were confronting them, and in greatly superior force. For three days Smith awaited their attack: then, since Mutlak, though ready to help the Jawasmi in defence, was apparently unwilling to take the offensive, he disembarked his troops and sailed away. And what of Said and his Omanis? They must have hoped to see the British fatally embroiled with the Wahabi, but, if they were disappointed, they were not betrayed. They could have withdrawn with the British; but, though the Wahabi were certain to attack them as soon as their allies had gone, Said, who throughout his life showed himself a better judge of policy than of fighting, stood his ground. The Wahabi onslaught was immediate and overwhelming. But Said found refuge with his routed men in the fortress of Sohar, some fifty miles to southward, whence, having withstood a short investment by the Wahabi, they finally returned to Muscat.[1]

But even Muscat was no longer safe for Said. He was in greater danger now than ever before or after in his life. The Wahabi army which had gathered at Baraimi and been directed thence to Ras al Khyma and Shinas had been dispatched by the Emir Ibn Saud from Nejd not merely, as before, to raid and terrorize the Omani country but to subjugate it once for all to Wahabi rule and the Wahabi faith. Mutlak was now moving west through the Batineh, pillaging the land and massacring its inhabitants; and, though Said hurriedly strengthened the defences of the forts he still retained, they could not be relied on, nor perhaps could Muscat itself, to stand a protracted siege by all the Emir's forces. There seemed only one hope, the British; and in January 1810 Said sent a desperate appeal to Bombay. 'I am expecting', he wrote, 'under the auspices of Heaven, your ships and victorious troops . . . having in view the annihilation of the deluded Wahabi tribe who are the foes of us both.' 'They have twice or thrice', he added, 'solicited a restoration of peace and harmony, but in consequence of my connexion with the British Government I would not accede to their wish.' This afterthought was as unwise as it was untrue, and Minto and his Council pounced on it when the Bombay Government submitted the letter to them. It was Said's obvious intention, ran their reply to Bombay, to antagonize the Wahabi against the British

[1] C. R. Low, *History of the Indian Navy* (London, 1877), i. 325–35. Miles, ii. 316–17. Duncan to Said, 7.ix.09 (B.P.S.C. 8–29.ix.09, pp. 8320–6). Bunce's instructions, ibid., pp. 8310–19.

by pretending that the latter were co-operating with him, in the hope that he 'may actually kindle a war and thereby secure to himself the aid he has solicited'. Nothing should be done to encourage 'the belief of our being a party in the war in which he is engaged with the Wahabees, against whom various considerations render it at present inexpedient and indeed impracticable to afford him effectual assistance, however desirable it might be on abstract grounds of policy to support the independence of Muscat'. He should be told that 'it is unnecessary to regulate his reply to any overtures on the part of his enemy by a reference to his connexion with the British Government', that that Government 'is no further interested in the existing contest between him and the Wahabees than as it is solicitous for the welfare and prosperity of the Imam', and that it recommends him 'to grant the terms of pacification solicited by the Wahabees if consistent with the honour and security of the State of Muscat . . . '—a chilling reproof, more in Malcolm's style than Minto's; but there was a real risk of entanglement with the Wahabi, and the need of firmly checking Said's designs was no longer offset by the danger of driving him into the arms of France. When this dispatch was drafted in August, Bourbon had already fallen and Île de France was about to fall.[1]

Meantime the Omani were making a stubborn resistance. Throughout the autumn and winter of 1810 Mutlak raided and burnt and slew, but nowhere could he enforce a general submission to Wahabi rule. With one or two exceptions all the towns that were equipped with forts and garrisons repulsed his attack. But Said was no match for Mutlak in the open field. Emboldened by the arrival of 1,500 Persian troops sent at his urgent request by the Governor of Fars, he offered battle; but the Persians—such at least was the Omani version—'wheeled their horses round and retreated without fighting', whereupon, it must be inferred, the Omani followed suit. A little later Mutlak, seeking a decision, marched against Muscat itself and

[1] Said to Duncan, 30.i.10; G. of B. to Supreme Govt., 17.vii.10; Supreme Govt. to G. of B., 10.viii.10 (Bengal P.C. 11.viii.10; B.P.C. 18.ix.10).

attempted to carry its impregnable defences by storm. He was repulsed and withdrew, but, when Said rashly pursued him, he rounded on him in the Maarwal Valley and defeated him with heavy loss. Then, for an interval, the pressure on Oman was reduced. Away in the West Mahomet Ali was about to launch from Egypt his first attempt to wrest the holy cities of Mecca and Medina from Wahabi control. 'The wretched army of the Wahabees', Said reported joyfully to Duncan, 'at every fortress it approached, experiencing defeat and discomfiture, was compelled to retreat. . . . They have fled with the utmost precipitation and confusion. . . . Through God's grace the affairs of this detestable race are on the decline.' And he added his congratulations on the news of the fall of Île de France. 'Thanks to the Almighty, mankind has thereby been relieved from the vicious propensities of those tyrants [the French].' But, despite this show of confidence, Said knew he was not yet out of danger; and one of his diplomatic agents, Sheikh Majid, was soon renewing at Bombay the old appeal for military aid. Duncan's term of office had expired, and it fell to the acting-Governor, George Brown, to make the old reply. He repeated the main point of Minto's dispatch. Said should come to terms with the Wahabi, in his own interests and without reference to the British who have never been attacked by the Wahabi and are determined on neutrality. But he added a new point by way of a further deterrent—or was it, perhaps, a faint intimation that British neutrality was not, after all, immutable? In the 'doubtful contingency', he wrote, of a force being sent to maintain 'the security of the State of Muscat', Said must realize that he would have to pay the whole cost of it.[1]

Events in the West soon showed that Said's forebodings had been justified. Early in 1812 the invading Egyptians were caught in a defile on their way to Medina and after three days' fighting put to rout with the loss of all their guns. It was a blow from which even the impetuous Mahomet Ali would need time to recover, and it seemed more than likely that, as soon as the

[1] Said's agent to Duncan, 10.iv.11; Said to Duncan, 10.v.11; Brown to Said, 20.xi.11 (B.P.C. 13.iv, 7.vi, and 4.xii.11). Miles, ii. 318.

heat of the summer was past, the Wahabi would descend again on Oman. Once more, therefore, Said dispatched an agent to Bombay with the usual prayer. And once more it was unheeded. Brown wrote in the friendliest terms, assuring Said of 'the sincerity of a connection which has now been so happily preserved for upwards of fourteen years', and informing him that his agent had been permitted to purchase military stores from the government department. But of an active alliance against the Wahabi, of sending troops for the defence of Muscat, there was not a word.[1]

For the moment, however, it seemed that Said would need no help. The autumn drew on, and the Wahabi did not come. Then in November Mahomet Ali struck again. This time he was more successful. Medina quickly fell, and, not many weeks later, he was master of Mecca too. Said might well have thought himself quite out of danger now; but, while the Egyptians were occupied in consolidating their hold on the Hejaz, the Emir Ibn Saud determined to seek compensation by a last attempt to subjugate Oman. In the spring of 1813 Mutlak was advancing once again from Baraimi on Muscat. Said met him at Masna'ah, about sixty miles from the capital, but now he did not take the risk of battle. Given time, he thought, he must be safe; so he requested a personal interview with Mutlak and persuaded him to withdraw from Oman with the huge bribe of 40,000 dollars. But he had wasted his money. Mahomet Ali was involved in intrigues at Mecca, and Ibn Saud had one more fling at Oman. In November Mutlak, recalled from his temporary disgrace, took the field again. He was approaching Muscat from the west when, in an encounter with the upland tribes, he was shot dead. Deprived of their greatest general, the Wahabi broke up and retreated. It was a stroke of luck for Said, and it was final. In April 1814 Ibn Saud died, and, not long after, a great Wahabi army was crushingly defeated by the Egyptians. A humiliating peace afforded the new Emir Abdulla a breathing-space, but in 1818 the Egyptian forces penetrated right through the desert into Nejd, took and destroyed its capital, Darayyah, and sent Abdulla to Constantinople, where the Sultan ordered his

[1] Brown to Said, 17.vi.12 (B.P.C. 1812, pp. 1380-1).

execution. It took the Wahabi twenty years to recover from this blow. It was not till 1845 that once again they invaded Oman.[1]

For this great relief Said owed nothing whatever to his British 'friends', but it was they who delivered him from his other danger. The Jawasmi had quickly recovered from the punishment administered by Colonel Smith. They restored their stronghold at Ras al Khyma and from 1811 onwards renewed their depredations on British shipping. In 1814 they were making captures as close to Bombay as the coast of Kathiawar and Sind. In 1815 they raided several ports in the Red Sea and preyed on the traffic between India and Mocha. Off Muscat itself, in that year, they caught a British merchantman and massacred her crew, and also fell in with, and nearly captured, Said's frigate, *Caroline*, of 40 guns, Said himself being on board and wounded in the fight. In 1816 the Resident at Bushire, Bruce, was sent with a frigate and two cruisers to Ras al Khyma to demand redress, but obtained no satisfaction. For two more years, nevertheless, the Governments at Calcutta and Bombay continued the old policy of patience, mainly for the old reason, but then at last the collapse of the Wahabi power set them free to deal with the incorrigible pirates firmly and finally without fear of complications elsewhere in Arabia. In May 1819, accordingly, Lieutenant Sadleir was sent to Muscat to repeat the role of Bunce in 1809. Said received him with the utmost courtesy, but evaded any definite commitments. His reason apparently was that the joint action proposed was not only with his friends, the British, but also with the Egyptians whom he regarded as potential enemies. Maybe, too, he doubted whether the British-Indian authorities had really at last made up their minds to fight. So he procrastinated and talked at large and refused to be cornered till Sadleir gave it up and rode off across the desert in pursuit of the Egyptian army. But when in November a force of 3,000 men, more than half of whom were British, under the command of General Sir W. G. Keir, actually

[1] B.R. 183-5. Miles, ii. 319-20. Dodwell, 45-9.

left Bombay, convoyed by nine warships, Said, of course, no longer hesitated. He joined them at Kishm with three ships and 4,000 men. As in 1809, the first blow was struck at Ras al Khyma, but now no more was needed. The Jawasmi knew their game was up. The Wahabi were no longer at their backs; and, as the strength of the expedition showed, the British were no longer to be satisfied with half-measures. On January 8, 1820, the famous 'General Treaty' was signed by the two leading chiefs, and in the course of a few weeks by eight others, declaring in its first article that 'There shall be a cessation of plunder and piracy, by land and sea, on the part of the Arabs who are parties to this contract, for ever'. Unlike its predecessor, this treaty was observed, mainly owing to the vigilance of the British squadron now permanently stationed at Kishm. Acts of piracy became rare and were promptly punished, until in the course of a generation the old curse of the Persian Gulf had been virtually extinguished.[1]

The expedition had a sequel in which Said was concerned. The Beni Bu Ali, a warlike tribe occupying the easternmost corner of Oman, having accepted the overlordship and the faith of the Wahabi, had long been a thorn in Said's side. At the time of the expedition, as it happened, they had not only been detected in acts of piracy but had murdered the interpreter of a British brig sent to make inquiries. Said seized this opportunity. He pleaded for prompt military action, and it was partly at least on his account that, in November 1820, six companies of sepoys with six guns, under Captain Thompson, now Resident in the Gulf, were dispatched from Muscat to Sur, accompanied by Said with about a thousand men. The result was disastrous. The combined force, advancing inland, was met by the Beni Bu Ali and completely defeated, the British-Indian section of it losing 6 officers, 270 men, and all its guns. The Government of India had never sanctioned this minor expedition, and it promptly recalled Thompson, but it felt bound, 'for the support of our

---

[1] B.R. 188. G. F. Sadleir, *Diary of a Journey across Arabia* (Bombay, 1866), 133-8. Low, i. 352-63. Miles, ii. 323-4. Wilson, 207-8. Treaty, B.R. 76.

national character', to make good such a severe and humiliating reverse. In March 1821 a large force under General Smith defeated and decimated the tribe, destroyed their habitations, and carried off most of the survivors to captivity in Bombay. Eighty of them unhappily fell into the hands of Said, who, with a vindictiveness towards his enemies he more than once displayed, starved them to death in one of the Muscat forts. The Bombay prisoners, on the other hand, were restored to their country two years later, with Said's reluctant consent, and provided with a government grant for the rebuilding of their villages.[1]

7

With the downfall of the Beni Bu Ali the first of the two periods into which Said's reign divides, the Muscat period, reached its climax. The young Seyyid—he was still only thirty—was now the undisputed master of all Oman. Of his external enemies, the Wahabi were broken, the Jawasmi suppressed. Inside Oman, the most troublesome of the tribes had been wellnigh wiped out. He might never be rid of personal intrigues; in later years his departure from Muscat for any length of time meant almost certain trouble; but so strong was his position now, so high his prestige, that in 1824 he could safely undertake the pilgrimage to Mecca. By that act he set the seal on his rise to power and proclaimed it to the Moslem world. The pious journey was also a triumphal progress. The mission sent to greet the pilgrim by Mahomet Ali, the courtesies paid him by the Turkish Governor at Jedda, the audience granted him by the Sherif himself, and the public admiration of his personal bearing and his princely retinue, alike acclaimed him the greatest ruler Oman had yet known.[2]

But Said was not now content with Oman. As with other rulers in history, so with him, the attainment of national unity and security at home was a prelude to expansion oversea; and

[1] B.R. 189–91. Low, i. 371–3, 381–3. Miles, ii. 326–7. According to B.R. 191, 'His Highness the Imam cut down the date groves and turned the watercourses' of the Beni Bu Ali in the course of the second expedition. Said and his prisoners: Badger, lxxi. 344.
[2] Miles, ii. 328.

Said, who had never forgotten, still less renounced, his hereditary claim to the overlordship of the Arab communities on the East African coast, now felt strong enough at last to assert it. A reconnoitring expedition, dispatched soon after the extinction of the Beni Bu Ali, had made it clear that a good deal of force would be needed. Mombasa, in particular, was not going to submit without a struggle. But Said was prepared to use all the resources of Oman to obtain an African dominion which would both raise still higher his political prestige and greatly improve his commercial and financial position. By the time of his pilgrimage he had already opened his attack on Mombasa.[1]

It was not only the strength of his domestic situation that seemed to justify this African adventure. No difficulty, no objection seemed likely to be made in this quarter by either of the two sea Powers who had recently contested the control of the Indian Ocean. Said's relations with the French were once more cordial. Taking quick advantage of the peace and of the amicable attitude of the British towards post-war France, he had concluded in 1817 a commercial treaty with the Governor of Bourbon, conceding 'most-favoured-nation' rights to either party. Nor, in any case, did it seem probable that the French were now harbouring any designs on East Africa which could conflict with his. As to the British, who were now, of course, unquestionably more important and formidable than the French, they were friendlier than they had ever been. The collapse of the Wahabi had swiftly brought about a frank recognition of a common interest between his little principality and the Government of India and, still better, active co-operation in its defence. On three occasions he and his Omani had fought side by side with British or Indian troops. On the last of these, it is true, the outcome had been unfortunate. It had so sharply reminded the Government of India of the risks of being implicated in the furtherance of Said's local ambitions that, though he accompanied the second expedition against the Beni Bu Ali, he was not permitted to bring any of his own forces with him. But that affair as a whole had not injured him. If there had been some

[1] See pp. 221, 233, below.

political loss, there had been a notable personal gain. In that first disastrous battle he had displayed, says the official résumé, 'great coolness and courage throughout', and he had been wounded in an attempt to save the life of a British artilleryman. It was his knowledge of the country, moreover, that had enabled the defeated force to make its way safely back to Muscat. For those services the Government of India had presented him with a sword of honour.[1] But Said was far too shrewd to misinterpret such symptoms of personal popularity with the British-Indian authorities. They had had, they still had, a common interest with him in the peace and security of the Persian Gulf; but, if anywhere in the neighbourhood of the Indian Ocean their interest instead of squaring should conflict with his, their friendship would certainly be strained and might easily be broken. But what conflict could there be in East Africa? The British, it seemed, were even less interested in that coast than the French. Their trade with it was trifling. Officially, they seemed scarcely aware of it. At Muscat he would always be in contact with Bombay; but once over in East Africa, if he chose to go adventuring there, he would surely have passed quite beyond the range of British interests or activities.

Said was unaware that just at this period the British Government, not only in India but in London itself and at Mauritius, had begun to be both interested and active in that hitherto neglected East African field. No desire for commercial exploitation, still less for territory, was prompting it. Its sole motive was humanitarian. The British crusade against the Slave Trade was now in process of extension from West Africa to East. And for that reason, so far from losing touch with his British friends by going there, Said was to find himself for all the rest of his life in closer contact with them than he had been before. It might be said, indeed, that Said and the British, with very different objects and in very different ways, entered the East African world together.

[1] The presentation in July 1821 by Dr. Jukes on the way to Teheran is described by J. B. Fraser, *Narrative of a Journey into Khorasan in 1821-2* (London, 1825), 19-20.

VI
BRITISH RECONNAISSANCES
1792–1812

I

THAT Britain entered the East African field so late and with so limited an objective was not due to any weakening of the forces that made for imperial expansion. On the morrow of the collapse of the first British Empire in the American Revolution the foundations of a second were being laid;[1] and the work was not retarded, it was stimulated and facilitated, by the long French wars—by the strategic and economic lessons of Napoleon's attempt to master the world and by the undisputed command of all the seas with which Britain emerged from the conflict. New 'colonies of settlement' were founded in Canada, Australia, New Zealand, and South Africa. New fields of commercial exploitation were sought out in South America, the Pacific, and the Far East, and the trade-routes safeguarded by new naval stations or ports of call. And nowhere was this process of accretion and protection more marked than in the Indian Ocean. It was made impossible, under the conditions of the time, for France or any other Power to revive Napoleon's plan of attacking British India oversea. The restored French posts in India itself, Pondicherry and Chandanagore, were 'demilitarized' by Article XII of the Treaty of Vienna.

'His Most Christian Majesty, on his part, having nothing more at heart than the perpetual duration of Peace between the two Crowns of England and of France, and wishing to do his utmost to avoid anything which might affect their mutual good understanding, engages not to erect any fortifications in the establishments which are to be restored to him within the limits of the British sovereignty upon the continent of India and only to place in those establishments the number of troops necessary for the maintenance of the police.'[2]

The sea-approach to India had been similarly protected. Cape

---

[1] A detailed study of British imperialism from 1783 to 1833 is being made by Professor V. T. Harlow, who kindly drew the author's attention *inter alia* to the Bulama incident briefly described below.

[2] *S.P.* i (1812–14), 162.

Colony, Ceylon, Mauritius, and the Seychelles had been captured and were retained. When the retrocession of the Dutch East Indies seemed to have resulted in the blocking of the path to China, a loop-hole was found and occupied at Singapore. The retrocession of Bourbon and the Madagascar posts was innocuous, since Mauritius was retained and Bourbon had no harbour. Access to the Persian Gulf was secured by the *entente* with Muscat. Access to the Red Sea was soon to be secured by the occupation of Aden. Nothing more was wanted, nothing in Asia, nothing in Central Africa. As regards the Indian Ocean and the route to the Far East, the only piece of Africa essential to the framework of the new British Empire was its southernmost extremity.

Nor was African soil desired in the early nineteenth century for its economic any more than its strategic value. From the commercial standpoint it had become again what it had been before the growth of the Slave Trade, little else than a gigantic obstacle in the way of ships bound for the golden East. In part of the shores of the Gulf of Guinea, British public opinion, it is true, was more interested than ever before. The long, exciting, and triumphant campaign against the Slave Trade had fixed attention on the coast whence most of the slaves were shipped across the Atlantic. And for a variety of interconnected reasons this interest long survived the abolition of the British Slave Trade in 1807. There was, first, the British diplomatic and naval effort, continued for more than fifty years, to suppress the foreign or smuggling Slave Trade. The methods and effects of the blockade were debated in Parliament. Captains' and commissioners' reports were printed and published. Dramatic incidents were described in the newspapers. And with this humanitarian interest was linked a new activity both in religious and in commercial quarters. Pitt had preached as earnestly as Wilberforce that besides the negative duty of stopping the enslavement of Africans there was the positive duty of helping them towards civilization; and Wilberforce, like Livingstone after him, put 'legitimate' commerce second only to Christianity as an instrument to that end. So, while missionaries spread out and worked and died along the coast from Sierra Leone to Calabar, merchants retained their old foothold on the Gambia and the Gold Coast and established a new one in the 'Oil Rivers'. Finally, associated with these philanthropic and economic interests, was that of science. The exploration of the African interior began.

Sooner or later, of course, the idea of territorial expansion, of colonization, was bound to emerge from this complex of interests. One new colony, indeed, had actually been founded. In 1787, when the crusade against the Slave Trade had only just begun, the crusaders themselves, with Granville Sharp at their head, created the colony of Sierra Leone as a home for emancipated slaves. How the other motives led in the same direction is well illustrated by the activities of the Association for the Discovery of the Interior Parts of Africa, which was formed on June 9, 1788. Its primary purpose conformed with its name. It was an earnestly scientific body. Sir Joseph Banks was a member of its first committee. Its 'plan' was an elaboration of the simple text that 'the map of the African interior is still but a wide extended blank'. It was for the cost of exploration that subscriptions were invited and received. And the achievements of the society in exploration were historic. Enough to say that among the men it sent to Africa were Ledyard, Hornemann, and Mungo Park. But, if it served science well and so served the world, the reader of its detailed and always interesting *Proceedings* soon discovers that its members naturally sought to serve their country too. In the early days of their collaboration they put it on record that 'of all the advantages to which a better acquaintance with the inland regions of Africa may lead, the first in importance is the extension of the commerce and the encouragement of the manufactures of Britain'. Some ten years later the desire for economic expansion had propagated a desire for colonies. In 1801 the society submitted to the Government a proposal 'for the establishment of a commercial and military station on the banks of the Joliba or Niger'.[1]

[1] *Proceedings of the Association for Promoting the Discovery*, &c. (London, 1810), i. 6, 11, 201; ii. 25.

British Reconnaissances

The idea of colonization in West Africa was certainly in the air at that time. In the course of the American War a penal settlement had been established on the Gambia for convicts who could no longer be transported to the American colonies. The climate had proved so deadly that the experiment had quickly been abandoned; but, none the less, in 1785 a select parliamentary committee recommended another attempt in West Africa, more to the southward, somewhere between Angola and Table Bay. There was here, said the Committee, 'a vast tract of country' between the Portuguese and Dutch settlements, with fine rivers and a good harbour, and a rich vein of copper ore in the mountains of the interior. A colony in that quarter would serve as a port of call for 'Indiamen', as a base for whale-fishing in the South Atlantic, and as a strategic post in time of war. A sloop was sent by Government to survey the coast, and that was the end of the airy project. Fortunately for the convicts and for the future of Australia no 'Botany Bay' was founded in West Africa.[1]

In 1792 another and more respectable colonial enterprise was launched. A society was formed in London for the colonization of Bulama, an island off the coast of Portuguese Guinea, some 120 miles south of the Gambia. Its object was to apply the 'positive policy' of Pitt and Wilberforce: to promote 'the civilisation of the Africans and eventually put an end to their slavery', and, as a means thereto, to develop the agricultural resources of the island. 'The produce of the West Indies might be readily raised at Bulama by free natives, and thus forming a contrast to the vicious habits of the slave-dealing Europeans, contribute towards the civilisation of those regions.' A memorial on these lines was submitted to Dundas, and a deputation was received by Pitt himself, who said 'he had no objection to our proceeding on our enterprise'. Its nominal head was Mr. H. Dalrymple, who had seen military service at the reduction of Goree in 1779 and had subsequently travelled along the coast;

---

[1] Select Committee on Convicts: *H. of C. Journals*, xl. 1784–5, 1161–4. Holland Rose, *William Pitt and National Revival* (London, 1912), 434–5.

but its moving spirit was Philip Beaver, a naval lieutenant of 26, whose restless and romantic temperament was ill suited to an inactive life at home in peace-time. In April, 275 men, women, and children set out in two brigs and a small schooner on a venture as ill-conceived, as dangerous, and as certain to fail as anything recorded in colonial history. The unhappy colonists arrived at Bulama in May, already discontented and divided, and alarmed by the murder of a party which had landed on the way to 'stretch their legs' ashore. The island was duly purchased with the assistance of an American 'slaver' from a local chief, and the work of clearing the ground and building a blockhouse was begun. Then came the 'rains', four months of tropical downpour and disease and death. The occasional visit of a sloop provided welcome stores but also a means of desertion; and the morale of the fast-diminishing community was further sapped by the menacing attitude of the natives from neighbouring islands. The only gleam of light in the tragic story was the Elizabethan heroism of Beaver, himself at one time nearly dead of fever, always in danger, sleeping every night in his clothes with arms within reach, obstinately refusing to admit defeat, declining to obey the summons home when war broke out with France in 1793, 'having', as he pleaded to the Admiralty, 'the direction of a small colony whose very existence depends upon my presence'. When at last, in the spring of the following year, the hopeless enterprise was given up, there were only two colonists left at Beaver's side.[1]

The difficulties of colonization in West Africa had been plainly revealed by this disastrous experiment, but the idea was not yet dead. About the same time as the survivors returned to England a weighty quarto volume was published in London entitled *An Essay on Colonisation particularly applied to the Western Coast of Africa*. Its author was Mr. C. B. Wadstrom, a Swedish traveller, who had visited the coast with a

---

[1] Capt. P. Beaver, R.N., *African Memoranda relative to an attempt to establish a British Settlement on the Island of Bulama in 1792* (London, 1805), *passim*. Capt. W. H. Smyth, R.N., *Life of Captain Philip Beaver* (London, 1829), 47–107.

fellow countryman, Dr. Sparrman, Professor of Physics at Stockholm. They had both become ardent exponents of colonization as the best method of economic development even in the tropical world. It was Sparrman's information and enthusiasm which had determined the choice of Sierra Leone for the Emancipators' colony in 1787. They both gave evidence before the Privy Council Committee on Trade in Africa in 1788-9; and when asked 'whether they thought that by any and what encouragement the natives of that country might be induced to cultivate cotton, indigo, sugar-cane, &c.', they both unhesitatingly replied that it could be done by planting colonies. The volume of 1794 expounded and expanded the same theme, with theoretical disquisitions on the philosophy of colonization and systematic directions, none the less precise for being academic, as to the organization and administration of a model colony.[1]

Nothing came of this propaganda. At the end of the French War and for more than a generation after, the only British colonies in West Africa were Sierra Leone and the old trade-posts on the Gambia and the Gold Coast. But these footholds on the coast were gradually strengthened and enlarged, mainly as the result of the persistent effort to suppress the Slave Trade. Thus the growing importance of Sierra Leone, which had been transferred in 1808 from Company control to Crown Colony government, was primarily due to the fact that it provided a base for the naval patrols, an official centre for adjudicating on captured slave-ships, and a dumping-ground for rescued slaves. Similarly, when at a lengthy interval another Crown Colony was established in West Africa, the reason was again the Slave Trade. Lagos, now the capital of Nigeria, was annexed in 1861 simply because, after patient trial of other methods, it seemed to be the only way of extirpating the gang of slave-smugglers it harboured. So, if there was no active 'imperialism', no sweeping territorial acquisitions, in West Africa, the British connexion was maintained; and by the

[1] C. B. Wadstrom, *An Essay on Colonisation*, &c. (London, 1794), *passim*. See also *Privy Council Committee's Report*, 1789.

middle of the century it was strong enough to resist the suspicions and anxieties which were beginning to affect public opinion as to the size and cost of British obligations oversea. When, after 1870, the tide turned, when a new wave of European expansion flooded the whole coast and swept far inland, the old British footholds were still there to serve as bases for the extension of British rule side by side with that of other nations.

In East Africa the same sort of British connexion was to be built up in course of time on the same sort of foundations, and it was to result, in the era of 'partition', in a similar extension of British rule over vast spaces of the continent. But at the end of the eighteenth century and far on into the nineteenth the process had not begun. East Africa was barely known in England. Whereas from the days of Hawkins onwards British ships had taken an increasing part in the export of slaves from West Africa, it was very rarely that they sought their victims beyond the Cape and then not farther north than Madagascar. The *Good Hope* is recorded to have gone to East Africa for slaves in 1686. The *Mercury* took slaves from Natal to Virginia in 1719. 'We bought in a fortnight's time seventy-four boys and girls: these are better slaves for working than those of Madagascar, being stronger and blacker.'[1] But, apart from these occasional 'slavers', almost the only British ships which had traversed East African waters from the time of Lancaster's visit to Zanzibar were, it seems, ships like Lancaster's, bound for India and stopping on the way for water and provisions; and almost the only place they had so stopped at was Johanna. Rumours, indeed, had reached England of trade to be got in East Africa. In 1792, for example, a public meeting at Liverpool, with John Tarleton, the mayor of the city and its M.P., in the chair, carried a series of resolutions protesting against the continuance of the East India Company's monopoly in the East because, amongst other weightier reasons, the Company

[1] W. H. Ingrams and L. W. Hollingsworth, *School History of Zanzibar* (London, 1925), 79. G. Mackeurtan, *The Cradle Days of Natal* (London, 1930), 74–5.

had done nothing 'for opening new sources of traffick on the Eastern coast of Africa'.[1] But these Liverpool business men, eager to beat the Company with any stick they could lay hands on, probably knew nothing of conditions in East Africa or of what the value of its potential trade might be. To the Company, at any rate, it did not seem high enough to divert them from the profitable fields they knew. There seems, indeed, to have been practically no British trading in East Africa at all—at Zanzibar or Kilwa or Mombasa or Pate. An exhaustive search through the log-books of merchantmen at British ports might reveal an adventurous voyage or two in those uncharted seas; but in all the fragmentary and scattered information from which an attempt has been made in this book to sketch an outline of East African history in the eighteenth century, once and once only, in an Arab manuscript chronicle of Mombasa, is a British ship discovered at anchor in a harbour on the coast.[2] When, in the last year of the eighteenth century, a British naval squadron put in at Zanzibar (as will presently be related), its officers were told that 'there had not been an English ship in Zanzibar within the memory of the oldest inhabitant'. And when, twelve years later, Captain Smee visited the island (as will also appear), he found that only 'one English vessel had touched' there since the squadron of 1799.[3]

Naturally, French ships are often in the picture; they had colonized the neighbouring Mascarenes. And once at least there are Dutch ships: Cape Colony was not so far away. But it was those Dutchmen, it will be remembered, that Captain Morice of Port Louis feared might compete with his countrymen in the East African field, not the British. It will be remembered, too, how anxious M. Cossigny was to afford the British no excuse for pushing their trade and domination into one of the few corners of the world in which they had not yet interfered. And so the old Portuguese preserve north of Cape

[1] Liverpool meeting, 23.xi.92. B.M. Add. MSS. 38228 (Liverpool Papers), f. 149.
[2] For 'Captain Cook' at Mombasa, see p. 218, note 1, below.
[3] Bissell's *Journal* (as cited p. 165, note 1, below), 37; *T.B.G.S.* vi. 47.

Delgado remained virtually a French preserve till the very end of the century. Then, in fairly quick succession, East African waters were thrice 'invaded' by British ships—by Commodore Blankett's squadron in 1798-9, by the East India Company's cruiser *Ternate* and schooner *Sylph* in 1811, and by the frigate *Nisus* in 1812. These were not merchantmen, they were ships of war; but their presence did not mean, as might be supposed, that the British Government had at last discovered a 'national interest' in East Africa and was bent on imperialist designs. Why these 'invaders' came and what they did stands on record and can be quickly told.[1]

2

The first 'invasion' was an incident of the war. It was not directed at the East African area. It was merely a passage through it towards an objective farther north.

On July 9, 1798, a naval squadron of three ships, *Leopard*, *Daedalus*, and *Orestes*, was dispatched from Portsmouth to the Red Sea to do what it could to frustrate Napoleon's designs to attack India from Egypt. The commander of the squadron was Commodore Blankett, who, as it happened, took a keen interest in the expansion of British trade side by side with British sea-power in all quarters of the world. Madagascar and the adjacent islands were the only part of East Africa which he, like many other seamen, had so far seen. He had stayed on or off Madagascar for a fortnight some ten years previously, and had been impressed by its size and fertility and abundance of cattle, 'the finest in the world', fish, vegetables, fruit, and timber— so much impressed that he saw in it the ideal solution of the old problem of the convicts. In a memorandum submitted to Lord Hawkesbury, the most active member of the Government in the development of overseas trade, he urged the purchase from the natives of a suitable site on the coast of Madagascar for a penal settlement. Apart from the convicts it should not be a colony—that would mean the departure from England of better and more useful members of society than convicts—

[1] Morice and Cossigny, p. 82, above.

but only a commercial and strategic post. 'It would serve', wrote the Captain, as he then was, 'as an *entrepôt* between Europe and Asia, and as a place of refreshment for all ships going to and from India.' It would be a valuable naval base in any future war. And under British enterprise its products could be widely distributed about the Indian Ocean—timber, salt, iron, and slaves to the Cape; rice, salt, provisions, dairy produce, and slaves to Mozambique, Sofala, Malindi, and other coast towns; salt, provisions, gum, and timber to India—while cutlery, brass-ware, fire-arms and powder, brandy, pins, needles, and all sorts of beads would be imported from England for sale to the natives of Madagascar.[1] (It may be observed in passing that Blankett had not yet been affected by the humanitarian movement, then just beginning to gather way in England, which was soon to inflame the conscience of the country, and nowhere more fiercely than in the Navy, against the Slave Trade.) The proposal, like many others of those days, was stillborn. War came without a British base in the western waters of the Indian Ocean to counteract Île de France or to safeguard British India and its trade from attack by sea.

The squadron, taking a course well south of the Cape, sighted Madagascar on October 18, and on November 5 it lay anchored at Johanna. This island, one of the hilly and verdant Comoro group, had long been known to Englishmen—it was, in fact, the only place in all East Africa they did know— because, as has been noted, their ships had often broken the Indian voyage there to take in water and provisions.[2] The connexion was highly valued by the islanders; they imitated English fashions and adopted English names. Austin Bissell, first lieutenant on the *Daedalus*, whose journal of the voyage has been preserved, was startled to hear the visitors to his ship introduce themselves as the Duke of Buccleugh, the Duke of

[1] Blankett's 'proposal', 19.v.1789. B.M. Add. MSS. 38224 (Liverpool Papers), ff. 130–1; kindly communicated by Professor V. T. Harlow.
[2] See p. 55, above. In the late seventeenth and early eighteenth centuries, British and French pirates occasionally operated from bases in the Comoros as well as in Madagascar. The undeservedly notorious Captain Kidd visited Johanna and Mohilla in 1697.

Richmond, the Marquis Cornwallis, Lord Augustus Fitzroy, and so forth. They produced 'very fine certificates of their honesty'; but Bissell, who had had his linen washed ashore, thought them undeserved.

'It is really ridiculous to call them honest, for they can and do steal and cheat as much as any other nation. They mostly profess the Mahometan religion: but those that we saw were not very rigid, and they can, when they choose, drink a glass (if not a bottle) of wine with as much composure as an Englishman.'

But, honest or not, the visitors were bound to feel some sympathy with the people of Johanna. They were told that every year, for more than ten years past, the island had been raided by a fierce and powerful tribe from the north-west coast of Madagascar. Every autumn they would gather at Bambetoke Bay to the number of four or five thousand, armed with muskets bought from French or Arab traders, and, embarking in a vast fleet of canoes, paddle across the 180 miles of sea between them and their prey. Usually, after laying waste the country-side, looting and burning and killing, they had gone home; but this year they had made a temporary lodgement in the island.

'On our arrival here [writes Bissell] we found that these Madagascars had made a descent on the east side of the island and taken possession of a town from whence they often sallied out, committing every kind of depredation, taking their bullocks and all other kinds of provisions whenever they thought proper, and the whole strength of the Johannese could not drive them out. Indeed on a former occasion they landed close to the town of Johanna, and destroyed a small village by fire (having first plundered it of everything), leaving every soul, men, women, and children, to perish in the flames. Their cruelty, when they take the Johanna men prisoners, is dreadful; they either cut them in pieces at the time or mutilate them in such a manner as to prevent their taking up arms against them in future.'

At the entreaty of the Sultan, Blankett sent the brig *Orestes* to bombard the town. If the invaders could be driven from the shelter of its walls, said the Sultan, his troops could attack them. The *Orestes* duly cannonaded the town for two hours, and some of the Malagasi quitted it. But the Johannese attack never materialized, and the *Orestes* sailed away. Blankett was not the only British officer to find (as will be seen) that the salvation of Johanna was beyond his power.[1]

Soon after leaving Johanna (November 11) the squadron found its progress impeded not only by the 'monsoon', blowing hard from east-south-east and driving them shorewards, but also by the strong south-westerly current. It took sixteen days to beat up to Barawa, the first coast town they sighted. ('The town seemed well-built, and on one of the islands stood a lighthouse of a tolerable height: but we were too far off to make any very accurate observations.') For the next ten days the ships were 'always under a press of sail', trying to beat to windward but failing to make way against the current. On December 18, 'finding we lost ground, though we had all sail set with a fine breeze', they anchored five or six miles off the mouth of Rogues' River, as the Juba was then called. They had lain there nearly a week, taking soundings and making observations of the river's mouth, when on Christmas Eve an unexpected tragedy occurred. Early in the morning four boats put off to try to obtain water ashore near the river-mouth; and one of them, from the *Leopard*, with Lieutenant Mears, an interpreter, and nine seamen aboard, was caught broadside on in the surf and upset. Mears and his men got ashore and were collecting the contents of the boat when a party of natives, armed with spears, appeared and 'approached them in a humble courteous manner'.

'Being nearly exhausted with fatigue in getting through the surf and heat of the sun, he [Mears] was induced to walk up from the beach towards a tree with some of his boat's crew, where they all sat down. The natives now came down to them in numbers from behind the sandhills; and they had been there but a short time before they began to strip Mr. Mears and his men of their clothes, and shortly afterwards let fly their spears at them. Lieutenant Mears, the interpreter, and two men fell; two escaped unhurt to the beach and joined their comrades, and another man (Michael Murphy) was dreadfully wounded in the shoulder and ran for some distance with the spear in his back, the natives pursuing them.'

[1] A. Bissell, *A Voyage from England to the Red Sea*, &c., published 'at the charge of the East India Company' by A. Dalrymple (London, 1806), and included in Dalrymple's *Nautical Memoirs*, vol. i, no. 7.

Meantime, the other three boats were keeping close in but were unable to get through the surf. One plucky seaman, William Lannigan, swam ashore, and tried to help the wounded Murphy to escape; but, Murphy collapsing from loss of blood, they were both captured. The six survivors

'ran along the beach, and threw away their clothes, piece by piece, as they could get them off, the natives still pursuing them. All the boats followed along the shore in hopes of finding a smooth place to take the men off . . . and a little after sunset took them off in a small bay . . . ten miles from where they began running. . . . perfectly naked and dreadfully burnt with the sun.'

On the same morning another of the *Leopard*'s boats, which had been sent to look for a lost grapnel some five or six miles up the coast, also 'got into the surf and filled'.

'While the boat's crew were endeavouring to get her afloat, the savages came down in numbers. Some threw their spears at the men, while others were running off with such of the boat's materials as they could get hold of which had been washed on shore. They killed two of the seamen, and a third, wounded, was drowned in the surf. Mr. Philip Boger, boatswain of the *Leopard*, escaped death by shooting the savage with a pistol while aiming his spear at him. They were fortunate enough to shoot a second, and then they all ran away to the back of the sandhills, leaving some of their spears behind them. The men's bodies were immediately attacked by the large birds of prey with which this coast abounds.'

On December 28, assuming Murphy and Lannigan to be dead and wisely deciding against any punitive operations, Blankett continued on his course. The first British 'invasion' of East Africa, as in fact in an innocent sense it was, had been repelled with loss.[1]

On the morning of departure from Rogues' River three dhows were sighted northwards and chased under the lee of some islands. Lieutenant Bissell, who had been moved from the *Daedalus* to take Mears's place on the *Leopard*, was sent with two 'well-armed' boats to investigate, and found the dhows to be from Muscat bound for Zanzibar. Not far off, on the main-

[1] Bissell, 15–20.

land, was a small town, with herds of cattle and plenty of goats near by; but, though the squadron was now short of food, and though the natives on the beach were 'constantly waving for us to land', 'we had too dearly experienced their treachery before', observed Bissell, and he returned to the *Leopard* without landing. Towards their Arab visitors, apparently, the natives were not hostile; for, when Bissell paid a second visit to the dhows to try to obtain information as to where water and supplies could be found, the Arabs told him that some natives had come on board in his absence, and tried to persuade them to join in seizing and murdering him and his men.

For the next fortnight the squadron continued to struggle against wind and current, some days gaining ground, other days losing it, till at last Blankett was reluctantly convinced that his men would starve before they got to any Red Sea port. On January 17, therefore, having transferred the *Daedalus*'s stores to the *Leopard* and *Orestes*, except for a few days' supply, he ordered her back to the Cape. It was hoped that the full moon would bring a change of wind and current; but both continued unabated; the wind blowing 'very strong at times', the current running two knots and more. For twenty days they lay at anchor, not many miles north of Rogues' River, waiting for an improvement which never came. All the bread, flour, and spirits were now gone, and the men were subsisting on rice, a little meat, and three pints of water a day. At length, on February 14, Blankett despaired of his task and turned back to seek food and water at some southward port. But his trials were not over. During the next night the *Leopard* ran fast aground on a sand-bank, and it took six hours of hard work with anchors, boats, and sails to get her off, making two or three feet of water an hour. On the 17th they anchored for the night off Mombasa, observing 'the Moorish colours', the scarlet flag of Muscat, flying over the Fort. On the 20th they reached Zanzibar and were piloted next day into the harbour. In six days the ships had covered the same distance southwards as it had taken them more than two months to cover northwards.[1]

[1] Idem, 20–31.

Bissell's first impression of Zanzibar, like Lancaster's two hundred years before him, was its wealth in all the 'refreshments' the *Leopard* and *Orestes* so badly needed. Plenty of good water was obtained at 'Fresh Water River'; and 'we got', says the journal, 'very fine bullocks, goats, poultry, rice, coconut oil etc.' 'Their fruits', it goes on, 'are very delicious and they have all kinds.' The only drawback was the cost. As the Governor, who, as Bissell notes, was appointed by the Imam of Muscat, maintained 'a monopoly of the sale of all kinds of articles, we paid exorbitantly dear for them'. The amount he received at the end of the ships' stay was roughly 2,500 dollars (about £550).

Bissell was quick to notice Zanzibar's connexion with the Mascarenes. 'They have a great deal of trade with the French for slaves and coffee, and many of them talk that language in consequence.' But they were by no means unfriendly to their British visitors. Some of the Arabs, indeed, invited the officers to, but not into, their houses, and, 'seating them in a little recess, entertained them with fruits and every nicety possible, while some of their slaves were employed in loading a boat with coconuts, poultry, eggs, and everything that was to be had'.

Among other points which Bissell observed was the annual immigration of the 'Northern Arabs', which is still a regular feature of the life of Zanzibar. 'The small trading-vessels from Muscat and the Red Sea, after discharging their cargoes, which are chiefly dates, always dismantle and move into an inner harbour at the back of the town and wait the return of the "monsoon".'[1]

At last the wind began to change, and on March 5 the two ships started again for the Red Sea. During their stay at Zanzibar the news had come by a boat from Pate 'that some Englishmen were still at Juba'. The course was set, therefore, for the old anchorage in the hope that Murphy and Lannigan were alive. They reached it early on March 10, and were encouraged by the spectacle of 'a vast crowd' of natives on the top of a hill, waving a flag. That afternoon, a native boat came

[1] Bissell, 31–7.

out with Murphy aboard. He and his mate, it seemed, had been taken to a town a little way up the river, and fairly well treated by their captors, who had employed them 'in sewing together their women's ragged clothes and cutting sticks for boiling their victuals'; but one night, after a dispute as to whose property Lannigan was, 'one of the savages came, while he was asleep, and cut his throat, but fortunately not effectually'. 'It had been intended', Murphy explained, 'that they should both be sent for sale to the slave-market at Pate'—a forewarning of which accounted, no doubt, for their survival being known there and so reported at Zanzibar. But now the ships had come back, the natives were hoping to obtain a substantial ransom. Meantime, they were holding Lannigan as a hostage.

At daybreak next morning, accordingly, two boats 'well-armed' and two cutters crossed the bar and proceeded up river to the town, where Murphy was landed and presented to 'his master' some of the coloured handkerchiefs, gilt buttons, rings, and other trinkets with which the boats had been loaded. A long haggle ensued. At noon a boat was sent back to the ships for money, arms, and ammunition. They were duly handed over. More haggling, and then, at length, near sunset, the deal was done. Lannigan was brought down to the boat 'pinioned, with many of their spears pointed to his breast to prevent his escape'. His captors would not come near the boat, but intimated that the seamen were to put the ransom on the beach and withdraw. Then, releasing their prisoner, they seized their booty and ran off into the bush.[1]

On March 12 the ships continued their voyage up the coast, making better headway than before, but still obstructed by occasional adverse currents. Passing Barawa and a town not marked on their chart, presumably Merka, they sighted the 'remarkable mosques or pagodas' of Mogadishu on the 19th. 'We stood close in to the town and saw many fishing-boats on the beach and a number of inhabitants', and, a little way off, 'herds of cattle and goats and a number of camels travelling southward'. The wind was now back again in its old

[1] Idem, 38–41.

south-easterly quarter, and it was not till April 8 that they came abreast of Cape Guardafui. On the 11th they were off Aden, and on the 14th reached Mocha, their goal, at last.

It had been a thoroughly unpleasant voyage. Only two of the three ships had been able to complete it. A lieutenant and six men had lost their lives at the Juba. The difficulty of navigation had been equalled by the difficulty of getting water and provisions. No wonder, perhaps, that there is no praise of East Africa in Bissell's journal, nor any proposals in Blankett's reports for a British connexion of any kind with a country so manifestly inferior to Madagascar. The impact on the 'invaders'' minds of this first 'invasion' may be judged from Bissell's summing-up at Mocha.

'Thus terminated one of the most perplexing and tedious voyages ever made by any ships. It is, I believe, the first attempt ever made to beat up the coast of Africa against the Easterly Monsoon, and it is to be hoped nobody will ever attempt it again.'[1]

3

One of the other two 'invasions', the later in time, was also an invasion by the British Navy; but, whereas Blankett's voyage had been only an incident of war, and his only interest in the coast that of a passer-by, the voyage of the frigate *Nisus* in 1812 was specifically directed to East Africa—to the one and only place in it in which, as has been observed, a certain British interest had been created. Some seven years after Blankett's visit to Johanna the islanders had been relieved at last of the annual visitation of the Malagasi raiders. The warrior queen of Bambetoke, an inveterate enemy of Johanna, had died; the succession was disputed; and the militant energies of the tribes concerned were absorbed in a protracted civil war. But early in 1812 it was reported by an Arab trader at Johanna that peace was imminent; and, dreading the prospect of a renewal of the old scourge, the Sultan dispatched an English-speaking islander to appeal for help to his particular friends, the British, now

[1] Bissell, 41–7.

established at the Cape. Sir John Cradock, Governor of Cape Colony (1811–14), promptly responded. He sent the *Nisus* to Johanna with a gift of 100 muskets, two brass swivels, and ammunition, and an assurance that the two brigs-of-war stationed at Mauritius would do what could be done by visiting the islands from time to time and overawing the Malagasi to protect them from attack. The commander of the *Nisus*, as it happened, was the hero of Bulama, now Captain Beaver, who, his disobedience of 1793 forgiven, had among other services in the war taken part in the capture of the Cape, Ceylon, and Mauritius. Besides his own reports on the voyage, a full description of it was published some years later by James Prior, surgeon on the *Nisus*, in a small but very interesting book whose fame has been completely overshadowed by its author's biography of Burke.[1]

As they sailed northwards both Beaver and Prior were impressed, as they were bound to be, by the evidence of Portuguese decay. They found Sofala, with a few 'black troops' in its little fort, still keeping alive on the export of slaves, ivory, gold-dust, and rice to Mozambique. Sena, they heard, was more important, 'a considerable town, well inhabited... and having a governor second only to that of Mozambique', and a flourishing 'Portuguese factory', whither the natives brought slaves, ivory, gold-dust, herbs, and gum in exchange for cloth, hardware, trinkets, and fire-arms. The banks of the Zambesi, however, were not wholly in Portuguese control, parts of them on both sides being under independent native rule. Prior must have read about the old Arab colonies on this part of the coast, for he was surprised to find the Arabs gone and little trace of their settlements left. Mozambique itself he reckoned to contain about 600 Europeans and half-castes, the same number of free

[1] J. Prior, *Voyage along the Eastern Coast of Africa*, &c. (London, 1819). The envoy from Johanna was well known to British visitors to the island who called him 'Bombay Jack'. He returned home in the *Nisus*, and his relations with the officers were cordial. Prior says that they wanted him to dine at their table, but being 'aware of the prejudices of the lower order of Europeans against persons of his colour', he could not be induced to do so (29).

Africans, and between 4,000 and 5,000 slaves. The fort, despite its poor condition, was, as it still is, an impressive building, 'a proof', notes Beaver, 'that the Portuguese were once a great and enterprising people'. The present colonists seemed indolent dispirited folk, hated by the natives of the mainland and never quite sure of their safety from attack. Parts of the coast had recently been raided with impunity by Malagasi slave-hunters, and, not long since, the peninsula of Mozambique had been itself invaded by mainland Africans and 'everything within their reach carried off or destroyed'. The character of the Governor, Don Antonio Manuel de Mello Castro e Mendoza, with whom Beaver had two conversations, was scarcely such as to inspire confidence in an emergency. He had just completed his three-year term of office, and the Englishmen were told that he had done nothing to improve agriculture or trade, had seldom visited any part of the colony outside its capital, and indeed had hardly ever left his house for fear of sunstroke or fever; yet now he was retiring to Madeira with a fortune of 300,000 dollars (about £80,000). There is no reason to suppose that the last assertion was mere gossip; Livingstone was to find the same thing in the same place half a century later. Nor can there be much doubt as to whence the money came. One business alone was flourishing when all else was 'ruin and dirt and devilment'. Not long since, so Prior was informed, the export of slaves had reached a total of 10,000 a year. They had gone both to South America and to the French and Dutch islands in the Indian Ocean. 'Indeed, throughout the East, the common term for an African is Mozambiquer.' But the recent British conquest of the Mascarenes and the vigilance of naval patrols had reduced the annual output to about 3,000—'quite enough to shock any mind but that of a slave-trader'. So, all in all, the Englishmen were not very kindly disposed towards the Portuguese, and the Portuguese returned the compliment. 'I am afraid we are not in great favour here', says Prior: 'a British man-of-war seldom is'—mainly because of the now notorious British hostility to the trade on which so many Portuguese subsisted, but also because 'an Englishman's mind is supposed to be filled with designs against their commerce' in general.[1]

At Johanna, naturally enough, the reception of the *Nisus* was more cordial. Its decks were soon thronged with aristocrats. The Dukes of Portland and of Hamilton came aboard this time, and Mr. Pitt, and Lords Rodney and Howe, and—a new creation since 1798—Admiral Blankett. Some of them 'inquired affectionately after their namesakes in England, begged their compliments on our return, and promised the best reception should they at any time visit Johanna . . . . One of the most inquisitive expressed his joy that his Royal Highness, the Prince Regent, made so good a governor as he termed it; and to our utter astonishment asked whether an *illustrious reconciliation* had yet taken place.' The Sultan Allawah, who had succeeded to the throne two or three years after Blankett's visit, overflowed with praise of 'his friend, good King George, Sir John Cradock, Captain Beaver, and the whole English nation'. For his future security from Malagasi raids he trusted, he told Beaver, 'in our interference'. If they continued, he would abandon the island. 'I cannot live here with my lands desolated, and see my women and children perish with hunger; and, if I leave it, all my miserable people will follow me.'[2]

They were right to cling to the British, these poor islanders: they had no other friends. And they were right to mourn the departure of the *Nisus*. For British friendship was of little use unless embodied in guns and men. The only effective protection of Johanna from its enemies was a cruiser permanently stationed in its harbour or a handful of troops in its fort. And, though Beaver and Prior were evidently sorry for the islanders, anything like an occupation of Johanna, on however small a scale, does not seem to have crossed their minds. Prior extols its beauty and fertility, and mentions its trade in coco-nut oil, rice, and tortoise-shell with the Persian Gulf. But there is nothing in

---

[1] Prior, 25–45. Smyth, 254–60. Prior reckons the value of the gold-dust annually exported at about £16,000.

[2] Prior, 46–50. Smyth, 261–2. Prior's whole account of Johanna and his personal experiences there is as amusing as it is informing.

his narrative about opportunities for British commerce, still less for British colonization.

Beaver's orders were to continue the voyage to the Seychelles and thence return to the Cape by way of Mauritius. From Johanna, therefore, he proceeded up the coast, and, being in need of timber for spars, he put in at Kilwa. 'It is almost new ground', notes Prior, 'to English enterprise and inquiry. The Sultan, or King of the country, has hitherto heard of us only as enemies, and felt the report to be partly true in the loss of his trade with the French, particularly the traffic in slaves.' The French, indeed, had apparently been Kilwa's 'only visitors', but with them there had been such 'constant intercourse' that most of the Kilwa folk spoke French 'tolerably well'. The beginning of the connexion in 1777[1] was still well remembered, and in memory of 'the first adventurer from Mauritius' a little island in the harbour was called Morice Islet. The slaves which Morice had wanted could still be procured from far inland, or, at need, by raiding a neighbouring village; but 'at present the demand is confined to the Arabs who do not take many'. Apart from slaves Kilwa had nothing to sell but ivory and tortoise-shell. Prior was again struck, as he had been farther south, by the evidence of depopulation. On a short excursion on foot along the coast he saw 'only four huts and one human being, a pretty black girl, in the space of twelve or fourteen miles'. Yet about eight miles from Kilwa he lighted on the ruins of what must once have been a considerable town—a mosque, a cemetery, a building larger than anything in Kilwa except the Sultan's palace, all broken down and overgrown by the jungle.

'The youth of the trees, the half-obliterated traces of ancient footpaths, the scattered vestiges of human haunts and habitations, the cemeteries and ruins, all proclaim this district to have been once open and populous. The ruins are evidences of a former people; they were comparatively rude, perhaps, though infinitely more civilised and industrious than the present race. But whither have they gone? What has become of their descendants? There have been no formal emigrations, no pestilences, no destructive wars, no

[1] See pp. 76–83, above.

native tyrants or foreign masters till lately: the soil cannot have become suddenly unfruitful: yet the neighbouring country, the town [Kilwa], and even the whole kingdom is wonderfully depopulated since Da Gama's time.'

There are some bold assertions here. Prior was unaware, for instance, of the irruption of the Zimba in 1587 and the massacre they wrought at Kilwa. But his solution of the problem is probably the right one—that the causes of depopulation were first the coming of the Europeans and the decline of Arab trade in the Indian Ocean before their 'superior power', and then the Slave Trade, sweeping away 'the wretched inhabitants whom it will now be impossible to replace'.[1]

At Kilwa as at Johanna Prior seems indifferent to British 'interests'. The only suggestion of acquisitiveness is his unstinted praise of the harbour, a 'grand basin, deep enough for the largest ships, and capable of containing nearly the whole navy of England'. But Beaver, this time, is more expansive, and in the pages of his journal, at any rate, he indulges in a little political speculation. Not that he wants, like Morice, to plant a colony at Kilwa. Bulama perhaps had taught him a lesson, and now he is middle-aged. But he contemplates something like a British protectorate. Seyyid Said's Governor was away, as it happened, on a visit to Zanzibar; and the Sultan—Beaver calls him Yousoufou—confided to the Captain his longing to throw off the rule of Muscat. That started a chain of reflection in Beaver's mind. 'The English character', he observes, 'cannot yet be very popular at Kilwa.' It is only known through the French, who naturally do not overpraise it. And yet, he goes on,

'I see no difficulty in sincerely attaching this people to the British. Yousoufou, I know, wishes to drive the Arabs [of Oman] off his territory, but without some powerful protection is afraid of the consequences. He, however, makes silent and cautious preparation, and has several cannon, with small arms and powder, concealed in his house: even the muskets and ammunition I gave him [to obtain timber], he landed in the night. Now to fix, to rivet the affections of the Kilwans, I would, at the written solicitation of the Sultan, put the Arab Governor and his garrison into a boat and send them to

[1] Prior, 66–9, 75–7.

Muscat with this message to their master—"That the Sultan of Kilwa, having entered into a treaty of amity with the British nation, had complained of the great grievances suffered by his subjects from Governors appointed by the Imam of Muscat, and requested its aid to prevent the same;—that the British had, therefore, at the entreaty of their ally, seized those who had dared to infringe on the independancy of Kilwa, and returned them to their native country, determined in future to guarantee the rights of Sultan Yousoufou." After this message I am inclined to think we should hear of no more Arabs at Kilwa; and for thus rendering him independent, all I should require on the Sultan's part would be a scrupulous fulfilment of the contract I made with him; that is, that he should supply us annually with four hundred large spars for which he should regularly receive the stipulated price. Do this, I say, and the Kilwans will be attached to the British for ever.'

Twelve years later, at another point on the East African coast, another British naval officer was to betray a similar contempt for international propriety, a similar disregard of the Imam's title to the government of an overseas dependency, a similar indifference to the policy of the British authorities in India. But Captain Owen's high notions issued, as will appear, in action; Captain Beaver's lay sterile in his journal. The reason or one reason may, perhaps, be inferred from Prior's dry comment. The Sultan, he says, might be given the British protection he desires 'without difficulty or expense as the name alone would ensure his quiet: should the timber, however, not prove valuable, this measure would be of no advantage'.[1]

From Kilwa the *Nisus* sailed on to Mahe without calling at any other port. So Prior's brief comments on some of the other coast towns are not from his own observation. He mentions 'the small independent state of Mombasa' which had recently 'repulsed an attempt of the Imam of Muscat to subjugate it ... the people possessing more fierceness and spirit than the Kilwans'. Mafia, once ruled by Kilwa, is now subject to Muscat under a Governor appointed by the Imam and pays an annual tribute of 6,000 dollars (about £1,500). 'Melindi and Barawa have not been visited by the navigators of the nineteenth century; and all the information we have gained is that they are

[1] Smyth, 278–80. Prior, 66, 79.

British Reconnaissances

independent and, wishing to remain so, cordially detest and exclude strangers. I commend their wisdom.' The 'fruitful island' of Pemba is 'partly subject to Muscat, partly to Mombasa, and a third part independent'. More interesting and informative is the account of Zanzibar.

'Producing several species of grain, abundance of bullocks, goats and poultry, it forms the great depôt of the Imam's colonial commerce and power. The population is considerable, and the sum of 50,000 dollars [about £12,000] is raised annually as tribute. The Governor is not only viceroy over the other islands but chief merchant in his own, no others being permitted to dispose of their merchandise till his bargains are made and permission purchased. The fort is said to contain many guns, but with the present soldiers would not resist two hundred English troops for two hours, were it attacked. Mauritius in the French time maintained constant intercourse with this island for slaves, ivory, and gold-dust. The people are partial to that nation, and lately were little less than hostile to the English.'[1]

Taken as a whole, Prior's description of East Africa betrays no more than an intelligent observer's interest in a country he has never seen before. Naturally so. It was, after all, a backwater: its political importance altogether secondary, its trade meagre, the resources of its hinterland unknown. Only one part of it really impressed him as it impressed Blankett and all other new-comers, and that part lay a little detached, was a little different in the character and history of its people, from the mainland.

'Madagascar is in itself such a magnificent country; its outline so commanding, its extent so considerable, its resources so varied and extensive in all the vast essentials requisite to constitute a great kingdom that it is amazing it has not been more firmly grasped and held by France who by means of its energies, judiciously directed, might have rendered many of our advantages in India nugatory.'

But that, Prior admits, would have needed an 'elaborate, firm and conciliating plan' of colonization. Failing that, 'the most prudent step for us or any other European power in the vicinity'

[1] Idem, 80–1. The 'Viceroy's' other 'islands' are presumably Mafia, part of Pemba, and Kilwa.

will be to maintain trading-posts only, 'by sufferance of the natives, neither trenching on the power of the chiefs, nor assuming any claims to any portion of territory'.[1]

4

The motive of the third 'invasion', which occurred a year earlier than the visit of the *Nisus* to Johanna and Kilwa, was different from that of either of the others. In 1811 Captain Smee and Lieutenant Hardy were sent to East Africa by the Bombay Government on what was called 'a voyage of research' with a threefold objective.[2] First, they were to obtain such general information as they could about the physical features and population of that almost unknown coast and the quite unknown interior. Secondly, they were specially to examine the rivers, in particular 'Rogues' River', the mouth of which, but no more, had been observed by Blankett. Seton, it appears, had heard of it at Muscat and had reported to Bombay that it was of 'immense extent', was called the Nilo, and was said to flow from the same source as the Nile and to be navigable as far as the city of Gunamma, a nine-weeks' journey, whence 'immense quantities' of slaves and ivory are brought down to a point near the coast, thence taken overland to Barawa, and 'either disposed of there or sent to Zanzibar'.[3] It is clear from the reports rendered of the expedition that the interest in this river and in other rivers was mainly an interest in the possibility of trading up them with the interior. The third objective— which was the subject of Smee's 'first and most anxious enquiry' when he landed—looks odd enough in the light of later knowledge. Mungo Park had disappeared into the Western Sudan in the spring of 1805. His death on the Niger in the following winter was not known till 1812. Friedrich Hornemann, similarly, had set off south-westward from Egypt and reached

---

[1] Prior, 60.
[2] A series of reports on the voyage are printed in the *Transactions of the Bombay Geographical Society*, vi (1844), 23–61.
[3] Ibid. vi. 31, note. This river is now known as the Juba.

British Reconnaissances 179

Fezzan in 1800, but had not been heard of since. Evidence that he had died somewhere in the Nupe country was obtained in 1822. In the absence of news it was thought at the time of Smee's voyage that one or both of these explorers might conceivably have wandered eastwards and might emerge from the dark interior on to the Indian, not the Atlantic Ocean. Smee, therefore, was to ask if anything had been heard of them on the coast.[1]

He sailed from Bombay on January 2, 1811, convoying two merchantmen bound for Mocha as far as Socotra, whence he made for Cape Guardafui. From January 16 to February 6 he sailed down the coast, usually two or three miles out, observing how bare the land seemed of man or beast or plant, until, after Mogadishu and still more after the mouth of the Juba, the whole prospect changed and he looked enchanted on 'richly-clothed islands', 'beautiful inlets', 'a delightful continent rich in all the charms of luxuriant vegetation', indicating 'a degree of natural wealth equal to the most favoured regions of the known globe'. But, like Blankett, he found it an awkward coast for navigation. All the way down to Zanzibar the north-east 'monsoon' kept blowing; and, since this made it dangerous to anchor in open water near the land, Smee was unable to stop and go ashore and learn more about the country until he got to Pate and with a local pilot's aid crept into a safe anchorage between the islands. Mogadishu, therefore, he only saw at some two miles' distance—a 'not very considerable' town, he notes, like those on the Arabian and Persian coasts, its 150 or 200 houses 'apparently built of stones and mud, of a low square form, with small doors and windows and flat roofs', and rising high above them the four mosques he had sighted ten miles off. Merka is 'small and has no safe anchorage off it'. 'Barawa town is composed of about 100 huts, and is as defective in its port as Mogadishu.' The harbours of Mombasa might have been more favourably mentioned; but, carried past by wind and current, Smee seems to have missed those narrow openings. One thing there he could not miss. 'The fort stands at a short

[1] Ibid. vi. 58.

distance from the shore on a steep woody ridge, said to be an island, and has three flagstaffs on it.'[1]

If Smee's only acquaintance with the townsfolk of the coast was at Pate, where he lay at anchor from February 7 to 10, the impression he got was fairly typical. He was more likely, perhaps, at Pate, where domestic strife seems to have been a permanent and incurable disease, to be in doubt as to which of two rival Sultans he should approach; but the squalor, the ignorance, the suspicion, the greed, the hostility he found at Pate he might just as well have found at Mogadishu or Lamu or Mombasa. His choice of Sultan was determined by 'a crowd of armed savages' who met his boat and led him to 'a large unshapely heap of mud, called the Palace of Sultan Hamed'. Hamed received him 'in a long dirty yellowish-coloured gown, with a greasy turban on his head and filthy loose slippers on his feet'. He could tell Smee nothing he did not know about the lost explorers or the rivers of the country. 'To our interrogations about the unfortunate Mr. Park and his associates he only answered, "How can I speak of the man? I never saw him".' He supposed the source of the 'immense' Rogues' River to be 'in our country', i.e. Europe. He knew that 'a great number of slaves were brought down it to Barawa; but as to the towns, state of the country, or people which dwell on its banks, he said he was totally ignorant'. Hamed, indeed, was not interested in Smee's questions but only in what he could get out of him. After hours of wrangling, during which the safety of Smee and his party was at times distinctly uncertain, five muskets and two pistols with powder and flints were extorted. It is not surprising that Smee, when at last he rowed away at sunset, had formed a poor opinion of Pate. 'The port of Pate', he sums it up, 'has little or no trade on account of the intricacy of its harbours and the nefarious conduct of its inhabitants.'[2]

Zanzibar, where Smee and his companions arrived on

---

[1] *T.B.G.S.* vi. 29–31, 40, 58. The author of the journal of the voyage was neither Smee nor Hardy but a third officer, unnamed. Smee appends a concise report of his own.
[2] Ibid. vi. 35–8, 61.

February 25 and stayed till April 9, presented a very different picture. They thought the island 'extremely delightful', with its covering of green growth, its picturesque coco-nut trees, its abundance of fruit,[1] its plentiful and fair-priced bullocks and goats, its varied and delicious fish, its springs and streams of pure water flowing all the year, and especially—for they were seamen—its 'remarkably smooth and safe' harbour. The town seemed 'large and populous', mostly consisting of huts, it is true, but with 'a good number of stone buildings in it belonging to the Arabs and merchants', and a fort on the beach, partly of Portuguese, partly of Arab construction. As to the political position there was no dispute. 'The sovereignty of the island belongs to the Imam of Muscat who appoints the Governor and to whom the revenue derived from its commerce and land-tenures devolves.' The Governor at that time, Yacout by name, was of an unusual type. He was not a leading Arab, imported from Muscat or chosen from the local community, but a eunuch who had belonged to one of Said's uncles, and was now a special favourite of Said. 'He lives like a beggar and tyrannically extorts from the inhabitants large sums which with his own savings he faithfully transmits [to Said] as the price of his continuance in the government. The people who live under his sway detest and despise him.' One of the chief sources of Yacout's income was the 'premium' of 10 dollars paid him by the French slave-traders for each slave exported from Zanzibar. Naturally, therefore, Smee found him 'warmly in the French interest'. He refused, indeed, to credit the report of the capture of Île de France which happened to reach Zanzibar by a ship from Surat while Smee was there, and, throughout Smee's stay, he showed himself 'extremely inimical', forbidding the Zanzibaris to provide him with lodgings ashore and trying to prevent their visiting his ship.[2]

[1] 'Pineapples of the most delicious sort are growing everywhere wild, and heaps of oranges and guavas etc. for want of consumers are left to rot on the ground.' Mangoes, lemons, limes, plantains, bananas, and pomegranates are also grown, and onions and sweet-potatoes. Sugar-cane is plentiful, but the art of making sugar is unknown. Ibid. 48.
[2] *T.B.G.S.* vi. 42–4, 48–9, 57.

The report on the results of his voyage which Smee submitted to Bombay was disappointing. He had heard nothing of the explorers: 'their fate is entirely unknown on this coast'. He had discovered little about the rivers. He had found no promising opening on the coast for British commercial enterprise. Such trade as existed was in the hands of Arabs from Muscat and other ports and 'a few adventurers from Cutch and the coast of Sind'. At Zanzibar the prospects were not much brighter. Its main exports were slaves, ivory, bees-wax, and tortoise-shell, mostly obtained from the mainland; its chief imports cloth, china, and earthenware from Cutch and Surat, iron, sugar, and rice from Bombay, and dates from the Persian Gulf. 'We were told that the demand for European goods on the continent was very great, and, if the natives had any return to make besides ivory and slaves, I have little doubt but we might here find an extensive and lucrative vent for numerous articles of our manufacture.' But there was no such return; and it is not surprising to find that Smee's prospecting expedition awakened no new economic interest in East Africa, no increase in the number of British merchantmen in its waters.[1]

There were two primary features of commercial life at Zanzibar, however, observed at close quarters by Smee, which were matters not indeed of British trafficking and profit but of British interests of another kind. These were the position of the 'banyans' and the prevalence of the Slave Trade.

'A considerable number of Banians', Smee noted, 'reside in the town, many of whom appear to be wealthy and hold the best part of the trade in their hands.' But he found them suffering from the arbitrary extortions of Governor Yacout. The customs duty imposed by the Imam's orders was a regular 5 per cent.; but 'few, except Arabs, ever pay so little on their goods as the lawful sum', and, since Yacout made a habit of exacting payment in kind from the 'banyans' and seizing what he most desired in their cargoes at his own valuation, they paid on an average—so at least they complained to Smee—a total of at least 20 per cent. From time to time, moreover, the Imam

[1] T.B.G.S. vi. 44–5, 60.

levied a kind of land-tax for meeting an emergency; and, while Smee was there, as it happened, a ship arrived from Muscat with a demand for 25,000 crowns (about £6,000) 'to assist the Imam in opposing the Wahabi'. Of this sum, said the 'banyans' from Surat, Yacout had fixed 3,500 crowns as their share and threatened them with imprisonment if they failed to pay. This was provocative information to lay before an officer in the service of British government in India, and the upshot was all that the complainants could have hoped.

'As these people [runs the report] were trading under the English flag, and were in fact British subjects, Captain Smee did not conceive that a foreign prince had any right to tax them, especially as they had already paid the customary port-dues. Impressed with these sentiments he made a representation to the Hakim [Governor] who in consequence withdrew his claims but privately threatened the merchants with a double imposition after our departure. To prevent this it was determined to leave the *Sylph* [which it had been deemed advisable to convert into a brig] to countenance them during their stay and convey them across to India at the breaking up of the rainy season.'

This is the earliest evidence to hand of the link which, however ignorant of East Africa and disinterested in it the British authorities in India might be, had connected them in some degree with its coast from the moment when the merchant-folk of western India, who from time immemorial had gone trading there, were brought under British rule. That link was to endure and be strengthened. It still holds to-day.[1]

As to the Slave Trade, it appears from Smee's report that a great number of slaves obtained from the mainland were employed in Zanzibar, some 150,000 (he roughly estimated) out of a total population on the island of 200,000; and that the number exported oversea was greater than from any other East African port. He put it at from 6,000 to 10,000 a year, shipped mainly to Muscat, India, and the Mascarenes. Those who remained in Zanzibar in Arab ownership Smee counted fortunate. 'The Arabs', he says, 'are justly famed for the mild treatment of their slaves. They are not overworked, are allowed to live on

[1] Ibid. vi. 43-4, 50, 61.

their master's estate and grow their own food, and seem fairly happy and contented.' It is the process of their sale that stirs Smee's indignation; and since his account of slave-marketing at Zanzibar, soon to become notorious, is the first of several accounts given by British eyewitnesses, it merits full quotation.

'The advocates of the Slave Trade ought to witness the market of Zanzibar, after which, if they possess the slightest spark of generous feeling, I will answer for an alteration in their present opinions. The show commences about 4 o'clock in the afternoon. The slaves, set off to the best advantage by having their skins cleaned and burnished with coconut oil, their faces painted with red and white stripes which is here esteemed elegance, and their hands, noses, ears and feet ornamented with a profusion of bracelets of gold and silver and jewels, are ranged in a line commencing with the youngest and increasing to the rear according to their size and age. At the head of this file, which is composed of all sexes and ages from six to sixty, walks the person who owns them. Behind and at each side two or three of his domestic slaves, armed with swords and spears, serve as a guard. Thus ordered, the procession begins and passes through the market-place and principal streets, the owner holding forth in a kind of song the good qualities of his slaves and the high prices that have been offered for them.

'When any of them strikes a spectator's fancy, the line immediately stops, and a process of examination ensues which for minuteness is unequalled in any cattle-market in Europe. The intending purchaser, having ascertained there is no defect in the faculties of speech, hearing, etc., that there is no disease present, and that the slave does not snore in sleeping which is counted a very great fault, next proceeds to examine the person: the mouth and teeth are first inspected, and afterwards every part of the body in succession, not even excepting the breasts etc. of the girls, many of whom I have seen handled in the most indecent manner in the public market by their purchasers: indeed, there is every reason to believe that the slave-dealers almost universally force the young females to submit to their lust previous to their being disposed of. The slave is then made to walk or run a little way to show there is no defect about the feet; after which, if the price is agreed to, they are stripped of their finery and delivered over to their future master. I have frequently counted between twenty and thirty of these files in the market at one time, some of which contained about thirty [slaves]. Women with children newly born hanging at their breasts and others so old they can scarcely walk are sometimes seen dragged about in this manner. I observed they had in general a very dejected look; some groups appeared so ill fed that their bones appeared as if ready to penetrate the skin.

'From such scenes one turns away with pity and indignation; and, while he execrates the conductors of this infamous traffic, blushes that his country should ever have sanctioned such iniquity, and remembers with exultation the men who freed her from so great a disgrace.'[1]

Many similar descriptions by later British observers of the methods of the Slave Trade in East Africa have been printed. In each case it is impossible to doubt the strength and sincerity of the writer's feelings, impossible to suppose that they were prompted by British self-righteousness or an insular contempt for foreign customs or an arrogant itch to interfere with other people's practices rather than by a simple instinctive humanity. And, since in those early years of the nineteenth century there seemed to be no political interest involved, no need for new strategic acquisitions, no tempting prospect of commercial expansion, that simple humanity was to be the principal reason for the British Government's intrusion into East African affairs a few years after Smee's visit to Zanzibar.

[1] *T.B.G.S.* vi. 44–6. It is not clear whether the account of the slave-market was written by Smee himself or by the fellow officer whose description of the voyage down the coast is printed with Smee's formal report.

VII

BRITAIN AND THE SLAVE TRADE

I

OF all the sea-going peoples of Europe, if the British people became in the course of the eighteenth century the greatest culprits in the matter of the Slave Trade, they were also the first to recognize their guilt and mend their ways. In 1807, in the midst of their desperate struggle with Napoleon, the Slave Trade was made illegal by Act of Parliament for any British subject or in any British ship; in 1811 it was made a felony punishable by transportation; and so rigorously was the law enforced by the British Navy that by the end of the war British 'slavers' had practically ceased to exist. Nor was that all. The Abolitionist crusade, led by Wilberforce and his allies, had so deeply stirred the public conscience that, not content with abandoning their own part in the Slave Trade, the British people strove, with a unanimity and a determination not easily to be realized in these days, to secure its complete suppression throughout the world. It was due to the pressure of British diplomacy that Portugal, on receipt of an indemnity of £300,000 from Britain and the cancellation of a 'war-debt' of over £400,000, bound herself by treaty in 1815 to limit the operations of her slave-traders to a field between the southern half of the African coasts and her transatlantic colonies; that Spain, similarly bribed with £400,000, signed a treaty in 1817 providing for the complete abolition of the Trade in 1820; and that France in 1818 enacted a law prohibiting the Slave Trade, though not making it a criminal offence. But those hard-won successes had little practical result. By the fourth decade of the nineteenth century the volume of the trans-Atlantic Slave Trade had surpassed the highest figures of the eighteenth. And the reason was plain. The demand for slaves was steadily increasing, and the men who made their fortunes by supplying them were not to be deterred by prohibitions and penalties which existed merely on paper. For many years the only Power which fully carried out in practice the obligations it had undertaken by law or treaty for the abolition of the Trade was Britain. For many years the only weapon used effectively and consistently for the purpose was the British Navy. And, while British cruisers from 1807 onwards could deal swiftly and drastically with British slave-smugglers, they could not interfere with shipping under foreign flags unless and until the foreign Governments concerned permitted them to do on their behalf what they would not do themselves. Years of diplomatic controversy were needed, volumes of official dispatches were penned, before the 'reciprocal right of search' was established in an effective form. And even then, even as late as 1860, there was still one fatal gap in the network with which Britain had tried unceasingly for half a century to hem in the western coast of Africa. Bitterly mindful of British molestation of their shipping in the past, the United States still refused to concede the right of search; and, when all other flags had failed them, the slave-smugglers could still bring their wretched cargoes safe to port by hoisting the Stars and Stripes.[1]

Through all those years the British fight against the Slave Trade was never identified with one party only or with any one section or group in public life. The humanitarians, of course, were in the forefront with voice and pen, but they were not alone. The movement had started as a national crusade. It became a national tradition. Opinions might differ as to the methods of the campaign or even, at one period of pessimism, as to the chances of ultimate success; but the mass of the British people, from the time of Wilberforce to the time of Livingstone, never ceased to hate the Trade. There was one distinct class of Britons, however, who hated it with a peculiar intensity. Most officers and seamen of the British Navy underwent a period of service sooner or later in the ships detailed to patrol the African coast or to waylay the smugglers at the end of their voyage on

[1] For a general account of the Slave Trade policy of Britain and the other Powers concerned, see W. L. Mathieson, *Great Britain and the Slave Trade, 1839–1865* (London, 1929), and R. Coupland, *The British Anti-Slavery Movement* (London, 1933).

the other side of the Atlantic; and they were thus brought face to face with the bestial realities of the Trade. They saw the horrible conditions in which the slave-ships, loaded with their human freight, accomplished the notorious 'Middle Passage' —the tight-packed shelves in the hold, the chains, the whips, the indescribable filth. They saw the unhappy creatures whom they released from captured ships, usually too bewildered to realize their freedom, often dumb with misery and terror, often sick, often dying. They saw them sometimes thrown in scores into the sea to drown by 'slavers' hoping to escape the penalties of capture. And such sights kindled in them an almost passionate loathing of the whole diabolical business. The task of its suppression, though it needed skill and patience and could be dangerous enough to health and life, was a strange task for men who had sailed under Nelson and 'Nelson's captains', with no glamour or glory about it, a wearisome and rather sordid task, akin to policemen's work or scavengers'. But innumerable reports in the Admiralty records bear witness to the keen, the almost fiery, temper in which, year after year, they 'carried on'. For their elders of the war-period the function allotted in the scheme of things to the British Navy had obviously been to fight the French. To these their successors in the years of peace its function seemed no less clear—to kill the Slave Trade. God-fearing British seamen of those days had no doubt about their mandate. And in the execution of it (as will be apparent in a later chapter) they were capable, when their blood was up, of regarding somewhat lightly the difficulties and hesitations and even at times the orders of mundane authority.

2

The example set by Britain in 1807 was not quickly followed. In so far as the war permitted, all the other Atlantic nations continued to pursue the trade. In the East African field the most active were the Portuguese. Unlike the French, they were able to carry on the trade unmolested by British cruisers in the later years of the Napoleonic War. A British naval officer on the Cape station reported in 1812 that ships came regularly every year from Rio de Janeiro to Mozambique, bringing provisions and taking back slaves, gold-dust, and gum.[1] In the same year, as has been told, the officers of the *Nisus* found that the export of slaves from the Portuguese part of the coast had been recently reduced in volume from about 10,000 a year to about 3,000, mainly owing to British activities in the Indian Ocean and particularly to their capture of Île de France and Bourbon.[2] But the South American part of the business continued briskly enough. It was reported by the British *chargé d'affaires* at Rio de Janeiro that in the course of the year 1817 four ships arrived there bringing 1,880 slaves from the port of Mozambique. In 1818 five ships arrived from Mozambique and three from Quilimane bringing 2,416 slaves between them. That the notorious hardships of the 'Middle Passage' were aggravated by the long voyage round the Cape was evident from the fact that 541 slaves had died on the voyage in 1817 and 1,110 in 1818. In one ship 238 died out of a cargo of 464, and in another 339 out of 807.[3] But, abominable as it was, this traffic was not illegal. In 1815 Portugal had consented only to confine her share of the Trade to exporting slaves from Africa south of the Equator and importing them into her 'transatlantic possessions', and in 1817, under further British pressure, only to stiffen the regulation of the trade with Brazil and to concede the 'reciprocal right of search'.[4] For some time after the war, therefore, while Portuguese 'slavers' could only smuggle slaves into Cuba, they could import them openly and honourably into Brazil. It was not indeed till 1830—some years after Brazil had

[1] Capt. Lynn to Rear-Admiral Stopford, 21.v.12: G. M. Theal, *Records of South Eastern Africa* (London, 1898–1903), ix. 16.

[2] See p. 172, above.

[3] *S.P.* viii (1820–1), 134, 155. Capt. Owen mentions (1823) a captain of a Portuguese slave-ship of exceptional humanity who 'generally saved about four-fifths of his miserable cargo to land at Rio, the calculated average of mortality during the passage being half the original number. To bring one-third to market is considered a profitable voyage': W. F. W. Owen, *Narrative of Voyages to explore the shores of Africa, Arabia, and Madagascar* (London, 1833), i. 196.

[4] Treaty of 1815, Articles i, iv. Treaty of 1817, Articles iii–viii. Hertslet, *Treaties of Commerce and Navigation* (London, 1840), ii. 73–95.

repudiated her colonial status and set up as an independent empire—that Portugal 'abolished' the Trade altogether.[1] So for fifteen years the British cruisers were compelled to let those crowded slave-ships round the Cape unhindered. There was even a doubt as to whether the British authorities at Capetown were not obliged to help them on their way; as to whether the rules of international intercourse might not apply even to men so near akin to pirates as these 'slavers'. But when in 1818 the question was put to the Colonial Secretary, Lord Bathurst, by Lord Charles Somerset, Governor of Cape Colony, and referred to the Law Officers of the Crown, they rose to the occasion. The British Abolition Acts, they pointed out, prohibited British subjects from aiding and assisting in the Slave Trade 'directly or indirectly'. 'It appears to us, therefore, that within the spirit, if not within the words of this enactment, it is illegal for any person (and of course for the Governor) to afford assistance to Portuguese slave vessels touching at the Cape for the purpose of enabling them to carry into effect more conveniently the transport of slaves from Africa to South America . . . though such traffic is permitted by the laws of Portugal . . . . We consequently think that supplies either of articles of food or of money cannot safely be afforded to Portuguese ships for the purpose of enabling them to carry on this trade.' Assistance or relief was only permitted under the Acts if the crew and the slaves were suffering from 'stress of weather, peril of the sea or other inevitable accident', and 'the extent of such relief and assistance should be measured and limited by the necessity and urgency of the case'. This report was duly forwarded to Lord Charles Somerset with instructions to abide by it. Beyond that nothing whatever could be done.[2]

With Spanish slave-ships likewise, which occasionally oper-

[1] An Act for the punishment of 'slavers' was passed in 1831: Mathieson, op. cit. 21.

[2] Law Officers' Report: *S.P.* viii (1820-1), 132-3. Somerset-Bathurst dispatches, *Records of Cape Colony* (Capetown, 1902), xii. 1-4, 7-12, 29-32, 36. A serious outbreak of smallpox in Capetown in 1812 was caused by infection from a Portuguese slave-ship. Prior, 4-5. For continuance of the Portuguese Slave Trade after 1820, see p. 226, below.

BRITAIN AND THE SLAVE TRADE

ated in the East African area, the British Navy could not interfere as yet. The promise made by Spain in 1817 to abandon the whole of her slave trade did not come into effect till 1820.

Meantime, direct news of the Trade was reaching London from British agents on the spot. It has been observed that before the war Britain had acquired no posts in East African waters; that British shipping, *en route* for India, had set its course straight from the Cape or merely touched at the Comoro Isles and passed on. But the capture of the Seychelles group of islands in 1794 and of Île de France in 1810 and their retention after the war as British possessions under a single colonial administration had given Britain her first footholds on the African side of the Indian Ocean.[1] In 1819 the islands were transferred from the naval control of the 'Indian Station' to that of the 'Cape of Good Hope Station';[2] thereafter, under the direction of the naval commander-in-chief at the Cape base, British warships were regularly visiting Port Louis and Mahé and patrolling the intervening waters; and, since the suppression of the Slave Trade was now the British Navy's main concern, it was from the captains of those ships and their commander at the Cape as well as from the Governor of Mauritius that the news of the French Slave Trade came to London. For Bourbon, its centre, lay right in the track of their patrols— about fifty miles west-south-west of Mauritius.

This French traffic was less exposed to British interference than the Atlantic trade, and it had been vigorously maintained during the greater part of the war. A naval report as late as 1809 spoke of the French privateers of Port Louis being 'all fitted up for slaves' which were bought at Zanzibar and Kilwa with the proceeds of their British prizes. An English merchant whom they captured and dropped at Zanzibar stated that during his stay of several months on the island 'the port was never without a French vessel, sometimes two or three, waiting for

---

[1] Seychelles became a separate Crown Colony in 1903.
[2] *S.P.* viii (1820), 907. Admiralty orders that one ship be stationed at Mauritius, especially to assist the Governor in suppressing the Slave Trade: ibid. 911.

cargoes collected along the coast'.[1] A dispatch from Lord Caledon, Governor of the Cape (1807–11), in 1810 gave further information of the French liaison with Zanzibar.

'The Isles of France and Bourbon receive their slaves principally from Madagascar but occasionally from Zanzibar. The island of Zanzibar is tributary to the Imam of Muscat who farms it out to black merchants connected with the French. . . . One of the chief advantages is derived from the contiguity of the island to the mainland whence the negroes are brought who are sent either directly to the French islands under the Arab flag or indirectly by going in the first instance to Madagascar.'[2]

That Arab flag was useful, especially in the later years of the war, when French sea-power had been eliminated from the Indian Ocean. Under French colours the trade, which Captain Smee found still flourishing at Zanzibar even after the fall of Île de France, would have been highly dangerous.[3] The traffic with Kilwa, as Prior found, was also well maintained.[4] And when the war was over, though the recrudescence of the Trade was relatively far less in these waters than in West Africa after the restoration of Senegal and Goree to France,[5] slave-smuggling into Bourbon from Madagascar and the mainland steadily continued. In this case it was really smuggling, at any rate after January 8, 1817; for on that date the French Government issued an *ordonnance* prohibiting the importation of slaves into French colonies; and in April 1818 this interdict was confirmed and extended by an Act of the French legislature which prohibited French subjects from any participation in the Slave Trade. But, unlike the severe and effective British Act of 1811, this Act prescribed no heavier penalties than the confiscation of the ship concerned and the suspension of its officers from service for ten years. The French Government, moreover, stiffly refused to concede to British cruisers the 'reciprocal right of

[1] Capt. Tomkinson to Vice-Admiral Bertie, Jan. 1809 (Theal, *R.S.E.A.* 1–3). [2] Caledon to Vansittart, 27.vi.10 (ibid. 13).
[3] See p. 181, above.
[4] See p. 183, above. For French traders at Mozambique in 1812, see p. 194, below.
[5] See the Anglo-French diplomatic correspondence: *S.P.* viii (1820–1), 259–387.

BRITAIN AND THE SLAVE TRADE 193

search'. The results, therefore, were disappointing. The Act was not indeed wholly inoperative: in 1818 and 1819 eight French slave-ships were seized and brought to Bourbon for adjudication, and six of these were condemned and confiscated;[1] and at least one Governor of Bourbon (as will presently appear) made every effort to suppress the Trade. But that was not enough. For several years to come French slave-ships were still at work in the Indian Ocean.

Portuguese, Spanish, French—there was still one more European Power involved. To the incessant, though always courteous, pleas and protests on the Slave Trade question addressed by Castlereagh to the French Government through the British Ambassador, French ministers were able on two occasions to make a neat rejoinder. In July 1818 the Duc de Richelieu informed Sir Charles Stuart that 4,000 Negroes had recently been imported into Mauritius and that *un bâtiment anglois* had been caught attempting to import 240 into Bourbon. And in June 1819 the Marquis Dessolles drew attention to the capture at Bourbon of 'un bâtiment armé à l'Île de France et faisant sous pavillon anglais la contrebande des Noirs'.[2] But in those two cases—and there were only two—the guilty persons, though doubtless British subjects, were probably not Britons. The strength of public opinion in Britain and the severity of the penal Act of 1811 had driven all but the most desperate British slave-smugglers from the seas;[3] but public opinion in Mauritius was more like that of the West Indies. The leading Europeans

[1] Official French list: *S.P.* viii (1820–1), 362.
[2] Ibid. 317, 322. If there had been other instances, the French Government would certainly have cited them. For the case of the *Favorite*, see pp. 345–60.
[3] A few British subjects continued after 1807 to finance the Trade by underhand methods at foreign ports and even at London and Liverpool, but they rarely ventured on voyages themselves, and their operations practically ceased after the Act of 1811 (Mathieson, op. cit. 5). Similarly with the slavers' crews. Théodore Canot, who was deeply engaged in slave-smuggling on the west coast for several years after the war, states that a fugitive cabin-boy was 'the only English subject I ever knew to ship in a slaver'. In this instance there is no reason to doubt Canot's word. His father was French, his mother Italian. (*Memoirs of a Slave-Trader*, first published 1854, reprinted, London, 1929, p. 66.)

of the island were French planters who, like their *confrères* in Bourbon, required slaves for the cultivation of their estates and had been accustomed, as has been seen, before the war to obtain them from Madagascar or the African mainland.[1] That the maintenance of slavery and the trade that fed it was their first consideration had been clearly shown by their attitude to the Revolution. When the news of it arrived in 1790 Port Louis was willing enough to follow Paris. A representative popular assembly was established. Even Jacobinism, when it came, was tolerated: a powerful Jacobin club was formed in 1793. But in 1794 it was reported that the National Convention had decreed the abolition of Slavery and the Slave Trade in all French colonies, and at once a strong reaction set in against the Revolutionary régime. Paris was far off and could be defied. The Jacobin leaders were deported to France; and when, in 1796, two agents of the Directory arrived to proclaim and carry out the emancipation of the slaves they were compelled after three days to leave the island with their task undone. Two years later a revolutionary movement in the garrison was quelled by sending 800 of the troops back to France.[2] Not till the rise of Napoleon, who restored colonial slavery in 1802, had the planters felt that their labour-supply and livelihood were safe again; and it is easy to understand their anger and alarm when, only eight years later, they discovered that British annexation meant the end of the Slave Trade. The resentment of these new British subjects in Mauritius was even more bitter than that of the old British subjects in Jamaica after 1807. Indeed, at the outset of the new régime, they openly continued to get what slaves they could from East Africa and Madagascar. Prior, touching at Mozambique in 1812, observed a number of Frenchmen from Bourbon *and Mauritius* who were 'in high favour here at present owing to speculations in slaves, a trade which still flourishes in those islands notwithstanding all our vigilance'.[3]

[1] At the time of the British occupation there were 60,000 slaves in Mauritius. P.P. 1826, xxvii, No. 295, p. 5.
[2] Lucas and Stubbs, op. cit. 139. Contemporary account in Grant, op. cit. 527–32.　　　　　　　　　　　　　　　[3] Prior, 33.

BRITAIN AND THE SLAVE TRADE 195

In thus defying the well-known principles of the British Government and Parliament, the Mauritian slave owners and traders claimed to be legally justified. The right to continue the Trade, they argued, was included in the 'laws and customs' which had been safeguarded by the terms of the capitulation; and this claim was actually supported by the Governor, Sir Robert Farquhar, who was not only anxious to placate the anti-British attitude of the island planters but seems almost to have shared their views. 'Without a fresh importation of slaves', he wrote to the Secretary of State in February 1811, 'these islands, as I have been given to understand and have been led to believe, cannot continue in cultivation and produce, but must become deserts.' And to the argument grounded on the capitulation he added another:

'I believe it has been generally agreed that a British Act of Parliament does not extend to a colony unless that colony be specially mentioned either by name or general inclusive words; and that an Act made previously to the acquisition of a colony . . . will not, generally speaking, bind the colony acquired subsequently.'

Lord Liverpool's reply was prompt and forcible.

'I cannot sufficiently express my surprise that you should have supposed it possible that when the Parliament of the United Kingdom had thought proper upon general principles to abolish the Slave Trade with respect to all the ancient colonies and established settlements of Great Britain, it could have been in their contemplation that this trade should be suffered to exist with respect to those islands or foreign possessions which the fortune of war might place under His Majesty's dominion. . . . As it appears to His Majesty's Government to be of the utmost importance that no time should be lost in correcting the extraordinary misapprehension into which you appear to have fallen upon this subject, I shall send several copies of this letter by the East India fleet which is on the point of sailing from this country.'

A copy of the Act of 1807 was enclosed and Farquhar's attention drawn to the penalties imposed. A few months later, a copy of the Act of 1811, making participation in the Trade a felony, was likewise forwarded to Mauritius. But Farquhar had already climbed down. 'Every possible step has been taken by this government', he wrote in October 1811, 'to enforce the Slave Act with the utmost rigour'; and for the rest of his term of office, which lasted till 1823, with a break from November 1817 to July 1820, he scarcely drafted a dispatch without asserting his zeal for the abolition of the Trade. But he made no secret of its difficulty and especially the lack of any effective support from public opinion in the island. The colonists hated the 'new order of things which strikes at the root of their most valuable individual interests'. Some of the officials were negligent, if not worse. Even the judges could not be relied on to enforce the penal provisions of the law. In 1814, stimulated perhaps by a firm dispatch from Liverpool's successor, Bathurst, declaring that the best way to treat the recalcitrant colonists was to remove 'any hope that the general laws of the Empire can be either violated with impunity or relaxed in favour of any particular colony', he suspended five judges from office. A more positive measure was the appointment of agents to watch and at need take action at the Seychelles and in Madagascar. Information thus obtained led to the capture in 1816 by H.M.S. *Tyne* of two schooners with 201 slaves in transit from Tamatave and Foulpointe to Mauritius. Yet the smuggling persisted. By 1817 the slave-population had risen far above the limits of any possible natural increase. And, though Farquhar was perhaps too sweepingly condemned by Buxton and his anti-Slavery colleagues, it is a strong point against him that, on his return for two years to England at the end of 1817, the more rigorous policy of his successors, General Hall and General Darling—further suspensions of officials, the suppression of the 'Conseil Général des Communes' (a body created to advise the Governor on commercial questions), searches of private estates, restrictions on fishing-boats, and so forth—substantially reduced the inflow of smuggled slaves. The Commissioners sent out in 1827 to inquire into the operation of preventive measures at Mauritius, the Cape, and Ceylon reported that 'the check given to the Slave Trade in 1818 tended to diminish the numbers [of slaves smuggled into Mauritius] in the following years; and, although projects were subsequently formed and vessels fitted out by

BRITAIN AND THE SLAVE TRADE 197

persons now resident in the colony . . . no direct importation of an entire cargo of Negroes has taken place in Mauritius since March 1821'.[1]

But, though reduced in volume, the smuggling Trade was still active, far more active than in the West Indies; and in the Mauritius debate of 1826 Buxton made a deep impression on the House of Commons by reading official figures which showed that in the course of the past year more than ten times as many smuggled slaves had been detected and freed at Mauritius as in all the other British colonies together. The fact was that the suppression of smuggling was far more difficult there than anywhere else. Farquhar, indeed, did not exaggerate the peculiarity of the situation of the colony—'with a population constituted as this is, with an extensive slave market close at hand, the settlement of a neighbouring power within a night's sail of it, surrounded by clusters of islands favourable to the daring enterprise of smugglers, and occasionally visited by cruisers only at long intervals'. Judge Smith, who presided over the Admiralty Court, was no less pessimistic.

'While the inferior departments of the police are either so corrupt or so negligent or so feeble that the last prisoner who escaped paraded the streets daily for a length of time without interruption, and while a vast majority of the population considers the abolition of the Slave Trade as an act of injustice to themselves, and every individual who engages in it as a meritorious character, and everyone whom we condemn as a martyr in a good cause, I repeat that no governor or

[1] Claim to continue Slave Trade: Farquhar to Liverpool, 11.ii.11 (*P.P.* 1826, xxvii, No. 295, p. 6); Liverpool's reply, 2.v.11 (ibid., p. 7). Act of 1811: L. to F., 14.ii.12 (ibid., p. 9). Farquhar's activities: F. to L., 26.x.11 (ibid., p. 8). Public opinion: F. to L., 1. ii. 12; Bathurst to F., 25.i.13 (ibid., pp. 11, 20). Suspension of judges: F. to B., 22.i.14 (ibid., p. 31). Captures: F. to B., 10. ix. 16, and captains' reports (ibid., pp. 104–5). Rise of slave-population: Hansard, 1826, xv. 1031. Commissioners' Report: *P.P.* 1829, xxv, No. 292, pp. 17, 27. Details of action by Hall and Darling in *P.P.* 1826, xxvii, No. 352. Buxton's attack on Farquhar, Hansard, 1826, xv. 1031. F.'s reply: ibid. 1037–47. F. attacks the Abolitionists in language akin to that of the West Indian planters in a letter to the Colonial Office in 1826: *P.P.* 1829, xxv, No. 337. The author is also indebted to an unpublished thesis on 'The Slave Trade at Mauritius, 1810–29', by Miss M. K. Jones.

judge, however great their talents or however animated their zeal, will ever in my humble opinion be able by any exertions individually on their part to overcome such difficulties.'[1]

It was this conviction which led Farquhar to the same opinion on the suppression of the Slave Trade as that which was increasingly held by British statesmen, and in later years especially by Palmerston, namely, that in East as in West Africa the exportation of slaves from their homelands could be more easily and effectively prevented than their importation into other countries. Among the efforts, therefore, which he made to erase the bad impression his first dispatch on the Trade had created at the Colonial Office, was an attempt to block the flow of slave-smuggling to Mauritius at its nearest source. He had failed (as has been seen) to prevent the British Government acquiescing in the restoration of the trading-posts in Madagascar to their founders;[2] but mainly, no doubt, owing to the prestige of victory, British influence in the island was still stronger than French. The greater part of it had come under the control of the shrewd and capable Radama, who in 1810 had succeeded to the chieftainship of the Hovas, the dominant tribe in the interior, and who in 1817, so powerful had he become, declared himself 'King of Madagascar'. And Radama, who seems to have shown a genuine anxiety to acquire the benefits of European civilization in so far as they did not threaten his independence, showed a marked preference for the new masters of Mauritius as against the old masters of Bourbon. In 1817 he readily accepted Farquhar's proposal to appoint a resident British agent at his court. In 1820 he warmly welcomed the pioneers of the London Missionary Society, who wisely set themselves, with quick and gratifying results, to teach not only the English language and the art of reading and writing but also industrial crafts. The French Roman Catholic missionaries, on the other hand, Radama refused to admit. French traders, he explained, were free to enter his country, but, as he had already admitted

[1] Buxton: Hansard, 1826, xv. 1026. Farquhar to Bathurst, 15.x.15 (*P.P.* 1876, xxvii, No. 295, p. 122). Smith to Hall, 6.ix.17 (ibid., No. 352, p. 9).   [2] See p. 141, above.

Protestant missionaries, he did not desire teachers of what he understood to be a different religion. Whether this explanation was wholly candid or not, it could find some justification in other chapters of African history; but, not unnaturally, French historians have regarded it as evidence of the perfidious intrigues by which Sir Robert Farquhar was recovering the hold on Madagascar denied him by the interpretation of the Treaty of Paris.[1]

Certain it was, at any rate, that these developments in Madagascar had greatly lightened Farquhar's task of diminishing the export of slaves therefrom. He could deal with one paramount native ruler who could answer for most of the east coast of the island, and with that ruler he was on the friendliest terms. On October 23, 1817, accordingly, a treaty was signed at Tamatave providing for the 'entire cessation and extinction, through all the dominions of King Radama and wherever his influence can extend, of the sale or transfer of Slaves or other persons whatever to be removed from off the soil of Madagascar into any other country, island or dominion of any other prince, potentate or power'. To compensate for the loss of revenue involved Radama was to be paid £2,000 a year.[2] In 1818, with a view to checking inter-tribal warfare as a means of feeding the Slave Trade, the export of arms and gunpowder from Mauritius into Madagascar was prohibited, and in 1819 Governor Milius of Bourbon promptly accepted the suggestion that he should enact a similar prohibition for his island. Milius, indeed, went farther. He prohibited also the export of horses for the equipment of slave-raiding cavalry in Madagascar; and even proposed

[1] L. McLeod, *Madagascar and its People* (London, 1865), 47–8. A. You, *Madagascar, colonie française* (Paris, 1931), 29–30. R. de Comte, *Des différentes phases de l'occupation française à Madagascar* (Montpellier, 1908), 97–8. L. Brunet, *L'Œuvre de la France à Madagascar*, 336–7.

[2] Text of the Treaty: P.P. 1821, xxiii, 'Slave Trade at Mauritius', 4–5. Besides the £2,000, Radama was to receive annually 100 barrels of gunpowder, 100 English muskets, 10,000 flints, 400 soldiers' caps, stocks, red jackets, shirts, pairs of trousers, and pairs of shoes, 12 sergeants' swords and belts, 400 pieces of white cloth, 200 of blue cloth, one full-dress cloth coat with two epaulets, cocked hat, and dress boots, and two horses.

to General Darling, who was governing Mauritius in Farquhar's absence, that their respective warships should exercise a reciprocal right of search, little knowing that he was reversing the role of his own Government in Paris, on which the British Government had strongly but quite vainly pressed precisely that same proposal.[1] These measures were followed by further negotiations with Radama. In 1820 the Treaty of 1817 was renewed with an additional article providing for twenty of Radama's subjects to be sent to England and Mauritius for training in handicrafts; and in 1823, since no promises, however honest, to suppress the export of slaves could be made effective without the exercise of force on sea as well as land, another treaty was concluded permitting British cruisers to seize slave-ships in Madagascar waters and prescribing the procedure of adjudication and confiscation. The results were satisfactory. The Commissioners of 1827 were able to report that the restrictions imposed on slave-smuggling at all the ports under Radama's control had proved effectual. Only in the south of the island, beyond the scope of his authority, was the traffic still prevalent.[2]

3

There was one corner of the East African world to which the repression of the Slave Trade in Madagascar brought immediate relief. The brief visit of the *Nisus* to Johanna in 1812 had proved, as it was bound to prove, an ineffective deterrent to the Malagasi raiders. They had not been in the least 'overawed'. From 1813 onwards the raids were resumed. Though not on

[1] *S.P.* viii (1820–1), 331, 353–4.
[2] Text of additional article: *P.P.* 1821, xxiii, 'Slave Trade at Mauritius', 5–6. Text of Treaty of 1823: *P.P.* 1826, xxvii, No. 352, pp. 163–4. It was calculated that the Treaty deprived Radama of an annual revenue of 60,000 dollars (about £14,000) from the tax on all slaves passing through his territory, and also of the profits he had made on the sale of prisoners of war. Owen, ii. 109. For relations with Radama, especially the conduct of General Hall and the lapse of the Treaty of 1817: *P.P.* 1826, xxvii, No. 352, pp. 54–6, 71–3, 75, 119, 146. Radama's remarkable efforts to introduce civilization are described by Farquhar to Wilmot, 6.vi.23 (ibid., pp. 148 ff.). Missionaries: McLeod, op. cit. 60–1. Commissioners: *P.P.* 1829, xxv, No. 292, p. 20.

their old scale, and directed now more specifically to slave-catching than to general destruction, they were still a grievous infliction and seemingly inescapable. To no one, therefore, were the efforts made by Farquhar and Radama to suppress the whole business of slave-trading more welcome than to the people of the Comoros; and, though 'slaving' was still occasionally practised on the islands by piratical Arabs, the operation of the Treaty seems at last to have stopped the raids from Madagascar. At any rate the Sultan of Johanna, replying to a friendly letter from Farquhar in the spring of 1821, expressed his gratitude for what had been done to save his people from the miseries of which 'my dilapidated towns and deserted villages are sad evidences'. And he went on to beg for the continuance of an old friendship which had proved so useful to his little realm.

'Your unequivocal acknowledgment of the existence of our alliance is particularly interesting to me at this time because so few English ships have touched here latterly that I began to be apprehensive lest His Britannic Majesty should have forgotten that the prosperity of my people depends entirely upon his protection of intercourse [sic] with the British nation. Your Excellency's friendly letter has, however, dissipated my fears; and I now flatter myself that in future I shall enjoy frequent opportunities of proving my attachment to the British nation by facilitating the refreshment, repairs and commerce of British ships.'[1]

Northwards of Mozambique, however, the Radama Treaty had made little difference. French 'slavers', as has been seen, were still trafficking with the Arab ports along the coast; and at Zanzibar, the central entrepôt of all the coastal trade, the Arab merchants, while they sold most of their slaves northwards to Asia, were willing to do business also with European buyers in the south. Some of the ships captured in the act of smuggling slaves into Bourbon had sailed from Zanzibar. And in the same dispatch in which Farquhar assured the Colonial Secretary of the proved efficacy of the Radama Treaty in the south he reported that the Trade in the north had been shown by recent

[1] 'King' of Johanna to F., 26.vii.21, enclosed in F. to B. 4.xii.21 (C.O. 167, 58).

events to be far more extensive than he had imagined. Rumours had reached him that the French 'slavers' were conspiring to take advantage of the restrictions imposed by the treaties with Britain on their Spanish and Portuguese rivals, that twenty-four slave-ships were being fitted out by a company at Nantes for East African waters, and that a secret depot for slaves was to be established in Providence, a small and rarely visited island between Madagascar and the Seychelles. At his request, therefore, Captain Fairfax Moresby of H.M.S. *Menai* had sailed from Port Louis to investigate; and this officer's report had shown that, though there was as yet no depot, a brisk trade in slaves under the French flag was traversing the area between Madagascar and Zanzibar. He had learned of eight ships sailing under French or Arab flags southwards from Zanzibar during the three weeks of his cruise, each laden with between 200 and 400 slaves. Of these he had captured between Bourbon and Providence one French brig with 340 slaves, *Le Succès*, 'a most beautiful vessel' which had 'arrived at Bourbon from Nantes in June last, quite new', and chased another French brig through the archipelago northwards. He had discovered also that no less than 20,000 slaves were herded in the Zanzibar market awaiting sale, and that French agents, aware of the fertility of Zanzibar and its excellent harbour, were 'busy in that quarter'. Moresby had added —what Farquhar doubtless knew—that Zanzibar was 'subject to the Imam of Muscat', who was 'closely allied in commercial and territorial interest with the English East India Company'.[1]

The moral was plain. The Imam must be persuaded like Radama to co-operate with Britain in the suppression of the Trade. But Farquhar could not deal alone with Said as he had with Radama. To negotiate with a Moslem prince of the Arabian mainland, representative of an ancient civilization and one in which Slavery and the Slave Trade were deeply rooted, was a different matter from negotiating with a chief, however enlightened, of a negroid tribe in Madagascar. Said, moreover, though hitherto a stranger to the Government of Mauritius, was an old

[1] F. to Bathurst, 14.iv.21; Moresby to F., and memorandum, 4. iv. 21; F. to M., 5.iv.21 (C.O. 167, 58).

Britain and the Slave Trade

acquaintance, a protégé indeed, of the Governments of British India. Farquhar, therefore, when he opened the question of a treaty with Said, wrote also to the Governor-General, Lord Hastings, asking him to bring pressure to bear on the Imam to stop the Slave Trade from his 'ports and subordinate dependencies of Zanzibar, Kilwa, and other petty factories on the East coast of Africa'. 'Were this measure accomplished,' he added, 'this hemisphere would for the future be cleared entirely of that pollution which has stained it from the earliest times.' Hastings's reply was wholly sympathetic. The Government of Bombay, he wrote, was to make a strong representation at Muscat on the question of 'this criminal and disgraceful traffic'.[1]

Thus the attack delivered on the Arab Slave Trade in East Africa in 1820 was a combined attack from south and east, from the British Government at Mauritius and the British Governments at Calcutta and Bombay.

4

From time immemorial, as recorded in an earlier chapter, African slaves had been imported into India by Indian and Arab merchants; and after the great extension of British rule in the eighteenth century they were still imported not only into the Indian States but also into the British Presidencies, and for service not only in Indian households but in those of British and other European residents. There was no reason, after all, why a British merchant in Calcutta in those days should not own slaves as much as a British planter in Jamaica or indeed a retired British 'West Indian' in England; and it is no more surprising to find advertisements of 'Coffrees' (as they were called) wanted or for sale in a Calcutta than in a London newspaper.[2] But, whereas no slaves were to be found in England

---

[1] F. to Hastings, 28.ix.21; G.-G. in C. to F. 18.viii.21; enclosed in F. to Bathurst, 4.xii.21 (C.O. 167, 58).

[2] *Hickey's Gazette*, for example, in 1780 contained the following among other similar advertisements: '*Wanted*. Two Coffrees who can play well on the French horn ...'; '*To be Sold*. A Coffree boy that understands the business of a butler, kidmutgar and cooking.' Quoted by D. R. Banaji, *Slavery in British India* (Bombay, 1933), 6.

after the Somerset Judgement of 1772, and the Slave Trade with the British West Indies was practically extinguished after 1807, the inflow and sale of slaves in British India, if checked, were by no means stopped. In Bengal, an official report of 1812, which appears from other evidence to have taken an optimistic view, admitted that at least a hundred slaves were still being shipped by Arab traders to Calcutta every year; in 1823 an article in the *Calcutta Journal* described Calcutta as a 'mart in which the manacled African is sold like the beast of the field to the highest bidder'; and again in 1823 an editorial in the same paper asserted that 'a hundred and fifty eunuchs have been landed from the Arab ships this season'.[1] On the west coast, so much nearer to the Arab and African sources of supply, the importation of slaves was greater and lasted longer. They were still being landed at Karachi as late as 1842.[2]

It must not be supposed that the British officials in India were indifferent to this state of things. Neither they nor their superiors in London were untouched by the great current of humanitarianism which had swept the British people into the anti-slavery crusade.[3] They belonged to the multitudinous company of public servants whose duty it was, in various ways and various parts of the world, to execute the public will—ministers in Whitehall, ambassadors at foreign capitals, consuls at foreign ports, colonial governors, officers and seamen of the Navy. If Slavery itself lingered longer in British India than in other British possessions, the reason was plain and respectable. It was a cardinal principle of British-Indian policy to abstain as far as possible from interference with the beliefs and customs of the Indian peoples; and Slavery had been maintained for ages past in India by Hindu usage as well as by Moslem law. Thus the historic Act of 1833, which ended Slavery in the British

[1] Banaji, 73–5.
[2] Idem, 75. For the Trade in the thirties, see p. 500, below.
[3] Charles Grant of the 'Clapham Sect', after seventeen years' service in Bengal, was a member of the Court of Directors from 1794 till his death in 1823, and in several years was chairman or deputy chairman. For Charles Metcalfe's vigorous repression of the local Slave Trade when Resident at Delhi, see Banaji, 345.

Colonies, was expressly not extended 'to any of the territories in the possession of the East India Company or [for similar reasons] to the Island of Ceylon or [because it was still under the Company's control] to the Island of St. Helena'.[1] In the Government of India Act of the same year, however, a clause was inserted requiring the Governor-General in Council 'to take into consideration the means of mitigating the state of Slavery and ameliorating the condition of Slaves, and of extinguishing Slavery throughout the said territories as soon as such extinction shall be practicable and safe'.[2] Nor were the results of this requisition long delayed. In 1843 the Government of India enacted the abolition of the legal status of Slavery, which so effectively cut its roots that it was practicable in the penal code of 1860 to make it a penal offence to own as well as to trade in slaves.[3]

But this caution in dealing with Slavery had never been observed with regard to the Trade. The Abolition Act of 1807 had applied to British subjects wherever they might be domiciled; and the Act of 1811, which made participation in the Trade a felony punishable by transportation for fourteen years or by three to five years' hard labour, specifically covered persons residing in territories under the government of the East India Company.[4] As the Judicial Department in Bengal pointed out in 1817, this implied that Parliament 'meant to provide for the effectual abolition' of the traffic between East Africa and India, 'which was in fact of a nature and tendency scarcely less objec-

[1] 3 & 4 W. IV, c. 73, lxiv. St. Helena was transferred to Crown Colony government in 1834. An interesting example of the use to which African slaves could be put is afforded by the Third Ceylon Regiment, which in 1811 consisted of nearly 800 Africans, purchased mostly at Goa for about £30 a head, freed on purchase, and then enlisted. The slaves had come originally from Mozambique and Zanzibar. Communicated by Mr. C. W. Dixon from an unpublished thesis on Sir Thomas Maitland.
[2] 3 & 4 W. IV, c. 85, lxxxviii. This clause was inserted in the House of Lords, mainly at the instance of the Duke of Wellington, in place of a clause directly abolishing domestic slavery. Hansard, 1833, xx. 446–7.
[3] The legal status was similarly abolished in Ceylon in 1844.
[4] 51 G. III, c. xxiii, clause i.

tionable than the trade which had been carried on between the western coast of Africa and the West India islands'.[1] But the British-Indian Governments had not waited for the initiative of Parliament. In 1805, two years before the British Act of 1807, the Bombay Government issued a regulation declaring that 'the importation and exportation of slaves for the purposes of traffic at the port of Bombay and at the other ports subject to the immediate authority of this Presidency stand prohibited'.[2] In 1807 this injunction was stiffened by the requirement of a declaration from masters or owners of all ships except the Company's that they were not carrying or intending to carry slaves, and by the imposition of a fine of 500 rupees for an infringement of the prohibition.[3] In 1811 a similar measure was enacted in Bengal. Regulation X of that year 'for preventing the importation of slaves from foreign countries and the sale of such slaves in the territories immediately dependent on the Presidency of Fort William' provided that importation should be punished by imprisonment for six months and a fine not exceeding 200 rupees or another six months' imprisonment, and required that 'captains and supercargoes of vessels, with the exception of the Honourable Company's ships, importing at Calcutta shall, previously to being permitted to land any part of their cargo or goods, execute a bond, rendering themselves liable to the payment of a penalty of rupees five thousand in the event of their disposing of any persons as slaves'.[4] In 1813 this regulation was adopted also in Bombay.[5]

The results were the same as elsewhere. Prohibitions and penalties might check the inflow of slaves into British India, but they could no more stop it—as the facts recorded above bear witness—than the statutes of 1807 and 1811 could stop it at Mauritius. No British-Indian enactment, moreover, could affect the steady trade with the Indian States, especially those which

[1] I.O., General Letter from Jud. Dept., Bengal, 29.x.17, par. 162.
[2] Bombay regulation of May 14, 1805. As to exportation, Indian girls were exported as slaves to Muscat and other Middle Eastern ports.
[3] Bombay regulation of Sept. 22, 1827: Banaji, 302.
[4] Bengal Regulation X, Aug. 6, 1811.
[5] Bombay regulation of May 5, 1813.

bordered on the Arabian Sea. Karachi was only some 500 miles from Muscat. It was as obvious, therefore, at Bombay as at Port Louis that it was more effectual to attack the Trade at its export than at its import end. And that meant Muscat: for the exporting centre for African slaves was Zanzibar, a dependency of Muscat, and most of the exporters were subjects of the Imam. Some years, therefore, before Farquhar found that his campaign against the Trade had to be extended northwards to Oman, the British-Indian authorities had been looking for the same reason in the same direction: but, knowing more of the local conditions, they were more acutely conscious than Farquhar could be of the difficulty of taking action. The suppression of the Arab Slave Trade, of that steady traffic in Africans which from the dawn of history had streamed across the sea to Oman and the adjacent coast-lands, might seem, indeed, to be quite beyond the scope of 'practical politics'. It would not only deprive many of Said's subjects of their livelihood and Said himself of a large part of his revenue. It would threaten the existence of Slavery itself. For one of the worst evils of Slavery is its interference with the normal balance and relationship between the sexes: the natural increase of slave-populations has never kept pace with their masters' needs: it has always had to be supplemented by a constant flow of recruits from outside. So it had been in the West Indies, and so it was in Oman. To the Arabs, therefore, as to the West Indian planters, Slavery and the Slave Trade seemed parts of one indivisible system. And it is important to realize that the extinction of Slavery—an institution sanctioned not only by immemorial usage but by the specific injunction of the Koran, and a seemingly indispensable element in Arab society—was at least as inconceivable to Arabs at this time as it had been to English planters in the middle of the eighteenth century. If any Arab ruler of those days had been mad enough to interfere with his subjects' ownership of slaves in order to soothe the unintelligible susceptibilities of foreign infidels, he would instantly have paid for it with his throne or with his life. Too hasty an attempt, therefore, to compel Said to suppress the Trade would be futile and dangerous. He would be obliged to resist it:

friendly relations would no longer be possible: the whole situation in the Persian Gulf would be disturbed. Often enough, in the course of their long crusade, British Governments at home were compelled to accommodate their humanitarian zeal to the exigencies of international relations: and so it was now with the Governments at Calcutta and Bombay. 'Policy' perforce came first and philanthropy second.[1]

Thus, while, as has been seen, measures against the importation of slaves had been taken at Bombay as early as 1805, it was not till the political importance of friendship with Muscat had been diminished by the destruction of French power in the Indian Ocean that the first tentative approach was made to Said. The Mascarenes were captured in 1810; Java in 1811; and early in 1812 the Government of Bombay informed Said of the prohibition of the Slave Trade in British India, furnished him with a copy of the Bengal regulation of the previous year, and requested him to 'give publicity to the purport of it throughout your dominions in order that your subjects, who are so much in the habit of frequenting the port of Calcutta, may not by its infringement incur the penalties of that ordinance'.[2] There the matter rested till in 1815 the Bombay Government felt that a more direct, if still cautious, attack might be opened. Sir Evan Nepean accordingly addressed a personal letter to Said in which, after a tactful allusion to the fact that 'the inhuman traffic' had been carried on in the past by European as well as Asiatic peoples,

'it is gratifying to me [he continued] to be enabled to assure your Highness that this commerce, so repugnant to every principle of humanity, has been annihilated in almost all the civilized world: and,

[1] The dependence of the Arabs on slave-labour is clear from the large number of slaves they possessed. Brucks estimated about 1840 that the slaves in Oman were probably one-third of its total population of 800,000 (B.R. 633). Smee guessed the population of Zanzibar in 1811 at 200,000, of which he thought as many as three-quarters were slaves (p. 183, above). Rigby states that the 'great bulk' of the population of Zanzibar in 1860 were slaves (*Report*, 9). Salil-ibn-Razik records that the Imam Seif-bin-Sultan had 700 male slaves (Badger, 93).

[2] Secretary to Bombay Government to Said, 4.iii.12 (I.O., B.P.C., vol. 32, 1812, pp. 388–90).

Britain and the Slave Trade

anxious as I am that one so intimately connected with the Company's Government should not only be exempt from the imputation of tolerating it but should also have the merit of interdicting it within the limits of his authority—having, moreover, lately learnt that a vessel with a vast number of slaves on board from Zanzibar to Muscat has been taken by the Jawasmi and every soul on board barbarously put to death—I feel the strongest inducement to recommend to your adoption an example so worthy of imitation as that which the abandonment of this Trade by the principal powers of Europe affords, under an assurance that your acquiescence in this proposition will be extremely gratifying to the British Government.'[1]

The meaning of this somewhat cumbrous language was clear enough to Said. Not only his friends at Bombay but their superiors in England did definitely desire the abolition of the Slave Trade: but they were not prepared, it seemed, in 1815 any more than in 1812, to take a strong line about it; and until the awkward request was put to him with less circumlocution and in a firmer tone, he decided to ignore it. No answer to Nepean's exhortations appears in the records. Nothing was done. And when, after another five years, the next move was made against the Slave Trade, it was directed not against Said but against his enemies, the Jawasmi, and not against the Trade as a single distinct iniquity but as a form of the piracy with which, as has been seen, the British Governments in India were at that time finally coming to grips.[2] The pirates and the 'slavers' of the Persian Gulf, in fact, were indistinguishable; and, when their power had been broken once for all by the campaign of 1819, they were compelled to pledge themselves in the General Treaty of 1820 to abstain from the Slave Trade together with piracy, or rather as a special form of piracy. 'The carrying off of slaves, men, women or children', ran Article XI, 'from the coasts of Africa or elsewhere and the transporting them in vessels is plunder and piracy; and the Arabs who accept the Peace shall do nothing of this nature.'[3] But this clause of the Treaty could not easily be enforced. Like the Bombay and Bengal regulations or Farquhar's attempts to prevent the

---
[1] Nepean to Said, 26.vii.15 (I.O., B.P.C., 1815, pp. 3685–8).
[2] See pp. 149–50, above.   [3] Text in B.R. 76–8.

smuggling of slaves into Mauritius, it attacked the Trade at its import rather than its export end. Once more it was clear that the only hope of really suppressing the Trade lay in preventing the slaves' being shipped from Zanzibar and other African ports.

Thus the appeal from Mauritius for co-operation in a further assault on Muscat was in complete accord with the ideas and intentions of the authorities at Calcutta and Bombay. But, whereas in 1815 Said had been invited to consider a wholesale abolition of the Slave Trade, it was wisely decided by all the parties concerned in 1821 to limit the scope of the new attack. The reasons which precluded Said from acquiescing in the abolition of the Trade in its entirety applied mainly to the domestic or 'internal' branch of it—the supply of slaves to his own subjects for their own use. The case for maintaining its export or 'external' branch was not nearly so strong. To stop the export of slaves eastwards to the Gulf of Cutch or southwards to the Mascarenes and Mozambique would mean a certain loss to individual 'slavers' and to Said's revenues: but it would leave the main body of the Trade untouched and would have no effect at all on the maintenance of Slavery itself in Oman. The Government of Bombay could ask Said, therefore, to suppress this 'external' Trade—with which alone it was itself directly concerned—not only without dangerously threatening Said's financial or political position, but without incurring the charge of unwarrantable interference in the purely domestic affairs of his dominions. The Government of Mauritius was in exactly the same position. Farquhar desired that the whole of the Arab Slave Trade should be brought to an end as soon as possible; but his immediate concern was only to cut off the southward branch of it, the smuggling of slaves into European ownership in Bourbon or Mauritius. In the autumn of 1821, accordingly, after further correspondence between Farquhar and Mountstuart Elphinstone (who had succeeded Nepean in 1819), a double request—from Mauritius and Bombay—was made to Said. As previously, an 'earnest recommendation' was submitted that he

should suppress the whole of a trade which all the Governments
of Europe had agreed to suppress and thereby make a name for
himself which all posterity would honour. But this time it was
suggested that Said might find it 'inexpedient or impossible' to
go all that length. In that case, to quote the Bombay letter,
'immediate interference' was solicited in the operation of the
'external' Trade. He was asked to issue 'peremptory orders' to
all the local governors of the territories under his control to hand
over any British subjects found in pursuit of the Trade to the
next British warship that touched there, to report the movements of any slave-ship owned by British or French subjects in
the Persian Gulf, and to direct his officials everywhere 'to prevent all dealings in slaves from being carried on by European
agents'. If the earlier part of this letter had been courteous—
indeed the official translator at Bombay noted that 'the
epithets applied to the Slave Trade are softened down in the
Arabic'—the latter part was firm. This time, it was clear to
Said, his British friends were not merely indulging in pious
hopes: they meant business.[1]

5

To Said this recrudescence of British humanitarianism must
have been far from welcome. He was only asked, it is true, to
prohibit the 'external' Trade. Yet it was not easy for him to
make even that limited concession. His fierce Arab subjects,
especially those who were making money from the southward
and eastward Trade, would bitterly resent this British interference in their seas: any submission to it at all would lower
their ruler's prestige. And would the matter end there? Were
not the British bent in fact on destroying the whole of the Slave
Trade and even Slavery itself? Would not this concession be
regarded as merely a first instalment? It would mean, moreover, a substantial loss to Said's revenues. No exact figure can
be given for the duties paid to him on the 'external' part of the
Trade. He himself, as will be seen, estimated their annual

[1] Govt. of Bombay to S., 7.viii.21 (I.O., B.P.C. Oct. 1821, xii. 6495).
F. to S. S., 11.v.21, enc. in F. to B., 4.xii.21 (C.O. 167, 58).

value at this time at about £9,000;[1] but fifteen years later he is said to have raised his estimate—in the light of actual experience but also, no doubt, with a desire to obtain the maximum of credit for the sacrifice he had made—to about £23,000.[2] Yet, if it was hard to grant the British request, it was still harder to refuse it. If the continuance of the Slave Trade were in danger, it was the more needful to retain and increase the 'legitimate' trade with British ports in the East. And the political argument was as strong as the commercial. Since 1811 the British had been masters of the Indian Ocean. Quite recently they had firmly asserted their great power in the Persian Gulf. By crushing the Jawasmi they had done the one thing needed, after the collapse of the Wahabi, to secure Said's position in Arabia. No one else could help him as they could to maintain it in the future. Theirs in fact was a friendship he could scarcely do without, and blunt opposition to their wishes on a matter which they took so curiously to heart might strain or even break it.[3] To yield, on the other hand, would confirm it. He would have put the British in his debt: he might be able, perhaps, later on to play on their sense of gratitude. And so, reluctantly, he yielded. He would do what he was asked this time; but no doubt he told himself, a little anxiously perhaps, that this first instalment must also be the last.

He wrote, accordingly, to Elphinstone and Farquhar declaring his willingness to do all he could to restrain his subjects from the Trade with Europeans and with India, and they at once replied congratulating him on his decision. He had adopted, said Elphinstone, 'a line of conduct which must cause the fame of your Highness' humanity and generosity to be more widely

[1] See p. 213, below. Miles (ii. 328) puts the loss, *if the prohibition were strictly enforced*, at between £5,000 and £6,000.
[2] B.R. 641.
[3] 'I have little doubt,' wrote Bathurst to Farquhar, summing up both motives, 'but that, when the Imam shall have maturely weighed the solid advantages which both himself and his subjects may fairly expect to derive from the protection which has been held out to their commerce with the British possessions in the East, he will no longer delay fulfilling the earnest wishes of Great Britain to which he is principally indebted for his political existence.' 12.vii.22 (C.O. 168, 6).

spread among the Nations of Europe than was the case even before its being adopted'. 'Your Highness', said Farquhar, 'will have the glory of exhibiting to the Nations of the World that your Nation yields to none in the early adoption of those principles of honour, justice and humanity which have been recognized by the Sovereigns of Europe as the grounds of the annihilation of the Slave Trade.'[1] Well-meant rhetoric, no doubt, but not very much, one suspects, to Said's taste. Those 'principles of honour' and the rest of it—why would the British talk like that? 'Annihilation'—an alarming word. But Said had already been careful to safeguard himself. He had told Elphinstone downright that the complete suppression of the Slave Trade in his dominions was impossible—'the reason is as clear to your Excellency as the sun and moon'—and he had taken the opportunity of a visit recently paid him by the British Resident in the Persian Gulf to explain very carefully what he could and could not do.

'His Highness [reported the Resident to Bombay] informed me that he was most anxious at all times to meet the wishes of the British Government to the utmost of his abilities and that therefore he felt peculiarly distressed that he could not in this instance do so so freely as he wished by abolishing Slavery and the Slave Trade throughout his territories as it affected his subjects in a religious point of view. Slavery being allowed according to the Mohammedan creed, therefore any infringement by him in this case would seriously militate against his personal safety and authority. But he had issued the most positive injunctions to his lieutenants at Zanzibar and the other ports on the African coast hereafter not to allow slaves to be sold to French, Portuguese and American vessels or to any Christian people whatever, although this prohibition subjected him to an annual loss of duty to the amount of forty to fifty thousand dollars.'[2]

Conceivably Said hoped that by this prompt issue of orders he might avoid committing himself to a more formal and permanent bond; but Farquhar had already sent him a draft outline of an agreement and was determined to secure his signature.

[1] S. to G. of B., 13.xii.21; G. of B. to S., 22.i.22; F. to S., 15.iii.22; copies enclosed in F. to Bathurst, 29.ii.22 (C.O. 167, 62).
[2] Bruce to G. of B., 20.ii.22 (C.O. 167, 62).

In the early summer of 1822 he wrote to Captain Moresby, asking him to proceed to Muscat and conclude a convention with the Imam on the lines he had drafted.

'You will make him sensible that we by no means wish to innovate on any of his religious practices or observances relative to Slavery, which is recognized and encouraged by the Mahometan faith. It is not the practice of Slavery or the disposal of slaves in his own dominions that is in question. It is the slave traffic alone for exportation which it is our object to annihilate. . . . I am sensible that the abolition of this traffic must occasion a considerable defalcation in his revenues, and you will let him see that we duly appreciate the disinterestedness, but at the same time it will save him from many inconveniences and subjects of misunderstanding and dispute and embarrassment, as H.M. ships would, of course, feel it a duty to intercept all illegal traffic.'

The East India Company, he added, might possibly 'find a mode of remunerating the Imam'; but Moresby must on no account commit the Government of Mauritius to any expenditure not previously sanctioned from home.[1]

Moresby was delighted with his mission. As good a hater of the Slave Trade as any of his colleagues, he had chafed at the legal difficulties of interfering with its European practitioners and had made the most of the greater liberties allowed him by the treaty with Radama in the neighbourhood of Madagascar. It 'has proved', he now told the Admiralty, 'the best preventative from that hitherto great mart for slaves; and, if I can succeed in the mission to Muscat, more will be effected than has been done since the existence of the Abolition Acts'.[2]

[1] Farquhar to Moresby, 3 and 10.vi.22 (Adm. i. 2188). Farquhar also wrote again to Said, 10.vii.22 (enclosed in F. to Bathurst, 25.ix.22). C.O. 167, 63.
[2] Moresby to Adm., 9.vi.22 (Adm. i. 2188). Moresby's zeal was recognized in England. Wilberforce wrote (28.v.22): 'I have heard from several quarters of your generous and indefatigable exertions for the suppression of the Slave Trade on the eastern side of Africa, and feel no small gratification in assuring you that your public spirit and philanthropy have obtained for you the respect and regard of many in this country. . . . When you return, I hope you will allow me the pleasure of paying my personal respects to you.' In a letter from Admiral Sir Fairfax Moresby's grandson to *The Times*, 1.viii.1933.

Britain and the Slave Trade 215

He did succeed. On September 22, 1822, Said signed a treaty which, together with some supplementary articles signed a few days later, declared that 'all external traffic in slaves' from his dominions and dependencies' should be abolished, that the sale of slaves by any of his subjects 'to Christians of every description' was prohibited, that Arab ships violating these engagements would be seized and confiscated by the Imam and their owners and officers punished as pirates, and that any such ship might be similarly seized by British cruisers if found to the south of Cape Delgado, 'His Highness' most southern possession in Africa', or to the east of a line drawn therefrom to a point sixty miles east of Socotra and thence to Diu Head at the western end of the Gulf of Cambay. The 'Moresby Treaty' also provided for the appointment of a British agent at Zanzibar or on the African coast 'for the purpose of having intelligence and watching the traffic in slaves with Christian nations'.[1]

In accepting these stipulations Said had made the best of a bad job. He had kept his concession strictly limited. He had warned the British that he could never go farther. And unquestionably he had pleased them. He had scored, moreover, a pretty point in the diplomatic game. The treaty implied the recognition by the British Government of his claim to 'overlordship' in East Africa. No doubt it was loosely drafted. No doubt Captain Moresby knew next to nothing about the real state of affairs on the African coast. But he had been ready to set his name to articles which spoke of Said's 'dependencies'—of the country as far south as Cape Delgado as in his 'possession' —of 'all his Governors' as implicitly exercising effective control over ports along the coast—and even of 'Arab ships' in those coastal waters as if they were all flying his flag. In view of the actual limitation of Said's power in East Africa in 1822, in view

[1] Text in B.R. 653–7. In a further agreement the Imam stipulated that only ships of His Majesty's Navy and not those of the East India Company should be entitled to seize slave-smugglers (p. 657). R. F. Burton, whose historical statements are often untrustworthy, ascribes to Moresby the offer of compensation to Said (£2,000 a year for three years) which was in fact made about twenty years later by Palmerston. (*Zanzibar*, i. 293; and see p. 505, below.)

of his open and unfinished conflict with Mombasa, those implications in the treaty were obviously of no small diplomatic value. Nor was the economic aspect of the settlement wholly to Said's disadvantage. The continuance of the highly cherished privilege by which his merchant-ships were treated in the ports of British India on the same footing as ships owned, manned, and built by British subjects could now be taken for granted; and at the very beginning of the negotiations he had adroitly obtained the same concession from Farquhar at Mauritius.[1]

To the British, for their part, the treaty gave as much as they had hoped to get. At the least it was a good beginning, and it promised within its narrow limits to be as effective as the Madagascar Treaties. For Said, it seemed, was as anxious as Radama to honour his signature. When Commodore Nourse, commanding at the Cape, visited Zanzibar at the beginning of 1823, 'I found the Imam of Muscat', he reported, 'had issued the most positive orders forbidding the traffic in slaves with any Christians whatsoever; and from all the intelligence I could obtain those orders had been most strictly attended to by the Governor of Zanzibar.'[2] That was all to the good, but orders from Muscat could be broken by hardy smugglers at Zanzibar as easily as orders from Lisbon at Mozambique; and far the most useful feature of the treaty from the British point of view was the right it gave to British cruisers to back up Said's orders like Radama's with their guns. Openly and in due legal form Britain's fifty years' war with the Arab Slave Trade had begun.

[1] In February 1822, before Moresby was sent to Muscat, Farquhar reported to Bathurst: 'The Imam has lately sent a ship of his over to trade at this port. The captain was the bearer of a very civil letter to me from the Imam requesting that the vessels might be put upon the same footing here as in other British ports to the eastward, and intimating at the same time his desire to meet my views as far as possible in any manner I might point out with reference to the abolition of the Slave Trade. I deemed it politic to accede to his request.' F. to B., 29.ii.22 (C.O. 167, 62).

[2] Nourse to Admiralty, 5.i.23 (*P.P.* 1823, vol. xviii). See also the report of the Commissioners of 1827, quoted p. 196, above.

VIII
OWEN'S PROTECTORATE

I

It is time to consider what in fact was Said's 'dominion' in East Africa and what were his 'dependencies' when he signed the Treaty of 1822.

For over a century, ever since the whole coast north of the Rovuma was wrested from the Portuguese by Seif-bin-Sultan, the Imams of Muscat had claimed the 'overlordship' of all the Arab towns. Seif himself had appointed governors or *liwali* at the more important of them, selecting for the purpose the heads of the leading local families—the Mazrui at Mombasa, the El Harthi at Zanzibar, the Nabahani at Pate—and backing them where necessary with garrisons of his own troops. But the Arabs of Africa had welcomed the Arabs of Oman only as deliverers from the Portuguese, not as new masters in their place; and when, after Seif-bin-Sultan's death in 1711, Oman began to drift into one of her recurrent periods of weak rulership and civil strife, the spirit of independence revived along the African coast. An opportunity for its assertion presented itself when in 1741 Ahmed-bin-Said was rewarded for delivering Oman from the Persians by his election to the throne. That meant the inauguration of a new dynasty in place of the discredited Yoruba; and Mahomed-bin-Othman, the Mazrui Governor of Mombasa, made this a pretext for renouncing allegiance to Oman and declaring himself an independent sheikh. 'The Imam', he was reputed to have said, 'is a man of the same standing as myself. He has usurped Oman. I have usurped Mombasa.'[1] Ahmed's response to this challenge was swift and characteristic. He sent five trusted Omani to Mombasa who pretended they had quarrelled with the Imam and deserted him, and, being welcomed accordingly by Mahomed, they murdered him and seized Fort Jesus. His brother, Ali-

[1] From an Arabic MS. history of Mombasa obtained by Capt. Owen and printed in his *Narrative* (London, 1833), i. 414–22. The translation has been modified. No Mazrui would have called himself 'a common man' as in the text.

bin-Othman, managed, however, to escape, and, assisted—so the Arabic narrative has it—by the captain of an English merchantman which happened to be in Kilindini harbour, he rallied his townsfolk, recovered the fort, and ruled as Sheikh in his brother's place.[1] Thus Mombasa's independence was reasserted, and most of the other coast-towns, Pate leading, soon followed her example. In 1777 the French slave-trader, Morice, reported that all the towns were independent except Zanzibar and Pemba.[2] He may have overlooked Mafia, which was certainly under Said's control in 1812.[3] Kilwa seems to have retained its freedom since the withdrawal of the Portuguese, till, about 1780, it was seized by the Imam, and an Omani governor and garrison installed.[4] In four places, then, Said's 'dominion' was a reality in 1812—at Kilwa, Mafia, Pemba, and above all Zanzibar, 'the great depot of his colonial commerce and power', where the rule of Muscat, ever since it had replaced the rule of Portugal, had remained unbroken.

But all up the coast northwards of Zanzibar Said's claim to 'overlordship' was little more than a claim. A rival authority, indeed, had more real power there than he had. Not content with recovering their own independence the Mazrui of Mombasa had steadily extended their rule over some 150 miles of the coast, as far as Malindi to the north and as far as Pangani to the south. Some time between 1812 and 1822 they succeeded also in annexing Pemba or part of it. If Said was ever to control the coast, he would have to grasp the nettle which had so often stung the Portuguese. But he had neither time nor strength for fighting the Mazrui while he was engaged in consolidating

[1] According to the Arabic narrative 'the people of Mombasa used to call the Captain of the English ship Muzugh-Kighugh'. Owen (420 n.) and Strandes (300) suggest that his name was 'Cook'. The Swahili word *mzungu* means 'European'. He is described as 'intimate with Ali-bin-Othman'; advising him after his escape from Fort Jesus to attempt its recovery; promising, if he failed, to take him off in his ship, the *Bombay*, and return next year with other ships to attack the fort; showing him how to surprise the fort by making a high ladder; and finally, when the Muscat men held out in a bastion within the fort, landing a gun from his ship and making a breach in it. [2] Morice MS. 50, 170.
[3] Prior, 80. [4] See p. 83, above.

his position in Arabia. In the early years of his reign he had to be content with holding on to what he had got. Meantime, however, he neglected no opportunity that offered itself of at least asserting his formal claim to 'overlordship' anywhere along the coast. This happened first when he had been barely a year on his throne. In 1807 the Mazrui of Mombasa in one of their expansive moods had taken advantage of a disputed succession to the Sultanate of Pate, pushed their own candidate on to the throne, and obtained from him an agreement that Pate should in future be regarded as a dependency of Mombasa. They then attacked Lamu, where the defeated candidate and his party had taken refuge, but were repulsed with heavy loss. Thereupon, in fear of another assault, the people of Lamu sent an envoy to Muscat to claim their overlord's protection—an opening which Said, though then at the worst of his troubles with the Wahabi and Jawasmi, could not neglect. He selected one of his Omani notables and sent him as his Governor to Lamu with instructions to fortify the town.[1] A few years later another opportunity offered. The death of the Sheikh of Mombasa in 1814 revived the dispute as to the Sultanate of Pate, and the claimant backed by the 'anti-Mombasa' party proceeded to Muscat to seek Said's aid. Again Said responded to the implicit acceptance of his suzerainty. In 1817 he dispatched a fleet to Pate with four thousand men. This assault was twice repulsed; but the town was captured at the third attempt through the treachery of the 'anti-Mombasa' faction within the walls. The ruling Sultan was deposed, but he was permitted to return to

[1] *History of Pate*, translated from Swahili by A. Werner, *Journal of the African Society*, 1914-15, 291-3. C. P. Rigby, *Report on the Zanzibar Dominions* (Selections from the Records of the Bombay Government, No. lix, N.S., Bombay, 1861), 30. In Sir John Kirk's copy of this report, against the account of the fight at Lamu there is the following pencil note, based doubtless on his own observation: 'The sands of Shela are still covered with the skulls of hundreds of those who then fell.' Sir Frederick Jackson in his *Early Days in East Africa* (London, 1930, p. 7) says that the sands in 1884 were 'almost completely white with the bones of Lamu-ites who had been butchered in thousands at some remote period. Who the invaders were or where they came from is not known.'

Mombasa together with the troops which the Mazrui had sent to support him under the leadership of Mbaruk, nephew of Suliman-bin-Ali, whose standing in the clan was second only to the Sheikh's. Thereupon, Said's protégé, backed by a garrison of his troops, was duly elected Sultan under his own 'sovereign authority'.[1]

Meantime that authority had been brusquely repudiated by Mombasa. The new Sheikh, Abdullah-bin-Ahmed, on his accession had duly dispatched a ceremonial present to his overlord, but it consisted of a suit of armour, a few bullets, a little gunpowder, and an empty corn-measure;[2] and, as if to mark its meaning, the donor proceeded to attack Barawa and reduce it to subjection. About the same time a deputation from Pemba arrived at Muscat to beg Said to expel their Mazrui masters, whose tyranny had become so unbearable that they even promised, it is said, to pay Said for their liberation a poll-tax of two crowns (about 9 shillings) a head and a 5 per cent. duty on all their produce. Such an insult from Mombasa and such an appeal from Pemba must have strained Said's patience, but he knew that the only effective response was a direct attack on Mombasa, and for that he was still not quite prepared. Again, however, he could do something. He issued an edict forbidding any of his subjects to trade with the rebel city and sent instructions to his Governor at Zanzibar to drive the Mazrui out of Pemba. A small expedition was dispatched to assist him to execute this task in 1822, the year of the Moresby Treaty. The Mazrui fought bravely. So great, indeed, was the courage shown by their leader, Mbaruk, that from that time on he was regarded

[1] Miles, ii. 329–30. T. Boteler, *Narrative of a Voyage of Discovery to Africa and Arabia* (London, 1835), i. 373–4; from the account given to Boteler by the deposed Sultan in 1823. The *History of Pate* (p. 293) records a quarrel between its Sultan and Said in 1820 which was settled in 1821.

[2] According to one tradition Mombasa had admitted the suzerainty of Oman about forty years before this date, under pressure of a personal visit by one of Ahmed-bin-Said's sons: and in that case the 'present' may have been given every year *pro forma*. But the Mazrui declared (truly or untruly) in 1823 that they had never acknowledged the 'overlordship' of Oman since the reign of Seif-bin-Sultan; see p. 257, below.

as the hero of his people. Mazrui children were 'taught to lisp his name', and songs were sung not only in Mombasa but among the neighbouring Nyika about 'the wars of Mbaruk'. But the superior numbers of the Imam's force compelled the Mazrui to admit defeat. Mbaruk and the more militant of his followers withdrew to Mombasa. The rest accepted Said's sovereignty. Two subsequent attempts by the Mazrui to recover a foothold on the island having been defeated, Pemba became thenceforward, like its consort Zanzibar, an obedient dependency of Oman under governors appointed by Said. Nor was that the only achievement of the expedition of 1822. It was not strong enough to touch Mombasa, but it could do something to strengthen Said's authority at other points on the coast. It visited Pate and confirmed its Sultan's allegiance; it assisted Barawa to recover its independence of Mombasa; and it obtained from the Sultans of Barawa, Pate, and some of the other towns an acknowledgement by 'formal act' of the sovereignty of Seyyid Said.[1]

And now, it might well have seemed, the final struggle between Muscat and Mombasa could not be long delayed; but before another year had passed the course of events was suddenly diverted by the intervention of a third party. The Mazrui knew well enough that their day of reckoning was imminent. Said would soon be at their gates with all his forces. Even their famous fortress, survivor of many a stubborn siege, might well fail to protect them, alone and unaided, against a potentate so famous in the Arab world. But there was one power in the Indian Ocean greater than Said's—the power which had helped him to rise so high. Might it not be wise, then, for Mombasa to follow the precedent set by her old enemy, Malindi, two centuries ago? If she could not keep her independence, might not the Christians from Europe prove less instant tyrants than their Moslem kinsmen at Muscat? Once before, it is true, the Mazrui had acted on this idea and nothing had come of it. After Said's first intervention on their coast, in 1807–8,

[1] Rigby, op. cit. 30. Ingrams, op. cit. 155–9, based on unprinted native histories of Pemba. The Mbaruk folk-songs: Owen's *Narrative* (as cited p. 227, n. 1, below), i. 426.

their Sheikh had gone in person to offer the overlordship of Mombasa to the British Government at Bombay, who had politely declined it. But the premonitory events of 1822 impelled them to try again.

2

It was in April 1823, little more than six months after the signing of the Moresby Treaty, that the Governor of Bombay received the Mazrui's new appeal for the protection of Mombasa from the claims and penalties of Said's 'overlordship'. 'His object', wrote the Sheikh Abdullah-bin-Ahmed of the Imam's recent operations, 'is to get possession of my country. To him I will not give it but to the King of England.... Dispatch a flag to me that the nations may know that the kingdom is held of you, and write to the Imam to abstain from any aggression on the kingdom of Mombasa, for that it is subject to the King of England.'

A remarkable offer—no less than the free transfer of an Arab colony to the British Crown—but it was not so very attractive in 1823. The British authorities, whether at the India House or at Bombay, knew little and cared nothing about Mombasa in those days. Blankett, Beaver, and Smee had all ignored it. Of its strategic value, its potential military strength, its magnificent harbour they were still unaware. The trend of their policy, moreover, at that time was strongly against further territorial acquisitions even within India and still more on other coasts of the Indian Ocean. They had their eyes on the gates of the Red Sea. Nowhere else had they any desire to occupy foreign soil, not even in the Persian Gulf and most certainly not in East Africa. But apart from such general considerations the requirements of their Arab policy were enough to put the Mazrui's offer out of court. If Said's territorial ambitions in the Persian Gulf had been in question, it might well have seemed legitimate to put a veto on them lest they should set the Middle East on fire; but there was no such good reason for British interference in East Africa. Mombasa was not Bahrein. The Mazrui had no friends or allies. Their downfall would have no effect in Arabia except to strengthen Said's prestige. Policy, in fact, could be no excuse for the acceptance of the Mazrui's bribe; and honesty demanded its rejection. How could the British, who had professed to be Said's friends and on the strength of it had recently obtained from him a treaty they desired, suddenly take sides against him in an old dispute and snatch from his imminent grasp the 'plum' among all the African towns he claimed as his 'dependencies'? On all counts, indeed, the offer seemed clearly unacceptable, and Elphinstone drafted a cold reply to Abdullah-bin-Ahmed's letter. 'It is contrary to our policy', he wrote, 'to enter on such intimate connections in Africa as those proposed by you; and, moreover, fidelity to our engagements with His Highness the Imam of Muscat would prevent our acceding to your proposal.'

But that was by no means the end of the matter. Six months later came another appeal. Abdullah had died, wrote two leading Mazrui, but their policy was unchanged. 'We now request that you will relieve us from the rule of Seyyid Said and receive from us in gift half our revenue and that you will dispatch one of your officers to us.' And with this letter came another from 'Ahmed-bin-Sheikh and the whole of the inhabitants of Mombasa', enumerating the produce of which they offered half —'elephants' teeth, shells, Chundroos wheat, cattle, sheep, gowaree, rice and other grain'. 'Consider us from this day as subjects of the King of England, bound to observe all His Majesty's ordinances and anxious to provide to the best of our ability whatever he may need.' Though any price, no doubt, was worth paying for deliverance from Said's vengeance, this offer of tribute shows how really desperate the Mazrui were. But that, of course, could make no difference to Elphinstone's decision. His second answer was in the same terms as his first.[1]

At Mombasa, in the meantime, hopes were high. Surely, thought the Mazrui, this second offer, gilded as it had been with the promise of ivory and grain and cattle, would not be rejected; and they were confidently awaiting their envoys' return—they

[1] I.O., B.P.C., 24.iv. and 1.xii.23 (English translation of Arabic letters made at Bombay). The second Mazrui appeals are dated Sept. 18, 1823. The spelling of 'Mombasa' often varies in these documents.

even went so far in anticipation as to manufacture a Red Ensign of their own—when on December 3, 1823, just two days after Elphinstone had signed his second refusal, a British ten-gun brig, H.M.S. *Barracouta*, anchored at Mombasa, engaged under Captain Vidal's command on an Admiralty survey for the purpose of correcting and supplementing the existing charts of the coast from the Gulf of Oman to Natal. It was an unexpected chance, and Sheikh Suliman-bin-Ali, Abdullah's successor, made the most of it. He sent his nephew, Mbaruk the hero, with a large retinue, to pay his respects to the captain and in the name of the ruler and people of Mombasa to request his permission for the hoisting of the British flag. Vidal must have realized at once that a matter of such high politics was beyond his competence; but he asked time to consider the request, and next day he ordered Lieutenant Boteler—he was indisposed himself—to visit the Sheikh and tell him that the question must await the decision of Captain Owen, the commander of the expedition, who would shortly be calling at Mombasa. On landing Boteler was instantly surrounded by a mob of inquisitive men and boys: but he was presently rescued by Mbaruk and his suite and escorted to Fort Jesus. At the ancient gate he noted de Seixas's historic inscription and its contrast with the dirt and dilapidation of its present surroundings. The masonry of the walls was patched and crumbling; and the space inside them was 'a mass of indiscriminate ruins, huts and hovels' in which the Sheikh and his Mazrui retainers, some two hundred men, women, and children, lived. He was received in the old guardroom by Sheikh Suliman, venerable, tall, and thin, with an anxious but 'mild and pleasing' expression, and a number of notables of whom the most important was apparently the 'Hereditary Prince of Malindi', a short, slight, keen-eyed elder, of a negroid complexion. Presently the Sheikh and the Prince and one or two others withdrew with Boteler into a small chamber on the rampart. The door was carefully shut, and then the Sheikh laid bare his fears and hopes. He told how time and again his little community had fought to save its freedom from foreign subjugation; how the love of liberty had thus been graven on their hearts;

how unbearable now was the thought that they were going to lose it. So bitterly did the Imam resent their attempt to defend their native soil that he would certainly take away their powers of self-government and probably their lives as well. And he was so powerful that with all their courage they could not hope to hold him long at bay. So 'they had unanimously resolved to give up their country to the English who, though differing so widely in religion and customs, yet ever protected the oppressed and respected the shrines of liberty'. An offer of cession had been sent to Bombay, but no answer had yet come, and every day they were expecting to sight the Imam's fleet. In this dilemma would not the captain save them by hoisting the British flag above the fort? Two or three other speakers spoke in the same vein: and then the old Sheikh broke in again. Holding out their home-made ensign, he declared that this was all they needed. Even if it were not backed by British troops, 'still, beneath its protecting shade we may defy our enemies. As the lamb trembles at the lion's roar, so will the Imam shrink from that which is the terror of the world.'

It is clear from his own account that Boteler was moved. The scene had touched his imagination. The sordid environment, the poverty and wretchedness of the ragged crowd that thronged the open windows of the guardroom, and, in sharp contrast, the glittering decoration of their arms—these were the people who had defied and defeated the Portuguese in the days of their imperial power and who had repelled again and again the avid grasp of Oman, till now, the strength of the Imam having risen and their own declined, they were about 'to taste the bitter cup of slavery'. In such a mood Boteler had quickly responded to the passionate eagerness of the speakers; but there was nothing he could do. He gave his message. They must wait for Owen. At once the torrent of argument and entreaty burst out again. So vehement were the Arabs that 'I began to think', says Boteler, 'they intended to *make* me hoist the flag'. But his firmness presently calmed them, and, having promised that Captain Vidal would come ashore if he were well enough, he was allowed to return to his ship.

Next day both Vidal and Boteler landed. There was another conference in the fort, but the spirit had gone out of it and the result could only be the same. When it was over, the Sheikh invited the two officers to dine with himself, the Prince of Malindi, and Mbaruk, and a feast was spread that almost recalls the entertainment of Ibn Battuta at Mogadishu—meat, fowls, and eggs prepared with sugar, and all manner of sweetmeats, and rice cooked in coco-nut water. When the party of five had finished, the remnants 'quickly vanished before the active fingers of the surrounding Arabs who, although of the highest rank, did not scruple to vie with each other in obtaining the largest share and the choicest bits'. When courtesy permitted, the guests made their farewells and withdrew. On December 7 the *Barracouta* sailed away, and Suliman and his fierce tribesmen sat down to await the coming of the man who, they were assured, had real power to give them the protection of 'the terror of the world'.[1]

William Fitzwilliam Owen was a seaman of character and repute, a brother of Sir Edward Owen, who was at this time Commander-in-Chief in the West Indies, and destined himself to rise to the rank of Vice-Admiral. Like most of his fellow officers, he regarded the destruction of the Slave Trade as the special task which, now that the French wars were over, had been assigned to the British Navy; and in the course of his voyage northwards from the Cape of Good Hope he observed with increasing impatience the evidence of a busy Slave Trade with which he and his frigate were unable to interfere. First came the Portuguese. All up the coast from Delagoa Bay, the southward limit of the territory they claimed to rule, a regular traffic was still being carried on, at Inhambane, Sofala, Angoche, Mozambique, Ibo, and, in greatest volume, at Quilimane.

'From eleven to fourteen slave-vessels [Owen recorded in his journal] come annually from Rio de Janeiro to this place, and return with from four to five hundred slaves each on an average.... They

[1] T. Boteler, *Narrative of a Voyage of Discovery to Africa and Arabia* (London, 1835), ii. 1–12. Owen, i. 403–12.

are purchased with blue dungaree, coloured cloths, arms, gunpowder, brass and pewter, red coloured beads in imitation of coral, cutlery, and various other articles. The free blacks of the country and "banyans" carry on the trade inland for the merchants; and the arrival of one of those people among the tribes with his pedlar's stock is the signal for general warfare when the weak become victims of the strong.... To contain the slaves collected for sale every Portuguese house has an extensive yard or enclosure, called a Barracon, generally surrounded by a lofty brick wall....'[1]

What a contrast with Cape Colony! If only, Owen must have thought, this vast province were also British! But it was Portuguese, and had to be respected as such, though it was only at those slave-ports and at one or two posts up the Zambesi that there was any 'effective occupation' or pretence of government.[2] Beyond the limits of Portuguese dominion it was

[1] Owen to Sir G. L. Cole, 4.viii.25 (*P.P.* 1826, xxvi, No. 331, pp. 4–6). W. F. W. Owen, *Narrative of Voyages to explore the Shores of Africa, Arabia and Madagascar* (London, 1833), i. 292–3. This book is mainly based on Owen's journal, but it also inserts at intervals the journal of Lieut. Boteler (published separately in 1835), who was in the *Barracouta* which with the sloop *Albatross* accompanied the *Leven* frigate. The chronology of the joint narrative is confusing. Owen's main movements in the *Leven* were as follows: Capetown, July 1822; Delagoa Bay, Sept.; Ste. Marie, Dec.; Johanna, Jan. 1823; Delagoa Bay, March; Simonstown, April; Delagoa Bay, July; Mozambique, Oct.; Bombay, Nov.; Muscat, Dec.; Mombasa, Feb. 1824; Delagoa Bay, April; Mauritius, May; Madagascar and Comoro Isles, July to Oct.; Mombasa, Nov.; Seychelles, Dec.; Mombasa, Jan. 1825; Zanzibar, Feb.; Seychelles, March; Madagascar, April; Mozambique, May; Mauritius, June; Delagoa Bay, Aug.; Capetown, Sept.

[2] The government was so weak that, when Commodore Nourse, C.-in-C. at the Cape, happened to put in at Mozambique at the end of 1822, he had landed a party of marines at the Governor's urgent request to protect him from a mutinous company of his native soldiers (Nourse to Admiralty, 5.i.23; *R.S.E.A.* ix. 18). For evidence that weakness, as so often, could be combined with cruelty, see Owen's description of some natives being flogged almost to death with knotted thongs of bull's hide, heavy stakes, and branches of thorn at the order of the commandant of the Portuguese post at Delagoa Bay, who 'stood by the whole time, encouraging his soldiers not to relax their exertions in the application of the torture'. *Narrative*, i. 124–5. Similar evidence of Portuguese weakness and lethargy was observed by Prior in the *Nisus* five years earlier. See p. 171, above. For a similar state of affairs about 1860, see Coupland, *Kirk on the Zambesi* (Oxford, 1928), *passim*.

another matter, and more than once Owen found himself longing for the power to establish peace and good government and, above all, freedom from the Slave Trade in this neglected corner of the world by the simple process of annexation. When he called at Johanna (January 1823) he observed, like Bissell and Prior before him, the attachment of the islanders to their old British connexion and their longing for British protection against slave-raids; and 'how easily', he thought, 'it could be given'! Writing a year later to the Admiralty, he drew a rosy picture of the fertile Comoros, and frankly propounded the idea which Beaver had committed only to his journal. 'These islands are capable of vying with Madeira for wine and with the Moluccas for spices and with the world for cotton, coffee, sugar, oil and fruits. . . . The finest ship's timber and spars of teak. . . . New sources open to the enterprise and industry of our countrymen . . . .' Why, he asks, had we refused protection? 'The presence of a single Englishman in authority would prevent the continuation of any traffic in slaves. . . . A company of men and a schooner of 4 guns would have governed all those islands under Mauritius in peace, security, prosperity, and happiness.' The cost would be repaid ten times by trade.[1]

At Delagoa Bay, a few weeks later, the seductive idea of annexation was thrust again into Owen's mind. The native chief of Tembe, a district on the shore of Delagoa Bay, next door to the southernmost Portuguese outpost, claimed—and it was true—that he was independent of Portuguese control, and definitely offered the 'full sovereignty' of all his lands to the British Crown. 'I, King Kapell, do declare that I am induced to make this cession by the advice of my chiefs because I find my state and people too weak to defend themselves against the aggression of either Africans or Europeans.' Owen was sorely tempted. He had no authority to accept the cession. In any case, of course, an acceptance could only be provisional until it

---

[1] Owen to Admiralty, 10.iii.24 (Adm. i. 2269). *Narrative*, i. 177–86. Boteler interviewed the 'King' at Johanna, and gives a similar account to Prior's (see p. 173, above)—'Lord Rodney' is still to the fore—but denounces the islanders in general as thieves, rogues, and cowards.

was confirmed in London: and, as the event showed, Owen was right to suspect that the British Government would hesitate to burden itself with such a trivial and seemingly useless acquisition. He refused. Kapell was importunate. Owen refused again. But at last he succumbed. He accepted the cession provisionally, and on March 8, 1823, he hoisted the British flag. Once the deed was done, he made the best of it. To the Admiralty he explained that, 'so far from having moved this [cession] myself or from having offered any inducement to the King of Tembe to do it, I have constantly evaded it'; but that, as a matter of fact, the country offered great prospects for the trade of Britain. 'It opens all the interior of Africa where millions of people are ready to receive clothing and civilisation from her.' To Philip, the famous missionary, he stressed the opportunities for working through the 'peaceable and tractable' people of Tembe to influence all the neighbouring tribes and for dealing 'a fatal blow to the last efforts of slave-dealing in these seas'. But it was all no use. Some interest was taken in commercial circles at Capetown—a few adventurous traders actually took ship for Tembe—but nowhere else. Bathurst inquired of Lord Charles Somerset, Governor of the Cape (1814–26), whether an 'establishment' at Tembe would be 'advantageous to Great Britain in a general point of view'; and received a discouraging reply, pointing out that the place was extremely unhealthy and that communication with it overland was quite impossible. So the matter dropped—and that was the main reason why half a century later, when Delagoa Bay had become more attractive, the British claim to its southern shore was rejected in the famous arbitration.[1]

The annexation or 'protection' of Tembe, however, even if he could have been certain of its confirmation, could do little to

[1] Kapell's declaration, with Owen's disavowal of 'inducement' appended: *R.S.E.A.* 25–8. Owen to Philip, 1823 (ibid. 23). Bathurst to Somerset, 10.x.23; S. to B., 22.iv.24 (ibid. 35, 45). In August 1823 Owen accepted a similar cession from Chief Makasane of territory adjoining Tembe. These cessions were the main basis of the British case in the arbitration of 1875. The 'treaty' and Owen's dispatches with a proclamation by Nourse are printed in *P.P.* 1875, c. 1361.

placate Owen's growing hatred of the Slave Trade. It was off the raiders' beat. The main lines of traffic lay north of it. The cession, nay, the seizure of the Portuguese slave-ports, of Mozambique or Quilimane—that is what Owen would have liked. And there will presently be evidence to show that, as he sailed up that desolate maltreated coast, he felt that almost any method of rescuing it from the clutches of the Trade would be acceptable.

It was the same story north of Cape Delgado, except that the 'rulers' of the coast were Arabs instead of Portuguese. At most of the ports he visited Owen found that slaves were being exported—at Mikindani, Lindi, Kiswere, Kilwa, and, of course, at Zanzibar. Some of the slave-ships were Portuguese, despite the provisions of the Treaty of 1815 limiting their participation in the Trade to their own colonies; some were French; but most of them were Arab dhows. And, since some of those dhows belonged to subjects of the Imam of Muscat and were trading not only with Asiatic markets in the north but also with European markets in the south, the Moresby Treaty was evidently being broken. The Arabs, moreover, it appeared, handled the slaves with a more callous brutality than European 'slavers'.[1] And Owen, no doubt, soon learned, as Moresby just at this time was learning, that the horrors of the slaves' sea-voyage across the narrow waters between the coast ports and Zanzibar were often worse than those of the notorious 'middle passage' over the broad Atlantic.

'The Arab dhows [wrote Moresby] are large unwieldy open boats without a deck. In those vessels temporary platforms of bamboos are erected, leaving a narrow passage in the centre. The negroes are then stowed, in the literal sense of the word, in bulk, the first along the floor of the vessel, two adults side by side, with a boy or girl resting between or on them, until the tier is complete. Over them the first platform is laid, supported an inch or two clear of their bodies, above a second tier is stowed, and so on till they reach above the gunwale of the vessel. The voyage, they expect, will not exceed 24 or 48 hours; but it often happens that a calm or unexpected land-breeze delays their progress—in this case a few hours are sufficient to decide the

[1] Owen to Cole, 4.viii.25 (*P.P.* 1826, xxvi, No. 331, pp. 4–6).

fate of the cargo. Those of the lower portion of the cargo that die cannot be removed: they remain until the upper part are dead and thrown over. From a cargo of from 200 to 400 stowed in this way, it has been known that not a dozen at the expiration of ten days have reached Zanzibar. On the arrival of the vessels at Zanzibar the cargo are landed. Those that can walk up the beach are arranged for the inspection of the Imam's officer and the payment of duties. Those that are weak or maimed by the voyage are left for the coming tide to relieve their miseries.'[1]

Owen had not sailed farther up the coast than Zanzibar when, burning with pity and anger at what he had seen and heard, and exasperated by his impotence to stop it, he took his frigate, H.M.S. *Leven*, to Bombay for refilling and supplies; and there, as it happened, he fell in with the Mazrui envoys. To Owen their offer of 'dominion' to the British Crown seemed almost providential. Its acceptance, he ventured to inform the Governor, was 'the surest if not the only certain means of putting a full stop to the diabolical traffic in slaves', and he expressed his regret that the chance was to be missed and the people of Mombasa left to their fate simply because the Government was unwilling on principle to interfere with Seyyid Said's designs. Elphinstone, it appears, was unable to convince the gallant captain that the politics of the Middle East were a matter of some complexity and delicacy, and that the diplomatic relations between Muscat and Bombay were best left in expert hands. Owen sailed for Oman to continue his survey with his mind made up to take action on his own responsibility.

He arrived at Muscat on Christmas Day, and quickly obtained an audience of the Imam, whom he described in his *Narrative* as 'about forty years of age, with mild and gentlemanly manners and very communicative'. The interview opened with the presentation of a letter from Elphinstone, explaining to Said the importance of Owen's survey and asking him to show Owen 'all kindness and attention' at Muscat and also to give him letters to his 'subordinate officers' on the African coast, directing

[1] Quoted by Buxton in H. of C., 9.v.26 (Hansard, xv. 1826, 1034).

them to supply him with 'such pilots, boats and provisions as he may require'. At the close of the audience there was an exchange of gifts, Owen presenting the Imam with 'an Arabic copy of the Scriptures' and receiving in return 'a superb sword, the blade of Damascus steel, and the handle richly mounted in gold'. If this exchange had been the other way about, it might almost have symbolized the preceding curious discussion, happily recorded in full in Owen's report to the Admiralty. For Owen, it appears, took a high line from the start. He at once protested warmly against the violations of the Moresby Treaty which he had himself observed on the African coast. Said's response was no less quick and direct. He gave Owen full authority to punish such offences on the spot without reference to Muscat. But when he went on to assert his claims to British friendship, Owen retorted with something like an ultimatum. There was only one key to British friendship, he told Said, and only one 'sure way to the empire of East Africa at which he was aiming', namely, the *complete* abolition of the Slave Trade, with Moslem as well as with Christian markets, within three years! He would shortly be touching at Mombasa, he continued, where he expected that the people would ask for the protection of the British flag. 'I should feel it my duty to my King to grant it to them, in which my principal motive would be the suppression of that hellish traffic.' The Imam, he hoped, would not think such action 'intended to operate against his just interests in any way': and indeed, if he would only promise to suppress the import and export of all slaves throughout his dominions, then Owen would refuse the request for protection and use his influence to persuade the men of Mombasa to submit to their overlord's authority. Said's astonishment and indignation at such an abrupt and imperious challenge may be imagined, but he was far too well versed in oriental diplomacy to answer it in kind. He would be happy, he replied, to see the dominions of England extend from the rising to the setting sun, and it would give him sincere pleasure if the British would take Mombasa. 'I thought', notes Owen at this point, 'I observed symptoms of insincerity.' 'But to put down the Slave Trade with

Mahometans', continued Said, 'that was a stone too heavy for him to lift without some strong hand to help him.' 'In short,' says Owen sourly, 'his power and his purse are upheld by this infamous commerce: his soldiers and his servants are supplied by it, and the Red Sea and Persia and some parts of North India pay him immense sums annually for slaves to be cut for the seraglios and other faithful services for which those of the East Coast are held in the highest esteem.'[1]

Owen's feelings in the matter almost burn the paper they were written on; and, as feelings, they do him credit. But consider also Said's. How could he have imagined that an Owen would follow a Moresby or have foreseen so incongruous a sequel to those quiet and friendly conversations of a year ago and to the sacrifices he had thought himself so wise to make for the sake of British gratitude? And what could have been more galling than this sudden and utterly unexpected intrusion into a field which he regarded as exclusively his own and over which, after long years of patience, he was now ready to assert his mastery? It so happened, indeed, that just before Owen's visit he had dispatched another small fleet to blockade Mombasa. But what could he do? He dared not risk an open quarrel with an officer of the British Navy. He could only submit and then use all his art to make the most of his submissiveness in higher quarters in the hope that Owen's actions would be disavowed. By one ship, therefore, he sent a message to his lieutenant off Mombasa telling him to leave the Mazrui alone and—a neat stroke of diplomacy—to put himself and his squadron under Owen's orders, while another ship carried to Bombay a letter to the Governor protesting, in the name of injured innocence and loyal friendship ill repaid, against Owen's conduct.

3

Owen, meantime, had sailed off along the Arabian coast to continue his survey. Skirting the north shore of Socotra, he struck the African mainland near Cape Guardafui: then, bending

[1] Owen's report to the Admiralty, 8.iii.24 (Adm. i. 2269). 'Cut' presumably means 'castrated'. *Narrative*, i. 342.

southwards, he put in at Mogadishu, where, he notes, 'the inhabitants appeared extremely jealous of strangers'.

'Our officers upon landing were subject to a species of imprisonment, being immediately shut up in a house, but with liberty to ramble about according to their inclinations within it. The only knowledge they gained of the town was, therefore, from the terrace of their place of confinement. This restraint was most respectfully but firmly enforced, and to evince their friendly disposition towards us, a camel, a bullock and a goat were brought to the beach for our use.'

In the course of this constricted visit Owen learned from his hosts that the settlement imposed by Said on the coastal towns north of Mombasa in 1822 had broken down. In 1823, they said, a squadron of the Imam's ships had called at Mogadishu, and its commander had ordered the chiefs to wait on him and receive the Imam's commands. 'Two of the principal people accordingly went on board with some trifling presents, when he immediately sailed and put them in prison at Zanzibar, there to remain until they could produce two thousand dollars for their ransom.' 'In consequence of this unjust measure,' Owen continues, 'Mogadishu, Merka, Barawa, Pate and Mombasa had before our arrival entered into a league against the power of the Imam.' Owen, it is evident, had quickly taken sides. It does not seem to have occurred to him that the league against Said *may* have been engineered, perhaps by Mombasa, before the incident; that Said *may* have got wind of it and arrested the chiefs of Mogadishu in an attempt to nip rebellion in the bud. Anyway, Owen departed with the intention of undoing 'this act of treachery' when in due course he should arrive at Zanzibar.[1]

At Lamu Owen went ashore to visit the Governor, Seif-bin-Hamed, a cousin of Said's. He presented him and several of his principal officers 'with copies of the New Testament in Arabic, with which they were much pleased' and in return sent him a quantity of fine fruits. Later, the Governor was received with military honours on board the *Leven* and dined with Owen. In the course of their conversation Owen explained that the Imam

[1] Owen, i. 357–9.

had authorized him to make arrangements for the prevention of the Slave Trade from Lamu to Mozambique and Madagascar. Seif replied that he had already published the Imam's edict permitting any British warship to seize dhows taking slaves to ports southwards of Kilwa, and he invited Owen 'to give what orders he pleased' for the treatment of ships proceeding northwards. He also informed Owen that Pate with all its dependencies had put itself under the Imam's protection; and, scenting perhaps the trend of Owen's mind on East African politics or possibly forewarned from Muscat, he shrewdly added that it seemed desirable for the whole coast to be united under the Imam's government. 'For not until then will the British have power to put an effectual termination to the Slave Trade.'[1]

At last, on February 7, 1824, more than a month since leaving Muscat, Owen sighted Mombasa. At the moment of his arrival, the Omani ships were in the act of bombarding the fort. Its guns were vigorously replying. Over it flew the home-made British flag. As the *Leven* drew near, the engagement was broken off. The blockading ships ceased firing. The Mazrui hauled down their flag. But two days later it was rehoisted, and this time with official sanction. For Owen was a man of his word. Promptly, but not without full discussion, he arranged with the eager Sheikh Suliman and his council of chiefs the formal establishment of a British protectorate. The terms of the convention gave the Mazrui all they asked and more, perhaps, than they had hoped to get—a British guarantee of their authority not only over Mombasa but also over the whole area which they claimed as dependent on it. The second clause provided 'that the sovereignty of the state should continue to be exercised by the Chief of the Mazrui tribe and be hereditary in his family', and the first 'that Great Britain should reinstate the Chief of Mombasa in his former possessions'—a phrase which was interpreted by the Mazrui and admitted by Owen to cover in particular the island of Pemba and the ports of Lamu and Pate, and, more generally, the line of coast as far south as the River

[1] Owen, i. 364-6.

Pangani. The next two clauses provided 'that an agent of the protecting Government should reside with the Chief', and, by way of payment for protection, 'that the customs-revenue should be equally divided between the two contracting parties'. Since no regular customs-system then existed, it was laid down by Owen for the execution of this last clause that 5 per cent. should be levied on exports and imports belonging to the people of Mombasa and 10 per cent. on the rest.[1] The last two clauses completed the British side of the bargain. They contained no explicit statement of what Owen himself describes as 'a formal gift without reservation of any kind to His Majesty of the country of Mombasa and all its dependencies': apparently that was regarded as implicit in the promise of protection. The fifth clause provided 'that trade with the interior be permitted to British subjects', and the sixth 'that the Slave Trade be abolished at Mombasa'. To each clause a discussion of some hours' duration was devoted; and if at the end of the whole debate Owen did not know all that was in the Mazrui's minds, the Mazrui probably knew all that was in Owen's.[2]

So Owen did what he had said he would do, swiftly, simply, and efficiently, on his own sole responsibility, with no notion as to what his own Government would think of it, yet in open defiance of what he knew to be the policy of the Government of Bombay, and—the most striking point—with a purity of motive rarely to be found in high international politics. Both he and his fellow officers, it is true, were impressed by the natural advantages of Mombasa, both commercial and strategic. Lieutenant Boteler, indeed, had made an enthusiastic note in his journal on that 'perfect harbour', whence 'English manufactures, brought out in large vessels, could be retailed from Mombasa to the whole line of coast'—a prophetic vision of modern Kilindini and its busy quays.[3] And in the plea he sent home for the confirmation of the protectorate Owen made the most of the case for retaining a position which he claimed to be politically more valuable than

---

[1] Capt. Moorsom to Commodore Nourse, 20.iii.24 (Adm. i. 69).
[2] Owen to Admiralty, 8.iii.24 (Adm. i. 2269). Owen, *Narrative*, i. 367–8.   [3] Boteler, ii. 13–14.

Mozambique. 'The most easily defensible spot in East Africa
... easy of access ... a spacious and secure harbour.' And last
came that old and potent argument which was one day to influence so strongly the course of British expansion in Africa—
the risk of a rival nation seizing an opportunity which Britain
had neglected. The Mazrui chiefs, wrote Owen, if British protection had been denied them, 'meant to have sent to Bourbon
to invite the French': and a French Mombasa would prove
'a more serious thorn in the side of India than ever Mauritius
or Pondicherry has been'. A forcible case, forcibly put: yet
no one can read Owen's long and fervent dispatches without
being convinced that those economic and political interests
were altogether minor matters in his eyes. He only mentions
them because he fears that the first and highest motive for
annexation, the suppression of the Slave Trade, may not be
enough by itself for his superiors. Without question it was
enough by itself for him. It is a detailed description of the Slave
Trade on the coast that takes up most of his long report. It is
the thought of destroying the Slave Trade that lifts his language
to heights of ardour in which his patriotism becomes almost
indistinguishable from his religion.

'Why has my country refused the glorious duty of extending its
protection to these poor creatures who sought it? ... The presence
of a single Englishman in authority would prevent the continuation
of any traffic in slaves to attain which on this coast we pay a hundred
times more in our endeavours to dam the torrent than would be
necessary to possess ourselves of the source and turn the stream, and
this without force or injustice.... Solely by the confidence felt by all
classes on these coasts in the generous character of my nation, I have
been able to restore peace and prosperity to thousands by a single
affirmative monosyllable.... Shall we refuse to use the power God
has given us?... As easily as I have performed this one little act by
the pure effect of national character, so could I place every foot of the
coast under British dominion.... I would recommend our Government to treat with the Imam of Muscat for all his dominions in East
Africa, offering him in perpetuity precisely the exact nett revenue he
now derives from it.... This single measure would place all this
country from Mogadishu to Delgado at once in our possession, and
with the possession the Slave Trade ceases for ever.... It is to me

as clear as the sun that God has prepared the dominion of East Africa for the only nation on the earth which has public virtue enough to govern it for its own benefit.... I have taken my own line to the honour of God and my King and to the benefit of my country and of all mankind.'[1]

Indeed there is no doubt about Owen's motive, and certainly the Mazrui were not allowed to doubt it. At the very outset of the proceedings at Mombasa, when, in the name and presence of two hundred chiefs and some two thousand people, the Sheikh made the formal offer of his country to the King of England, Owen came at once to the point. He would not accept the gift, he would not hoist the flag, he would have nothing at all to say, until they had arrived at 'a perfect understanding about the Slave Trade, the total suppression of which (he explained) would be his only inducement, as he believed it would be with his superiors, that could obtain for them definitively British protection and government'. The Mazrui, no doubt, were as startled as Said had been by such abrupt and direct diplomacy; and they must have wondered, rather angrily, why in the world this queer Christian seaman was so fiercely bent on putting a stop to an old and ordinary occupation which seemed to them as innocent as it was profitable. But they had no choice. It was ridiculous: it was impracticable: but they had to promise to abolish the Slave Trade unless they wished to be abandoned to Said's vengeance. So they promised; and Owen at any rate was convinced, if not of their good faith, at least of their goodwill. And perhaps at the moment he was right; for it was the moment of their deliverance from the ugly spectre that had haunted them for the last ten years. 'We have the hearts of the people', wrote their deliverer: they are 'intoxicated with delight at finding themselves at ease under a British flag'.[2]

4

On February 13, 1824, Owen left Mombasa to continue his cruise down the coast. He intended in due course to call at Port Louis, where he hoped to persuade Sir Lowry Cole, who had

[1] Owen to Admiralty, 8 and 10.iii.24 (Adm. i. 2269).   [2] Ibid.

recently succeeded Farquhar as Governor of Mauritius, to accept and confirm his convention pending the final decision in London, and to detach a small body of troops from the garrison of the island to occupy Fort Jesus. He therefore took with him in the *Leven* 'Prince' Mbaruk, with his brother and a suite of twelve, as an 'embassy' to the Government of Mauritius with authority to conclude the act of cession. Mbaruk's credentials, signed by Sheikh Suliman-bin-Ali and 'the most ancient of the chiefs', declared that 'whatever arrangements are made by Mbaruk will be our law'.[1]

Owen first touched at Pemba, where Mbaruk and his party went on shore. From the outset of the negotiations at Mombasa the Mazrui had been specially insistent on their claim to the possession of that island; and Owen, mindful of the formula to which he had committed himself in the first clause of the convention, was doubtless anxious to do what he could to satisfy them. But he found the island firmly held by Said's Government, and he remembered, rather late in the day, 'the very ancient friendship between the British nation and the Imam'. On that account, as he explained in a letter to Captain Moorsom, who was cruising in the vicinity in H.M.S. *Ariadne*, he contented himself with explaining the situation to the Governor and urging him to respect the persons and the property of the people of Mombasa who had continued living in Pemba since Said's acquisition of it.[2] Then, re-embarking Mbaruk, he sailed

[1] A translation of the document is enclosed in Cole's dispatch to Bathurst, 19.vi.24 (C.O. 167. 72).
[2] Owen's *Narrative*, i. 369. Owen to Moorsom, 21.ii.24 (Adm. i. 69). The Pemba affair is mysterious. According to the *Narrative*, i. 369, Owen promised to convey 'Prince Mombarrok' and fifty of his men to Pemba, and duly landed them there. Nothing is said of their return to the ship; and 'Prince Mombarrok' next appears on board the *Leven* at Mauritius (ii. 25). That Mbaruk was accompanied by his brother and a suite of twelve appears from a claim afterwards submitted by Owen to the Admiralty for his expenses in entertaining them on the *Leven* (Owen to Admiralty, 7.x.21: Adm. i. 2271). What happened to the fifty? Said's squadron of five small ships, which had been bombarding Mombasa, accepted Owen's orders, accompanied him to Pemba, and was sent to seize in Said's name three ships that were slave-trading on the coast under European flags. (*Narrative*, i. 370.)

on to Zanzibar, where he interviewed the Governor, Abdullah, and impressed on him his views about the Slave Trade. He also raised the question of the two imprisoned chiefs from Mogadishu, and 'directed' Abdullah to liberate them, 'which from either fear or respect he did'. From Zanzibar Owen continued his course southwards, without much assistance from his pilots, whom he suspected Abdullah to have chosen for him because they knew little of that part of the coast. Passing Lindi, the 'vast stream' of the Rovuma, and Ibo, he reached Mozambique on March 5. Thence he sailed on to Delagoa Bay, where, finding that the Portuguese had taken down the British flag at English River, he promptly rehoisted it. Finally, on May 21, he reached Mauritius. On the 23rd, as the outcome, doubtless, of informal conversations, he reported in writing that an ambassador from Mombasa was on board the *Leven*, whose object was 'to make a full and free cession of the most beautiful little kingdom in Africa to His Majesty if he will graciously condescend to accept its sovereignty'. 'In the meantime', the letter continued, 'for strong reasons I accepted the cession on the spot till His Majesty's pleasure should be known, promising on my part to use the little influence my situation may give me with Your Excellency to prevail on you to occupy Mombasa as soon as possible, awaiting His Majesty's pleasure for its final disposal.'[1]

Sir Lowry Cole, and Commodore Nourse, who happened to be at Port Louis and who, as Commander-in-Chief at the Cape, had a general responsibility for naval operations all up the coast, were thus suddenly confronted with an awkward and delicate problem. After some discussion and delay, on June 4 Mbaruk was received on shore with military honours. 'I had no alternative', Cole reported to Bathurst, 'but to receive Prince Membarrok, the chief of the embassy, and to direct that himself and suite should be accommodated and provided for during their stay here in a suitable, yet economical, manner.'[2] Then he and Nourse sat down to thrash the matter out with Owen. The

[1] Owen, i. 359, 369–74; ii. 18–25. Owen to Cole, 23.v.24, enclosed in Cole to Bathurst, 19.vi.24 (C.O. 167. 72).
[2] Cole to Bathurst, 19.vi.24 (C.O. 167. 72). Owen, ii. 25.

eager conviction with which the latter pressed his case for annexation may be imagined; but the evidence to hand was not all his own, nor all in his favour. One of Nourse's officers, Captain Moorsom, had touched at Mombasa in H.M.S. *Ariadne* on February 28, had stayed there till March 11, and had given an unfavourable account of the Mazrui in his report to Commodore Nourse. They refused, he wrote, either to repair the dilapidated walls of Fort Jesus or to allow a British garrison to occupy it. 'Not a soldier shall come there', they declared. Nor were they satisfied with the results of the convention. The cession, they argued, was conditional on their being reinstated in Pemba, Pate, and Lamu. On the possession of Pemba they specially insisted and they wanted to attack the island. 'Our flag fettered their actions while it had not recovered their rights.' In fact 'those half-caste Arabs' had no notion—or, one suspects, pretended to have none—of what in fact the cession of their country meant. They had 'sought the protection of the English from the spoliation of people of their own faith'—no more than that. Despite Owen's lengthy explanation of each clause of the convention, they had no idea—or so it seemed—'that other British subjects are to enter into competition with them for the produce of the country'. On the other hand, 'a great point has been gained by the prohibition of the expatriation of the natives —the abolition of the Slave Trade—which was what Captain Owen had chiefly in view; and Mr. Reitz [who had been left in charge as Commandant] reports that in this the Arabs seem disposed to act with sincerity and good faith'. If Mombasa were retained, Moorsom had finally suggested, a colony for freed slaves might be established there as at Sierra Leone. But a British garrison seemed essential. 'Without such, our flag will be prostituted to the protection of those who are to be viewed in no better light than free-booters.'[1]

In view of this disquieting report Cole suggested, and Owen agreed, that specific questions should be put to Mbaruk. Did the 'King' and chiefs of Mombasa definitely wish to cede the full and unconditional sovereignty of their territory to the

[1] Moorsom to Nourse, 20.iii.24 (Adm. 1. 69).

British Crown? Did they assent to the occupation of Fort Jesus by a British garrison? Did they agree that half the revenue was to be paid to the British authorities? If no full cession were desired, would they accept British 'protection' with 'a British agent or agents to administer justice and regulate the revenue and customs'? The answers, written in Arabic and signed by Mbaruk and two of his own compatriots, were, literally translated, as follows:

> '1. The King of Mombasa and all his councillors and all his chiefs in the territory of Mombasa have voluntarily undertaken to become subjects of the King of the English, and all their country will be under the King of England, and he will have half of the revenues.
> '2. The Governor who goes to Mombasa may reside within the Fort, but, if he wishes to reside within the Town, he may; or, if he wishes to reside by himself within the Fort, we agree; and, if he wishes his suite to reside within the Town, he may do as he pleases.
> '3. With regard to the income of the territory of Mombasa, this subject may be suspended till our arrival in the land of Mombasa.
> '4. With regard to the towns of Pate, Lamu, and Pemba which have been taken from us by Seyyid Said-bin-Sultan, we wish to have them back, and we are awaiting the answer from the King of the English respecting our said places which Said-bin-Sultan has taken without any right.'

There is no need to suspect the sincerity of these answers. The first is straightforward enough. The third is not an evasion: Mbaruk told Owen that 'in time of perfect peace the revenue used to amount to between 4,000 and 5,000 dollars a month for Mombasa only' (roughly £12,000 a year); and a more definite reckoning could only be made on his return. The second seems rather more equivocal. It was unpleasant, no doubt, to contemplate the continued presence of British soldiers in Fort Jesus. The Sheikh and his chief supporters lived in it themselves. Its occupants would always be masters of Mombasa. Yet Owen must have made it clear that there could be no concession on this point, and in the rough translation he made of the answers for Cole to read, there was no ambiguity about it. 'The garrison may reside either in or out of the Fort as they please.'

A further request on Mbaruk's part, which does not appear in the Arabic text, is included in Owen's version—an interesting request because it foreshadows the modern principle of 'indirect administration'.

'They wish it to be understood that in receiving a British garrison it is in the confidence that His Majesty will govern the Arabs and Africans by their own laws, and not deprive the chiefs of their dignities and honours, and that they will be consulted on all matters touching their own interest.'

Lastly, the fourth answer, revealing that, as Owen had discovered before he left Mombasa, the motives prompting the cession had grown into something more positive and acquisitive than the first urgent need of protection from Said, was summarized and explained by Owen as follows:

'Mbaruk has added a clause to his categorical answers that their object in ceding the sovereignty of the country and admitting a British garrison is the hope that His Majesty will demand restitution of Pate, Lamu and Pemba of which they have been unjustly divested. Pemba is the garden and granary of Mombasa at present and is said to be the most fertile island known. Mbaruk expresses a desire to address His Excellency on the subject of Pemba in particular and also to write to England about it—in short, but restore that island to them and you may seat yourself in Mombasa on any footing or terms you please.'

But Cole, it need hardly be said, was not going to concern himself with Pemba, still less with Pate and Lamu. It was difficult enough to decide what advice he should tender to the Colonial Office about Mombasa, especially as he was not quite so sure as Owen—and the sequel was to justify him—of the value of Mbaruk's promise to hand over Fort Jesus. The result of his deliberations is best given in the words of the carefully phrased dispatch he wrote to Bathurst on June 19.

'I have refrained from taking upon myself to accept the cession of Mombasa without previous instructions from home, as your Lordship will perceive by this accompanying copy of a letter which I have written to His Highness Suliman-bin-Ali, the Chief or Ruler of Mombasa; and for the same reasons I should have declined detaching a military force from this garrison for the occupation of that island, had not the weak state of the two regiments stationed here rendered it next to impossible. . . . On a liberal and extended view of the situation of Mombasa, I am inclined to consider it as presenting a favourable means for putting down the Slave Trade as well as for opening a commerce with the eastern coast of Africa which might ultimately be of advantage to the mercantile interests of Great Britain and could not but tend to the civilisation of that part of the world.

'With these impressions, therefore, if I ventured any suggestion, it would be that H.M.'s protection should be afforded to the Island of Mombasa, that a British commercial Agent or Agents should reside there, and that a vessel of war belonging to the squadron on this station should be employed on that coast to co-operate with the Agents. Indeed it appears to me that this is precisely the sort of protection which the people of Mombasa are desirous of obtaining from H.M. Government; and, from all I learn on the subject, not only are those people disposed but even anxious that the Agents alluded to should have the power of administering justice among them and should be charged with the collection of the revenue and customs dues—half the amount thereof being paid to the Chiefs who on these conditions would relinquish all traffic in slaves.

'If an arrangement of this sort could be made, the expense of which would, I should think, be more than covered by the dues to be collected, H.M. Government would possibly find their advantage in it; but, as to the military occupation of Mombasa, I am not sufficiently informed on the matter either to recommend such a measure to your Lordship or to say that the Chief and people of the island are disposed to admit such a proceeding. Their great object seems to be to secure our protection against the power of the Imam of Muscat with whom, it appears, they have long been at war; and, notwithstanding Captain Owen's strong opinion on the subject, I have great doubts whether these people are prepared to make an unconditional cession to His Majesty.

'There is, however, one point which seems to be deserving of the particular consideration of Government, and that is, should H.M. decide on withholding his protection from the Island of Mombasa, the determination of the Chiefs is to throw themselves on the French for support against the Imam of Muscat; and, as the island possesses a very fine harbour and is in other respects advantageously circumstanced both as to climate and productions, it might hereafter in the hands of the French become a great annoyance to our trade in the East.

'I have only further to apprise your Lordship that Prince Membarrok will return in a few days to Mombasa, and that Commodore

Owen's Protectorate 245

Nourse will make arrangements for continuing to that island the protection afforded by Captain Owen until H.M.'s pleasure shall be known.'[1]

Nourse agreed with Cole. The object of the people at Mombasa, he reported to the Admiralty, was 'to relieve themselves of the Imam's attempts at dominion over them'. From the British standpoint he submitted that the occupation of Mombasa would provide 'an opening for the total extirpation of the abominable traffic in slaves'. But he recommended a commercial rather than a military establishment, provided that it was 'supported by frequent and certain visits of the smaller English men-of-war'.[2]

Cole's decision was communicated forthwith to Mombasa.

'I cannot take upon myself [he wrote to Suliman] to accept the cession of Mombasa until I shall receive instructions to that effect from my Sovereign. I must likewise acquaint Your Highness that I am unable to detail any military force from this garrison for the purpose of occupying Mombasa; but Commodore Nourse, the naval Commander-in-Chief on this station, will make arrangements for continuing the same protection as has been afforded to Your Highness' country by Captain Owen until the intentions of the British Government shall be known: and I shall take an early opportunity of writing to the Imam of Muscat stating that the island of Mombasa has for the present been taken under the protection of His Britannic Majesty.'[3]

[1] Cole to Bathurst, 19.vi.24, enclosing the questions to Mbaruk, his answers in Arabic, and Owen's English version and note (C.O. 167. 72).

[2] Nourse to Adm., 28.v. and 21.vi.24 (Adm. 1. 69).

[3] Cole to Suliman, 19.vi.24; copy enclosed in Cole-to-Bathurst of the same date (C.O. 167. 72). Cole's letter to Suliman was presumably drafted in English and then translated into Arabic. The English version he sent to Bathurst is probably identical with his original draft. Cole also sent a copy of the letter to Bombay, whence it or another copy of it was sent to London and is now in the India Office. This Bombay copy is also in a file of documents on the Mombasa affair sent from Bombay to Mauritius and preserved in the Mauritius Archives. It is different in wording from the Cole-to-Bathurst version. So it looks as if Cole sent an Arabic version to Bombay which was translated back into English there. One minor difference is in the last paragraph: Said is to be told that Mombasa is under British 'authority' *vice* 'protection'. More startling is the omission of the negative in the first paragraph. The Bombay copy reads: 'I have to tell you that I consent to accept your country

It only remained to inform Bombay. 'I have been induced', wrote Cole to Elphinstone, 'to acquiesce in the measures taken by Captain Owen until His Majesty's pleasure shall be known.' He had reported this, he added, to the Secretary of State, and had also informed the Imam of Muscat of 'the arrangements that have been made for the protection of Mombasa and its dependencies' and requested him 'to discontinue hostilities against that State until His Majesty's pleasure on the proceedings of Captain Owen shall be signified'.[1]

Thus ended the conclave at Mauritius; and when Owen left for Madagascar on July 16, he could assure himself that at least he had got something of what he wanted. He had persuaded the Governor of Mauritius to recognize his unauthorized protectorate as at least a provisional *fait accompli* and to write a dispatch to the Colonial Office which at least put the case for its permanent confirmation. Could he have really expected more? Did he really think that Cole would send a force of British regulars from Port Louis to take Pemba, Pate, and Lamu from Said's Governors and annex them to the provisional protectorate? ... Mbaruk, of course, was frankly and outspokenly dissatisfied. One evening, Owen records, the Governor sent his carriage to take the 'ambassador' out to dine with him and Owen at his country house at Reduit among woods and waterfalls. But Mbaruk was 'less pleased with the novel scenes to which he was introduced than disappointed that nothing was determined upon respecting his country, and expressed a desire to extend his voyage to England'. It was a disgruntled 'embassy', therefore, that embarked in due course in a small ex-slave-ship, the *Wizard*, and followed the *Leven* back to the mainland.[2]

Owen had sailed from Mauritius to Madagascar, and on his

on the terms you have proposed.' In the Mauritius copy 'consent to' is crossed out, and 'cannot' inserted. The mistake, though curious, must have been accidental. It is impossible, with the other documents in mind, to suspect Cole of double dealing.

[1] Cole to Elphinstone, 1.vii.24 (I.O., B.P.C., 25.viii.24). The author has been unable to find a copy of Cole's letter to Said.
[2] Owen, ii. 26–7.

way thence to Mombasa he called (September 1824) at Johanna and obtained from 'King' Abdullah a promise to assist the British efforts to suppress the Slave Trade. But Abdullah explained that his authority was impaired at the moment by the fact that the three other islands of the group had revolted. 'If', he added, 'by British influence I could be put in possession of the other three islands, I should have no difficulty in suppressing the Slave Trade entirely.' The same plea, in fact, in a smaller field as the Mazrui had made or as Said, no doubt, would have made if he had been asked. 'Let the British lion roar my subjects into submission, and I will make any promises you wish.' But Owen's impetuosity had lost its edge. He told Abdullah that he would 'represent his proposal in the proper quarter'.[1]

5

Mombasa, meantime, had not been left with nothing but a flag to protect it. Owen had appointed Lieutenant Reitz, aged twenty-one, as Commandant and set him in charge of the protectorate with an 'establishment' consisting of Midshipman Phillips, a corporal of Marines, and three seamen and with particular instructions to secure 'the entire destruction of the hell-born traffic in slaves'.[2] The young administrator soon discovered that the gratitude of the Mazrui was not to be relied on. Owen, indeed, had only reached Pemba when he was overtaken by letters from Reitz saying that the Mazrui seemed disposed to forget their obligations now that they no longer feared the vengeance of Muscat.[3] Captain Moorsom, likewise, as has appeared, was not favourably impressed by the Mazrui. But Reitz was quite undaunted. Inexperienced though he was and almost alone, he handled his difficult and rather dangerous protégés as coolly and firmly as if he had had a British regiment at his back. On one occasion he even interfered with the manner in which the Sheikh collected his personal revenue. On another he insisted that a fifteen-year-old relative of the Sheikh, who had light-heartedly cut open an aged 'banyan's' head with his

[1] Idem, p. 41.   [2] Owen to Moorsom, 21.ii.24 (Adm. 1. 69).
[3] Owen, *Narrative*, i. 371.

sword, should be flogged and imprisoned and pay ten dollars compensation to his victim.[1] But unhappily, like many of his fellow-countrymen after him, he did not know or did not care about the dangers of the climate; and he decided to carry out Owen's orders to explore the protectorate without waiting till the rainy season was over. Suliman and the other chiefs tried to dissuade him, but, the weather having temporarily improved, Reitz set out on an overland march to the Pangani River on May 4, with a suite of seventy, headed by a brother of Mbaruk. The day after their departure rain fell again in torrents, and on the night of the 6th it caught them in the open with no shelter but the rocks. By the 15th, when they reached Tanga, several of the Arabs were down with fever; but Reitz had so far escaped it, and, against the Arabs' advice, insisted on completing the last stage of his journey—a stretch of twenty-five miles to the mouth of the Pangani—by water in an open boat. The rain was drenching, the wind against them, and the sea far from smooth. The boats accompanying Reitz gave up and returned to Tanga; but Reitz kept his own crew going till after nine hours' labour they reached the river-mouth. There he was baffled. Against the ebb-tide and the river current, swollen by floods inland, the exhausted oarsmen could make no headway. One of them collapsed. There was nothing to do but wait in the dark and the rain which—to quote the narrative based on Reitz's diary— 'like one sheet of water enveloped them'. Their anchor held against the swirling current, but they were 'in constant dread of the huge trees that, floating down the river, threatened from time to time to sweep them to destruction'. At last day dawned, and, helped by the change of tide and a favouring breeze, they pulled into the river and landed at Pangani, where they found that the flood had swept a channel clean through the village, carrying away the huts in its path. Next day, May 14, Reitz's diary stopped. Exhausted by fatigue and exposure, he was gripped by fever, presumably malaria and already in his blood. The anxious Arabs decided to carry him back as fast as possible to Mombasa. On the 29th, just as they came in sight of

[1] Boteler, ii. 200.

the town, he died. He was buried, in the presence of all the leading Arabs, in the ruined Portuguese cathedral at the spot where the altar had once stood. He possessed, says Boteler, 'an uncommon share of wit and good-humour together with a pleasing frankness of manner that made him respected and beloved by his companions, as also by the Arabs who ever after spoke of him in the highest terms of admiration'.[1]

For the next three months Midshipman Phillips was acting-commandant. During his administration an Arab slave-dhow was captured off the port, and, despite the protests and promises of the agitated Mazrui, it was duly confiscated. The slaves on board, in accordance with Moorsom's idea, were settled as a freedmen's colony on a little plantation, now known as English Point, which the hereditary Prince of Malindi in the rosier days of the convention had given to the British saviours of Mombasa. 'This little negro establishment', reported Lieutenant Boteler when he returned to Mombasa in October, 'presented a picture of perfect content; each individual had a portion of ground to cultivate, the proceeds of which, together with other supplies, supported them in a manner far superior to that which they had been accustomed to.'[2]

Young Phillips was not left long alone at his post. Commodore Nourse visited Mombasa in September to examine the situation for himself, and appointed Midshipman Emery as acting-lieutenant and commandant.[3] Then, on October 23, the *Barracouta* arrived, and the *Leven* on November 2. Like Reitz and Moorsom, their officers found the Arabs less agreeable than they had been when Said's fleet was in the offing. Boteler was particularly disgusted at the heartless cruelty with which they treated the 'helpless and unprotected' 'banyans'. The leading chiefs did not

[1] Idem, pp. 175–85, repeated in Owen, ii. 140–8.
[2] Boteler, ii. 187.
[3] Suliman-bin-Ali wrote to Bombay that he asked Nourse what had been decided about the cession, and that Nourse replied that 'he could say nothing more on the subject than had been already communicated to me by Captain Owen'. Suliman to Elphinstone, Oct. 1824; copy in Mauritius Archives, Dispatches Received, ii.1825.

scruple to borrow from them constantly and heavily without a thought of repayment, with the result that the 'banyans' made up for their losses by extortionate charges in their dealings with the lower classes of the population. Nor was their good faith in the vital matter of the Slave Trade as certain as it once had seemed. Without the sympathy of his fellow Arabs it is unlikely that the onetime owner of the slaves who had been freed and settled at English Point would have dared to attempt their recovery. But he did dare—and at the time when the *Leven* and *Barracouta* were actually in the harbour. He sent a band of his Swahili retainers and slaves to raid the 'colony' by night in the hope that the disappearance of the slaves would be attributed to marauding Nyika from the neighbourhood. Fortunately the slaves' cries were heard on the ships, and a party of seamen was dispatched to rescue them. An ugly incident; but, whatever their real feelings on the matter, Suliman and his elders were not prepared to quarrel with Owen about it. The instigator of the raid had covered his tracks; but one of the raiders, a valuable slave, had been caught in the act; and, under Owen's eye, he was tried and sentenced to be flogged and banished to the Seychelles.[1]

On December 2 both ships set sail again to perform their last task in these waters—an inspection of the Seychelles and a final study of the coast northwards of Mombasa. A few weeks were spent at Mahé and its fellow islets, and then on January 3, 1825, Owen was back again at Mogadishu. At the request of his friends at Mombasa he had brought with him in the *Leven* a Mazrui chief, 'Prince' Rashid-bin-Hamed, and his suite, charged with a 'mission', which, though Owen does not state its object, was intended, it may safely be assumed, to bring pressure on the Chief of Mogadishu, backed by the presence of the *Leven*, to accept the alliance, if not the domination, of Mombasa. But nothing came of it. The people flocked in hundreds to the beach: but the Chief was 'in the country', says the *Narrative*, without hint that this evasion of the mission was anything but

[1] Boteler, ii. 197. Owen, ii. 151–3.

accidental; and in his absence 'the people, ever jealous and suspicious, would not allow the prince or our officers to walk through the town. . . . Accordingly the prince returned on board, and we continued our course to the southward.'[1]

At Barawa their reception was very different. 'The Chief', says Owen, 'came on board with several attendants to pray for a flag and to be taken under British protection as a dependent or ally'—one wonders which—'of Mombasa; to which Captain Owen acceded on condition that he would use his endeavours towards the abolition of the Slave Trade.' In his final report on the Trade, drafted in the following August, Owen describes his agreement at Barawa as similar to the Mombasa Convention which entailed the prohibition of 'any traffic whatever in slaves'.[2]

The *Leven* called next at Lamu (January 17), where Owen merely records that the Governor, Seif-bin-Hamed, dined on board and was persuaded to liberate 'an unfortunate slave who had been imprisoned and almost starved for serving his master, the ex-Sultan of Pate, with too much fidelity'.[3]

On January 20 the *Leven* was back at Mombasa, where the *Barracouta* presently rejoined her. The seven-months' cruise had fulfilled its scientific purpose, and from Owen's account its political aspect might seem slight and innocent enough. But that was not the opinion held at Muscat. Every move of Owen's since his disturbing visit at the end of 1823 had been closely watched; and the reports of Said's officials and agents on the coast had been highly coloured. As soon indeed as the British warships first touched on the coast, they had shown a quick distrust of their intentions. Ten days before Owen paid his explosive visit to Muscat, and thus before any definite threat to the integrity of Said's dominions had been made, the Governor of Zanzibar wrote anxiously to report that the Englishmen had hoisted their flag there—which was true enough, but the flag or

---

[1] Idem, p. 178.
[2] Idem, pp. 178–9. Owen to Cole, 4.viii.25 (*P.P.* 1826, xxvi, 'Correspondence on the Slave Trade at Mauritius, &c.', 6).
[3] Owen, ii. 179.

flags had only been tied to some trees by an officer of the *Barracouta* to serve as marks for the survey.[1] And, of course, after the Muscat interview and Owen's subsequent operations on the coast, the suspicion and irritation had steadily increased. By now the atmosphere at Said's court must have been burning hot, and there was nothing to cool it in the angry accounts which soon reached Muscat of Owen's latest little cruise. Writing to Said on March 2, Seif-bin-Hamed, the Governor of Lamu, has more to report than the dinner-party on the *Leven*.

'I have to inform you that Captain Owen has returned here and that his conduct towards me has been highly improper since my remonstrating with him respecting the Agent whom he left in this quarter and whom he had authorised to hoist British colours on the towns belonging to your Highness. . . . We little expected that the British Government would ever have treated us in the manner this Captain Owen has done.

'Captain Owen has left this for Mauritius, and God knows whether he means to return here or not. His improper behaviour towards us has increased every year, and as we know that you entertain a high esteem and friendship for the British Government, we should be sorry to become the cause of any misunderstanding between you by checking Captain Owen in his unbecoming and unfriendly career, but we are anxiously waiting to receive instructions from your Highness for our future guidance.'[2]

A further account of Owen's activities was sent to Said by another of his leading officials, Nasor-bin-Suliman, who had recently been appointed Liwali of Pemba. His letter was written on March 12 from Faza at the eastern end of Pate Island.

'I have to acquaint your Highness that Captain Owen arrived at Mombasa and took on board the son of Rashid-bin-Hamed with five other principal inhabitants of that port, from whence he proceeded to the Seychelles, Mogadishu and Barawa where he hoisted British flags. At Lamu he demanded from your Highness' Liwali, Seif-bin-Hamed, the surrender of Ozi, Siu, and Jezeer. These are now the only places, with the exception of Pate and Lamu, that are free from Captain Owen's control. Those which he previously took from us

[1] Said to Elphinstone, 29.x.24 (Mauritius Archives, Dispatches Received, ii.1825). Owen, i.428.
[2] Seif to Said, 2.iii.25, translated from Arabic (Mauritius Archives, Dispatches Received, ii.1825).

have been given up to their inhabitants and freed from all allegiance to the Imam, whereby the revenue of Pate and Lamu, which, as you know, was almost entirely derived from those places, has been considerably diminished.

'It would appear from Captain Owen's conduct that he has secret instructions from the British Government to get possession by some means or other of half [the revenue of?] Mombasa. He has made this proposal to the people of that place, but has not yet succeeded in his object. He has appointed in different parts of Mombasa eight Agents, all of the British nation.'[1]

There is exaggeration, no doubt, in this version of events, and misunderstanding, wilful or otherwise. The little party of seamen at Mombasa—there were no other members of the 'British nation' at this time on the coast—would have been startled to learn that they were the appointed agents of an acquisitive 'economic imperialism'.

But there is a last paragraph in Nasor-bin-Suliman's letter which, exaggerated or not, can scarcely be a complete invention.

'On his return to Mombasa Captain Owen put in at Faza where I went on board and found Mbaruk and two hundred men. After some conversation Captain Owen proposed that I should deliver into Mbaruk's charge the whole of the subordinate *bunders* [ports or landing-places] of this island. I refused to comply, stating that I had no authority for such action, but that the Imam's chief Liwali, Ahmed-bin-Seif, at Zanzibar could probably give a more satisfactory reply to his demand. He accordingly proceeded thither, but has failed in obtaining the object of his wishes, and has returned to Mombasa. It is particularly desirable that something should be done to put a stop to these proceedings. Otherwise the people of Mombasa will gradually become masters of the whole of this part of your Highness' dominions, and that will mean a serious loss to your revenue.'[2]

No mention of this incident appears in Owen's *Narrative*. Of his political activities during the twelve days he spent at Mombasa he only records that he 'held several councils, and formed many salutary laws for the government of the natives'. (It is tantalizing not to be told what they were.) 'He also promised to write to the Imam and request him to give back

[1] Nasor to Said, 12.iii.25 (Mauritius Archives, Dispatches Received, ii.1825). Some roughnesses in the translation have been smoothed out.
[2] Nasor to Said, as in preceding footnote.

Pemba to the Mombassians.'[1] But, if much is left unsaid, there is no reason to suspect Owen of a disingenuous concealment quite foreign to his frank and self-confident character. Throughout his book those political questions are treated incidentally and summarily, probably for the good reason that any full account might be regarded by Government as improper. And, though without Owen's version of the facts the exact truth is now undiscoverable, the general tenor of it is evident enough. Wherever he went, it is obvious, whether calling at the seaports on the coast or arguing with Cole and Nourse at Mauritius, whether acting single-handed or with Mbaruk and a band of Mazrui at his side, he was trying his utmost to fill up the loophole in the execution of his Convention. In its second clause he had rashly undertaken that 'Great Britain should reinstate the Chief of Mombasa in his former possessions', and he had admitted that the phrase was meant to cover Pemba, Pate, and Lamu. As long as this side of the bargain was unfulfilled, what was to stop the Mazrui from losing patience and repudiating their side? His personal influence seems never to have failed him on the spot; but what would happen when he had gone? What, above all, would happen to the Slave Trade?...There was only one sure way, indeed, of making good what he had done in East Africa—the acceptance of his protectorate by the British Government. And for that he was still hoping when on February 2, 1825, the *Leven* left Mombasa for the last time, followed three days later by the *Barracouta*. The Arabs gave them a cordial farewell.[2]

On his way south Owen called again at Pemba and had 'several interviews respecting the administration and politics of the country with Nasor-bin-Suliman, the Governor'. No doubt

[1] Owen, ii. 181.
[2] Idem, pp. 181–2. Owen does not mention the parting; but Boteler, always more given to personal detail, says: 'With many a hearty farewell, we bade a final adieu to our Arab friends of Mombasa, and, as we steered through the narrow channel in going out, returned the salute of the crowd that had assembled on the castle battlements to take a last view of us as we passed.'

Owen's Protectorate

he pressed once more the claims of the Mazrui, if not for the island itself, at least for the lands they owned there; and perhaps it was as well that the gallant captain had no idea of the sort of letter Nasor would be writing about him to Said a few weeks later. As it was, their relations were to all appearance of the friendliest, and the Governor gave his visitor a parting gift of six bullocks and eighty fowls.[1]

It was much the same at Zanzibar, where Owen arrived on February 7. He had dealings there not only with the Governor, now Ahmed-bin-Seif, but with one 'Seyyid Mohammud of Muscat', whom Said, it would seem, had sent to Zanzibar as a special confidential agent. With him, records the *Narrative*, Owen 'made the necessary arrangements for preserving the peace of north-east Africa until the British Government should have come to a determination respecting the acceptance of the territory.... Until then Captain Owen desired that no force or illegal interference should be attempted by the Imam's officers' —a last effort to safeguard his protégés at Mombasa.[2] It appears, also, though Owen does not record it, that by way of a final attack on the Slave Trade he made the Governor a strange proposal, half menace and half promise. He said, reported Ahmed to his master, 'that, unless His Highness consented to abolish the Slave Trade at every port under his authority on the coast of Africa, he would be deprived of the whole of his possessions in that quarter, but that, if he agreed to this measure, the settlements of the Portuguese should be taken from them and added to his dominions'. The Imam, added Ahmed, might do well to accept this offer, 'as the territory was of considerable extent and value'.[3]

From Zanzibar Owen returned to the Seychelles and thence by way of Madagascar and Mozambique to Mauritius. As it

[1] Idem, p. 181.   [2] Ibid.
[3] Report of Resident in Persian Gulf to Bombay Govt. on conversation with Said, 14.v.25 (Mauritius Archives, Dispatches Received, ii.1825). Ahmed's letter, reporting Owen's proposal, was shown to the Govt. of Bombay by Said's *Vakil*: G.-in-C. Bombay to Court of Directors, 24.vi.25 (ibid.).

happened, it was during the month he was there that the blow he had been dreading fell. A dispatch arrived from Lord Bathurst directing that no further steps should be taken at Mombasa. How Owen tried, even yet, to evade or at least to postpone the undoing of all he had done will be presently described. But it must have been in less than his usual sanguine mood that on July 19 he sailed away southwards to begin another scientific task, the survey of the Gambia in West Africa, having done all he could in East Africa to bring the major part of the old Arab settlements within the orbit of the British Empire. It is fitting that one of his last acts in East African waters should have witnessed to the fierce incentive which had spurred him to go crusading on his own. At Cole's request he drafted and left in his hands a concise account of the continued prevalence of the Slave Trade, Portuguese, French, and Arab, all up the coast as he himself had observed it.[1]

6

Four years before Owen first hoisted the British flag at Mombasa a more famous Englishman had been guilty of a similar audacity five thousand miles away on the opposite side of the Indian Ocean. At the beginning of 1819 Stamford Raffles, an official in the service of the East India Company, had established, with the consent of the local Sultan, a British post at Singapore. A sharp controversy had ensued. In some quarters Raffles had been fiercely denounced as a piratical disturber of the peace. But he had been supported by the Governor-General of India, Lord Hastings, under whose rather vague instructions he could claim indeed that he had acted; and finally, if uneasily, the British Government had recognized the *fait accompli*. By that decision the main course of the history of the next century in that corner of Asia was determined. Stage by inevitable stage, the greater part of the Malay Peninsula came directly or indirectly under British rule. And there can be little doubt that, if Owen's action had been similarly confirmed, the history of

[1] Printed in *P.P.* 1826, xxvi, 'Correspondence on the Slave Trade at Mauritius, &c.', 4–6.

East Africa would have been similarly changed. But the circumstances, of course, were very different. Owen had acted entirely on his own initiative. So far from being authorized by the Company's Government in India he had cut straight across the policy it had pursued for the past fifteen years. At Singapore, moreover, the rights of local sovereignty, though a matter of dispute, were less obscure than at Mombasa. Suliman's appeals and Said's protests to the Government of Bombay were in open contradiction. The Mazrui statement of the historical facts was vehemently brief and precise. Seif-bin-Sultan, they declared, had captured Mombasa from the Portuguese and established the Mazrui there; but the Mazrui did not acknowledge the authority of Ahmed-bin-Said, and the people of Mombasa had never submitted to any ruler of Oman save only Seif-bin-Sultan, before whose time Mombasa had no connexion with Oman at all. As to Seyyid Said's other claims on the coast, he had taken possession, by force or fraud, of Pate and Lamu, which were allied with Mombasa, and of Pemba, which was 'part of the Mombasa territory'. 'It is commonly notorious', wrote Said on the other hand, 'that the people of Mombasa are dependents of Oman and that their Liwali derives his office from Oman; but for some time past we have winked at their acts, and this they have ascribed to weakness on our part.'[1]

It was, in fact, a good straight issue; and it seemed as if on paper the Mazrui had the best of it. Nothing could be found in the records at Bombay to substantiate Said's claim to Mombasa after the death of Seif-bin-Sultan and the change-over to the Albusaid dynasty.[2] But this quasi-legal point, it need hardly be said, was not the main factor in the minds of the Governments at Calcutta and Bombay. Two other points had greater weight: first, the value of Mombasa in British hands as a means of abolishing the Slave Trade—and that might be a matter of doubt—and, second, the desirability, in policy as well as in good

[1] Statement of Salim-bin-Rashed Mazrui, enclosed in Govt. of Bombay to Court of Directors, 15.xii.24 (I.O., Bombay Political Letters Received, Feb. 1823–Nov. 1825). Said to Elphinstone, 29.x.24 (ibid.).

[2] Memorandum by the Persian Secretary, Bombay: ref. as in preceding footnote.

faith, of meeting Said's wishes—and as to what they were there was no doubt at all.

Said's diplomacy had been patient, but assiduous. He let eight months go by after Owen's departure from Muscat, waiting to see what he would do not only at Mombasa but elsewhere; and then, when his cup was full, he made his full and formal protest to the Governor of Bombay. First, without disclosing his plans at Muscat, he said, Owen had gone off and taken sides with the rebels at Mombasa and prevented the Omani force from taking lawful possession of it. Next, he had visited Pemba, taking Mombasa people with him, and in 'threatening and unbecoming language' demanded the surrender of the island to Mombasa. And then, at Zanzibar, he had 'expressed himself in a very unbecoming manner, saying that he had found friends in the men of Mombasa, but that I had not behaved to him as a friend'; and had wanted to hoist the British flag above his residence. Is all this as it should be? 'If it was done by the direction of the Sirkar, there is no objection. The country is yours. Everything I have is at the service of the Sirkar. If the Captain acted on his own authority, I have only to beg that you will be good enough to make answer to him.'[1]

A few weeks later Said received Cole's letter of June 19 informing him of the result of Mbaruk's embassy to Mauritius.[2] It was not what he had hoped. If Owen had not got what he wanted, neither had he. Owen's actions, it was clear, were not regarded as personal vagaries of no political importance which could be disavowed and undone forthwith by the Governments of British India or Mauritius. The possibility of a permanent British occupation of Mombasa was serious enough for it to be discussed and decided in London. And, lest in London his case should be neglected, Said promptly drafted a memorial to King George in which he reasserted his right of dominion over Mombasa, Lamu, Pate, and Pemba and repeated his account of Owen's incursion. In this version he specially stressed Owen's attempt to intimidate the Liwali of Pemba into surrendering the

[1] S. to Elphinstone, 29.x.24; ref. in footnote, p. 257, above.
[2] See p. 246, above.

island to the Mazrui—'he used expressions which it is not becoming to repeat'—and he appended to it a new grievance. Owen's 'deputy' at Mombasa, Mr. Reitz, had 'seized a vessel with every person and thing on board, belonging to subjects of mine and bound from Zanzibar to Muscat' and had written 'to my Liwali at Zanzibar that he was instructed by Captain Owen to seize every vessel belonging to me having negroes on board bound to Moslem countries'. This was contrary, as Said quite correctly pointed out, to the Moresby Treaty, which had not prohibited the Slave Trade within his own dominions.

'I have heard that the aforesaid deputy has seized two other ships belonging to my subjects: but I have hitherto abstained, out of the sincere attachment and goodwill I bear to Your Majesty's Government, to make any representation of my case; and I have allowed Captain Owen to act as he pleased towards my subjects until I could appeal to the justice of Your Majesty.'

With his usual tact Said submitted this memorial to Bombay with the wish that it should only be forwarded to England if the Governor approved.[1]

About this time Colonel E. G. Stanners, Resident in the Persian Gulf, paid a visit to Muscat and heard the whole story from Said's own lips. Arab interests may have biased him, but his sympathies were at once with Said rather than Owen. Said's loyalty to the British cause justified him—so he felt and so he reported to Bombay—in expressing his regret at what had happened and his belief that it had been quite unauthorized by Government. He went farther. He assured Said that 'the British Government were incapable of giving their sanction to any act of injustice or oppression, particularly to the prejudice of so old and faithful an ally'; but 'I was careful', he adds, 'to avoid expressing any opinion on the case and recommended him to await with patience the result of the reference to England'.[2] That report was made in February 1825. In the middle of May Stanners wrote that he had seen the Imam again and was

[1] Address to His Majesty the King of England, from His Highness the Imam of Muscat, 6.xii.24: ref. in footnote, p. 257, above.

[2] Stanners to Govt. of Bombay, 1.ii.25 (I.O., Bombay Political Letters Received, Feb. 1823–Nov. 1825).

forwarding at his request the disquieting dispatches he had received from his officials on the coast. The ultimatum delivered at Zanzibar[1] had particularly alarmed him. What was he to do if Owen persisted in his demands for the surrender of Omani territory? How was he to reconcile 'the respect with which he was bound to treat all British authorities with the preservation of his most important interests?' To which Stanners replied that his wisest course would be to inform Captain Owen that he had referred the matter to England.[2]

Elphinstone, therefore, was fully seized of Said's point of view when he set forth in a careful minute what immediate action his Government should take and what advice they should submit for the final settlement in London. On the first head, Stanners was to inform the Imam that Owen's action had taken the Government of Bombay entirely by surprise; that the decision of His Majesty's Government could not be predicted; but that the Imam's case would be fully explained and he might trust in no injustice being done to so sincere a friend of Britain. Stanners at the same time was to be warned—in allusion, no doubt, to the sympathetic assurances he had already given Said —to be 'careful to say nothing that may embarrass us or compromise His Majesty's Government, should it decide on retaining Mombasa'.[3]

Elphinstone's opinion on that second and ultimate question was incorporated verbatim in a dispatch from the Governor-in-Council to the Court of Directors.

'Judging from this partial information the Imam's right to Mombasa seems very questionable, but, even admitting it to be so, he appears to have reason to be dissatisfied with our Government. He has always been our faithful and cordial ally and not only has co-operated with us in all our attempts to put down piracy in the Persian Gulf, but has on more than one occasion refrained from enterprises that promised to be profitable to him, because we represented

---

[1] See p. 255, above.
[2] Stanners to Govt. of Bombay, 14.v.25, as in p. 259, note 2, above.
[3] Elphinstone's Minute: Govt. of Bombay to Court of Directors, 15.xii.24 (I.O., Bombay Political Letters Received, Feb. 1823–Nov. 1825).

to him that his engaging in them would be inconsistent with our Policy. He has also agreed to a considerable pecuniary sacrifice first, at the request of this Government, by forbidding the purchase of slaves by Europeans in his dominions, and afterwards by placing still narrower limits to that traffic in his agreement with Captain Moresby. In return for this friendly conduct he has received many assurances of goodwill from our Governments both in India and at home. It must therefore have occasioned much surprise to him to find us appear in a point so remote from our own possessions and connections for the purpose of undertaking the protection of a people with whom he had for some time been engaged in open war and over whom he pretended to the rights of sovereignty. The Imam's surprise must have been increased from the measure being the result of a visit from some of our vessels which had been recommended to him by this Government as employed on the duty of surveying and to the operations of which he had been requested to afford every assistance.

'It may, however, be considered as inexpedient to recede from the engagement entered into by Captain Owen, unless the Imam's right to the sovereignty which has been offered to His Majesty could be proved. If his right is not proved, it would also be advisable to consider how far the possession of Mombasa could be made instrumental to the abolition of the Slave Trade on the Eastern Coast of Africa. But if Mombasa is retained from whatever motive, it seems both just and politic to offer some indemnity to the Imam to whose interests we have certainly not shown that attention which he is entitled to claim from us.'[1]

A cautiously balanced dispatch. The possibility of maintaining the protectorate is by no means ruled out; nor is the motive of Owen's action ignored. But it is made clear enough that the dominant consideration in the mind of the Bombay Government is not the suppression of the Slave Trade but Policy—a policy which demands a fair deal for Said.

This dispatch was submitted to the Board of Control and communicated by them to Bathurst; but, before it had left Bombay, the Home Government had made its decision. It accorded with Elphinstone's ideas, but the factor which mainly determined it was not the claims of Said, still less the yet more doubtful pretensions which, it was suggested, Portugal

[1] Ibid.

might dig up from the ruins of her imperial past. What chiefly influenced ministers was the actual situation at Mombasa, as to which they had before them the direct but by no means concordant information of two eyewitnesses, Owen and Moorsom. It is improbable that Liverpool and his colleagues would have accepted Owen's passionate and sanguine plea for his protectorate at its face-value even if it had stood alone. As it was, Moorsom's more temperate account of his visit to Mombasa exploded one of the main assumptions on which Owen's case was grounded —the delight, the positive intoxication, of the people at finding themselves under the British flag. The Mazrui could never have imagined that by their truculent talk to Moorsom they were sealing their own fate. Yet so in fact it was. Not even to help the fight with the Slave Trade was the British Government prepared to force British 'protection' on a people who could only be induced to respect the obligations it entailed by the presence of a British garrison or regular visits by British cruisers.

The decision was promptly transmitted to Cole in a brief dispatch from the Colonial Office. After acknowledging the receipt of Cole's report on Mbaruk's 'embassy' and observing that reports had also reached London from Owen and Moorsom, Bathurst continued:

'Whatever measures His Majesty's Government might have commanded to be adopted in the event of the inhabitants of Mombasa unequivocally desiring to place themselves under the protection of Great Britain, regard being had to the claims of the Imam of Muscat and the claims which Portugal might also possibly advance to the sovereignty of that territory, yet, as subsequently to the period of the cession which is alleged to have been made of the island to Captain Owen, it has been reported by Captain Moorsom that there did not appear on his proceeding to Mombasa any general disposition on the part of the inhabitants to belong to Great Britain, it is His Majesty's pleasure that no further measures should be taken upon the subject.'[1]

The purport of this was obvious enough. The offer of the protectorate was rejected. But, if Bathurst or any of his col-

[1] Bathurst to Cole, 9.xi.24 (C.O. 168. 8).

leagues had gone into greater detail, a good deal of further correspondence would have been avoided. 'No further measures', he said; but what of the undoing of what Owen had already done? The British flag was still flying at Mombasa over Lieutenant Emery and his little 'establishment'. Their removal was clearly implicit in the Government's decision. Specific orders to that effect, one would suppose, should have been sent from the Admiralty to Commodore Christian, who on Nourse's death in September 1824 had succeeded to the naval command at the Cape: but—can it have been sheer oversight?—those orders were not sent. Even so, Christian and Cole might well have given effect in their own way to the Government's unmistakable intention. They could have evacuated Mombasa at once if they had wished. But they did not wish. And the reason is not far to seek. By an odd coincidence the *Leven* with Owen on board was, as has been seen, at Mauritius, on the very eve of her final departure from East African waters, when Bathurst's dispatch arrived. Naturally Cole communicated the tenor of it to Owen, and Owen, unwilling to abandon his darling project without one last struggle, drafted a formal reply to Cole, with the request that he should forward it to the Secretary of State. 'I can only lament', he wrote, 'that a decision which, if not in some way altered, will give up the people of that kingdom to wars, discord, and misery has been founded on a misunderstanding of the real disposition of that people.' How could Moorsom, ignorant of Mombasa and the ways and language of its inhabitants, learn as much of their true mind on one brief visit as he (Owen) had learned? What more unequivocal expression of their real wishes could be desired than the act of cession itself? As to withdrawal, Commodore Christian would no doubt act 'as he may judge proper'; but the departure of the British garrison would put an end to the peace which all parties at Mombasa were at present pledged to maintain. And what, finally, would happen to the freed slaves located there? 'If our party be withdrawn, these unfortunate people will again be reduced to slavery.' This last point was at least a substantial reason for delay; and in a year's time 'I hope to be able to offer to His Majesty's ministers all the living evidence they may require from me to enable them to decide as they please'.[1] No doubt Owen pressed these views more fully and vigorously on Cole in conversation, and no doubt, when he called at the Cape a few weeks later on his way to West Africa, he pressed them likewise on Christian. At any rate he got his way. For both Cole and Christian, though they questioned the wisdom of Owen's high-handed conduct—Christian indeed went so far as to say, in a letter to Cole, 'It is most unfortunate that the Establishment was ever made'[2]—were nevertheless inclined to accept the protectorate as a *fait accompli*; and, since the disposal of the freed slaves was a real difficulty, they were willing to hold their hands while the point was referred to Whitehall. So the delay Owen wanted was accorded him. Months passed. Cole did nothing. Christian did nothing. The British flag still flew above Mombasa.

7

The Mazrui, meantime, were getting restless. The menace of Said's vengeance still darkened their horizon. To protect them from it they did really want to keep the flag—though, as they had so imprudently betrayed to Moorsom, it was only the flag they wanted and nothing else, no garrison, no British traders, no obligations except the payment of a subsidy. So, knowing nothing, it seems, of what had happened in England, they determined, towards the end of 1825, to bring the question to an issue by a direct appeal to the highest authority. In February 1826 a letter from Sheikh Suliman arrived in London. It was addressed to King George IV and it proposed to cede to him Mombasa and half its revenue. But this straight offer was as unavailing as Owen's protest. Both came too late. George IV's ministers were not disposed to change their minds. The dispatch from Bombay had stiffened their dislike of Owen's adventure. The possibility of external complications seemed now more serious. 'The jealousy with which the Imam of Muscat has viewed the late proceedings of Captain Owen' was now better

[1] Owen to Cole, i.vii.25; Cole to Bathurst, 3.vii.25 (C.O. 167. 78).
[2] Christian to Cole, 10.v.26 (C.O. 167. 83).

understood.[1] So Bathurst promptly instructed Cole 'to take an early opportunity of intimating to the Sheikh that His Majesty could not accept such a proposal as that which has been made to him without compromising the good faith of the British Nation with other powers with whom it has been long united in the most cordial amity'.[2] Meantime the curious omission of the previous year had been made good. In the autumn of 1825 Admiralty orders had gone out to Christian to withdraw Lieutenant Emery from his post.[3]

It seems, however, as if nothing could go smoothly in this queer business of Mombasa. Christian duly received his orders in April 1826; but he did not like them. The period of inaction had not softened his regret that the protectorate had ever been established, but it had not weakened either, it had fortified, his feeling that it was best to leave bad alone and not make it worse by trying to undo it. And since Christian, it seems, was as ready as Owen to take a line of his own and to risk the displeasure of his masters in Whitehall, he sought—and found—excuses, if not for disobeying his plain orders, at least for postponing their execution. The first was the old one—the unsolved difficulty of disposing of the freedmen. The second was more audacious. The dispatch had only ordered the withdrawal of Lieutenant Emery: it had said nothing about the rest of the 'establishment'! Thus armed, the Commodore drafted a reply to the Admiralty in which he not only asked for more explicit instructions but reopened the whole question of Mombasa. Sir Lowry Cole, he wrote, agreed with him in thinking that the occupation of the town had proved 'a powerful check on the revival of the Slave Trade, as it is from that part of the African coast that the

---

[1] Bathurst to Cole, 26.xii.25 (I.O., Bombay Dispatches, 52).
[2] Bathurst to Cole, 17.iii.26 (C.O. 168. 8 and 9).
[3] Admiralty to Christian, 23.ix.25 (Adm. 2. 1587). The orders referred to the appointment by the late Commodore Nourse of Midshipman Emery 'to act as civil governor and commandant of the island of Mombasa', and went on: 'My lords having disapproved of this appointment, I am commanded by their lordships to signify their direction to you to recall Mr. Emery from the above situation.' That was all.

islands to the eastward are chiefly supplied'. He was afraid, moreover, that the Imam of Muscat, if the 'establishment' were removed, would 'forcibly take possession of the port and put to the sword the whole of its inhabitants', and that the 'moral effect' of the British Government's surrendering a 'protected people' to their fate might be incalculable.[1]

This bold dispatch was dated May 1, 1826, and when Cole received a copy of it before the month was up, still influenced perhaps by Owen's eloquence, he informed Christian that he approved the 'reference back' to England.[2] But that was all the support that Christian got. His notification of the further postponement of the evacuation did not reach Bombay till September, and by then (as will appear) Elphinstone had already informed Said of the British Government's decision. Some hard things must have been said about naval officers who meddled in politics and evaded their orders; but, since the Commodore at the Cape was quite beyond the scope of his authority, Elphinstone could do no more than send him a dispassionate restatement of the case for evacuation. There was no reason, however, for serious anxiety at Bombay, no real danger of any change of policy in London. Ministers were not tempted by Christian's dispatch to reconsider, still less to reverse, their decision; it only induced them with due deliberation to make it effective. Late in November—just two years after the resolution 'to take no further measures' had been adopted—the Colonial Office requested the Admiralty to direct Commodore Christian 'to convey the free blacks to the Cape of Good Hope and place them under the protection of the Governor of the Colony'. The Admiralty at once complied. Yet, even now, the line taken was strangely indirect and incomplete. Christian was simply told to remove the 'free blacks' to the Cape 'as desired by Lord Bathurst'; and since he had already been instructed to remove Emery, no doubt that was enough, no doubt it meant complete withdrawal from Mombasa, and it was impossible for him to plead that he had received no orders about the little British

[1] Christian to Admiralty, 1.v.26 (Adm. 1. 70).
[2] Cole to Christian, 28.v.26 (C.O. 167. 83).

garrison. None the less, it is odd that no simple, direct order for evacuation was ever sent.[1]

By that time, however, it was not needed. The thing had been done. Yet another naval officer had taken a line of his own.

In the summer of 1826 Commodore Christian instructed Captain Arland to proceed to Mombasa in the sloop *Helicon* with dispatches for Lieutenant Emery. Arland was expected to report on the situation at Mombasa—for Christian was anxious, no doubt, to learn that all was well with the young commandant and his companions—but he was not authorized to take any action whatever. And for the first five days the *Helicon* spent at Mombasa, taking in firewood and water, no action seemed required. All was still. The British flag drooped languidly over a scene of tropical calm. On the fifth day (July 22) Emery himself, having been informed in his dispatches of Christian's decision to postpone the evacuation until he had received further orders from home, sat down and wrote in reply that he was glad to hear of the postponement. It would, he said, ensure for a little longer the local suppression of the Slave Trade and stave off the danger—a real danger in his opinion—of the French occupying Mombasa in our place. Moreover, those Indian 'banyans' who had come in increasing numbers from Bombay, Cutch, and Surat to settle at Mombasa, trusting in the protection of our flag, would be given time to remove their property to a place of safety before that protection was withdrawn. In all this there was no note of uneasiness. The longer, indeed, the evacuation were delayed, the better, it seemed, would Emery be pleased. That did not mean, of course, that he regarded his lonely post as an easy or a congenial one. He knew, as he afterwards admitted, that he was not popular with the Arab chiefs. In particular they had bitterly resented his having 'insisted on equal justice between Arabs and Indians trading under British protection'. But 'this jealousy', he thought, 'had subsided'.

[1] Bathurst to Admiralty, 22.xi.26 (C.O. 168. 10). Admiralty to Christian, 23.xi.26 (Adm. 2. 1588).

There was nothing, in fact, to make his position more uncomfortable than it had always been.[1]

Next day his eyes were opened. Ever since the Mazrui had been informed of the rejection of their offer by King George, their mood had become more desperate and defiant. A significant change, moreover, had recently occurred in their leadership. The aged Suliman, whom even Owen had regarded as incompetent—'a dotard of eighty' he had called him[2]—had not been the natural or most suitable successor to his nephew Abdullah: he had only been chosen as Sheikh in 1823 because the title of Salim-bin-Ahmed, Abdullah's eldest brother, had been disputed by the notorious Mbaruk, a younger brother: and it was perhaps a symptom of the rising tide of Arab feeling that, in the first half of 1826, Suliman's tenure of office, which had always been regarded as provisional, was terminated, and by the general consent of the Mazrui, including Mbaruk, Salim was elected in his place.[3] It was this new Sheikh, therefore, a man (as will presently appear) of courage and resource, who on July 23 summoned the leading Mazrui to a council in the Fort and carried by a unanimous vote the four following resolutions:

(1) The chiefs consider that they never ceded the Fort to the British Government.
(2) That they do not consider themselves amenable to a British subject as a Governor.
(3) That they acknowledge Mr. Emery in no other light than as the receiver of half the amount of port-duties.
(4) That they consider the Treaty has not been fulfilled inasmuch as the island of Pemba has not been restored to their territories.

On receipt of this ultimatum—it was nothing less—Emery at once consulted his superior officer, Arland, who decided to convene a *durbar* at Emery's house. Salim and his kinsmen obeyed the call, but held grimly to their resolutions. They denied downright that they had ever ceded their country to the British. They would only tolerate Emery, they declared, as 'a civil resident without any powers of government'. Agreement was obviously

---
[1] Emery to Christian, 22 and 30.vii.26 (Adm. 1. 70).
[2] Owen to Adm. 8.iii.24 (Adm. 1. 2269).
[3] Guillain, i. 576, 583–4. Miles, ii. 331.

impossible, and the *durbar* broke up, leaving Arland with the conviction that, whatever he had done in the past, Emery with his tiny garrison would be unable to exercise any 'real power or influence' in the future. Emery himself admitted as much; but he had not realized that he was not merely powerless but in personal danger till a friend in the town whom he trusted sent secretly to tell him that Sheikh Salim and several other Mazrui chiefs were plotting to murder him as soon as the *Helicon* had sailed. . . . The disillusionment was complete. Those Arab hearts which Owen had imagined to be overflowing with affection for the British saviours of Mombasa were seething now with murderous resentment.[1]

Arland was thus suddenly confronted with the necessity of making a quick and grave decision. As he confessed in his report to Christian, he felt the weight of his personal responsibility. He had only been instructed, he said, to deliver the dispatches: he had received no orders about the establishment. But British naval officers, however junior, in those days before their ships on all the seven seas had been tied with invisible threads to Whitehall, were accustomed to dealing with emergencies on their own account. Nor was Arland, it seems, in any doubt as to what his decision had to be. 'Considering the situation of the British flag being in the hands of a tribe of lawless Arabs, the possibility of insults being repeated against the Commandant of the Establishment, also the personal safety of British subjects and property being endangered, together with the prospect of the speedy reduction of the Establishment—all these things combined resolved me to decide on withdrawing it.' In this Emery concurred. 'He could not remain at Mombasa'—so he put it, at Arland's request, in writing—'except in command as ordered by Commodore Nourse.' And again, in his report to Christian, he could not remain, he wrote, 'for the honour of the British flag if its protection was imagined to be *paid for* and its colours *only hired*'.[2]

[1] Emery to Arland, 23 and 25.vii.26; Arland to Christian, 8.ix.26 (Adm. 1. 70).
[2] Arland to Christian, 8.ix.26; Emery to Arland, 25.vii.26; Emery to Christian, 30.vii.26 (ibid.).

The decision was promptly carried out. On July 25 Arland issued a proclamation declaring that, whereas the treaty had been violated and the chiefs had refused to accept a protectorate, the British Establishment would be immediately withdrawn. Thereupon the flag was hauled down, and Emery and the garrison—one sergeant and one private of marines and four seamen—embarked on the *Helicon*. Of the 'free blacks', who numbered about sixty, some thirty odd could not be found; they had hidden themselves, it was said, because the Arabs had told them that a dreadful fate awaited them on the ship. Twenty-seven men, women, and children, however, were safely taken on board. There was nothing more to do. It was no occasion for ceremonious farewells. The anchor was weighed and the *Helicon* set on her course for Mauritius.

As he sailed away Arland received what might perhaps be regarded as a parting message from the Mazrui to their protectors. His interpreter told him that he understood an invitation was on its way to the French at Bourbon to send, not indeed their flag or a garrison, but traders to do business at Mombasa—business, it might be supposed, which did not exclude the Slave Trade. Whether such an invitation was actually sent it is impossible to say; but in any case it was ingeniously malicious to set the rumour of it afoot at the moment of the British withdrawal. The Mazrui had had the last word.[1]

Christian wisely accepted the *fait accompli* and reported accordingly to the Admiralty and to Bombay. Moorsom, he now saw, had been right and Owen wrong. The infatuated Mazrui had themselves exploded all his pretexts for delaying the evacuation. 'They have no just claim', he wrote, 'to any protection from me.' And with those words the strange story of 'Owen's Protectorate' appropriately ends.[2]

[1] Arland to Christian, 8.xi.26; Emery to Christian, 30.vii.26 (Adm. 1. 70).
[2] Christian to Admiralty, 16.x.26 (ibid.). Christian to Govt. of Bombay, 5.ix.26; G. of B.'s reply, 13.ix.26 (I.O., B.P.C., Oct. 18–Nov. 22, 1826).

IX

THE FATE OF THE MAZRUI

I

THE evacuation of Mombasa was a triumph for Said, who for more than two years had patiently endured the frustration of his designs in East Africa. The Bombay Government had done their best to temper his indignation: as recorded in the preceding chapter, they had told him at the outset of the trouble that Owen's action was quite 'unexpected' by them and that no injustice could be intended towards so old and tried a friend. But Said had not been wholly reassured. He had tried indeed to obtain a more certain guarantee. At the interview with the British Resident in the Persian Gulf in December 1825 in which he had complained of Owen's further interference in his East African dominions, he had intimated that 'he considered his connexion with the British Government in the light of an offensive and defensive alliance'. But that, of course, had not been allowed to pass at Bombay. The agreement, Said had been told, 'was merely intended to convey a general notion of strict friendship'.[1] 'Sincere friends', 'strict friendship'—that was all he had got; and, though he might believe that the Bombay Government honestly meant those words when they used them, he could not be sure how they would be interpreted in far-off London. Who, indeed, could tell what those unaccountable Englishmen might or might not do in their crazy hatred of the Slave Trade? So it was with 'great satisfaction' that Said acknowledged the news of the decision promptly communicated to him from Bombay—though he shrewdly added that 'it still left him uncertain whether the British Government might not again interpose at some future period'.[2] Finally, in October 1826, the British Resident in the Persian Gulf was sent to inform him that the flag and the 'establishment' had been removed and also—it could scarcely be omitted—to impress on him 'the anxiety of the British Government that the people of Mombasa

---

[1] B.R. 193. [2] I.O., B.P.C., Sept. 6–Oct. 11, 1826.

should not suffer for their temporary connexion with us, and the policy of his endeavouring by means of conciliation to prevent their completing the projected connexion with France'.[1] Said knew what that meant. Forgive the Mazrui? It was at most a request. The projected connexion with France? That was probably Mazrui bluff and he would call it. In plain fact his hands at last were free.

2

The Mazrui were not kept long in suspense. Before the end of 1826 an ultimatum arrived from Muscat ordering them to submit to their overlord and surrender Fort Jesus and the town. Disobedience, it was clear, would be followed by the attack in force which had so long been dreaded. To obey, on the other hand, without question or condition was not only more than Mazrui pride could bear, it would be akin to suicide: for Salim and his kinsmen were under no illusion that, if once they put themselves at Said's mercy, their old record of contumacy and rebellion, aggravated by their long and provocative liaison with the British, would go unpunished. The obvious, the only course was to temporize—and strengthen their defences. So Salim wrote to Said, saying that the people of Mombasa were willing to acknowledge his formal suzerainty and even to resume the payment of the tributary customs duties, but they were not prepared to evacuate the fortress. To confirm the sincerity of this compromise, Salim offered to send two of his kinsmen to discuss it with Said at Muscat. To this Said made no immediate answer. In the course of 1827 he was engaged in intrigues among the Arabs of the 'Pirate Coast' and in negotiations for his marriage with a daughter of the Prince of Shiraz. He was

[1] Govt. of Bombay to Resident, P.G., 12.x.1826 (I.O., B.P.C., as in preceding note). Said was also informed of the evacuation by Cole, and replied: 'I am pleased beyond measure that the English Government has abandoned the Settlement of Mombasa and removed its flag from thence. I consider this measure to have been dictated by a feeling of delicacy towards myself, and am grateful to the King of England and to your Excellency on that account.' S. to C., March 1827 (Mauritius Archives, vol. F. 2, No. 42).

The Fate of the Mazrui

also carefully preparing to deal with Mombasa as he, not Salim, chose. So when at last, at the end of 1827, the envoys sailed for Muscat, they met near Socotra a fleet of ten or eleven ships bearing south, with some 1,200 troops on board and with Said in his flagship, the *Liverpool*, in command. Said gave the envoys a friendly reception. Only to use force when intrigue had been tried and had failed was one of his invariable rules, and he succeeded, it was said, in corrupting one of the envoys with a bribe of 300 piastres. At any rate, on arrival at Mombasa, Said waited for three days to allow the effect of his sudden descent in person with such formidable forces to sink in. Then, no offer of submission coming, he opened a bombardment of Fort Jesus and the town. Still no sign of submission. Evidently Said would have to land his troops and attempt to storm the fort. For this, of course, in the last resort he had come prepared: but before committing himself to the risks and losses it must involve he had one more try at diplomacy. He suspended the bombardment, and invited Sheikh Salim and his brother Mbaruk to negotiate on board. On condition that two of Said's kinsmen were put ashore as hostages, they agreed. The condition was accepted, and a secret conference ensued. The Mazrui, it appeared, were still willing to bargain. They offered Said the same sort of agreement as they had made with Owen. They would admit Said's overlordship and pay him half their customs revenue if he would confirm the hereditary claim of their family to control the local government and recognize Sheikh Salim as Governor. There remained the crucial question of Fort Jesus, and on this the Mazrui now thought it safe to compromise. Sheikh Salim and his family would remain in the fortress, but fifty of Said's soldiers would be admitted to share it with them. On those terms, on January 11, 1828, a peace treaty was concluded. Said, together with the Mazrui chiefs, swore on the Koran to observe it. Then Said sent in his fifty men . . . and then, by guile or stealth, he inserted bit by bit another fifty, and another, till they were two hundred strong. Thereupon they turned Salim and his kinsfolk out into the town and barred the gate against them. . . . So Said was master at last of the fortress. He visited it in person, gave orders for the repair of its walls, and installed a garrison of 350 Arabs and Baluchis. Two or three weeks' peace assured him that the work he had come to do had been well done, and he sailed off to Zanzibar.[1]

It was Said's first sight of the African coast, his first visit to the island colony which had shown such unusual loyalty to Oman; and it may well be that the idea of shifting the centre and the balance of his realm from Muscat to Zanzibar now first came into his mind. At any rate he lingered there for three whole months till in April Muscat brought him hurrying home. Saüd, Bedr's nephew, had broken into rebellion and seized the persons of Said's eldest son, Hilal, and one of his nephews. Said's return dispersed the storm. The young men were ransomed. A reconciliation with Saüd was patched up. But the incident had shown how dangerous it was for Said to leave Muscat for any length of time.[2]

Meanwhile the situation at Mombasa had dramatically changed. Before leaving Zanzibar Said had taken two steps to safeguard his position. Most of the Arab towns along the coast, impressed by Said's swift and signal triumph at Mombasa by whatever means achieved, had kept quiet, accepting Said's overlordship without demur. But Mogadishu, away in the freespirited north, had defiantly refused submission. Said, accordingly, had bidden the Governor of Zanzibar to proceed to Mogadishu with the ships and men that had been used against

[1] The fullest account is by Guillain (i. 584–9), who visited Zanzibar and the coast in 1846–8, and was supplied with the Arab documents. Miles (ii. 332–3) is very brief, and dates the treaty and occupation of Fort Jesus in 1832, which, though Miles was working on contemporary official reports, must be wrong in view of (a) a letter from Said from Mombasa, dated Jan. 17, 1828, announcing the occupation of Fort Jesus, preserved in the Zanzibar Archives (text in Said-Ruete, 52) and (b) the log of the American brig *Virginia* for Sept. 3, 1828, as cited p. 275, opposite. As to Said's stratagem, according to Guillain (i. 588) parties of Said's men entered the fort each day on the pretext of visiting their comrades and left some of their number behind at the conclusion of the visit. Said-Ruete (54) suggests that Said interpreted the treaty as permitting the introduction of 50 at one time and not stipulating for withdrawals!

[2] Guillain, ii. 189–90.

The Fate of the Mazrui

Mombasa and to punish it for its recalcitrance. Those orders had been obeyed. The town had been bombarded, and, on its evacuation by its inhabitants, occupied and sacked by a landing-party. On the departure of the fleet, a letter of apology and submission had been sent to Muscat.[1] Said's second step was riskier and less effective. He had instructed the Governor of Pemba, Nasir-bin-Sultan, an old enemy, as it happened, of the Mazrui, to take command of the garrison in Fort Jesus and assume the Governorship of Mombasa in Sheikh Salim's place. But to this second flagrant violation of the treaty the Mazrui refused to submit. They told Nasir to leave the place within twenty-four hours (May 1828); and, when he shut himself up in Fort Jesus and began to bombard the town, they rose, with the whole population at their back, and, surrounding the fort, set themselves to starve it into surrender.[2]

Throughout the hot summer months and into autumn the siege dragged on. In September one catches a sight of it, by chance, through American eyes. On the third of that month Captain Henry Leavitt, master of the brig *Virginia* of Salem which had come up from Madagascar and Zanzibar in the hope of doing a little trade at Mombasa and Lamu, made the following entry in his log:

'On nearing the eastern side of Mombasa Island which must [be] approached very close, were fired upon from a small stone fort and by near 200 or 300 men from the beach. We immediately hauled on a wind and attempted to beat out, but, there being a fresh breeze from S.E. and a large sea rolling in together with the flood tide, we found it impossible to gain any ground. The fire of musketry continued pretty brisk till we anchored, when it ceased. Several bullets passed through our sails. . . . Went ashore and learnt that the Mombasa inhabitants had revolted from the Imam, and had shut up the Arab garrison in the castle, and had fired upon us under the idea that we were an Arab brig of war.'[3]

The siege lasted into December, and then, in the last straits of hunger, the garrison surrendered. They were allowed to

---
[1] Guillain, i. 590. Miles, ii. 334.
[2] Miles, ii. 336. Guillain, i. 591–4.
[3] Log-books: Essex Institute, Salem, Mass.

depart unharmed, but Nasir was thrown into prison. A frigate sent by Said in the hope of raising the siege arrived too late. Mombasa was once more as independent as it had ever been.[1]

3

Said, of course, was not going to allow his East African designs to be thus frustrated by the Mazrui, but for the moment he was occupied elsewhere. He had impetuously declared war on the Sheikh of Bahrein—an island he coveted all his life as avidly even as Mombasa. An assault at full strength in November had been badly handled and repulsed with heavy loss, Said himself being wounded and barely escaping capture. Some months of desultory sea-fighting ensued, till in May 1829 the Government of Bombay, anxious to restore peace in the Persian Gulf, instructed its representative to offer mediation. But this move, which was more welcome to Said than to the Sheikh of Bahrein, only served to protract an uncertain truce, and it was not until the British Resident, after months of fruitless negotiation, had withdrawn from the dispute that at the beginning of December peace was finally concluded. Freed from this entanglement, Said turned at once on the Mazrui. Before this year was out, a second large-scale expedition, eight ships and 1,400 men, was launched against Mombasa.[2]

The Mazrui were in a defiant mood. They knew that the release of their prisoner, Nasir, one of Said's most trusted officials, would be his first demand, so at the news of the fleet's approach they cut his throat. It was a clear hint to Said that no friendly accommodation was to be expected this time, and the preliminary exchange of messages was acrid. Each party accused the other of breaking the treaty. Said demanded the restoration of Fort Jesus. Salim told him to come and take it. Then Said attempted landings at two opposite points on the island simultaneously. Both were beaten off with heavy loss. For a week he tried and tried again. Not a foothold was gained. The losses mounted up. Force was evidently useless, and Said opened negotiations. His envoys offered Salim a renewal of the

[1] Miles, ii. 336. Guillain, i. 591–4.   [2] B.R. 198.

old treaty, and Salim, showing prudence in victory, accepted it provided one clause was deleted. He had learnt his lesson: he would not admit another fifty of Said's men within Fort Jesus. Said acquiesced. He could not expect, and he could not, it seemed, enforce, better terms. He made peace, determined to break it at the first good chance, and sailed away to Zanzibar.[1]

Once more he lingered on the island. It seems probable that the idea of making his home there was now taking definite shape, and maybe it was during this second visit that he began to build himself a palace by the sea and to lay out plantations of clove-trees and rice. But this second holiday was interrupted precisely as the first. At the end of April 1830 he was urgently recalled to Muscat.

The trouble that awaited him was largely of his own making. Before setting out against Mombasa he had thought to safeguard the internal peace of Oman by treacherously seizing and imprisoning his young cousin, Hamil, whose gallantry and liberality had dangerously endeared him to the tribesmen. Therein he had overreached himself. Soon after his departure, Jokha, Hamil's martial sister, had set herself at the head of a rebellion: Hamud, another of Said's many cousins, had joined in it; and only the arrival of two British cruisers, sent in response to an urgent appeal to Bombay, and a firm warning addressed to Hamud by the British Resident at Bushire had prevented an attack on Muscat itself. As it was, Said was unable to recover all he lost. The important town of Sohar, in particular, halfway up the Batineh, remained in Hamud's possession; and an attempt by Said to recover it in February 1831 was repulsed with heavy loss. His power, indeed, in his own Oman seemed ebbing, and the African dream faded for the moment into the background. When the north-east monsoon began to blow in the autumn, it carried no further expedition for the conquest of Mombasa, but only three of Said's smaller ships to maintain a blockade of the port till the change of wind in the following spring.[2]

[1] Guillain, i. 594-6.
[2] Miles, ii. 332. Guillain, i. 193-5, ii. 597.

Some time before the blockade was lifted Said left Muscat for East Africa, and there he stayed, mostly, no doubt, at Zanzibar, till September. Conflicting records leave it uncertain whether during those months he made another attack on Mombasa; but it is certain enough that, if he did, he failed again.[1] It is certain, too, that his absence from Muscat had its usual result. He had scarcely left, indeed, before the Omani tribes were up in arms again and at each other's throats, instigated this time, it seems, not so much by hostility towards Said himself as by sectional rivalry and jealousy of Said's deputy. Again it was only by the firm intervention of the British Resident and the dispatch of a naval force to Muscat that peace was restored and Said's authority re-established; and it is not surprising that, when he returned in September from Zanzibar, he was advised by the British Resident to stay at home for the future and govern his own country himself. Nor was it only internal schism that now threatened the stability of Oman. The decline of Said's prestige occasioned by his disastrous attack on Bahrein, by his long absences in Africa, and by the two resulting insurrections had upset the uneasy balance of Arabian politics. The Wahabi in particular had seized the opportunity of renewing their old designs of aggression and aggrandizement. And Said, so low now had his fortunes fallen, was incapable of resistance. In the course of 1833, on the advice of the British Resident, he humbled his pride and purchased a promise from the Wahabi to respect the integrity of his realm by a renewal of the old payment of an annual tribute, disguised as *zukat* or 'religious tithe', to the amount of 5,000 German crowns (over £1,000). That the Wahabi accepted the bribe, that they did not press their advantage home up to the very walls of Muscat, was partly due, no doubt, to distractions elsewhere; but it was mainly due to the fact that, if Said had no friends left in Arabia, he still had friends at Bombay. 'It could not be concealed', wrote the Assistant-

[1] That Said went to East Africa in 1832 and returned to Muscat on Sept. 10 may be accepted from B.R. 204–5. Miles (ii. 332) fills the interval with the first attack and the Treaty of 1828; Said-Ruete (64) with the second attack and the renewed Treaty of 1830. Guillain (ii. 597) leaves 1832 blank.

Resident in the Gulf, looking back to this critical period some ten years later, 'that our influence alone prevented his immediate downfall.'[1]

4

Fate had decreed, it seemed, that Said should never maintain his authority in both parts of his realm at the same time. With the regularity of a seesaw his fortunes in Arabia and in Africa had gone up and down. Triumph at Mombasa had meant danger at Muscat. Recovering his hold on Muscat, he had lost Mombasa. And with that lop-sided arrangement Said could not now be satisfied. The balance of his ambitions lay, if anything, the other way. Almost certainly by now he had made his great decision to shift the head-quarters of his realm from Muscat to Zanzibar. He had set his mind and staked his future on a new Omani dominion in East Africa. And for that the undisputed ownership of Mombasa was essential. Fallen from its old estate, it was still the key to the coast, its harbour far the best and most easily defended, its fortress the one impregnable stronghold in all East Africa. It was almost as idle, indeed, for Said to dream of creating a new dominion in East Africa with Mombasa in the hands of the Mazrui as to dream of maintaining his old dominion in Oman with Muscat in the hands of the Wahabi. The possession of Mombasa had become in fact the crucial issue of Said's career. And yet, it seemed, he could not decide that issue: his forces were not strong enough unaided to storm Fort Jesus and eliminate the Mazrui. And where could he hope to get assistance from outside? He had no friends in Arabia or its neighbourhood. The British certainly would not help him. Had not the Bombay Government asked him to forgive and conciliate the Mazrui? Nor would they agree to his reviving his old connexion with the French. Had they not warned him about Bourbon?

There seemed, indeed, only one place in all Said's world where he might possibly obtain the help he needed—the great island in the south. At an early stage of his operations in East

[1] B.R. 203–6.

Africa Said had realized the importance of Madagascar and had entered into a friendly correspondence with Radama. But there had been changes since those days. Radama, as has been recorded, had strengthened his hold on the island, declared himself 'King', and obtained the recognition and support of the British at Mauritius. In 1825, two years after the conclusion of the second Slave Trade Treaty, he had at last secured the submission of his only dangerous enemy, the Sakalava, and sealed the bargain by marrying Ranavolana, the daughter of their chief. He then turned on the French, who had openly encouraged the Sakalava in their resistance, tore down their flag at Fort Dauphin, and drove their traders to seek refuge in Bourbon. Three years later he died, and his widow, Ranavolana, had secured her election to the vacant throne. It had soon become apparent that the new Queen was not kindly disposed towards Radama's European friends. The British Agent had been seized, put to torture, and expelled from the capital; and, though the missionaries were allowed for a few years longer to remain at work in the numerous schools they had established, in 1835 a royal edict was issued forbidding the teaching of Christianity, and in 1836 the missionaries left the island. Nor had Ranavolana shown herself much more friendly to the old allies of her tribe; and most of the French as well as the British traders had fled from the island in 1828. The French Government had been naturally unwilling to abandon their interests in Madagascar. A squadron from Bourbon bombarded Tamatave and re-hoisted the French flag in 1829, and in 1830 the militant ministers in Paris, who achieved so quickly and firmly in that year the conquest of Algiers, had planned a full-scale expedition to Madagascar when their activities were cut short by the 'July Revolution'. In 1831 a more peaceful method of recovering the lost ground had been tried: Ranavolana had been offered a French 'protectorate'. But she had promptly made it clear that she was able to protect herself and desired no dealings of any sort with any European nation. In 1832 she had declared that native law would henceforth be applied in every detail to European immigrants. Another general exodus of Europeans had inevitably followed. Those who had remained and defied the new decree had been put to death, French and British alike, by the inexorable queen.[1]

It was to this powerful and independent sovereign that Said turned for help in his sore need. In the autumn of 1833 an embassy from the ruler of Oman arrived at Antananarivo. It brought to the widowed Queen a startling offer—no less than Seyyid Said himself for a second husband. But the embassy had a further purpose. It sounded the Queen's ministers as to whether they would lend Said two thousand soldiers for an attack upon Mombasa; and it is difficult not to believe that this was the only serious object of the mission. Said, it is true, had failed to bring off his previous negotiations for the hand of a Persian princess; and no doubt a connubial alliance with the Queen of Madagascar would greatly heighten his prestige and enlarge the scope of his designs in East Africa. But surely he cannot have expected that Ranavolana, the strong-minded, not to say arrogant, occupant of Radama's throne, would consent to leave Antananarivo for distant Muscat or even Zanzibar and take a place, however eminent, in a Moslem ruler's harem. Still less, surely, could Said have thought of migrating to Madagascar and playing the part of consort to its Queen. No: it was the soldiers that he wanted; and the offer of his hand was a bit of flattering diplomacy which might make it easier to get them.[2]

Before the embassy returned with the answer, a chance—or so it seemed—of obtaining help in another and even more distant quarter suddenly cropped up, and Said snatched at it. In the autumn of 1833 a representative of the Government of the United States arrived at Muscat for the purpose of negotiating a commercial treaty with the ruler of Oman. He was warmly welcomed by Said, and, as will be more fully described in a later chapter, the treaty was quickly concluded.[3] But in the course of the negotiations—so at least it was reported to the Government of Bombay and credited by them—Said made an un-

[1] McLeod, op. cit. 74–89. You, op. cit. 30. L. Brunet, *L'Œuvre de la France à Madagascar* (Paris, 1903), 10, 338.
[2] B.R., Capt. Hart's Report, 277–8.   [3] See pp. 367–9, below.

expected proposition. He offered the Americans the right to erect commercial establishments or 'factories' at Zanzibar or at any point on the African coast on one condition—that they would lend him armed assistance for the capture of Mombasa.[1] Nothing, of course, came of it. The American Government was no more anxious than the British to engage in such a distant adventure, and even Owen's zeal had not gone the length of open warfare. So when in November 1833 Said sailed south to attack Mombasa for the third or fourth time, he had only his own Arabs and Baluchis to rely on. At Lamu, on his way down the coast, as it happened, he met his ambassador returning from Madagascar with letters from the Queen and from her ministers. Those departed missionaries, it appeared, had worked to good purpose; for all the letters were written in English, and, since neither Said nor any member of his suite could read them, their contents would have remained a tantalizing mystery if there had not been by chance at anchor off the port a British merchant-brig whose master—another stroke of luck in those days—could read.

'Thus it was [records Captain Hart, R.N., who visited Zanzibar a few weeks later] that His Highness became acquainted with the reply to his royal love from the Madagascar Queen. . . . The Queen said she had been made happy by hearing from one who had long been in friendship with her father, and she hoped always to hear of his welfare and wished he could pay a visit to Antananarivo. In case he did not do so, she would be very much obliged if he would have the kindness to send her a coral necklace of a thousand dollars, and she would order the money to be paid whenever it was landed. She hoped the friendship would increase and that opportunities would offer for their becoming better acquainted.

'The Ministers were also glad to hear of His Highness, and wished much that he would come and show himself or send some of his men-of-war which should have every attention paid to them. They could not offer the Queen because by their law it was contrary for her to marry, but there was a young princess which he might have. As for the men, he might have as many as he pleased.'

When the master of the brig came to tell this tale of a royal romance—and how often and with what gusto he must have

[1] Miles, ii. 335.

told it!—he made much of Said's disappointment. 'Why was there not more said about love in the Queen's letter?' The master did his best to console him. 'She had said as much as she could say in a first letter.' But one suspects that the *rusé* Arab diplomat was neither surprised nor disheartened by the tenor of Ranavolana's missive; that on the other hand he was delighted at the last words written by her ministers. One suspects, too, that he regretted the accident by which an Englishman had become privy to his dealings in that matter of the soldiers. For he seems to have felt that the calling in of forces other than his own to aid him in attacking Mombasa would be resented by his old friends in Bombay. He delayed to take advantage of the offer from Madagascar, and when, soon after his arrival at Zanzibar, he was visited by Captain Hart, he put the straight question to him.

'The Imam told me [says Hart] that the Mombasa people were in [a] state of rebellion and asked, if he were to send to Madagascar and get troops, whether the English would like it. I told him the English would not interfere between him and his subjects and that he could act as he pleased to subdue a rebellion in his own dominions. But he repeated "Will they *like* it?" That I could not tell.'

It is easy to imagine how strongly Said was tempted. 'An Arab will not fight,' Hart comments bluntly on this conversation, 'whilst those Malambo people from Madagascar are said to be good soldiers and desperate fellows.' And, though Said, of course, would never have admitted it, he knew in his heart that his own troops would never take Mombasa. He was fresh, indeed, from a further proof of it. On leaving Lamu he had carried out his projected attack. Yet once more he had thrown his Arabs and Baluchis at the impregnable island. Yet once more they had been beaten off; and after a week of inconclusive fighting Said had sailed on to Zanzibar, digesting as best he could the hard fact that without the help of other troops than his own he would never be able to force his way into Fort Jesus. At that particular moment, therefore, the temptation beckoning to Said from Madagascar must have been doubly difficult to resist; and it is remarkable testimony to his dread of a breach with the

British that he dared not yield. A month later, in compliance with the ministers' invitation, he sent the frigate *Piedmontese* to Madagascar; but it brought back no Malagasi soldiers. There is no evidence that he ever employed them.[1]

5

If Said had in fact obtained those soldiers and stormed Fort Jesus with their aid, the British authorities in Bombay and London would probably have shrugged their shoulders and recognized the accomplished fact. But his anxiety to do nothing to excite their suspicion or resentment was natural enough. He had not forgotten Owen; and British cruisers were still to be seen at times along the coast, helping in the execution of the 'Moresby Treaty'. Might not the Mazrui change their minds and ask again for the British flag? And might not another British captain prove as mad and masterful as Owen? And if in that event Bombay still backed its old friend at Muscat, would London still back Bombay?

Such apprehensions on Said's part would have been greatly accentuated if he could have known what was actually about to happen in London. A few months after his talk with Captain Hart nothing less than the 'Owen policy' with variations was again being pressed upon the British Government and by none other than Owen himself. Ten years, if they had dimmed his memory a little, had not diminished his ardour and ambition. In September 1834 he was in England and out of active service, and he wrote to Palmerston, then in his fourth year of office as Foreign Secretary, explaining that in 1824 and 1825 the Imam of Muscat had entrusted him with 'authority in his East African dominions second only to his own'. 'With his entire concurrence [*sic*] I accepted, subject to the approval of His Majesty's Government, the cession of Mombasa and all its dependent territory.' But 'the back-handed policy of interested parties prevented His Majesty's Government from acceding to the wishes of all parties concerned'; 'my little garrison' was withdrawn; and, owing to

[1] B.R., Captain Hart's Report, 277-8. Guillain, i. 597-9. Miles, ii. 336. For Hart's mission, see p. 373, below.

the Imam's efforts to capture Mombasa and to compel other towns on the coast to pay tribute, 'those beautiful countries have ever since been deluged in blood'. The Imam's character, nevertheless, was 'amiable, liberal and just', and one of three policies should now be adopted towards him. (1) 'Unreserved friendship . . . using our moral influence to confirm his authority everywhere on the whole line of coast and to modify his government [so] as to make it a blessing to his people.' (2) 'To accept the voluntary subjugation [to Britain] of the Mombassians and others who are now at war with the Imam, but on terms of friendly relations with him.' (3) 'To extend British government and British protection to all who ask it and have a right to dispose of themselves.' The third course would doubtless be incompatible with the maintenance of friendly relations with the Imam, but not the first or second. And in case either of those should be adopted, 'I beg to offer you my services as Consul-General for Eastern Africa and for South Arabia in the Indian Ocean, either to be attached to the person of the Imam or to a local residence at any point required'. 'Such a nomination', Owen boldly concludes, 'would, I have cause to believe, be agreeable to the Imam himself.'[1]

Palmerston referred this characteristic document to the two other departments concerned and received—it is not surprising —discouraging replies. Thomas Spring-Rice, who was Colonial Secretary for a few months in 1834, 'did not think that any advantage would accrue from the employment of Captain Owen in the manner suggested'.[2] The reply from the Board of Control was more vigorous. It had not been forgotten at the India House any more than in Bombay how impudently and clumsily Owen had thrust his fingers into the complex and delicate web of Arab politics; and fresh irritation had recently been provoked in those same quarters by the fact that the Admiralty had sent Captain Hart to Zanzibar without troubling to inform, still less to consult, the Indian authorities. His mission, it is true, had

---

[1] Owen to P., 8.ix.34 (F.O. 54. 1). To avoid confusion 'Imam' has been inserted for Owen's 'Sultan'.
[2] C.O. to P., 26.ix.34 (ibid.).

been only to inquire about the commercial treaty which Said was reported to have made with the United States; but a sharp remonstrance had gone from the India House to the Admiralty, pointing out the danger of negotiations with an Arab prince conducted independently by a department which—it was implied—knew nothing at all about him or his position in the Eastern world.[1] And now, in commenting on Owen's letter, the Board of Control took a very high line indeed. They virtually requested Palmerston to keep his hands off the Indian Ocean. 'No communication', they declared, 'with States like that of Muscat should be held except through the Governor-General of India in Council.' They then made short work of Owen's proposals. The appointment of a Consul-General would be 'very undesirable'. It would flatly contravene the principle just asserted, since a consular official 'would not be an officer of the Government of India nor under its control'. 'The policy', moreover, 'on which the appointment has been advocated by Captain Owen is at variance with that which in the opinion of the Indian Home Authorities should be pursued in respect to the Imam of Muscat, the bordering Arab tribes, and the states generally in the East.'[2] A rather provocative note, but Palmerston ignored the challenge. In minor matters, indeed, he was quite content to leave the affairs of Muscat to another department, and, when an application was made to the Foreign Office for an introduction to the Imam in 1836, he made the following pencil note on it: 'He should address himself to the Board of Control with whom our relations with the Imam rest. P.' But Palmerston, of course, or for that matter any other Foreign Secretary, could never admit the Indian claim to a monopoly of diplomatic action in the Indian Ocean; and he certainly intended if occasion should arise—as it did arise before long—to deal with Said or anybody else himself and not through the Government of India.[3] As to the immediate question at issue, on the other hand, he fully shared the Board's aversion to any more adven-

[1] Secret Committee to Admiralty, 27.viii.34 (F.O. 54. 1).
[2] India Board to Palmerston, 27.ix.34 (ibid.).
[3] Application: 2.v.36 (ibid.). See Chap. XV, below.

tures in East Africa whether they aimed at confirming Said's authority or offering protection against it, and he hoped, no doubt, that he had heard the last of Owen when he told his secretary to inform him, in plain, brief terms, that 'His Majesty's Government do not contemplate making any such appointments' as he had proposed.[1]

But he had not heard the last of him. Four years later a plea for the 'Owen policy' appeared once more on his table at the Foreign Office, and this time it came from a quarter he could not altogether disregard. Thomas Fowell Buxton, who had succeeded Wilberforce as the leader of the anti-slavery crusade, had convinced himself that the Atlantic Slave Trade could never be suppressed by the naval patrols alone. The only hope, he now believed, was to cut off the supply of slaves at the source by planting European settlements in Africa itself and developing a 'legitimate' trade in other natural products than human beings —a development of the 'positive policy' which, first preached by Pitt and Wilberforce, had inspired the ill-fated experiment at Bulama in 1792 and was presently to inspire the more elaborate but equally disastrous Niger Expedition of 1841.[2] The same doctrine, it seemed to Buxton, applied to East Africa, and he was deeply interested when in the autumn of 1838 a Quaker friend reminded him of the story of 'Owen's Protectorate' and reported to him the opinions of a certain Montgomery Martin who had been serving at that time as surgeon in the *Barracouta*.

'Martin says that Commander Owen who founded the settlement and governed it, who was much beloved by the natives, who likes the country, is a very fine clever fellow, though rather eccentric and half an Arab himself; he is now on a small island off New Brunswick, not sent there by Government, but King of it for his own pleasure; and he has no doubt he would willingly go to Mombasa as Governor.'

Buxton promptly passed on this somewhat equivocal testimonial to Lord Glenelg, now Colonial Secretary and the mouth-

[1] F.O. to Owen, 29.ix.34 (ibid.).
[2] Bulama: see pp. 157–8, above. Niger Expedition: W. L. Mathieson, *Great Britain and the Slave Trade*, chap. i; R. Coupland, *Kirk on the Zambesi*, 31–8.

piece of the humanitarian movement in the Cabinet, with the comment that Mombasa might be 'as important with regard to a portion of the East coast as Fernando Po is to the Western, and its attainment especially at the present moment far less difficult'. Might not Said be induced to give it or sell it to Britain as part of the commercial treaty which was then in process of negotiation?[1] Glenelg was sympathetic, and he sent on Buxton's letter together with Surgeon Martin's 'opinion' to the Foreign Office.[2]

The result was a mild explosion. Palmerston heartily disliked Buxton's new ideas of annexation. They were not only, he thought, impracticable; they were a danger to the cause he was fighting to uphold at least as stubbornly as any of the humanitarian leaders. For they were undermining public confidence in the tedious and costly system of naval blockade which Palmerston, in the belief that it was the only real means of suppressing the Trade, had been labouring for years to make more effective by extorting concessions as to the 'right of search' from foreign Governments. His reply, therefore, showed little tenderness towards Glenelg's or Buxton's opinions. Mombasa, he wrote, had been 'definitely evacuated' in 1826, and it was obviously impossible to set up 'a government establishment . . . in the territory of an ally'. The Commercial Treaty, moreover, about to be concluded with the Imam, would enable British merchants to settle anywhere they wished in his dominions.

'But, after all, this settlement scheme of Buxton's seems to Melbourne and myself a wild and crude idea. In order to extirpate the Slave Trade by commercial settlements you must begird with them the whole circumference of Africa. . . . As long as there should remain any great extent of coast unprovided with those commercial settlements you would not have cured the evil. But what an expensive and slow process it would be to stud the coast of Africa with 'factories', even if there were no political difficulties in the way!

'No doubt the extension of commerce in Africa is an object to be aimed at, but I am inclined to think that such extension will be the effect rather than the cause of the extinction of the Slave Trade. It is

[1] For the Treaty of 1839 see pp. 481–2, below.
[2] Glenelg to Palmerston, with enclosures, 10.ix.38 (F.O. 54. 2).

Europe and not Africa which takes the lead in the intercourse between those two quarters of the globe. We want to sell our commodities in Africa and we send them thither. The Africans who want to buy will pay us in whatever way we like. If we insist on having slaves, slaves they will produce. If we prefer being paid by elephants'-teeth and gold dust, those articles will be collected. . . .

'If then we can prevent Europeans from bringing slaves away from Africa, we shall at once convert the Trade into one of barter of commodities, and it is obviously far easier to catch and condemn slave-ships, supposing all the nations who have flags to have combined for the purpose, than to make the line of circumvallation of settlements and 'factories' which Buxton proposes. The reason why the Trade is so extensive is not that slave-ships elude the vigilance of our cruisers, but that this vigilance is rendered unavailing by want of Treaty Power.'[1]

Three weeks later Palmerston returned the documents to Glenelg with a brief covering note which finally quashed the scheme. Mombasa, it said, was now an acknowledged part of the Imam's dominions. He would not make us a gift of it, and Parliament would not consent to purchase it.[2]

That really was the last of Owen. He fades out of East African history into the mists of the North Atlantic, keeping his flag flying on his little private island.[3] But it was not the last of Owen's ideas; for behind his extravagant and egotistical presentation of them lay a durable core of truth. Buxton, up to a point, was right. The treaty-system and the naval patrol could and did diminish and restrict the Slave Trade in West Africa, but could not and did not eliminate it. Slave-smuggling did not completely stop till slaves were no longer saleable. And time was to show the same results on the east coast. 'The shortest and simplest form of check we shall ever be able to impose [on the Arab Slave Trade]', reported the Political Agent in the Persian Gulf to the Government of Bombay in 1842, 'is to obtain possession of the sea-ports or line of coast of Africa whence the slaves are exported and to prevent the arrival there of slaves

[1] Palmerston to Glenelg, 24.ix.38 (F.O. 54. 1).
[2] P. to G., 14.x.38 (F.O. 54. 2).
[3] Owen became a Vice-Admiral on the retired list in 1854 and died at St. John's, New Brunswick, in 1857.

from the interior or the sale of them.'[1] True enough, in East Africa as in West, though to a far less extent, slave-smuggling continued long after the system of treaties and patrols had been completely organized, and it was not wholly suppressed until not only the 'line of coast' but its hinterland too had been annexed and occupied by European governments.[2] And if up to to-day or yesterday slaves were still occasionally smuggled across the southern waters of the Red Sea, if a British naval patrol was still needed there to check it, the reason is simply

[1] Colonel Robertson to G. of B., 4.iii.42 (B.R. 645, note).

[2] The last slave-ship known of in East African waters was wrecked off Wasin Island, about sixty miles south of Mombasa, in the summer of 1899. The following account of the incident has been communicated by Sir Claud Hollis, G.C.M.G.: 'In 1899 I was Acting District Officer in charge of the Vanga District (the most southerly district of what in those days was the East Africa Protectorate), the headquarters of which were at Shimoni, immediately opposite Wasin Island. I was on the point of going to bed one night when the Sergeant of the East African Rifles (there were no police in the out-districts in those days) reported that news had just been received from Wasin Island that a large Arab dhow had been wrecked on the bank or reef on the South-West end of the island. It was raining hard at the time with a high wind blowing and one could hear the breakers booming on the reef. I started off at about 11 p.m. with the Goan Customs Officer and about 15 Askari in my large sailing boat, but we had to land at Wasin town on the north side of the island as it was too rough to leave the sheltered channel. We walked across the island to the fishing village Kunguni, and thence through the bush to the reef, but it was too dark to see anything, so we had to wait till morning, as we only had a few fishermen's dug-outs, and they could not put out in the rough sea. The dhow broke up about 5 a.m., and the master, some of the crew and (if I remember rightly) 13 out of 56 "passengers" were either washed ashore or rescued by my men and the people of Wasin in the dug-outs which they had managed to launch. It was not long before I learnt that the dhow was conveying slaves and not passengers to Muscat, and I arrested the master and crew. The dhow, which had left Bububu (Zanzibar) the night before without papers, belonged to a Muscat Arab who was the master, and the crew consisted partly of Arabs and partly of negroes from Arabia. The slaves had been kidnapped by an old dodge. They were induced by payment of double wages to carry at night loads of coconuts to the beach at Bububu, where they were seized and put on board. After the ship-wrecked people had been fed and rested, I arranged for them to be taken overland to Mombasa. The master and crew were tried in the High Court, and sentenced to varying terms of imprisonment. The captured slaves were sent back to Zanzibar and returned to their homes.'

that Europe, though it had directly or indirectly annexed the coast, held it lightly and did not hold the Abyssinian hinterland at all. Theoretical logic, in fact, was on Owen's and Buxton's side. Subsequent history has proved it. But in the common sense of the matter, in its 'practical politics', Owen and his school were surely wrong and Palmerston surely right. For it is difficult to believe that the British people, determined as they were to kill the Trade, could ever have been persuaded in those days that the only way to kill it was to embark on a gigantic programme of territorial annexation. They might find themselves forced, all other means failing, to occupy a single and specially atrocious smugglers' nest like Lagos; but the 'annexationist' logic was not logical at all, it did not provide for the complete cessation of the Trade, if it were content with piecemeal occupation here and there, with chasing smugglers out of one nest into another. It required, as Palmerston said, the occupation of 'the whole circumference of Africa'—and indeed a deep slice of the interior as well. A vast West African empire? No statesman of the time, it is safe to say, not Wilberforce himself if he had lived another twenty years, could have led the British people to the conquest of it. Still less in regard to remote, unknown East Africa could Englishmen of 1840 conceive the imperial dreams of 1890. Many years were to pass and much was to happen before the first tenuous connexion with that coast into which Britain had been drawn by her pursuit of the Slave Trade could develop to its last intimate stage of annexation.

6

When Palmerston finally rejected the 'Owen policy' in the autumn of 1838, he spoke of Mombasa as 'now an acknowledged part of the Sultan's dominions'. It was true. The long conflict was over. After eight years of frustrated effort Said had got his way at last, not by force—his own troops could never have stormed Fort Jesus and he had not obtained more daring soldiers from Madagascar or elsewhere—but by fraud.

It might have been supposed that the Mazrui were as much a match for Said at the one kind of game as at the other; but in a final spasm of their old reckless stupidity they had given themselves away. On the death of Sheikh Salim in the spring of 1835, incapable of breaking the Arab habit of disputing the succession, they had split into warring factions. Salim's son, Rashid, seized the fort; his opponents, including two of Salim's brothers, held the town. For over a year the deadlock lasted. It was not till the end of 1836 that the dispute was patched up and Rashid's succession generally recognized by the population. Meantime, however, some of the Arabs and Swahili of the town who were not members of the Mazrui clan, disgusted at the interminable quarrel, had conceived the fatal idea of asking Said to intervene. He leapt at the chance. In December 1836 he led his last expedition against Mombasa. But this time, instead of making another futile attack on the fort, he proceeded by intrigue and bribery to reopen the breach which had just been closed by Rashid's election. It was easy work. Rashid's rivals among the Mazrui had never in their hearts accepted the settlement; they saw themselves deposing him with Said's help. And the other Arabs and the Swahili were all the more ready to accept Said's gold because they knew his old feud was not with them but with the arrogant Mazrui. So, bit by bit, Rashid's adherents melted away until he realized that even the possession of the fort could not long avail him when the bulk of the population were against him and—worst of all—his own Mazrui were divided. So, in February 1837, when Said offered to throw over his own allies and confirm Rashid's appointment as Governor of Mombasa provided that he resided down in the town, he accepted the terms which his father and his father's predecessor had so often rejected. Said's troops, five hundred strong, took possession of Fort Jesus.[1]

First point, and the decisive point, to Said. But he had not finished the game, and he meant to finish it. Once before he had held the fort and lost it again. He could not yet feel that Mombasa was safely and permanently his. So he invited Rashid to

[1] Guillain, i. 601-5. Miles, ii. 339-40.

The Fate of the Mazrui

Zanzibar and offered him three choices. Would he accept a gift of 10,000 piastres and a life-pension of 300 piastres and together with the other leading members of his family take up his residence in Zanzibar? Or would he take the Governorship of Mafia with its emoluments? Or, still more tempting, the Governorship of Pemba? These were liberal offers; but all of them meant exile from Mombasa, the stage on which for generations past, right back into the days of Portuguese dominion, the Mazrui had played their part in history. Rashid refused the offers. Of all the other leading members of the clan who had come with him to Zanzibar, including his two uncles and rivals, not one questioned his decision.[1]

Said concealed his disappointment. He continued to treat Rashid and his kinsmen as honoured guests and sent them back to Mombasa with the customary presents. Two months later, Khalid, Said's second son, followed them thither and carried out his father's orders. He received Rashid and the other notables in the friendliest manner when they came to pay their visit of courtesy on board his ship. Two days later he went ashore and held another *durbar* outside the gate of Fort Jesus. At the conclusion of their formal interviews first Rashid alone and then some twenty-five to thirty of his leading kinsmen, singly and in twos and threes, were invited into the fort for a political discussion. Inside the gate they were seized, gagged, and bound by Said's garrison, carried off to the ships, and conveyed to Zanzibar. Thence, after a month of suspense, they were dispatched by Said to Bunder Abbas. Some of them, it is said, were dropped overboard on the way. Those who survived the voyage were thrown into prison. They were never heard of again. British officials on the Gulf believed that they were starved to death.[2]

Thenceforward Said was the undisputed master of Mombasa. The rest of the Mazrui, on hearing of the capture of their leaders,

[1] Guillain, i. 605–6. Miles, ii. 340. A piastre was worth between four and five shillings.
[2] Guillain, i. 607–8. Miles, ii. 340.

fled to the mainland; and little more was heard of their once famous name until in 1895 the descendants of those fugitives followed with hereditary recklessness another Mbaruk and another Rashid into a futile rebellion against British rule.[1]

[1] For the dispatches on this rebellion, including a brief memorandum by (Sir) Arthur Hardinge on the history of the Mazrui, see *Correspondence respecting the recent Rebellion in British East Africa*, 1896 [C.–8274].

X
SEYYID SAID AT ZANZIBAR: ECONOMICS

1

THE capture of Mombasa in 1837 cleared the way at last for that master-move of his long career which Said had evidently been contemplating for several years. It was significant that, probably during his second visit to Zanzibar in 1830, he had begun to build himself a sea-side palace (Bet-el-Mtoni) some five miles from the town, and a little later he had built another in the town itself (Bet-el-Sahil). Between 1832 and 1837 he had spent as much time at Zanzibar as at Muscat; and now in 1840 he practically transferred his court to Zanzibar. There was no formal announcement of the move. He still visited Muscat from time to time: he could not help it. But in fact his 'permanent' residence was at Zanzibar. He had decided to make it the new capital of the Omani realm.[1]

It was a strange and a daring decision. To shift his home and throne from Oman to an island across 2,500 miles of sea, not easily navigable by sailing-ships except at the fixed periods of the 'monsoon', was not only a startling break with the immemorial traditions of Oman's history; it was to risk, it was almost to invite, those internal dissensions in Oman which had already shown themselves to be the wellnigh automatic sequel to his departure from the country. Why, then, did he do it?

The physical attractions of East Africa were obvious enough. To escape from the torrid heat of Muscat, one of the fiercest spots on earth for four months of the year, to the equable warmth of Zanzibar, from the drought and dust of almost rainless Oman and its labouring well-wheels to a land of seasonal rainfall and running springs, from glaring brown rock and yellow

[1] Hart reported the current belief that Said was contemplating the transfer in 1834. B.R. 280. Krapf dates the transfer definitely in 1840: *Travels*, &c. (London, 1860), 123. Bet-el-Sahil was destroyed in the bombardment of Zanzibar in 1895. The ruins of Bet-el-Mtoni are still standing. Photographs in Said-Ruete, op. cit.

sand to verdure and fertility—all that in itself must have been as tempting to Said as it had been long ago to the first Omani settlers on the African coast.[1] But these were not the only contrasts. At Muscat Said was caught fast in a ferment of intrigue which might be checked by his personal presence and prestige but never stopped. Ring on ring of potential enemies encircled him—his uncles and his cousins, the outlying tribes of Oman, the faithless Jawasmi, the arrogant Wahabi. At Zanzibar he was in another world. The loyalty of the local Arab 'colonists' was notorious, and when Said first landed at Zanzibar in 1828 they had received him with tumultuous enthusiasm as the head of the house to which for a century past, ever since the beginning of the Omani conquest, they had maintained unbroken allegiance. Unlike some of their kinsmen on the coast, they had preferred the overlordship of Muscat to that of Mombasa; and in response their Muscat overlords had protected them more than once from Mazrui aggression. There were self-seekers and double-dealers among them, notably the chiefs of the el-Harthi tribe; but they were not likely to give trouble as long as Said lived. Nor had he anything to fear in other quarters. The native population of the island paid him its tribute as submissively as ever.[2] In the neighbouring coast towns, once the Mazrui had been disposed of, there was no prospect of any formidable challenge to his peace or power. No restless hinterland lay at his back—only the unknown spaces of torpid Africa. To take refuge, then, as it were, in that remote little island, with

[1] C. P. Rigby, British Consul at Zanzibar from 1858 to 1861, giving evidence before a House of Commons Committee: 'I often said to the Sultan (Majid), "You Arabs come down here because you find a very pleasant and fertile country preferable to your own barren deserts."' *Report of Select Committee on East African Slave Trade*, 1871, 420, Q. 576. For a contemporary description of Muscat, see Capt. Taylor in 1818, B.R. 10; J. B. Fraser in 1821, *Narrative*, 7; Capt. Owen in 1824, *Narrative*, i. 336–9; Col. Hamerton in 1855, B.R. 238–9. All agree as to the heat and smell and the meanness of the buildings. Fraser, for instance, writes of the 'small and ill-built houses and huts of date-tree leaves of the most wretched description, hardly sufficient to give shelter from the weather, all huddled together in the greatest confusion.... That of the Imam, though a building of stone and lime ... is still poor enough.'

[2] See p. 321, below.

those of his relatives and his notables he chose to have about him, to set that gulf of sea between his new home and feverish Arabia, must have been as tempting an idea as it was dangerous. And suppose the danger materialized, suppose his migration meant the loosening of his hold on Oman. Arabs had always been migrants. Time and again in the past Said's ancestors had folded their tents and sought new grazing-grounds across the desert. Might he not acquire in Africa a wider power, a richer patrimony, than all he had inherited in Asia?

Once that idea had lodged in Said's mind, the obvious advantages of Zanzibar, strategic and commercial, must soon have led him to his great decision. It possessed a commodious harbour, seven to nine fathoms deep, ringed by islets and coral-reefs. Its supply of fresh water for a voyage was the best on all the East African coast. And, no doubt, though Muscat was almost unassailable by land, the fact that Zanzibar could only be approached by sea was a further attraction in Said's eyes. For, like other Arabs of an earlier and greater age, Said was more a sailor than a soldier. The story of Mombasa has sufficiently exposed his weakness in the field. His military operations, despite his personal courage, had usually miscarried; they had ended sometimes in humiliating defeat; and his political triumphs in Arabia had been achieved more by astute diplomacy and British backing and good fortune than by the force of Omani arms. Some of his people were good enough fighters, but not all. 'As great a coward as a Muscatee' was an Arab saying of the time. And, had they all been as brave as their ruler, Arab custom would not have permitted their maintenance and training as regular troops. The tribesmen would follow their leader to war; but for a permanent force Said had only as many foreign mercenaries, mostly Baluchi or Persian, as he could afford or thought it worth while to employ, and in 1855 that was only some 1,500. A fleet that could be quickly manned with Arab seamen and Indian 'lascars' was a readier and trustier weapon, and Said had begun early to forge it. In 1834 his navy, gathered at Zanzibar, consisted of one British-built line-of-battle ship, the *Liverpool* (1,800 tons and 74 guns), three frigates (36, 26, and 24 guns), two corvettes, and a brig, with a bunch of armed dhows; and Captain Hart, who saw and listed it on his visit to Zanzibar in that year, observed that it appeared 'to constitute his [Said's] great pleasure and amusement'. On board the flagship 'he conducts everything himself; gets her under weigh, shifts her berth, or brings her to anchor, by giving every word of command'. Said, it seems, was happier, more at home, on the quarter-deck than in the saddle.[1]

Whether this fleet was an effective instrument of war it is difficult to say. Said mainly used it for convoying troops or for bombarding or blockading hostile seaports. There is no record of its having ever fought a full-scale naval action. What other fleet was there in the Indian Ocean, except the pirates of the Gulf, for it to fight? It was natural enough that Captain Roberts, the American Commissioner, who had visited Cochin China and Siam on his way to Muscat in 1833, should be impressed by the relative strength of Said's navy. It was larger when he saw it at Muscat than when Hart had seen it at Zanzibar. Besides the *Liverpool*, he counted five ships of over 30 guns, one of 24, one of 22, two of 18, and two of 12; and he observed that the officers had 'good chronometers' and had been trained, at Bombay for the most part, in taking lunar observations. Judging by these appearances, he roundly asserted that Said possessed 'a more efficient naval force than all the native princes combined from the Cape of Good Hope to Japan'.[2] Captain Hamerton, on the other hand, who seems, when he first came to Zanzibar as British Consul in 1841, to have somewhat underestimated Said's power and prestige, was inclined to

[1] Hart's Report: B.R. 281–3. Number of troops: Brucks, ibid. 633. 'Lascar' crews: Owen, *Narrative*, i. 340.
[2] E. Roberts, *Embassy to the Eastern Courts of Cochin China, Siam, and Muscat, 1832–4* (New York, 1837), 361–3. Captain Geisinger of the *Peacock* in which Roberts sailed wrote home of Said's visit to the ship: 'He examined every part of the ship and expressed himself in strong terms of admiration at what he considered her fine condition etc. The Sultan, having made several voyages in his own ships of war to his possessions in Africa and elsewhere, is considered to be a good judge of anything relating to naval affairs.' C. O. Paullin, *Early Voyages of American Naval Vessels to the Orient*, 720.

scoff at his 'building ships and keeping them to rot at their anchors' and asserted that his fleet was only dreaded in so far as it was thought to have British sea-power at its back.[1] But Said's dominant interest was not the fleet; it was trade. 'I am nothing but a merchant', he said with a smile to a French traveller who visited him not long before his death; and there was more than mock-modesty in the remark.[2] Power, prestige, security—these, no doubt, had been Said's major aims; but to attain them wealth was needed, and for wealth an increase of public and private revenue, and for that a growth of trade. If Said was a great deal more than a merchant, it was to trade that he devoted most of his thought and energy for the latter half of his long life; and it was the prospects it offered of a great development in trade that more than anything else determined Said's move to Zanzibar. Direct taxation, it must be remembered, was almost unknown in the Arab world; and, apart from such 'tribute' as Said levied from the Zanzibar natives or paid himself to the Wahabi, almost the only source of public revenue was customs and excise duties on external and internal trade. Thus, according to the rough estimates made by Captain Brucks, who surveyed the Arabian and African coasts for the Bombay Government between 1829 and 1835, three-quarters of Said's revenue, which was put at about 600,000 German crowns (about £137,000), consisted of customs dues.[3] The next largest item (80,000 crowns) accrued from a similar tax on the 'internal' Slave Trade, i.e. the trade between different parts of Said's dominions. The bulk of the imports, inanimate or animate, on which these taxes were levied, were not 'consumed' on the spot: they were re-exported to Egypt, inner Arabia, Persia, and India; and the volume of this through-trade was at least as great at Zanzibar as at Muscat, because Zanzibar was the

[1] H. to Palmerston, 5.i.42 (F.O. 54. 4). See also p. 473, below.
[2] 'Ses affaires, c'était là toute sa vie, et il s'en préoccupait bien autrement que de sa dignité royale, ou, pour mieux dire, sa dignité royale avait surtout cette valeur de lui créer une position commerciale unique dans le monde.' A. de Gobineau, *Trois ans en Asie* (Paris, 1905), 99.
[3] For 'German crowns' or 'Maria Theresa dollars', see p. 304, below.

natural entrepôt and outlet for most of the exports from East Africa.[1] Thus, while the low cliffs at Mombasa and the narrow inlet to the harbour made it strategically stronger than the flat coast-line of Zanzibar, its commercial position was far weaker. It lay away to the north. Its hinterland soon merged into the barren and thinly populated Nyika. Behind that were the Taita, Kamba, Kikuyu, Masai, and similar tribes about the highlands and lakes of Kenya, then the Galla of the Abyssinian foot-hills, and away in the coastal deserts of the north the Somali, all fierce fighters. Never, it seems, did slave-traders from outside gain a foothold there, and the amount of ivory or other goods that came down from the interior to Mombasa was relatively small.[2] Zanzibar, on the other hand, was central; the fertile maritime belt on the opposite coast was deeper and better peopled; and inland towards the Great Lakes, spreading slowly farther and farther westward and south-westward, lay the slave-hunter's paradise. If Said's mind was set on the development of trade, neither Muscat nor Mombasa nor any place in his dominions was as well suited as Zanzibar to be the centre of his operations.

2

It was trade, then, above all else, that drew Said to Zanzibar, and Said drew with him from Muscat not only many of his own Omani subjects who were of little use for trade but many also of those Indian merchants and bankers and shopkeepers who from time immemorial had been the mainstay of all oversea trade in the Indian Ocean. Already at Muscat Said had done all he could to attract these indispensable 'banyans'; there were over a thousand of them residing there before he moved to Zanzibar; and when the English traveller, Palgrave, visited the

[1] Brucks reckoned Muscat's customs revenue at 180,000 crowns and the total revenue from Zanzibar (exclusive of Slave Trade receipts but presumably inclusive of the native 'tribute' or poll-tax) at 220,000.
[2] Consul Rigby reported in 1861: 'No slaves are brought [to Zanzibar] from the coast of Africa to the north of Mombasa, the tribes being too fierce and warlike, and the Galla and Somali tribes are never made slaves.' *Report*, 9. For Mombasa trade, see p. 242, above.

place in 1863, seven years after Said's death, and observed its rapid decline from the 'golden times' it had enjoyed some thirty years before, he ascribed it mainly to the less favourable treatment accorded to the 'banyans'.

'Sa'eed knew that, whatever might be the energy and enterprise of his own born subjects, their commercial transactions would never attain real importance except by the co-operation and under the lead of Indian merchants, and accordingly used every means in his power to allure the Banians of Cutch, Guzerat, and the Concan to Muscat, and by absolute toleration, special immunities, and constant patronage rendered the port a half-Hindoo colony. Nor had ever a government more useful, more steady-working, and more inoffensive *protégés* than the Banians proved themselves to Oman: interfering with no one, seeking nothing beyond their direct line of business, unobtrusive, courteous, and above all far more skilled in the mysteries of the ledger and the counter than ever Arab was or will be, they made the good fortune of Muscat and were its favourable genius.'[1]

It was the same at Zanzibar. His Arab subjects might resent their coming, might be jealous of these intruders doing profitable business which they ought to do themselves, might talk bitterly of their dishonesty and avarice, as thriftless borrowers all the world over have always talked of alien money-lenders. But to Said no immigrants were more welcome to his new and fast-growing capital than 'banyans'. He could not make his people treat them as he treated them himself. An American naval officer, calling at Zanzibar in 1835, observed that the 'banyans'—there were already between 300 and 400 of them—were 'despised by the Arabs and obliged to submit to insult and indignity'.[2] But Said made what amends he could. He gave the

[1] W. G. Palgrave, *Narrative of a Year's Journey through Central and Eastern Arabia* (London, 1865), ii. 369–70. J. B. Fraser also commented on the Hindu business men at Muscat in 1821 who numbered about 1,000 and were protected and encouraged by the Imam. *Narrative of a Journey into Khorasan* (London, 1825), 6.

[2] W. S. W. Ruschenberger, *Narrative of a Voyage round the World during the years 1835, 1836, and 1837* (London, 1838), 42. Captain Guillain, when at Zanzibar between 1846 and 1848, took the Arab view, and denounces in his book the greed, vindictiveness, and dishonesty of the 'banyans'. 'Ce sont les plus rusés commerçants de ces contrées, et peut-être du monde entier . . . . Ne consommant rien qui n'ait été

fullest toleration to their faith. He laid no dues or restrictions of any sort on them. He took them into his own service and even into his confidence. 'Some of them', reported Brucks, 'have great influence with the Imam who finds it greatly to his interest and the benefit of his revenues to give them every encouragement.'[1] The financial side of the government itself was entrusted largely to them; and the key-post, the collection of the customs, was always held by a 'banyan'. Nor were these Hindus, who mostly came from Cutch and Kathiawar, the only immigrants from India. Moslems, also, of the Khoja and Bhora sects from Cutch, Surat, and Bombay settled at Zanzibar in equal or greater numbers. 'A very thrifty and industrious people', according to Rigby, they took their share in trade and shopkeeping and could compete at times with the richer and more powerful 'banyans' even in 'big business'. Unlike the 'banyans', moreover, who never brought their wives with them from India and always looked forward to returning thither as soon as they had made enough money to retire, the Moslems were mostly true settlers: they made permanent homes for themselves and their families at Zanzibar; and by the end of Said's reign a new and still spreading quarter of the town had grown up, populated entirely by them. The Moslems from India, therefore, must be reckoned with the Hindus in the business community of Said's capital. Nor was it only at Zanzibar that Indians settled. Each Arab coast town had its little group of Indian traders. There were said to be as many as forty to sixty of them 'constantly resident' in the neighbourhood of Kilwa in 1843. Apart from the Slave Trade they did good business with the natives as small retailers. 'As they [the natives] do not know the use of money', notes Christopher, 'they are dealt with in barter very much to the advantage of our Indian subjects.' Thus, on the mainland as well as at Zanzibar, the Indian invaders of East Africa prospered and

apporté de ses pays et convertissant tous ses bénéfices en espèces métalliques qu'il y envoie, le banian est, pour les contrées où il trafique, un parasite qui prend toujours et ne rend rien.' Op. cit. ii. 123-4. For the ill treatment of the 'banyans' by the Arabs of Mombasa, see pp. 249-50, above.   [1] B.R. 631.

multiplied under Said's régime. In 1844, when Said had been settled at Zanzibar only four years, there were over one thousand of them. In 1860 there were between five and six thousand.[1]

But if Indian immigrants were thus welcomed and favoured, they were given no *exclusive* commercial privileges. The founder of Zanzibar, like the founder of Singapore, believed in free trade. In one part of his dominions only did Said take any steps to protect his own and his subjects' trade from external competition. Along the stretch of coast between Pangani and Kilwa he prohibited the export of ivory and gum-copal under any flag but his own.[2] Apart from that he claimed no monopoly and conceded none; and one of his first and wisest moves was a drastic assault on the multiplicity, uncertainty, and irregularity of the customs and other port dues which irritated and discouraged merchants from oversea. Customs varied, it appears, from one of his ports to another. Duties might be charged at will on exports as well as imports. Payments of varying amount were required for pilotage and anchorage. And, as a matter of course, the port officials demanded and received their bribes. At the time of Captain Smee's visit in 1811, the Governor of Zanzibar himself had taken the lead in the business of extortion. All this tangle of obstruction to the easy flow of trade was steadily cut down by Said until in course of time he had reduced it to a system so simple, uniform, and liberal as to be almost complete free trade. No harbour dues or pilot dues were levied, or any other charge on shipping or navigation, or duties of excise on internal production, or even export duties. The one and only tax was a flat 5 per cent. import duty paid on all goods, except bullion, landed, or transhipped from one vessel to another, at any port in Said's dominions. If bribes were still solicited, they could no longer be enforced.[3]

Another measure for easing and simplifying trade was an

[1] Rigby, 4. Christopher, *T.B.G.S.* vi. 378. Numbers of Indians: Hamerton, *1844 Report*, 5; memorandum by Cogan, 29.i.46 (F.O. 54. 10); Guillain, ii. 80; Rigby, 4.

[2] See pp. 386, 423, 481, below.

[3] Rigby, 19. No duty was levied on cargo landed or transhipped from a vessel under repair. Smee's evidence, see p. 181, above.

expansion of the currency. When Said came to Zanzibar the only coins in circulation were 'Maria Theresa dollars', also known as 'German crowns', and Spanish dollars which were both rated at 4½ or 4¾ to the English sovereign. Broken sums were paid in somewhat varying measures of holcus grain. It was a great step forward, therefore, when about 1840 Said obtained from Bombay 5,000 dollars' worth of the small copper coins of British India, called 'pice', and put them into circulation at the rate of about 135 to the dollar. At the end of his reign Spanish dollars had disappeared, and 'Maria Theresa dollars', though still the standard currency and still being minted at Vienna from the die of 1780 for use in East Africa, were beginning to grow scarce, while Indian pice had spread so widely up and down the coast that they too were often unobtainable and had risen in value to 110 or 130 to the dollar according to the supply.[1]

Still more important in their results were the constructive measures which Said adopted to increase the volume of trade. These fell into three main divisions, and in each his policy was again a wise policy and again successful.

He set himself, in the first place, to stimulate the export of the chief products of the African mainland—ivory, slaves, gum-copal, coco-nuts, copra, and palm-oil. Most of them needed little attention. The bulk of the gum-copal was extracted from the soil a few miles inland, and an inferior quality was found in Zanzibar Island itself.[2] The products of the coco-palm were similarly within easy reach in the plantations on the coast. But ivory and slaves could only be obtained by long, costly, and sometimes dangerous expeditions into the interior; and, though it is not known how systematic or comprehensive Said's methods were, it is certain that during his reign the whole system of

[1] Rigby, 26. R. H. Crofton, 'A Century of Currency', in *Zanzibar Gazette*, Oct. 24, 1925. For the 'Maria Theresa dollar', see C. R. Fay, *Imperial Economy* (Oxford, 1934), 107, and M. Fischel's entertaining monograph, *Le Thaler de Marie-Thérèse* (Paris, 1912), reviewed by J. M. Keynes in *Economic Journal*, xxiv (1914), 257. The dollars are still current in Abyssinia, the Red Sea coast, Aden, and the Sudan. The Royal Mint issued 150,000 in 1936. (*The Times*, 7.vi.38.)

[2] Rigby, 21.

inland trade was extended and elaborated far beyond the more or less casual operations in which the Arabs of the coast had been engaged for ages past. More and bigger caravans were organized and they penetrated deeper into the continent. New trade-routes were explored. New trading-settlements were founded. For all this there is copious evidence. The European discovery of the Great Lakes occurred in the years immediately succeeding Said's death in 1856. Burton and Speke first saw Lake Tanganyika and Speke Lake Victoria Nyanza in 1858. Livingstone first saw Lake Nyasa in 1859. And from the records of their wanderings through Tanganyika, Nyasaland, and North-East Rhodesia (as now those lands are known) a clear view can be obtained of the Arab exploitation of the interior at the close of Said's reign.

The principal route, which has naturally become with some deviations the line of the modern railway from the coast to Lake Tanganyika, started from Bagamoyo opposite Zanzibar, ran south-west to Kisaki (or Zungomero), and then went north-west through the rising uplands to Tabora,[1] then as now the nodal point of trade and communication in the interior. A second route or group of routes led from Kilwa and other ports south of Zanzibar towards Lake Nyasa. One of them, followed by Livingstone in 1866, ran up the River Rovuma and across the highlands at its source to Mataka's, the 'metropolis' of the Yao tribe, not far from the lake. Thence it branched to two lakeside villages, Losewa and Ngombo, where some thirty small dhows were stationed for the transport of goods, principally human, from the opposite shore.[2] A third main route ran from Tanga past Mount Kilimanjaro to Burgenej and thence towards Victoria Nyanza.[3] These trade-routes were used, no doubt, by the Arabs of the coast before Said's time. Prior was informed in

[1] The large and straggling African town was called Unyanyembe. It lies a mile or two north of Tabora, which as the centre of the provincial administration has long overshadowed it. The Central Railway runs from Dar-es-Salaam through Tabora to Kigoma on Lake Tanganyika near Ujiji. There is a branch line from Tabora to Mwanza on Lake Victoria.
[2] Livingstone, Last Journals (London, 1874), i, chaps. 3 and 4.
[3] Krapf, 487 note.

1812 that most of the thousands of slaves exported from Kilwa in earlier days had been obtained 'from a considerable distance in the interior'; and in 1850 the Swahili captain of a dhow in which Krapf was sailing down the coast told the missionary that 'many years ago he had journeyed with a caravan from Kilwa to the country of the Yao near Lake Nyasa' where slaves had been obtained from beyond the lake.[1] But after 1840 there was evidently a great increase in Arab enterprise; the routes extended farther inland and carried far more caravans than ever before. Burton was always inquiring as he moved from place to place about the development of Arab trade, and the information he obtained was sometimes fairly definite in point of time. A wealthy and widely travelled Arab at Tabora told him, for instance, that about fifteen years ago—i.e. about 1842—'the line of traffic [on the main route from Bagamoyo] ended at Usanga and Usenga', roughly one hundred miles west of Tabora; and he learned elsewhere that Ujiji, on the shore of Lake Tanganyika, about another hundred miles farther on, was 'first visited by the Arabs about 1840'.[2] Now by 1858, when Burton and Speke were there, Ujiji had become a regular outpost of Arab trade. Caravans from Tabora were frequently coming and going, and new routes had been developed up and down the lake. Southwards there was an Arab settlement on Kazenge Island, close to the western shore, whence caravans penetrated to the south beyond the River Marungu even, it was said, as far as Kasembe and the Katanga copper-mines, and to the west into the Urua country, where Livingstone was to find them ten years later collecting slaves and ivory on the upper reaches of the Congo. 'It will be seen', says Speke, 'that the Zanzibar Arabs have reached the uttermost limits of their tether; for Urua is half-way across the continent, and in a few years they must unite their labours with the people who come from Loanda on the opposite coast.'[3] Northward, also, new routes had been

---

[1] Prior, 80. Krapf, 419.
[2] Burton, *Lake Regions of Central Africa* (London, 1860), i. 324, ii. 57.
[3] J. H. Speke, *What Led to the discovery of the Source of the Nile* (London, 1864), 199, 229, 241. Burton, op. cit. 151.

opened up. From Ujiji and Uvira at the northern end of Lake Tanganyika Arabs had made their way through Ruanda to Bunyoro. From Tabora they had reached Victoria Nyanza in the neighbourhood of Mwanza and following up its shore had finally attained Kampala, the capital of the kingdom of Buganda. A Swahili or half-Arab trader from the coast entered Buganda in 1848. A Baluchi deserter from the ranks of Said's mercenaries took service with King Suna (c. 1832–57) a few years later. The first pure Arab to be seen in Buganda was Snay-bin-Amir of Tabora, Burton's informant mentioned above: he made the journey to Kampala in 1852. At that point Arab penetration stopped. To push farther north, to follow down the Nile, to make contact in the end with other Arabs in the Sudan, was impossible. Suna forbade it.[1]

Thus, in the course of fifteen years or so, the field of commercial exploitation had been extended westwards beyond all the three Great Lakes by those pioneering caravans in quest of slaves and ivory. Burton, Speke, and Livingstone often saw them, winding in single file along the narrow track through forest and jungle and high grass—the native guide at the head bearing a scarlet flag, if the travellers hail from Zanzibar, to show that they are under Seyyid Said's protection;[2] then the long straggling line of slaves, some of them old and tried, others newly bought or kidnapped, all carrying on their heads the bundles of all shapes and sizes that made up the baggage-bales of cloth, bags of beads, and coils of wire for buying with, tusks that have been bought, grain and rice and fowls for the hurried

[1] Burton, ii. 116, 120, 176, 186, 193. Speke, 229, 255. H. B. Thomas and R. Scott, *Uganda* (Oxford, 1935), 7. 'Buganda' is the correct spelling of the better-known 'Uganda'. Burton and Speke refer to Kibuga, which is the native town adjoining Kampala. That the penetration of the country west of Lake Tanganyika began about the end of Said's reign is confirmed from another source. H. Brode in *Tippoo Tib* (London, 1907), 17–19, puts it from oral evidence about or a little before 1856 to 1859.

[2] 'When all is ready, the Kirangozi or Nyamwezi guide rises and shoulders his load which is ever one of the lightest. He deliberately raises his furled flag, a plain blood-red, the sign of a caravan from Zanzibar, much tattered by the thorns.' Burton, i. 346.

meal in the early morning and the lazier one at night; at intervals along the line a few Swahili or trusted slaves with guns; and last the Arab merchant or company of merchants who finance and command the whole adventurous enterprise. On the shorter trade-routes a caravan might be only a few score strong; but for the long dangerous journeys far inland fifty Arabs or more might join forces and the whole party might number one thousand men and over. The expansion of Arab trade on such a scale was a new experience for East Africa. The steady progress of those big, determined, well-armed bands was usually irresistible. 'When two bodies meet', says Burton, 'that commanded by an Arab claims the road.'[1] That scrap of scarlet bunting weaving its way through the dry brown 'bush', penetrating deeper and deeper into the unknown, signalized the first real 'invasion' of the East African interior.[2]

And it was a little more than invasion. In a very limited and localized sense it was occupation too. The progress of the caravans, especially in rough country or wet weather, was very slow. The journey from Tabora to Ujiji, for example, though only about 100 miles, was rarely done in less than twenty-five days. When the season of heavy and steady rain set in, swelling the rivers and streams and converting soft stretches of low ground into bog, movement was almost impossible. The caravan season, therefore, was normally the dry period between the end of the 'greater rains' in April or May and the beginning of the 'lesser rains' in October or November; and since that period was

[1] Burton, ii. 351.

[2] Krapf observed that caravans starting inland from Mombasa were from 600 to 1,000 strong, but those starting from Bagamoyo or other ports for Nyamwezi and the lakes 'consist generally of from three to four thousand men that they may be strong enough to defend themselves on the way from the attacks of hostile tribes'. Krapf, 364, 421. Burton's estimate is lower. 'It is impossible to average the numbers of an East African caravan which varies from half a dozen to 200 porters under a single merchant. In dangerous places travellers halt till they form an imposing force; 500 is a frequent figure, and even bodies of 1,000 men are not rare. The only limit to the gathering is the incapability of the country to fill more than a certain number of mouths. The larger caravans, however, are slow and cumbrous, and in places they exhaust the provision of water.' *Lake Regions*, i. 341.

not long enough for an expedition to the Great Lakes or beyond, allowing time for trading and in suitable country for slave-raiding, the long-range Arab merchants and their dependants were accustomed to settle down somewhere up-country during the wet weather and to stay away from their homes on the coast or at Zanzibar for two years and sometimes more. Here and there, accordingly, little Arab 'colonies' grew up along the inland trade-routes. One such colony was founded at Sena long before Said's time,[1] but no more of them are heard of till the founding of Tabora, probably about 1830. It stood in the heart of the central uplands at a natural cross-ways of trade, and the growth of that trade soon made it the largest and most famous of the colonies. When Burton and Speke saw it in 1857-8, it was not what they could call a 'town'. It had no fixed bounds or centre or any regular street. It consisted of a number of separate little hamlets, a group of four Arab houses here, another group of six there, and so on, each group surrounded by a cluster of native huts. The average number of Arabs in residence was twenty-five. At the height of the season most of them were 'scattered in trading trips', leaving sometimes only three or four behind. They lived, says Burton, 'comfortably and even splendidly'.

'The houses, though single-storied, are large, substantial, and capable of defence. Their gardens are extensive and well-planted; they receive regular supplies of merchandise, comforts and luxuries from the coast; they are surrounded by troops of concubines and slaves whom they train to divers crafts and callings; rich men have riding-asses from Zanzibar and even the poorest keep flocks and herds.... There are itinerant *fundi* or slave-artisans—blacksmiths, tinkers, masons, carpenters, tailors, potters, and rope-makers—who come up from the coast with Arab caravans.... The traveller can always recruit his stock of country currency—cloth, beads and wire—his requirements of powder and ball, and his supply of spices, comforts, and drugs without which travel in these lands usually ends fatally.'[2]

Speke, who was less interested in Arabs than in Africans, is more laconic. To live at Tabora in a substantial house provided

---

[1] See pp. 30, 50, above.   [2] Burton, i. 326-34.

by Sheikh Snay-bin-Amir, enjoying the generous hospitality with which the explorers seem always to have been treated by the Arab merchants, 'surrounded by an Arab community, felt like living in a civilised land'.[1]

The Arabs were evidently making money. Snay-bin-Amir himself was a notable example of the profit to be won in East Africa, as in other lands and at other times, by colonial pioneering. He had started life as a confectioner at Muscat. Fifteen years of trading had made him one of the wealthiest Arabs in all East Africa. The house he had built at Tabora and the guest-house, the storehouses of 'currency goods' and ivory, the slave-compound—it was a village in itself. Nor was it only Arabs or half-Arabs who prospered on the inland trade. In the interior as on the coast, where there were Arabs, there were also Indians; and the story of Musa Mzuri, the leading Indian at Tabora, to whom as well as to the Arab merchants the British explorers carried a personal letter of introduction from Said's successor at Zanzibar, is even more remarkable than Snay's. Born at Surat, a Moslem of the Kojah sect, he was driven by poverty to follow his elder brother to Zanzibar. The pair of them were employed at first by the Governor to make trading journeys on the mainland, but after a while they essayed a little gamble of their own in the ivory trade. They bought a small stock of beads, set out inland, and returned with a load of tusks weighing—so the story went—some 28,000 pounds. His brother's death left Musa all the profit. He went from strength to strength. He was ahead of the first Arabs in exploring the country westwards of Tabora. When Burton and Speke saw him, he had become at the age of forty-five or so the pre-eminent man of business, the Ludha Damji, of the interior.

'He is the recognized doyen of the commercial body, and he acts agent and warehouseman. His hall is usually full of buyers and sellers, Arab and African; and large investments of wire, beads, and cotton-cloths, some of them valuable, are regularly forwarded to him from the coast.'

'His gains', adds Burton, 'are principally represented by out-

[1] Speke, 254–5.

lying debts; he cannot, therefore, leave the country without an enormous sacrifice.' But why should he? Except in ancestry, he was the real aristocrat of Tabora. The Arabs respected him —and owed him money. He travelled with greater pomp than they. His house was the best in the place, 'almost a village, with its lofty gates and spacious courts, full of slaves and hangers-on'.[1]

Besides Tabora in this central part of East Africa there were Arab 'colonies' at Masansa (Msene), some fifty miles north-west of Tabora, and at Ujiji. Both had their Arab residences, their store-houses, and their clumps of huts like Tabora, but they were on a smaller scale. Ujiji had promised, when the Arabs first frequented it, to become a large and prosperous lake-side settlement. But 'the climate', Burton was told, 'proved unhealthy, the people dangerous, and the coasting-voyages frequently ended in disaster'. When Livingstone spent so many dreary months there in 1870–1, it was little more than a trading-post where goods were brought in and stored to await the flying visits of caravans from Tabora.[2] No doubt there were several such trading-posts—Burton describes one at Zungomero— scattered here and there along the trade-routes, but, though a few Arabs or Swahili lived in them to mind the store-houses and to provide caravans with 'trade goods' at a higher price than they could be got on the coast, they could scarcely be called 'colonies'. Adventurous Arabs, finally, sometimes built themselves houses and settled down by themselves with their retainers in some isolated spot. Speke was the grateful guest of one such Arab, Sheikh Hamed-bin-Sulayyim, on Kazenge Island, close to the western shore of Lake Tanganyika. He had a substantial, comfortable house with a spacious veranda where he would sit 'surrounded by a group of swarthy blacks, gossiping for hours together, or transacting his worldly business in

---

[1] Burton, i. 323, ii. 223–6. Burton describes Musa as 'thin-bearded, tall, gaunt, with delicate extremities and with the regular and handsome features of a high-caste Indian Moslem.... His clean new dress, perfumed with jasmine-oil and sandal-wood, his snowy skull-cap and well-fitting sandals, distinguish him in appearance from the Arabs.' For Ludha Damji, see p. 325, below.

[2] Idem, ii. 56–7. Livingstone, *Last Journals*, vol. ii, chap. vi.

purchasing ivory, slaves or any commodities worthy of his notice'. But so lonely a life could be dangerous. Hamed, as it happened, was just off, with an escort of armed slaves, on a trade-trip to Urua when Speke visited him. He never came back. He and all his party, so Speke learned later, were murdered by the natives.[1]

Such was the Arab invasion of inland East Africa as it was immediately after the end of Said's reign, a much bigger, more methodical, more profitable, more far-reaching invasion than anything the Arabs had attempted since first they came to the coast. And it can be no mere coincidence that the Arab exploitation of the interior began thus to change its character and to swell in strength and scope about the time that Said moved his home and court from Muscat to Zanzibar. The change, it seems more than probable, was largely the result of the move and of the new commercial policy which had mainly inspired Said to make it. His own interest in the business and his own example—for Said, as will be seen, took an active part in trade on his own account—must have done much to kindle the new spirit of commercial enterprise. The sense of security and confidence, moreover, which sets trade expanding, must have been enhanced by Said's assertion of his authority on the coast and the revival of his political prestige. There, at Zanzibar, at the very centre of the Arab community in East Africa, was an Arab prince whose name and fame were known not only in Arabia and the Middle East but in India and in Europe and even in America.

In this part of Said's commercial policy there was, of course, no novelty. It was only an extension, though a great extension, of the network of inland trade which the Arabs had begun to spin from the time when they first colonized the coast. Like them Said was content with middleman's and carrier's business. He devised no more ambitious schemes of economic exploitation. Although, at the very end of his reign, a successful experiment

[1] Speke, 229–41.

was made in the cultivation of sesamum on the coast between Malindi and Lamu,[1] he did nothing else to increase production on the mainland. And, in accordance again with the local Arab tradition, it was no part of his policy to take possession of new lands in order to grow new crops. Here and there some acres of African soil must have been bought or leased or seized from local tribes for the establishment of the permanent settlements. But neither Said nor any of his 'subjects' attempted to conquer, annex, or occupy any large tract of the country behind the coast. The old methods, applied with new vigour and courage, seemed profitable enough. The streams of ivory and slaves converging on Zanzibar steadily increased in volume.

More original and even more remarkable in its results was the second item in Said's economic programme—the exploitation of Zanzibar itself. The low ridges of the island are covered for the most part with a rich red loam beneath which the honeycombed coral-rock provides ideal drainage. But at the time of Said's first visit, though the tangle of wild luxuriant growth betrayed the rare fertility of the soil, only a small fraction of it had been cleared and cultivated. The natives had been content with a few palms and patches of grain; the Arab settlers had shown their usual indolent indifference to the use of land. But Said was an unusual Arab. Soon after his arrival he decided to make the experiment of planting clove-trees on a large scale. Cloves, as he knew, were a luxury which the world could scarcely do without. Cloves had provided one of the principal ingredients in the historic spice-trade between Europe and the East. The immensely profitable exploitation of the East Indies by the Dutch had been largely based on cloves. But the supply had rarely equalled the demand. Cloves, it appeared, would only grow in peculiar and quite unknown conditions of climate or soil. In some highly fertile places the seed would refuse to germinate. In others a tree might grow for a few years and then suddenly wither away. Till near the end of the eighteenth century, indeed, cloves had only been known to prosper in the Moluccas—the original 'Spice Islands'—and neighbouring isles

[1] Rigby, 22.

of the East Indies. But in 1770 Pierre Poivre, Intendant of Île de France, who, like Sir John Kirk in a later age at Zanzibar, was an expert in botany as in administration, obtained by stealth some clove-trees and seeds from the Moluccas and planted them in Île de France. The trees and most of the seedlings perished, but a few of the latter survived. The experiment was repeated in Bourbon. In 1785 the director of the Jardin Impérial des Plantes, now known as the Royal Botanical Garden, at Pamplemousses informed the Governor that clove-trees were beginning to do well in Bourbon. Plants were also sent to more distant French colonies such as St. Domingue and Cayenne, but their export to foreign possessions was jealously controlled. Somehow or other, however, from Île de France or Bourbon the precious seeds or seedlings came to Zanzibar. Who actually introduced them and exactly when is uncertain and unimportant. What was important, indeed momentous, was Said's decision to make clove-culture the primary industry of Zanzibar. Setting an example on his own plantations, he insisted on all the landowners in the island planting cloves instead of or in greater numbers than coco-nut palms, even (it is said) under threat of confiscation. He did the same thing in Pemba. He tried it on the opposite mainland at Bagamoyo, but there the trees would not grow. The twin-islands, however, were enough. As chance would have it, their soil or their climate or both fulfilled the cloves' mysterious needs at least as effectively as the Moluccas themselves. The results for Said and for Zanzibar were prodigious. The plantations, which at the time of Hart's visit in 1834 were still 'in their infancy', were producing by the end of Said's reign an average annual crop of about seven million pounds, and the value of the cloves exported every year came next to that of the ivory and the slaves. To-day Zanzibar and Pemba produce about four-fifths of the whole world's consumption.[1]

[1] Rigby, 22. B.R. 280. Ingrams, *Proceedings of the Royal Society of Arts and Sciences, Mauritius*, 1932, 50–2. Pearce, *Zanzibar*, 295–7. Guillain (ii. 49) ascribes the introduction to a Creole of Île de France or Bourbon about 1800. The Germans attempted but failed to cultivate cloves in Mafia, a coral island like Zanzibar and only fifty miles

The third and last part of Said's commercial policy was the natural complement of the others. To absorb the increased products of East Africa he had to find new markets. And, whereas before his time the export trade from the coast had been more or less limited to the lands that fringed the north-east corner of the Indian Ocean from Aden to Bombay—Egypt, Arabia, Persia, Cutch, and Kathiawar—it now began again to reach out, as in old days, to the rest of India and beyond it into the Far East. Not only in Bombay and Calcutta but in the Dutch East Indies and even in China agents of Arab trade were soon installed once more.[1] But Said, who had acquired in the course of his career a shrewd working knowledge of the main political and economic factors in the contemporary world, quickly realized that the best market for some of his chief products—not for slaves, indeed, but for ivory and cloves—was in Europe and North America. Subsequent chapters will show how eagerly he welcomed the first European and American traders who visited Zanzibar, how willingly he negotiated commercial treaties with their Governments—with that of the United States in 1833, of Great Britain in 1839, of France in 1844—and how gladly he assented to the establishment of their consulates at his doors. He may well have suspected that this new economic interest might lead one day to political interference. As regards the British, he knew that it would mean a closer watch on the Slave Trade, a constant pressure to reduce its scope still further, and a consequent diminution in that source of his revenue; but, on the other hand, the presence of a British consul would be an additional attraction and safeguard to the invaluable 'banyans', the majority of whom came from British India and could claim the rights of British subjects. In any case, he was more than ready, he was anxious, to run any of the risks which these new commercial contacts might involve. And again he was right, at any rate for the term of his own life

---

away. For recent developments, see Professor R. S. Troup's *Report on Clove Cultivation in the Zanzibar Protectorate*, Zanzibar, 1932. From 1920 to 1930 the average annual production of cloves in Zanzibar was 3,133 tons, in Pemba 6,435 tons.   [1] Gobineau, op. cit. 97-8.

and a generation after. At the date of his death the markets of Europe and the United States were absorbing, directly or indirectly, more than a third of the African products that passed through and out of Zanzibar.[1]

3

A policy so enterprising and far-sighted achieved the results it deserved. They can be seen materializing in the rough estimates of revenue and trade made by Captain Hart and Captain Brucks in and about 1834 and by Consul Hamerton in 1844 and 1855, while the far more detailed and reliable report of Consul Rigby, though it is based on the figures for 1859, three years after Said's death, may fairly be taken to illustrate the final outcome of his work.

First, as to the volume of trade. It has been observed that, before Said moved his court from Muscat, the trade coming in and out of Zanzibar in other 'goods' than slaves was meagre. A little ivory and gum-copal from the mainland and a few home-grown cloves were exported in Arab dhows to Arabia, Persia, and western India. The imports were 'chiefly dates and cloth from Muscat to make turbans'. But already the bigger ships and bigger money of the first American traders were beginning to dwarf the business of the 'country vessels'.[2] The French connexion followed, and the German, and lastly and slowly the British. During 1857 ninety European and American vessels called at Zanzibar with a total burden of 27,653 tons. In 1859 Zanzibar exported more ivory, more cloves, and more gum-copal than any other place in the world. The value of the ivory exported in that year was £146,666, of the cloves £55,666, of the gum-copal £37,166. Sesamum was exported to France to the value of £20,800, and cowries to West Africa, for use as currency, to the value of £51,444. The total exports for the year stood at £609,020. The chief imports were American cottons (£93,744), Indian dyed cloth (£53,777), English cottons (£37,711), rice (£38,444), Venetian beads (£21,879), and muskets (£18,840). All

---

[1] Rigby, 23. The bulk of the goods sent to Bombay went on to England.   [2] See Chap. XII, below.

of these, except the rice and some of the muskets, were used for barter in the African interior where no coinage was as yet in circulation. The total imports may be set at about £760,000. The aggregate trade of Zanzibar amounted, therefore, in 1859 to about £1,371,250.[1]

The growth of the customs revenue naturally reflects this astonishing growth of trade. Before Said came to Zanzibar, the *total* revenue it paid him, including receipts from the Slave Trade and the 'tribute' from the Hadimu, was probably not more than sixty thousand crowns—say £10,000.[2] By 1834, owing doubtless as much to Said's visits to Zanzibar and to stricter methods of collecting and 'farming' the customs as to the rapid increase in trade, the *total* revenue from Zanzibar was said to have risen already as high as 150,000 or even 220,000 crowns and to be increasing every year.[3] Neither Hart nor Brucks, who give these figures, stayed long at Zanzibar or made a special study of its finances, and the information supplied to them by the local Arabs was almost certainly exaggerated; but it seems safe to put the Zanzibar customs revenue at not less

[1] Rigby, 21–3. This invaluable report, which has been reprinted as an appendix to Mrs. C. E. B. Russell's *General Rigby, Zanzibar and the Slave Trade* (London, 1936), contains one mistake. In Kirk's copy there is the following pencil note in his handwriting against the totals of exports and imports: 'False, as Ivory is reckoned twice. J.K.' Kirk's authority is conclusive, and the rest of the report may be presumed to be correct. The false figures have been adjusted in the text above by subtracting the value of the ivory *exported* from the total *exports*. But, since the value of the ivory *imported* is not stated and may have been greater or less than that of the ivory *exported* in that year, the figure given for the total imports (£908,911 according to Rigby) is a rough estimate, but probably fairly near the mark.

[2] In 1810 Lord Caledon, Governor of Cape Colony, reported that the Imam of Muscat was said to have received 40,000 Spanish dollars (= crowns) as 'rent' from Zanzibar in 1807 (Theal, *R.S.E.A.* 13). Smee in 1811 put the revenue from Zanzibar at 60,000 dollars *plus* 'additional levies' (*Transactions of the Bombay Geographical Society*, vi. 60). Fraser at Muscat in 1821 reckoned the revenue from Zanzibar and other ports outside Oman at 30,000 to 40,000 dollars (*Narrative of a Journey to Khorasan*, 15). Hart's figure for the period before 1833 is 'about 30,000 or 40,000 dollars' (B.R. 281).

[3] Hart, B.R. 279–81. Brucks, B.R. 632.

than £20,000. Hamerton's estimates, which, since he was in close personal touch with Said after 1841, are more authoritative, give no separate figures for Zanzibar, but the customs revenue derived by Said from *all* his dominions may be reckoned from them at about £40,000 in 1844 and about £75,000 in 1855.[1] In 1847 the customs of Zanzibar and the East African dependencies alone yielded nearly, and in 1859 over, £40,000.[2] Thus it may be roughly calculated that in the twenty years of Said's rule at Zanzibar the amount of customs revenue he obtained there was increased at least eight-fold. There was also the annual 'tribute' of about £2,500 from the Zanzibar natives; and at least 25 per cent. of the total must be added for receipts from the Slave Trade.[3] Moreover, while the whole of this public revenue was at Said's autocratic disposal, he obtained also a large private income from his own commercial operations. A merchant-prince in the fullest sense, he did more trade himself, as he owned and cultivated more land, than any of his subjects. Before he left Muscat he was trading regularly with Madagascar, Mauritius, Bourbon, and the chief ports of India,[4] and he maintained and strengthened these commercial threads at Zanzibar.[5] Hart found him in possession of 'twenty merchant-ships of different kinds' in 1834.[6] In 1847 he determined to start trading direct with Europe, and in 1849 Hamerton reported that one of his ships was bound for London and another for Marseilles, each laden with cloves.[7] Guillain guessed the profits of all this trade

[1] A. Hamerton, *Report on the Affairs of the Imaum of Muscat*, 1844, p. 3. B.R. 238.

[2] Guillain (ii. 251) gives the sum for which the customs for Zanzibar and all the 'coast' except Pemba were farmed to the 'banyan' Jairam Sewji in 1847 at 175,000 dollars, and adds 12,000 for Pemba, making a total of about £38,000. For 1859 Rigby (p. 19) says: 'The customs are farmed to an Indian Banyan for the sum of 196,000 German crowns per annum.' The amount collected was presumably, on the average, substantially greater. [3] See p. 212, above, and p. 509, below.

[4] Fraser, op. cit. 16. [5] Brucks, B.R. 632. [6] B.R. 279.

[7] H. to Palmerston, 3.i.49 (F.O. 54. 13). Among memories of her childhood at Zanzibar Said's daughter, Salme, recalled his 'elaborate system of barter'. 'Once a year a fleet of his sailing vessels laden with native produce, especially cloves and spices, started for British, French, Persian, Indian, and Chinese ports, by means of the agents there em-

—it was mainly carrying-trade—to be about 100,000 dollars a year, and added another 50,000 for Said's clove-plantations.[1] It may be assumed, moreover, that some of the caravans which started inland from Bagamoyo were financed by Said. The total revenue, therefore, at his disposal must have far exceeded his expenditure, which was limited to the upkeep of his navy and merchant-ships, the pay of his Baluchi troops and his police who together numbered two thousand at most, the salaries of a few officials, the maintenance of his residences and those of his family, the provision of an extensive harem, and the hospitality and gifts required of a prince. Fraser estimated his annual surplus in 1821 at 100,000 dollars.[2]

Another reflection of the growth of trade was the growth of Zanzibar itself. There had been nothing but a fishing-village on its site when, early in the eighteenth century, the reigning chief or 'Mwenyi Mkuu' of the Hadimu, Hasan by name, established his 'capital' there. The good harbour, the fresh water, and growing trade attracted Arab colonists and Indian merchants. When Smee saw it in 1811, the village had grown into 'the only assemblage of habitations on the island that deserves the name of town', but, though there were 'a good number of stone buildings belonging to the Arabs and merchants', it still consisted mainly of huts. By 1830 it had attained some importance as the head-quarters of the Imam's administration in East Africa, but in size or structure or civic celebrity it could not compare, of course, with Kilwa or Mogadishu in their old golden days. Its population, slaves included, may have been over 5,000: there is not enough evidence even for a plausible guess. As Hamerton reported in 1844, 'such a thing as a census

ployed exchanging the home commodities for foreign': Emily Ruete, *née* Salme-binti-Said, *Memoirs of an Arabian Princess* (London, 1888), 85. For voyages to Europe or other long distances Said employed European skippers: Guillain, ii. 245.

[1] Idem, ii. 251.
[2] Fraser, 17. Said asked Hart in 1834 to take 7,000 dollars in his ship to Bombay: B.R. 282. Rigby, who was British consul at Zanzibar from 1858 to 1861, believed that Said left a fortune of 'several million dollars': *Report of Select Committee on the East African Slave Trade* (1871), 45.

of the population was never known or heard of by these poor people'. But quite certainly after Said's arrival the number rapidly increased. By 1848 it was already up to 25,000. In 1859 there were about 60,000 people in Zanzibar, far more than any town on the coast contained, far more than Mombasa, nearly ten times as many as Mozambique, the capital of Portuguese East Africa. For the first four or five months of every year, moreover, between the north-east and the south-west 'monsoons', some 3,000 or 4,000 'strangers', fierce slave-trading Arabs from the north, poured in to swell the population. Spreading new quarters had been built, new public buildings, mosques, dwelling-houses, shops. Before Said's reign had ended, Zanzibar had attained the girth and dignity of a capital town.[1]

All in all, Said's achievement in the economic field, under the conditions of his time and with the means at his disposal, must be rated high. Muscat, when he left it, was of no great significance in the commercial world, and he himself as prince or private person was relatively poor. In the brief space of twenty years he made Zanzibar one of the three or four focal points of trade in all her western Indian Ocean and multiplied his revenue ten times.

[1] Hasan, Ingrams, and Hollingsworth, *School History of Zanzibar*, 69–70. Smee, *T.B.G.S.* vi. 43. Rough figures for the population of the island as a whole are Smee's in 1811, 200,000; and Hamerton's in 1844 (with Pemba), 450,000 (*S.P.* xxxiii, 1844–5, 674). The only clue to the size of the population of Zanzibar town in Smee's report is untrustworthy. He says that he was told that 15,000 people died in an epidemic of small-pox in the town alone, but adds in a footnote that his informant was 'rather given to exaggeration', and suggests 5,000 as 'more probable'. One thousand or less seems more probable still. The figure for 1848 is Guillain's rough estimate: ii. 78. The figure for 1859 is reliable, being Rigby's, *Report*, 25. For Mozambique, see p. 171, above, and for the coast towns, pp. 329–30, below. For a description of Zanzibar town by a Moslem merchant in 1852, see Col. Sykes, quoting Lt. Ferguson, in *J.R.G.S.* xxiii (1853), 106.

XI
SEYYID SAID AT ZANZIBAR: POLITICS

1

SAID was more than a merchant. Trade and wealth were means to other ends. How was his personal and political position affected by the move to Zanzibar? What manner of authority did he exercise in his new realm? And what was its extent? How far did he realize the dream of an Omani empire in East Africa?

With the greater part of his subjects in Zanzibar and the adjacent isles, the original native population, Said had little to do. The Arabs of his day spoke of them comprehensively and contemptuously as the *Mukhadim* or 'slave-folk'. But they were not slaves, nor of a single tribe. The Hadimu were scattered along the east coast of Zanzibar and in the southern part of the interior. The Tumbatu lived along the north-west coast, opposite the little island whence they get their name. The Pemba were the aborigines of Pemba. Each of those tribes had its ruler, but the chief of them was the ruler of the Hadimu, the Mwenyi Mkuu, who no longer lived at Zanzibar, but in 'a large castle' in the centre of the island. Over all these people Said exercised no more than the function of an overlord. The Mwenyi Mkuu collected a poll-tax of 2 dollars from the head of each family and handed over to Said as 'tribute' about 10,000 dollars a year, retaining a residue of 2,000 dollars and upwards for his own revenue. Otherwise these natives were allowed to manage their own affairs. They were a primitive, peaceful folk and seem to have given no trouble. It is said that Said once quarrelled with the Mwenyi Mkuu and imprisoned him in the fort at Zanzibar, and that he escaped the first night and was permitted to resume his office. But it was not on these people that Said's position depended. The real business of his government was with the immigrant or colonial community, concentrated in Zanzibar city and its neighbourhood: the Arabs, the

Indian business men, the half-castes, and the slaves, who outnumbered their masters by two or three to one.[1]

As regards his relations with this community it is clear from the accounts of contemporary European observers that Said obtained at Zanzibar the personal peace and security which were unobtainable at Muscat. Family dissension, it is true, pursued him to his new home. He could not be rid of it as long as his first-born, Hilal, lived in the same place.[2] But at Zanzibar such feuds were confined within the palace walls, whereas at Muscat the infection of them might spread like a plague among the restless tribes of Oman. The secret, indeed, of Said's new position was its remoteness from those tribal Arabs. Colonial life is notoriously free from the vested interests and social schisms of the mother country; and most of the few thousand Omani colonists who had preceded and followed Said to Zanzibar had lost or loosened their connexion with the ancestral animosities and ambitions of their homeland. At Muscat Said's exercise of power was always tempered by the need of considering and, if need be, conciliating the leading notables of his realm, uncles and cousins of the inner circle, powerful and unruly Sheikhs of the country-side, many of them potential rivals and enemies and even aspirants to his own throne. But at Zanzibar Said was almost alone in his glory. Only the proud and ambitious chiefs of the el-Harthi tribe, who numbered about eight hundred and had many slaves, ever questioned his authority, and that was only when he was himself away.[3] The other Arab Sheikhs on the island were little more than local landlords, accepting without demur the supremacy of Said, the biggest and wealthiest landlord of them all. Even in the management of their own property they took his orders. It will be remembered that he compelled them to plant cloves on their land by threatening its confiscation: and it was said that, when in the course of

[1] Ingrams, *Zanzibar, its History and its People*, 30–2, 147–53. Rigby, 19–20. Burton, i. 272, 410. Rigby says the poll-tax was considerably reduced by Sultan Majid and Burton puts it at 1 dollar in 1859. The greater part of Ingrams's work, cited above, is devoted to a full and scientific account of the aborigines.

[2] See pp. 453–4, below.   [3] See p. 456, below.

his continual enlargement of his own estates he coveted a plot belonging to one of his subjects, he forced the unhappy owner to exchange it for land he did not want elsewhere.[1] As to politics, he allowed no meddling. No body of official advisers, no council of elder statesmen, was allowed to share in his secrets and decisions. When Captain Guillain visited Zanzibar in 1846, he found only one man besides Said entrusted with the work of government, Suliman-bin-Hamed, who had been Governor of Zanzibar before Said transferred his court there and was retained in office after the transference. He was a distant relative of Said's, but one whose loyalty was above suspicion; and when Guillain tried to discuss politics with him, he changed the subject, for fear, as the Frenchman thought, of displeasing his master. About ten years later, when Said was sixty-five and nearing the end of his long reign, there was still—so Captain Hamerton reported—only one man at Zanzibar who 'interfered in affairs of government', and it was still Suliman-bin-Hamed. 'Not a clever man', says Hamerton, 'but a kind good sort of person'—a description which illumines and explains those long years of faithful service.[2]

But, if Said had in fact monopolized his own government, he did not hold himself aloof from his people. A *baraza*, the local name for a *durbar*—immemorial tradition of oriental rule, however absolute—was held two or three times a day. Every Arab of standing attended. If they had any complaints to make, presumably they made them. But that was all. 'They do not interfere in the government,' notes Hamerton dryly; 'but, if called on by the Imam, they would do as desired.'[3] And this submissiveness, almost unnatural in Arabs, was certainly not due to fear. Said could be ruthless enough in dealing with his external enemies, but towards his own people of the island his leniency and benevolence became almost proverbial. Except for the crime of murder, no Arab was put to death by him in Zanzi-

[1] Guillain, ii. 51.
[2] Idem, pp. 26–7. B.R. 237–8. Guillain describes Suliman as a healthy and noble-looking Arab of 57 in 1846. He was a wealthy man, the biggest landed proprietor in the island after Said, and also engaged in trade.   [3] B.R. 238.

bar. Nor, apparently, were there any undercurrents of disloyalty beneath the tranquil surface. Secret intrigues or open rebellions never ceased in Oman; but there seems to have been only one serious incident of the kind at Zanzibar, and that one came to nothing.[1] And the explanation of this unusual peace is not far to seek. The coming of Said, at the height of his fame, to Zanzibar must have intensified its traditional devotion to his throne. Its sequel had been the conversion of a mean and obscure townlet into more than a second Muscat. Said had made Zanzibar; and the Zanzibar Arabs, proud and contented participants in its growth and prosperity, had less than no reason to quarrel with its maker. 'His Highness the Imam', observed Captain Hart in the early days of the new régime, 'possesses absolute power, and his word is law.' And so it was to the end.[2]

The administrative structure of this patriarchal absolutism was very simple. There were no departments, no ministers. Except for the Governor, there were no important administrative officers.[3] Even the collection of taxes was in unofficial hands, for the one and only tax, apart from the *Mukhadim* tribute, levied throughout Said's dominions was the customs duties, and these (as has been mentioned) were always 'farmed out' by Said to a leading member of the Indian mercantile community, usually on a five-year contract, on the payment of a lump sum calculated on an estimate of the annual yield. The contract was first obtained by the house of Wat Benia for 70,000 dollars, but it passed soon after to Jairam Sewji, and with him or his firm it remained till long after Said's death.[4] The contractor was called the 'Customs Master', and, though

[1] For Hilal, the pro-French 'party', and the el-Harthi see pp. 453-6, below.

[2] B.R. 280.

[3] According to Smee, in 1811, before Said's removal to Zanzibar, the 'whole establishment' consisted of the Governor, an assistant or councillor, and three Arab officers to command the garrison. *T.B.G.S.* vi. 43.

[4] Kirk's *Administration Report* for 1870, and personal information obtained at Zanzibar by Mr. R. H. Crofton.

he was not in form a member of Said's government, his power was actually greater than any one's save Said's. Twenty years after Said's death an English scientist described the Customs Master and his fellow 'banyans' as 'the real ruling power' at Zanzibar.[1] And in commerce and finance they probably were. Sewji had his agents at every port on the coast where customs were paid to Said, and, since he issued no regular 'returns', he could make good use of the opportunities for corruption, peculation, and extortion enjoyed by collectors of customs on many of the world's frontiers. He continued, moreover, to carry on his firm's private trade in which, of course, he was greatly assisted by his office; and, though he was said to have habitually complained that Said had the best of the bargain, receiving from him more than he collected, he made a great fortune. Rigby, who was British consul at Zanzibar from 1858 to 1861, was asked by the old man to make his will, and records that he left 'three million dollars in hard cash', i.e. about £650,000. Ludha Damji, the confidential agent of Sewji's firm, who acted as Customs Master on its behalf, was well known in Livingstone's day as the leading merchant in all East Africa: and it is significant, perhaps, that, when Seyyid Majid gave H. M. Stanley an audience in 1871, Ludha Damji, 'a venerable-looking old man with a shrewd intelligent face, sat on the right of the Sultan'.[2]

The judicial system was no less primitive. 'Nothing like a court house or a court of justice exists in the Imam's territories', wrote Hamerton in 1855. The Korân was the only code. No lawyers were allowed to plead. In civil cases the kadi or quasi-ecclesiastical judge, of whom there were two, listened to the opposing parties and then gave immediate judgement. 'The kadis', reported Rigby in 1859, 'are persons of no character, are

[1] J. Christie, *Cholera Epidemics in East Africa* (London, 1876), 345.
[2] Rigby, 19. Evidence before the H. of C. Select Committee on the East African Slave Trade: Report, 1871, p. 45. Guillain, ii. 29. Burton, i. 271–2 (who betrays his usual inaccuracy in detail). H. M. Stanley, *How I found Livingstone in Central Africa* (London, 1872), 37. Other references to Ludha Damji will be found in Livingstone's *Last Journals* and in most European accounts of Zanzibar at that time.

not at all respected by the people, and bribery is said to be very common.' Appeals, however, were always allowed to Said, from whom 'alone', so Hamerton reported in 1844, 'a poor man can obtain justice', or in his absence to the Governor. All criminal cases of a grave sort were tried by Said himself in public *baraza*, lesser cases being left to his son Khalid or to the Governor. Neither in criminal nor in civil cases was any written record kept. Capital punishment was only inflicted on murderers. If the family of his victim consented, a convicted murderer could avoid execution by paying them 'the price of blood'. A beating, a fine, or imprisonment was the usual penalty of crime. Prisoners were confined, both sexes together, in the fort, since no regular jail existed. They could buy or be given food and amused themselves by talking to any visitors who came or by playing cards with the guards. Only in serious cases were they put in irons. No specific term of confinement was ever awarded, but release could easily be obtained by bribing the kadi or some other influential Arab. Runaway slaves were punished by being chained up by the neck in some public place till their owners claimed them. 'Twenty to thirty slaves', says Rigby, 'of both sexes and of all ages, including even little girls, are frequently fastened by the neck with heavy iron collars to one chain.' But in general the penal system was not unusually barbarous. Confessions were sometimes extorted from suspected persons by burying them up to the neck on the sea-beach till their heads were covered by the rising tide. But the use of this or other forms of torture seems to have been rare.[1]

No regular courts, no regular jail—and no regular police. 'The Imam has only about two or three hundred troops which he brought from Muscat', observed Hart in 1834, 'but there appear to be a great number of police, armed with spears.' These spearmen, however, probably belonged to Said's nondescript little army. Rigby at any rate declared, some twenty years later, that the only men employed in maintaining order, patrolling the streets by night, arresting criminals, and guarding

[1] Hamerton, in 1844, *Report*, 5; in 1855, B.R. 241. Rigby, 6–8. Guillain, ii. 237. Burton, i. 263.

them in the fort were the Baluchi or Mekrani (coast-Arab) mercenaries.[1]

Altogether, then, it was a primitive form of government. The most powerful sovereign in the north-west corner of the Indian Ocean and one of the most famous princes in the Arab world, Said ruled his people by methods and machinery almost as archaic and rudimentary as those of some desert Sheikh in the days of Abraham. Similarly, in his personal life there was no outward show of his standing or his wealth. His habits were extremely frugal. His dress was the plain Arab robe and coloured turban. He wore no jewels. His palace in the town was 'a kind of double-storied white-washed barrack, about 140 feet long, roofed with dingy green-red tiles'. His palace in the country, where he mostly lived, was no less unpretentious—a bare, straggling, ugly building: 'pauperish and mouldy', the caustic Burton called it. His bodyguard consisted of twelve swarthy Mekrani, dressed in the discarded and threadbare uniforms of Bombay sepoys. The whole *ménage*, in fact, was plain and rude. To European visitors who had heard of Said's fame it seemed almost shabby, and British officials from Bombay were struck by the sharp contrast it afforded with the pomp and glitter of a Prince's court in India.[2]

The very simplicity of the setting may have made the central figure all the more striking, and it seems that no European could make Said's acquaintance without being deeply impressed by his personality. It was not only his quiet and unaffected courtesy, his generous hospitality, the care he took to meet all his visitors' needs at Zanzibar—a task in which he was efficiently assisted by his secretary or major-domo or general factotum, Khamis-bin-Osman, a remarkable half-caste who could speak

[1] B.R. 281. Rigby, 7. In 1811 Smee observed no Baluchi troops at Zanzibar, but only some 400 or 500 armed slaves, belonging to the Governor, serving under three Arab officers. *T.B.G.S.* vi. 44.

[2] J. R. Wellsted, *Travels in Arabia* (London, 1858), 5–6. Burton, i. 31, 256, 265. Guillain, ii. 31. B.R. 241. Krapf (123) describes the audience-chamber in the town palace as 'pretty large and paved with marble slabs' and with a 'stately chandelier' hanging from mid-ceiling.

English, French, Portuguese, Hindustani, Malagasi, and Swahili as well as Arabic, and who, oddly enough, had served on board the *Leven* and accompanied Owen to England. But it was something more than Said's friendliness and attentiveness that won all strangers' hearts, something more, too, than that venerable and kindly aspect which grew on him with age and greying hair. Let three Europeans who saw him at different periods of his life speak for themselves. Captain Hart in 1834—'He is a tall, stout and noble-looking man, with a benevolent countenance, clear, intelligent, sharp-eyed, and remarkably pleasant and agreeable in conversation.' Captain Guillain in 1846—'Il est rare de réunir à un si haut degré que le sultan Said la majesté de la taille, la noblesse de la physionomie, et la grâce parfaite du geste.' William A. Shepherd, in 1856—'His fine manly open face, with broad brow, large grey eyes, tight close mouth, hedged round with silvery moustache and beard . . . in all this there is so much of firmness, honesty of purpose, kind feeling and decision of character, combined with his genuine welcome and warm grasp, that your esteem is won at once. . . . One of the noblest-looking men I have seen in the East.' A remarkable consensus of opinion, and all the other testimony on record is much the same. A benevolent and venerable patriarch, a devoted lover and parent, the father of his people—it is a charming, almost a romantic picture, and as portraying him in his home or among his loyal Zanzibari it may be true to life. But of the Said of the outer world, the Arab politician, the fighter at grips with his foe, the youth who won his throne by murder, the man who tricked and made away with the Mazrui, the likeness seems imperfect.[1]

[1] B.R. 277. Guillain, ii. 10, 34–5, 220. W. A. Shepherd, *From Bombay to Bushire and Bussura* (London, 1857), 51–4. An interesting collection of personal testimonies is given in Said-Ruete, Appendix A, 151–81. An intimate domestic picture of Said as one of his daughters remembered him many years after his death is given in the *Memoirs of an Arabian Princess*, cited in a previous footnote. 'So far as I can remember, my father had only one principal wife from the time I was born; the other, secondary wives, numbering 75 at his death, he had bought from time to time. . . . Every one of my father's children—there were 36 when he died—was by a secondary wife, so that we were all equals' (10).

2

To describe the character of Said's rule on the African mainland is a more difficult task. Its extent, to begin with, was not defined by any fixed frontier. Said himself seems never to have set a northward limit to his 'dominion' on the coast. No doubt, if occasion had arisen, he would have claimed the whole of it up to Cape Guardafui or beyond it, just as, when occasion arose in 1855, he claimed the Kuria Muria Islands off the South Arabian coast.[1] Southwards, it will be remembered, he secured the recognition in the Moresby Treaty of Cape Delgado as the limit of his 'possessions'.[2] But in this there was no more reality. It was the farthest south he could go. It was the more or less recognized frontier of Portuguese Mozambique.[3] But, whatever his claims, there was no other external power to dispute them; and though, as will be seen, his authority over the intervening strips of the coast-belt and the native tribes that occupied them was irregular and incomplete, there was no question, after the fall of Mombasa at any rate, as to his overlordship of all the Arab colonies from Mogadishu to Lindi.

They were not jewels in his crown, those crumbling relics of a greater Arab age. The descriptions of them given by Owen and Boteler when they surveyed the coast in 1823-4 make startling reading side by side with the accounts of Ibn Battuta or Duarte Barbosa. Mogadishu, that 'exceedingly large city', with its 'big palaces' and 'great mosque' and crowded pilgrims, was still important, 'the only town of any importance' on the northern part of the coast; but nothing more than the empty shell of its ancient glory had survived.

'At a distance the town has rather an imposing appearance, the buildings being of some magnitude and composed of stone. The eye is at first attracted by four minarets of considerable height, towering above the town and giving to it an air of stilly grandeur. But a nearer approach soon convinces the spectator that those massive

[1] See p. 527, below. Claims in the north in 1842: p. 510, below.
[2] See p. 215, above.
[3] For the limits defined in the Treaty of 1849 see p. 515, below. For claims in Madagascar see p. 440, below.

buildings are principally the residences of the dead, while the living inhabit the low thatched huts by which these costly sepulchres are surrounded.'[1]

Of the 'great town' of Barawa nothing but a few stone houses remained. Pate was only a pack of 'wretched mud habitations' huddled round the ruins of the old fort, 'miserable indeed to the eye of an Englishman'.[2] Lamu was a little more respectable, 'one of the best stations upon the coast', with a population of five thousand (including slaves) and 'much commerce'. In the centre of the town was a fort, 100 yards square with walls from 40 to 50 feet high; and there were a few 'superior' houses made from the ruins of earlier buildings.[3] Malindi, on the other hand, lay desolate. One of the pillars set up by the Portuguese along the coast as monuments and landmarks still stood beside the sea, the sole memorial of that 'noble city'.[4] Of 'most beautiful and best-built' Kilwa, with its 'fair houses' and streams and orchards, the fort alone remained intact. Part of the old city walls were still 'in a tolerably perfect state' and there were some 'ponderous relics' of other buildings.[5]

Twenty years later Guillain made the same coast-voyage and told the same pathetic story—Mogadishu, 'a mass of crumbling ruins'; Merka, a clump of 'broken-down houses' whose regular layout 'contrasts with the savage aspect of the surrounding huts and bush'; Barawa, 'a *pêle-mêle* of stone houses, mud-walled thatch-roofed cottages, and native huts'.[6]

Once proud and wealthy little city-states, now mean drab townlets or villages—such were the coastal centres of Said's colonial realm. Nor could his rule afford them any prospect of recovery. The great Arab age had departed long ago. No one could bring it back. And Said himself could never have dreamed of restoring the ancient glories of the coast. Where were the men? Where was the money? Greatly as he increased his revenues, they must have been a pittance beside the wealth of

---

[1] Owen's *Narrative*, i. 357. The four minarets were doubtless the 'four towers' observed in passing by Vasco da Gama.
[2] Boteler's *Narrative*, i. 373–5.
[3] Owen, i. 364–5. Boteler, i. 378.   [4] Owen, i. 400–2.
[5] Idem, ii. 4–5.   [6] Guillain, ii. 526; iii. 138, 167.

Kilwa or Mogadishu at their zenith. Zanzibar alone absorbed all he could afford to spend on public works; and, as it rose, the coast towns sank still farther. All, indeed, that Said wanted to do with them, perhaps all he could do, was to stimulate the trade that flowed down to them from the interior and through them to Zanzibar and oversea. And the primary, almost the only, direct administrative function of his overlordship was to secure the customs dues payable to him at every port. In each of the towns he installed a Governor, sometimes a local Sheikh, sometimes a man of his own from Zanzibar or Muscat, and furnished him with a show, but only a show, of military force. Along the whole coast there were only about four hundred of his 'Baluchis' in 1846; and of these some hundred and fifty were then in occupation of Fort Jesus.[1] At Lamu there were about thirty, at Pate twenty-five, at Kilwa half a dozen, and at the other places two or three apiece. Even in those decayed seaports the Arabs had not altogether lost the free spirit of the desert: many of them showed courage as well as ferocity in their trading ventures among the natives of the interior; and it is clear that Said's Governors, with only a handful of poor soldiers at their call, did little governing. On Said's behalf they may have heard appeals from the judicial decisions of the local Sheikhs; but, in general, though Said was in theory the overlord and the Sheikhs his vassals, they were in practice and in the normal course of events the almost unchecked masters of their own little parcels of the coast. They paid their feudal 'tribute' in the shape of the dues on their trade; and that was practically all that Said and his deputies required of them.[2]

Only at Mombasa and the little ports to the south of it was Said's power as real as it was at Zanzibar. His Governor at Fort Jesus, with a substantial garrison at his back, was more than a

[1] The strength of the garrison varied from time to time. Lieut. Christopher, visiting Mombasa in 1843, reported only twenty 'Beloochees' in the fort: T.G.B.S. vi. 377. Krapf, on the other hand, found 400 'Beluches' there in 1844: 119. Guillain says 250 in 1846: ii. 238.

[2] References to Governors: Owen, i. 366 (Lamu); ii. 6 (Lindi). Garrisons: Boteler, i. 375 (Pate); ii. 4 (Kilwa). Size of garrisons: Guillain, ii. 238.

collector of customs. He, not the local Sheikh, was the ruler. His post was the most important in Said's African service; and when Krapf came to Mombasa in 1844 it was held by Ali-bin-Nasir, who ranked so high in Said's entourage that he had twice been sent as his representative to London. More than once he figures in Krapf's journal, entertaining him at the fort on his arrival, taking a benevolent interest in his mission, assisting him to deal with certain difficult native chiefs—it is all the Governor and no one else.[1]

The coast towns, similarly, between Mombasa and Pangani, which had been under Mazrui domination, had passed into Said's effective control. At Tanga, for example, as at Mombasa, the Governor concerned himself not only with the port but also with the interior. It was to him that Krapf applied for 'permission' to make his journey into Usambara—which, as it happened, the Governor declined to grant without written orders from Said himself.[2] South of Pangani there is little evidence to show the extent of Said's authority. Kilwa, as has been seen, was still proud enough in her decline to remember her great days, to boast of her unbroken line of Sultans, and to resent an outsider's interference. But she had submitted; Said's Governor had been duly installed; his garrison had occupied the ancient fort; and, whatever part he played in the domestic affairs of the town, he made it his business to deal with strangers.

'He appeared always in fear of us [recorded Owen]; and upon Lieutenant Owen one evening landing near the fort to obtain the latitude by the stars, an alarm was given, and the old Governor was seen hurrying half-dressed down to the spot at the head of a dozen or two Arabs, armed with swords, matchlocks, and every other kind of weapon ancient or modern that could at the moment be mustered: these were drawn up in a line a short distance off, where they patiently awaited the departure of the boats.'[3]

[1] Krapf, 118, 128, 181. Missions to London: pp. 480, 508, below.
[2] Krapf, 368.
[3] Owen, ii. 5. Establishment of Omani control: p. 218, above. When Christopher visited Kilwa in 1843, he interviewed the Sultan, not the Governor: *T.B.G.S.* vi. 377. That Said's authority was not very strong and did not extend inland is clear from Hamerton's objection to Burton and Speke starting on their expedition from Kilwa 'on account of the

At Lindi, likewise, far down towards Cape Delgado, it was the Governor, not any local Sultan, whom Boteler asked for leave to survey the place.

'On landing he was met by several Arabs, and a great array of the natives carrying assegais and bows and arrows. . . . They conducted him to the Governor whom he found seated on a bench at the gate of a small whitewashed fort.'[1]

Much less effective had been Said's attempt to extend his 'dominion' still farther south, not of course into Portuguese Mozambique but into the area of Madagascar, from which the anti-European attitude of Queen Ranavolana seemed to have combined with their own mutual suspicions to keep both France and Britain, for the time at least, aloof. Said's dubious proposal for linking Madagascar itself with Zanzibar in 1833 by marriage with its formidable queen has been recorded.[2] A few years later he tried to secure a foothold on the island of Nossi-bé, which lies just off the western coast of Madagascar, about 100 miles from its northern tip. It was ruled by the Sakalava, a tribe which had so far escaped, but constantly dreaded, conquest and domination by the Hovas. When, therefore, in 1838 the famous Imam of Muscat offered them his protection, it was gratefully accepted by Queen Seneekoo, and a treaty was signed by her ministers under which she surrendered 'all her dominions on the island of Bookeen' (the native name for Nossi-bé) to Said and agreed to pay him 30,000 dollars and the usual 5 per cent. duty on the exports and imports of the island, while Said for his part undertook to 'take charge of the fort and protect us on the sea side and generally protect us as he does his other subjects'.[3] At some time, moreover—whether before or after the conclusion of this treaty is uncertain—a number of colonists from Zanzibar had settled at Nossi-bé: their descendants are still living there and

opposition to be expected at a port so distant from the seat of government where the people, half-caste Arabs and Swahili, who are only under a nominal control, still retained a violent hostility to strangers'. Burton, i. 5.

[1] Owen, ii. 6.
[2] See pp. 281–2, above.
[3] Said to Palmerston, 1.v.41, with copy of treaty (F.O. 54. 4).

claim to be Zanzibari. But Said, it seems, was slow to act on the treaty. He appointed no Governor. He did not even garrison the fort. He merely hoisted his flag. And his delay proved fatal. Before two years were up, the French (as will appear in a later chapter) had given the island more substantial and more lasting protection.[1]

So much for the south. Northwards of Mombasa Said's authority was weaker. It is true that at Lamu, about 150 miles from Mombasa, and at Pate next door to it he had established his 'overlordship' and the fiscal control it implied long before the fall of the Mazrui,[2] and had maintained them against Mazrui claims and intrigues. When Owen visited Lamu in 1824 he had found a cousin of Said's, Seif-bin-Hamed, installed as Governor.[3] 'Like the generality of Arab Governors', Boteler observed, 'he made but little display of his official dignity, and could never be distinguished from those by whom he was surrounded except on the entrance of an Arab who always first saluted him. He was generally to be found sitting in the guard-house, receiving the duties levied on goods embarked or landed, out of which, I was informed, his allowance as Governor was paid.'[4] He probably did little outside the guard-house or apart from the receipt of custom, and his guards were doubtless more for show than for service. But at any rate, after Said's occupation of Mombasa as before it, this important commercial centre remained submissive to his suzerainty.

It was otherwise at Pate on its island less than fifteen miles away. Not only was Pate constantly at war with Siu, a rival town at the other end of the island, but it was as constantly riven by internal strife; and in both conflicts the battle-cry of independence from Said's authority was freely and frequently raised by one side or the other. In 1839 there was an actual rising. The Governor and his handful of Baluchis were murdered, and Said's overlordship was denounced and repudiated by the local Sultan. It was a challenge which could scarcely be evaded, but Said took it quietly. He attempted no punitive measures.

[1] See pp. 439–48, below.   [2] See p. 219, above.
[3] See pp. 234–5, above.   [4] Owen, *Narrative*, i. 381–2.

He sent no ships or men to enforce submission and install a new Governor. He only extended the authority of his Governor at Lamu to cover Pate. Intrigue, not force, was his weapon, and it did not fail him. Having obtained from the Sultan's brother a promise to restore the old relationship, he declared him the rightful ruler of Pate. Secret agents and silver did the rest. Public opinion turned steadily against the Sultan till presently it was possible for the Governor of Lamu to intervene and peacefully to set Said's 'pretender' in his brother's place. Said, it might seem, had recovered his hold over Pate, and by relatively cheap and easy methods: but it remained to be seen how long an authority grounded on the shifting sands of popular faction could last.[1]

Farther north Said's 'dominion' was still more tenuous and insecure. South of the River Juba the old Arab colonists had remained Arab or half-Arab;[2] and despite their local pride and independence the idea of a common and not over-burdensome allegiance to a famous Arab prince was at any rate not intolerable. But north of the Juba, along the coast of what is now Italian Somaliland, the Arab colonies, as their old power gradually declined, had fallen more and more under the ascendancy of the natives of the interior. The Somali were far more akin to the Arabs than were the Bantu tribes to the south, and far more militant and better organized; and only some twenty miles inland from the isolated seaboard-towns was a large, fertile, and well-peopled district, watered by the Webi Doboi river flowing parallel with the coast. Its inhabitants had steadily interpenetrated and ultimately swamped the maritime belt. When Christopher in 1843 and Guillain in 1847 visited Mogadishu, they found it more a Somali than an Arab town. In a population of about 4,000 there were only about thirty families of Arab origin and a few Indian traders. The rest were Somali, who had established themselves in the half-ruined houses of the Portuguese and greater Arab period. Unlike the Swahili of the southward towns, who were armed, like Arabs, with sword and dagger, these Somali carried spears and bows and arrows; and, though

[1] Guillain, iii. 98–100.   [2] Except at Siu, which was half Somali.

they all professed to be Moslems and should therefore have been able to read the Korân, they knew little or no Arabic. Mogadishu, in fact, was virtually an outpost of a Somali 'kingdom' with a population of some 150,000 centred in the Webi Doboi country. Its real master was the Sheikh at Geledi, a warrior chieftain who at need could mobilize at least 20,000 spears.[1]

Naturally, therefore, this Somali part of the coast was the last part over which Said attempted to exert his overlordship. No governors or garrisons had been installed at Mogadishu or Barawa or Merka by 1823 as they had been at Lamu and Pate: Owen and his colleagues dealt only with the local Sheikhs. In 1828, after his first occupation of Fort Jesus, Said dispatched his fleet to make a demonstration at Mogadishu which resulted in its formal acceptance of his suzerainty; but it was not till about 1840, on the eve of his migration to Zanzibar, that he sent a mission to the three Somali ports to fix the customs duties he had long established farther south.[2] At Barawa he attempted more than that: he appointed a Governor. But the result was disappointing. The Governor soon forgot he was Said's officer and began to pursue an independent policy for his own profit. British and American merchants were presently complaining at Zanzibar that duties had been levied on their trade at Barawa in flagrant violation of the commercial treaties which Said had recently signed. As if to prove, moreover, how slight was Said's hold on all that coast, a Somali force descended in 1841 on one of his ports—which of them is not recorded—massacred a number of Said's subjects who were doing business there, and 'took away all the money in the place'.[3]

In the light of all these facts it is not surprising that, when the first British official appointed to Zanzibar took up his residence there in 1841, he should quickly have discovered that Said's 'dominion' in Africa meant something much less than domination. Except at one or two points like Kilwa and Mombasa,

---

[1] Guillain, ii. 514–50, iii. 1–63. Christopher, *T.B.G.S.* vi. 379–400. G. and C. both visited Geledi.   [2] Guillain, i. 590; ii. 529.
[3] Hamerton's consular report, 5.i.42 (F.O. 54. 4).

Hamerton reported to the Foreign Office, the Imam had no more than a nominal authority on the coast, 'nor', he added, 'is his personal popularity at all what we supposed it to be'.

'I told him that, if he did not bestir himself and make it appear that he had some title to the places on the coast of Africa, I feared all would pass away from him as Nossi-bé has. He has no form of government at the different places on the coast. In fact the Imam's affairs are in a miserable state. His country, I told him, is now becoming better known to Europeans, and it will be necessary for him to conduct things differently. The truth is *he has more than he can manage.*'[1]

At this early stage of their acquaintance Said seems to have realized that Hamerton's advice was as friendly and disinterested as it was frank. He did bestir himself, but cautiously and step by step. First, he ordered his scarlet ensign to be hoisted at each of the ports which recognized his overlordship.[2] Then, after waiting for a year, in the spring of 1843 he at last appointed a Governor for Mogadishu. In deference to the independent spirit of its people, he chose a Somali, not an Arab, and sent no garrison, but only a couple of soldiers to mount guard at the customs-house. It was something, no doubt, that the Somali acquiesced in the appointment: but Said cannot have been very confident that this forward move at Mogadishu would be ultimately more successful than it had been at Barawa. And in fact (to anticipate a moment) it was not. The new Governor soon quitted his post and retired to his own Somali country inland. When Guillain came to Mogadishu in 1848 he found 'an old Arab' in the Governor's place, who was rather the agent of Jairam Sewji, the Customs Master, than Said's representative.[3]

Said's next step was more vigorous. He might never, indeed, have taken it, he might have been content with his flags and his new governorship, if the coast had kept quiet. But just at this time the old trouble at Pate broke out once more. The success of Said's diplomacy had been transient; the tide had soon turned again; and in 1843 the new Sultan brusquely repudiated the suzerain to whom he had owed his office. It was not, as has

---

[1] Hamerton's report, 5.i.42 (F.O. 54. 4). For the French occupation of Nossi-bé see pp. 439–43, below.
[2] Ibid. This was at the end of 1841.   [3] Guillain, ii. 529–30.

been seen, a new challenge, and Said no doubt would have preferred to meet it again as he had met it before. He was reluctant to use force. He had only used it once on the coast—at Mombasa; and it was not his Baluchis who had captured Fort Jesus. But whether he felt that Pate's disorder had now proved itself too deep-seated for any gentler cure, or whether he recognized that in his most dangerous enemy at Pate, one Fumo Bakari, the real power behind the Sultan, he had met his match at intrigue, or whether Hamerton's warning was still haunting his mind and stinging his pride, he decided on a military expedition, and that on a large enough scale not only to crush the revolt at Pate but to convince her sister-towns all down the coast that Seyyid Said was their overlord in more than name. The call went out from Muscat for Omani volunteers; and emissaries, bearing bags of silver, were sent to invoke the aid of the chiefs along the Arabian coast. At the end of December a squadron of ten ships of varying size left Muscat for Zanzibar with some twelve hundred fighting men on board. A few hundred island-Arabs and Baluchis joined up at Zanzibar, and a few hundred more at Lamu. Early in January 1844 a little army of 2,000—a bigger force than any Said had launched against Mombasa—landed at Faza, a few miles from Siu, with Hamed-bin-Ahmed, Said's most trusted general, in command.[1]

The sequel was another of those fiascos in which, whether owing to misfortune or mismanagement, Said's military enterprises were so often involved. Half-way to Siu, Hamed's first objective, his army was caught unprepared for battle by the enemy and put ingloriously to rout. Hamed rallied his men at Faza, but he could not induce them to advance again. After three weeks' inaction he sailed away, leaving instructions for the building of a fort and its occupation by a garrison of a hundred Baluchis.

To have used force unsuccessfully was worse than not to have used it at all, and Said resolved to try again. 'Presents in money to a considerable amount', reported the Assistant-Resident in

[1] B.R. xxiv. 215. Salil-ibn-Rasik (Badger), 360. Rigby, 31. Miles, ii. 344. Guillain, iii. 100.

the Persian Gulf in the autumn, 'have been sent up by His Highness the Imam from Zanzibar to all the maritime chiefs.'[1] In December nine hundred men were collected at Muscat, conveyed to Zanzibar, and reinforced with local troops and light artillery. Hamed was once more in command, but this time Said himself accompanied the expedition in his frigate *Victoria* as far as Lamu. In January 1845 a landing was made again at Faza, and again the march on Siu was begun. And then, as before, came disaster, but far worse than that of the previous year. Riding to the rear of his advancing troops in order to hurry on the guns, Hamed was caught in an ambush and killed. The news completely broke the spirit of his men. They broke and ran for the ships. 'All the soldiers fled', wrote the triumphant annalist of Pate; 'they ran into the mangroves and died in the mud. The Siu women, when they went for firewood, saw them and struck them with axes.' Some three hundred men in all were killed or drowned. All the guns were lost. 'And when Said heard of the death of the general and this defeat of his troops, he arose and got into a boat and went off to his ship, and he spoke to no one till he reached Manda.'[2]

The humiliation, indeed, was as deep as any Said suffered in all

[1] B.R. xxiv. 215.
[2] The Pate version of the two campaigns, with some repetition and embroidery, is in the Swahili *History of Pate* (*J.A.S.* 1914–15), and in Stigand, *Land of Zinj*, 91–3. The Omani version, naturally brief, is given by Salil-ibn-Razik, 355, 360. The most reliable European account is that of Guillain (iii. 99–102), who obtained his information on the spot between 1846 and 1848. The summary account in B.R. (xxiv. 215, 217) and Miles (ii. 344), derived from Persian Gulf officials, describes only one expedition, that of January 1845, and includes some details (e.g. the numbers and composition of the troops obtained from Muscat) which fit in better to the campaign of 1844 as recorded by Guillain. Miles puts the disaster in March 1844. Rigby (*Report*, 31–2), writing in 1860, also mentions only one expedition which he dates in 1843. Both Rigby and B.R. say that Ali-bin-Nasir, sometime 'envoy to England', was killed as well as Hamed; but Guillain does not mention this, and Krapf noted in his journal (128) that on March 13, 1844, he was received at Mombasa by the ex-envoy, then Governor. Burton's version (i. 298), published in 1872 from notes made in 1856, distinguishes the two expeditions, but ascribes the disaster of the second to the first and is otherwise more picturesque than accurate in detail.

the changing fortunes of his long career. And what could he do to efface it? His sea-power was still unchallengeable, and he used it to blockade Pate; but it was a half-hearted business, only one brig and a few dhows took part in it, and there can have been little hope of its bringing the exultant rebels to terms. A year went by, and the situation was unchanged. Then, in 1847, Said reverted to the methods of diplomacy which—he doubtless told himself—he ought never to have discarded. The Kadi of Zanzibar, who happened to be a native of Pate Island, was sent to negotiate with the Sultan of Pate and the principal neighbouring chiefs. He did his work better than Hamed. Seyyid Said, he explained, was still a formidable enemy, but he had no desire for vengeance or indemnity. All he wanted was the restoration of the old position—the formal acceptance of his overlordship, the reappointment of a Governor, and the payment of the usual dues on trade. For that—and what a small price it was!—Pate would purchase Said's friendship and his protection from all outside interference.... Maybe the Sultan and people of Pate had tired of the long quarrel. Maybe, despite their victories, they feared a third attack. Maybe the time had come for another turn of public sentiment. At any rate, the Kadi's arguments prevailed. Peace was patched up. A Governor was re-installed, but with only five men for escort. The duties were paid once more.[1]

What, then, had Said accomplished on the coast in the six years since the new British consul had warned him that he would lose his so-called dominion in Africa if he did not 'bestir himself'? Less than nothing. The flags had been useless in themselves. The two new governorships had both proved failures. The great assault on Pate, so far from strengthening Said's prestige, had, for a time at least, impaired it. Indeed, the one bright feature on the scene was the fact that the Siu disaster had not led to a general revolt. Said's 'dominion', in fact, in 1847 remained more or less as Hamerton had depicted it in 1841

[1] Guillain (iii. 102–3); wisely discounting the description, given him at Zanzibar, of these proceedings as a great diplomatic triumph. Rigby (30) says that Said bought back his captured guns.

or as Krapf, who (as will be seen) was familiar with part of the coast, less pessimistically described it in 1844. 'The Arabs and Africans', he wrote, 'submit to his [Said's] nominal pretensions so long as their own old arrangements are not too stringently interfered with. They receive the Sultan's Governors and pay the dues which he levies from their ports; but beyond that Seyyid Said seems to have no hope of their further obedience and subjection.'[1] And what, after all, would he gain by further obedience and subjection, by interfering in the local administration, establishing his own courts, setting up in fact a 'form of government', the absence of which struck Hamerton with his knowledge of direct British rule in India as so surprising? To make his 'dominion' real in that sense would not swell the volume of trade or multiply the customs dues; and it would necessitate a military effort which, to judge from what happened at Pate, was almost certainly beyond his strength. No: all Said wanted was to *keep* what he had got. The elimination of the Mazrui had enabled him to make the whole coast from Somaliland to Cape Delgado his exclusive commercial and fiscal preserve. He need fear no trespassing therein by any Africans or Asiatics. But there were two European peoples whose encroachments he might well dread. If either the British or the French should desire to control, occupy, annex the African coast, he could not prevent them. Hence the supreme importance of the British recognition of his 'dominion' in the Moresby Treaty, and, still more, its unequivocal confirmation in the abandonment of 'Owen's Protectorate'. It might be said—Hamerton indeed had hinted—that its unusual and insubstantial character invited the attention of any Power bent on territorial aggrandizement. That was a real danger, but it lay far ahead. As long as Said lived, and long after, the 'dominion' *was* recognized, and on that account, as a matter of international relations, it was real. So Said was content.

And for the same reason the peoples of the coast towns, except for occasional demonstrations of independence, were content. They too were aware of the possibility of European

[1] Krapf, 124.

encroachment. They knew far less than Said about the power or the policies of European governments, but they could not miss the meaning of the coming and the going of the British at Mombasa. The kadi at Pate was right. If they could protect themselves from European occupation by saying their towns 'belonged to the Imam', 5 per cent. on their exports and imports was not a big price to pay.

Thus Said's 'dominion' served its purpose both for the 'overlord' and for his 'subjects'. But it was a queer political institution, unique in European experience, unknown to international law. It defies definition in customary terms, and perhaps the best description of it is that given by Guillain, who had reason to know what he was writing about. 'It is neither suzerainty nor sovereignty: it is rather a kind of protectorate, constituting the protected town dependent but not subject.'[1]

3

'The influence of the Imam', reported Hamerton to Palmerston in 1848, 'extends but a very short way into the interior from any part of the coast'.[2] It has been shown that the British Consul underestimated the real value of Said's overlordship at the sea-ports. Did he likewise understate the extent of his 'influence' among the native tribes inland?

Certainly not in the north. Above the Juba Said had no influence whatever, not even on the coast. The Somali and Galla who encircled the Arab or half-Arab towns were fiercely independent. It was as much as his life was worth, or at any rate his liberty, for a merchant of Zanzibar to land on that inhospitable shore between one port and another. Nor was it dangerous only for Arabs. The murder of a landing-party from Commodore Blankett's squadron in 1798 has been described in an earlier chapter.[3] Some thirty years later the crew of a boat from a British whaler, having lost their ship in pursuit of a whale, reached land about sixty miles north of Mogadishu after nine days at sea. The officers and two of the men died of exhaustion.

[1] Guillain, ii. 528.   [2] H. to Palmerston, 15.xii.48 (F.O. 54. 12).
[3] See p. 165, above.

The five survivors were carried off and sold for slaves. Evidently the Somali had no fear of Europeans or of the reprisals which their ill treatment of them might provoke. Why should they? Since Blankett sailed up the coast, the only British warships they had seen were those of Owen's little squadron till Christopher's brig arrived in 1843.[1]

It was much the same along the Galla section of the coast. The Arabs of the seaports, Boteler observed, 'dare not venture into their [the Galla's] country and their trade with them is carried on entirely in the towns'.[2] And Owen's pilot told him that Arab voyagers 'never attempted to land' except at the ports, 'as the enmity of these savages is so great that they are constantly on the watch to entrap them'.[3] On one occasion, in 1823, a large dhow from Zanzibar was driven ashore by stress of weather. In a very short time every plank and cord in it had been torn out and carried off by Galla 'wreckers'. The master and crew were marched away up country where they were sold for slaves, and a year went by before they got a message through to Zanzibar and obtained their freedom with a ransom of 2,000 dollars.[4]

Akin to the Galla, but not frequenting the coast as they did, were the fighting tribes located in and about the highlands of Kenya. These also were too fierce and formidable for Said or his Governors or urban 'subjects' to have any dealings with them. The story of Krapf's heroic attempt to penetrate their country attests the risk any strangers ran unless they were well armed and in substantial numbers, and there are several references in his journal to two specially dangerous tribes, the Masai and the Kwavi.[5]

[1] Christopher, 379–82. At Barawa Christopher was approached by a man 'of very unpromising appearance' who claimed that he had rescued the seamen from slavery by a ransom of 30 German crowns and produced a statement, written by the harpooner, 'acknowledging the great kindness and attention shown him by the bearer'. As the claim was supported by the people, Christopher paid over the 30 crowns on his Government's behalf. What happened to the seamen is unknown.
[2] Owen's *Narrative*, p. 292.   [3] Ibid., p. 355.   [4] Ibid., p. 402.
[5] The Masai were called Kwavi on the coast. Krapf mistook an internal feud for a quarrel between separate tribes. See A. C. Hollis, *The Masai* (Oxford, 1905), pt. iii.

'Their manner of life [he notes] is nomadic, and when they find water and grass, there they often camp for months together. They live entirely on milk, butter, honey, and the meat of black cattle, goats, and sheep, and on game which they hunt down, having a great distaste for agriculture, believing that the nourishment afforded by cereals enfeebles and is only suited to the despised tribes of the mountains, while to feed on meat and milk gives strength and courage. When cattle fail them, they make raids on the tribes which they know to be in possession of herds. . . . They undertake expeditions for hundreds of leagues to attain their object, and make forays into the territories of the Kamba, the Galla, the Chagga, and even of the Nyika on the sea-coast. They are dreaded as warriors, laying all waste with fire and sword, so that the weaker tribes do not venture to resist them in the open field, but leave them in possession of their herds, and seek only to save themselves by the quickest possible flight.'

It is fortunate, Krapf adds, that the Masai and Kwavi are mortal enemies. United, no other tribe could resist them, not even 'the savage Galla'. As it is, they each strike terror into all East Africans, 'the Swahili with their muskets not excepted'. After that it is not surprising to find Krapf altering the course of a journey projected by his colleague, Rebmann, because 'the savage Masai are occupying the route'.[1]

As to Kenya, then, Hamerton was right. Said's 'influence', whether exerted by his Governor at Fort Jesus or through Arab or Swahili caravans, did not permeate the Masai country. But in the near neighbourhood of Mombasa the Governor had more than influence. Not regularly nor formally, but none the less forcibly when occasion called for it, he exercised a ruler's function over the weak and unwarlike Nyika. Krapf again is witness. 'We complained', says the journal, 'of the conduct of

[1] Krapf, 358–9, 361, 195. On his way from Pangani to Vuga in 1852, Krapf was told at Kisara, a village above the Kerenge valley some thirty miles from the coast, that 'only a few days before some 800 Masai had passed through the valley on their way to carry off the cattle of the Zigua; for as the Zigua are enemies of King Kimweri [of Usambara, see p. 345, opposite] he does not prevent the Masai from traversing his country, although I suspect this permission is given more from fear than policy; for no East African nation dares offer resistance to the Masai and Kwavi', 381–2. (For the sake of uniformity, the prefix 'Wa' has been omitted from the names of tribes as spelt by Krapf.)

the chiefs of Great Rabai to the Governor, and asked him to remove the obstacles thrown in the way of our journey. He promised to grant the request and gave us a letter and soldiers who are to communicate his orders to the chiefs.'[1]

Similar control was exercised, one may suppose, by the Governor of Tanga, but only within a relatively narrow radius of the town. For immediately to the west of Tanga lay an organized and powerful native state, the kingdom of Usambara. According to the traditional history, which in this case goes farther back than in most inland areas of mid-Africa, a certain Bega migrated from the Ngura district, about eighty miles from the coast opposite Zanzibar, to the Usambara mountains which begin to rise from the maritime plain some twenty-five miles from Tanga and reach heights of over 6,000 feet. The people of this beautiful and fertile country, the Shambaa, accepted Bega as their 'King'; and he founded his capital in the heart of the mountains at Vuga. Bega was succeeded by his son Buga, and he in turn by his son Sheluge, who extended the bounds of the kingdom north-eastwards towards the present frontier between Kenya and Tanganyika. The southern boundary seems always to have been the River Pangani. The next king, Kimweri, son of Sheluge and great-grandson of Bega, was the greatest of the line. Born about the beginning of the nineteenth century, he proved himself in his younger days a bold warrior and a strong and efficient ruler. By 1840 he had conquered not only the greater part of the Pare Mountains, stretching some eighty miles north-westwards towards Kilimanjaro, but also the plain between Usambara and the sea. Thus, when Krapf visited Kimweri at Vuga in 1848 and 1852, he found his kingdom extending some 60 miles from north to south and some 140 miles from north-west to south-east and containing, so he estimated, at least half a million people. Kimweri appears to have contemplated still further expansion south of the Pangani, but there he had been checked by the Zigu, who had been the first tribe of this part of the coast to obtain fire-arms from the European and American merchants of Zanzibar and had used them with effect against

[1] Krapf, 181.

the spears and arrows of Usambara. Not only had they repulsed Kimweri's invasion; they had crossed the Pangani about 1840, laid waste the coastal plain, and destroyed the villages and plantations clustered on the fertile slopes of Mount Tongwe.[1]

The kingdom was divided into districts, each of which was put in charge of a 'Governor', who was usually but not invariably one of the many children born to Kimweri by his numerous wives. Thus Krapf found sons of the King installed as 'Governors' at Chumbi, Dofa, Kisara, and Utinde. He also speaks of his daughters 'ruling' the villages of Kadango, Pombe, and Nugniri. But this administrative decentralization detracted nothing from Kimweri's absolute authority. 'Simba wa Muene' his subjects called him, 'Lion of Heaven' or 'the only true lion'—'by way of contrast with the Governors of districts who as smaller lions dwell in the mountains of Usambara'.[2] Each Governor was required to have at court a representative, called a Mlau, through whom and not directly, even if the Governor were Kimweri's son, all state business was transacted.[3]

The central government was simple. Beside the Governors' Mlaus Krapf only mentions three officials, the Mdoe or Vizier, the Mboki or Military Chief who commanded the standing army in the King's absence, and, on a lower footing, the Mbereko or Captain of the Bodyguard. Among minor members of the court the royal physician, Osman, an Arab or half-Arab from Zanzibar, seems to have enjoyed a special measure of his master's confidence.[4]

The primitive financial system was wholly under Kimweri's control. Revenue was obtained by levying a direct tax or 'tribute' on this or that district from time to time. When Krapf landed on the coast in 1852, he was met by the Mdoe, who with the Governors of Chumbi and Dofa and an escort of soldiers had been sent to collect the tribute at Pangani. He noted that the inhabitants of the four villages at the mouth of the river,

---

[1] Krapf, 275, 374, 378, 381–6, 389. O. Baumann, *Usambara und seine Nachbargebiete* (Berlin, 1891), 186–7.
[2] Krapf, 272, 369–89.   [3] Idem, 369–89, 401.
[4] Idem, 369, 390.

numbering about 4,000, paid 200 yards or pieces of American calico, worth only from 50 to 60 dollars; and he was told that 'this tribute is exacted only once in every two or three years when the Vizier comes to the coast'. Having obtained their cloth, the officials departed for Madanga, a village some ten miles inland, where also they were to obtain the tribute before returning to Vuga.

'At break of day the war-horn sounded, and a soldier ran up and down the village shouting with a loud voice, "Get ready, ye Sambaa soldiers, the Mazambe, the Kings (the Vizier and the two Governors) are about to depart." The whole village was at once in motion; for the people were glad of their departure, the soldiers having behaved to them with violence and robbed them of poultry and other things, and the owner of the house in which I was had buried his valuables out of fear of the soldiery.'

Having witnessed the collection of revenue, Krapf happened also to be present at its allocation. Summoned one day to Kimweri's presence, he found him engaged in dealing with the tribute which the Mdoe had duly brought in—the calico from Pangani and some oxen and sheep from Madanga. 'Of the 200 pieces of cloth the King retained 100 for himself and his wives, giving forty-two to the Vizier and his soldiers, thirty-three to the headmen of Vuga, and twenty-five to the Mbereko and his servants.' The Mboki, it seems, did not figure on this 'Civil List'.[1]

Krapf also witnessed Kimweri dispensing justice. When the Vizier was collecting tribute at Mringano, one of the villagers had killed three of his military escort and fled into the forest. Since he could not be found, his children and kinsmen had been arrested and brought to Vuga. After hearing the Vizier's report, Kimweri pronounced the following sentence: 'The kinsmen shall be confined in the state-prison until the criminal is discovered and slain; and his children shall be sold as slaves.' Messengers were then dispatched to all the Governors ordering them to make a search for the criminal and to send him, if caught, to Vuga.[2]

Taken with Krapf's reference to the conduct of the soldiers at

[1] Idem, 369, 375, 396. [2] Idem, 396–7.

Pangani, this case suggests that Kimweri, like many other autocrats in history, permitted a certain licence to his troops on whom his power rested. But that did not mean loose discipline. Krapf observed that the soldiers were quick to obey orders because they knew that the invariable penalty of disobedience was to be sold for a slave.[1]

Kimweri seems indeed to have been a highly efficient autocrat. 'He does not always exercise his power to the utmost', Krapf remarks: 'he mostly demeans himself gently towards his subjects, but only to make them bear with his despotism all the more patiently.' But despotism it certainly was, and stringent at that. None of Kimweri's true African subjects—the Swahili of the coast, it will be seen, were treated differently—was allowed to ride on horse or donkey, to wear expensive clothes, or to travel far from home. And Krapf hints at worse, because more arbitrary, forms of tyranny. 'The Sambaa', he notes, 'do not care to amass riches; for in doing this they would live in constant dread of provoking the jealousy and covetousness of the King and his governors.' But, if the despotism was there, so, it seems, was the patience. Krapf, it is true, mentions a case of a village in rebellion in the Chumbi district: the soldiers of his escort were summoned to assist in its suppression. But he evidently regards a conversation he had with a native as revealing more truly than any minor symptoms of unrest the general attitude of the people. 'Are there', he asked, 'any liberated slaves in Usambara?' 'With us', was the answer, 'no one can free a slave, for we are all slaves of the King who is our Muungu (God)'[2]—a case of mistaken identity such as has often enough occurred in the history of less primitive societies.

To Krapf's sober and orderly mind this despotism was clearly attractive, if only in comparison with the feebleness and disorderliness of the tribal government with which he was familiar in the neighbourhood of his mission-station near Mombasa. Directly he crossed the frontier of Usambara he was struck by the efficiency of the arrangements made for the transport and care of strangers. Freedom alone was denied them. A stranger

[1] Krapf, 385. [2] Idem, 371, 384–5.

could not enter the kingdom or leave it without the King's personal permission. His every movement was prescribed: he must follow the routes and keep the time-table laid down for him. But, granted these restrictions, his path was smooth enough. An official was told off to guide him—in Krapf's case no less a man than the Mdoe. Soldiers carried his baggage. Free food was furnished at every village. No wonder that Krapf, who had known, like many a European traveller after him, the weariness of haggling for porterage and food, exclaims that 'never before had a journey been made so easy for me'. And arrived at Vuga he found himself waited on by the Mbereko who brought a sheep and other provisions: 'for he adds to his military functions that of providing foreigners and visitors with food and drink whether the King is in Vuga or absent from it'. In return for all this kindly, if masterful, treatment the stranger was expected to make a present to the King.[1]

But in Krapf's view these particular arrangements were only part of the general efficiency of Kimweri's government. On his first visit to Usambara, at the end of his first day in it, before he had seen Kimweri and been influenced, perhaps, in his favour by the friendliness accorded to himself and to his project of founding a mission in the country, Krapf noted down his most immediate and marked impression. 'The tranquillity and respect with which the people accosted me, not one of them begging anything, soon showed me that in the territory of King Kimweri there must reign such order as is sought for in vain among the republican communities of the Nyika and Kamba.' He felt the same wherever he went. He makes the same comment in almost the same words at the outset of his second visit. 'As regards security', he says a little later, 'I do not believe that one could be safer in any European country than in Usambara, provided it is not in a state of war.' Again, 'the great difference between monarchical Usambara and the unbridled republicanisms of the Nyika and Kamba struck even my two Nyika servants who could not sufficiently extol the order prevailing in the land'. And, apart from the use of the

[1] Idem, 370.

word 'republic' as a term of abuse, there is little to quarrel with in Krapf's admiration of Kimweri's rule. There is a stage in the political development of all societies, African or other, at which a vigorous despotism may be the only means of securing unity and maintaining peace and order, and these are specially difficult tasks in a land of mountains and mountaineers. 'The social condition of Usambara would be a critical one', Krapf finally and truly observes, 'if its inhabitants were not ruled by the iron hand of their monarch; for every petty magistrate or chief would revolt upon his mountain and strive to be independent.' 'It were well', he cannot forbear from adding, 'if those quarrelsome and drunken republicans, the Nyika and the Kamba, could feel, at least for a time, the power of an African lion-king!'[1]

Kimweri died about 1860, and his kingdom did not long survive him. But the fame of it was remembered among its subjects, not without pride, nor only by the people of the mountains. The following passage occurs in a report on the development of 'Indirect Rule' in Tanganyika by Sir Donald Cameron from 1925 onwards—a policy which involved the re-establishment of the old tribal organization. 'In Usambara the chiefdom known to early explorers as the important Kingdom of Vuga has been restored after an abeyance of some forty or fifty years, and so popular was this measure that a portion of the tribe living in Tanga District insisted on their inclusion in the Native Administration.'[2]

Over a fellow-monarch as powerful as the King of Usambara Said could assert no overlordship. But their political relations had somehow to be adjusted as soon as Kimweri extended his frontier to the coast between Vanga and Pangani. That section had been claimed as part of their 'dominion' by the Mazrui at

[1] Krapf, 274, 370, 377–8, 385. Burton and Speke paid a surprise visit to Vuga in 1857, but they only stayed a day and had one short interview with Kimweri at which they presented their letter of introduction from Said's successor, Majid. Speke, 182–4.
[2] *Report to the Council of the League of Nations on the Administration of Tanganyika Territory for 1927* [Colonial No. 32], 98.

Mombasa, and their claim had passed to Said. Tanga, an old-established Arab seaport, lay in the centre of it. The chief caravan-route to the interior started farther south from Bagamoyo, but Pangani, whence the river valley penetrated the hill-country right up to the slopes of Kilimanjaro, was a busy centre of the export trade in slaves.[1] And all up the coast Swahili and 'banyan' merchants were trafficking in ivory, cereals, and cattle as well as slaves, each of them in some sense under Said's over-lordship, each of them a thread in the economic network radiating from Zanzibar. Here, then, was a conflict of authority which might well have led to ceaseless friction. But, since Kimweri could be as cautious and practical-minded as Said himself, a tacit compromise was found in what might almost be called, in the language of European politics, a 'condominium'. Tanga, of course, and its immediate neighbourhood remained the preserve of Said's Governor. But elsewhere along the maritime strip Kimweri appointed head-men, called Diwans, 'to uphold his influence', says Krapf (who was respectfully received by the Diwan at Mtangata, twelve miles south of Tanga), 'among the Swahili on the coast whom he considers to be his subjects'. But the appointment of a Diwan had to be confirmed by Said, 'who makes the candidate a present that he may not lose sight of the Sultan's interests should they run counter to those of the King of Usambara. Thus the Diwan must receive the assent of the sovereign by sea as well as of the sovereign by land.' His appointment confirmed, the Diwan was permitted by Kimweri certain privileges of office enjoyed by no one else. He could wear a special sort of sandal. He could carry an umbrella of state. He could walk about preceded by a band of music. What precisely were his functions Krapf does not say. Presumably he would report and at need get aid from Vuga if Kimweri's authority were questioned. But there was little to question. The Swahili of the coast were not taxed. They were exempt from those stringent prohibitions regarding riding and clothes and travel which applied to all Kimweri's other subjects. Indeed, these latter distinguished the Swahili from themselves as

[1] Krapf, 373.

the 'Wangwana', the 'free people'. And the reason for the difference was plain enough. 'Kimweri knows perfectly well', writes Krapf, 'that the Swahili, through their connexion with the Arabs, might become dangerous to him if he were to treat them with similar rigour.' And Said for his part was quite ready to concede to Kimweri at distant Vuga the same sort of nominal authority as that which the Somali chiefs, for example, conceded to him at still more distant Zanzibar, provided it implied no interference with his taxation of the coastal trade. Ivory, next to slaves, was the most important export, and he exacted duties rising from two dollars to twelve on every 'frasila' (36 pounds) according to the distance it had come from the interior. As everywhere else in this African world it was economic, not political, aggrandizement that Said sought, commerce, not conquest. And again Krapf sums it up in a sentence: 'In a general way he does not trouble himself about this coast except in so far as regards its trade.'[1]

South of the Pangani away down to the Portuguese frontier there was no organized African state like Usambara with which Said's economic exploitation of the coast could conflict. He had a Governor at Buyeni, just below the river; and all the seaboard tribes, says Krapf, including the militant Zigu, main-

[1] Krapf, 384-5, 416-17. The account given by Krapf in the *Travels*, published in 1860 and followed in the text, is better informed than the following earlier description of the coast, written in 1850: 'The Imam of Muscat has not an inch of ground on the coast between the island of Wasin and the Pangani River: this tract in fact belonging to King Kimweri of Usambara down from 4° 30' to 5° 30' S.' Quoted by W. H. Sykes, *R.G.S.J.* xxiii, 1853, 106. There seems to have been some transient disagreement between Said and Kimweri early in 1853. The missionary Erhardt wrote home in April that Said, 'after a long conversation about Usambara, offered me most kindly a letter to Kimweri'. He had had letters from his agents on the coast saying that 'the difficulties with Kimweri had been solved and the country would soon be quiet again'. The trade-route from Tanga inland had been interrupted by a Zigua raid, and Said went on to say that 'he would erect a fort near Mnt. Tongwé and place a garrison on the road between the coast and the capital of Kimweri'. Speke's observation in 1857 of a fort 'on a hill called Tongwé' near the Pangani River with a garrison of 25 Baluchis (op. cit. 174) is evidence that he did so. Erhardt to Venn, 9.iv.53 (F.O. 54. 15).

tained friendly relations with the Swahili and were 'directly or more or less indirectly subject' to Said.[1] Naturally this control was most effective in the district nearest to Zanzibar and in the neighbourhood of the great caravan-route which debouched at Bagamoyo; and it was on the route some eighty miles inland from Bagamoyo that arose the one occasion on record—there may, of course, have been others—on which Said himself used force against a native African community.

Among the officers of the French corvette, *La Dordogne*, which was cruising off the East African coast in 1843 under Captain Guillain's command, was an ensign of twenty-five, named Maizan, who became fired with the idea of crossing the continent from the Indian Ocean to the Atlantic. Having obtained official sanction of his enterprise at Paris and Bourbon, he arrived at Zanzibar at the end of 1844 on the ship which brought the first French consul, M. Broquant, appointed under the commercial treaty recently concluded between the French Government and Said. At Zanzibar the young adventurer tarried for eight months in order to learn Swahili, but mainly, it seems, because he could not make up his mind about the route and organization of his expedition. He accumulated, meantime, so much baggage and so many scientific instruments of gleaming metal that Consul Hamerton warned him of the risk he would run in travelling through savage Africa with such valuable and attractive belongings. But Maizan seemed deaf to warnings. He did not even ask for one of Said's invaluable 'passports', and declined the guides he offered to supply him. Yet all might have been well if in accordance with his final plan he had set off for the interior with a big Arab caravan bound for Nyamwezi. But he let it start without him. And then, suddenly, soon after the early rains of 1845, he took a boat for Bagamoyo, and went quickly to his fate.

The lengthy delay at Zanzibar had meant, of course, that rumours of Maizan's project had spread far. Long before he started, it was known along the coast and up the inland routes

[1] Krapf, 418–19. Ivory from near the coast above Tanga paid 2 dollars, from Usambara and Chagga 4, from Unyamwezi 12.

that one young Frenchman, and one alone, was planning a journey into the interior. There is no reason to suppose that a plot was hatched for his destruction by Arabs or Swahili on the coast in the belief that he was bent on exploring the ground for French trade or even annexation. In any case those heavy boxes, those fascinating instruments were strong and direct enough temptation for any chief who dared to rob a white man. And Maizan, it appears, had been told that one particular chief, P'hazi Mazungere, who lived a few leagues up the caravan-route, was a notoriously reckless brigand. This time he listened to the warning and attempted to circumvent P'hazi's country: but after twenty days' wandering from Bagamoyo he found himself back on the route at the village of Degelamhora, only three days' march or some eighty miles from the sea. There P'hazi caught him with only a few porters and his young Malagasi servant. He tied him to a fence and cut his throat. Curiously enough he spared the servant's life; and presently surrendered him to Said for a ransom of 100 piastres. And this was still more curious: for the servant could and did retail at Zanzibar the full details of the crime.[1]

When the news reached Bourbon, Commandant Romain-Desfossés, the senior naval officer on the station, went at once to Zanzibar and informed Said that his Government required him as overlord of the coast to arrest the murderer and hand him over to justice. Said promised to do all he could. The commandant sailed away. And nothing happened.... It was not

[1] The best account is that of Guillain (ii. 15–19), who, as will appear, was sent to Zanzibar in the following year to exact reparation and who was therefore equipped with all the information obtained by the French Consul at the time. Krapf's summary account (421) agrees in the main with Guillain's. Burton visited Degelamhora in 1857, twelve years after the event, and claims precedence for the version he obtained from the villagers on the spot, though it differs markedly from Guillain's (*Lake Regions*, 73–7: cf. *Zanzibar*, London, 1872, i. 56). When Speke visited the neighbourhood again in 1860 he met a sub-chief, Hembe, who claimed to have been the murderer, but said that 'the fault did not rest with him, as he merely carried out the instructions of his father ... a Diwan on the coast'. *Discovery of the Source of the Nile* (London, 1863), 29–30.

any doubts as to the success of a little punitive expedition that made Said hesitate. P'hazi was not the Sultan of Pate or the King of Usambara. He and his tribesmen could easily be dealt with by a small force of 'Baluchis'. But in that area above all others Said was reluctant to make trouble. The effect of an armed invasion from Zanzibar, however small its scale, on the tribes all up the great caravan-route was incalculable. It might seriously imperil the smooth transit of his precious caravans. It might sever for an indefinite time the chief artery of the commercial system he had so patiently created. It might set currents of fear and hate towards all Arab intruders running far and wide in the interior. Said decided to do nothing unless the French forced his hand. . . . They soon did force it. Consul Broquant naturally reported his inaction, and when in the autumn of 1846 Captain Guillain was sent in the *Ducouëdic* to visit Zanzibar and the northward coast towns, the Maizan affair was one of the matters he was instructed to settle promptly and finally with Said.[1]

Nothing could have been friendlier, Guillain reported, than Said's reception; but, when he recalled the promise made to arrest P'hazi and, pointing out that the recent treaty with France gave any Frenchman the right to go freely about his territories,[2] pressed for its fulfilment, Said coolly denied that he had ever promised more than he could perform and said he could not arrest P'hazi because he had no authority over him. 'He and his people are not my subjects,' he declared, 'nor is his country part of my dominions.' If that were so, Guillain answered, Said must not be surprised if the French navy took action on its own account to secure the satisfaction due to it. Said, no doubt, was expecting that ultimatum, and he could not ignore it. He knew what the French had done at Nossi-bé.[3] He dreaded what they might do, if occasion or excuse were offered, all up *his* coast. But to submit at once was not in accordance with the rules of his diplomacy. He answered Guillain in much the same way as he had answered Owen in that

[1] Guillain, ii. 20–1. See p. 451, below.
[2] See pp. 423, 481, below.   [3] See pp. 439–40, below.

famous interview at Muscat.[1] He would be very glad if the French would do what he could not do himself and punish P'hazi as he deserved. When, however, the faithful Suliman-bin-Hamed reported, as he was meant to do, the gist of a long talk he had had with Guillain—the ease with which a naval landing-party would achieve the 'impossible' task; the change it would bring about in the high opinion which the French Government now held of Said's power and prestige and the extent of his authority; the proof which his inaction would afford of a lack of goodwill towards France—then Said saw that the time for evasion was past. He informed Guillain that the requisite action would be taken, and this time he kept his word. Two or three hundred 'Baluchis' were dispatched to Degelamhora. P'hazi they failed to catch: he had escaped into the 'bush'. But, as Said wrote to Romain-Desfossés, 'they killed every one they could, and left the villages in ruins'. P'hazi's chief 'minister', who had assisted in the murder, was brought to Zanzibar and handed over to the French Consul. For nearly two years he was kept in chains opposite the consulate. Then he was moved to the fort and ironed to a gun. He died about ten years later.[2]

The moral of this incident was plain. Said's attitude to the African chiefs and tribes inland was much the same as his attitude to the Arab coast towns. He would have no trouble with them if he could help it. Peace, not war, was the condition of good trade. If fighting tribes were to be found here and there with whom no peace was possible, it was wisest to tell the Arab merchants that, if they ventured into their country, they could expect no help from him. As to the weaker tribes, he had no appetite for conquest, no desire to impose his rule. He would no more interfere with the affairs of an African chief than with those of a sultan of an Arab seaport—unless his claim to a general and loose, *but exclusive*, overlordship were seriously threatened from within or without. Hence his relations with the inland Africans were at once distant and friendly; and it is

[1] See p. 232, above.
[2] Guillain, ii. 36–43, 91–3. Krapf, 421. Burton, *Lake Regions*, i. 77–8.

significant that the member of his court whom Hamerton picked out as having 'much influence with the pagan chiefs on the coast of Africa' was that 'kind, good sort of person', Suliman-bin-Hamed.[1] But naturally to Guillain as to Hamerton this kind of relationship, though in fact it served its purpose with the Africans as with the Arabs, seemed something far short of 'dominion'. 'Il faut dire', wrote the Frenchman, with the Maizan affair in his mind, 'que l'autorité de Syed Said sur les chefs des peuplades qui avoisinent la côte est plus nominale qu'effective, et qu'il a grand besoin de ménager leur susceptibilité pour qu'elles ne gênent pas la circulation des caravanes qui de l'intérieur se rendent à Zanzibar, en traversant leur territoire.'[2]

The caravans—they dominate the picture; and it was through them that Said did in fact enjoy a sort of authority in the interior, a quite peculiar sort, indirect but more than nominal, and more effective than his European critics realized. For it is evident from the narratives of the great explorers that the Arab traders exercised a certain power at any rate in the main field of their operations between the coast and Lakes Tanganyika and Nyasa. At their settlements and as they moved along the trade-routes, they were, as a rule, the masters of the country round. A strong slave-raiding caravan, such as has been described in the preceding chapter, could usually go where it pleased and do what it liked. Generally speaking, the only danger—and it was sometimes a real one—was to cross the path of some fighting people like the Masai in the north or the Zulu or Matabele in the south, engaged on a long-distance raid.[3] The less warlike tribes, scattered in little villages, could make no effective resistance to the strangers' muskets. Arab adventurers, indeed, could and sometimes did depose the local chiefs and set up for a period as 'Sultans' in their place. But such usurpations were rare. Even at Tabora, their largest and most important settlement, while they governed their own community them-

[1] B.R. 238. [2] Guillain, ii. 17.
[3] Krapf speaks of caravans of 600 to 1,000 being often attacked in the Masai country and 'nearly all slain' (364).

selves, the Arabs made no attempt to govern the natives of the district. They recognized their independence outside the settlement, and paid them tolls for the transit of their trade. One occasion is known in which they interfered. About 1860 they took part with a native faction in ejecting the local 'Sultan' who had been duly appointed by the paramount chief of the tribal group, but had unwisely raised the tolls. It is not till after Said's time that there is any record of a combined and formidable movement of native tribes against the alien invaders from the coast. The control, in fact, exercised by the Arab traders, though nearly always indirect, intermittent, and irregular or (so to speak) peripatetic, was none the less a real control.

Now all those traders were nominally Said's subjects. They acknowledged his overlordship no less than their kinsmen of the coast. At Tabora, as at the coast towns, Said seems to have appointed a leading Sheikh as his personal representative or governor.[1] But Tabora was several weeks' march from the sea in the dry season and for nearly half the year it was almost inaccessible. It was impossible, therefore, for Said to make his power felt there as he could by means of his fleet along the coast. None the less, the Arabs in the interior, whether at settlements like Tabora or Ujiji or wandering far inland, seem generally to have obeyed their overlord. It was only in small matters, after all, that he was likely as a rule to require their obedience; and the evidence of their attitude is mainly derived from the reports of missionaries or explorers such as Rebmann or Livingstone as to the practical value of a *firman* or passport from Said or his successors. The inland Arabs, it appears, professed a deep respect for their distant sovereign's wishes and did all they could to help a stranger commended by him to their care. Nor

---

[1] Burton and Speke do not mention a Governor. Burton says the Arabs need 'some man to take the lead'. 'About fifteen years ago Abdullah-bin-Salim, a merchant from Zanzibar, with his body of 200 armed slaves, kept the whole community in subjection: since his death in 1852, the society has suffered from all the effects of disunion' (*Lake Regions*, i. 329). But Stanley was received by 'the Governor, Said-bin-Salim' in 1871 (*How I found Livingstone in Central Africa*, London, 1872, p. 258).

was this submissiveness in little things surprising. Deference cost nothing. Disregard might have cost much. For, though those Arabs in the interior might be far beyond Said's grasp for years at a time, sooner or later most of them returned to the coast and many of them to Zanzibar itself. It was from Zanzibar that the biggest and richest caravans set out for their long speculative journeys. The 'banyans' of Zanzibar, Said's protégés and instruments, financed them. And in their houses there, hostages or pledges under Said's eye, they left their wives and children, their goods and chattels. A rumour reaching Zanzibar that this or that caravan-leader had treated a letter from his overlord with indifference, though he were hundreds of miles away, might well mean his ruin.[1]

It may be said, then, that, however rare its exercise or limited its purpose, Said's authority over the Arabs and their Swahili associates in their wanderings or at their settlements in the interior was as real as his authority over the coast towns. And somehow or other the fact of this authority was communicated to the African mind. As the caravans pushed deeper and deeper inland, there spread with them through all the tribes the name and fame of the mighty prince to whom all these rich and well-armed traders and their followers owed allegiance. The shadow of the throne at Zanzibar thus lengthened out for hundreds of miles westward from the coast. And it was more than a shadow. Behind the power of the caravans lay Said's power; and, though it has often been construed too literally, there was some truth in the proverb, first spoken in Said's day and still repeated in ours:

> *When one pipes at Zanzibar,*
> *they dance on the Lakes.*

Such, in the mere outlines that can now be drawn, was Said's rule in the interior of Africa. It may be defined as a system of economic penetration with only the minimum of political

[1] The Arab caravan-leaders 'obtained credits from big Indian merchants domiciled at Zanzibar which they repaid when they returned from their *safaris*. The goods taken on credit—such as *merikani*, beads, Manchester goods, flintlock rifles, powder and shot—were exchanged by them for ivory and slaves.' O'Swald (as cited p. 382, note, below), 41–2.

activity required to supply the export trade. It was operated by Said himself in his capacity as a merchant and by his subjects as private individuals or groups. It was directly controlled by the State—and the State was Said—only in so far as its commercial proceeds were made to contribute their quota to the revenue. But indirectly, and especially in the vital matter of finance, Said could probably make his will prevail when and where he wished. Like his 'dominion' on the coast, it was, as has been said, a peculiar system. No label can be found for it in the conventional vocabulary of politics. To call it an 'empire' would be absurd. Could it even be described in the technical terms of a later day as 'effective occupation'? That question was asked and answered a generation after Said's death, and a full discussion of it must be reserved for a later volume; but this much may be said here—that Said's occupation of the midland area was at least as real an 'occupation' and at least as 'effective' as the only other example of alien rule in East Africa in his time, the Portuguese occupation of adjacent Mozambique. It is as easy, indeed, to make too little of Said's achievement as to make too much. Whether he 'possessed' the coast or not, he did bring the whole of it—from Mogadishu to the Rovuma—within the range of a single political and economic system. Never before had all the Arab colonies submitted to one Arab overlord. Never before had they established so wide and deep a contact with the inland country. And all the threads of that far-reaching web led back to Said's tax-collectors and the strongest of them to Said himself. Simple and loose as it was, the system admirably served the purposes of its maker, and the making of it sets Said-bin-Sultan among the great figures of Arab history.

XII

TRADERS FROM AMERICA AND GERMANY

FROM the account of Said's 'dominion' in the preceding chapter it might seem as if at the climax of his reign East Africa from the Red Sea to Delagoa Bay had been finally 'partitioned' between Europe and Asia. South of the Rovuma the Portuguese retained the dilapidated remains of their old empire, while over the northward coast, now lost to them beyond recovery, Said had imposed at least as wide and real a measure of control as was theirs in Mozambique.[1] But there were other Europeans than the Portuguese, not indeed in occupation of East African soil, but frequenting East African waters. Besides the British cruisers busy with the Slave Trade, there were merchant-ships from at least four maritime states of the Western world. Their number steadily increased throughout Said's reign. Foreign houses of business established themselves at Zanzibar. Foreign consuls were appointed there. And since (as has been seen) the encouragement of this external trade was an essential part of his economic policy, Said not only welcomed this growing contact with Europe and the West; he did all he could to encourage and extend it. It served his ends. It greatly enlarged his revenues. And, no doubt, he was only hastening a process which could not have been long delayed. But there were risks in it which threatened his throne and his 'dominion'. Elsewhere, and notably on the opposite side of the Indian Ocean, European trade had been the prelude to European rule; and though the danger did not in fact materialize till Said had been dead for thirty years, the commercial invasion of his realm, side by side with the missionary and humanitarian invasion, marked the beginning of another revolution in East African history.

[1] For evidence of the deplorable character of Portuguese administration in Mozambique at this period see Owen's *Narrative*, i. 123, 190, 286, and the violent censure of the American Captain Roberts in his *Embassy to the Eastern Courts of Cochin China, Siam and Muscat, 1832–4* (New York, 1837), 370.

Represented now by more persistent agents than the Portuguese, Europe was re-entering the field.

I

The first and for a long time the most numerous commercial invaders were not Europeans of Europe. One of the most interesting results of the American Revolution was the intrusion of American enterprise into the honey-pot of oriental trade round which the sea-going peoples of Europe had been buzzing for two centuries, but which had been barred off from British colonists by the mercantile system and the East India Company's monopoly. The maritime community of Massachusetts, shrewd and bold men of business, first-rate ship-builders, skilled and adventurous navigators, and seamen as brave and hardy as any in the world, were quick to seize the chance so long denied them; and their stout little ships, of about 300 tons burden on the average, were soon at work in almost every corner of the Indian Ocean, the China Sea, and the South Pacific, bringing back direct to their home-ports, at enormous profit, tea and silks and china-ware and 'nankeens' from Canton or sugar and rice and spices from India and the Malayan islands or coffee from Mocha. Before the end of the eighteenth century the volume of American trade over this vast area had already outstripped that of every other nation except Britain, and the merchants of New England had even begun to undersell the East India Company's Chinese tea and silk in European markets. In this swift and triumphant campaign, one of the most remarkable in the history of commerce, Boston took the lead, closely followed by Salem, then an old-fashioned seaport of some eight thousand inhabitants. By a tacit understanding these two rivals divided the new field between them. The Boston ships mostly set out round Cape Horn, sailed thence up the coast to Alaska where they loaded furs, so crossed to China, and came home through the Indian Ocean. The Salem ships went out by the Cape of Good Hope, avoiding Table Bay for fear of getting wind-bound, and thence, touching at Madagascar or the Mascarenes, to Arabia, India, the East Indies, and the South Pacific

Isles.[1] Returning the same way, they sometimes met their Boston compatriots off Java Head and sailed home in their company. The dividing line was occasionally crossed. A Boston ship might try its luck at Calcutta or a Salem ship at Canton, but on the whole the trade south and west of China was monopolized by Salem, and Salem merchants were soon well known at Calcutta, Bombay, Madras, and Rangoon, coming and going year after year and sometimes settling down as permanent residents in charge of business houses of their own. A certain Thomas Lechmere of Salem, for example, became an alderman of Bombay.[2]

The obstacles and accidents of world-war from 1793 to 1815 and the unfortunate Anglo-American conflict of 1812–15 checked and diverted this new stream of commerce; and, when peace came, ocean trading began to yield to manufacture the dominant place in the life of Massachusetts. Boston alone was still a great seaport at the end of this economic revolution. The rest, Salem among them, rapidly decayed. Already in 1815 Salem had lost more than two-thirds of the trading-fleet she had owned in 1807. But she struggled on. One Salem ship made twenty-one voyages to Calcutta between 1815 and 1837. Others stubbornly continued the famous Salem pepper trade with Sumatra. Others again explored the fringes and by-ways of the Eastern field in the hope of finding some rich new vein of trade whereby Salem might fortify her waning vigour. Thus it was that a Salem ship sailed up-stream to Saigon in 1819 and opened the first American trade with Cochin China: and thus it was that Salem ships, a few years later, began to turn off from the main Cape-to-India route up the side-track which most of their predecessors except the Portuguese had virtually ignored, and to

[1] In a note kindly prepared for me by Mr. S. W. Phillips of Salem, a keen student of the invaluable commercial archives at the Essex Institute, it is stated that a Salem ship called at Île de France in 1789 and that in 1805 eight Salem ships landed over two million pounds of coffee from Mocha. About 1833, 101 American ships of nearly 40,000 tons burden were engaged in trade with Java and the neighbouring islands in a single year. Roberts, op. cit. 7.

[2] For this paragraph see S. E. Morison's fascinating *Maritime History of Massachusetts, 1783–1860* (London, 1923). For the China trade see also K. W. Porter, *J. J. Astor*, Cambridge, Mass., 1931.

nose their way up the East African coast. Only one or two merchant-ships from New York and other ports followed their lead. But they were accompanied, at least as far north as Zanzibar, by several American ships of quite a different class. The Indian Ocean was one of the recognized areas for whale-hunting, and for some time past American 'whalers', mostly from New Bedford, the centre of the industry, had begun to frequent the southern half of the East African coast.[1] American 'slavers' also were not only busy on the west coast. A British naval officer reported in 1812 that Americans had been in the habit for some time past of visiting Mozambique and 'still continue to do so every year in the months of June and July, and smuggle slaves to the Brazils and Spanish America'.[2]

From 1820 onwards, therefore, the presence of American ships in East African waters is frequently recorded. Owen observed three American ships in Bombetoke Bay and was impressed by the busy trade that was going on ashore at Majunga.[3] Nathaniel Isaacs, pioneer of British colonization in Natal, when on the voyage out to the Cape in 1829, was asked by an American skipper at St. Helena about the prospects of East African trade. In 1830 and again in 1831 the American brig *St. Michael*, of 150 tons, was trading muskets for ivory near Durban and selling powder to the Portuguese at Mozambique. In 1831 Isaacs counted at one time in Delagoa Bay nine American ships, eight of which were 'whalers', and two British. In the same year he encountered two American trading-ships on the west coast of

---

[1] Morison, op. cit., chaps. xiv, xx. American as well as British whalers were frequenting Delagoa Bay as early as 1798: G. M. Theal, *History of South Africa*, London, 1910, iii. 333. American ships were trading as far up the coast as Mozambique about 1804: Prentout, 445.

[2] Capt. Lynn to Rear-Admiral Stopford, 12.v.12: Theal, *R.S.E.A.* ix. 16.

[3] 'Notwithstanding the great distance the Americans come and the delay they are subject to in procuring the cargo, they still find the trade lucrative. . . . [They] have established small shops, where they retail a variety of assorted goods which they give in exchange for the minor articles of trade which the natives bring in for sale. They also purchase or erect a large wooden building with a yard or pound attached, wherein they slaughter their bullocks and jerk the beef' (*Narrative*, ii. 101–2).

Traders from America and Germany

Madagascar, one coming out from home, one returning from Mocha; and found residing at Majunga an American commercial agent, Mr. Bates, 'who has had a knowledge of the trade' ever since the American Captain Forbes discovered the place in 1819. American merchants, it appears, were doing 'a lucrative trade' at that time with the Arabs not only in Madagascar ports but also at Zanzibar, selling muskets, powder, and cloth, and buying hides, tortoise-shell, and beef, which last was salted and shipped to Cuba for feeding slaves. Pursuing his journey north, Isaacs put in at Lamu, using the sailing-instructions given him by an American shipmaster. Lamu, he points out, is a free port for any trade, 'but few have visited it except the enterprising Americans whose star-spangled banner may be seen streaming in the wind where other nations, not excepting even my own country, would not deign to traffic'.[1]

A more direct impression of this minor trafficking up the coast may be obtained from the log-book and journal kept by one of those 'enterprising Americans', Charles Millet, master of the brig *Ann* which sailed from Salem on March 12, 1826, laden with cotton goods mainly, but also tobacco, nails, and glass mirrors. Rounding the Cape and passing the east coast of Madagascar, Millet made straight for Mocha, which he reached on June 20, 106 days' sailing from Salem. There he stayed, loading coffee, till the beginning of 1827 when he sailed south on the look-out for other cargo. In the autumn he worked his way right up the line of Arab seaports, using a copy of Owen's map and acknowledging in his journal the correctness of his survey. At

[1] N. Isaacs, *Travels and Adventures in Eastern Africa* (London, 1836), 5–6, 343–4, 355–61, 391–2. G. Mackeurtan, *The Cradle Days of Natal* (London, 1930), 153, 159, 327. For the salt-beef trade see also Hart's Report (1834): 'One of the principal ports is Majunga . . . where a whole fleet may lay in six or seven fathoms, sheltered from all winds. Bullocks are plentiful in this place and very cheap. About eight years since, the Americans carried on a most lucrative trade from this port in buying bullocks at two dollars a head, which they killed on the spot and salted the meat and also the hides and took the hoofs and horns, and the latter selling for the original price of the bullocks left the meat for clear profit which they sold for an enormous price at the Havannah when they had lost their supplies from South America.' B.R. 279.

Lindi he was told (Nov. 17, 1827) by.'the natives' that 'this is the first American vessel that has ever visited this place'. 'Found it', he notes, 'to be a place of no trade except in slaves. I was informed that there was [sic] 300 arrived on this day from the interior for sale. The French carry on a great trade for slaves at this place from Bourbon. Finding there was nothing to be done to advance the object of my voyage, weighed anchor.' Next day he put in at Kiswere, forty miles to the north, and found it similarly confined to a trade in which he had no wish to share. 'A French schooner came in while we were there for slaves.' On November 24 he reached Zanzibar. 'Went on shore, and ascertained that grain, the article I was in want of, could not be had at this place, and was informed that it can be had at Mombasa.' Four days later he anchored in Mombasa harbour, and 'found a French schooner lying here from Bourbon after slaves'. At Hosea, a little north of Mombasa, he 'remained three days, endeavouring to trade for grain, but found the people rather unfriendly and disposed to cheat and deceive us'. Proceeding northwards he was pursued by some 'piratic dhows' which he assumed, probably wrongly, hailed from Muscat. 'Outdistanced all but one, which frightened off by getting guns out.' Early in December he was at Lamu, where, as will be seen, he got plenty of the grain he chiefly needed. At Merka, on the way to Barawa, he 'found the people very friendly'. From Barawa he turned south again on January 24, 1828. On May 9 in the next year he brought back home to Salem a cargo of Mocha coffee; 1,210 bags of *jonaree* (corn), 60 bags of rice, and 217 'elephants-teeth', shipped at Zanzibar; 1,124 bags of *jonaree*, 10 bags of *dhole* (lentils), and 21 'elephants-teeth', shipped at Lamu; and an assortment, gathered at various places, of bullock-hides, goatskins, sheepskins, gum arabic, gum copal, myrrh, beeswax, turtle-shell, dates, and ostrich-feathers.[1]

[1] Log-book and Journal of the *Ann*: Essex Institute archives, Salem. Another Salem brig, *Virginia*, visited Madagascar, Zanzibar, Mombasa, and Lamu in 1828. Christopher observed in 1843 that Barawa 'for fourteen years has been a welcome port to European and American traders, several of whom have resided on shore for days at a time'. *T.B.G.S.* vi. 381.

2

Small as they were at the moment, these new lines of trade in the Indian Ocean and the South China Sea seemed to the energetic Americans who first pursued them to be capable of wide expansion; and one of those pioneers, Captain Edmund Roberts, wrote to Mr. Woodbury, Senator for New Hampshire, to solicit the interest and support of the Federal Government. His case was convincing. The enterprising American traders whose ships were scattered over the Eastern seas clearly deserved some token of their Government's sympathy and support. As Roberts put it later, 'Not a single vessel of war is to be seen waving the national flag over our extensive commerce from the West of Africa to the East of Japan.'[1] And so, in due course, Mr. Woodbury having in the meantime been appointed Secretary of the Navy, Roberts was requested by the Government to go out as its 'Special Agent' to Cochin China, Siam, and Muscat and negotiate commercial agreements with their sovereigns for the promotion of American trade. In March 1832, accordingly, the United States sloop *Peacock* sailed from Boston and, having rounded Cape Horn, crossed the Pacific, traversed the Far East, and arrived at Muscat on September 18, 1833. His business concluded, Roberts left for home by the Cape route on October 2, and in the course of November the handful of British settlers at Port Natal were excited and intrigued by the unprecedented appearance in their bay of an American warship with a 'political commissioner' on board. Were the Americans, they asked, intending to plant a colony on the coast?[2]

The negotiations at Muscat had been smooth and successful. To Said, indeed, the arrival of this official mission from the United States was highly gratifying. It promised an expansion in his overseas trade. It flattered his pride to have attracted the attention of the great nation of the New World and to be treated by its President as his equal. It opened the prospect of a new political friendship which, however much he trusted his older

[1] Roberts, op. cit. 7.
[2] Report of Dr. A. Smith of Cape medical staff: Mackeurtan, op. cit. 329.

British friends, might be useful some day, even perhaps to play off against them. And, as has been mentioned in a previous chapter, he had a special reason at that moment for desiring any help he could get from outside.[1] When, therefore, Roberts presented himself, armed with a letter from President Jackson, he received him with every mark of honour and goodwill, and he made no difficulty at all about the commercial negotiations. 'The Sultan', wrote Roberts, 'at once acceded to my wishes by admitting our commerce into his ports upon the same terms as his most favoured friends, the British, to wit, by paying a duty of five per cent. on the cargo *landed* and free from every other charge whatever on imports or exports or even the charge of pilotage.'[2] Accordingly, on September 21, a Treaty of Amity and Commerce was signed 'between the United States of America and His Majesty Syud Saeed bin Sultan of Muskat and his Dependencies'. Article I, in the common form, pledged the signatories to 'perpetual peace'. Article II prescribed that American citizens should be free to come and go and buy and sell in all the Sultan's ports without any interference by him or his officers as to the fixing of prices or otherwise, with this peculiar postscript —'that the articles of muskets, powder and ball can only be sold to the Government in the island of Zanzibar, but in all other ports of the Sultan the said munitions of war may be freely sold without any restriction whatever to the highest bidder'. Article III imposed the 5 per cent. duty on cargo landed from American ships 'in full consideration of all import and export duties, tonnage, licence to trade, pilotage, anchorage, or any other charge'. Articles IV and VI absolved American citizens from the payment of any other duties as traders or residents than those paid by subjects of 'the most favoured nation'; and Article VIII bestowed a similar 'most-favoured-nation' privilege on vessels of the Sultan resorting to any port in the United States. Articles V and VII provided for assistance to be given to Americans suffering shipwreck or taken by pirates. The last

[1] See p. 282, above.
[2] E. Roberts, *Embassy to the Eastern Courts of Cochin China, Siam and Muscat, 1832–4* (New York, 1837), 360.

and ninth article was not the least important; for it not only established a permanent diplomatic connexion between the contracting parties, but introduced in an interesting form the historic principle of 'extra-territorial rights'.

'The President of the United States may appoint Consuls to reside in the ports of the Sultan where the principal commerce shall be carried on, which Consuls shall be the exclusive judges of all disputes or suits wherein American citizens shall be engaged with each other. They shall have power to receive the property of any American citizen dying within the Kingdom, and to send the same to his heirs, first paying all his debts due to the subjects of the Sultan. The said Consuls shall not be arrested, nor shall their property be seized, nor shall any of their household be arrested, but their persons and their property and their houses shall be inviolate. Should any Consul, however, commit any offence against the laws of the Kingdom, complaint shall be made to the President who will immediately displace him.'[1]

In 1833 the day when the sensitive nationalism of politically backward peoples would bitterly resent such European impositions as 'Capitulations' or 'Unequal Treaties' was still far off, and it doubtless seemed to Said a natural and quite inoffensive condition of the agreement, and one which would relieve him of a tiresome and delicate responsibility, to grant to a foreign official a power of jurisdiction over his fellow-citizens at his ports. At any rate, for the reasons given above, he was well satisfied with the treaty, and there was more than the usual sincerity in the oriental exuberance of the letter which Roberts carried back from him to 'the most high and mighty Andrew Jackson, whose name shines with so much splendour throughout the world'.

'On a most fortunate day and at a happy hour I had the honour to receive Your Highness's letter, every word of which was clear and distinct as the sun at noonday and every letter shone forth as brilliantly as the stars in the heavens. . . . His Highness may depend that all American vessels resorting to the ports within my dominions shall know no difference in point of good treatment between my country and that of his own most happy and fortunate country where felicity ever dwells. . . . I offer most sincerely and

[1] Text in B.R. 262–4.

truly to His Highness the President my entire and devoted services to execute any wishes the President may have within my dominions or within any ports or places wherein I possess the slightest influence.'[1]

About the same time Said entrusted Captain Waters, the master of a homeward-bound Salem brig, with a letter which he asked him to have published in America inviting her citizens to come and trade in his dominions.[2]

If Said was satisfied, so, of course, was Roberts. His countrymen had hitherto been generally obliged to pay as much as 7 per cent. on exports as well as imports together with 'anchorage money' and 'presents' to port officials; and now, for the mere asking and with nothing of real value offered in return—for not many Muscat ships were likely to visit the United States—he had obtained for them the same favours as those which the British had at least done something to win. To Roberts, moreover, it seemed a substantial advantage to have established a friendly and regular connexion with an Asiatic ruler so powerful commercially and politically in the Indian Ocean as Said. He observed that ships from Muscat were trading as far afield as Gujarat, Surat, Bombay, Calcutta, Ceylon, Sumatra, and Java; and he was not a little impressed by the size and efficiency of Said's navy.[3] Nor was there anything in the treaty with which the authorities responsible for the foreign policy of the United States could quarrel. In June 1834 it was smoothly ratified by the President and Senate;[4] and in 1835 Roberts was back again at Muscat to exchange the ratifications. This time an alarming mishap—the grounding of the *Peacock*, the warship which was taking him to Muscat—afforded Said an opportunity of yet more signal demonstrations of friendship. The ship had stranded off the inhospitable Arabian coast near the island of Masirah between two and three hundred miles from Muscat. It was a dangerous situation. A gale would destroy the ship, and the boats were only sufficient to save one-third of the crew.

---

[1] Dated Oct. 7, 1833, Muscat. English translation from Arabic in Roberts, op. cit. 430.   [2] B.R. 281: see p. 378, below.

[3] Roberts, op. cit. 362: see p. 298, above.

[4] W. S. Ruschenberger, *Narrative of a Voyage round the World etc.* (London 1838), i. vii.

Meantime they were exposed to a burning sun, their water-supply was small, and, worst of all, their efforts to shift the ship were obstructed by an increasing swarm of dhows full of pirates who—so at least thought Commodore Kennedy—were bent on seizing the ship and killing all aboard as soon as they were strong enough. Only from Muscat could help be got, and Roberts volunteered to try and get it. Embarking in a 20-foot boat with a midshipman and six men, he succeeded in eluding the pirates' pursuit and reached Muscat on the third day. Said took instant action. In less than two hours of Roberts's arrival a new sloop of Said's, the *Sultaneh*,[1] was ready to sail for Masirah with food and water; a courier was well on his way to Sur with orders for the Governor to proceed at once with 6 dhows and 300 men to protect the *Peacock* from the pirates till the *Sultaneh* arrived; and 150 of Said's own troops were prepared to mount their camels and ride overland to the scene of danger in case the Commodore and his company were forced to seek safety on shore. As it happened, after two days' effort, and then only by jettisoning stores, spare spars, and half the guns, the *Peacock* had been got afloat, and, creeping back in a leaky state to Muscat, met the *Sultaneh* coming to her aid some fifty miles from port. But 'the good Sultan's' efforts 'to serve our country through us', as Kennedy put it, had deeply impressed the Americans, and there was more to come. Said put a furnished house at Roberts's disposal, fed him from the palace kitchen, and supplied the *Peacock* with abundance of meat, fruit, and vegetables. He 'laid us all', says Kennedy, 'under obligations which can never be forgotten'. To cap it all, when his visitors had gone, he sent boats to Masirah, recovered the eleven guns they had thrown overboard, and shipped them after them to Bombay free of charge.[2]

[1] The *Sultaneh* was armed then or later with 20 guns bought from the United States: Said-Ruete, 127.
[2] Said-Ruete, 137. Kennedy's report, *U.S. Navy Department Archives*, Captains' Letters, 1835, i, printed in *U.S. Naval Institute Proceedings*, xxxvi, No. 3, and C. O. Paullin, *Early Voyages of American Naval Vessels to the Orient*, 720–1. When the *Sultaneh* visited the United States a year or so later, her crew was subjected (at which port is not

Finally, on December 6, 1836, the President informed the Senate that the ratifications of the treaty had been duly exchanged—a treaty, he said, which promised 'great advantages to our enterprising merchants and navigators'.[1]

3

The swift conclusion of this new *entente* did not, of course, escape the notice of Said's older friends. The British Resident in the Gulf at once informed the Bombay Government of the Treaty of 1833 and of the reported offer by Said to permit the Americans to make a settlement on the African coast if they would help him to reduce Mombasa. The idea of an American colonization in this part of the world, fantastic as it may have seemed at Washington, was not new. In the summer of 1796 the American merchant ship *Hercules*, bound from Calcutta to London with a cargo of rice, was wrecked on the coast of Kaffraria near the mouth of the Umzimvubu. The master, Captain Benjamin Stout, with most of his crew, got safe ashore, was received in the friendliest manner by the natives, and finally made his way overland to Capetown. Stout's interesting account of this experience was published in London in 1798 and again in 1810 and 1820, together with a dedicatory letter to President Adams, extolling the beauty and economic value of the country he had traversed and recommending an American settlement on the coast of Kaffraria. It would 'amply repay the expense', since it would provide the people of America in profusion with 'several articles essential to their commerce which they cannot find at home'. Failing this, Stout looked forward ungrudgingly to the expansion of British colonization up the coast from the

---

on record) to a disagreeable experience. 'They were tormented continually by the mob crowding to see the Arabs, looking on them as a curiosity. Their privacy was intruded on; they were pulled by the beards and otherwise insulted.' Hamerton to Palmerston, 10.ii.42 (F.O. 54. 4), reporting that Said frequently speaks of this 'ill usage of his people', and asking that similar incidents should be prevented when the ship about to take Said's envoy to England comes to London.

[1] *Journal of the Senate of the U.S.A.* (Washington, 1835), 24th Congress, Session 2, p. 8.

Cape—a move which would, he argued, give Britain ('whose prosperity has ever had the second place in my affections') control of Madagascar and bring her greater profit than that from all her possessions in the Indies, East and West.[1] President Adams, of course, ignored this appeal, if indeed he ever read it. But, despite the extreme improbability of the young United States, with its own vast continent still unoccupied and unexplored at its feet, embarking on a colonial adventure far oversea, British settlers in Cape Colony continued for years to dress up and parade this bogy. The anxiety occasioned by the voyage of the *Peacock* in 1832 has already been remarked. Eight years earlier Dr. Philip, the famous missionary, who in the matter of national prejudice might well have taken a lesson from Captain Stout, had bitterly deplored the prospect of 'the vindictive and enterprising spirit of America' materializing in an African colony. 'It is pretty generally known', he wrote from Cape Colony to a friend, 'that the American Government has for several years past been on the look-out for a favourable port between their own shores and India.' Delagoa Bay had been considered. 'It must appear on reflection that in the hands of America it might afford that power the means of doing great injury to our India trade and to this colony.' In the event of war, they might arm 'the savage tribes' and incite them to attack us.[2]

Needless to say, the British Government took no such melodramatic view of American ambitions; but the news of Roberts's mission and the treaty, quite apart from the repetition of the old rumour about a settlement, suggested that inquiries should be made as to what exactly the Americans were doing on that side of the Indian Ocean. On Admiralty orders Captain H. Hart, R.N., in H.M.S. *Imogene*, paid a visit to Said at Zanzibar in February 1834. His report, while it confirmed the growth of American trade, was reassuring on the political side. As far

[1] B. Stout, *Narrative of the Loss of the 'Hercules'* (1820 edition, under first title *Cape of Good Hope and its Dependencies*), 18–19, 21–6, 30–2. Details of the three editions in S. Mendelssohn's *South African Bibliography* (London, 1910), ii. 444–6.

[2] Philip to P. G. Brink, 13.iv.24. Theal, *R.S.E.A.* ix. 44–5.

as he could learn, no American colony was contemplated in East Africa.[1] But the rumours of such a colony smouldered on. The return of the *Peacock* rekindled them, and the initiation of American mission-work in the south fanned the embers. In 1834 the first agents of the American Board of Commissioners for Foreign Missions arrived in South-East Africa; and by 1837 four mission-stations had been established in Natal and Zululand.[2] No scrap of evidence suggests that this bold enterprise was not wholly innocent of politics, but it was enough to inspire all sorts of circumstantial stories. In the summer of 1835 Rear-Admiral Campbell reported from the Cape that 'the Americans intended to form a settlement somewhere in the neighbourhood of Delagoa Bay and that an American frigate and two store-ships were expected for this purpose this year'. From the Admiralty this report was handed on by way of the Colonial Office to the Foreign Office, where it was treated to a douche of common sense.

'He [Lord Palmerston] is inclined to doubt the existence of an intention on the part of the American Government to make the settlement in question, as it has not hitherto been the policy of that government to form colonial establishments, the whole annual increment of population and capital of the United States having found ample bent in the unsettled and uncultivated tracts in the interior of their own territory.'

Palmerston went on to say—in ignorance, no doubt, of Owen's 'treaties' in 1825, in the light of which British ministers in later years were to assume a different attitude—that, if indeed such a project was contemplated, no just objection could be made, since 'the Crown of Great Britain does not assert any rights of sovereignty in Delagoa Bay'. The authorities at the India

[1] B.R. 281. An anti-American writer in the *Edinburgh Review* (1835, lxi. 358) put his own interpretation on Hart's mission. He had been sent 'to demand explanations', and 'thus was frustrated, *we presume*, the scheme of conquest concerted by the Sultan with the Americans'.

[2] Mackeurtan, op. cit., chap. xiii. For the American Mission Board and extracts from missionary reports see J. Bird, *Annals of Natal* (Pietermaritzburg, 1888), i. 198–229.

House were equally unperturbed. 'It does not appear to the Secret Committee that the supposed intention of the Americans is likely in any way to affect the interests of the British Government in India.'[1]

But colonial opinion on the spot was more excitable. These missionaries, wrote an imaginative settler to the *Grahamstown Journal* in February 1836, were a pretext for the foundation of a great American Empire in Africa. Why, he asked, should 'the dexterity of America' be 'permitted to forestall our markets, seize our ports, and under our very nose acquire in Africa a means of wealth and power which England indolently relinquishes'?[2] Such hysteria was premature. Early in 1838 the strained relations between native blacks and immigrant whites in Natal reached breaking-point. In February Piet Retief and his companions were massacred by the Zulus. By the middle of the year the last American missionary had abandoned hope and left the country. Only two of them resumed their hazardous task a few years later: Aldin Grant, in the service of the Cape Government, and Newton Adams, as founder of the Adams Mission Station which still stands to-day near Amanzimtoti. And this could scarcely be described as the foundation of an American empire. In the north, similarly, the talk of American colonization took a little time to die away. At the beginning of 1838 the Company's agent at Muscat reported another visit by an American warship;[3] and at the end of 1839 Captain Cogan, who (as will appear later) had been commissioned by the British Government to negotiate with Said a commercial treaty similar to that he had concluded with the United States, informed the Foreign Office that American influence at Zanzibar was still increasing and that the rumour of Said's intention to cede a port on the coast for the use of American whalers and merchantmen was again current.[4]

[1] Adm. to C.O., 30.vi.35; Palmerston to C.O., 29.vii.35; Secret Committee to India Board, 28.vii.35; India Board to C.O., 3.viii.35 (C.O. 48. 163).
[2] Quoted by Mackeurtan, op. cit. 329.   [3] F.O. 54. 3.
[4] Cogan's memorandum on the Imam's government, 9.xii.39 (F.O. 54. 3).

4

It may be safely assumed that the idea of an American colony in East Africa was never seriously considered in any authoritative quarter in the United States. The dispatch of a sloop to 'show the flag' and make commercial agreements in distant corners of the world was a simple, an inexpensive, and at the worst a harmless act; but it was a very different matter for the Government of the United States to commit itself to an imperial responsibility so uncongenial, so remote, and leading to such incalculable ends as an African colony on the Indian Ocean; nor was there any section of public opinion, commercial or philanthropic, anxious to influence it in that direction. As an American trader said to Captain Hart in 1834, 'There are not ten people in my country who know where Zanzibar is or ever heard of it.'[1] Apart from the whaling industry of New Bedford, almost the only American citizens who could have been interested in the subject were the merchants of Salem, already far gone in its decline, and there is no evidence that they desired or even contemplated a colony. Why should they? The Arab ports were open to them on reasonable terms. Their trade, indeed, in this new East African backwater was growing as fast as they could wish. Between September 1832 and May 1834, of the 41 foreign ships, including 'whalers', which called at Zanzibar, 32 were American, the British coming second, at a long remove, with 7. And of the 32 American ships, 20 came from Salem and only 3 apiece from Boston and New York.[2] It was not so varied a trade, of course, as that with the Far East. Apart from ivory, gum-copal, which was mainly used as a base for varnish, had become the chief and most profitable export since 1831. In that year John Bertram, master of the *Black Warrior*, happened to arrive at Zanzibar just when one of Said's ships was about to sail with a cargo of gum-copal for India, whither he had been accustomed to send it for cleaning and sale. Bertram promptly

[1] B.R. 281.
[2] Ruschenberger, op. cit. i. 66. Cf. Hart's Report: 13 foreign ships at Zanzibar in 1833, of which 9 were American and 4 British. B.R. 280.

bought the cargo, and, having arranged with Said for similar purchases in future, shipped it back to Salem. To deal with the subsequent steady inflow of the gum a factory to clean it and prepare it for market was presently erected in Salem near Hawthorne's 'House of the Seven Gables', and from 1845 onwards, aided by the discovery of a new and cheap method of cleaning the gum, it was handling one and a half million pounds a year. Bertram, meantime, had resigned his mastership and set up a business at Zanzibar which carried on till near the end of the century.[1]

Thus East African products helped to nourish Salem in her decline; but the search for them on that distant coast was a long and laborious business. 'These ships', reported Hart of the Americans, 'have great difficulty in collecting a cargo, and their plan is to touch upon different parts of the coast and leave one or two of their crew behind with an interpreter whilst they visit some other parts or come to Zanzibar which is the great mart and *rendezvous*.' So limited a trade, moreover, could only be profitable if it were more or less monopolized by one small group of merchants; and the intrusion of outsiders into their preserve was naturally resented.

'The English brig [wrote Hart] is a great annoyance to them: it is her first voyage to this coast, and she has brought out a cargo of goods, the whole of which she has disposed of, and is now about to return with a full cargo of copal, gum, ivory and drugs with a little gold-dust and tortoiseshell. The latter, the Master gave me to understand, the Americans knew nothing about and that he expected to clear for his owners 170 per cent. The Americans and this man (who is a clever, industrious, active, close-handed fellow, and understands perfectly what he is about) are upon perfect good terms with each other, though it is evident they are very jealous of him, and it is only his extreme good humour that prevents their quarrelling. Copal, gum and ivory are the only return cargoes; they are therefore all looking out for the same thing.'[2]

If the goods they wanted had not been so scarce, there would not have been much cause for jealousy. When, in 1841, four years

[1] Mr. Phillips's note. See also Morison, op. cit. 222.
[2] B.R. 281.

after the American, the British Government established a consulate at Zanzibar, its first occupant, Hamerton, found that Said and the 'banyans' had encouraged or at least permitted 'a monopoly of the trade in favour of the Americans and to the exclusion of our merchants', and he had some difficulty in obtaining the same privileges for British merchants as those enjoyed by the Americans.[1]

But it was not only the competition of other countries of which the Salem traders were jealous. When Captain Waters presented to his owners the letter of invitation to Americans in general which Said had asked him to take home for publication, 'No, Mr. Waters', they said: 'if we allow this to be published, everybody will hear of the place, and we shall lose our trade.'[2] So Salem's monopoly was preserved. Mr. Richard Palmer, the first American consul to take up his duties at Zanzibar in accordance with the new treaty, came from Salem: so did his four successors, Messrs. R. P. Waters, C. Ward, W. G. Webb, and McMullen. And the three American business houses established in Zanzibar by 1856—Messrs. Bertram & Co., Messrs. Rufus Green & Co. and Mr. Samuel Masury—were all from Salem.[3] Thus, when the romance of the China trade was half forgotten, this clinging contact with one distant tropical island still tinged the life of Salem with a dash of colour from the Old World. Many of her citizens were living or had lived at Zanzibar as merchants, agents, clerks; and their houses were bright with rugs and wicker-baskets and fans and ivory-work brought back from Africa. In the Peabody Museum there are sundry curious exhibits presented by ships' masters in the twenties when the trade was new—a necklace of cloves from Madagascar, bows from Sofala, sandals from Zanzibar; and

[1] Hamerton to Palmerston, 21.v.42 (F.O. 54. 4). See p. 477, below.
[2] As reported to Hart by Salem traders at Zanzibar: B.R. 281.
[3] Burton, op. cit. i. 313, 318. Said-Ruete, op. cit. 126. Burton says that Masury, whose sagacity and probity he praises, left Zanzibar about 1858 and died shortly afterwards. Among other Salem merchants at Zanzibar, Mr. Phillips mentions M. Shepherd (Bertram's first partner), T. Deland, D. Pingree, R. Brookhouse, G. West, B. H. West, E. Emmerton, and N. L. Rogers.

there, too, hangs, not inappropriately, the only existing portrait of Seyyid Said.[1]

As chief exporters the Salem merchants were also chief importers, and of their imports the white cotton cloth woven in the Massachusetts mills soon took the lead. This 'coarse unbleached cotton-cloth', reported Consul Hamerton in 1848, 'has come into universal use in Arabia and the coast of Africa, and is fast driving the British and Indian manufactured articles of this kind out of the market'. Greatly desired by the inland natives, this cloth was soon being carried by the Arab caravans far into the interior, where it became the principal article of barter, almost indeed a kind of currency. Itinerant traders purchased their provisions or rights of way with it. The natives themselves paid their chiefs tribute in it. And, if British and Indian cotton goods were never actually excluded, the American stuffs, being, it seems, of better and more lasting quality, easily kept their lead. As early as 1850 and long afterwards, the native name for cotton cloth was *merikani*: the word is still sometimes used to-day. Nor was East Africa the only market. Re-exported from Zanzibar, American cloth began to penetrate Arabia and Persia and to cut out the British cloth which in this case had preceded it.[2]

5

So, all in all, the pursuit of the East African side-track proved a profitable venture, small in its results compared with the old China trade, but displaying in Salem's declining days an energy and enterprise worthy of her prime. From those bold beginnings in 1829 the available figures show a steady yearly rise to a peak in 1859. In that year, of 80 foreign ships calling at Zanzibar with a total burden of 23,340 tons, 35 were American and their tonnage 10,890. Of the aggregate trade of Zanzibar, which amounted to about £1,370,000, the American share was about

[1] Mr. Phillips's note. Said-Ruete, 126. The author visited the Essex Institute and Peabody Museum in 1933.
[2] Hamerton to Palmerston, 15.xii.48 (F.O. 54. 12). Burton, *Lake Regions*, i. 149. *Merikani* in 1905, Eliot, op. cit. 224. Ruschenberger, op. cit. i. 65–6. For cloth as tribute see p. 347, above.

£200,000. The value of the American cotton goods imported was about £94,000, of the Indian £54,000, of the British £38,000.[1] At all points, in fact, the Americans—and that means primarily Salem—had easily maintained their lead over all rivals for thirty years. But even Salem could not withstand the devastating effects of the Civil War, especially on the cotton trade; and after 1861 her business at Zanzibar declined as fast as it had risen. By 1870 the American figures had fallen by more than a half, and the British, German, and French had overtaken them.[2]

For East Africa, likewise, the American connexion, while it lasted, was not unprofitable. In *merikani* the Africans had obtained the commodity they most wanted, and it was of better quality than European or Indian merchants supplied. Minor goods from Salem—tools, nails, mirrors, and so forth—did no one any harm. Muskets, perhaps, were of more dubious virtue. Krapf, indeed, deplored the trade in them, and he was not thinking only of their use against his friend Kimweri. Their diffusion would, he predicted, make it increasingly difficult for Arab and Swahili caravans from the coast to penetrate inland; and what would happen then to the European firms at Zanzibar? 'They will discover too late that they would have done better if they had foregone the quick profit made in the traffic of firearms and had only brought harmless articles of commerce into the East African market.'[3] No doubt Krapf felt that firearms which could hinder Arab trade could also stop the spread of other influences from the coast, including mission-work. But what of the Slave Trade? Could Krapf have grudged the inland tribes guns to use against slave-hunters' guns?

Zanzibar, too, made its profit from the American connexion. The success of *merikani* hit the Lancashire manufacturers and the re-exporting firms in Bombay more than the 'banyan' middlemen on the spot. Through them, at Zanzibar or at the coast-towns, the Americans did most of their buying and selling. And for Said, finally, there was a double gain. In his public capacity he obtained increasing revenues from the increase of

[1] Rigby, 22–5; see p. 317, note 1, above.
[2] Kirk's notes in his copy of Rigby's Report.   [3] Krapf, 383.

American trade. Privately, as has been seen, he engaged in it himself, and with at least one of the American merchants he was on the friendliest terms. Nor had he any serious difficulties with the American Government. Once the treaty had been concluded, Washington took no interest in Zanzibar. Unlike the British Government, it had no call to worry Said about the Slave Trade, nor could it be reasonably suspected, like the French, of nursing any territorial ambitions in East Africa. Only one instance of strained official relations is on record, and that was a petty affair. Consul Ward complained in 1850 that no salute had been fired by Said's guns on the Fourth of July, and, when Said replied that, except on one occasion when a special compliment was paid to Queen Victoria, his guns had never fired except to answer a salute first given by foreigners, Ward took a high line and referred the dispute to Washington. The State Department wisely consulted Michael Shepherd, Bertram's partner, then at home at Salem, to whom Said also, as it happened, had written to explain his quarrel with the consul. Doubtless Shepherd advised a reconciliation in the interests of trade, and the incident, it seems, was closed when the captain of the gunboat *Susquehannah*, which called at Zanzibar in 1851, presented to Said a friendly letter from President Fillmore himself.[1]

6

The American incursion into East African waters dated from the War of Independence. Another current of white man's enterprise, which was also to find its way in time to Zanzibar, was set flowing by the Napoleonic War. In 1815, all over Europe, trade and industry were suffering from more than

[1] Ward to Said, 5.vii.50: stating his grievance, demanding a special salute to the American flag by way of reparation, and threatening otherwise to close the consulate. S. to W., 6.vii.50: explaining his case and offering to refer the matter to the British and French consuls and abide by their decision. S. to Shepherd, 24.ii.51, referring to a previous letter on the dispute and trusting in Shepherd's 'good sense'. C. C. Jowett, Washington, to Shepherd, 14.v.51: referring to the gunboat's voyage and asking for advice as to how Said should be treated. These letters are preserved at the Peabody Museum, Salem, Mass.

twenty years of disturbance, restriction, and destruction; and among other mercantile communities the cities of the Hanseatic League, which were as dominant in German overseas trade as the ports of New England in American, were soon searching for new commercial openings in the outer world. Thus in 1822 the *Mentor* left Bremen for a two years' voyage round the world by South America, the Sandwich Islands, China, the Philippines, Singapore, and so home round the Cape. The supercargo of the *Mentor* in the service of the Preussische Seehandlung was Wilhelm O'Swald, who started a firm of his own at Hamburg in 1831. It was to trade partly with the Baltic ports and Archangel, but also with the new markets discovered overseas: and in 1844 the schooner *Alph*, in which O'Swald's firm had a part interest, called at Zanzibar on the return voyage from the Red Sea. The prospects of trade in this quarter seemed so promising that the firm acquired two brigs of their own to pursue it. The first was lost in the Channel: the second arrived at Zanzibar in 1847. In 1849 the first of the many branches of Wm. O'Swald & Co. which are still at work to-day in the East African field was established at Zanzibar.[1]

O'Swald found the agents of another German firm on the island, Messrs. Horn acting for A. J. Herz & Sons. They were also from Hamburg, whose merchants were to enjoy a similar monopoly to that of Salem. In 1844 Herz & Sons, after some two years' trading in West Africa, had made a curious and profitable discovery, namely, that cowrie-shells could be obtained at Zanzibar in any quantity, of a good size, and at a low price. Now cowries were in general use as currency in dealings with West African natives, but hitherto the traders on that coast had only been able to obtain a supply from the Maldive Islands, through Liverpool. The opening was unmistakable. Herz promptly sent a ship to Zanzibar which brought a cargo of cowries to West Africa and returned to Hamburg in 1846 with

[1] *The Story of the House of O'Swald, 1831–1931* (Hamburg, 1931), 7–10. A copy of this brochure, privately printed in German and English, and illustrated with interesting old prints and photographs, was kindly given to the author by the company.

a big profit to its credit. O'Swald soon followed this lead and before long he had headed Herz. Between 1850 and 1878, when cowries were beginning to go out of use in West Africa, his firm shipped about 27,000 tons of them.[1]

A third Hamburg firm at Zanzibar in those early days was Messrs. Hansing, and a little later came a fourth, Messrs. Müller. Cowries, of course, were only one line of their trade. Like the Americans they exported ivory, gum-copal, hides, cloves, and so forth from East Africa, and imported a vast variety of goods for sale or barter. The first cargo, for example, which the *Afrika* brought to Zanzibar included iron, copper and brass wire, padlocks, nails, knives, scissors, crockery, tumblers, mirrors, beads of three sorts, umbrellas, hats, soap, tin pots, lamps—and muskets, gunpowder, flints, swords—and gin, porter, wine—and as many other things again. All in all, the Hamburg firms did well. By the end of Said's reign they had secured the fourth place on the list of foreign trade with Zanzibar. In 1856 twenty Hamburg ships, of some 5,400 tons all told, called there; and in 1859 the value of the goods imported and exported by the Hamburg houses was over £100,000.[2]

7

To Said, no doubt, these German invaders of his African realm were as welcome as the American. They were evidently quite as innocent of ulterior designs. They might, it is true, have been suspected far more reasonably than the Americans of territorial ambitions. For the German States had no open and

[1] O'Swald, 10. A. Coppins, *Hamburg's Bedeutung auf dem Gebiete der deutschen Kolonialpolitik* (Berlin, 1905), 58. In 1850 Krapf visited Chole Island, south of Mafia, and noted: 'In Chole there has lately sprung up an important trade in cowries, of which there is an abundance on this coast, these shells being bought by traders from Zanzibar, who dispose of them to Europeans there, by whom they are sent to the west coast of Africa where, as is well known, they form the currency. We were told that two measures of cowries were given for one measure of rice.' Krapf, 422. Cowries at Lamu: Boteler, i. 386. As currency in Uganda: Speke, *Journal of the Discovery of the Source of the Nile*, 551.

[2] Rigby's Report, 23–5. O'Swald, 36–9. Coppins, 58–9. Burton, *Zanzibar*, i. 320–1.

barely peopled continent at their doors, and the stream of emigration, which after the long impoverishment and immobility of the Napoleonic Wars began to pour out in increasing volume to seek a freer and more prosperous life elsewhere, was perforce directed overseas, mainly to North and South America. If, therefore, O'Swald and his fellow-traders at Zanzibar had known and reported home that there were highland areas in East Africa where an experiment in European colonization might at least be tried, it is just conceivable that the advice given to his countrymen by List, the economist, in 1841, 'to buy lands in far countries and settle them with German colonists'[1] might have inspired a German interest in Said's 'dominions'—but only just conceivable, in view of the hesitation and distrust with which German policy, nearly fifty years later, at last embarked on 'imperialist adventures'. And in actual fact, of course, in Said's time such a territorial interest was impossible. When he died, only one European, Krapf, had seen Mount Kenya; only two, Krapf and Rebmann, had seen Kilimanjaro; and none had set eyes on Lake Tanganyika. Nor, apart from colonization, could Germans be suspected, like Englishmen or Frenchmen, of thinking of naval bases as they sailed up the coast: for in those days the German States had no navy worth the name.

So Said had no cause to fear the German traders, and he showed them the same personal attention and offered them the same commercial privileges as the Americans. But, whereas the merchants of Salem had been fortified by a commercial treaty and a consulate at a very early stage of their operations, the merchants of Hamburg had to manage without such formal and official aids for some ten or fifteen years. But in 1855 Wilhelm O'Swald submitted a petition to the Hamburg Senate 'for the better protection of German interests in Africa'. He pointed out that the Hamburg statistics did not include the large amount of trade which the Zanzibar firms were doing with other ports than their home-port, and asserted that the amount of North German capital invested in Africa was no less than £600,000.

[1] M. E. Townsend, *The Rise and Fall of Germany's Colonial Empire* (New York, 1930), 33.

It may well have been due to O'Swald's influence—he was one of the leading men in Hamburg, and his second son, Wilhelm Heinrich, was afterwards Burgomaster—but in 1859, the year, as it chanced, of his death and three years after Said's, at length a Treaty of Amity, Commerce and Navigation was concluded between the aforesaid William Henry O'Swald, plenipotentiary of the Hanseatic Republics of Lübeck, Bremen, and Hamburg, and Said's son and successor, Majid, 'in consideration of the extensive and fast increasing trade and navigation' between the Republics and his dominions.[1]

Most of its clauses reproduced those of the American Treaty in much the same words. It prescribed the same general freedom of trade, the same single and universal duty of 5 per cent. on goods landed, and the same 'most-favoured-nation' treatment; and it provided similarly for the appointment by the Senates of the three Republics of consuls whose status was to be the same as that enjoyed by the consuls of the most favoured nations. But there were one or two significant provisions which had not been included in the American Treaty but were now reproduced from the treaties which Said (as will be seen) had made with Great Britain in 1839 and with France in 1844. Thus, while Americans had only been accorded the right to reside in the Sultan's dominions, Hanseatic citizens, like French or

[1] O'Swald, 18–20. The proposal for a treaty was accompanied by a letter to Sultan Majid from Albrecht O'Swald, elder son of Wilhelm. 'The letter with which Your Highness honoured me came into my hands . . . I certainly shall never forget all the friendship and favours Your Highness bestowed on me during my stay at Zanzibar . . . I also feel very grateful that my brother Wilhelm has been honoured and favoured with Your Highness' friendship, and I hope that Your Highness may bestow the same on my brother's successors. By this mail the Senates of Lübeck, Bremen and Hamburg, forming the Hanseatic League, send a letter to Your Highness with their compliments and proposals to sign a treaty with Your Highness, my brother Wilhelm being appointed a Commissioner to negotiate, conclude and sign the said treaty. . . . In the expectation that the said treaty will be concluded and signed, I request Your Highness to grant me the particular favour to be appointed Your Highness' Consul General in this place. My beloved father sends his highest respects and wishes for Your Highness' welfare in all things.' Hamburg, 1.ii.59. Zanzibar Museum.

British subjects, might purchase, sell, or hire land or houses therein. Certain privileges, again, which Said had conceded to the Americans without return had now been made reciprocal. The Hanseatic Treaty, like the British and French, empowered the Sultan to appoint his consuls, and entitled his subjects to trade and reside, in the countries concerned; and though these, no doubt, were largely matters of form, nevertheless they signified the recognition of complete diplomatic equality between the little Arab state and the nations of the Western world.[1] One other important provision in the Hanseatic Treaty had no precedent in the American but only in the British and French Treaties—a provision which embodied the only exception to Said's general system of free trade. In the fourth article, corresponding to the tenth in the British Treaty and the eleventh in the French, the Sultan undertook 'not to permit the establishment of any monopoly or exclusive privilege of sale within his dominions except in the articles of ivory and gum copal on that part of the east coast of Africa from the port of Tangate [Mtangata], situated in about $5\frac{1}{2}$ degrees of south latitude, to the port of Quali [Kilwa], lying in about 9 degrees south of the equator, both ports inclusive; but in all other ports and places in His Highness the Sultan's dominions there shall be no monopoly whatever'.[2]

In accordance with this treaty, Johann Witt, of the O'Swald firm, was appointed Consul for the Hanseatic League in 1860:[3] and thereafter the German share in the trade of Zanzibar continued steadily to grow. By 1870 it had surpassed the American and French and stood second only to that of British India.[4]

[1] It seems probable that Albrecht O'Swald was appointed Consul for Zanzibar at Hamburg: see note, p. 385, above.
[2] Text of Hanseatic Treaty: *S.P.* 1 (1859–60), 1118–23. Texts of British and French Treaties, B.R. 250–6, 266–71. See p. 487, below.
[3] The succession of German Consuls at Zanzibar up to 1884 is as follows: (1) Johann Witt, Jan. 1860–Nov. 1868; (2) Theodor Schultz, Nov. 1868–June 1875; (3) Robert Veers, June 1875–Nov. 1877; (4) Emil Grallert, Nov. 1877–1884. (Information kindly supplied by the German Foreign Office.) The Hanseatic Consulate established in 1860 was taken over by the North German Confederation in 1868 and by the German Empire in 1871. [4] Kirk's notes in Rigby's Report.

XIII
THE MISSIONARY INVASION

I

THE Hamburg merchants were not the only Germans in East Africa in Said's reign. European science and European religion were attacking Africa side by side with European trade; and among the explorers and the missionaries who were beginning at this period to uncover piece by piece the veiled spaces of the continent Germans were well to the fore. In North Africa the crossing of the Sahara and the Libyan and Nubian deserts, the exploration of Northern Nigeria and Abyssinia, the pursuit of the Blue and the White Nile southwards from their junction were largely the work of such men as Hornemann (1798), Rüppell (1824), Barth (1850), and Vögel (1853). In South Africa the German contribution was mainly to the mission field. The Moravian Brethren started work in Cape Colony before the middle of the eighteenth century; the Rhenish Society began to operate in Natal in 1829 and the Berlin Society in 1836; and missions from Hanover and Hamburg were established inland between the Orange and the Vaal in the fifties.[1] But many of these German achievements were not initiated or directed or financed by Germans. The work of the Hamburg merchants in Africa may be rightly described as national: they were all representatives of German commerce: but of the German explorers Hornemann was employed and salaried by the African Association in London and Barth by the British Government. Similarly, the German missionaries Krapf and Rebmann, the first Europeans to explore equatorial East Africa at any distance from the coast, were agents of a British institution, the Church Missionary Society.

Johann Ludwig Krapf was born in 1810—three years before the birth of Livingstone—at the village of Derendingen near

[1] The inclusion of German-speaking Austrians and Swiss would add to the explorers the Swiss Burckhardt (1813) and the Austrian Russegger (1837), and to the missionaries Knoblecher, an Austrian, who opened the first Christian mission in the Sudan at Gondokoro in 1850.

Tübingen, the son of a prosperous farmer. In 1824 his youthful imagination was captivated by an address on mission-work delivered by the rector of his school, and in the next holidays he made his way on foot to the famous missionary centre at Basel. His reception confirmed his choice of a career. A few years later he was admitted to the Basel Missionary College. In 1829 he was ordained, and in 1836 Mr. Dandeson Coates, 'lay-secretary' of the C.M.S., who had come to Basel in quest of workers, appointed him to a vacant post on the staff of the Abyssinian Mission under Isenberg and Blumhardt. He worked first at Adowa and then in Shoa among the northern Galla. In 1843 the work in Abyssinia was brought to an end by the hostility of its rulers, incited—so Krapf, a stout Protestant, believed—by the jealousy of his Roman Catholic fellow-workers with French political designs in the background: and, while his colleagues went to Egypt and the East Indies, Krapf, who had often contemplated attacking the Galla from the south, obtained permission to proceed to East Africa. Sailing from Aden and visiting Mombasa and other ports on his way, he arrived at Zanzibar on January 7, 1844.

Naval chaplains, no doubt, had been seen at Zanzibar from time to time in passing, but Krapf was the first Christian minister since the fall of the Portuguese Empire to come to mid-East Africa with the intention of making his home there. The little European community seems to have welcomed his arrival. He was 'hospitably received' by the British Consul, Hamerton; and the American Consul, Waters, took him and his wife to live in his house.[1] Still more important for the success of his mission, he was given a 'most friendly' reception by Seyyid Said, to whom Hamerton presented him on the second day after his arrival.

'When the consul appeared with me at the entrance of the palace, the Sultan, accompanied by one of his sons and several grandees, came forth to meet us, displaying a condescension and courtesy which I had not before met with at the hands of any oriental ruler.

[1] J. L. Krapf, *Travels, Researches and Missionary Labours during an eighteen years' residence in Eastern Africa* (London, 1860), 121–2.

... I described to him in Arabic my Abyssinian adventures and plans for converting the Galla. He listened with attention and promised every assistance, at the same time pointing out the difficulties to which I might be exposed.'[1]

A softer man than Krapf might have flinched from those difficulties—and the dangers too—and might have yielded to the promptings of Consul Waters, who had quickly become 'a zealous friend of the mission' and urged Krapf to remain at Zanzibar, preparing himself for the invasion of the mainland by the study of the native languages and in the meantime preaching to the Europeans, working amongst the Indians, and founding schools for the Arabs and Swahili of the island.[2] These long-range tactics were to be adopted twenty years later by Bishop Tozer after the initial disasters of the Universities' Mission;[3] but Krapf was of more impetuous temper, and early in March he was off to Mombasa, with such a 'passport' from Said in his pocket as a Christian missionary could hardly have expected from a Moslem ruler.

'This comes from Seyyid Said. Greeting to all our subjects, friends and governors. This letter is written on behalf of Dr. Krapf, the German, a good man who wishes to convert the world to God. Behave well to him and be everywhere serviceable to him.'[4]

The injunction was obeyed. The Governor of Pemba, where Krapf touched *en route*, instructed him about the 'monsoon', plied him with questions as to the politics and religion of Europe, and asked for an Arabic copy of the Bible. The Governor of Mombasa, Ali-bin-Nasir, who had recently been in England as Said's envoy, was as anxious to help as Said himself, and the townspeople visited Krapf's lodgings 'in great numbers' to pay their respects to this new kind of Englishman—for English, no doubt, he seemed—who had not come like Owen and Reitz and Emery with a garrison and a flag, but alone and armed only with his faith. Krapf had not expected such a welcome. At Takaungu, thirty miles north of Mombasa, where he had put

---
[1] Krapf, 123. [2] Idem, 122.
[3] See the author's *Kirk on the Zambesi* (Oxford, 1928), 257–8.
[4] Krapf, 127.

in on his way down to Zanzibar, he had heard the English bitterly denounced for leaving the Mazrui at the mercy of the treacherous Said and surrendering the people of Mombasa to his rule, 'as they had voluntarily become the subjects of England and been mildly governed by the English for three years'.[1] But at Mombasa itself, where the facts of Emery's virtual expulsion were doubtless better remembered, there seemed to be no such grievance. After all, it was only the Mazrui who had suffered, and their ejection had put an end to the dubious delights of independence—the constant faction-fights, the wars with neighbouring states, the haunting fear of Muscat—and started a new age of peace and growing trade under Said's easy overlordship. Quite apart, therefore, from what had really happened twenty years ago, it was difficult to keep alive a grudge against England at Mombasa, and Krapf was at once impressed with 'the friendliness of the people and officials towards Europeans, especially the English'—so much impressed that he decided to plant his first mission-station close to Mombasa and to work up towards the Galla through the local natives, the Nyika.[2]

Full of high hopes, he took up his quarters for the time being in the town, but like many another missionary in Africa he soon found that Nature was less friendly than the natives. Within a few months he lost his wife, whom he had fetched from Zanzibar, and his infant daughter too, and nearly died himself of fever. But he struggled on alone, learning Swahili and exploring the neighbouring country, till in the summer of 1846 he was joined by his 'dear and long-expected fellow-labourer', Johann Rebmann, a Württemberger like himself, born at Gerlingen in 1820, but trained at the C.M.S. College in Islington and ordained in England. Both of them were soon down with fever —Rebmann was seriously ill for a month—but by the end of August they were established in healthier surroundings at their chosen station at Rabai Mpia[3] about fifteen miles inland from Mombasa and some 900 feet above sea-level. There they worked steadily for a year, building their house, planting a garden, and preaching to the Nyika, while Krapf worked also at his Swahili

[1] Krapf, 115.   [2] Idem, 129.   [3] New Rabai.

grammar and dictionary and at translating into that language the whole of the New Testament—a monument, surely, of stubborn industry.[1]

Meantime the original idea of penetrating into the interior had not been forgotten. That it would be dangerous was obvious enough. The Arab and Swahili traders at Mombasa declared that the barren wilderness which began a few leagues inland was invested by predatory bands of Galla and Kwavi.[2] It was only three years ago and only a hundred miles or so to the south that Maizan had been murdered.[3] Said, indeed, with whom Krapf had another interview when he visited Zanzibar in March 1847, was a little uneasy at hearing that the missionaries had moved even so short a distance from the coast as Rabai. It would have been better, he said, to stay safely in Mombasa, for the Nyika were 'bad people'. But when Krapf retorted that even the cannibals of the South Sea islands had been known to become 'quite different men' under the teaching of the Word, Said tactfully acquiesced. 'If that be so', he said, 'it is all right. You may stay among the Nyika as long as you wish and do whatever you please.'[4] If Said had known of the projected inland expedition, he would have been still more anxious, remembering Maizan's fate and the trouble it had caused him with the French, but presumably he would have realized that with or without his blessing the missionaries would 'do what they pleased'. So thought, no doubt, his deputy at Mombasa. Whatever his inner convictions may have been, Ali-bin-Nasir, when informed that the first inland venture had been decided on and that Rebmann was to undertake it, did all he could to help. He provided another 'passport', and, when two of the Nyika chiefs at Rabai suddenly interposed a veto on the expedition, he sent them a sharp order—not to be disobeyed at such close range—to withdraw their opposition.[5] And so on October 14, 1847, Rebmann set out on the first of the travels which were to emblazon his name on the great record of African exploration.

On this first occasion his aim was not ambitious, no farther

[1] Krapf, 107–60. [2] Idem, 222. [3] See pp. 353–4, above.
[4] Krapf, 166. [5] Idem, 181. See p. 344, above.

indeed than the district of Taita, about a hundred miles from Mombasa, where an eastward outcrop of the mountain-mass of Kilimanjaro rises from the low maritime belt to 6,000 feet and upwards. Following much the same line as that of the modern Uganda railway, Rebmann emerged from the vegetation of the coastland and crossed the stony wilderness. He saw nothing of the dreaded brigands. He suffered only from the direct rays of the sun—he was between three and four degrees south of the Equator—and from sore feet. On the fifth day he reached Mount Kadiaro on the outskirts of Taita. He found the natives not unfriendly and considered the locality to be a promising mission-field. On October 25 he was back at Rabai. It had been an uneventful and easy journey, only important in history because it is the first recorded intrusion of a European into the interior of mid-East Africa.[1]

In the following year Rebmann started on a longer, more hazardous, and more famous expedition. This time the Governor of Mombasa had been more concerned for his safety; for the explorer proposed to go beyond Taita into a country that was exposed, so Ali-bin-Nasir told Krapf, 'to many dangers from Galla, Kwavi and Masai as well as wild beasts'. But, if go he would, he must at any rate make no attempt to climb Kilimanjaro. 'People who have ascended the mountain', he said, 'have been slain by the spirits, their feet and hands have been stiffened, their powder has hung fire, and all kinds of disasters have befallen them.'[2] A little puzzled by this mysterious warning—for the Governor had seen something of the world and could scarcely be supposed to share the idle superstitions of the natives—Rebmann, on April 27, 1848, set out for the second time into the unknown. It was the season of the 'long rains', and his progress was hindered by a constant and heavy downpour, but in ten days' time he had passed Mount Kadiaro and was traversing the fine uplands which led to what he called the 'Jagga' (Chagga) country. 'How splendid the whole landscape',

[1] Rebmann's own account of the journey is printed in Krapf, 221-9. No Portuguese exploration in this area is recorded.
[2] Krapf, 191-2.

his diary exclaims, 'with its rich variety of mountain, hill and dale, covered by the most luxurious vegetation! I could have fancied myself in the Jura mountains near Basel or in the region about Cannstätt in the dear fatherland.' And then on May 11 he was confronted with a portent of nature which there was nothing in Germany to match.

'This morning we discerned the mountains of Jagga more distinctly than ever; and about ten o'clock I fancied I saw the summit of one of them covered with a dazzling white cloud. The guide called the white which I saw merely *beredi*, "cold"; it was perfectly clear to me, however, that it could be nothing else but snow.'[1]

Thus European eyes first looked on Kilimanjaro. What Rebmann called the Jagga mountains was in fact a single huge volcanic massif, its sides clothed, belt on belt, with a riot of vegetation warmed by the tropical sun and watered from the glaciers above, and with forests climbing higher and higher, until at last they thinned beneath the frost and left the vast two-crested dome of the summit sheathed only in snow and ice. Years were to pass before all its secrets were revealed. It was not till 1867 that the English missionary, Charles New, first attained the lowest edge of the snowfield, not till 1889 that the German scientist, Dr. Hans Meyer, first reached the top, and not till 1921 that its height was finally fixed at 19,321 feet.[2] It

---

[1] In *Inner Africa Laid Open* (London, 1852) Cooley ridiculed Rebmann's description of the snow-mountain as mere imagination and the natives' accounts of it as 'a fireside tale'. In an appendix to his book, published in 1860, Krapf stated that he had seen the mountain himself more than once from a distance, and gave further evidence in support of Rebmann's description of it. 'He slept at the base of the mountain and even by moonlight could distinctly make out snow. He conversed with the natives in reference to the white matter visible upon the dome-like summit of the mountain, and he was told that the silver-like stuff, when brought down in bottles, proved to be nothing but water, and that many who ascended the mountain perished from extreme cold or returned with frozen extremities which persons unacquainted with the real cause ascribed to the malignant influence of *djins* or evil spirits.' Krapf, 543–4.
[2] New gives a graphic account of his climb in his *Life, Wanderings and Labours in Eastern Africa* (London, 1873), chaps. xx, xxi. See also C. Dundas, *Kilimanjaro and its People* (London, 1924), chap. i.

rises abruptly from its foot-hills: twenty miles away the levels are down to 3,000 feet and less: so that, seen from a distance of fifty or sixty miles, the whole mass seems to tower like a huge broad column far up into the sky. Rebmann was a little too close to appreciate its full grandeur, but it was quite sufficiently impressive, and his emotions must have been akin to Livingstone's when, seven years later, he first saw that other wonder of the African world, the Victoria Falls.

On May 13 Rebmann reached 'the little kingdom of Kilema', about two days' march from the mountain, his feet so bruised and torn by his rough journey that he could not leave his hut for a week. He stayed there till May 26, an object of friendly curiosity to 'king' Masaki and his tribesmen, and then followed his path back to Mount Kadiaro, whence by a new and more southerly route over the Shimba plateau he reached Mombasa on June 11.[1]

It was now Krapf's turn; and on July 12, 1848, he set out southwards to visit Kimweri, 'king' of Usambara (of whom something has been said in an earlier chapter),[2] and to examine the possibilities of a mission-station in his country. Ascending and crossing the Shimba uplands by way of Kwale and then traversing a dreary expanse of 'wilderness', he reached the River Umba on July 21, and three days later passed the boundary of Kimweri's territory at Fugoni. On July 28 he received a message from the 'king', summoning him to his capital at Vuga. The route thither led upwards through the foot-hills of the Usambara Mountains which rise to heights of 6,500 feet at some fifty miles' distance from the sea: and Krapf was fascinated, like Rebmann, by the beauty of the 'East-African alpine land'. 'The cool water trickling from the granite rocks, the little hamlets rising above the mountain-ridges, the many patches of Indian corn, rice, bananas, and sugar-cane, the numerous cascades, the murmur of the river Eugambo, the mountain-masses in the distance. . . . It will be a noble land when Christian culture shall hallow it!' On August 6, after

[1] Rebmann's journal in Krapf, 230–47.   [2] See pp. 345–50, above.

The Missionary Invasion

some days of toilsome progress, 'up hill and down dale and across rivers', Krapf reached Vuga and, finding that Kimweri was at Salla, his 'second capital', he pursued him thither, and on August 10 he obtained audience of the Lion of Usambara, a far more powerful personage than Masaki of Kilema.[1]

The half-caste Arabs or Swahili of the place, so Krapf asserts, had done their best to poison Kimweri's mind against the Christian stranger. He should refuse to see him, they had said, and send him back straightway to the coast. But Kimweri had told them that the missionary was his guest and under his protection; and it soon appeared from his conversation with Krapf that it was 'obviously his wish to enter into closer relations with Europeans'. He promptly agreed to the suggestion that 'teachers of the glad tidings' should come to his country. 'He wished, too, for skilled people, especially a good medical man.' He would not allow Krapf to take any boys away to be taught at Rabai: but, 'if I would return to his country, he would entrust me with young persons to instruct'. He repeatedly pressed him to promise to come back within three or four months, and on his departure he presented him, since he refused to accept slaves or ivory, with five goats for food on his journey.

On Kimweri's advice Krapf started for home by an easier route south-eastward, beneath the heights on which the Amani Institute now stands and across the line now taken by the Tanga–Moshi railway, to the River Pangani. On August 19 he reached Pangani village, on the coast, where he was 'kindly received by a friendly *banyan*' and astonished the local Swahili with the scarcely credible story that he had made the journey from Mombasa to Vuga by land. From Pangani he sailed to Zanzibar. He was warmly welcomed there by Hamerton, who put him up at the consulate, and he had another friendly interview with Said, who displayed an eager curiosity about Kilimanjaro. On September 1 he was back at Rabai, joyfully telling Rebmann of the hopeful outlook in Usambara, of its peculiar merits as a site for a mission-station, its grand surroundings, its fine climate, its easy approach from the sea. 'We encouraged

[1] See p. 348, above.

each other anew to pray and to labour for the conversion of Eastern Africa, where in so many places the portals open for us to begin the blessed work.'[1]

The next journey was Rebmann's. On November 14 he started on another march to 'Jagga-land', and this time he pushed on westward beyond Kilema, much against the wishes of Masaki, to Machame, a district on the south side of Kilimanjaro between ten and twenty miles from Moshi. Its paramount chief, Mamkinga, 'the greatest of the kings of Jagga-land', though disappointed to find that Rebmann was not a wizard and a rain-maker, was as friendly as Kimweri. 'He assured me frequently', says Rebmann, 'of his great affection for me, and would have kept me much longer with him, had I not entreated him to allow me to return. Indeed he would have been well pleased if I had at once settled down at Machame, in which event he would have given me his own son for a pupil.' Rebmann got back to Rabai on February 16, 1849, and in consultation with Krapf it was decided that he should at once return to Machame and take advantage of Mamkinga's friendship to push on with his help into the country of Unyamwezi. He left Rabai, accordingly, on April 6. The wet season was just beginning; it poured with rain all day and sometimes all night; the track was waterlogged, the rivers swollen; and it was not till May 15 that Rebmann reached Machame, exhausted and depressed by cold and damp. An ominous delay ensued. For ten days Mamkinga ignored his presence, and, when at last he came to see him, it was clear his mood had changed. It was not pious instruction he wanted now, but more tangible gifts, nor were those which Rebmann offered adequate. Bit by bit his precious bales of *merikani*, with which alone he could hope to buy his way and a welcome among the Nyamwezi, melted away. His chance of further exploration thus destroyed, his strength undermined by the exposure he had suffered on his march, Rebmann fell ill with fever and dysentery. He only asked Mamkinga now for permission to go home; and even this was refused till June 6. Next day he and his handful of

[1] Krapf, 266–82.

Nyika porters crept away, bullied and robbed to the end. They had to pay with a last strip of cloth or thread of beads even for the privilege of being spat on by their hosts—the customary method of saying 'good-bye'. Nor were their troubles yet over. Anxious to avoid the country of Masaki, whose hostility had only been restrained on the previous journey by fear of Mamkinga, they diverged from their old track in a southward direction and soon found themselves in the thick bush or 'jungle' nurtured by Kilimanjaro's melting snows. For several days they hewed a way through it with their axes. They crossed unfordable streams by felling trees over them. At last, a week from Machame, they reached open country, but it was 'wilderness', devoid of food and almost of water. Their little stock of beans would not have saved them from starvation if they had not found wild honey and a number of birds' nests full of young. On June 21 they reached Kadiaro. A week later, at the very end of his tether, Rebmann reached Rabai.[1]

He found that the mission staff had been reinforced during his absence by the arrival from Europe of J. J. Erhardt and Johann Wagner, but both of them had been struck down by fever on the morrow of their landing at Mombasa and were still lying dangerously ill. At the end of July Wagner died. After weeks of uncertainty Erhardt just pulled through. It was a sad and anxious summer for the two senior missionaries. Projects of further exploration were necessarily laid aside. But in the autumn, Erhardt having quite recovered, Krapf began to plan another journey. In which direction? So far they had probed the hitherto unknown interior to the west and south-west. The north-west remained, the line of Krapf's original ambition, leading to the southern flank of the Galla country—and beyond that whither? Might he not discover located somewhere in that direction those lost fragments of Christian tribes of which he had heard tell in Shoa? Might he not even find that loadstar of every African explorer of his day, the sources of the Nile? Such triumphs, of course, were not to be won at once. The first

[1] Rebmann's journal in Krapf, 248-64.

stage was to prospect the Ukamba country, which stretched far to the north from the line of Rebmann's march to Kilimanjaro till it reached, so Krapf had learned, the River Tana. It happened that Chief Kivoi of a Kamba tribe living in that area had recently come trading to Mombasa and had visited the mission at Rabai. It was arranged, therefore, that Krapf should make his way to Kivoi's village and push on with his help to the Tana. So, on November 1, 1849, he set forth along the line of the Taita route. A few days out he fell in with a small caravan of Kamba traders, and proceeded thenceforward in their company. By November 9 he had left Mount Kadiaro behind him to the south-east and reached Mount Maungu,[1] whence he had his first glimpse of the Kilimanjaro snows. Here he heard alarming news. 'Three days before, the Masai had been seen near the River Tsavo: they had killed several Kamba and had made an incursion into Galla-land.' There was truth, then, apparently, in the Arab traders' yarns; but Krapf continued his march till on November 14, after suffering severely from lack of water, he reached the Tsavo—to be famed in later days of railway building for its dangerous lions.[2] Two days later Krapf enjoyed a clear view of 'the whole of the eastern side of Jagga-land and its enormous mountain-mass as well as the transparent white crown on the dome-like summit of Kilimanjaro'. Presently he had crossed the River Athi and was climbing the Yata Hills above the Athi Plains about forty miles east of Machakos. On November 22 he reached the River Tiva and four days later arrived at Kivoi's village, which lay a few leagues from Kitui.[3]

Kivoi was pleased to see Krapf and to accept the gifts he brought. He had not believed, it seemed, that Krapf had really meant to make such a hazardous journey; but, finding he had come so far and was still set on penetrating farther to the Tana and the Kikuyu country beyond it, he offered to take him with

[1] Maungu is now the eighth station out from Mombasa (Kilindini) on the Uganda railway.
[2] See Col. J. H. Patterson's well-known book, *The Man-Eaters of Tsavo* (London, 1908). Tsavo is the twelfth station on the railway, 136 miles from Mombasa, 1,525 feet above sea-level.
[3] Now the centre of an administrative district of Kenya Colony.

The Missionary Invasion 399

a party he was to lead thither in the following month in quest of ivory. It was a tempting offer, for Krapf's appetite had been whetted by hearing of a second snow-mountain away in the north, named 'Kegnia' (Kenya), and by seeing a party of Kikuyu folk who performed one of their leaping and stamping dances in the village. But the arrangements Krapf had made with Rebmann did not provide for this extension of his present journey, and on December 3 he took a friendly leave of Kivoi, promising shortly to return. That morning, as it happened, the clouds which hung over the highlands had cleared away, and from a hill near the village Krapf 'could see the Kegnia most distinctly, and observed two large horns or pillars, as it were, rising over an enormous mountain to the north-west of the Kilimanjaro, covered with a white substance'. The homeward march was uneventful, except for occasional thirst. He reached Rabai on December 21.[1]

2

Three years passed before Krapf fulfilled his promise to return to Ukambani. At the beginning of 1850 he decided to pay a visit to Europe. His health demanded a draught of northern air, and he was anxious to urge in person on the C.M.S. the new plans he had made for its East African mission. But before leaving he carried out a long-cherished project of inspecting the whole coast down to Cape Delgado. On February 4, in a small dhow hired at Mombasa, he started southwards, accompanied by Erhardt, and, hugging the shore and landing at every little port, he reached the River Rovuma on the 26th. It was not, of course, a technical survey of the coast like Owen's in 1823–6,[2] nor had it a political objective like Guillain's in 1846–8;[3] but it was none the less instructive. Krapf marked the relics of the greater Arab age—especially Kilwa-el-Muluk,[4]

---

[1] Krapf, 283–99, 544. Krapf gives the native name as Kima ja Kegnia, Mount of Whiteness, but the word may be derived from the Masai 'erukenya'—'mist'. The native pronunciation 'Kane-ya' has been now discarded by English usage in favour of 'Keen-ya'.
[2] See Chap. VIII, above.   [3] See p. 451, below.
[4] Better known by its Swahili name, Kilwa Kisiwani, Kilwa on the Island.

'Kilwa the Mistress', with nothing to show for her name but a cluster of Swahili huts, the ruins of one great mosque, and battlements crumbling into the encroaching sea, and overshadowed now by Kilwa Kivinje, twenty miles north on the mainland, 'a metropolis of the Slave Trade' and a flourishing place in its way, with over 10,000 inhabitants. He noted the methods and the limitations of Said's overlordship—the Governors, the little garrisons, the customs-houses. At Tanga he talked to one of Said's soldiers who had been to London in one of his trading-ships and, falling ill there, had spent the better part of two years in the 'marine hospital'. At Mtotana, a tiny haven north of Simba island, he saw a Swahili who had taken service with Maizan and seen him murdered. At most points, but particularly southwards of Pangani, he heard of the ravages of the Slave Trade among the inland tribes and observed how that stretch of coast had been moulded into bights and bays as if 'purposely to harbour slave-ships'. He found, however, that the Moresby Treaty, though evaded by occasional smugglers, had driven the European 'slavers' from the coast.[1] Finally, he obtained geographical information of the first importance. Evidence gathered at the starting-points of the trade-routes running westward through Unyamwezi and again farther south confirmed the reports he had previously heard that they led to great inland waters, known as Tanganyika in the north and Nyasa in the south, and it may have been at this time that he was told that these waters did not form, as geographers had hitherto supposed, one vast, long, inland sea but two separate lakes. At the mouth of the Rovuma he was informed that the river had its source in Lake Nyasa and noted in his journal the desirability of exploring it in a small steamboat as far as it was navigable. Eleven years later, in the course of the Zambesi Expedition, Livingstone came to the same place, having heard the same report, and attempted the desired exploration in the *Pioneer*; but the water was too shallow for a steamer, and in 1862 Livingstone and Kirk pushed up the river in a boat until, about 120 miles from the sea and less than half-way to Lake

[1] See p. 499, below.

THE MISSIONARY INVASION 401

Nyasa, the channel was blocked by shoals and rocks.[1] From the Rovuma Krapf sailed north again, calling at Zanzibar and enjoying Hamerton's 'usual hospitality', and arrived back at Mombasa on March 20.[2]

Three weeks later, leaving Rebmann and Erhardt at Rabai, Krapf left for home by Aden and the 'overland route'. The news of his and Rebmann's discoveries, that of Kilimanjaro in particular, had long preceded him, and he found himself not, of course, a popular hero like Livingstone on his return from his far greater and more dramatic exploit, the crossing of Africa in 1855–6, but a man whose name was known and honoured by the professional geographers and their exalted patrons. He was summoned to Windsor for an audience with the Prince Consort, who expressed a warm interest in his mission and its achievements and entrusted him with some complimentary gifts for Seyyid Said. At Berlin, likewise, Krapf had a notable reception. He was welcomed by the aged Baron Humboldt and invited to dine with King Friedrich Wilhelm and the Queen. They rained questions on him—before all others, 'Was the crown of Kilimanjaro really snow?'—and at parting the King invested Krapf with the gold medal of the order *pour le mérite*.[3]

But those were gilded interludes, and Krapf's main business in Europe was to submit to the C.M.S. Committee his long-pondered design for extending the mission-field in East Africa. It was a spacious design—nothing less than the establishment of a chain of mission-stations right across the continent along the equatorial belt. Secretary Venn and the Committee were on their guard against 'grand schemes' involving 'the lives of missionaries and the expenditure of sacred funds', and they set

[1] R. Coupland, *Kirk on the Zambesi*, 188–9, 240–6.
[2] Krapf, 411–31, 496.
[3] E. Stock, *History of the Church Missionary Society* (London, 1899), ii. 130. An account of Rebmann's discovery of Kilimanjaro had been published in the *Church Missionary Intelligencer* (May, 1849), and attention was drawn to its outstanding geographical importance in the president's address to the Royal Geographical Society in 1849 and again in 1850 (*R.G.S. Journal*, xix, p. lxxvii; xx, p. lx). It is curious that the R.G.S. never awarded a 'Royal Premium' or one of their medals to Rebmann or Krapf.

themselves 'rigidly and faithfully to try the question whether these extensive aims were the dreams of enthusiasts or the sober calculations of wise men'. Their decision was a tribute to Krapf. He was instructed to return to his post, but not to settle down there, gathering a school of converts round him in the normal missionary manner, but 'to branch out far and wide, witnessing to the Truth in successive tribes and countries'. And he was at once to make a beginning of the great chain. New posts were straightway to be founded in the districts which he and Rebmann had prospected, one in Usambara and the other in Ukamba or in 'Jagga-land'. For these purposes the staff was to be increased. Three missionaries and three lay-brethren were to return with Krapf to Rabai.[1]

So Krapf left England, early in 1851, with his hopes and happiness at their zenith. And thereupon the decline began. One of the three new missionaries had been withdrawn before starting: a second absconded at Aden: and it was only with missionary Pfefferle and the three lay-brethren, Hagermann, a carpenter, Kaiser, a farm-worker, and Metzler, a smith, that Krapf reached Mombasa in April. Then savage Africa showed her teeth again. The four new-comers were quickly down with fever. In a few weeks Pfefferle was dead, and Kaiser and Metzler were soon sent back to Europe as the sole chance of saving them from the same fate. Only brother Hagermann made a good enough recovery to justify the risk of his remaining at Rabai.[2]

[1] Krapf, 210, 300. *History of the C.M.S.* ii. 131–2. Krapf had conceived the idea of the chain in 1844 during his first year on the coast. 'I estimated at some 900 leagues the distance from Mombasa to the River Gabon in Western Africa, where the Americans, before the occupation of the French, had founded a mission and laboured successfully. Now, if stations with four missionaries were established at intervals of 100 leagues, nine stations and thirty-six missionaries would be needed, probably at an annual expense of from £4,000 to £5,000. If every year progress were made from west and east, I calculated that the chain of missions would be completed in from four to five years.... After I had forgotten these ideas, they were re-awakened in the years 1849 and 1850 during my visit to England.' Krapf, 134.

[1] Krapf, 210–11. *History of the C.M.S.* ii. 132–3.

Krapf took the disappointment in the grand manner of his calling. 'Though I too should have to fall,' he wrote, 'it does not matter; for the Lord . . . will carry on and complete His cause in His own good time. The idea of a chain of missions will yet be taken up by succeeding generations and carried out; for the idea is always conceived tens of years before the deed comes to pass.'[1] Meantime he and his old companions could continue their work of preparing the ground for the first links of the chain, and to that end Krapf started off on July 11 for Ukamba. Except a brush with a band of robbers near the Tsavo River, no serious incident occurred on the outward march till the Yata uplands had been climbed. At the village of a friendly chief in that district Krapf decided to stay for a time, since it seemed a suitable site for the projected station, lying as it did on a main caravan-route and in easy touch with Mombasa and Rabai. But the delay was too much for the loyalty of his Nyika porters. On the arrival of a caravan bound for the coast they deserted their master and hurried off on its tracks for home. Thus left alone with his two Nyika servants, Krapf continued his journey to Kitui. On August 4 he was warmly welcomed by his 'old friend', Kivoi, who renewed the promise to take him farther into the interior. There happened to be a native in the village whose home lay close to Mount Kenya, and Krapf's anticipations of the discoveries awaiting him were whetted by talk about the mountain. It was capped, said the native, with 'a white substance, producing very great cold'; and water continually flowed out of it, descending the mountain and forming a big lake in which the River Tana took its source.

Some time elapsed before Kivoi was ready for the expedition, and it was not till August 24 that, in a party of fifty odd, they started, heading north-west towards Kikuyu-land. Soon after the start Krapf could clearly see the mountains that rim the Kenya Highlands—a 'magnificent view' across the Tana valley —but he was never to climb them. On the third day out the party was attacked by a body of marauding natives more than twice its strength. Its path barred ahead, its retreat cut off,

[1] *History of the C.M.S.* ii. 133.

subjected to a rain of poisoned arrows, the caravan broke up in confusion. Krapf had just turned to fly when Kivoi, who had been at his side, fell dead. Fortunately there was a forest not far off to which some of the fugitives were running, and Krapf, the arrows whistling past him, ran after them. When he reached the shelter of the forest the other fugitives had disappeared. He ran on alone. Presently he came to a glade along which some of the robbers were carrying off the loot of the caravan. Shying away, he ran for another ten or fifteen minutes through the trees till he emerged on to a grassy plain. He lay down exhausted. He had injured his hip in a fall, he had no food, and he was desperately thirsty. At some distance he observed a line of lofty trees which might mark, he thought, the bed of the Tana River. There was nobody to be seen. Thirst drove him to risk the venture over open ground. He crossed it undetected and was soon rejoicing in the cool waters of the river, some 6 feet deep and 150 broad.

Thus hunted and helpless, the first European came to the upper reaches of the Tana. Sixty miles westward of the point whereabouts Krapf slaked his thirst now stands Nairobi, the capital of Kenya Colony, with some four thousand European residents. Twenty-five miles northward, on the edge of the highlands, lies Fort Hall, the centre of a district studded now with the farmhouses and the coffee and sisal plantations of European settlers.

For the rest of that day Krapf stayed hidden in the bushes by the river. At nightfall he set out back across the plain. Stumbling over the rough ground, impeded by thorn-bushes and tall grass, losing in his frequent falls the little stock of water he was carrying, he was soon again exhausted and again tormented by thirst. But, drawing strength from prayer and from the example of others in like straits—he thought especially of Mungo Park—he struggled on through the dark. Dawn found him several miles from the river. In the course of the morning he heard monkeys chattering near a dried-up stream, and, looking about, he discovered a water-hole which they had dug. Later, he fell in with a Kamba man and woman, fugitives like himself from

Kivoi's party; and for the rest of the day and all the next night they journeyed on together, stopping only for a snatch of sleep. Early on the following morning they sighted people in the plain whom they thought to be their enemies and took to their heels. Krapf, who had eaten nothing since the attack on the caravan except a bit of dried cassava-root given him by the Kamba woman, could not keep pace with his companions. But there was no pursuit, and that afternoon (August 29) he reached the outskirts of the Kamba plantations and the village of one of Kivoi's kinsmen.

Krapf's troubles were not over. Most of the fugitives had got home. Kivoi's death was known. The white man, it was openly said, was a wizard: he ought to have protected Kivoi: he should be put to death. On the second day he was taken under escort to another village, and for three more days he was kept there in the chief's hut. Convinced that Kivoi's relatives were determined to murder him, Krapf resolved to attempt an escape. In the early hours of September 4 he unpiled the logs which barred the opening of his hut without awaking his sleeping warders and made off along the path to Yata. From dawn till dark he lay hidden in long grass, within earshot of Kamba working in their fields. All the next night he hurried on, often falling as before into holes or over stones and torn by thorns, 'those relentless tyrants of the wilderness'. Another day of hiding—he was nearly detected by some women gathering wood—and another night of stumbling, ill-directed flight, and then Krapf realized that he would never get to Yata without help. He was weak from lack of food. He had only found water at long intervals. A remembered landmark of the outward march showed him how short a distance he had covered. He decided to give himself up and ask to be taken to Kivoi's own village. A Kamba was soon met with and showed him the way. In the afternoon (September 6) he reached the village and was received with seeming friendliness by Kivoi's brother and chief wife. There he stayed three days, nursing his cuts and bruises, and fighting a mild attack of fever. Nobody in the place would help him. He was obliged to beg for food. But he got the impression that his life was no longer in serious danger. He asked, therefore, that he might be conveyed to Yata, in payment wherefor he would send back part of the goods he had left stored there. The request was grudgingly granted, and on September 13 he reached the village he had chosen for the mission. His two Nyika servants were there and his stock of goods unpilfered. And now, it appears, Krapf proposed to settle down as if nothing had happened and as if his health was still robust and begin the work of the new station. But it chanced once more that a party of Nyika were returning to the coast, and both Krapf's servants insisted on accompanying them. Alone among the alienated Kamba, deprived of his only friend among their chiefs, unable by himself to maintain contact with Rabai, Krapf was reluctantly convinced that he too must go. 'Can I be blamed', asks the journal, 'if I renounced for the time the Ukamba mission?'

The journey down was as uneventful as the journey up; but there was shortage at times of food and water, and Krapf was near the end of his strength when on the evening of September 28 Rebmann and Erhardt, who had heard some weeks before a circumstantial report of his murder, were joyfully surprised to see their colleague limping home.[1]

These harsh experiences had not cooled Krapf's zeal for exploring the interior, but they had convinced him that the first link of the equatorial mission-chain should be forged not in Ukamba but in Usambara. Early in February 1852, therefore, he set out to pay a second visit to 'king' Kimweri in order to make sure of his promised consent to the establishment of a mission in his country. This time he decided to take the shorter and safer route from Pangani. The Governor of Tanga, to whom he applied for leave to make the journey, refused to give it without Said's written orders—a piece of punctilio which involved a detour to Zanzibar and back—but on February 20 Krapf reached the river-mouth, where he found that Kimweri's 'royal vizier' and one of his sons, apprised of his coming by the messengers he had sent ahead, were waiting to conduct him to Vuga. So his

[1] Krapf, 317–50.

path was smoothed. 'Never before', notes the journal, 'had a journey been made so easy for me'; and, with nothing to trouble him but a passing touch of fever or the theft of a night's sleep by a plague of ants or the breath-taking steepness of the mountain-paths, he vastly enjoyed the upward march through scenery that reminded him again of Switzerland or the Black Forest. On March 8 he came to Vuga. Kimweri was away but sent a message of warm welcome and an assurance that a mission-settlement would be permitted, and when he arrived in person a few days later it was soon evident that, unlike his fellow-monarch in Machame, he had not changed his mind. Again the Moslem faction, headed by Osman, Kimweri's Arab physician from Zanzibar, did their best to thwart Krapf's purpose. 'Wherever a European once plants his foot', Osman warned the king, 'the whole country must soon fall into his hands.' So formidable, indeed, seemed these intrigues that Krapf let it be known that unless the Moslems held their peace he would 'denounce them to the English Consul at Zanzibar and have them punished in an exemplary manner'—a threat which may have over-estimated Hamerton's power on the coast but which, looking on to Sir John Kirk's day, was as prophetic as Osman's warning. Krapf, as a matter of fact, had no reason to be anxious. His interviews with Kimweri, who lay as a rule on a bed, being old now and very stout, were consistently friendly, and at last, on the day of Krapf's departure (March 19), the king bestowed on him, with due form and ceremony, the right to establish a missionary-settlement on Mount Tongwé.[1]

It was with a consciousness, therefore, of having saved something from the wreck of his great hopes that Krapf returned to Rabai on April 14 by way of Pangani and Zanzibar. Usambara had made amends for Ukamba; and early in 1853 Erhardt was sent to establish the new station. But Krapf was not destined to take a further part in it. That summer his health broke down completely. He was only forty-three, but it was evident he would not live much longer if he stayed in Africa, and on September 25 he bade Rebmann a sorrowful farewell and

[1] Krapf, 367-405.

sailed away for Europe. It had been a hard decision but a wise one. His life was prolonged for twenty-eight years, during most of which he lived in his Württemberg homeland, steadily pursuing the linguistic studies which were to form the basis of our modern knowledge of East African speech. Three times in those years he saw Africa again. He went twice to Abyssinia, as guide and introducer of a C.M.S. mission in 1855 and as interpreter with Napier's army in 1867: and in 1861 he revisited his own old field in charge of a mission-party sent out by the United Methodist Free Churches which he helped to make its home among the Nyika near Rabai. He must have welcomed such new efforts, for the old, it seemed, were petering out. Africa had rejected Erhardt as it had rejected him. Ill health had driven him from Usambara after only a few months and out of Africa for good in 1855. Even that first link of the chain had snapped. Only Rabai remained, and Rabai was only a base with the sedentary, static functions of a normal station. Rebmann was still there when Krapf saw him for the last time in 1861, and there he stayed, faithfully preaching to the Nyika, till at last in 1875, after nearly thirty years of exile, he was brought home, blind and broken.[1]

3

The figures of these early-Victorian missionaries stand at the very front of the stage on which this book is set. They were true 'invaders' of East Africa. Before they came American and German business-men had invaded the East African area and, settling in its island outpost, had skimmed its coast for trade: but Krapf and Rebmann invaded the mainland itself. Since the Portuguese were swept away southwards in the seventeenth

[1] Krapf, 402–84. *History of the C.M.S.* ii. 135. Erhardt prepared a detailed map of the country between the coast and the 'inland sea', based on his personal explorations and the information he had obtained from natives. Its publication in England in 1856 was one of the factors that prompted the expedition of Burton and Speke in 1857 which penetrated to Lake Tanganyika and led to Speke's subsequent discovery of Lake Victoria Nyanza. Speke visited the latter lake again with Grant in 1862 and proved it to be the source of the Nile.

century they were the first Europeans—for Owen's 'establishment' at Mombasa had been a brief and passing incident—to make their homes on the coast for many years. And they were the first Europeans of all time to penetrate to Kilimanjaro and the outskirts of the Kenya Highlands. Nor was the objective of their 'invasion' limited in space or time. They contemplated, as has been seen, a steady advance right through the continent. 'A missionary', Krapf once noted in his journal, 'often shares in common the desires and aspirations of a great conqueror';[1] and indeed, Krapf's chain of missions was akin in principle to Seyyid Said's chain of trading-posts and Cecil Rhodes's 'Cape-to-Cairo' railway. Nor were these missionaries to come and go like raiders. Their chain was meant to grip the people of Africa as firmly as a railway grips its soil; and that first settlement at Rabai was the beginning of a permanent 'occupation' of the country. At the present day there are some fifteen to twenty missionary societies, the C.M.S., of course, among them, operating in Kenya, Tanganyika, and Uganda: there are scores of mission-stations: there are hundreds of mission-schools. Of native education in those territories no less than nine-tenths is in missionaries' hands.

The founding of the Rabai mission, therefore, marks the first appearance of a dominant and permanent factor in the process of invasion; and it is of primary historical interest to observe how the various peoples and persons concerned reacted to it.

Of the East Africans themselves it was the Nyika with whom the contact was closest and most continuous, and the Nyika were maritime folk, too long associated with the Arab or Swahili civilization of the coast to be regarded as unadulterated or typical East Africans and too close to Mombasa with its Baluchi garrison to ignore the fact that Krapf and his colleagues enjoyed the favour and protection of the Governor. They seem, however, to have treated the missionaries with a natural friendliness. Though they were slow, very slow indeed, to accept their teaching, they listened to it: and if the elder tribesmen betrayed from time to time a mild anxiety lest the new doctrines should

[1] Krapf, 184.

prove incompatible with the tribal traditions on which their own authority was based, there was only one case of serious friction, and never persistent antagonism. Anywhere near the coast, indeed, the Rabai brethren seem to have moved freely and safely among the natives. Inland, of course, it was different. The Kamba proved far less friendly, and their enemies—unidentified in Krapf's narrative but apparently a relatively small and casual band of robbers—were not deterred from attacking Kivoi's caravan by the presence of a strange white man with a gun.[1] If Krapf or Rebmann had fallen in with the organized militant tribes of the highlands, if they had crossed the path of a Masai raid, they would probably have never told the tale. The attitude of two of the inland chiefs, on the other hand, was remarkably benevolent. If Mamkinga was interested only in the white man's goods and was as treacherous as he was greedy, it is difficult to doubt that Kivoi's and Kimweri's friendliness was sincere or that the latter at any rate really desired the establishment of a mission in his country. Krapf was sure of it. 'It is certain', he wrote after his last departure from East Africa, 'that the king of Usambara is now, as previously, disposed to admit missionaries to his country and will allow them to select their own locations.' And he added: 'In time of peace a missionary can safely roam about the country everywhere if he has but secured the friendship of the king.'[2]

The attitude of the Arab traders and their half-caste or Swahili associates can be assessed with more precision. It was definitely hostile, and with good reason. No Europeans had yet moved among the native tribes with whom they did their inland trade. European intrusion might presently lead to European

[1] The gun was not of much use. Krapf had loaded it before the attack, and when the fighting began his companions, who were armed, like the enemy, with bows and arrows only, implored him to fire. 'I fired twice, but in the air: for I could not bring myself to shed the blood of man.' In his flight to the forest he fell and broke the butt. He subsequently used the barrels for carrying water, stuffing the mouths with grass and bits of cloth cut from his trousers; but this stuffing was torn out by thorns and twigs as he fled through the jungle and the precious fluid escaped. Krapf, 320–6. [2] Krapf, 405.

competition. Those American and German merchants, once the paths had been opened and found to be not too dangerous, might prefer to dispense with the costly middleman and go and buy their goods themselves. And in any case, the nosing white men would learn too much about the character and methods of the trade. Englishmen, especially, would find more fuel to feed their zeal against the Slave Trade; and missionaries with their tiresome ideas of right and wrong might question the honesty with which trade in other lines than slaves was conducted and upset the simple natives' minds. It was a reasonable anxiety, and certainly Krapf personally justified it. In Usambara he made it his business to explain to Kimweri and his people how the Swahili—as he called all the low-class Arabs and half-castes of the coast—cheated them and to advise them to trade direct with Zanzibar. When he left Usambara for the last time he took one of Kimweri's officers, the *Mbereko*, with him to the island so that 'he could see with his own eyes things as they were and report accordingly to his master at Vuga'; and the *Mbereko*, no doubt on Krapf's advice, also took the opportunity of seeking 'to form connexions with the European merchants at Zanzibar so as to obviate the necessity of disposing of the products of Usambara through the agency of the cheating Swahili'. On this account, says Krapf, 'I was naturally a thorn in the side of the Swahili.'[1] Very naturally indeed!

If Krapf had meddled thus directly and injuriously with the middlemen's trade on the coast at an earlier stage of his career in East Africa, it is conceivable that the attitude of the middlemen's suzerain at Zanzibar would have been little friendlier than theirs. For Said not only had to take some account of his people's feelings: he was a middleman himself, financing caravans which brought him goods from the interior to be sold again oversea.[2] But Krapf, as it chanced, never saw Said again after he had engineered his 'exposure'; and every time he had seen him —from the day when he received his 'passport' onwards—he had been treated with a marked and active kindness duly reflected by Said's deputies at the coast-towns. And so, when Krapf got

[1] Krapf, 404.   [2] See p. 319, above.

home and looked back on his work for Christianity in Africa, he could gratefully re-affirm what had struck him at its outset as a paradox—it was a Moslem ruler who had made it possible.

'How little could I suppose, when beginning my journey, that in the distant south of Africa an Arabian prince was preparing for me a way to the heathen! Yet so it was; for without the conquest of Mombasa by a prince as well inclined as the Imam of Muscat to Europeans and especially to the English, the establishment of a missionary station in Nyika-land could never have been effected.'[1]

It was true: and Said's conduct in this matter has been sometimes cited as a striking proof of his enlightened and magnanimous attitude towards other religions than his own. Certainly Said was tolerant. The Hindu 'banyans' in his realm were as free as Christians to follow their creed. But Islam has never been so fanatical or militant in East Africa as elsewhere; and religious toleration was, after all, an essential complement of Said's desire to foster contact with the outer world. He wanted to keep on good terms with his indispensable 'banyans'. He wanted to attract Europeans to Zanzibar, 'especially the English'. And without denying that Said, compared with other Arab rulers, was signally broad-minded or that his friendliness to Krapf accords with the general tradition of his courtesy and benevolence to strangers or that he was naturally and keenly interested in the more secular side of the missionaries' work, the exploration of his little-known 'dominions', it should be remembered that Krapf was commended to his care by Consul Hamerton. If Hamerton had disavowed him or discountenanced his plans in East Africa, Krapf, it is safe to assume, would have got little help from Said.

Hamerton's support, in fact, was as essential to the success of the mission as Said's; and it was given, it may be guessed, with

[1] Krapf, 538. Cf. 498: 'That the present period of interference on the part of Seyyid Said, Sultan of Zanzibar, with the affairs of those coast-tribes is of great importance for our missionary labours is not to be denied.' Krapf similarly stresses Said's marked friendliness to himself and his fellow missionaries in a letter written in September 1850 to Lord Chichester, President of the C.M.S. F.O. 54. 14.

THE MISSIONARY INVASION 413

a dubious mind. For Hamerton had been trained in the service of the East India Company which, not so long ago, had regarded Christian missionaries in India with frank hostility. As soon as it became aware that nothing so inflamed the passions of the Indian peoples as their warring creeds, the Company had striven to avoid all ground for the suspicion that the English had come to India to propagate not only their trade and their power but also their religion. It was not till 1813 that Wilberforce, after twenty years of persistent effort, had secured for missionaries the same right as other Englishmen to be admitted into India under licence unless good cause to the contrary could be shown. By Krapf's time, however, the old controversy had lost its edge. There were no such quarrels in Hardinge's or Dalhousie's day as in Minto's.[1] But at its friendliest the Government of India still held aloof: it gave, it still gives, no official support to missionary work: and Hamerton, brought up in this tradition, may well have thought that Krapf's invasion of East Africa might lead to difficulties with the tribes of the interior and do more harm than good. But he was the accredited agent of the C.M.S., a body which had proved its power in high circles, and Hamerton, as has been seen, received him cordially and backed his application to Said. Some months later his attitude was officially confirmed. The appropriate strings had been pulled in London, and at the instance of Lord Aberdeen at the Foreign Office the Board of Control had issued instructions that the C.M.S. mission in East Africa was to be 'recommended to the Imam's protection'.[2]

Eight years passed and nothing happened, except the personal dangers to which the missionaries so coolly exposed themselves, to justify any doubts that Hamerton may have had as to the results of their activities or to ruffle his friendly relations with them. On each of his visits to Zanzibar Krapf mentions the Consul's ready hospitality; and in 1850 Palmerston wrote from the Foreign Office telling Hamerton that he was glad to have

[1] On Minto and Serampore see *Lord Minto in India*, 61–82, and for the whole subject A. Mayhew, *Christianity and the Government of India* (London, 1929).
[2] Aberdeen to India Board, 20.vii.44 (F.O. 54. 6).

heard from Krapf of his friendliness, and instructing him 'to continue to protect and support the missionaries'.[1] But in the spring of 1852, when his time in Africa nearly up, he made his last two calls at the island on his way to Usambara and back, Hamerton was not there. He had gone with Said to Muscat and did not come back till the end of 1853: and, when he did come back and received a dispatch from the Foreign Office informing him that the Hanoverian Protestant Missionary Society was sending a ship to East Africa and asking him to help, he replied in terms which must have surprised Lord Clarendon. 'I have cause to believe', he wrote, 'that this or any other missionary expedition will not be well received by the Imam or his people.' Their ideas about missionaries from Europe and their intentions in East Africa are much less favourable than they were—a change 'which, I regret to say, has been caused by Dr. Krapf'.[2] A disquieting accusation. What was it the good Krapf had done?

It was in February 1852 that Krapf and Erhardt had come to Zanzibar on their outward journey to Pangani. Let Krapf's own journal speak of the happy and innocent week he spent there.

'On the 13th I reached Zanzibar; but, as Major Hamerton had left for Muscat where there were political differences to be adjusted, I was in some perplexity as to a lodging; but was however soon relieved from it by the harbour-master, Jairam, who handed me the keys of the British consular residence. M. de Belligny, the French consul, also kindly invited me to take up my abode in the French consulate during my stay, and I experienced likewise much civility from his wife and from Mr. Kuhlmann, his secretary. This gentleman had a love, kindred to my own, for all that is in any way connected with the geography and history of Eastern Africa, which made my stay at Zanzibar a pleasant little episode in my life's history.'[3]

On their return journey in April the two missionaries paid another short visit to the island. They sheltered again under Hamerton's roof and in due course Belligny called on them. He

[1] Palmerston to Hamerton, 2.xi.50 (F.O. 54. 14).
[2] Hamerton to Clarendon, 14.ii.54 (F.O. 54. 15).
[3] Krapf, 368.

was welcome. They invited him to stay to dinner. There was more delightful talk about East Africa. After dinner, to quote Krapf's account, Belligny 'took up a map and said he had heard that a portion of this coast between Vanga and Pangani did not belong to the Imam'. Could Krapf, who had just come from there, say if this was so? Erhardt, if the story told to Hamerton was true, sensed the danger of such a question and advised Krapf not to answer it. But Krapf saw no harm in admitting what many Arabs at Zanzibar must have known and what Belligny himself would be able to discover any day if he took a trip to Pangani. So he briefly described 'king' Kimweri's status and authority, and how he appointed officials and periodically levied tribute on the coast. But he had forgotten his 'Swahili' enemies, and it was on this occasion, it will be remembered, that he had brought the *Mbereko* to Zanzibar with the deliberate intention of 'exposing' their dishonesty and ruining their trade. That little conversation was overheard, and soon a sinister rumour was spreading through Zanzibar. Krapf, it was said, had told the French Consul that Seyyid Said's dominions did not extend unbroken down to the Rovuma: that a stretch of it, many leagues in length and of high commercial value, was under the effective and unquestioned rule of the black chief of Usambara! And why was the question asked and answered? Because Belligny's people were about to execute the design which —everybody knew—they had long been contemplating. That Frenchman who had recently opened a trader's shop at Lamu had been sent there to inaugurate a French colony. An official mission was on its way from France to occupy the coast at large. And Krapf's journey to Vuga had been for the purpose of arranging for the cession of the country to the French without reference to its lawful owner, Seyyid Said. . . . For months the talk went on. When Said came back from Muscat in November it was poured into his ears. Hamerton, returning a year later, found the feeling it had excited still strong and bitter. 'The good old Imam', he reported, 'is very much distressed at all this.' And no wonder. For what could be more irritating and alarming than this disclosure to a French official of the weakest spot in the façade of his African realm? When Erhardt next came to Zanzibar, after Krapf had gone home, Said was careful to inform him, in the course of a very friendly conversation, that the difficulties he had had with Kimweri had been amicably settled, and that he was about to build a fort and garrison it in the disputed territory.[1] In the background of it all, moreover, though it was carefully not mentioned, was Krapf's attack on the middlemen's trade. What Said thought of that or what he would have said to Krapf about it if he had ever seen him again must remain a matter of conjecture. But Krapf himself was aware to what he owed the manufacture of the storm—'the envy and malice of the Swahili'. They had taken a quick and not ineffective revenge.[2]

Even more unfortunate than the effect of this affair on Said and the leading Arabs was its effect in British official circles. Hamerton himself was quite dismayed. He could not credit, of course, the popular version of the story, but the fact of the notorious question and its answer seemed established, and that was quite enough. For he had urged Said to help the missionaries on the ground that their activities would be purely religious and that they would never 'interfere in secular affairs'. 'This conduct of Dr. Krapf', he wrote angrily to Clarendon, 'has greatly lessened and injured my influence with the Arabs and shaken the implicit reliance they were accustomed to place in my word.' As a matter of fact, Said and his advisers were probably well aware that there was a good deal less reality in Krapf's interference in politics, about which they complained so much, than in his interference in trade, about which they made no complaint at all; and if Hamerton's training had not infused in him at least a tincture of official prejudice he might have seen Krapf's indiscretion in less glaring colours: he might even have detected the whole ingenious plot that had been woven round it. As it was, the wretched affair seemed just what he ought to have

[1] See p. 352, note 1, above.
[2] Krapf, 368–9, 404. Krapf to Venn, 3.iv.53; Erhardt to Venn, 9.iv.53; Hamerton to Clarendon, 14.ii.54; Hamerton to Govt. of Bombay, 3.vi.55 (F.O. 54. 15).

expected of a missionary, and when he reported it to the Government of Bombay the official reaction was the same. Even the highest circles at Calcutta bridled at the apparition, far away in Zanzibar, of the bugbear they specially and very properly abhorred—the missionary in politics. Dalhousie dispatched to London a stiff request that the Government should make the C.M.S. 'take notice' of this 'mischievous meddling in secular affairs'. . . . Poor Krapf! He had supposed, he pleaded in his defence, that the French Consul, with whom Hamerton himself had told him to make friends in the event of his own absence from Zanzibar, had been interested only in geography and not in politics. He humbly apologized. So did Secretary Venn. 'If Dr. Krapf had done any harm', he told the Foreign Office, 'he was most anxious to undo it.'[1]

The charge against Krapf, of course, was nothing more serious than 'talking politics', for nobody can have supposed that he had engaged in an intrigue for a French occupation of East Africa. His experiences in Abyssinia had given him the same sort of anti-French bias as that of his fellow-Protestant missionaries in Madagascar; and the only kind of European 'occupation' he actually desired was of limited extent and under the British flag. When he visited the 'ruined and deserted town of Malindi' he thought it 'might again be a populous and flourishing port, serving as an important missionary centre, were the English to occupy it as they had done Aden'. And at Malindi or Mombasa or ruined Kilwa he wanted, like Buxton, to see a colony of freed slaves established—a reproduction, as he says, of Sierra Leone, a revival of English Point.[2] With regard to wider projects of annexation than a naval base or a freedmen's colony, he took a neutral, an almost Laodicean, line. He supported neither of the factions into which British philanthropists were then divided as to whether or not the definite extension of British rule, in South Africa, for instance, or the South Seas, was an advantage to the humanitarian cause. One of the pieces of advice which he

---

[1] Hamerton to Clarendon, 14.ii.54; Govt. of India to Court of Directors, 3.xii.53: Venn's comments, 5.xii.54 (F.O. 54. 15).

[2] Krapf, 134, 152, 427.

addressed to young missionaries at the end of his work at Rabai was as follows:

'Expect nothing or very little from political changes in Eastern Africa. As soon as you begin to anticipate much food for missionary labour from politics, you will be in danger of mixing yourself up in them. Do not think that, because the East Africans are "profitable in nothing to God and the world", they ought to be brought under the dominion of some European power in the hope that they may then bestir themselves more actively and eagerly for what is worldly, and in consequence become eventually more awake to what is spiritual and eternal.... Europe would, no doubt, remove much that is mischievous and destructive out of the way of missionary work, but she would probably set in its place as many and perhaps still greater checks.'[1]

On the other hand, Krapf did not share the view that the extension of European rule should be opposed and obstructed because it would tend to facilitate and increase the intercourse between white men and black. He had too much common sense to imagine that any native people anywhere in the world could be somehow fenced off by an eternal barrier through which the only Europeans admitted would be missionaries. The first European of modern times to live in East Africa, he knew he would not be the last. His chief reason for devoting so much toil to compiling grammars and dictionaries of the native languages was 'the certain conviction that the time would come when Eastern Africa would be drawn into European intercourse'.[2] More traders, he was well aware, would come from Europe, and possibly settlers too. Rebmann, at any rate, when he first crossed the Shimba plateau, was as much impressed with its suitability for European homes as Livingstone when he first climbed the Shiré Highlands. It 'offers to the settler', he observed, 'the finest and healthiest situation with an extended view over the Indian Ocean and with continuous enjoyment of the fresh sea-air'—a rosier description than the real facts of the climate justified.[3] That this increasing contact with Europeans would not be an unmixed boon to the natives Krapf was also well aware. Already, it seemed to him, the growth of trade with

[1] Krapf, 512–13. [2] Idem, 141. [3] Idem, 242.

The Missionary Invasion

the outer world had meant a decline of native morals. If only, he exclaims, the goods which Europe buys from Africa could speak! 'How many slaves, how many women, how much palm-wine, how many objects for the gratification of lust and vanity are purchased by the Galla, Nyika, Kamba, and Swahili with the ivory which they bring to the coast!' But Krapf did not waste time—this is, indeed, the only instance in his book—in deploring the bad side of the contact between primitive and civilized peoples, nor in explaining its good side. The contact was inevitable. It was the missionary's task to make the best of it, counteracting the bad and confirming the good. And as to its probable sequel—a more formal occupation and the establishment of European government—Krapf was equally clear-sighted and equally hard-headed. 'Whether Europeans take possession of Africa or not', he said, 'I care very little, if at all.' What he did care about was the manner in which the Europeans, whether traders or prospectors, whether settlers or officials, behaved to the Africans. 'Hitherto,' he wrote, 'the more recent relations of Europeans with Eastern Africa have been always of a peaceful kind and calculated to efface the bad impressions which the conduct of the Portuguese in earlier times had left behind. The natives are pleased with and desirous of European intercourse, and if Europeans deal with them honourably and justly, it will never be otherwise.'[1]

The influence of personal conduct on the native mind—it is there, perhaps, the historian will detect the most definite and far-reaching result of this first missionary 'invasion'. Nowadays the mission-societies in East Africa are fulfilling functions far beyond the range of Rabai. In their monopoly, or something like it, of native education they possess an instrument which must have profound and incalculable results on the future welfare of the people. Krapf and his comrades and their earlier successors could do nothing like that. The teaching given at Rabai indeed was scarcely education. It was limited in scope. Its technique was primitive. It was little more than preaching. And its fruits were meagre. But if the Africans may not have

[1] Idem, 185, 513, 540.

been impressed by what those first missionaries said, they must have been impressed by what they were. Hitherto the natives of the coast had seen no white men since the Portuguese except passing traders and sailors and Owen's garrison. The natives of the interior had never seen a white man at all. They were to see many of them in due course of time, white men of all sorts, coming to their country with various and mingled motives. But these first 'invaders'—and others of the same kind were to follow them—had one motive only. They did not seek to make money from the natives. They did not covet their land or its produce. They did not even want to govern them. They only wanted to give them a new God and thereby make them better men. Though missionaries in Africa or elsewhere have not all been as wise as Krapf, though by bigotry or meddling or factiousness they have sometimes done more harm than good, all, or almost all, of them have been thus disinterested; and the knowledge of that in native minds has been not the least important factor in the slow and complicated process of adjusting the relations between white men and black.

XIV

THE FRENCH AT ZANZIBAR

I

AMERICANS and Germans were relatively new-comers in East Africa in Said's day. Far older and stronger was the French connexion, established long before the beginning of the Napoleonic War and maintained till near its end. The 'constant intercourse' of French traders with the Arabs was one of the things which most impressed the British visitors to the coast during the war. Bissell was struck by it at Zanzibar, Smee at Pate, Prior at Kilwa. At all three places Arab sentiment was warmly pro-French. At Zanzibar and Kilwa French was widely spoken.[1] Naturally, therefore, the break occasioned by the British occupation of the Mascarenes was only temporary, and soon after the restoration of Bourbon the old liaison was resumed. In 1817 a merchant of Bourbon visited Muscat to explore the possibilities of reviving the trade which had once linked Oman with Île de France, and he brought with him a complimentary letter to Said from the commandant of the island. Nothing would please him more, wrote Said in reply, than a renewal of his old ties of friendship with the French colonies. This interchange was fruitful; French trade with Muscat and Said's African ports increased; and in 1822 an agreement was concluded for its regulation.[2]

With this agreement the Bourbon merchants were content for a time, but when Said began to extend his commercial relations with other Western countries, when he negotiated a treaty in 1833 with the United States, far wider in scope than the Bourbon agreement of 1822, and, in particular, providing for the establishment of a consulate, and when (as will be related) a similar treaty was made in 1839 with Britain, it seemed clear that French interests would inevitably be overshadowed unless the same privileges and safeguards were obtained by France. The visit of a French warship to Muscat in 1838, reported to the

---

[1] See pp. 168, 174, above.   [2] Guillain, ii. 212. Miles, 323.

Bombay Government by its watchful Indian agent, may have been significant. In the next year, at any rate, a French consulate for Said's dominions was decided on in Paris, and in 1840 the official appointed to the post arrived at Muscat. The French Government may have imagined that this step could be taken without obtaining Said's explicit assent. A French Consul at Muscat was not an innovation. Might he not regard himself as the legitimate successor, after an interval, of Dallons? But in fact his reception was more like Cavaignac's. Said declared that he could not confirm the appointment unless the establishment of a consulate were incorporated *de novo* in a treaty. It has been suggested that his hesitation was due to the increasing tension between France and Britain on the question of Mahomet Ali; but the main reason was probably simpler. Said's treaties with the United States and Britain had flattered his pride and raised his prestige. He had dealt as an equal with the heads of two great nations. And, though he might never make much use of them, he had obtained the same commercial privileges as he had given. Naturally, therefore, he objected to unilateral action: what he wanted was a reciprocal agreement. To this the French Government, with the precedents before it, could scarcely demur; the unwelcome official was withdrawn, and a year or two passed while the clauses of the proposed treaty were drafted and discussed. But before committing himself to the final stage Said was determined to obtain the British Government's approval. Just at this time, as will presently appear, he had been greatly alarmed by French expansion in the neighbourhood of Madagascar and by reports of further French designs on his own African coast. If these designs were serious the French might pick a quarrel with him over the treaty and appeal to force; and that would mean, if he were left unaided, the swift collapse of his loose-knit and defenceless 'empire'. While, then, it was always important, it was now imperative, that in his transactions with a foreign Power he should do nothing to which objection could be taken by his British friends, and early in 1843 he confided his difficulties and fears to the British Consul. He was careful to explain that he did not like the French.

'They do not possess patience', he told Hamerton, 'and are not a long-suffering people.' They were pressing for a commercial treaty, and he was afraid they would not be satisfied with the terms of the British Treaty of 1839: they would resent exclusion from the trade in ivory and gum-copal on the Mrima. But they could not, of course, have more than the British. Would it displease the British Government if he gave them as much? . . . Hamerton promptly submitted the matter to the Foreign Office, and in due course received a short and sensible reply. Aberdeen had no desire whatever 'to interfere in the Imam's treaty of commerce with the French', since any concessions granted them would automatically extend to the British under the 'most-favoured-nation' clause in the Treaty of 1839.[1]

There was now no further obstacle to the completion of the business. On November 9, 1844, three French warships arrived at Zanzibar, bringing Captain Romain-Desfossés, commander of the naval division of Bourbon and Madagascar, with full powers of negotiation from King Louis-Philippe; and on the 17th a Treaty of Commerce between the Imam of Muscat and the Emperor of the French was signed by him and Saïd.[2]

Most of the nineteen articles of the treaty were practically identical in sense and generally in language with the corresponding articles of the British treaty. It mattered little that the French Consul's right 'to hoist the French flag over his house' should be solemnly affirmed. It might matter more that in the eleventh article, which, like the tenth article of the British treaty, provided for the reservation of the Mrima trade, an additional sentence was inserted: 'But, if the English or Americans or any other Christian nation should carry on this trade, the French shall in like manner be at liberty to do so.' Apart from these minor differences, there were three new articles which had no counterpart in the British treaty. Article IV, which was one day to prove a serious obstacle to British efforts

[1] French warship: F.O. 54. 3. Consulate at Muscat: Guillain, ii. 213; Miles, 341; and see p. 88, above. Hamerton to Aberdeen, 14. ii. 43; A. to H. 11. vii. 43; F.O. 54. 5.
[2] Guillain, ii. 213. R. H. Crofton, *The Old Consulate at Zanzibar* (Oxford, 1935), 16.

to suppress the Slave Trade, ran as follows: 'The subjects of His Highness the Sultan of Muscat actually in French service shall enjoy the same protection as the French themselves: but, if subjects of His Highness are convicted of any crime or punishable breach of the law, they shall be discharged by the French from whosesoever service they may be in and delivered to the local authorities.'[1] Article XVI provided for the restoration to the Consul of any French ship taken by 'other than Christian pirates' and brought into the Sultan's dominions. Article XVII gave the French the right of 'establishing *dépôts* or warehouses (*magasins d'approvisionnement*) at Zanzibar or any other place in His Highness' dominions'—a curious addition to the treaty, since Article III had already accorded the general right 'to purchase, sell or rent land, houses and *magasins*' anywhere.[2]

2

This time there was no delay in Said's confirmation of the French Consul's appointment. M. Broquant had accompanied Captain Romain-Desfossés to Zanzibar, and he received his *exequatur* as soon as the treaty was signed. On November 21 the French flag was duly hoisted over his house and a salute of twenty-one guns was fired by the corvette *Berceau* and by Said's frigate *Shah Allum*.[3]

Broquant's tenure of his post was short. When Captain Guillain visited Zanzibar in 1846 he thought the house which Said had insisted on putting at the Consul's disposal was dark, damp, and unhealthy, and deplored the fact that the British and American Consuls, with salaries far higher than the 15,000 francs allotted to their French colleague, could afford much better and more salubrious quarters. Whatever the reason, the unfortunate Broquant was soon attacked by fever and dysentery, and in the spring of 1847 he died. At Said's request Hamerton took charge of his possessions. 'In the death of M.

[1] Literal translation of French text.
[2] French text in Guillain, iii. 459–64. Both 'Imam' and 'Sultan' are used in the preamble, but only 'Sultan' in the Articles. English text (presumably Hamerton's translation from the Arabic), B.R. 266–70.
[3] Guillain, ii. 214. Crofton, 16.

Broquant', he wrote to the Bombay Government, 'I have to lament the loss of a sincere friend and most agreeable companion.'[1]

The next Consul was M. de Belligny, a French Creole from Ste-Domingue, whom Krapf (it will be remembered) found so friendly and hospitable and so keenly interested in the African coast. He remained at Zanzibar till the end or near the end of Said's reign in 1856 when he was transferred to Manila.[2]

Hitherto the base of the French trade had been in Bourbon, but the establishment of the consulate encouraged two rival firms of Marseilles, Vidal Frères and Rabaud Frères, to send resident agents to Zanzibar. At the time of Burton's visit in 1857 there were four Frenchmen in the island working for these firms—MM. Bauzan, Wellesley, Perronet, and Bérard—while two more—MM. Mass and Terassin—were at Lamu, where from 1852 onwards each firm had opened a local branch mainly for exporting sesamum.[3] A French report of 1847 stated that 'profits ranging from 75% to 100% could be made in Europe on Zanzibar produce', and advised French traders how to make the best of the round voyage. On the way out they should call first at Majunga on the Madagascar coast where goods could be sold for Spanish dollars and no duties need be paid except a present to the Sakalava king. The next call should be at Mozambique, where duties could be evaded by dealing on board ship, bribing some official, and slipping quickly away. At Zanzibar, or at Lamu if the prices at Zanzibar were too high, orders should be given for local produce to be ready in two or three months' time, and the interval should be spent in a voyage to Bombay for Indian stuffs or to Mocha for coffee.[4] Apart from ivory, gum-copal, and cloves, the French traders shipped mainly sesamum and other oil-bearing grains which were used—so Burton believed—for making *huile d'olives* in Provence. More

[1] Guillain, ii. 12–14; iii. 89–90. Crofton, 18–19.
[2] See pp. 414–15, above. Burton, *Zanzibar*, i. 313–14. M. Vignard, de Belligny's successor, died of sunstroke on the voyage from Aden. M. Cochet was then appointed.
[3] Burton, 319–20. For Lamu see also p. 415, above.
[4] Report summarized in *O'Swald & Co.*, 39.

than 8 million pounds of sesamum, worth over £20,000, were exported from Zanzibar in 1859. French imports were mostly of the same mixed kind as American or German, but there was one French speciality. As he sailed down the coast in 1850 Krapf was distressed to observe how fast the sale of French brandy was spreading among the Arabs and Swahili, Moslems though they were. It was 'everywhere asked for, even by the governors and their soldiers'.[1]

This trade may not have been all that was expected when Broquant hoisted his flag; but for ten years or so the French with their older connexion to help them did rather better than the Germans and a very great deal better than the British. In 1855 the tonnage of the French ships trading at Zanzibar amounted to about 5,500 as against 9,000 tons of American and 3,500 of German shipping. In 1857 French tonnage took the lead with 10,000, but in the next two years it rapidly declined, and in 1859 it was only 3,000 as against 10,000 for the Americans and 4,500 for the Germans. In his consular report on that last year Rigby noted a still steeper decline in the volume of French trade at Aden, and prophesied that 'the trade between France and Zanzibar will probably altogether cease in a few years as the American and Hamburg merchants are driving the French out of the market'. Burton, too, at about the same time observed that the two Marseilles firms were 'eating up each other' and were rumoured to be both in financial difficulties. But the complete collapse foretold by Rigby was avoided. By 1871, while the German tonnage retained its lead at 7,500, the French tonnage had risen again to 5,500.[2]

3

There was another branch of French trade in East Africa of which no account was taken in official estimates. The planters

---

[1] Burton, 319. Rigby's Report, 22. Krapf, 428, 430, and (for a French order for ivory) 404.

[2] Rigby's Report (with Kirk's notes: see p. 317, note 1, above), 24. Burton, 320. French imports were still higher than German in 1859, but consisted mainly of bullion.

The French at Zanzibar

of the Mascarenes still needed labour, and it was at least as difficult to stop slave-smuggling into French Bourbon as into British Mauritius. From 1815 onwards French 'slavers' were busy all up the coast. Some were engaged in the traffic round the Cape and over the Atlantic, but most of them were in quest of slaves for Bourbon. With or without the connivance of the Portuguese officials they obtained a steady supply from Mozambique: in 1827 they had a resident agent at Ibo. North of Mozambique the loyalty of Said and his Governors on the coast to the 'Moresby Treaty' prevented slave-trading at the ports under their effective control,[1] but at the southern end of Said's 'dominions', at little harbours and bays where his officials and soldiers were unknown and his authority merely nominal, there was a regular French trade in slaves. About 1826 some eight ships from Bourbon were making two voyages a year to Mongo Bay (or Mongorella) just north of the Portuguese frontier, at Mikindani, at Kiswere, and also, it was reported, at Lindi, where, at times at any rate, Said did maintain a Governor and garrison. Up in the north similarly there were stretches of the coast where Said's orders could freely be evaded. Offshore near Pate, in 1824, the natives in their canoes would not come near the *Barracouta* because they had suffered so often from French kidnappers. In order to check this trade in the north an interpreter, who had served with Captain Moresby for several years and had assisted in the conclusion of the Treaty of 1822, suggested in a report to Commander Christian that, if the Imam's permission could be obtained, Mombasa might be re-occupied. 'The Arabs of that place', he wrote, 'are doing what they can to induce the French to resort thither.'[2]

All this traffic, of course, violated French law. Slave-trading had been prohibited in 1818 and it was penalized by fine and

[1] See p. 499, below.
[2] Owen to Adm. 23 and 26.vii.25 (*S.P.* xv (1827–8), 373). Acland to Christian, ix.26 (ibid. 446–7). *Barracouta*, Owen's *Narrative*, i. 381. Report of Amease, the interpreter, 1826: (ibid. 447–8). Statement by a Dutch deserter from a French 'slaver' at Port Louis, 22.v.27 (ibid. 458–60).

banishment in 1827. But the French Government did little to enforce the law till 1831 when, as one of the immediate results of the 'Revolution of July', a sterner Abolition Act was passed and a treaty for which the British Government had long been pressing was concluded, providing for the reciprocal right of search. In 1833 the essential 'equipment article' was added by a supplementary convention.[1] To the Bourbon planters this evidence of a new determination to stamp out slave-smuggling was far from welcome; and their case seemed the harder when they compared it with that of their fellow-planters and fellow-Frenchmen in Mauritius. By 1830, it is true, slave-smuggling there had been suppressed; but successive Governors at Port Louis, confronted with the problem of conciliating new and unwilling subjects to British rule, had shown no lack of sympathy with the planters' demands for labour. Farquhar himself had needed a sharp rebuke from the Secretary of State to spur him to a whole-hearted attack on the Trade. Though Slavery as practised in the island was more cruel than in any other British colony, nowhere was local opinion allowed so obstinately to resist and obstruct the 'ameliorating' policy which the British Government and Parliament adopted between 1820 and 1830 as the only alternative to the drastic step of abolishing Slavery outright. When a newly appointed Attorney-General was mobbed in 1832 because it was known that his previous experience in St. Lucia had made him an 'anti-Slavery' man, Sir Charles Colville agreed with the planters that he ought to go and ordered him back to England. And when the final blow fell and the Emancipation Act of 1833 came into force in 1835, Sir William Nicolay attempted to soften its effect on the labour-supply by passing an ordinance compelling any unoccupied man or woman under sixty to 'take employment' and requiring children of eight or over to be apprenticed. Glenelg at the Colonial Office promptly disallowed this ordinance, but by then the planters had ceased to need it. In the interests of sugar-production the British Government had agreed to the introduction of the needed labour from poor and populous India. Indian traders

[1] Texts in *S.P.* xv (1827–8), 451–2; xviii (1830–1), 641; xx (1832–3).

and artisans had been crossing the sea to Port Louis since its earliest days, but from 1834 onwards a new class of unskilled labourers or coolies came pouring in. Over 25,000 had arrived when in 1839 further immigration was prohibited as the result of an inquiry by the Government of India which had revealed a number of abuses—the ships were too crowded, the men unsuitable (they were mostly fugitives from debt), the proportion of women far too low, the work on the plantations too exacting. In 1842 coolie-immigration was again permitted, under more stringent regulations, but so great was the influx—34,000 in fourteen months—that a limit of 6,000 a year was imposed. Finally, in 1847, under Earl Grey's régime at the Colonial Office, the system was re-examined and further conditions imposed to safeguard the coolies' freedom and facilitate their return to India if they wished. Thus, from 1834 onwards there was only one brief period, 1839 to 1842, when the planters of Mauritius were not assured of a reasonable supply of labour.[1]

The planters of Bourbon were in far worse case. The supply of coolies from the little French footholds on the coast of India was inadequate; and, while in 1844 the Government of India permitted coolies in British India to emigrate not only to near-by Mauritius but to far-distant British Guiana, Trinidad, and Jamaica, it prohibited their emigration to any foreign colony. Naturally the thoughts of the Bourbon planters reverted to Africa. If free labourers might legitimately be obtained from India, why not from Africa? The obvious answer was that in Africa the enlistment of free labour under contract might all too easily mean a revival of the Slave Trade in disguise. In the first place, unless the business of enlistment were most carefully and vigorously controlled by the Government, and every detail of the contract interpreted and explained, it would be impossible to ensure that the African was freely and willingly accepting service oversea for a period of years. Secondly, the supply of

[1] W. L. Mathieson, *British Slave Emancipation* (London, 1932), chap. ix. W. P. Morrell, *British Colonial Policy in the Age of Peel and Russell* (Oxford, 1930), chaps. vii and xi. For Farquhar and the Slave Trade see pp. 195–7, above.

Africans would almost certainly be provided not from the coast-towns and the adjacent villages but from the interior where there was no possibility of European control and the methods of obtaining 'free' labour would inevitably be the same as those of the Slave Trade. For these reasons the British Government consistently refused to permit the enlistment of labourers for service in the British West Indies from the independent territories on the West African coast, but under persistent pressure from the West Indian planters and their friends and agents in England, permission was granted in 1840 to Trinidad, and a little later to British Guiana and Jamaica, to import Africans from Sierra Leone. In a British colony the process could be and was very strictly regulated; but it was, none the less, a relief to humanitarian opinion in England when the experiment broke down for the simple reason that very few Africans in the colony could be induced to follow, however freely, the path across the Atlantic which so many of their kin had traversed in chains. In the West Indies, as in Mauritius, the labour crisis was overcome by Asia, not by Africa.[1]

This West African experiment, unsuccessful though it had been, was at least a precedent for the Bourbon planters; and unfortunately, about the same time, a lead was given them nearer home. From 1839 to 1842, as has been seen, Indian coolies were not obtainable in Mauritius, and in 1841 an attempt was made to obtain free labourers from Zanzibar. In August of that year Commander Allen, returning to Zanzibar from Mombasa in H.M.S. *Lily* with Hamerton on board, found two British ships in the harbour, the schooner *Joshua Carroll* under Captain Porter, and the brig *Maria* under Captain Turner. Both had come from Port Louis and were returning there. From what he learned ashore, Allen suspected that Porter, and possibly to a less extent Turner also, were after slaves. He searched the *Joshua Carroll*, and, finding it equipped with planks for making a 'slave-deck' and supplied with food and water for 150 people for a month but with no cargo, he dispatched it under guard to the Cape for trial in the Vice-Admiralty Court. The subsequent

[1] Mathieson, 118–23. Morrell, 154–5.

proceedings showed that he had made a very natural mistake. Captain Porter, it appeared, had been sent to obtain free labourers, and this, however undesirable, was not illegal. The *Joshua Carroll* was released forthwith, and the acting-Governor at Port Louis informed the Colonial Office that 'from the respectability of the charterers and the open and regular manner in which the vessel was dispatched there does not exist a doubt here that the undertaking was, what they state it to be, a legitimate attempt to obtain free labourers'.[1]

Action, meantime, had been taken to prevent the recurrence of the incident. As Hamerton explained to his chiefs in London and Bombay and to the Governor of Mauritius, now Sir Lionel Smith, there were no free labourers obtainable in Zanzibar or Pemba. The Arab estates were worked by their slaves. The native population obtained the means of subsistence from their village lands and would not be tempted by the prospect of earning wages oversea. The only labour, therefore, available for Mauritius was slave-labour. It was a common practice for the Arabs to hire out their slaves for staffing caravans on the coast and so forth, and they might well be willing to allow them to work for Mauritius planters for wages which they, the owners, would appropriate. All this was as clear to Said as it was to Hamerton. 'What shall I do about these ships?' he asked the Consul. 'There are no natives of these islands who would go to Mauritius of their own free will, even for 20 dollars a month; but many would send their slaves if they were certain of being able to recover whatever the slaves might earn.' Said may not have realized that this would mean the revival of Slavery in thin disguise on British soil; he may even have contemplated making a little money himself and supposed that the British Government would not object. If so, he was quickly undeceived. Hamerton straitly advised him 'not to countenance the measure', and, as usual, he acquiesced. The stoppage of the traffic at its other end was no less promptly brought about. On receipt

[1] Hamerton to Bombay Govt., 20.viii.41 (F.O. 54. 4). Allen to Rear-Admiral King, 24.viii.41; Col. Staveley to Lord Stanley, 15.i.42 (C.O. 167. 236).

of Hamerton's report Sir Lionel Smith issued orders 'that on no pretext whatever were labourers from the East Coast of Africa to be permitted to be introduced' into Mauritius, a step which Stanley at the Colonial Office 'entirely approved'.[1]

It is not surprising that the planters of Bourbon should have done what the planters of Mauritius had tried to do. Nor is it inexplicable that the French Government, unlike the British, should have failed to stop it. 'Free emigration', it is true, from the East African coast was almost indistinguishable from the Slave Trade except that its victims were more humanely treated both on the sea-voyage and on the estates in Bourbon. The 'emigrants' were obtained in the interior by the Arab traders as slaves, brought down to the coast as slaves, and sold to the French agents as slaves. They were then taken on board the French boat where, according to Lyons McLeod, who came out to Mozambique as British Consul in 1857 and closely studied the 'Free Labour Emigration System', the transition from slavery to free employment was brought about in the following manner:

'On reaching the deck of the French ship, the ceremony of engaging the slaves as "free labourers" is gone through by an Arab interpreter who asks them in the presence of the Delegate [a French official] whether they voluntarily engage to serve for five years at Réunion. The interpreter assures the Delegate that the slave is willing to become a "free labourer" at Réunion in every instance. The Delegate cannot speak the native language and does not know what question the slave is asked nor the nature of his reply, but being assured by the Arab that the slave is willing to go to Réunion, the French Delegate is satisfied.'[2]

[1] H. to Sir L. Smith, 17.viii.41; Staveley to Stanley, 15.i.42; Stanley to Staveley, 30.v.42 (C.O. 167. 236: 168. 26). Hamerton obtained information that Said had suggested to the supercargo of the *Maria* that he should send 200 of his slaves to Mauritius in one of his own ships in the belief that 'our Government would wink at a transaction of this kind'. When asked about it, Said said that it was one of his relations, a leading Arab in Zanzibar, who had proposed the scheme. H. to Priv. Sec. Governor, Mauritius, 16.x.41 (ibid. 410).

[2] L. McLeod, *Travels in Eastern Africa* (London, 1860), i. 307. McLeod was an anti-slavery zealot, but there is no reason to doubt his word. His account of the 'System' is confirmed at various points by Livingstone in his narrative of the Zambesi Expedition, and by General

A bad enough business; but it must not be forgotten how hard it was for the French Government to see Bourbon starved of labour when Mauritius, except for one brief period, got all it wanted. By 1859 there were 180,000 coolies in the British island and only 30,000 in the French. And after 1840–2, to Bourbon's need were added the needs of Nossi-bé and Mayotta, new settlements crying out for hands to work at new construction. The British Government was surely justified in refusing to permit the emigration and employment of its Indian subjects under conditions it could not itself control and enforce, but the French Government was only human if it regarded this refusal as dictated by no higher motive than a determination to exploit for British purposes alone the excessive share of lands and labourers which Britain had obtained by war. In the long dispute about 'free emigration' the French attitude was always clearly visible beneath its diplomatic covering, and in the end it was open and explicit. 'We will not stop getting labour from Africa unless you let us have coolies from British India.'[1]

The 'getting' began in 1843, two years after the affair of the *Joshua Carroll*. In April of that year Hamerton reported that a French brig-of-war had visited the coast and that Said had been induced to give permission for 'free labourers' to be procured from his 'dominions'. 'The slaves will have nothing to do with the matter', he commented, 'further than to say that they wish to be made free.' About the same time Lieutenant Christopher observed an unusual number of Arab dhows plying between Kilwa and Nossi-bé, but apparently he did not stop and search them as he was entitled to do under the Treaty of 1831.[2] In 1845 that treaty was set aside and a new agreement con-

Rigby (British Consul at Zanzibar, 1858–61) and the Rev. H. Waller (Universities' Mission to Central Africa, 1860–4) in their evidence before the Select Committee of 1871.

[1] W. L. Mathieson, *Great Britain and the Slave Trade* (London, 1929), 149–50. The French Government put the matter very clearly in 1857. 'Labour can only be carried on in the Isle of Réunion and in the French Antilles by negroes procured from Africa or by coolies. It is obvious, therefore, that, if the latter can be procured, the former will not be necessary.' S.P. xlviii (1857–8), 1150.   [2] T.B.G.S. vi. 377.

cluded under which the French Government undertook to maintain a substantial squadron on the African coast so that British assistance in the suppression of slave-smuggling might be dispensed with. It seems significant that the scope of this agreement was limited to West Africa, and Palmerston, at any rate, was convinced that the French had insisted on the restriction in order to have a free hand for developing their 'free emigration system' in Said's 'dominions'.[1] After 1848 there was greater need than ever to keep British busybodies at a distance. The Revolution of 1848 did more than change Bourbon's name to Réunion: it precipitated the long-dreaded emancipation of the slaves. Still more 'free' labour had now to be got by hook or by crook from outside. From Cape Delgado northwards the whole coast was ransacked. In Zanzibar itself slaves or *émigrés* were obtained from Arab slave-owners and shipped away from a quiet corner of the island. When Consul Rigby arrived in 1858 he found that the French 'slave vessels', as he bluntly called them, were escorted by warships. Seyyid Majid, Said's son and successor, would have liked to stop it, mainly because the tax he levied on the export of slaves throughout his 'dominions' was not payable on 'free emigrants': but, as he complained to Rigby, he could do nothing with French men-of-war. 'If I attempt to interfere, the French Consul immediately threatens me with the interference of his Government.'[2]

Still the supply from the Arab coastland was not enough, and in 1854 the Portuguese Government was induced to permit the extension of the 'system' to Mozambique. This was the more unfortunate because (as will be described in Chapter XVI) British efforts had succeeded just at that time in greatly reducing the smuggling of slaves from the Portuguese ports. The sale of them, indeed, had so far fallen off at the coast that it no longer paid the traders to bring big caravans down from the interior. Thus, while the new demand for 'emigrants' was met at first by

[1] Mathieson, 150.
[2] Rigby's evidence before the Select Committee on the East African Slave Trade in 1871: *Report*, 42–3, Q. 537–42, 549, 552. A notorious Spanish slave-trader, Buonaventura Mass, obtained over 400 slaves for Réunion at Kilwa in 1857. *Report*, 114.

the sale of 'surplus stock', it soon led to a brisk revival of business in the interior, with the active support of the Portuguese officials, who were as ready as the French to differentiate between *émigrés* and slaves and, if McLeod is to be trusted, received more than one-third of the purchase price of 30 to 40 dollars a head. When Livingstone came to the Zambesi in 1858 and penetrated inland in the course of the next five years he found the country round Lake Nyasa ravaged and depopulated by slave-raids mainly to meet the French demand. As late as 1863 some thousand *émigrés* in the year were being shipped to Mayotta and Nossi-bé.[1]

What could the British Government do? It was no use exhorting Said to cancel his agreement and prohibit 'free emigration' from his ports unless British warships were sent to fight the French warships. And it was the same with Portugal. Under strong pressure from the Foreign Office the Government at Lisbon prohibited the traffic; but when in execution of its orders the *Charles et George* with over a hundred Negroes and a French official on board was seized off Mozambique in 1858, Napoleon III sent two battleships to the Tagus. Again the only alternative to acquiescence was war with France. So, at last, in 1859 the British Government surrendered. Negotiations were opened for the importation of coolies from British India into French colonies under safeguards as strict as they could be on paper. Napoleon on his side agreed to stop the 'free emigration'. In 1861 the importation treaty was concluded. In 1864 the 'system' was finally abolished. If, for a few years longer, slaves still found their way to Réunion, Mayotta, and Nossi-bé, that meant no official palliation of the business: it was just smuggling as of old.[2]

4

Unlike the American and German invaders of the East African field in this period, the French invaders were not concerned with trade alone.

'Remember the precarious condition of our old French possessions

[1] McLeod, i. 306, 316. Mathieson, 166, 184–5. R. Coupland, *Kirk on the Zambesi*, chaps. vi and vii.
[2] Coupland, 85, 266–8. Mathieson, 168–9.

in the Indian Ocean, mere flotsam and jetsam saved from the lamentable shipwreck of 1815. Pondicherry, Chandernagore, and Karikal lay stifled under the pressure of the vast Indo-Britannic empire. Bourbon was not only eclipsed by her one-time sister, Île de France, and menaced by the emancipation of the slaves; she had no harbour. Madagascar was still too difficult a prize to grasp.'[1]

In those sentences from the preface of the book in which Captain Guillain, sailor, scholar, and patriot, described his travels and researches on the coast of East Africa from 1846 to 1848 lies the key to the political policy which, side by side with her commercial activities, France adopted or, rather, resumed some twenty years after the end of the Napoleonic War. Naturally she wanted something to off-set the losses of 1815; naturally she sought new footholds in the Indian Ocean; and it would indeed be comical if a British historian were to reprobate such attempts as an exhibition of rapacious imperialism. For almost all the old footholds, once Portuguese or Dutch or French, right round the coast and on the islands from Calcutta to the Cape, were now in British occupation or under British 'influence'. Was there anything, it might be asked, worth having left?

At the northern end of this western section of the Indian Ocean there was so far, it is true, no European settlement. From the Red Sea to the Persian Gulf the Arabs were still masters of all the Arabian coast. But French intrusion in that quarter would not only be fiercely resisted by the Arabs; it would certainly be disliked and probably be obstructed by Britain. If proof were needed that the British Government desired to maintain an exclusive 'sphere of influence' in this part of the Middle East, its reaction to Mahomet Ali's Arabian adventure in 1834–9 supplied it. There were only two commanding points, moreover, on the Arab seaboard, Muscat and Aden, the keys to the Persian Gulf and the Red Sea; and of these one was virtually in British hands after 1815 and the other actually so after 1839.[2]

[1] Guillain, i. xii–xiii.
[2] Mahomet Ali's advance to the Persian Gulf and the British occupation of Aden will be briefly described in Chapter XV.

The situation on the African coast southwards of the Red Sea was similar but not the same. It lay just outside the range of European policy. Even the British had not occupied any of its ports, nor even appointed political or commercial agents there. But southwards of the Somali country the Arab occupants of the seaboard were not as independent as on the Red Sea and in south-west Arabia. They were nominally subject to the Imam of Muscat; and, however vague and tenuous his suzerainty might be, it would be difficult, if not dangerous, to dispute it, since the British—it is always the British—were the Imam's friends. Before the war, it will be remembered, the idea of French expansion in that field had been mooted at Port Louis; but if another Morice had proposed between 1815 and 1840 to help any of the Arab coast towns to repudiate Said's authority and to establish a French protectorate or even a colony, the answer would still have been Cossigny's answer—a fight with Muscat might mean a fight with Britain.[1] For the first twenty-five years of the peace, accordingly, French interest in the African mainland was confined to trade. The preceding sections of this chapter have shown how the authorities at Bourbon renewed the old commercial ties with Oman, how French trade with Muscat and the African ports was revived and regulated by agreement, and how finally in 1844 a commercial treaty was concluded with Said on the same lines as his previous treaties with the United States and Britain.

There remained Madagascar, a 'prize' indeed, and one which France might hope to win without quarrelling with Britain. Surely French designs on that great island could not be questioned at Muscat or Zanzibar: its northernmost point lay south of Cape Delgado, the recognized limit of Said's 'dominions' on the mainland. Nor, it seemed, did Britain covet it for herself: otherwise the British Government would have contested the French interpretation of the Treaty of Vienna.[2] But, throughout the period covered in this chapter, Madagascar was, as Guillain said, 'too difficult to grasp'. Queen Ranavolana's

[1] For Morice and Cossigny see pp. 76-82, above.
[2] See p. 141, note, above.

hatred of all European intrusion did not abate.[1] In 1844 both French and British traders were once more expelled from Tamatave. As a punitive measure the town was bombarded in 1845 by a combined French and British squadron; but the only result was a massacre of native Christians.[2] The re-establishment of the old French posts on the seaboard of the Queen's realm could only be achieved, it was clear, by the use of force on a far bigger scale, by something like a war of conquest.

There was nothing left. Mozambique was preoccupied by Portugal. Farther south the British, now firmly settled in Cape Colony, once more barred the way. So, for the first phase of the peace, from 1815 to 1840, it seemed as if the new footholds France desired were not obtainable.

5

It was a seaman who revived at Bourbon the energy and enterprise displayed by La Bourdonnais at Île de France. In 1840 Admiral de Hill, Governor of Bourbon, commanding the French squadron in the Indian Ocean, set himself to discover the indiscoverable opening. Two areas, one north, one south, attracted his attention. On the coast beyond Mombasa and Lamu, up by the Somali country, Said's authority was said to be less effective than it was in the nearer neighbourhood of Zanzibar. Conceivably he might not object to French activity so far afield. At least the question might be put to him, backed perhaps with a little show of force; and, should he actually assent, it would be difficult for the British to find a plausible excuse for making trouble. In the south, again, every acre of Madagascar was not barred to France. Ranavolana, like Radama before her, had not subdued the whole huge island to Hova rule; and not far off the coast, yet quite beyond her reach since she possessed no fleet, lay a few independent little islets. Nossi-bé, for instance, near the northern end of the east coast was ruled by the Sakalava tribe. And about a hundred miles

[1] See p. 280, above.
[2] R. de Comte, *Des différentes phases de l'occupation française à Madagascar* (Montpellier, 1908), 103.

The French at Zanzibar

farther out at sea, in the centre of the Mozambique Channel, was the nearest of the Comoro Isles, governed by independent chiefs, who, though Arab or half-Arab in blood, owed no allegiance to Muscat. A naval base in such a commanding strategic position might almost make up for the loss of Port Louis.

In the summer of 1840 a French corvette of 22 guns arrived at Zanzibar; and, Said being then at Muscat, its commander addressed himself to his son Hilal and requested permission to establish 'a French agent' at Zanzibar and 'to erect a fort and buildings at Mogadishu and Barawa, where they said they wished to form a settlement'. Hilal, no doubt, protested that he had no authority in such a matter. At any rate the permission was not granted. Thereupon the corvette sailed south to Nossi-bé, and invited the Sakalava to accept a French protectorate. The offer—so at least it was reported at Zanzibar—was refused. Finally the corvette came to Muscat, and the requests made to Hilal were repeated to his father. Said evaded them, but with no easy mind. He was convinced that the French designs were serious, and, turning in his alarm to British friendship, he told the whole story to Captain Hennel, Resident in the Persian Gulf, who chanced to be at Muscat. Hennel at once communicated it to the authorities in London. 'The object of the corvette's visit to this port', he wrote, 'is unquestionably to persuade, if not to frighten, His Highness into making concessions and granting privileges to the French which he conceives to be in the highest degree detrimental to his own interests.'[1] By the same mail went a letter from Said himself to Palmerston at the Foreign Office. 'The French nation have their eyes on our possessions in and about Zanzibar. . . . Is it possible that you could restrain them and keep them from us and our posterity or do you advise us to agree to their demands?'[2]

Before a reply could be received from distant London, Said's anxiety was deepened by further news from Zanzibar. At the beginning of November he told Hennel that 'he had lately received

---

[1] Hennel to Secret Committee, 31.vii.40, communicated to Palmerston, 3.ix.40 (F.O. 54. 3).
[2] Said to Palmerston, 30.vii.40 (translation): ibid.

positive information from his son, Khalid, that two French frigates had arrived at the island of Nossi-bé from Bourbon, and that, having landed a number of people there, they had commenced building a fort and store-rooms without the slightest reference being made to the Governor of Zanzibar'. 'It was notorious', Said went on, 'that Nossi-bé belonged to himself and he could not but consider the conduct of the French as most unfriendly. . . . Unless some immediate check were given to them, he would before long be deprived by that Government of all his possessions on the African coast.' Was an answer from Lord Palmerston ever coming? . . . Hennel did his best to reassure him, and it was probably at his suggestion that Said dispatched a personal note of protest to the Governor of Bourbon. 'Your Excellency is aware', he said, 'that the inhabitants of the island in question belong to me and are my subjects. . . . What I therefore hope from your Excellency, considering the friendship subsisting between us, is that you will forbid your people from seizing my territories and possessions.'[1] In all probability this was the first de Hill had heard of Said's claim to Nossi-bé; and in any case the deed had now been done. When Said himself repaired to Zanzibar in the following spring, he at once dispatched an agent to Nossi-bé who reported the presence at the island of a French warship and a 'general' with four hundred soldiers and two hundred workmen and others. 'From what I learn', wrote Said to Palmerston, 'they are fixed there.'[2]

Palmerston, meanwhile, had not by any means neglected Said's appeal, but it was a question that needed careful handling. He knew nothing about Nossi-bé. It took some time, indeed, to identify its exact position on the map. But it was near Madagascar, it seemed: and though the French had maintained their interpretation of the treaty and re-established their old trading-posts in 1819, the time had not yet come to concede to France an exclusive 'influence' in the Madagascar area at large. Before the general expulsion of the Europeans, British traders had been

[1] Hennel to Secret Committee, 3.xi.41, enclosing translation of Said's letter to Governor of Bourbon (F.O. 54. 4).
[2] S. to P. i.v.41 (ibid.).

busy on the island as well as French, and British missionaries busier still. It was with the British, moreover, in Mauritius, not with the French in Bourbon, that Ranavolana's predecessor on the Hova throne had markedly made friends. Might not her successor do as Radama had done? But it was Muscat more than Madagascar that determined Palmerston's response to Said's appeal. He received it just when the long and difficult 'affair' of Mahomet Ali was coming to its dramatic end. On September 30, when he sent off his reply to Said, the tension created by his co-operation with Russia, Austria, and Turkey in defiance of France was still acute. It was not for another week or ten days that he knew the danger of war was past. And the reason of his firmness both on the big issue and on the little one was the same —the need of safeguarding the overland route to India. At one end of it were Beyrout and Aleppo, whence a British force was helping to eject the Egyptian army of occupation. At the other end was Muscat, where British interests were secured by the protection Britain afforded to Said and his 'dominions'. Palmerston's letter, therefore, was in rigorous terms. 'The British Government recommend Your Highness to refuse to comply with any demands . . . which may in your opinion be inacceptable . . . and rely on the support of England if circumstances should render it necessary for Your Highness to seek for her assistance.'[1] Ringing words, which must have done something to temper Said's fears; but they did not promise the fulfilment of his actual request that the French should be 'restrained'. Palmerston was not quite so impetuous and bellicose as popular tradition has depicted him. He could use strong language and yet display considerable patience. It was not, indeed, till five months later, when Hennel's second dispatch had reached London, that he decided to raise the question in Paris. On February 5, 1841, he instructed Lord Granville, the Ambassador, to invite the French Government's attention to the events of Nossi-bé.

'Your Excellency will state to the French Government that such a representation has been made by the Imam of Muscat between

[1] P. to S. 30.ix.40 (F.O. 54. 3).

whom and the British Government relations of friendship have long existed and with whom Great Britain has recently concluded a Commercial Treaty. His Majesty's Government are disposed to think that the Imam must have been misinformed, for they cannot suppose that the French Government would forcibly and against the Imam's will take possession of a portion of his territory, not as a measure of reprisal and hostility for any injury done or offence committed, but merely because the occupation of the place might be convenient to French interests; but His Majesty's Government would be very glad if the Government of France would enable His Majesty's Government to relieve the Imam from the apprehension which he appears to feel of hostile intentions towards him on the part of France.'[1]

Though the gist of this dispatch beneath its diplomatic phrasing was firm enough, Palmerston had no intention of picking another quarrel with France. At this moment, indeed, he was bent on a policy of reconciliation and renewed co-operation. Thus Granville, though he doubtless said to M. Guizot what he had been told to say, was careful not to press the question. Guizot, no less wisely, gave no answer. And Granville, wise again, made no further mention of the matter in his reports to the Foreign Office.[2] So six months safely passed, and when in September Palmerston renewed his inquiries, his tone had changed. For in the interval Said had provided further information about Nossi-bé which, so far from strengthening his case as he had doubtless hoped, had virtually destroyed it. In the first place he had submitted a version of a treaty he had concluded in 1838 with the ministers of Seneekoo, Queen of the Sakalava, under which she had surrendered 'all her dominions on the island of Bookeen' (Nossi-bé) to Said, and undertaken to pay him 30,000 dollars and the yield of a 5 per cent. duty on imports and exports, while Said on his part had promised to 'take charge of the fort and protect us on the sea side and generally protect us as he does his other subjects'. So far, so good. Said, it would appear, had had the same idea as the French. He had wanted to establish a foothold at Nossi-bé and he had got there first. But Said incautiously appended to the

[1] P. to G. 5.ii.41 (F.O. 54. 4).
[2] Pencil note on above draft dispatch.

The French at Zanzibar

treaty a copy of a letter he had recently received from Queen Seneekoo in reply to an inquiry from him as to the doings of the French. 'You refer to the French people who are with us', she had written. 'We do not want them, and I am sorry I have been obliged to allow them because your people were not with us....'[1] In those last words the truth was out. Said's assertions that Nossi-bé 'belonged' to him and that its people were his 'subjects' were based on a contract undertaken three years back and never carried out. It is possible that Seneekoo had fulfilled her part in it—there is record of beeswax being sent to Zanzibar by the Sakalava as' tribute'[2]—but it is certain that Said had neglected his. The Governor of Bourbon, therefore, was entitled to do in 1840 what Said himself had done in 1838; and, since he had not only made a bargain but quickly executed his share of it with ships and troops and workmen and a fort, his position now was immeasurably better than Said's. The Queen and her people may or may not have preferred the 'protection' of Oman to that of France, and French advances may have been harder to resist than Said's; but the conclusion could scarcely be evaded that now, in 1841, according to international usage, Said had lost his claim to a foothold on Nossi-bé and the French had made theirs good.

Palmerston, meantime, apprised of the uncertain nature of the ground, was preparing for a diplomatic retreat. He drafted a reply to Said which was markedly less robust than his previous letter. He had not known, he told him, that he claimed possession of any part of Madagascar; and he could give him no further advice until he had made inquiries.

'In the meantime I have only to observe that it cannot escape the sagacity of Your Highness that there is a material difference between territories which have for a length of time belonged to a Sovereign and districts which have only recently tendered their submission to such Sovereign and over which he has in fact never exercised any practical authority.'[3]

[1] Documents with Said's letter to Palmerston, 1.v.41 (F.O. 54. 4). For Zanzibari 'colonists' see p. 333, above.
[2] *Story of the House of O'Swald*, 39.
[3] P. to S. 13.viii.41 (F.O. 54. 4).

Secondly, he asked the Admiralty to order inquiries to be made by naval officers on the spot as to what precisely the French had done at Nossi-bé and what, if any, was Said's authority in the island.[1] Finally, he wrote to Lytton Bulwer, who had been *chargé d'affaires* at Paris since Granville's recent retirement, asking him what had been the outcome of the February dispatch, telling him that inquiries had been set on foot as to the validity of Said's claims, and bidding him to be cautious.[2]

This last advice was justified in the event. Bulwer, it is true, was not inclined to overlook or minimize French designs in the Indian Ocean, and he sent Palmerston an article from a Paris newspaper discussing a proposal to establish a French line of steamships from Suez to Bourbon and Madagascar. 'Sooner or later', it said, 'France may be called to play an important rôle in this Indian Ocean where the fate of England will be decided.'[3] The naval reports, on the other hand, cast doubts on the importance or long duration of the French occupation of Nossi-bé. The French flag was flying there, wrote Captain Allen, and the settlement was freely permitted by the natives. Some bamboo houses and stockades had been erected. But the neighbourhood was very marshy: already there was great sickness among the Europeans; and in his opinion a permanent settlement was impossible.[4] This view was confirmed by Consul Hamerton at Zanzibar. 'Close to the establishment', he wrote, 'is an immense bog which stinks in a most fearful manner, particularly after rain.' Nor was there any truth, he added, in the rumours of other places being occupied by the French. Said, in fact, had been needlessly alarmed. And anyhow he had no case against the French at Nossi-bé. Its people had requested—or had they, in fact, only accepted?—French protection because Said had not afforded it. He did 'nothing but send them a red flag'.[5] But, if Hamerton was right on the diplomatic issue, he had

[1] P. to Admiralty, 13.viii.41 (F.O. 54. 4).
[2] P. to Lytton Bulwer, 2.ix.41 (ibid.).
[3] Bulwer to P., enclosing cutting from *La Presse* of 30.v.41 (F.O. 27. 624). [4] Allen's report, 3.xi.41 (F.O. 54. 4).
[5] Hamerton's consular report, 5.i.42 (ibid.). For his appointment see pp. 482–4, below.

under-estimated French vigour and tenacity. In the summer of 1842 came another naval report. The French were still at Nossi-bé, and they had now occupied not only its neighbour, Nossi-cumba, but also Mayotta, a much larger and more important island out in the middle of the Comoro group. The Sultan of Johanna—the report continued—had refused to cede Mayotta to France and claimed to be under British protection, but the local chief had surrendered control of the harbour. Little had been done, however, at any of those settlements: very few houses had been built, and there had been eighty deaths.[1] Another report, made a year later, stated that there were then a hundred French soldiers and fifty 'drilled blacks' at Nossi-bé.[2]

These reports did not tell all the truth. About this time the energetic Governor of Bourbon was obtaining a French footing also in Nossi-mitsion and Anjouam by treaties with the local chiefs.[3] But the information was enough to convince the Foreign Office that French activities in those unknown islands between Madagascar and East Africa were serious and not likely to be abandoned because of initial difficulties with the climate. What, then, was to be done? The answer, for more than one reason, was 'Nothing'. In the first place, Franco-British relations were already strained again and by a dispute, as it happened, over a similar question on the other side of the world. Like King Radama of Madagascar, Queen Pomare of Tahiti, chief of the Society Islands in the South Pacific, had come under British influence through the establishment of the London Missionary Society in her island since 1797. She and her father were both converts to Christianity, and she regarded the leading missionary, George Pritchard, who came to Tahiti in 1824, as her confidential adviser in politics as well as in religion. In 1826 she asked to be put under British protection, but Canning politely refused. In 1836 and again in 1837 Pomare, like Radama, declined to admit French Roman Catholic priests; and on that account a French frigate visited Tahiti in 1838 and

[1] Naval Report, 10.vi.42 (F.O. 54. 4).
[2] Ibid. 10.vi.43 (F.O. 54. 5).
[3] G. Hardy, *Histoire de la colonisation française* (Paris, 1928), 172.

obtained an apology and an indemnity. Pomare then appealed for protection direct to Queen Victoria, but again the request was refused. In 1841, in the absence of Pritchard on leave and of the Queen on a tour, four Tahitian chiefs, at the instance of the French Consul, wrote to Louis-Philippe asking for French protection. In 1842 Admiral Du Petit Thouars arrived, and, going beyond the instructions he had received from Guizot, forced Pomare under threat of bombardment to ask for protection and thereupon proclaimed a French protectorate. In 1843 the French admiral returned and formally annexed Tahiti. In 1844 Pritchard, who since resuming his post in 1843 had used all his influence against the French, was arrested and deported. Public feeling now ran so high in England and France that war again seemed imminent; but Guizot and Aberdeen, who had succeeded Palmerston at the Foreign Office in 1841, were happily able to arrange a settlement behind the backs of the politicians and the public. The British Government received an indemnity for the treatment of Pritchard. The French Government maintained its protectorate.[1]

This alarming quarrel was the first reason for not picking another over the Madagascar islands. And the second reason was as good: the British had no ground at all for interference. If Said indeed had established his claim to any sort of effective authority in that part of the world, the British Government would have been justified in intervening on behalf of a sovereign who was admittedly its friend. *A fortiori*, if the British Government had indeed established the 'protectorate' over Johanna which its Sultans had more than once asked for,[2] it could properly have insisted that the Sultan's claims to suzerainty over the other islands should at least be examined and put to proof. But, as it was, the French had just as much right to occupy Nossi-bé or Mayotta as the British had to occupy Aden or Socotra; and it would have been, to say the least, illogical to accept a French protectorate in Tahiti and resist it in the Comoro Isles. So Palmerston's inquiries in Paris were not re-

[1] R. B. Mowat, *Cambridge History of British Foreign Policy* (Cambridge, 1923), ii. 182–5.   [2] See pp. 173, 201, above.

The French at Zanzibar

peated by Aberdeen; and the only step taken in the Comoro Isles was neither political nor economic, but purely humanitarian. It was suspected that the need of labour for the new French settlements in the neighbourhood might mean an increase in the Slave Trade, and in the autumn of 1844 an official representative, Josiah Napier, was sent from Mauritius to Johanna to negotiate a treaty with the Sultan on the same lines as the 'Moresby Treaty' with Said under which the people of Johanna would be prohibited from dealing in slaves with Europeans. The treaty was signed on November 8 by Napier and Sultan Suleem.[1]

Said's anxiety, meanwhile, had deepened. The news of the French advance in the south had alarmed and depressed him as much as anything in all his chequered career. It happened that the first British consul appointed for his dominions arrived at Zanzibar at that dark time; and at his first interview with Said, 'I found him', he reported, 'dejected and broken-spirited in consequence of his having a few days before received authentic information of the occupation of the island of Nossi-bé by the French.'[2] Then Palmerston's first encouraging letter had come, and then his second discouraging one, and then the news that Palmerston had gone out of office and Aberdeen come in. To make matters worse, Palmerston had begun, and Aberdeen was continuing, to press Said at this of all times to make a difficult, if not dangerous, concession to British sentiment about the Slave Trade, and that thorny business was the main reason for his sending Ali-bin-Nasir to England in 1842. But he instructed his envoy not to omit to raise with Aberdeen the question of French aggrandizement.

'Speak also to the Grand Vizier about the French and what we know of them with respect to the island of Nossi-bé. "And now the French have made us their enemies; and there is no doubt that, when they are able to do anything to hurt us, they will not delay it. But let the whole injury which may happen to us from the French be upon the English Government. And if this be disagreeable to you,

[1] S.P. xxxviii (1849–50), 809.
[2] Hamerton to Govt. of Bombay, 15.v.41, cited by R. H. Crofton, *The Old Consulate at Zanzibar*, 2.

and you abandon us, then we will repair our condition with the French in the best way we can. But this shall be by your consent."'[1]

It was the only weapon Said had, this threat to come to terms with France, and he was careful to blunt its edge. Of course it made no impression on the Foreign Office. There was no Napoleon now in the background. The British mastery of India and the Indian Ocean was undisputed. Was it likely that Said would change sides? So the question of Nossi-bé was ignored and Ali-bin-Nasir returned to Zanzibar with a great deal to tell Said about the Slave Trade but nothing about the French.[2] For five years Said accepted the rebuff, and then in 1847, when Palmerston was back again at the Foreign Office, he ventured on one more complaint about the Comoros. Palmerston was readier, no doubt, than Aberdeen to stand up to the French; but since, as has been seen, Said had no case, there was little he could do. One thing, however, he did. He 'minuted' on Said's letter: 'This communication seems to shew expediency of sending without delay a consular officer to the Comoro Isles'; and he added—there was French precedent for it, good or bad, in Tahiti—'the chiefs to be exhorted by consular agent to reject any offers from the French'.[3]

In this decision and in a promise that the naval Commander-in-Chief at the Cape should be instructed to send a warship to those waters from time to time, Said had to seek what cold comfort he could find.[4] Napier was appointed consul and he took up his duties at Johanna in February 1850.[5] On June 3 he signed with Sultan Suleem 'a Treaty of Peace, Friendship and Commerce between Great Britain and Johanna'. Following again the Muscat model—in this case the commercial treaty concluded with Said in 1839—it provided for 'most-favoured-nation' treatment for the trade of each party (Clauses II, III, IV, and VI) and for the reciprocal right of appointing consuls (Clause

[1] S.'s Instructions to Ali-bin-Nasir, Feb. 1842 (*S.P.* xxxi (1842–3), 650). [2] H. to A. 14.ii.43 (F.O. 45. 5).
[3] S. to P. 19.viii.47 (F.O. 54. 11).
[4] P. to S. 29.vii.48; P. to Hamerton, i.48 (F.O. 54. 12).
[5] H. to P. ix.50 (F.O. 54. 14).

The French at Zanzibar

VII). The opportunity was also taken of incorporating in the Treaty (Clause VIII) the supplementary article which had been added to the 'Moresby Treaty' enabling the Indian Navy as well as British warships to deal with slave-smuggling.[1] In the following October Napier died of phthisis. His successor was William Sunley, who reported in 1852 that, while few slaves from the African coast were now being imported into Johanna, some 300 had recently been landed in the neighbouring island of Mohilla. A British consul, as the next few years were to show, could not by himself prevent the continuance of the Slave Trade in one form or another, except in the neighbourhood of his consulate. Still less could he prevent by himself the steady process of French expansion. In due course over all the Comoro Isles, and later on over all Madagascar too, the French flag flew unchallenged.[2]

Thus, by a series of bold steps, the political position of France in the Indian Ocean had been substantially improved. The new acquisitions were small, but they might be made the basis of something bigger. Mayotta in particular, definitely annexed in 1843, seemed to offer great opportunities of further expansion. Its position made it an ideal centre for the development of an entrepôt trade between Europe, Africa, and Asia. Its strategic value was still more evident. Equidistant from Africa and Madagascar, it commanded the Mozambique Channel. A British naval captain, says Guillain, described it as 'a little Gibraltar'.[3]

6

The first move northwards, from Mayotta, was soon made. In the spring of 1843 Hamerton reported that a French brig had been visiting the coast and that several 'chiefs' had come to Zanzibar to tell their overlord that at Kilwa and other places the French had been trying to buy land. 'His Highness' had been 'terribly frightened'.[4] A few months later Hamerton had

[1] Text of Treaty: *S.P.* xxxviii (1849–50), 807–9. Addition to 'Moresby Treaty', p. 215, above.
[2] Sunley to Malmesbury, 28.x.52 (*S.P.* xliv (1853–4), 1255).
[3] Guillain, i. xi–xiv.   [4] H. to A. 27.iv.43 (F.O. 54. 5).

an illuminating conversation with the captain of a French merchantman. The French, he wrote home, have 'exaggerated ideas' as to the possibilities of trade on the coast, and their Government is determined to establish 'factories' at 'the Imam's African ports'. Almost all those ports had been visited and 'private agents' appointed at them.[1]

No wonder Said was frightened. If France was really determined to force an entry, he could do nothing by himself to prevent it. In response to Hamerton's warnings, it will be remembered, he had ordered his flag to be hoisted at all the ports which acknowledged his overlordship in 1841. It was in this year, 1843, and probably in view of the French activities, that he appointed a Governor at Mogadishu. And it was in 1844 that he made the first of his ill-starred attempts to obtain control of Pate.[2] But these were only measures to strengthen his 'suzerainty' on the coast, and his 'suzerainty' in itself was useless against determined French aggression unless the British acknowledged and upheld it. Fortunately, perhaps, for Said British interest in keeping the French away from the north was livelier, and the British case for interference stronger, than in the south. A French naval base anywhere from Mombasa northwards would menace the Red Sea route, and go far to neutralize the recent acquisition of Aden—as Guillain and doubtless many other Frenchmen were well aware.[3] For the moment the Foreign Office held its hand; but when in the winter of 1844 it was reported from Aden that a French warship was engaged in inspecting the northern part of the East African coast, the Commercial Treaty which Said had just concluded with France was carefully scrutinized; and it was suggested that the clause which permitted the French to build *maisons et magasins* anywhere in Said's 'dominions' might be given a sinister interpretation.[4] Early in 1845, accordingly, Aberdeen wrote to Lord Cowley, Granville's successor at the Paris Embassy, expressing the hope that the

[1] H. to A. 31.viii.43. (F.O. 54. 5).
[2] See pp. 337–40, above.
[3] See p. 457, below. Owen had pointed out the danger of a French base at Mombasa twenty years back: see p. 237, above.
[4] Article XVII of treaty: cf. Article III. Text in B.R. 266–71.

magasins were to be commercial only, not military or naval.[1] The question was duly put and promptly answered. Guizot told Cowley that he had not yet examined the treaty, but that 'the views of the present Government in entering into the engagement were simply commercial, and that it had never entered into their contemplation to build forts or establish depots for warlike stores in the territories of the Imam'.[2] Next year Captain Guillain arrived at Zanzibar. His instructions, as he explains in his published account of his mission—a highly interesting and informative work and indispensable, as previous pages of this book have shown, to any historian of East Africa—were to foster friendly relations, to prospect for further openings for French trade, to try to obtain an adjustment of the local currency in French interests, and to obtain satisfaction for the murder of Maizan. The Maizan 'affair', as has been seen, was ultimately settled; and on the monetary question Said agreed to fixing the exchange-value of the French five-franc piece, although it meant a depreciation of the Maria Theresa and Spanish dollars on which his own currency was based.[3] But Guillain had other business which was not for publication. In the summer of 1847, in the course of his cruise along the coast in the 18-gun brig *Ducouëdic*, he put in at Lamu and Barawa. The news of what he did there came quickly to Said's ears at Zanzibar and was as quickly communicated by him to the British Consul. The French captain, Hamerton reported to London and Bombay, 'has been tampering with the Chiefs and trying to induce them to sell certain ports to the Government of France. . . . The Chiefs did not consent as they said the place belonged to His Highness the Imam.'[4]

As long as the Arab rulers on the coast thus accepted Said's

[1] A. to C. 25.ii.45 (F.O. 54. 8).
[2] C. to A. 10.iii.45 (ibid.).
[3] Guillain (i. xiv–xv) represents his voyage as a reconnaissance preliminary to an economic conflict between Mayotta and Zanzibar to secure the entrepôt trade. For the currency problems see Guillain, ii. 43–6. Maizan, see pp. 353–6, above.
[4] Hamerton to Palmerston, viii.47 (F.O. 54. 12). Miles, ii. 345. Krapf's journal records two incidents arising from the *Ducouëdic*'s visit

'suzerainty' and as long as the British Government upheld the integrity of his 'dominions', Said might feel himself secure. But there were uncertainties about that first proviso. The old and friendly connexion of some of the coast towns with the French has already been remarked. And there were Arabs in Zanzibar itself who were openly or covertly pro-French. Said's withdrawal thither had not wholly freed him from the worst and most persistent pest of a ruler's life in Muscat. The ineradicable factiousness of Arab politics had pursued him to his island sanctuary. Despite his great prestige there were Arabs at his court—one of them had been Governor of Zanzibar and Pemba —who bitterly criticized his policy, who formed what might be described as an active, if covert, opposition, who, if they did not dare attempt an open revolt while he lived, were determined to get their way when he died. Naturally, since Said leaned so hard on British friendship, such a faction would be pro-French. 'There is a strong party here in favour of the French', Hamerton had reported in 1842. 'It is in constant communication with them and will no doubt seek their assistance on the death of the Imam.' Naturally, too, the motive of this intrigue was not disinterested patriotism. Just as the mainstay of the pro-French party at Muscat in Sultan's and Cavaignac's and Seton's day was those Arabs who made their living from trade with the French islands, so it was now in the time of Said and Guillain and Hamerton. And now there was a new factor, intensifying the old sentiment for France and the old antagonism to Britain. The trade which these factious Arabs wanted above all else to pursue at Zanzibar and all up the coast was the Slave Trade. France, they believed, would permit it.

to Mombasa. May 24, 1848: 'Whilst engaged in breaking stones near my hut two Europeans approached, and I found that they were officers from a French ship of war which was exploring the haven of Mombasa. One of them was a good botanist, and both were very friendly.' May 27: 'I heard with much sorrow that a French sailor had entered the house of a Mnika [i.e. one of the Nyika], and had attempted to take liberties with his wife. The Mnika wanted to lodge a complaint with me, but desisted when he heard that the French did not belong to my Kabila, my tribe or people.' Krapf, 194–5.

Britain, they knew, would not. So the series of French advances which had so frightened Said, the visits of French warships, the scrutiny of the coast, the efforts to obtain a foothold on it, had not frightened them. On the contrary, they had welcomed the intrusion of the French into their East African domain. They 'look upon their coming amongst them', Hamerton had written in 1843, 'as the re-establishment of the foreign Slave Trade'.[1]

An Arab intrigue would not be true to type if it did not penetrate the circle of the ruler's family; and it seems more than probable that the pro-French party made the most of the unhappy quarrel between Said and his eldest son, Hilal. Arab thrones, as Said had reason to know, were easily lost, and often enough in Arab history their occupants suffered from the impatience of their heirs. In Hilal's case this traditional uneasiness in his relations with his father was accentuated by a difference in character, tastes, and ambitions. Said, it has been seen, was a peace-lover: his dominant interest was trade and the prosperity to be won by trade; his military record was not glorious. Hilal was or would have liked to be a man of war, and therein he better fitted the usual conception of what an Arab ruler ought to be than his younger brother, Khalid, who had already made a fortune out of trade and was thoroughly unpopular with the Arab rank and file. That Hilal in these circumstances was courted and made use of by the pro-French party is likely enough. At least he was on the best of terms with M. de Belligny. His own half-sister, recording many years later the memories of her childhood at Zanzibar, refers to a 'sad report' that Hilal took to drinking, 'seduced by Christians and in particular by the then French consul'. It only needs the harem to complete the familiar picture. Khalid's mother was one of Said's favourite wives.[2]

In all these circumstances the domestic breach inevitably

[1] Hamerton's report, 5.i.42 (F.O. 54. 4); H. to Aberdeen, 31.viii.43 (F.O. 54. 5). For the earlier pro-French party see pp. 103, 106, 421, above.
[2] E. Ruete, *née* Salme-binti-Said, *Memoirs of an Arabian Princess*, 139.

widened, till in 1844 Said made up his mind to exclude Hilal from the succession. After consultation, no doubt, with Hamerton he wrote to Aberdeen informing him that Khalid was to take his place at Zanzibar and inherit 'all our possessions in Africa' which he defined as 'all places on the continent of Africa between Mogadishu and Cape Delgado together with the adjacent islands now subject to our rule'—while Thwain, his third son, was to take his place at Muscat and inherit his Asiatic possessions. The British Government would, he hoped, approve this arrangement and befriend these heirs of his as they had befriended him. Comment on this historic decision to partition the Omani realm must be reserved for a later volume. The immediate point is Hilal's double disinheritance. When he learned of it or guessed it, he did not acquiesce without a struggle: and Aberdeen, already embarrassed by Said's attempt to enlist his aid in a family dispute, was still more embarrassed by the sudden arrival of Hilal, who had slipped secretly away from Zanzibar to appeal, like his father, to the 'power behind the throne'. Aberdeen did what he could within the bounds of diplomatic etiquette. He treated Hilal as the guest of Government: he urged him to make it up with his father and wrote to Said to the same effect: and finally he sent him home in a British ship. Early in 1846 Hamerton reported the moving scene of the prodigal's return. The crowd at the harbour-side displayed great emotion—and so did Said. Never again, he declared, should Hilal and he be parted. He wept.... But it was no use. The tears were soon dry. As time went on, Arab public opinion, though Hilal remained its favourite to the end, became convinced that a real reconciliation was impossible. At last, in 1849, Said cut the knot. Hilal was banished from Zanzibar. He made his home at Lamu till in 1851, in the course of the pilgrimage to Mecca, he died at Aden.[1]

Meantime French activity on the coast seemed to have been suspended. A French trader had established himself at Lamu

[1] S. to A. 23.vii.44 (F.O. 54. 6); A. to H. 6.x.45 (F.O. 54. 7); H. to A. 10.ii.46 (F.O. 54. 10); H. to P. 2.xi.49 (F.O. 54. 13). Guillain, ii. 226. Miles, 346. Said-Ruete, 80–1.

by 1852, but his *magasin* was above or beneath suspicion.[1] Then, at the end of 1853, came another demonstration. Admiral La Guène arrived at Zanzibar in his flagship on December 4 and stayed in harbour there a month. His conversations with Said were doubtless courteous: they were certainly disquieting. 'Exceeding great fear of the French', wrote Hamerton to Bombay in the spring of 1854, 'has come over the people here.' It happened that Said was about to leave Zanzibar on one of his periodical visits to Muscat. Normally Hamerton would go with him: but now Said came in person to the British Consulate, accompanied by his son Khalid and 'all the principal Arabs of the town', and in their presence he solemnly told Hamerton that neither Khalid nor any of the leading Arabs would remain in Zanzibar if he left it unless Hamerton stayed behind. He 'placed his son's hand in mine and desired him in all difficulties to be guided by my advice and to do nothing without consulting me. The Arabs then rose and came and kissed my hand, saying "We are now satisfied through the favour of the Almighty and the powerful destiny of Her Majesty Queen Victoria all will go well with us".' In a subsequent private interview with Hamerton Said explained that Khalid and the notables had been imploring him for three days past not to ask the Consul to accompany him this time to Muscat because they were so frightened of the French. In a letter to the Government of Bombay Said was equally explicit. The reason, he wrote, for wanting Hamerton to stay at Zanzibar was that the French were 'pressing a quarrel on him'.[2]

There can be no doubt that Said was genuinely alarmed. It was not that he feared an overt French move on Zanzibar or any of his 'possessions': that would be too direct a defiance of British policy. But suppose the pro-French faction at Zanzibar, with the el-Harthi at its head and the resumption of the Slave Trade as its watchword, were to attempt in his absence some such daring *coup d'état* as they would never venture on if he

---
[1] See p. 425, above.
[2] I.O., Enclosures to Secret Letters from Bombay, April to Sept. 1854: H. to G. of B. 18.iv.54; S. to G. of B. 3.vi.54.

were there? Suppose they seized the government, brushed weak Khalid aside, acclaimed as their overlord his younger, bolder brother Barghash, who had taken Hilal's place in their intrigues—and then invited the protection of the French? It might not be easy for the British Government to undo a deed of Arab doing. There was more meaning, therefore, in that dramatic demonstration, in those emotional appeals for British aid, than might appear from Hamerton's account, and the event soon proved it. A few months after Said's departure Khalid died. As Hamerton knew, Said put his fourth son, Majid, next in the line of succession at Zanzibar, and in due course an order arrived from Muscat appointing Majid acting-governor 'over Zanzibar, the mainland of Africa and its islands', and letters to the same effect went out to Said's governors and dependent sultans on the coast. But in the meantime there had been trouble. The dissident Arab minority realized that Majid's appointment marked him as Said's successor. To acquiesce in it meant abandoning the claims of Barghash. If Said had not taken the precaution of making Barghash accompany him to Muscat, there might perhaps have been a rising. As it was, Majid was so perturbed by the rumours that reached him that he asked for Hamerton's advice. Hamerton reassured him and promptly consulted the *jemadar* of the Baluchi garrison, the only troops in Zanzibar, and arranged for the strengthening of the guard at certain points. The action was observed, particularly, no doubt, the British Consul's part in it, and the peace remained unbroken.[1]

Thus the only disquieting feature in the new network of relations with Europe which Said had so eagerly fabricated for purposes of trade was the political ambitions of France. He had nothing to fear from the Americans or the Germans or, as will be seen, from the British. He had nothing to fear from 'legitimate' French trade. The danger lay in the French desire for territorial expansion up the coast linked with the Arab desire

[1] Coghlan to G. of B. 4.xii.60; Majid to Coghlan, 14.x.60. *Proceedings of the Commission on the Disputes between the Rulers of Muscat and Zanzibar* (Bombay, 1861), 58, 116. H. to G. of B. 15.xi.54: Crofton, 23.

The French at Zanzibar

to resume the Slave Trade. The strength of the latter will appear in a later chapter. French expansion had been checked so far by Said's personal authority and the backing given to it by the British Government: but in some French minds at any rate the idea of compensation for the losses of 1815 by new acquisitions of territory or 'influence' in East Africa was at least as active in 1856 as it was when de Hill made his first move north from Bourbon in 1840. Indeed, the re-emergence of the old project for cutting a canal through the Isthmus of Suez had greatly reinforced it. In an eloquent exordium to the preface of his remarkable book, published in the year of Said's death, Guillain pointed out the immense opportunity which the cutting of a canal would offer to France if only her statesmen would act in time and act with courage. Two currents of European commerce and civilization would issue from the Red Sea—one eastwards to India and beyond, the other southwards to East Africa, bearing to that backward land 'an incalculable increase of vitality'. Despite French interests in Indo-China and the Pacific, the first was likely to remain under British domination. 'It is the English flag one meets at every stage on the long voyage from Aden to Japan or to New Zealand.'

'But the African branch of the great sea-way can be dominated by French interest, not only because we possess along this route Bourbon, Sainte Marie, Mayotta and Nossi-bé, but because, when we want Madagascar, we shall have it, an Australia all of our own, as well as a line of secondary posts established at intervals along the coast—carefully studied by French travellers in the last twenty years—of Zanzibar, the Gulf of Aden, and Abyssinia.

'It must not be forgotten [adds Guillain in a footnote] that the Red Sea also has its Gibraltar, the port of Aden, which commands the Straits of Bab-el-Mandeb. If the position which England has already acquired there is not neutralized by some suitable provision for guaranteeing a free passage through the Straits to every flag, the cutting of the isthmus of Suez, instead of opening to the ships of Europe a direct entry to the Indian Ocean, will merely have extended to the bottom of the Red Sea the *impasse* which closes the Mediterranean at its Egyptian end.'

To realize these aims, Guillain continued, two things were needed. First, it must be recognized that the productive capacity of East Africa is far greater than that of the French colonies in West Africa—Madagascar alone 'could supply all Europe with sugar, rice and ebony'—and that the canal will bring Mayotta as near to Marseilles as Goree. Secondly, the ground must be prepared at once, and for what better purpose than that could France employ her recently augmented naval power?[1]

[1] Guillain, i. xxv–xxxi.

XV

THE BRITISH AT ZANZIBAR

I

THE position of the British in the western waters of the Indian Ocean after the Napoleonic War was the reverse of the French position. Victory had given them all they wanted. Their control of India and the routes to it had been secured, it seemed, for an indefinite time to come. With the Cape and Mauritius in their hands, with their sea-power supreme in the Mediterranean, with a dominant influence at Muscat and in the Persian Gulf, their only political interest in East Africa was negative. As long as the French remained without a naval base along the coast or near it, the British needed nothing more than Port Louis. Nor was the economic interest in East Africa strong enough to tempt British commerce away from more profitable expansion elsewhere. British subjects from India continued their old-standing African business, which indirectly benefited British manufacturers; but there was no direct trade between Zanzibar and British ports. Practically the only British interest in East Africa, therefore, in the first decade of the peace was, as has been seen, humanitarian. Only the attack on the Slave Trade induced British governments to extend their relations with Seyyid Said from his Arabian to his African 'dominions', and the only immediate result was the 'Moresby Treaty' of 1822. The story of 'Owen's Protectorate' is significant. If Owen could have proved that a permanent occupation of Mombasa was the one way or even the best way to suppress the Arab Slave Trade, the upshot might have been other than it was: but in 1824, as in 1838, the treaty-system backed by preventive naval measures held the field as against the method of territorial annexation: and, that being so, Owen's other arguments, political and economic—the value of Mombasa as a naval base, the possibilities of its commercial development—made no mark at all.

In the course of the next two decades, between 1825 and 1845, the situation changed. The humanitarian interest is still dominant: indeed, it steadily grows stronger. But the political interest, though still negative, is keener, and a new, though transient, economic interest develops. The change is illustrated by the fact that from 1841 onwards a British political agent and consul was posted at Zanzibar.

2

On the political side the cause of this change lay in Asia, not in Africa. Once more the decisive question was the security of the lines of communication with the East; and, while the sea-route was now safer than it had ever been, it seemed from about 1830 onwards that India was again in danger of attack by land through the Middle East.

There was, first, the south-eastward expansion of Russia, conjuring up a spectre that was to haunt the Foreign Office for more than a generation. It was mainly the fear of Russia getting possession of Constantinople and thence extending her power over the Moslem peoples of Anatolia and Irak that committed British ministers to the policy of maintaining the integrity of the decaying Turkish Empire. It was the fear, again, of Russia moving south and east from the Caucasus that made Persia once more a diplomatic battleground. It was the Russian instigation of the Shah's attack on Herat in 1838 that induced the British Government to compel its abandonment by a naval demonstration in the Persian Gulf. It was the Russian alliance with Dost Muhammad that precipitated the ill-fated British invasion of Afghanistan in 1839. Thus the hinterland of the Persian Gulf had apparently become as important and dangerous a field of British foreign policy as it had been in the days of Minto and Gardane.

A second threat to the 'overland' approach to India came from France. The occupation of Algiers in 1830 in the teeth of British disapproval had greatly improved her strategic position in the Mediterranean; and to befriend and encourage Mahomet Ali was a natural expression of her old interest in Egypt and the East. But that astute and vigorous ruler was no mere instrument of French designs. Recognizing, indeed, both the gravity of British interests in Egypt as the bridge between East and West and the strength of British sea-power, he may be said to have been on the whole as much or as little in accord with British policy as with French. He had his own ambitions, and it was these which, in themselves, constituted a third threat to the stability of the Near and Middle East. By 1820 only the first steps in his career of conquest had been taken. He had secured the virtual independence of Egypt, mastered the Sudan, and, as has been seen on an earlier page, he had occupied the Hedjaz and its Holy Places, and, penetrating into the heart of Arabia, broken for a time the power of the Wahabi. Now, in 1831, he advanced on Syria, and by the end of 1833 he had wrested the whole of that historic province from Turkish rule. Nor was that enough. He wanted Irak also: for his designs had mounted to no less than the establishment of a new Moslem Empire from the Nile to the Euphrates and from the Mediterranean to the Persian Gulf. In 1834 Egyptian armies began again to penetrate inland through Arabia, obtaining the submission of the tribes and levying tribute. In 1838 a victory over the Assiri chiefs of Yemen extended Mahomet Ali's influence into the hinterland of Aden. In the same year another army under Kurshid Pasha reached Anaiza, midway across Arabia. In 1839 it reached the 'Pirate Coast', occupied the districts of Al Hassa and Katif, and made contact near Basra with the Egyptian fleet sailing round from the Red Sea. The expected advance on Bagdad did not take place, but the threatened occupation of Bahrein Island was striking evidence of the confidence with which the new Egyptian 'imperialism' was treading the treacherous ground of Middle Eastern politics. By the end of 1839, indeed, Mahomet Ali was in effective control of all Arabia except its southern and eastern coasts. To British observers this was disturbing enough in itself, but it took a yet darker colour from the belief that the all-conquering viceroy was the tool of France. Modern research, as suggested above, has modified this belief, but its prevalence at the time is not surprising. Some of Mahomet Ali's ablest officials were Frenchmen, including the head of his War Office and the reorganizer of his navy. And when reports reached

London that the activities of French agents had been resumed not only in Egypt, Syria, and Irak, but in India too, no wonder that it seemed as if all Napoleon's dreams had not been banished with him to St. Helena. It was a clear echo of Pitt's voice when Palmerston said that 'the mistress of India cannot permit France to be mistress directly or indirectly of the road to her Indian dominions'.[1]

The progress of science, meantime, had given an even greater strategic importance to the Middle East than it had had in Napoleon's time. The introduction of steamships had raised high hopes of shortening the intolerable length of the voyage to India by the Cape; and, while the pioneering effort of the S.S. *Enterprize* in 1825-6 had shown that the unbroken voyage round the Cape was not yet a business proposition, it was thought that something could be done on the water-sections of the 'overland' journey. In 1830-1 the route by Antioch through Irak was carefully surveyed, and in 1834 two flat-bottomed steamboats were assembled and floated on the upper Euphrates, one of which safely reached Basra. But the eventual triumph of the rival route by the Red Sea had already been determined when in 1830 the *Hugh Lindsay* steamed from Bombay to Suez in thirty-three days. Transit from Suez to Cairo and Alexandria was an easy and old-established affair; and in 1835 a regular service of French steamers was initiated between Alexandria and Marseilles. In the same year British mails began to be carried by steamships from Falmouth to Alexandria via Malta, and the building of several new ships was ordered both for the Mediterranean and for the Red Sea. In 1837 arrangements were concluded by the British Government and the East India Company for a monthly service between Bombay and England by way of Suez. The story of one of the world's greatest highways had thus begun; and, though it was not to attain its full importance till the opening of the Suez Canal in 1869, it was already clear to all but a few reactionaries that the Cape route to India was going to be largely superseded. Evidently, then, it was more vital than ever for British interests that no foreign

[1] H. Dodwell, *The Founder of Modern Egypt*, chap. v. Hoskins, chap. xi.

Power should be so placed as to be able to obstruct or to threaten from the flank the freedom of British transport between Suez and Bombay.[1]

Firm action was accordingly taken in 1839 to check the Egyptian advance. Palmerston instructed Consul-General Campbell at Cairo to warn Mahomet Ali that 'the British Government could not see with indifference' any move on his part towards Basra and Bagdad. The Government of India directed political officers in the Persian Gulf to take the same line. When, as the result of this uncompromising attitude, the Egyptians evacuated Bahrein Island, it was occupied by British-Indian forces as a base of operations. In the following year a blockade of the ports on the Gulf still in Egyptian possession was contemplated; but by that time Mahomet Ali's fortunes had passed their zenith. His very success had undone him. A decisive victory over a Turkish army on the Syrian frontier and the transfer of the Turkish fleet's allegiance from the Sultan to himself had thrown open the path to Constantinople by land and sea; and the Great Powers, however disunited, were agreed—even France was obliged to acquiesce—in preventing the complete collapse of the Turkish Empire. By general consent, therefore, in 1840 Mahomet Ali, while permitted to retain the government of Egypt and the Sudan, was compelled to abandon Syria. His troops had already evacuated most of Arabia. History was to regard him as the founder of a new Egypt, but not of a new Moslem Empire.[2]

3

More positive measures, meantime, had been taken by the British authorities in India to safeguard the new Suez route. To assist navigation a new and complete survey of the coasts and islands along the route was carried out between 1829 and 1834 by a number of naval officers, including Commander Moresby, a brother of Fairfax, and Captain Brucks. No less

[1] Hoskins, chaps. iv, v, and vii.
[2] H. Temperley, *The Crimea* (London, 1936), chaps. iii and iv. Dodwell, chap. vi. Hoskins, chap. xi. Miles, 342.

important was the question of coal-supply. Stocks of Welsh coal could be dumped at Suez—for Mahomet Ali never obstructed the development of the route through Egypt—and at Mocha as well as at Bombay. But so small were the new steamships and so heavy their fuel-consumption that an intermediate coaling-station was required. The most attractive, the most obvious site was Aden, one of Albuquerque's 'principal keys' to the Eastern world, the only one he had failed himself to acquire.[1] The prospects of securing a satisfactory depot there seemed favourable. It was not so long ago that the Arab ruler of Aden, the Sultan of Lahej, had gladly given British troops a refuge from the fiery furnace of Perim, had asked for a positive British alliance, and in default of it had signed a Treaty of Amity and Commerce (1802).[2] In 1808 Lord Valentia, who visited Aden on the way from India to the Red Sea, had written in strong terms to Canning of the Sultan's friendliness to Britain and the strategic value of the place. 'It is', he said, anticipating Guillain, 'the Gibraltar of the East, and at a trifling expense might be made impregnable.'[3] The experiment, accordingly, was determined on. A stock of coal was landed on an island in Aden harbour in 1829 for the first voyage of the *Hugh Lindsay*. There was no difficulty in obtaining the Sultan's consent, no political friction; but the depot was soon abandoned owing to the difficulty of obtaining the labour required for handling the coal.[4]

The next choice was Socotra. In 1834, on the instructions of the Bombay Government, Captain Ross obtained from the Sultan of Fartak, a chief on the Arabian mainland some 250 miles away who claimed possession of the island, an agreement permitting 'the landing and storing of any quantity of coals or other articles on any part of the sea-coast'. But the Sultan, doubtless realizing that the presence of the British would weaken and might soon destroy his own authority in Socotra, seems to have regretted his complaisance. The execution of the agreement was obstructed, and when in 1835 Commander

---

[1] See p. 47, above. [2] See p. 99, above.
[3] V. to C. 13.ix.08, quoted by Dodwell, 146.
[4] Hoskins, 196. Dodwell, 147.

Haines arrived with a force of marines and an offer to buy the island outright for 10,000 dollars, the Sultan stubbornly refused. So Haines, standing on the letter of the agreement, landed his marines at the points he wished to occupy. The occupation, however, was short-lived. The harbours were found to be shallow and unsafe, the water-supply bad and inadequate, and the climate very unhealthy. Before the end of the year a diminished and fever-ridden body of marines was on its way back to Bombay.[1]

To judge only from the map, an alternative to Socotra might have been Perim, an island of five square miles in the Straits of Bab-el-Mandeb at the very mouth of the Red Sea. But the British troops landed on it for a few months in the course of Admiral Popham's expedition in 1799 had soon discovered that its waterless rocks, its torrid heat, and its fevers made it quite unsuitable for permanent settlement. It was not occupied till 1857.[2]

No other islands existed at the point on the route where they were needed. The Kuria Muria group lay too far north and east. So the possibilities of Aden, which had again been explored by Haines at the time of the occupation of Socotra, were reconsidered, and the Government of Bombay were soon convinced that at Aden and nowhere else, whatever minor difficulties might have to be overcome, the needed coaling-station must be located. Early in 1837 an opportunity for action presented itself. A Madras-owned ship under British colours, carrying pilgrims bound for Mecca, ran ashore near Aden. The survivors were plundered and the wreck looted by the Arabs. It was reported on inquiry that the Sultan of Lahej had been concerned

[1] Hoskins, 188-9. Text of Agreement: Aitchison, vii. 191. The Bengal Government, having arranged a steamship service from Calcutta to Suez, contemplated a coaling-station on the Maldive Islands, and the objections of their 'King' were overcome by the gift of a silver watch and other presents; but, the islands being found to be lacking in harbours and surrounded by dangerous coral reefs, the project was abandoned. Hoskins, 123, 196.

[2] Idem, 196. C. P. Lucas and R. E. Stubbs, *Historical Geography of the British Colonies*, vol. i, 'The Mediterranean and Eastern Colonies' (Oxford, 1906), 75, 81.

directly or indirectly in the disposal of the loot. Some months later the Government of India authorized the Government of Bombay to demand satisfaction for what the Governor, Sir Robert Grant, brother of Lord Glenelg, had described as 'an insult to the British flag'. Haines was dispatched on this mission, and by the beginning of 1838 he had not only recovered the remnants of the cargo and secured compensation for what had been stolen, but he had also persuaded the Sultan to sign an agreement for submission to Bombay, ceding possession of the town in return for an annual subsidy. So far the proceedings had been friendly enough: it seemed indeed as if the Sultan's dread of a descent of Mahomet Ali from the north had decided him to commit himself to British protection. But he was old and infirm, and his policy was promptly repudiated by a vigorous anti-British party led by his son. He was soon impelled by them not merely to go back on the agreement, but to attempt the seizure of Haines's person and the destruction of the document. Apprised of the plot, Haines sailed for India, where his report of what had happened confirmed the growing conviction that Aden would have to be annexed. Haines was sent back with instructions to confirm the agreement; and when the Arabs, now virtually under the control of the Sultan's son, refused to parley, British and Indian troops were dispatched from Bombay, and on January 16, 1839, they landed and occupied the town and its environs with little loss to themselves or their opponents. Negotiations were thereupon resumed with the Sultan, who had fled to the mainland and was now ready again to come to terms; and on February 2 and 4 treaties of 'peace and friendship' were concluded, recognizing Aden as 'belonging to the English' and guaranteeing free intercourse and trade between the port and the interior.[1]

The anti-British faction were by no means content. Three times in the course of the next twelve months or so they attempted to regain the town by force. But they were held up

[1] Full details in *Parl. Pap.* 1839, No. 268. Text of treaties: Aitchison, vii. 136, 150. Hoskins, 197–207. Low, *History of the Indian Navy*, ii. 116.

by newly built defences, and after 1840 the British hold on Aden was not contested again till the time of the Great War.

There was little discussion of the *fait accompli*. Protests in Europe were ignored. Mahomet Ali was told to abstain from any interference with the tribes in the neighbourhood of what was now a British port. In England itself public interest in the matter seems to have been slight. One question was asked in the House of Lords. There was no debate in the House of Commons. A comprehensive Blue Book made it sufficiently clear that the failure to bring about an 'amicable arrangement' had been mainly due to the hostility of the dominant section of the Arab population. What would have happened if, while refusing to surrender Aden, they had given Haines no excuse for using force must remain a matter of speculation. As it was, the Governments of India and Bombay could congratulate themselves on having secured so easily and inexpensively the 'key' to the Suez route—a prize which was soon to be made still more precious by the cutting of the canal.[1]

Yet one more step was taken in 1840 to safeguard the British position in that area. The strategic value of Aden would be to some extent impaired if a rival sea-power were to establish a base on the opposite Somali coast, a bare and torrid country in which the British Government had only once shown any active interest apart from survey-work. The plundering of the *Marianne*, a British merchant-brig, by the Somali of Berbera in 1825 had led to the dispatch of a warship and the conclusion in 1827 of a treaty of 'friendship and commerce' under which the Sheikhs of the offending tribe had agreed to pay compensation for the damage done and to permit British ships to trade at any port under their control 'without impediment, injury or molestation'.[2] But the acquisition of Aden, followed as it was by the rumours, mentioned in the preceding chapter, of French incursions into the East African field, at once drew attention to this no-man's-land; and in the autumn of 1840 Captain Robert Moresby negotiated treaties with the ruling Chiefs at Tajura

[1] Dodwell, 151. *Hansard*, 1839, xlvi. 207. *Parl. Pap.* 1839, No. 268.
[2] Text in Aitchison, vii. 180–1.

and Zeila. Both treaties provided for freedom of trade on the payment of a 5 per cent. duty and for the encouragement of British commerce with the Abyssinian interior; and both bound the respective chiefs not to enter into any treaty or bond with any other European nation without previously informing the British Government at Aden. The Zeila Treaty included under this condition the giving of permission to other Europeans to settle in the territory or 'to pass through in any numbers'. As an additional safeguard the ruler of Tajura was induced to sell the Mashah islands, a little group in the mouth of the Gulf of Tajura, to the British Government 'for ten bags of rice', and the islet of Aubad near Zeila was similarly ceded. Thus, for the time being, international rivalry at the mouth of the Red Sea was forestalled. There were no other ports of importance in the neighbourhood in those days, no other bases for contesting the British mastery of the Gulf of Aden.[1]

4

The new importance of the Gulf of Aden in British policy detracted little from the old importance of the Persian Gulf. If any of the latter's ports should fall under foreign control, the safety of the waterway from Aden to Bombay would at once be threatened. The occupation of Aden, moreover, did nothing to lessen the danger, such as it was, of a Russian move on India. That could only be checked or diverted in Persia, and British pressure could only be brought to bear on Persia through the Persian Gulf. Aden, therefore, by no means overshadowed Muscat. Throughout the eighteen-thirties British policy was as much concerned with maintaining the integrity of Oman and keeping it within the sphere of British influence as it had been in Napoleon's day.

There was good reason again, therefore, for Seyyid Said to count on British support against his enemies, internal and

---

[1] Text of treaties in Aitchison, vii. 177–80. Zeila is now the most northerly port in British Somaliland (protectorate, 1885). Tajura is in French Somaliland and now overshadowed by its capital, Djibouti, on the opposite side of the Gulf.

external. Of the former the most dangerous at this time was Hamed-bin-Azan, the restless, ambitious, and deeply religious chief of Sohar, who had secured a strong personal hold on the fickle loyalties of the Omani tribesmen. He was implicated in the rising of 1832, which, as recorded on an earlier page, brought about the intervention of the British Resident at Bushire and the dispatch of a cruiser to Muscat. He headed the rising of 1834 when the prospect of his attempting to seize Muscat itself elicited another and more vigorous warning from Bushire. Hamed was plainly told that, unless he desisted from rebellion, he would be treated as an enemy of Britain. In 1836 he was persuaded to go to Muscat on a British warship and there to sign a promise to keep the peace. These repeated British intrusions into the domestic politics of Oman must have irritated Hamed, but they seem to have sobered him. Five years later, when Said, as so often now, was away in Zanzibar and the auspices seemed favourable for another bid for power, Hamed went in person to Bombay to entreat the Government not to intervene in the rebellion he proposed to raise. He was courteously received, but of course discouraged, so firmly discouraged that, soon after his return home, he made over the rulership of Sohar to his son and retired into religious seclusion. It was a relief to Said's mind, and he owed it almost wholly to his British friends. Only once again was Hamed troublesome, when in 1849 he was persuaded by his priestly advisers to resume the government of Sohar; and this time British aid was not required to deal with him. The historic precedent by which Said forty years earlier had won his throne was followed by his son Thwain, who was officiating as regent in his father's customary absence at Zanzibar. Acting—so it was generally and approvingly believed at Muscat—on his father's instructions, he proposed to Hamed a new treaty of peace, invited him to a friendly discussion of its terms, and, having lulled his suspicions by several inconclusive interviews, suddenly seized him and carried him off to Muscat, where he was imprisoned and after some months put to death by poison or starvation.[1]

[1] Miles, 334–48; and see p. 278, above.

After Said on British advice had made his peace with the Wahabi in 1833,[1] Oman was free from external pressure till the Egyptians advanced across Arabia in 1839. That they intended to occupy Muscat there can be no question. A substantial force was detached from the main army and moved south-east to Baraimi, whence the Wahabi had so often menaced Oman, and an ultimatum from its leader was received at Muscat, offering the choice of alliance or hostility. No answer was given; and when Said, who was at Zanzibar, returned in the autumn, he was more than encouraged, he was virtually instructed by the British Resident in the Gulf, to resist Egyptian aggression. He was suspected of having secretly offered to submit to Mahomet Ali's overlordship and pay him tribute if in return he were given the possession he had so long and obstinately coveted of Bahrein. If that was true, it may be pleaded on Said's behalf that, until he was certain of British protection against the unconquerable Egyptians, it was wise to make a bargain with them before it was too late. Be that as it may, he yielded at once to British pressure. He exerted all his authority in Oman to counteract the influence of Egyptian agents. He wrote to the Sheikhs of the tribes around Baraimi, exhorting them to maintain their independence. If Egyptian emissaries were still received at Muscat with outward courtesy, the purport of their communications was immediately betrayed to the British authorities. Finally, in April 1840, Mahomet Ali was directly charged by Consul-General Hodges at Cairo with designs on Oman; and when, after some equivocation, he admitted that he had intended to annex it, he was straitly told that the British Government forbade it. But by then, as has been seen, the danger was past. Before the year was out the Egyptians had evacuated most of Arabia.[2]

This revival of Muscat's old importance in the field of British-Indian policy had determined the Bombay Government to resume direct personal relations with Said. When peace put an end to Napoleon's designs, occasional visits to Muscat by the resident at Bushire or one of his assistants had seemed suffi-

[1] See p. 278, above.   [2] B.R. 218–21. Miles, 342.

cient, and Seton's old place at Said's side had been left vacant; but early in 1840 it was filled again by the appointment of Captain Atkins Hamerton as the Company's political agent in the dominions of the Imam. If that had meant residence in Muscat, Hamerton would have had no closer contact with East Africa than Seton. It will be remembered, however, that in 1840 Said practically transferred his seat of government to Zanzibar, and thither Hamerton was instructed to accompany him. This first invasion, therefore, of the East African field by a British political officer was not due to any new political interest in East Africa. It was merely at the outset an enforced change of residence by the agency concerned with the old political interest in Oman. The thread which had run so long from Bombay to Muscat had been extended to Zanzibar.[1]

5

Hamerton inevitably acquired a better knowledge of East Africa and a closer interest in it than Seton. Mere neighbourhood induced it. Said's own predilections encouraged it. But British policy at Zanzibar was as negative as it had been at Muscat. It was not aggressive; it aimed at no territorial acquisitions; its only purpose was the maintenance of the *status quo* as it stood in 1840 on the coasts of the Arabian Sea. That meant that Said's independence and the integrity of his 'dominions' were to be preserved as far as possible in Africa as in Arabia. If British Governments, satisfied with Aden, desired no naval base or colony on the East African coast, they were anxious that no rival Power should have one as a counterpoise to Aden. In foreign eyes, no doubt, a 'dog-in-the-manger' policy: in British eyes a natural precaution for maintaining in that corner of the world the stability of the international settlement which had emerged from the long ordeal of the Napoleonic War.

Previous chapters of this book have shown this policy in operation. On the one hand, the British Government was twice

[1] G. of B. to Secret Committee, 23.v.40 (F.O. 54. 3). B.R. 211.

pressed to annex Mombasa, in 1824 and 1838, and on both occasions it firmly refused.[1] At any time, indeed, there was nothing to prevent its occupying all the coast and Zanzibar as well if it had wished. France alone could have offered any serious resistance, and more than once in this period British ministers, anxious as they properly were to be friends with France, made it plain that they were not afraid of her. On the other hand, it has been shown how closely the movements of any foreign nation in East African waters were watched and how firmly territorial ambitions, actual or hypothetical, were restrained. But there were limits to this restriction. No attempt was made—it would have been absurdly high-handed to make it—to monopolize all East Africa. Only the 'dominions' of Britain's protégé, the Imam, were sacrosanct. The French Government's claim to its pre-war foothold in Madagascar was not contested.[2] When it was reported in 1835 that the Americans desired to make a settlement on what he supposed to be no-man's-land at Delagoa Bay, Palmerston saw no reason to object.[3] If he did object, and strongly, to the French occupation of Nossi-bé in 1840, it was only so long as he imagined it was part of Said's 'dominions', and, when Said's claim was found to be invalid, he promptly withdrew his objection.[4] But all up the coast northwards of Cape Delgado, where Said's overlordship was normally unquestioned, a persistent attempt on the part of France or any other Power to acquire a territorial footing would certainly have been resisted; and it was doubtless the knowledge of this that prevented the repeated French advances in that field from being in fact persisted in.

None the less, the possibility of a sudden descent on some coveted port and its occupation on some colourable pretext, presenting as it would all the awkwardness of a *fait accompli*, was always in Hamerton's mind. That Said could himself resist such a trespass on his property was obviously out of the question. His military weakness was betrayed by the failure of all his major operations, and in Hamerton's eyes at any rate his

[1] See pp. 262 and 287, above.   [2] See p. 141, above.
[3] See p. 374, above.   [4] See pp. 440–45, above.

navy was little better than a sham.[1] His only safeguard lay in establishing so sure a title to his mainland 'dominions' that an invasion of them could be reasonably denounced and firmly opposed by Britain as a plain infringement of international law or at least of international propriety. Hence at one of his earliest interviews with Said at Zanzibar Hamerton warned him that 'his country was becoming better known to Europeans' and pressed him to do something to assert and strengthen his overlordship of the coast.[2] The same anxiety explains his irritation at Krapf's guileless admission to the French Consul in 1852 that Said was not the real ruler of the coast between Vanga and Pangani.[3] Throughout his tenure of office, indeed, Hamerton was constantly worried by the presence of French ships or reports of French designs on this or that section of the coast. Guillain's lengthy visit, in particular, must have tried him. And the intrusion of any European, however innocent his purpose, into Said's preserve was a matter of anxiety lest as in Maizan's case it should lead to international complications. Thus in 1849 Hamerton was relieved, no doubt, to find good reasons for discouraging the airy project of a certain reverend Dr. Bialloblotzky, who came to Zanzibar with the intention of proceeding inland from Mombasa in quest of the sources of the Nile. He brought with him the backing of sundry German and Austrian scientists, but only twenty pounds to finance the expedition. Hamerton received him 'most hospitably', but, as the doctor complained to Palmerston, 'his personal kindness did not extend to my plans which he denounced as utterly impracticable, leading to my destruction, and likely to create bloodshed and troubles by which even the missionaries on the coast might become endangered'. Hamerton frankly told him that if he persisted in his project, he would feel it his duty to advise Seyyid Said to put a stop to any move inland. That was the end of it. Palmerston, though the well-known explorer, Beke, supported Bialloblotzky's appeal to him, refused to interfere.[4]

[1] See p. 299, above, and p. 476, below.
[2] See p. 337, above.   [3] See pp. 415–17, above.
[4] Dr. B. to P. 27.viii.49; P.'s minute, 31.x.49 (F.O. 54. 13). In a

It was this cardinal point of British policy—the maintenance of the *status quo*—that determined Said's attitude. He desired, as has been seen, to increase the volume of his trade with Europe and America. With none of the white folk who came to Zanzibar would he quarrel if he could help it. He kept up with Bourbon his earlier *entente* with Île de France. He was no less friendly with Americans and Germans. But the opinion of visitors like Krapf that his feelings for Britain were warmer or at least his professions of esteem more genuine was unquestionably correct.[1] It is true that now as in the old war-years he found the British to be difficult, importunate, and not over-generous friends. Now as then their backing in Arabia seemed at times to be somewhat coldly calculated lest it should impair British interests ranging farther than the bounds of Oman. Thus, in 1844, when the Wahabi, freed from Egyptian pressure, had recovered their ascendancy in central Arabia and, again invading the Batineh by way of Baraimi, demanded the payment of 20,000 dollars 'tribute', Said's appeal for military aid made some impression on the Foreign Office but none on the Government of India. When Aberdeen intimated to the India Board that 'more efficient measures' should be adopted by the authorities in India to support 'our ally' against Wahabi aggression, Lord Ripon replied that the Government of India was strongly opposed to a military expedition. Two British warships were already posted in the Gulf, and a landing of troops would 'involve us in hostilities of indefinite extent and duration and might also, especially after our recent occupation of Aden, give rise to a general, however erroneous, impression of our having conceived views of territorial aggrandizement for ourselves on the Arabian continent'. A firm statement of our attitude, it was suggested, would suffice.[2] This forecast proved right. The aggressiveness of the Wahabi was checked, no doubt, by finding

footnote to the presidential address to the Royal Geographical Society in May 1849, which alluded to Bialloblotzky's venture, the editor remarks that it had failed because the British consul at Zanzibar had objected to it and refused to help. *R.G.S. Journal*, xix (1849), p. lxxvii.
[1] Krapf, 538.
[2] A. to India Board, 8.viii.45; Board to F.O. 22.viii.45 (F.O. 54. 9).

The British at Zanzibar

a more formidable combination of Omani tribesmen gathered in defence of their country than they had expected: but they were checked also by a letter which the Resident in the Gulf addressed to the Emir Feisal, begging him, 'if he valued the friendship of the British Government', not to permit the invasion of Said's territories. Salutary likewise, no doubt, was the sight of the British warships patrolling the coast of the Batineh. The Emir wrote a conciliatory reply. The demand for 'tribute' was lowered to 5,000 dollars and at that level accepted by Thwain. The Wahabi forces then withdrew.[1]

With these results Said should have been more or less satisfied. British support, if not as vigorous as he would have wished, was effective. But on another issue, which seemed to him almost as important as Wahabi aggression, if not more so, he got no satisfaction at all. The desire to annex Bahrein had become, as has already been noticed, almost an obsession with him, and he was continually asking for it. In 1839 and again in 1842 he intimated that the 'restoration' of Bahrein was the one bribe which might induce him to meet British wishes with regard to the Slave Trade.[2] In 1844 Hamerton reported to Bombay that Said had tried at various times to get possession of Bahrein by intriguing both with the Wahabi and with the Persians, and, these failing, was pinning his last hope on British friendship.[3] Again Aberdeen, with the Slave Trade in mind, would have liked to acquiesce; but again the Government of India vetoed it. In the first place, it was pointed out, the Arabs of Bahrein would repudiate allegiance to Said and were confident of repelling an attack by him; and secondly, the Shah of Persia, to whom the island had long been tributary, would resent Said's intrusion and suspect that behind it lay insidious British designs of aggrandizement at Persia's expense. As before, Aberdeen accepted the expert opinion. Interference in the Persian Gulf, he admitted, would involve the risk of war with Persia.[4]

[1] B.R. 218. Miles, 344.
[2] Cogan to Carnac, vii.39 (F.O. 54. 3). See p. 509, below.
[3] H. to G. of B. 1.x.44 (F.O. 54. 8).
[4] A. to India Board, 16.v.45 (ibid.).

But what did Said care about that? It would have suited him well for Britain to fight Persia. He could render the most active aid in what was bound to be an easy victory, and might obtain Bahrein as his share of the spoil. In 1848 he actually proposed to push a dispute with the Persian Government over the rent he paid for territory leased to him to the point of blockading the Persian ports on the Gulf with his own fleet if the British Government would sanction it. 'His Highness', wrote Hamerton to Palmerston, 'has certainly a number of *empty ships of war*, but he has no seamen whatever to man them, and not a single man in his service who has the least idea of working the guns or handling a ship of war.' Said was powerless, in fact, by himself, and his request for British approval was really a request for British help.[1] And again, of course, that was denied him. Said was to be politely warned of the risks of his proposed expedition and the bad effects of a failure on his prestige, and to be told that the British Government 'earnestly hoped' he would not undertake it.[2]

It was a cautious, negative attitude, then, that his British friends displayed towards Said's anxieties and ambitions in Arabia and the Gulf. But it seems improbable that he harboured much of a grievance against them on that account. He must, after all, have understood the British desire for peace in the Middle East; and he can hardly have expected his plea for Bahrein, however importunate, to prevail. Nor can he have resented it very bitterly if British help against the Wahabi invasion seemed halting or half-hearted. He took it lightly enough himself. Grave as was the threat to the integrity of Oman and even the safety of Muscat, he remained at Zanzibar. In the autumn of 1844 he apparently thought it more important to gather forces for his second attack on Pate than for the defence of his Arab capital; and though the fighting at Pate was all over in January 1845 and no terms were made with the Wahabi till June, he still stayed at Zanzibar, instructing his son at Muscat by letter. No wonder that British officials in the Gulf, whose

[1] H. to P. 12.x.48 (F.O. 54. 12).
[2] P.'s minute, 31.v.49 (F.O. 54. 13).

endless task of keeping the peace was almost always made easier by Said's presence at Muscat, observed with irritation his 'increasing indifference to home affairs'. Indeed, it seems more than likely that Said had already come by now to care more about East Africa than Oman and that, as long as he could safely count on the British guarantee of his 'dominions' in the former field, he was not overmuch disturbed or offended if at times their backing in the latter seemed less certain.

Said's subjects were not all as clear-sighted as their master. When Hamerton arrived at Zanzibar in 1841 he was at once aware of a strong current of anti-British feeling. It betrayed itself at that time in a deliberate policy, in which even, it would seem, the 'banyans' concerned with customs-duties and commerce were taking a hand, of favouring and exalting the Americans at the expense of the British. More trivial but no less significant were the insults levied at the new British agent.

'On the first day of my arrival here I observed two pictures hung up on either side of the Imam's chair in the room where he holds his *durbar*: the subjects were naval engagements between American and English ships: the ship of England is represented as just taken by the Americans, and the English ensign being hauled down and the American hoisted at the masthead.'

At the *durbar* itself, moreover, the leading Arabs, members of Said's entourage, who were 'all', says Hamerton, 'ill-disposed towards us', treated him with 'marked disrespect, such as talking loudly in my presence of the power and wealth of America and the superiority of their sailors over the English'. So Hamerton was not surprised to find, when he promptly raised the question of the American 'monopoly', that these prominent Arabs 'extend all their influence with the Imam to allow it to continue'. It was only, indeed, with 'great difficulty' that he succeeded in winning Said over. But he did succeed. 'Our traders', he reported, 'are now permitted to participate in the trade and to enjoy equal advantages with the French and Americans.' And something had happened in the meantime to mend the Arabs' manners. H.M.S. *Lily*, engaged in hunting slave-ships down the coast, put in at Zanzibar. A British cruiser was then an infrequent spectacle—indeed the Zanzibari had not seen one in their harbour for nine years—and it had its effect. 'A wonderful alteration was to be observed.' The notables did Hamerton 'the honour of a call', and were full of 'civility and professions of respect and regard'. When Hamerton next visited the *durbar* chamber, he noticed that the offensive pictures had been replaced by pictures of the battle of Navarino.[1]

Favouring the Americans was a relatively harmless method of showing a dislike of the British. Favouring the French was a more serious matter. The preceding chapter has shown how strong the pro-French faction was at Zanzibar, how real and persistent the French desire to find a footing on the coast, and how genuine the fears it excited in Said's mind. If French designs were dangerous in themselves, they were doubly dangerous in that they were linked in Arab eyes with the restoration of the Slave Trade. Nor, of course, was it only the pro-French Arabs who hated the existing restrictions on the Trade and dreaded its further repression. Every Arab at Zanzibar, it is safe to say, would have clamoured for a full and free resumption of the Trade if the British had not forbidden it. Said himself would have wished it. That being so, the fact that Said committed himself and the loyal majority of his notables so unreservedly to British friendship despite the painful price they had to pay for it makes two points clear beyond dispute. It meant, first, that he put his political independence above the profits of the Trade. It meant, secondly, that he believed British friendship to be the surest safeguard for that independence he could find in a fast-changing world. He was certain—and more certain after the occupation of Aden—that the British had no positive political ambitions in East Africa.

6

Not much more positive than the new British political interest in East Africa was the new economic interest. To de-

[1] H. to G. of B. 20.viii.41; H. to Palmerston, 21.v.42 (F.O. 54. 4). Crofton, op. cit. 3.

scribe its origin and growth the narrative must go back to a few years previous to Hamerton's appointment.

Before the eighteen-thirties some British goods had been sold at Zanzibar and along the coast, and some East African exports had come to England; but most of this meagre business had gone through the hands of the Salem merchants; there had been practically no direct trade between Zanzibar and England; and the brig, which figures in Hart's report as the cause of 'great annoyance' to the American traders in 1834, must have been one of the first British merchant-ships to invade East African waters. Its master told Hart that he had disposed of the whole of the goods he had brought from England, that he was about to sail for home with a full cargo of ivory, copal, gum, drugs, and a little gold-dust and tortoise-shell, and that he expected a clear profit for his owners of 170 per cent.[1] If that news got about, it doubtless set British business-men wondering whether it was not worth while to pay attention to this neglected corner of the world. But what moved the British Government was probably not so much any evidence that good trade was being done by Americans and could be done by Englishmen as the fact that the American Government had concluded in 1833 a commercial treaty with Britain's old friend and protégé at Muscat and established a consulate at his new resort at Zanzibar.[2]

Said's mind was also bent on encouraging trade with England and putting it on the same formal footing as his trade with the United States. A desire that his *entente* with the Americans should not be misunderstood in London may have been the motive that prompted him to present his British-built frigate, *Liverpool*, to the Royal Navy. 'She is in very good condition', he told Hart in 1834, 'but too large for the service of Muscat. If the King of England will accept her, it will make me very happy.' He also expressed to Hart a wish to have an Englishman at Zanzibar.[3] In the same spirit he sent one of his most trusted

[1] Hart's Report, B.R. 281. Trade via Salem: *Edinburgh Review*, lxi (1835), 356.
[2] See pp. 368-9, above.
[3] B.R. 275-7. The ship was added to the Navy under the new name of the *Imam*.

officials, Ali-bin-Nasir, Governor of Mombasa, to London to present his congratulations to Queen Victoria on her accession. The envoy arrived early in 1838, accompanied by Captain Robert Cogan, an ex-officer of the Indian Navy. Cogan, it appears, having visited Zanzibar with the idea of opening a business there, had so won Said's confidence that he had been entrusted with the charge of the *Liverpool* on her farewell voyage and now brought with him Said's commission as his diplomatic representative in England. Palmerston pointed out that he could not recognize this appointment because Cogan was a British subject;[1] but he was interested in what Cogan had to say and obtained from him a memorandum in which he pointed out that Said's friendship was not a negligible asset and was easy to obtain. We had never courted him as the Americans and the French had done. The Government of India had often seemed indifferent to his interests in Arabia. Yet he occupied a central position in the Middle East, the more important since the development of the Suez route.[2] The upshot was all that Cogan could have wished. Ali-bin-Nasir, who was treated while in England as the Government's guest, was granted an audience by the Queen, and, accompanied by Cogan, dined and spent the night at Windsor. He was also taken to see Birmingham and Manchester.[3] When he returned to Zanzibar[4] he was presently followed by Cogan with the title—which this time could not be challenged—of 'Her Majesty's Commissioner and Plenipotentiary at the court of the Imam of Muscat' and with the task of negotiating a commercial treaty.

There was no hitch. Early in May 1839 Cogan reported that Said was in the friendliest mood. He had been delighted with the reception accorded to his envoy in London and with the

[1] Minute, 19.iii.38 (F.O. 54. 2).
[2] C.'s memo. and letter to P. 22.ii.38 (ibid.). Cogan suggested that, as 'Imam' had a religious significance, 'Sultan' should now be used as Said's title; and 'Sultan' was adopted in the text of the Treaty. But 'Imam' was retained in official correspondence for some years.
[3] P. to C. 27.viii.38; C. to P. 29.viii.38; P. to C. 29.viii.38 (ibid.).
[4] Lieut. Christopher conveyed him from Aden to Zanzibar as a guest of honour on board the *Tigris*: *T.B.G.S.* vi. 375.

portrait of herself the Queen had sent him. A few weeks later, on May 31, a 'Treaty of Commerce between Her Majesty the Queen of the United Kingdom of Great Britain and Ireland and His Highness Sultan Seyyid Said-bin-Sultan, Imam of Muscat' was signed and sealed by Cogan and Said.[1]

The most important articles of the treaty, which was three times as lengthy a document as the American Treaty, were the first three, and the ninth and tenth. The first provided for reciprocal freedom of trade, residence, and movement for subjects of each party in the territories of the other. Article II enabled British subjects 'to purchase, sell, or hire land or houses' in the Muscat dominions, and safeguarded their premises from unauthorized entry or search. Article III acknowledged the right of each party to appoint consuls in the other's dominions 'wherever the interests of commerce may require', such officers to enjoy the same status as the consuls of the most favoured nations. Article IX provided that no duty exceeding five per cent. should be levied on British goods imported in British ships into the Sultan's dominions, that this duty should cover all trade or shipping charges of any kind, and that no further duty should be levied on the transit of goods from one place to another. Article X declared that, apart from the 5 per cent. duty, trade between the British and the Sultan's dominions was to be 'perfectly free' and engaged the Sultan 'not to permit the establishment of any monopoly or exclusive privilege of sale within his dominions except in the articles of ivory and gum copal on that part of the East Coast of Africa from the port of Tangate (Mtangata) to the port of Quiloa (Kilwa)'—an acceptance on the British side of the one reservation Said had made in his free-trade policy in the interests of himself and his subjects.[2]

One other article, the fifth, illustrates, like the ninth article of the American Treaty,[3] the judicial privileges claimed for the citizens of 'white' States who might choose to reside in 'backward' countries. It laid down that the Sultan's authorities

[1] C. to P. 6.v.39 (F.O. 54. 3). C.'s memo. and letter to P. 22.ii.38 (F.O. 54. 2).
[2] See p. 303, above.   [3] See p. 369, above.

'should not interfere in disputes between British subjects or between British subjects and the subjects or citizens of other Christian nations'. A dispute between a British subject and a subject of the Sultan should be decided by the British Consul if the latter was the complainant, by the Sultan or his nominee if the former was the complainant. In the second case the Consul or his deputy should attend the trial. The remainder of the seventeen articles were of minor importance except the fifteenth, which renewed and confirmed the 'Moresby Treaty' of 1822 for the suppression of the Slave Trade and will be discussed in the next chapter. The ratifications of the Treaty were exchanged at Muscat on July 22, 1840.[1]

As regards the facilities accorded to British trade, the treaty did no more than confirm existing practice. No suggestion was made to Said that he should go back on his promise to treat no nation 'more favourably' than the United States or concede to his older friends any privilege denied to others. The treaty gave the same freedom to British traders as that given to American six years before. It fixed the same inclusive 5 per cent. duty. Nor was there anything new in the establishment of a consulate: an American consul had been flying his flag at Zanzibar for a year or more. Yet it was this provision of the treaty more than any other that was destined to advance British commercial activity and political influence at Zanzibar till in Sir John Kirk's day they completely overshadowed those of any other nation.

Soon after the signature of the treaty Said wrote to Palmerston about the appointment of a consul. 'We would beg you of your kindness to send us a steady wise man and a genuine Englishman: may your other men also, who are to reside in our country either at Zanzibar or Muscat or in any other places, be all true pure English and not of other nations.' Probably Said would have liked an Englishman whose simple purity had not been sullied by any previous contact with the East. However much he trusted men like Seton, he may well have preferred a

[1] Text of treaty in B.R. 251–6, and Aitchison, vii. 93–8.

new-comer, less inconveniently familiar with Arab ways and perhaps a little less stiff-lipped and high-handed than officials from British India were sometimes inclined to be. Certainly one of his reasons for desiring the treaty and the consulate was that it would create a direct relationship with the British Government in London. At the outset of his memorandum Cogan had observed that Said had been 'disappointed in the conduct of our Indian Government' for the reasons suggested above, and was looking to 'the fountain-head of our Empire'. But any hope Said may have entertained that by getting nearer to London he could get farther from Bombay was bound to be frustrated. At an early stage of the negotiations Palmerston had minuted that 'a consul ought to be appointed', and had shrewdly added, 'I think there would be an advantage in having some person from India acquainted with the language and customs. A stranger from England would find himself much thrown out for a long while.' Nor, of course, could there be any question of the British Governments in India disinteresting themselves in the matter. Such British trade as existed with Zanzibar was almost wholly British-Indian trade. And, still more important, however much time he spent at Zanzibar, relations with the Imam of Muscat were an essential ingredient of British-Indian policy in the Middle East. On its own account, as has been seen, the Government of Bombay was contemplating at this very time the reappointment of a political agent at Muscat; and naturally enough, as soon as the text of the treaty was available, the India Board protested against the prospect of a consul responsible, as consuls must be, to the Home Government and constituting therefore a separate and independent authority from that of the agent of the Government of India in the Persian Gulf, an anomaly which would prove particularly awkward in dealing with the difficulties and grievances of British Indians at Zanzibar.[1] A similar protest had been entered, it will be remembered, with regard to Owen's project of a consulate in East Africa in 1834;[2] and now as then Palmerston avoided any

[1] Board of Control to F.O. 8.ii.40 (F.O. 54. 3).
[2] See p. 286, above.

foolish quarrel between the Foreign Office and the Government of India. When the India Board proposed that the two rival authorities should be combined in one man and that the political agent, appointed by the Government of Bombay and paid by the Government of India, should also receive a consular commission from the Crown, he promptly accepted the compromise on condition that the two-faced official should correspond directly with the Secretary of State for Foreign Affairs as well as with the Government of Bombay.[1] In informing Said of Hamerton's appointment Palmerston took occasion to emphasize the importance of the intercourse between his dominions and British India. 'Her Majesty's servants trust', he wrote, 'that the Treaty will contribute more and more to promote that intercourse and to advance the prosperity and happiness of the inhabitants of the respective countries.'[2]

7

When Hamerton hoisted the British flag at Zanzibar in 1841 he found that the number of British Indians resident in the island or at the coast-towns within Said's 'dominions' in East Africa was already high; he put it in 1844 at about five hundred Hindu 'banyans' and between six and seven hundred Moslems. And he had soon discovered that most of the commercial business of East Africa was in their hands. 'The bulk of the trade in slaves, ivory and gum copal', he wrote in 1841, 'is carried on by the natives of India: the Arabs do little or nothing in it.'[3] And in 1844: 'As long as they [the Arabs] can procure slaves at a cheap rate to cultivate their cloves, from which they derive great profit, little is to be expected from them.'[4] And Rigby, who succeeded Hamerton in 1858, was equally disparaging.

'The soft climate [he reported in 1860], added to the custom of

[1] Hobhouse (President of Board of Control) to P. 14.iii.40; P. to H. 16.iii.40 (F.O. 54. 3).
[2] P. to S. 2.iv.40 (ibid.). Hamerton's commission as 'H.M. Consul in the dominions of the Imam of Muscat' was dated Dec. 14, 1841 (F.O. 54. 4).   [3] H. to G. of B. 28.ix.41 (ibid.).
[4] Report on the affairs of the Imam of Muscat, 5.ix.44 (Bombay Archives, No. 22 of 1844).

The British at Zanzibar

keeping so many slaves and concubines, has destroyed all the rough virtues usually attributed to Arabs, viz. manliness of character, energy and personal courage. Foreign trade has of late years introduced amongst them a taste for foreign luxuries. They have also imbibed a passion for spirituous liquors and the consumption is rapidly increasing. They are inveterate liars and so dishonest as traders that most of the foreign merchants avoid dealings with them, and in consequence all the trade of the port is passing into the hands of natives of India. . . . The ivory is consigned to them from the interior: the gum copal is purchased from the diggers by 'banyans' residing on the coast; and the entire cargoes of American and Hamburg vessels are purchased by them. . . . A good deal of the landed property is also mortgaged to them. Were the prosperity of the Zanzibar dominions dependent upon these degenerate Arabs, it might well be despaired of.'[1]

Thus the British subjects with whose interests the first British consul was concerned were nearly all Indians, hailing from western India, which had by now come almost wholly under British control either by annexation to the Bombay Presidency or by acceptance of British suzerainty and protection. To Arabs or Swahili in East Africa, uninstructed in the meaning of the British 'Raj', it must have seemed at first somewhat surprising that Hamerton should concern himself with others than his own white people. In a conversation with the Governor of Mbweni, near Pangani, Krapf was asked

'whether the English consul in Zanzibar protected only his fellow-countrymen or whether other persons came also within his jurisdiction and under his protection; to which I answered that every consul had to protect all the subjects of his sovereign; and that therefore the English Consul took under his protection the Banyans also because, though not his own countrymen, they were subjects of the British crown. This reply delighted the Banyan who was seated by the Governor's side.'[2]

Hamerton had not been many months at Zanzibar before his intervention on behalf of these British-Indians was needed. It appeared that Jairam Sewji, the Customs Master, himself a 'banyan', desiring to control the commercial operations of the

[1] C. P. Rigby, *Report on the Zanzibar Dominions* (Bombay, 1861), 8, 25.   [2] Krapf, 418.

lesser members of his caste and finding that their rights as British subjects obstructed the exercise of his arbitrary power, had attempted to compel the local 'banyans' to sign a declaration repudiating their status as British subjects and accepting that of subjects of the Imam. Many of them had refused. 'We would prefer', they said, 'to leave Zanzibar.' 'This prevented further force being used,' reported Hamerton, 'as the 'banyans' leaving the place would at once ruin the revenue.' Hamerton suspected, rightly or wrongly, that his American colleague, Waters, who, when he was the only consul at Zanzibar, had established a friendly liaison with the all-powerful Customs Master, was at the back of the business. He certainly had no suspicions of Said. He reported the matter to him officially and nothing more was heard of it.[1] But, though they retained their British status, the 'banyans' still needed consular protection from time to time. In 1845, for instance, Hamerton had to intervene to stop unauthorized charges being levied on them at some of the coast ports.[2]

Thus independent and thus protected, the 'banyans' did well. The value of the trade, import and export, between Zanzibar and India steadily rose. In 1859 it was over £333,000, the highest figure on the list. The trade with the United States came next at about £245,000.[3]

British business shared in the profits of this British-Indian trade since some of the cotton goods from India were of British manufacture.[4] Moreover, while, in the course of the next decade, British cloth and Indian cloth as well were being fast driven out of the African market by *merikani*, most of the other articles imported by American and German merchants—muskets, hardware, earthenware, cutlery, wire—were made in Britain. Indirectly, then, Britain was taking part in the commercial invasion of East Africa; but of direct British trade there was still

[1] H. to G. of B. 28.ix.41 (F.O. 54. 4).
[2] H. to Aberdeen, 24.iii.45 (F.O. 54. 7). [3] Rigby's Report, 23.
[4] In 1859, when there was still no direct trade between Britain and Zanzibar, British cotton goods to the value of £37,000 were imported. Rigby, 23.

practically none. The most profitable section of the coast, it is true, was partly closed to them, the section known at Zanzibar as the 'Mrima', which lay between latitudes 5°30' and 9°, i.e. roughly between Pangani and Kilwa. Along that stretch Said had set up the one monopoly in his commercial system—a monopoly for himself and his subjects in the export of ivory and gum copal.[1] This monopoly, as has been noticed, was specifically reserved from the general freedom accorded to foreign trade in the Treaty of 1839 with Britain and the Treaty of 1844 with France.[2] No such reservation had been made in the Treaty of 1833 with the United States, presumably because Said had not established his monopoly at that date. But though Said himself confessed, when pressed by Hamerton to declare that British traders had the same rights in his 'dominions' as American, that on this one point the American had the advantage, they had not in fact made use of it. In 1848 the only traders other than Said's subjects who were exporting the most valuable products of the Mrima were British-Indian traders, who, as the agents of Zanzibar business houses and with the connivance of Said and his customs officers, evaded the monopoly by the simple expedient of hoisting Said's flag.[3] But the Mrima was not all East Africa. When Christopher called at Barawa in 1843 he found that it had been since 1830 'a welcome port to European and American traders, several of whom have resided on shore for days at a time', but that Englishmen had so far not availed themselves of the opportunities awaiting them: in particular Christopher mentioned the Juba River as 'open to English enterprise'.[4] Nor had British ships, other than 'whalers', done much business yet on the coast to the south of Kilwa or in Madagascar waters. Thus, while from 1830 onwards American ships were frequently at Zanzibar—there were forty of them there between 1832 and 1834—and while John Bertram and other Salem merchants were often residing on the island, British ships were few and far between—only seven between 1832 and

[1] See p. 303, above. [2] See pp. 423 and 481, above.
[3] H. to P. 15.x.48 (F.O. 54, 12).
[4] *T.B.G.S.* vi. 381, 398.

1834—and till the time of Hamerton's arrival there were no British residents at all.

Hamerton was not the only Briton who came to live at Zanzibar in 1841. Captain Cogan, whose previous visits to the island have been recorded, had come to take more than a diplomatic interest in East Africa; and within a few months of the opening of the consulate he established the firm of Robert Cogan & Co. and installed Mr. Peters, the young son of a fellow-officer in the Indian Navy, as his 'resident partner'. Peters accordingly settled down in Zanzibar, and Cogan came out from England from time to time to help him. During his visit in 1842 he did at least one good stroke of business—or so he thought. 'Although three French gentlemen arrived at Zanzibar as a deputation from a party at Mauritius, offering to manufacture sugar for His Highness on an extensive scale, yet he preferred employing our firm, inexperienced in the matter, for that purpose.' Cogan interpreted this as a proof of Said's goodwill towards Britain: it was certainly no proof of his business sagacity. The production of sugar had long been the main industry in Mauritius; to make a beginning of it in Zanzibar would demand a familiarity with every stage of the process, planting, growing, cutting, crushing, which Cogan and Peters entirely lacked; and it is not surprising that no more is heard of extensive sugar-making. Nor, it appears, did the firm prosper in more normal trading-operations. With Americans, Germans, and French already busy in the limited field, there was little left for the new-comers; and, whether for lack of capital or of enterprise, Cogan & Co. made no new openings on the Juba or elsewhere. At last, after some years of disappointment, there seemed to be a chance of making big and easy profit. In 1845 it was reported at Zanzibar that Latham Island, a little islet some thirty miles southwards, was covered with guano, the excrement of sea-birds, greatly desired by European farmers for the enrichment of their fields; and Cogan, who felt himself entitled to trade on Said's gratitude for his services, asked to be given, over and above his salary of 20,000 rupees (£2,000) as Said's diplomatic agent, a concession for extracting and selling this guano. He obtained it; and in due course some Swahili labourers were sent to the bare flat bank, where they built a couple of huts to live in. But no ship came to load and take away the precious guano. Said had prohibited the shipping of 'native' labourers from Zanzibar on the ground that none but slaves were available;[1] and Hamerton accordingly had refused Cogan & Co. the requisite sanction. Cogan, of course, was up in arms; and his lawyers in London addressed a formal protest to the Foreign Office, demanding what rightful impediment there could be to the hiring of such free labourers from India, Madagascar, and the Comoro Islands who were always to be found at Zanzibar. Aberdeen replied that the prohibition had only applied to 'natives' of Zanzibar and the neighbouring coast, and that he would instruct Hamerton that he saw no objection to the hiring of 'free foreign labourers' if they existed, 'cautioning him at the same time not to lend his sanction to the hire of any person with respect to whom he has not clear and incontestable proof that he is bona fide a free person, working solely for his own profit', and directing him to obtain security for the return of every such person to the place whence he was shipped. Whether, as Hamerton suspected, Cogan was planning to get slaves or not, this official intervention put a stop to the enterprise; and a year or two later a tidal wave immersed the islet and swept the huts away.[2]

Cogan & Co. struggled on for a few years at any rate. Another British firm established at Liverpool with a capital of £70,000 for direct trade with East Africa was even more quickly discouraged. In 1847 it sent out Captain Parker in the *Anne*. He seems to have found no profitable opening in the field already occupied by Americans, French, Germans, and Indians, and to have concluded that the only chance of a substantial return lay in some special line outside the ordinary run of business. Just as Cogan & Co. were tempted by the guano on Latham Island

[1] See p. 431, above.
[2] Cogan to Forbes, 28.x.42 (*S.P.* xxxii (1843–4), 186). H. to Aberdeen, 24.iii.45; S. to H. 20.x.45 (F.O. 54. 7). Henderson & Co. to A. 27.v.46; reply, 27.vi.46 (*S.P.* xxxv (1846–7)). Guillain, ii. 4, note.

so Parker was tempted by the antimony which, he was told, was to be found not far inland from Mombasa. The sequel is recorded in Krapf's journal. On his way from Zanzibar to Mombasa, the missionary found himself on the same ship as the man of business, who, aware of his work among the tribes around Rabai, appealed for his assistance.

'Captain Parker wished me to accompany him to the Nyika and Duruma where he intended to purchase from the chiefs the mines of antimony which exist there, and to pave the way for working them; but, as I foresaw that the enterprise would displease the Sultan of Zanzibar, that the Nyika chiefs would suspect the missionaries of wishing to sell their country to the Europeans, and also that the powder and shot he thought of disposing of to the Swahili would do no good, I declined his proposal.'

The story is continued in the journal four days later.

'Mr. P. paid a visit to the Duruma chiefs, but found them so tipsy he could do nothing with them. He was so frightened by their demeanour and savage appearance that he gave them at once the presents which he had brought for them, and then quitted them without further parley.'

That was the end of Parker's pioneering. The *Anne* returned to Liverpool with a loss to her account; and the firm abandoned its East African adventure.[1]

All in all, then, Hamerton was obliged to report that direct British trade with Zanzibar was so meagre as to be almost non-existent. In 1847 only four British ships, their combined tonnage only 694, came to the island, importing hardware, earthenware, cotton goods, beads, wire, muskets, and gunpowder worth about £12,000, and exporting cloves, coco-nut oil, and hides worth £11,000.[2] And in that same year even this small business seemed to be seriously endangered by Said's decision to take part in the trade with Europe himself.[3] Peters and another British merchant, Pollock, now trying his luck at Zanzibar, submitted a formal protest to Said, declaring that his

[1] Krapf, 166–7. [2] Return of Trade for 1847 (F.O. 54. 12).
[3] See p. 318, above.

competition would make the position of European traders at Zanzibar impossible and might drive them to the Mrima. In a letter to the Foreign Office, explaining this protest, they complained that the Consul had 'not evinced the slightest sympathy or consideration for the position in which we are placed', and pointed out that, if the trade with Zanzibar were lost through Said's competition, British merchants would be shut out from East Africa altogether 'unless indeed the road [to the Mrima] be opened by the Americans under the protection of their superior treaty'.[1]

No notice seems to have been taken of this protest either by Said or by the Foreign Office; and Pollock and Peters can scarcely have expected any vigorous support from Hamerton. Personally he was not indebted to them; for Cogan had pressed at the Foreign Office for the appointment of Peters, though he was then only twenty-four, as the first British Conṣul, and, when the choice fell on Hamerton, had done his best to undermine his authority both with Said and with Palmerston.[2] And officially Hamerton's attitude was correct and creditable. If British business could not succeed without his interfering in Said's own commercial operations, it had better fail. And fail it soon did. Before the year was up, Cogan & Co. closed their doors. Not long after, Messrs. Peters & Pollock also faded out of the East African scene. In 1849 Hamerton reported that every one connected with the firm was dead or gone. There was no other British house of business at Zanzibar, nor any other Briton living there except the consul.[3]

Years passed without a change. Only two British ships called at Zanzibar in 1855, and only two in 1856. Three came in 1857, but their total tonnage was only 770. Thus, while American, German, and British-Indian trade was fast increasing at and after the end of Said's reign, and French trade, though beginning sharply to decline, was still substantial, British trade remained

---

[1] Memorial to S. in H. to P. 25.iii.47; Pollock and Peters to P. 24.iv.47 (F.O. 54. 11).
[2] Cogan to C.O. 16.vi.38 (F.O. 54. 3). For attacks on Hamerton see pp. 506, 510–11, 548–9, below.   [3] H. to P. iii.1.49 (F.O. 54. 11).

diminutive. The value of exports and imports in 1859 was roughly as follows: American £245,000, British-Indian £205,000, French £170,000, German £137,000, British £5,000.[1]

Hamerton, who died in 1857, was consul nearly all this time, and the first duty of a consul is to protect and advance his country's trade. What, then, it may be asked, was he doing? If Peters had had his place, with Cogan in the background, a more enterprising policy might perhaps have been attempted. The Foreign Office might have been bombarded with appeals for the abolition of the Mrima monopoly. Said himself might have been subjected at close quarters to constant requests for favours to British trade. An effort might have been made to open up new fields north of Mombasa. But Hamerton did none of these things; and his reasons were clear enough. He was political agent as well as consul, and he set his duty in the one office above his duty in the other. Politically, as has been seen, his main preoccupation was the fear lest increasing European contact with the coast should expose the weakness of Said's 'overlordship' and disturb the *status quo*.

'The East Coast of Africa [he wrote to Palmerston] is attracting the notice of the commercial men of all nations, particularly that part called the Mrima, and His Highness now entertains the greatest possible fear that without the assistance and kind consideration of the Governments of the Western World, changes most unfavourable to his interests will take place.'

It was not merely the loss to Said's revenue which the invasion of his preserve would entail. It was much more the threat to his prestige and authority. 'The Arabs look upon this territory as peculiarly their own place of trade. Should the Europeans and Americans proceed there, the influence of the Imam, even such as it is, would soon entirely cease to exist.' There would be danger, moreover, of friction between the Europeans and upland natives, coming to the coast to barter gum and ivory; and, before European trade with any part of the coast were extended, it would be desirable for Said to set up at his ports

[1] Rigby's Report, 23.

'establishments of a very different nature' from anything that yet existed, 'in order to protect the Europeans from the treachery of the Natives and to protect the Natives from the violent and unfair dealing of the Europeans'. Hamerton, in fact, was as anxious to keep white traders out of East Africa as he was to keep white explorers out or even, one suspects, white missionaries. He under-estimated, perhaps, the strength of Said's status on the coast, but not its vulnerability to such European intervention as might any day be provoked or excused by some unfortunate event. He did not want another Maizan 'incident', whatever the victim's nationality might be. He did not even want another such 'insult to the British flag' as had led to the annexation of Aden. Nor was he interested only, if mainly, in the integrity of Said's realm. That the British Government should concern itself with protecting, as far as might be, the natives of East Africa from Arab slave-raiders and traders was a familiar idea by now; but this is the first suggestion on record that they might need protection also from American and European, including British, merchants engaged in less nefarious forms of trade.[1]

To sum up, then, it may be said that if any economic interest in East Africa had been aroused in England at the time of the conclusion of the Commercial Treaty, it had soon evaporated. To the end of Said's reign and for some years after it the advancement of British trade—with one exception to be dealt with in Chapter XVII—was almost a negligible factor in British relations with Zanzibar.

[1] H. to P. 26.iii.47, 15.xii.48, and Trade Return for 1847 (F.O. 54. 11 and 12).

XVI

SECOND ATTACK ON THE SLAVE TRADE

I

THE opening of the British attack on the East African Slave Trade between 1815 and 1822 has been described in a previous chapter, and it will be remembered that it had to deal with two distinct but interconnected branches of the Trade—the 'Christian' and the Arab. Portuguese, French, and, to a diminishing extent, Spanish traders were exporting slaves both from Portuguese territory and from the Arab seaports farther north to the Mascarenes, South America, and the West Indies. Arab traders were exporting slaves from their section of the coast both 'internally', i.e. to any part of Said's 'dominions' in East Africa and Arabia, and 'externally', i.e. to Mozambique or the Mascarenes in the south and to the Arab, Persian, and Indian coastlands in the north and east. The 'Christian' Trade was attacked by pressure on the foreign governments concerned to make the Trade illegal and to promote the execution of the law by treaties with Britain for 'reciprocal right of search' and for the effective disposal of ships engaged in or equipped for smuggling slaves, by the strict application of the Abolition Acts in Mauritius, and by the treaty with Radama. The Arab Trade, south, north, or east, outside the limits of Said's 'dominions' was dealt with by the Moresby Treaty with Said, by the peace treaties with the Arabs of the Persian Gulf, and by the prohibition of the import of slaves into British India. The 'internal' Trade between ports under Said's rule or 'overlordship' was permitted to continue. Such were the lines on which the campaign began in the first quarter of the nineteenth century. How did it prosper, what success did it achieve, in the course of the second quarter?

As regards the 'Christian' Trade the Spanish share of it, which was never substantial, seems to have practically disappeared even before the effective Anglo-Spanish Treaty of 1835. And the far larger Portuguese share would have similarly disappeared if pledges or prescriptions on paper had sufficed. When by 1825 Brazil, the only colony into which Portugal was entitled to import slaves under the Treaty of 1815, had achieved its separation from the mother country, Portuguese legislation in 1830–1 abolishing the Trade and penalizing its practitioners was the logical but quite ineffectual sequel. It mattered little to Portuguese 'slavers' that they were now no longer sailing 'on their lawful occasions' but were smuggling, as long as the Portuguese authorities ignored or connived at it. The execution of the law was virtually left to British naval patrols; and, since the Portuguese Government stubbornly refused to sign a replica of the Spanish Treaty of 1835, the 'right of search', conceded in 1817, was only effective if a 'slaver' were caught with slaves on board. As if to justify this obstinacy it was made very clear on paper that Portugal could and would deal with the business herself. In 1836 the Secretary of State at Lisbon addressed a lofty epistle to Queen Maria II. It condemned the 'infamous' Slave Trade as a stain on modern civilization. It pleaded that the severest critics of Portugal's share therein had once been 'deeper in guilt' themselves—a thrust, of course, at Britain. But it admitted that action 'to repair the evil done and prevent its repetition' was demanded both by the honour and by the interests of Portugal.

'The dominions which we yet possess in that part of the world are as yet the most extensive, the most important, and the most valuable possessed by any European nation in Southern Africa. . . . The civilisation of Africa, of which so many powerful nations have despaired, is more feasible to the Queen of Portugal who holds in her hands the key of the principal gates at which it can enter and whose authority is obeyed in various parts of that vast continent at distances of more than two hundred leagues from the sea; and, as it was possible for the former Sovereigns of Portugal to open roads for civilisation, a step which no other Prince had ventured upon, so it will be possible to make that beneficial plant thrive and flourish in those regions.'

This letter was by way of preamble to a stern decree which, while it permitted planters in Portuguese territories to import ten fresh slaves apiece, thereafter finally and for ever abolished the Trade. Officials who suffered it to continue by negligence would be dismissed: those convicted of connivance at it would be sentenced to transportation. Slave-traders themselves would be condemned to the galleys for from two to five years.[1]

But in the thirties and forties as in the sixties words at Lisbon were only partially translated into acts in Africa, and Palmerston continued to harass the Portuguese Government until, as the result of the extraordinary Act of the British Parliament of 1839, permitting British cruisers to treat Portuguese 'slavers' precisely as if they were British, at last, in 1842, it surrendered and signed a treaty declaring the Slave Trade piracy and providing for the condemnation of ships equipped for, though not actually engaged in, carrying slaves.[2] And certainly, whether by Act or Treaty, the British naval patrols needed as free a hand as possible. That rigorous decree, it is true, was not wholly unobserved. The British Commissioners at the Cape, charged to watch the Trade, reported in 1844 that at least the Governor-General of Mozambique was 'honest', and in 1841 a Portuguese ship from Rio de Janeiro selling slaves at Quilimane was deflected from that port not only by the vigilance of a British cruiser but also by 'the honourable opposition' of the Governor. His successors, however, were not all so scrupulous. In 1843 several slave-traders, so far from being sent to the galleys, were residing openly in Quilimane, collecting slaves from Swahili or 'banyan' traders; and 'barracoons were established there and at other points on the coast, holding sometimes as many as three hundred slaves. In that year, the Commissioners' report continued, and one month of the next the Governor was said to have amassed some 60,000 dollars.[3] The next Governor frankly co-

[1] Decree of 10.xii.36 and letter to Queen (*S.P.* xxv (1836–7), 219–21).
[2] *S.P.* xxx (1841–2), 448. For the Act of 1839 (repealed as it affected Portugal in 1843) see W. L. Mathieson, *Great Britain and the Slave Trade*, 20–1; R. Coupland, *The British Anti-Slavery Movement*, 165.
[3] *S.P.* xxix (1840–1), 372; xxxiii (1844–5), 349–54. Cogan's memorandum of 5.xii.39 (not so authoritative as the Commissioners' Reports) stated that the 'Government of Portugal (presumably at Mozambique) openly levies a duty of seven Spanish dollars on each slave exported

operated with the naval patrol. The next absconded in a slave-ship, with five hundred slaves aboard, bound for Rio. The next was 'an honourable contrast' to other officials. The next was found to be part-owner of a captured slave-ship, and, after less than three years of office, returned to Lisbon with (it was said) 92 contos of reis (about £20,700). 'It is, of course, well-known in Lisbon', wrote the British *chargé d'affaires*, 'that the fortune he has made is derived from successful Slave Trade speculations.'[1] It is clear that at Quilimane successive Governors-General, who continued to help, and to be trusted by, the British captains who watched the coast, were unable to prevent vice alternating with virtue. And Quilimane was not the only infected spot. 'I have been credibly informed'—it is again the British *chargé d'affaires* writing—'that almost every Portuguese Governor on the east and west coast of Africa is more or less interested in the continuance of the Slave Trade. . . . Inadequately paid, they are enabled, almost without risk, to acquire a considerable fortune in the course of a few years.' Yet the only penal action recorded in execution of the decree of 1836 was at Ibo, whence the Governor was 'removed' by a new Governor-General in 1851.[2]

Under these circumstances the Trade from Portuguese East Africa could not be destroyed. Every year a certain number of slave-ships were caught and condemned—eleven, for instance, in 1846, five Brazilian, one American, and five Arab—but a greater number escaped the patrol. In 1848, indeed, the Commissioners reported that 'the usual proportion of the immense

(*S.P.* xxvii (1838–9), 886). In 1843 a small 'slaver' was captured by H.M.S. *Cleopatra* and taken to the Cape with 447 slaves on board. Owing to rough weather and overcrowding 177 of them died on the voyage and 63 more after landing. R. N. Lyne, *Zanzibar in Contemporary Times* (London, 1905), 38.

[1] *S.P.* xxxiv (1845–6), 642–3; xxxvii (1848–9), 334; xxxviii (1849–50), 318; xl (1850–1), 486, 489, 525.

[2] References to Governors-General as in preceding note. In 1846 the Commissioners reported that the Governor-General, hitherto reputable, was now said to be implicated in the Trade, but that this might be slander spread by disappointed 'slavers'. *S.P.* xxxiv (1845–6), 642. Howard to Palmerston, 28.viii.50 (*S.P.* xl. 489). Ibo, *S.P.* xlii (1852–3), 288.

number of negroes imported into Rio de Janeiro during the last twelve months has been furnished by the slave-traders in the Mozambique'.[1] In 1849 the Trade seemed to be actually increasing. But then, mainly owing to the naval watch kept off the places of export, a steady improvement began. The caravans, sometimes with as many as three or four thousand slaves, still came down from far inland to the coast; but there the great bulk of the slaves remained, herded in 'barracoons', while the traders waited in vain for a chance to ship them oversea. In 1851 some five thousand of them were reported to be thus detained at Quilimane and about the same number at Ibo. In 1852, similarly, there was little shipment. But, if the Trade was checked, it was not killed. In East Africa, in fact, as in West the trans-Atlantic Slave Trade did not completely cease till from 1865 onwards the abolition of trans-Atlantic Slavery put an end to the demand for slaves.[2]

The French share in the Trade along the coast has been described in Chapter XIV. It was seen that French 'slavers' were active till the laws enacted in 1831 and 1833 made it possible to repress them, but that unhappily the need of the Bourbon planters for labour led to the initiation in 1843 of the 'free emigration system' which in fact amounted to a revival of the Trade under official regulation. Under this system, till Said's death and for some years after it, the export of Africans from the coast for work on French plantations steadily continued.[3]

2

How far was Said concerned with this 'Christian' Slave Trade? He could not, of course, prevent its being fed from the African interior. What he could do and had promised to do in

[1] *S.P.* xxxvi (1847–8), 515; xxxvii (1848–9), 332.
[2] *S.P.* xxxviii (1849–50), 318; xlii (1852–3), 288; xliii (1853–4), 1191. R. Coupland, *Kirk on the Zambesi*, passim; *The British Anti-Slavery Movement*, chap. vi. The work of the British patrols after 1850 was not assisted by the refusal of the Portuguese Government to renew the triennial protocol permitting search for 'slavers' in 'bays, ports, creeks and rivers' in Portuguese territory (*S.P.* xliii (1853–4), 1355 ff.).
[3] See pp. 433–5, above.

execution of the 'Moresby Treaty' of 1822 was to prohibit his subjects from selling the slaves when they got to the coast to 'Christian' traders or shipping them to markets on 'Christian' soil. And since his orders to that effect were backed by British cruisers, empowered to deal with Arab slave-ships as if they were British, something, if not very much, had been done to check the southward traffic. European traders no longer thought it worth the risk to put in at Arab ports if in obedience to Said's decree the inhabitants refused to sell them any slaves. 'The bights and bays of this coast', wrote Krapf in 1850 at Kilwa, 'look as if they had been purposely constructed to harbour slave-ships, and formerly they must here have carried on their horrible traffic undisturbed and unseen. But now their occupation, at least in so far as regards European 'slavers', has been destroyed by the influence of the English.' There was still, however, a steady flow of smuggling into Mozambique and Madagascar by Arab or Swahili traders. In 1843 Aberdeen wrote from the Foreign Office to inform Said that Her Majesty's Government had heard, 'not without pain', that 'vessels from Your Highness' dominions are in the habit of supplying the market of Quilimane with human beings for sale' in violation of the Treaty of 1822. In 1846, as mentioned above, five Arab dhows were caught off Mozambique by British cruisers, and in that year Hamerton reported that 'the Imam's subjects have been in the habit of taking slaves from His Highness' African dominions' to various places in Madagascar, 'where they are collected by agents residing there until resold to the Portuguese and Spanish 'slavers''. In 1850 Krapf saw two dhows at Kiswere full of Africans. 'We were told that they were only sailors, but it was clear that they were slaves who under this pretext were to be transported to Mozambique.' But, if Krapf thus witnessed a violation of the 'Moresby Treaty', he also, on the same voyage along the coast, saw something of Said's efforts to enforce it. He anchored one evening off the village of Muitinge in Lindi bay and found that in the previous year the Governor of Kilwa had come on Said's orders with a body of troops and burnt the village to the ground 'to punish the inhabitants for having entered into relations with a Portuguese slave-ship'. Such punitive action on the coast was only taken once or twice in the course of Said's long reign for any other cause; and it confirmed the belief held by Hamerton and his chiefs at the Foreign Office in Said's genuine fidelity to his engagements.[1]

3

Far more substantial than this smuggling southwards was the traffic northwards. Cogan reckoned in 1839 that of the 40,000 to 45,000 slaves sold every year in the Zanzibar market about 20,000 went to Egypt, Arabia, Persia, and the Makran coast. The number landed at the Egyptian ports in the Red Sea was relatively small, since Cairo obtained its slave-supply mainly by slave-hunting among the Nilotic tribes of the Sudan. The British Resident at Bushire estimated about 1840 that the annual import of slaves at the Persian ports on the Persian Gulf and a few Arab ports on the other side was roughly 3,500, and that a still greater number were taken to the great slave-markets at Bussora and Bagdad for distribution in the Turkish Provinces. Others were sold at Muscat and in parts of Arabia outside Oman. Others again were carried along the Makran coast, some of them being sold here and there on the way to Sind, Cutch, Kathiawar, and even to Bombay. The prohibitory regulations imposed by the Bombay Government in 1805 and 1807 were often, it seems, evaded. Captain Hennell was informed by the Company's capable agent at Muscat, an Indian Jew, that

'the manner in which slaves are introduced into our Indian possessions is by the males being classed on board the Arab vessels on which they are embarked as part of the crew while the females are passed off as their wives. As a large portion of the crew of native boats is frequently composed of Negroes, it must, of course, be extremely difficult, if not impossible, for any examining officer to ascertain whether the Africans on board are bona fide seamen or

[1] Krapf at Kilwa, 427. Captured dhows, p. 497, above. H. to Aberdeen, 28.ix.46 (*S.P.* xxxv (1846–7), 638). Aberdeen to S. 2.viii.43 (*S.P.* xxxii (1843–4), 564). Krapf at Kiswere and Muitinge, 430, 427. Said's pacific policy on the coast, pp. 352, 355, above.

brought for sale. . . . The Agent further stated that a great number of Negro and Abyssinian slaves were yearly landed in Bombay, the females being dressed up as men, while others, he asserted, were passed through the guards by means of bribes.'

'The purchasers of such slaves', Hennell adds, 'are said to be generally from Lucknow and the Deccan.' But the Bombay regulations, though by no means proof against smuggling, must have greatly obstructed and diminished the traffic on British-Indian soil, whereas in Kathiawar and Cutch, being mainly composed of Indian States outside the bounds of British India, there were no regulations at all. The Political Secretary at Bombay, writing at the end of 1835, declared that his attention had been drawn to the question of the Slave Trade during his previous service as Agent at Rajkot by 'frequently observing African boys in attendance upon the Chiefs of Kathiawar' when they came to visit him. On inquiry he discovered that something like a regular trade in slaves, most of whom came 'from the dominions of the Imam of Muscat and from various ports in Arabia', was being carried on at all the ports of Kathiawar, including Portuguese Diu, and still more at those of Cutch. He wrote, accordingly, to the Jam Sahib of Nawanagar and other leading Chiefs of Kathiawar, 'denouncing the trade in human flesh as opposed to the laws of God and man', and from most of them received replies denying the existence of a regular trade in slaves in their territories, but undertaking to prohibit all import and sale of them in future. He recommended, further, that the Commander of the Indian Navy at Surat should be instructed to watch the coast of Kathiawar and Cutch, search all vessels, and detain any engaged or believed to be engaged in the Slave Trade; and that steps should be taken, if possible, to stop the Trade at Diu. Pressure was also brought to bear on Cutch, and early in 1836 the Raja issued a proclamation prohibiting the import of any more slaves into his country and declaring that slave-carrying ships would be confiscated and their navigators 'brought to condign punishment whether they belong to Cutch or to another country'. Thus along the whole curve of the Indian coast northward from Bombay the Slave Trade was outlawed except in Sind, with whose Emirs an agreement was not yet thought practicable.[1]

In view of the facts thus coming to light from 1835 onwards it was clear that the Treaties of 1820 and 1822 had not proved adequate to check the outflow of slaves from East Africa to many other parts of Asia than Oman, where alone their import was permitted. Between 1838 and 1851, therefore, a series of measures was adopted to stiffen up the system of control. In 1838 the leading Jawasmi Sheikhs were induced to supplement the Treaty of 1820 by an agreement authorizing British cruisers to stop and search any of their ships suspected of being employed in kidnapping slaves on the African coast and, if found to be so employed, to seize and confiscate them. The next move was an attempt to reduce the opportunities of misusing the licence given to the 'internal' trade between Said's 'dominions' in Africa and Oman in order to smuggle slaves into India. In 1839 Said was asked, and readily consented, to sign an agreement supplementing the 'Moresby Treaty' of 1822. Its first article narrowed the limits within which the 'internal' trade might be carried on. The line drawn in 1822 ran from Cape Delgado to Diu Head on the edge of the Gulf of Cambay. Its northern terminus was now pushed back some 500 miles westwards to Pussem (Pasni) on the Makran coast. The second article permitted British search and seizure outside this narrower field. The third article was a novelty. It was aimed at Jawasmi 'slavers', other than Said's subjects, and dealt only with the traffic on the Somali coast. Somali being Moslems and their enslavement therefore contrary to Moslem law, it was agreed that trading in them should be considered piracy and punished as such. This agreement of 1839 was also signed by the Jawasmi Sheikhs. Ten years later a loophole on

[1] Cogan's memorandum, 5.xii.39 (*S.P.* xxvii (1838–9), 886). For the slave-raids on the Upper Nile and British attempts to persuade Mahomet Ali to stop them see *S.P.* xxvii (1838–9), 723; xxx (1841–2), 594–6; xxxii (1843–4), 548–59. Report from Bushire Residency with Hennell's statement, B.R. 646–52. J. P. Willoughby *re* Kathiawar and Cutch, 1.xii.35 (B.P.C. Doc. 1835). Cutch proclamation and Sind: J. P. W. memo. 25.iv.35 (*S.P.* xxxii (1843–4), 181–2).

the Arabian coast, outside the entrance to the Persian Gulf but not under the control of Muscat, was filled up by an agreement obtained by Hennell from the Chief of Sohar to 'prohibit the exportation of slaves from the coasts of Africa and elsewhere' in his subjects' ships and to permit their search and seizure by British patrols.[1]

It remained to secure the adherence of the two major states on the Persian Gulf to this treaty-system. In 1847 the British ambassador at Constantinople reported to Palmerston that the Sultan had at last been persuaded 'to meet the wishes of the Queen and prove the friendly spirit that animates his conduct towards Great Britain' by prohibiting the importation of African slaves into his ports on the Persian Gulf. Some Ottoman vessels were to be ordered to the Gulf 'to cruise with those of Her Majesty in order to prevent a continuance of this infamous traffic within those waters'. In 1848 the Shah of Persia issued *firmans* to the Governors of Fars and Ispahan, directing that, 'with a view to preserving the existing friendship between the two exalted States', the importation of Negroes into Persian territory by sea should be 'entirely forbidden'. And in 1851 an agreement was signed permitting British cruisers, including those of the Indian Navy, to search Persian ships, and, if slaves were found aboard, to deliver them to the Persian authorities for condemnation.[2]

4

On neither coast of Africa could the attempt to destroy the Slave Trade by a system of treaties and patrols achieve complete success: it could only check it: it could make slave-smuggling dangerous but not by any means impossible. And British cruisers in the Indian Ocean, though less handicapped in their pursuit of smugglers by the misuse of foreign flags than British

[1] Treaties of 1820 and 1822, see p. 209, above. It should be noted that the 1820 Treaty did not prohibit slave-trading but only slave-stealing: see the interpretation in B.R. 637. Agreement of 1838, B.R. 668. Agreement of 1839, signed by Said, B.R. 658; signed by Jawasmi, 669. Sohar Agreement of 1849, B.R. 682.

[2] Wellesley to Palmerston, 1.ii.47 (*S.P.* xxxvi (1847–8), 689). Persian *firmans*, B.R. 684–5; Agreement, 685–6.

cruisers in the Atlantic, were in one respect at a serious disadvantage. Off West Africa, from about 1825 onwards, all slaves carried in European or American ships—and there were no others there—were contraband. The whole coast, therefore, could be put under blockade. But in East Africa this was impracticable. The 'Moresby Treaty' kept open a 'corridor' all up the coast from Cape Delgado to the Red Sea, the Arabian seaboard, and the Persian Gulf. The Articles of 1839 narrowed this corridor on its eastern side, but maintained it. And along it Arab 'slavers' had a right to sail provided they were bound for Muscat or any other port in Said's 'dominions', African or Asiatic. Since most of the British cruisers employed against the Slave Trade were needed on the Atlantic and only three or four could be spared for the Arabian Sea, the smugglers had a very good chance in any case of evading the patrol; and, even if sighted, overhauled, and searched, they had only to assert that they were bound for one of Said's ports, and then, at a safe distance, change their course to a Persian or Jawasmi port in the Gulf or creep along the Makran beyond the 'corridor' to India, and try at the end of the voyage by deceit or bribery to land their slaves in the teeth of the engagements undertaken by the Shah or the Jawasmi Sheikhs or the Chiefs of Kathiawar and Cutch or even perhaps to worm a way through the regulations at Bombay. Thus by 1840 it had become clear that the existence of the 'corridor' was the chief obstacle to a further reduction of the Trade; and it was decided to obtain from Said yet another concession and one far more onerous than that yielded in the 'Moresby Treaty'. He was to be asked—and, in the existing political situation in the Indian Ocean, he could be virtually compelled—to prohibit altogether the oversea export of slaves from his East African ports.

The attack was opened indirectly by the Foreign Office, but directly by the Government of Bombay. After studying the reports on the Bombay Government's efforts to suppress the Trade in the Persian Gulf, including the agreement of 1839 with the Jawasmi Sheikhs, Palmerston suggested in the summer of 1841 that the question should be raised afresh with the Sheikhs and also with Seyyid Said. It should be pointed out that the 'British nation' was deeply concerned in the abolition of the Slave Trade and that 'the British Government would be unable to justify itself towards the British nation' if it did not use the naval power it possessed in Indian and Arabian waters to secure that object. Having already shown their sympathy with this humane purpose by concluding various treaties for the reduction or limitation of the Trade, the Imam and the Arab Chiefs might now be asked to undertake a further engagement 'to forbid all slave trade by sea and to permit British ships of war to search, seize and confiscate all native vessels found with slaves on board wherever navigating'. The communication should continue on the following lines:

'To the Imam a promise might be made that he should receive an annual payment of £2000 sterling for three years as a compensation for the loss of duty he would sustain by the abolition of the Trade until his subjects should turn themselves to other kinds of more legitimate commerce, the customs duties in which would more than compensate him for the loss of his duty on slaves.

'To the Arabian chiefs it might be said that the fair construction of the Treaties already subsisting with them tends to the entire abolition of the Slave Trade in their ships and by their subjects: and that consequently the new Treaty would only place in clearer language what has already been agreed to: but that, if they prefer it, the British authorities would act upon the existing Treaties without requiring the signature of any new ones.

'But it would be desirable that the Imam and the Arabian Chiefs should be made to understand that the British Government is determined at all events to put this Slave Trade down, and is conscious that it has the means of doing so.'[1]

It was decided not to negotiate a new agreement with the Jawasmi Sheikhs, but in due course the proposed communication was addressed to Said from Bombay. In view of its drastic objective—nothing less than the complete cessation of the Trade by sea—and the firmness of its tone, it had better, perhaps, have gone from London. Said had always preferred to do business

[1] Lord Leveson to Board of Control, 8.vi.41 (I.O., General Correspondence Political, xiii. 331–5). Copy to Govt. of India, 19.vii.41. See also B.P.C. 17.xi.41.

with the British Government direct; it enhanced his prestige to deal on equal terms with the Secretary of State for Foreign Affairs, a vizier who stood at the Queen's side, rather than with a Governor at Bombay or even a Governor-General at Calcutta; and it better suited his diplomacy to treat with a distant minister than with officials of the East India Company who knew much more about the East and were occasionally a little too frank and forcible in their attitude to Eastern Princes. It seems, moreover, that the old idea of the Company as primarily a commercial concern and not over-scrupulous in using its power for profit was still alive; and, if Cogan is to be believed, this idea had been fostered in Said's mind, in all honesty perhaps, by the American Consul, C. P. Waters. 'He represented the East India Company as distinct from the Imperial Government of Great Britain and no better than aggrandizing freebooters whose creature, he said, Captain Hamerton was; and he talked of the interference and assistance of the United States if required by His Highness.' It was unfortunate, too, that, when Hamerton presented the letter from Bombay, an incident had recently occurred which had sharply wounded Said's pride. Hamerton had suspected that a ship, belonging to one of Said's subjects and then at anchor in the harbour of Zanzibar, was carrying slaves; and, a brig of the naval patrol being at hand, he had instructed its captain to board and search the ship. No slaves were found; and Said not unnaturally felt that the search, conducted as it was within view of his own palace windows, not only lowered his prestige in the eyes of the Zanzibari, but implied that his fidelity to the 'Moresby Treaty' was in doubt. As a matter of fact, in this as in other cases there were no suspicions of Said's honesty in British official quarters. Hamerton trusted Said as much as he distrusted his officials. Hennell, similarly, reporting on the smuggling of slaves into India in Omani ships, had stated his 'firm conviction that His Highness the Imam is not in the slightest degree aware that such a nefarious traffic is carried on by his vessels'. But Said could not know that his personal integrity was not in question, and the nasty incident had stung.[1]

[1] Cogan to Sir Charles Forbes, *S.P.* xxxii (1843–4), 185–6. B.R. 650.

So Hamerton found his task even less agreeable than he had expected. Said began by asking, in evident ill humour, what the Company had to do with these high matters; and Hamerton had to explain, not for the first time, that his advisers had misinformed him as to the position and power of the Company and that the Queen's request came with equal force from the Governor of Bombay as from the Foreign Secretary. Said confessed that Hamerton had often told him before that the 'Royal Government' and the Government of the Company were 'one and indivisible' and that he now believed it; but this admission was made with none of his customary calm and courtesy. 'The Imam's manner was most insolent. He muttered about one thing and another, and behaved in a way I never saw him do before.' But it was as easy for Hamerton as it had been for Owen or Malcolm in their day to put the helpless Said in his place. 'I at once assumed a high tone with him.' And Said, knowing what that meant, recovered, with an effort, his composure. 'After a little', he asked quietly if Hamerton would bring him an Arabic translation of the letter next day, and so put an end to the only openly unpleasant episode—he had observed the proprieties in his interview with Owen—in all the long record of Said's intercourse with agents of the British Crown.[1]

Said must have spent an uneasy night. Twenty years ago he had been confronted with the same dilemma; now as then there was no way round it, and this time it was far harder to do what he was told. It had seemed hard enough in 1822 to interfere with his people's slave-trading in the south and the north-east; but the volume of that traffic was far exceeded by the steady flow of dhows, during the south-west 'monsoon', bearing slaves from East Africa to Muscat and his other Arab ports. The loss to his revenue, the blow to his prestige, would be far greater. How could he tell his subjects that their most lucrative means of livelihood must be given up? How could he face those fierce 'Northern Arabs' who descended every winter on Zanzibar in quest of slaves? But in 1842 he had no more choice than in

[1] H. to Select Committee of the E.I.C. 9.ii.42 (*S.P.* xxxii (1843–4), 175–6).

1822. If anything, he had less. French friendship had never seemed, except at uncertain moments of the Napoleonic War, as useful to him as British; and just at this time, as has been seen, the French on their side had betrayed their acquisitive designs on East Africa by the occupation of Nossi-bé, while he on his side had incurred (so he thought) their enmity by asking the British to prevent it. . . . Next day, accordingly, his demeanour was all that Hamerton could have desired. 'How many lies people tell me! But you, by the Son of the Prophet, have never deceived me. . . . The letter is enough for me. It is as the orders of Azrael, the angel of death. There is nothing to be done but obey.' But would Hamerton advise him? He would like to send Ali-bin-Nasir again to London in the *Sultaneh* with letters for the Queen and the viziers, explaining the magnitude and difficulty of the sacrifice he had to make. Would that be wrong? Would Hamerton translate the letters into English? Would it give offence if he commissioned the American Consul's brother-in-law to navigate the *Sultaneh*? . . . Hamerton had no instructions to press the matter to an immediate issue, and no reason, therefore, to object to the proposed mission to England. In the following June Ali-bin-Nasir was in London with letters for Queen Victoria and Lords Aberdeen and Palmerston.[1]

In the letter to the Queen one short paragraph of business was embedded in a glittering cluster of oriental compliments.

'Now in these days came here to me his honour, Captain Hamerton, and he showed me a letter from Thy Majesty to Lord General Calcutta. And in it was thy desire that the traffic in slaves, the transportation of them by sea for sale, should cease and not continue. And I am a hearer of thy words, and in obedience to thy wishes. But be Thy Majesty informed that these countries will in consequence be totally and entirely ruined.'

The letters to Aberdeen and Palmerston, which were identical, reaffirmed his obedience to the Queen's will, ruinous though the result would be; but asked them to 'assist me and intercede for me with Her Majesty and the Government'.[2]

[1] H. to Secret Committee, as in preceding note.
[2] S. to Queen, A. & P. 11.ii.42, Hamerton's translations from the Arabic: *S.P.* xxxii (1843–4), 176–80.

For the detailed presentation of this case at the Foreign Office Said gave Ali-bin-Nasir full instructions in writing. He was first to plead that ever since the agreement of 1808—permitting the occupation of Bunder Abbas by British troops if required as a precaution against a French invasion[1]—'being now nearly thirty-four years ago', Said had never opposed British wishes, and for twenty-two of those years he had been treated 'with perfect honour and respect'. But for the last twelve years—the instructions did not explain that this was the period of the first British attack on the Slave Trade—he had 'received treatment the reverse of what it was before', though he was 'not aware of any fault, nor conscious of any blame'. With this preliminary Ali-bin-Nasir was to point out that, while the request to prohibit the Slave Trade by sea would be obeyed, 'the whole of the inhabitants of the country will be injured, and the revenue will entirely disappear'. All other branches of trade were linked with the Slave Trade. If no slaves came down to the coast from the African interior, no ivory would come, since it was the slaves who carried it. If neither slaves nor ivory can be obtained, traders will no longer come to Zanzibar, selling beads and other goods from Arabia and India; and 'there will no longer remain any purchasers of the goods which come from Europe such as cotton, cloth, &c.; for the people of Zanzibar are satisfied with little; and, if this takes place, there will no longer be any revenue at all'.

The question of pecuniary compensation was to be evaded. As regards the offer of £2,000 a year for three years it should only be remarked that the diminution in the revenue would be at least five times that sum. But there was something (as has been observed) that Said wanted more than money. 'If the Great Vizier says to you, "What will satisfy Said with regard to the loss which has come upon him?" say to him, "The decision as to this rests with you; but, if it be possible, retake possession for him of his island of Bahrein; I think Said will be satisfied with this as compensation for his loss."' Nor was that all. After his envoy's departure from Zanzibar it had occurred to

[1] See pp. 129–31, above.

Said that only to ask for Bahrein, which he was unlikely to obtain, was not to take full advantage of the situation. There was nothing he wanted on the southern or central section of the African coast: his 'dominion' was recognized as reaching Cape Delgado; but might he not take this opportunity of defining, and possibly expanding, its limits in the north? He wrote, accordingly, direct to Aberdeen, explaining that 'the territories bequeathed to us by our ancestors in East Africa extend a great distance along those shores, but from Cape Guardafui to Berbera there is no controlling authority on the coast, nor is there protection for its inhabitants'. He had thought, therefore, of 'extending our government' over that area with a view to providing the requisite protection and opening 'the road to commerce into the interior'. He expected Her Majesty's Government would approve of such a step. If not, might he be informed? It can scarcely be supposed that Said had any genuine intention of planting governors and garrisons from his meagre and not very formidable forces among the fierce Somali. He had not yet attempted it nearer home at Mogadishu. All he wanted, probably, was the British Government's recognition of his formal claim to 'overlordship'. One day it might prove useful.[1]

Said made one more request, a small one. By the end of his reign, as will appear, he was to come to know and to like Hamerton better; but at the moment the memory of the incident in the harbour, aggravated doubtless by that 'high tone' at the interview, was still rankling. Ali-bin-Nasir was to express Said's belief that Aberdeen could not approve of the present behaviour of British agents at Zanzibar and Muscat towards him, and his hope that in future, provided he had done no wrong, they would treat him 'kindly, and not harshly and irritably'. This attack on Hamerton was renewed while Ali-bin-Nasir was in England. It chanced that Cogan paid one of his recurrent visits to Zanzibar a few weeks after Said's 'scene' with Hamerton. His reasons for disliking the latter have been

[1] Instructions to Ali-bin-Nasir: *S.P.* xxxi (1842–3), 648–50. S. to A. 19.vi.42 (ibid. 650).

recorded, and in conversation with Said he encouraged, one suspects, the idea that a new and friendlier British Consul might be found. At any rate, on his return to London he wrote to Sir Charles Forbes, a retired Bombay merchant of some influence, recapitulating Said's complaints of Hamerton's conduct, which 'had on various occasions bordered on insult', and expressing with studied moderation his own judgement on the matter.

'Captain Hamerton I believe to be a kind-hearted energetic man with considerable talent, particularly as a linguist; but he is considered quick-tempered and overbearing in his conduct towards the prince and people of Zanzibar which, they say, has led to the unsettled state of our affairs at that place and may still lead to more serious results. Captain Hamerton's services and acquirements could in my opinion be better employed elsewhere by the Indian Government.'

This letter, as Cogan probably suggested, was passed on by Forbes to Aberdeen.[1]

Ali-bin-Nasir, of course, was careful to submit these various propositions and requests to Aberdeen with due modesty and tact. 'His Highness is well aware', he wrote, 'of the strength of the British Government by sea and land, and that, when exercised in the cause of justice and humanity, its power must, under God, be irresistible; but he confidently trusts that it will not be put forth to oppress the weak and unoffending.' It may be doubted, however, if Said or his envoy, however submissive their demeanour, expected to get much from the Foreign Office: and it was little enough they got. In the first place, Aberdeen refused, not unnaturally, to accept Said's estimate of the loss to his revenue which a further restriction of the Slave Trade would involve. On the contrary, he maintained that Said would ultimately gain by it. 'If in the first instance some sacrifice of revenue should be necessary, the loss will speedily be compensated by the establishment of a legitimate commerce, far more profitable to the revenue and beneficial to the population of His Highness' dominions than the

[1] Instructions, *S.P.* xxxi (1842–3), 649. Cogan to Forbes, 28.x.42; F. to A. 24.xi.42 (*S.P.* xxxii (1843–4), 182–8).

inhuman one which now occupies its place.' But to meet the temporary loss of duties levied on the Trade Aberdeen, less shy of the subject than Said, asked Said to state 'without delay the terms upon which he would be willing to take a share in the proposed measures'—a straightforward, if slightly indelicate, way of putting it. As to the other forms of compensation, while Said's request for the 'restoration' of Bahrein was ignored, his designs on the Somali coast were given a very diplomatic blessing. 'Her Majesty's Government can have no objection to Your Highness taking the proper steps for extending your government . . . along all that part of the eastern coast of Africa which comprises the territory bequeathed to Your Highness by your ancestors'—which, since it adroitly avoided the vital point as to whether in fact Said possessed an inherited claim to the particular piece of coast in question, was not what Said wanted. As to his third and last request (for a request it was), the removal of Hamerton, Aberdeen, of course, said nothing: more evidence and from less prejudiced quarters would be needed before the charge against him could deserve consideration.[1]

With these concessions, such as they were, went the firmest possible restatement of the British Government's desire or demand for the new restriction of the Trade.

'There is a continual, an increasing, and a most earnest desire in Her Majesty, in the Government, and in the people of this country for the total extinction of this odious traffic—the daily occasion of incalculable misery to the human race. His Highness has shown a benevolent wish to cultivate the enlightened arts of peace, to interchange kindly offices, to promote good-will wherever his influence extends or his arms have penetrated: [but] nothing can so tend to exalt the opinion of His Highness in the country or to rivet the bonds of friendship which exist between the sovereigns and subjects of Great Britain and Muscat as an unwearied endeavour of His Highness by every means in his power to extinguish the revolting custom of the Slave Trade.'[2]

[1] Ali-bin-Nasir to A. 3.xi.42; A. to S. 9.xi.42; A. to Ali-bin-Nasir, 12.vii.42, 6.viii.42, 9.xi.42 (*S.P.* xxxi (1842–3), 642–51). For the decision not to remove Hamerton see p. 549, below.
[2] A. to Ali-bin-Nasir, 9.xi.42 (*S.P.* xxxi (1842–3), 651).

Second Attack on Slave Trade

Ali-bin-Nasir left England at the end of November and, travelling by way of Egypt and the Red Sea, he was back at Zanzibar in February 1843. It was clear at once to Said that the British Government was not to be diverted from its insensate persecution of the Slave Trade, and so, as on other occasions, there was nothing for it but to submit with as good grace as possible. 'We are desirous', he wrote eventually, 'that your Lordship should understand that we look up to the British nation and we feel that we are part of it.' The Queen's will shall be done. The loss of revenue 'we will sacrifice to your wishes'. But there was one point which had not yet been mentioned in the negotiations, a point of supreme importance to Said, a point he had certainly not overlooked but had shrewdly kept in the background till the appropriate moment. The object of prohibiting the export of slaves from his African 'dominions' was, as he now defined it, to prevent their being taken to Arabia, Persia, and the Red Sea. But, if more than that was intended, if *all* transport of slaves by sea were forbidden, then the maintenance of slavery in Zanzibar itself and his other islands off the coast would soon become impossible, and in the coast towns it would be much more difficult than it was at present to keep up the supply of slaves. Said, therefore, pleaded that 'the free sale and transit of slaves on the coast between the ports of Lamu and Kilwa, including the islands of Zanzibar, Pemba and Mafia, shall be continued as it now is with these places, and that this agreement shall be confirmed to our heirs and successors'. To make this concession was to weaken the practical effect of the new restriction. As long as those dhows and *buglas* were allowed to leave port at all with slaves aboard, the patrols would still be faced with their old difficulty in preventing smuggling. Most of the 'slavers', perhaps, would only go where they were supposed to go, to Zanzibar or up and down the coast; but some would slip away to forbidden fields in Asia. To refuse the concession, on the other hand, meant that the attack on the Slave Trade would become, indirectly at any rate, an attack on Slavery itself. For several months the question was discussed. At Aberdeen's request Hamerton supplied a brief account of

Slavery in Zanzibar. Of the 450,000 which he estimated as the total population of the two islands, only about one-fifth 'are considered free'. 'The people are growing rich, and able to buy more slaves to cultivate cloves.' Sugar was also being increasingly planted and would require still more slaves. Though the annual death-rate among agricultural slaves was as high as 22 to 30 per cent., they were generally well fed, rarely ill treated, seldom, if ever, flogged. A slave was supposed to be protected by the law equally with a free man, and his evidence would be accepted in court. The only really inhuman feature of the business was the treatment not of the living slave but of the dead. When he first came to Zanzibar, Hamerton found that the bodies of slaves were never buried, but just thrown on the beach. 'I have seen fifty dead Africans, men and women, lying on the beach and the dogs tearing them to pieces as one sees the carrion eaten by the dogs in India.' At Hamerton's earnest entreaty Said had put a stop to this and had all dead slaves buried. On the whole, then, unpleasant as Slavery in any shape might be to British eyes, it might have been worse than it was at Zanzibar: it had been worse not long ago in the British West Indies: and, even if Hamerton's picture had been much blacker than it was, Aberdeen could scarcely have thought the time was yet ripe for forcing on an independent Moslem prince what had not been forced on Christian British planters till 1833. So the concession was made, without any commitment, of course, as to Said's heirs and successors; and towards the end of 1844 the draft of an agreement incorporating it was dispatched to Hamerton for submission to Said. 'Her Majesty's Government', wrote Aberdeen to Said, 'claim no right to interfere with the passage of slaves in your ships between the ports and islands on the coast of your African dominions.'[1]

A little more delay, and then, at last, on October 2, 1845, the Agreement 'for the termination of the export of slaves from the

---

[1] H. to A. 14.ii.43 (F.O. 54. 5). H. to A. 2.i.44; S. to A. 8.iv.44; A. to S. 21.xii.44; A. to H. (with draft agreement), 21.xii.44 (*S.P.* xxxiii (1844–5), 674–9). Bodies on beach: H. to G. of I. 2,i.42, cited by R. H. Crofton, *The Old Consulate at Zanzibar* (Oxford, 1935), 5–6.

African dominions of His Highness the Sultan of Muscat' was signed by Said and Hamerton. The text of its four articles was as follows:

'I. His Highness the Sultan of Muscat hereby engages to prohibit, under the severest penalties, the export of slaves from his African dominions, and to issue orders to his officers to prevent and suppress such trade.

'II. His Highness the Sultan of Muscat further engages to prohibit, under the severest penalties, the importation of slaves from any part of Africa into his possessions in Asia, and to use his utmost influence with all the chiefs of Arabia, the Red Sea, and the Persian Gulf, in like manner to prevent the introduction of slaves from Africa into their respective territories.

'III. His Highness the Sultan of Muscat grants to the ships of Her Majesty's Navy, as well as those of the East India Company, permission to seize and confiscate any vessels the property of His Highness or of his subjects carrying on the Slave Trade, excepting such only as are engaged in the transport of slaves from one part to another of his own dominions in Africa, between the port of Lamu to the north, and its dependencies, the northern limit of which is the north point of Kiwayu Island, in 1° 57′ south latitude, and the port of Kilwa to the south, and its dependencies, the southern limit of which is the Songo Mnara or Pagoda Point, in 9° 2′ south latitude, including the islands of Zanzibar, Pemba and Mafia.

'IV. This agreement to commence and have effect from the 1st day of January, 1847, of the year of Christ, and the 15th day of the month of Moharram, 1263, of the Hejira.'[1]

Three 'additional articles' were also agreed and signed, providing that ships belonging to Said or his subjects were not to be searched between Lamu and Kilwa, nor anywhere if they were bound from the Red Sea or Arabian Sea for Said's 'dominions', and that Said should not be held responsible without sufficient proof for the smuggling of slaves from Africa in violation of his orders. Said made no secret of the reason for

---

[1] *S.P.* xxxv (1846–7), 632–3. Spellings in the text: Lamoo, Kuyhoo, Keelwa, Songa Manata, Bemba, Monfea, Imaum.

thus protecting ships from the north from interference. It was to ensure the continuance of the supply, mainly from Mocha, of Abyssinian girl-slaves and eunuchs for Zanzibar and the other Arab towns in East Africa.[1]

There remained the question of compensation. Said realized that he could not have Bahrein. 'Whatever causes any inconvenience to Her Majesty', he told Aberdeen, 'we do not wish for.' But money he evidently wanted. He repeated to Hamerton the case which Ali-bin-Nasir had put to Aberdeen—the loss of the duty on slaves (one dollar a head) previously imported into Zanzibar for re-export oversea and the loss of import-duties on goods brought to Zanzibar by traders from the north wherewith to purchase slaves. He reckoned the probable total diminution of revenue at between 35,000 and 40,000 dollars (about £8,000). But in writing to Aberdeen he still would not name a sum. 'Know that the whole of our present revenue is insufficient to defray our expenditure; then what shall we do when we lose the half of what we now receive? Her Majesty and your Lordship are our masters: the matter rests with you, your benignity is spread over the whole world, and from you I shall not experience loss.' The record of the sequel seems to have been lost among other more important documents; but it may be hoped that the British Treasury confirmed at least the original offer of £2,000 for three years.[2]

To legalize the execution of the agreement an Act of Parliament was passed in 1848, authorizing naval officers 'to visit and detain in any seas', outside the limit set for the coast-trade, 'any merchant vessel belonging to the subjects of the Imam of Muscat which shall upon reasonable grounds be suspected of being engaged in the export of slaves' from the Imam's African dominions or their importation from Africa into his possessions in Asia; providing for the trial of such vessels in Admiralty and Vice-Admiralty courts; and directing the payment by the Treasury of bounties to the officers and men concerned on slaves

[1] *S.P.* xxxv (1846–7), 630–2.
[2] S. to A. 27.ix.45; H. to A. 4.x.45 (*S.P.* xxxv (1846–7), 628–31).

taken on such ships and on their tonnage. A similar Act of 1849 implemented the agreements with the Jawasmi Chiefs.[1]

5

The new agreement was to take effect on January 1, 1847, and a few months earlier Hamerton felt it incumbent on him to warn the Foreign Office not to expect too much from its operation. Arab and Swahili 'slavers' had been realizing immense profits from the overseas trade. They bought their slaves at Zanzibar or on the coast at from 2 to 5 dollars a head, and they sold them in Madagascar for 25 to 30 dollars. At Muscat their profit was only 20 per cent., but at Basra or Bushire it was never less than 50 per cent., and in Kathiawar it ran up from 50 sometimes as far as 200.[2] These branches of the Trade, wrote Hamerton, were 'such a source of wealth to the Imam's subjects that his orders, it is much to be feared, will have but little effect in even lessening the evil'. To enrich himself in this manner seemed to the Arab to be directly sanctioned by the Koran and to be prevented from doing so to be 'the greatest possible oppression that could be used against him'. It might be hoped that the new agreement would at any rate convince those Arabs who had been trading with Madagascar in virtual, if not literal, violation of the Moresby Treaty[3] that 'south of Cape Delgado vessels under his Highness' flag ought not to be in any way engaged in transporting slaves from one place to another'. But, whatever the agreement meant, they would one and all, in their hearts and, as far as they could, in their acts, repudiate it. 'His Highness the Imam'—and this was the most significant thing that Hamerton had to say—'is *the only man* in his dominions who wishes to meet the views of the British Government on the slave question.' How could it be expected, then, that he could make that wish effective?

'He does not possess the means of enforcing the suppression of the export of slaves from his dominions further than giving orders to that

[1] 11 & 12 Vic., cap. cxxviii; 12 & 13 Vic., cap. lxxxiv. Instructions to naval officers for the execution of these Acts: B.R. 679.
[2] Madagascar figures in Hamerton's letter, cited p. 518, n. Persian Gulf: B.R. 649. Kathiawar: Willoughby's memorandum, cited p. 502, n. 1, above. [3] See pp. 497, 499, above.

effect. He has not a single ship in what is called "commission": he has neither officers nor seamen, only five empty ships. But even if he had ships in commission with proper equipment, they would not enforce his orders. Indeed, the probability is that, notwithstanding what orders they might receive from the Imam, his officers would certainly be bribed and most likely do a little business in the Slave Trade on their own account.'

Execution of the agreement, therefore, would still depend almost entirely on the exertions of the meagre naval patrol; and not an Arab, except the Imam, would try to facilitate its task. On the contrary, the right of search and seizure would always be disputed. Hamerton had talked to many Arabs on the subject, and they had all maintained that 'their saying the slaves on board were passengers and not for sale should be considered satisfactory'. Even the Imam was disposed to argue that the cruisers should not interfere with a 'slaver' unless 'actually found in the act of selling slaves'.

A disheartening outlook; its only bright spot Said's loyalty. That at any rate Hamerton acknowledged, and in generous terms. 'His Highness', he wrote, 'will have great difficulties to encounter, but he will do all in his power and make every sacrifice; and he is entitled to and well deserves every possible consideration from the people and Government of England.' He would get little from his fellow-countrymen. 'He has been looked up to not only by his own subjects, but by all the Arabs generally, as the person who should protect and guarantee to them what they all consider as their dearest interest—the right to carry on the Slave Trade.' And now he had betrayed them. No wonder he seemed to Hamerton 'in great distress of mind on this slave question'.[1]

Palmerston returned to the Foreign Office in 1846, and it was he, not Aberdeen, who received Hamerton's gloomy report. He found it provocative. He wrote to Said, brusquely dismissing the idea of limiting in any way the legal operations of the patrol. No British commander can avoid dealing with slave-ships 'as their proceedings may deserve'. 'Your Highness' sub-

[1] H. to A. 28.ix.46 (*S.P.* xxxv (1846–7), 637–8).

jects may not have as yet all of them understood that slave-trading is a criminal act, deserving severe punishment; but it is so considered in England, and the British Government is only following out its unavoidable destiny by employing all the means in its power to put an end to the Slave Trade.' To Hamerton he dispatched an irritable preachment.

'You will take every opportunity of impressing upon these Arabs that the nations of Europe are destined to put an end to the African Slave Trade, and that Great Britain is the main instrument in the hand of Providence for the accomplishment of this purpose: that it is in vain for these Arabs to endeavour to resist the consummation of that which is written in the book of fate: that they ought to bow to superior power, to leave off a pursuit which is doomed to annihilation, and a perseverance in which will only involve them in pecuniary losses and in various other evils; and that they should hasten to betake themselves to the cultivation of the soil and to lawful and innocent commerce.'[1]

Hamerton was instructed to hold this kind of language in his communications with Said and his subjects, but he may well have doubted its efficacy. For a time, indeed, it seemed as if his pessimistic forecast was to be justified. Smuggling overseas continued. In 1850 Krapf found at Kilwa that the old stream of slaves was still flowing in full volume down from Lake Nyasa to the coast and thence not only up the coast but also oversea. The caravans started every March and reached Lake Nyasa, 'the chief seat of the East African Slave Trade', in a fortnight or three weeks. They came back in November to Kilwa, through which 'ten to twelve thousand slaves are said to pass yearly on their way to the various ports of the Swahili coast and to Arabia. We saw many gangs of six to ten slaves chained to each other.' 'Slavers' bound for forbidden Arabia sailed round the eastern side of Zanzibar 'so as to evade the Sultan's police'. And, if they were caught, the captain simply declared that the slaves were sailors. Again, three years later, at Mogadishu Krapf saw twenty Arab ships engaged in smuggling slaves to Arabia.[2] But already before 1853 the tide had turned at last and

[1] P. to S. 17.xii.46; P. to H. 18.xii.46 (*S.P.* xxxv (1846–7), 639).
[2] Krapf, 423–4, 112.

turned sharply. If Hamerton had been too pessimistic in 1846, perhaps he was too optimistic when he reported in 1850 that while many slaves were still being carried in Persian and Jawasmi ships from the Red Sea to the Persian Gulf, the export northwards from East Africa had fallen off beyond all expectation. 'There certainly is not one-fifth part of the Slave Trade carried on from the Imam's African dominions which used to be a few years ago.'[1]

Not one-fifth? Had it been one-half, the change would have been startling enough. But Hamerton had no doubt about the cause of it. It was not any late flowering of Said's executive authority. 'The Imam has not an officer in the service who pays the slightest attention to his orders relative to the suppression of the Slave Trade.' It was simply the greater freedom given to the patrols. 'It is the fear of the English ships-of-war which alone prevents the subjects of the Imam from carrying on the Slave Trade openly as they formerly did.' And, if this was so, Said deserves his word of credit. For he had not only ceased to raise petty difficulties about the right of search and so forth: he had done all he could to help the work of the patrol. One instance, in the year of Hamerton's heartening report, illustrates his goodwill. In 1850 Commodore Wyvill, Commander-in-Chief at the Cape, reported that a loophole had been found in the Agreement of 1845 and that slaves were being shipped to Mozambique from little ports between Songo Mnara and Cape Delgado; and at his instance Hamerton obtained from Said written authority for British ships to suppress this trade and with that object to enter harbours and penetrate the creeks and backwaters in which that section of the coast abounded, and to destroy the 'barracoons' which had been built there. In due course Said received Palmerston's 'sincere thanks' for this real concession; and meantime Wyvill had made prompt use of it. Said had granted it on May 6. By June 7 the 'barracoons' at Mnasi and Kionga had been destroyed.[2] One more example of Said's loyalty may

[1] H. to P. 20.viii.50 (*S.P.* xli (1851–2), 412).
[2] H. to P. 20 and 22.viii.50; Wyvill to H. 1.v.50; S. to H. 6.v.50; H. to W. 8.v.50; W. to H. 8.v.50 (*S.P.* xli (1851–2), 411–16). P. to H. 18.ix.50 and 8.ii.51 (*S.P.* xl (1850–1), 463).

be cited. It seems—and it is evidence in support of Hamerton's optimism—that the slave-owners in the nearest Asiatic coastlands were becoming alarmed by the shortage in the supply of slaves. Early in 1850 emissaries were sent to the African coast towns to incite the Arabs to disregard the intolerable restrictions imposed by the British infidels on their lawful and remunerative trade. One of them, a Turkish Arab, came to Zanzibar, where he claimed to have been deputed by the Sherif of Mecca himself 'to remonstrate with the Imam for the injury he had inflicted on the Moslem world' by his acquiescence in the British campaign against the Slave Trade.

'This man's arrival here [reported Hamerton] has caused much excitement; he has been telling the people that such conduct on the part of the Imam is in every way contrary to the Koran and the Mahomedan religion. . . . He is looked on by the people here as an inspired man, a most holy person; but the Imam has paid him little attention, and told him he would do all in his power to meet the views of the British Government as long as he lived.'[1]

All credit, then, to Said: but Said, of course, would never have acquiesced in the attack on the Slave Trade, still less have aided it, if he had been a wholly independent sovereign in a world in which the power and policies of Europe had no place. But all his life he had been practically at the mercy of British or French interests. At one time, during the long war, he had been able to balance them or play one off against the other. But since 1815 he had been forced to choose definitely between them. It was not, as has been seen, an easy choice. His submission to the wishes of the British Government was bitterly resented at Zanzibar. It increased his difficulties in Oman. It threatened his reputation in every Moslem land. It is not too much to say that only a prince who had reigned so long and won such high prestige could have done what he did without losing his throne or his life. Those difficulties and risks were greater in 1845 than in 1822, for the new restrictions on the Slave Trade hit his subjects far harder; but the reason for his accepting them was also stronger. He was more certain now that British friendship was

[1] H. to P. 21.viii.50 (*S.P.* xli (1851–2), 413).

the best available guarantee for his independence and the integrity of his 'dominions' in East Africa: and he was more certain now that he could only retain British friendship by acquiescence in the British crusade against the Trade. If he had had any doubts as to the strength and solidarity of British public opinion on the question, Ali-bin-Nasir, after six months in England, would have quickly dissipated them. And if he had been tempted for a time to be evasive and even obstructive, the return of Palmerston, arch-enemy of the Trade, to the Foreign Office had soon induced a wiser submissiveness. It is significant that in 1842 he was making difficulties with Aberdeen over the right of search, while in 1850 he freely conceded it beyond the letter of his agreement. And it may be that not on Said only, but on his subjects too, Palmerston's high language had had its effect. Was it only the wider range of the cruisers and a growing dread of their guns that had brought about so steep a fall in the volume of the Trade? Or was it also a conviction that the British really meant what they said and could do what they wished; that indeed the destruction of the Trade was 'written in the book of fate'?

But, when all has been said for Palmerston and for Hamerton and for the vigilant patrols, the ultimate credit for the success of the second campaign against the Arab Slave Trade lies with the British people, whose fidelity to the humanitarian tradition had inspired it and whose taxes had paid for it. And it is worth stressing once more that this form of interference in East Africa, this kind of philanthropic 'invasion', was not merely disinterested; it was impolitic. It created for British interests, political or economic, the same sort of difficulties as it created for Said. Ten years before the first attack had opened with the 'Moresby Treaty', Prior and Smee had noticed that the new British attitude to the Slave Trade was alienating the Arabs and strengthening their preference for the French. In 1846, when the second attack was on foot, Captain Guillain declared that the British attempt to block up the Arabs' main source of wealth had roused 'a rancorous and implacable hatred'. And, reflecting thereon, he was moved to pay a remarkable tribute to the British people. France, he says, should envy England the honour of having taken the lead in the campaign against the Slave Trade. He sees no trace in it of 'that Machiavellian egoism of which that great nation is accused'. At the most it might be suggested that philanthropic zeal was fortunately not incompatible with material profit.

'But, even if such an insinuation were not quite gratuitous, one must none the less acknowledge an incontestable merit, a manifest greatness, in a people which, as one whole body, government and governed alike, is passionately bent on redressing the social crime of Slavery, and pours out its money, its ships, and its sailors and involves itself, day after day, in quarrelling and bloodshed in order to achieve its noble mission.'[1]

[1] Guillain, ii. 124, 52–3.

XVII
THE KURIA MURIA ISLANDS

I

It has been pointed out in previous chapters that British policy in the area of Said's rule was not acquisitive. The claims of British trade were never pressed. No occupations or annexations of territory were desired by the British Government. Its primary interest was the abolition of the Slave Trade. But 'philanthropic zeal was not incompatible with material profit', and that negative record does not mean, of course, that British ministers or the public opinion behind them were not concerned with business, nor anxious to obtain legitimate commercial profits, in any corner of the world. The reason why British merchants were not to the forefront in East Africa was, it seems probable, because they were occupied in more fruitful fields elsewhere. And when, as it happened, at the very end of Said's reign, an opportunity presented itself on the outskirts of his 'dominions' for a commercial enterprise which, though limited in scope, seemed to promise a very high return on the capital expended, British business men were quick enough to seize it; and, since their operations were expected to benefit an important section of the British people, British ministers were ready enough to back them, even if it meant a little territorial addition to the British Empire.

Twenty-five miles from the southern coast of Arabia, some 800 miles by sea from Aden and some 500 miles from Muscat, a submerged chain of mountains breaks through the Indian Ocean in five isolated conical peaks. These are the Kuria Muria Islands. The largest of them, Hellaniya, is eight miles long. Two of the smaller ones, Kiblia and Haski, are about two miles and one mile in length. All the islands consist of barren rock, scorched by the Arabian sun. They can never have sustained more than a negligible population, and when (as will appear) in 1854 they were visited by a British naval officer, he found a mere handful of Arabs even on the largest of them. His description of the ten he saw on one side of Hellaniya—four men, three women, and three children—was as follows:

'They have no huts, scarcely any clothes, and subsist entirely upon fish. They dwell in the clefts of the rocks with no furniture whatever except a mat or two. They have no boats. They cannot read or write. They have no idea of time, dates, or even their own ages. They merely keep account of the moon's age and revolution for religious purposes as they are staunch Mohammedans. They speak and understand Arabic and have also a language of their own, not intelligible to my interpreter. They smoke tobacco and are capital swimmers. They were all born on the island, and, although the men sometimes go to Muscat or Zanzibar or even Bombay, their tenacity of home is invincible. One man in reply to a question from me said: "It is our home, and as long as there is a fish to be caught on the island, we prefer it to all the comforts and luxuries of any other spot in the world."'

On the other side of the island the officer found a few more people of the same sort. All of them were friendly, but they were in some distress and alarm because, as they told him, a band of Arabs had recently come over from the mainland in canoes and stolen three or four of their children.[1]

This visit would not have been paid to the islands, nor would they have figured in this narrative, if in the previous year a certain Captain Ord, master of a merchant-ship owned by a Mr. C. G. Cowie of Liverpool, had not touched at the islands, probably to take in water, and discovered that on one or two of them at any rate there was something on their barren rocks more valuable than any vegetation. It was guano, the droppings of generations of sea-birds, dried by sun and wind, widespread and thick. Ord knew a good thing when he saw it. As soon as he got home he instructed his solicitor to write to the Foreign Office, suggesting that the islands should be occupied by Britain and claiming in that event a lease for the removal of the guano as a reward for its discovery. 'I don't see how we can help,' minuted Clarendon on this letter; 'for it is clear we have no right to those islands and not clear who has, nor consequently to whom application for this concession could be made.' As it

[1] Capt. Fremantle to Clarendon, 18.vii.54 (F.O. 54. 16).

happened, however, guano was a matter in which the British agricultural community at that time was keenly interested. It was the best of manures, but, owing to the shy and secretive habits of wild birds, it was hard to find. The supply with which, it was believed, the plains of Tibet were covered was unobtainable. The only substantial and available source was Peru. And unfortunately the Peruvian product had been 'cornered' by a group of merchants who kept up the price of it in England as high as £15 a ton. It seemed worth while, therefore, to follow up Ord's assertions and to make inquiries at Zanzibar. A dispatch went out to Hamerton asking whether the Imam claimed possession of the islands and 'whether any jurisdiction or act of sovereignty has ever been or still is exercised over them'. It was thought that, in justice to Ord, the utmost secrecy should be observed about his find. Not a word was said to Hamerton about the guano.[1]

A few weeks after sending this inquiry, and long before an answer could be received, the Foreign Office seems to have made up its mind that the guano was somehow or other to be acquired. Specimens of it brought home by Ord had been tested and found to be as rich or richer than the normal supply from Peru. It was suggested, therefore, to the Admiralty that, since the islands were 'uninhabited and apparently unclaimed as part of the territory of any country... protection and assistance should be given by one of H.M.'s ships of war to Captain Ord towards securing these islands for the British Crown'. The Admiralty agreed. It happened that H.M.S. *Juno*, commanded by Captain Fremantle, was about to sail for Australia. It would not divert him greatly from his course to do what was needed in the Arabian Sea. Fremantle accordingly was summoned to the Foreign Office and given his instructions. He was to go first to Zanzibar, and find out from Hamerton whether the Imam claimed possession of the islands. If so, he was to propose, with Hamerton's assistance, that the Imam should cede the islands,

---

[1] J. Bell to C. 20.viii.53; C.'s minute, 14.ix.53; F.O. to Bell, 17.ix.53; C. to H. 20.ix.53 (F.O. 54. 16). Peruvian guano: Hansard, cxliv (1857), 1031, 1951.

since to himself they were 'evidently of no value at all', whereas they were valuable to Great Britain 'as a coaling-station between Bombay and Aden'. 'The matter of the existence of the guano should be sedulously kept entirely out of sight.' 'If the Imam should demur to a gratuitous cession', Fremantle was 'to offer up to a maximum of £10,000 for them'. ('£5,000 or £10,000', Clarendon had minuted, 'would perhaps make the Imam's mouth water in exchange for what is valueless to him.') The bargain, however, was not to be concluded until Fremantle had visited the islands and inspected the quantity and quality of the guano. If the Imam had not claimed the sovereignty, he was to cross to the mainland, inquire of the inhabitants as to the ownership, and treat on similar terms with such 'chief' or 'proprietor' as he might discover. If no owner could be found, and if the guano had proved to be valuable, he was to take possession of the islands in the Queen's name. Finally, having accomplished his task, he was to call at Bombay, explain to the Governor what he had done, and ask that one of the Company's ships should visit the islands from time to time.[1]

These instructions were drafted on February 14, 1854. On the next day Hamerton at Zanzibar dispatched his answer to Clarendon's inquiry as to the ownership of the islands. 'They are considered', he wrote, 'by His Highness the Imam as a dependency of Oman . . . I heard, when last at Muscat, that these islands were frequently claimed by various tribes on the Hadramaut coast, but that they were for a length of time claimed by the Imam of Muscat and his claim acknowledged by the tribes adjacent; but there is always uncertainty and difficulty amongst Arabs on these points.' It is a pity that the Foreign Office had not waited for this dispatch before giving Fremantle his instructions; for, after dealing with Said's claims, Hamerton proceeded to explode Ord's pretensions to have discovered the guano and to make unnecessary and indeed ridiculous the 'sedulous' and rather unpleasant secrecy in which the

[1] C.'s minute, 2.xii.53; F.O. to Adm. 21.xii.53; C. to Addington, 2.ii.54; A. to C. 2.ii.54; Adm. to F.O. 11.ii.54; F.O. to Adm. 14.ii.54 (F.O. 54. 16).

matter was to be wrapped up. The islands, it appeared, were quite 'well-known to the Bourbon and Mauritius people'. Ships from both were in the habit of calling there for guano, and Hamerton had 'heard that a company of French merchants from Bourbon wanted to buy the exclusive right to take guano from these islands, but that the tribes refused to enter into any terms with them'. The Frenchmen had also, it appeared later on, applied to Said more than once for the cession of the islands, but each time he had refused. 'He much disliked Frenchmen to be near his Arabian possessions.' Nor was it only Europeans who knew of the guano and exported it. Arabs from the Red Sea 'take many cargoes of it to Makalla and other ports'. They used it specially for cultivating tobacco.[1]

Hamerton's next dispatch (June 26, 1854) reported the arrival of the *Juno*. Since the Imam was not at Zanzibar, he had written a letter which Fremantle would give him at Muscat.

'I made no allusion to guano, but gave him (the Imam) to understand that England wished to possess these islands in order to prevent them coming into the possession of any other nation and that they would be useful as coaling-stations for British steamers and as a naval station for stores. This His Highness will understand; yet I do think he will surmise the guano a thing to be considered. He quickly sees through things of this nature. He is a very extraordinary old gentleman, certainly the most clear-sighted Asiatic I have met with during the twenty-nine years that I have had much intercourse with Eastern chiefs and princes. Nevertheless, I am quite certain, was it told the Imam that guano was the chief consideration, it would not in the least influence him in his line of conduct, nor prevent his meeting the wishes of the British Government as far as lay in his power.'

In conclusion, Hamerton ventured to warn the Foreign Office of the inadvisability of 'hurried or informal negotiations' with the local Arabs on a territorial question of this kind. Sheikhs might personally be willing to do business, but their authority depended on their whole-hearted championship of their people's rights.[2]

---

[1] H. to C. 15.ii.54; 10.iii.57 (F.O. 54. 16).
[2] H. to C. 26.vi.54 (ibid.).

The Kuria Muria Islands

Meantime Fremantle was carrying out his orders. Since Said was at Muscat, he decided to visit the islands before instead of after beginning to negotiate for their cession. He sailed, accordingly, direct from Zanzibar to Hellaniya. His description of the handful of wretched Arabs he found there has been given on a previous page. He was unable to investigate the amount or quality of the guano, which lay, as a matter of fact, on two smaller members of the island-group, Kiblia and Haski; but from what Hamerton had told him, especially about the desire of French business men to acquire it, he felt justified in assuming that it was sufficiently valuable to make the proposed bargain with the Imam worth concluding. That the Imam was the man to bargain with seemed clear. The Arabs told him that they 'look up to and acknowledge the Imam of Muscat as their chief and sovereign to whom all the coast adjacent belongs'. One of them produced a document signed by the Imam's brother-in-law, requiring any one who might visit the islands to treat the inhabitants well 'under pain of His Highness's displeasure'. Further evidence of the connexion with Muscat was the fact that, when any of the islanders went there, they were welcomed by an Arab notable who was commissioned, it seemed, to look after them and to provide them with the necessaries of life.[1]

So far Fremantle's task had proved simple enough, and the last part of it was the easiest of all. He arrived at Muscat early in July, obtained an interview with Said, and presented Hamerton's letter. The sequel is best told in his own words.

'He received me with marked attention and with that courtesy and affability of manner which characterise his intercourse with English people. To show his eagerness to give a prompt reply to any communication from Her Majesty's Government, after a short interval he caused the room to be cleared and read Major Hamerton's letter. He did not hesitate a minute to return an answer which was an affirmative in the fullest sense, delivered in language most modest in all that concerned himself and most flattering in all that related to Her Majesty and her Government. He seemed rejoiced to have in his power the means of conferring the smallest obligation on a nation for

[1] F. to C. 18.vii.54 (F.O. 54. 16).

whose friendship he entertained so much respect. .... He concluded by saying that, if Her Majesty required any other portion or the whole of his dominions, whether in Arabia or in Africa, he would be equally cheerful to surrender them into her hands.'[1]

Thirty years earlier another British naval officer had interviewed Said at Muscat and discussed the ownership of one of his possessions. On that occasion, likewise, Said had been 'mild and gentlemanly'. 'It would give him sincere pleasure', he had said, 'if the British would take Mombasa.'[2] Owen had not believed him, and he was right. Said certainly did not want to give up Mombasa. Fremantle, on the other hand, clearly thought that Said's willingness to cede the Kuria Muria Islands was genuine. But was it? Said knew about the guano. He knew it was worth a lot of money. He could not exploit it, it is true, with his limited resources in organization and shipping, as quickly or fully as a British Company. But Clarendon and his advisers, who personally knew nothing of Said's commercial enterprises, were surely wrong in their hasty and convenient assumption that the islands were 'of no value at all' to him. And, guano or no guano, princes, or peoples for that matter, have seldom positively wanted to be relieved of territory, however small or barren. But in this case Said did not protest against Fremantle's proposal as he had against Owen's as soon as his back was turned; and the only uncertainty is not that he yielded the favour asked of him honestly and without hesitation, but whether or not he wished that his British friends had not asked it. At any rate, having made up his mind, he determined to do the thing in style, to make the best possible impression on the Foreign Office. When Fremantle in accordance with his instructions suggested that the British Government would be willing to pay a reasonable sum for the islands, Said refused even to consider the notion. 'He utterly shrank from all idea of compensation.' More than that, he actually 'offered to send a vessel to take all those people away from the island if I wished it, and would have allotted a spot of land near Muscat for their residence and subsistence'. But the Foreign Office had not contemplated, and Fremantle

[1] F. to C. 18.vii.54 (F.O. 54. 16).   [2] See p. 232, above.

was far from desiring, that the surrendered site should be forcibly cleared of its human encumbrances. 'Knowing their attachment to their simple and independent mode of life, I begged he would on no account disturb them.'[1] Nor, finally, did Said ask for time before the agreement was formally concluded. A short Deed of Cession was rapidly drafted, and on July 14 it was signed and sealed by Said with Fremantle as witness.

'From the humble Said-bin-Sultan to all and everyone who may see this paper, whether Mahomedans or others:

'There has arrived to me from the powerful nation [England] Captain Fremantle, belonging to the Royal Navy of the Great Queen, requesting from me the Kuria Muria Islands, *viz.* Heilaniya, Kiblia, Soda, Haski and Gurzond; and I hereby cede to the Queen Victoria the above-mentioned islands to be her possessions or [those of] her heirs and successors after her. In proof whereof I have hereunto affixed my signature and seal on behalf of myself and my son after me, of my own free will and pleasure, without force, intimidation, or pecuniary interest whatsoever.

'And be the same known to all to whom these presents may come.'[2]

Said had done his last favour to the British Government and done it handsomely. It seems unfortunate that his generosity could not be reciprocated when, very soon afterwards, he pleaded for help to assert his valuable rights at Bunder Abbas.

2

On the receipt of Fremantle's report and a copy of the deed, the Foreign Office, having done its share of the business in bringing about the cession, handed over the control of the new British possession to the Colonial Office in October 1854. Sir George Grey, who had become Secretary of State earlier in that year, was not altogether easy as to the manner in which the business had been handled. He submitted to Clarendon the question 'whether the gratuitous cession of the islands by the Imam could in justice and fairness be held to be binding, pro-

[1] F. to C. 18.vii.54 (F.O. 54. 16).
[2] English translation of Arabic text. Aitchison, vii. 102–3. The spelling of the names of some of the islands has been changed.

cured, as it has been, by a studied concealment of the value of what was ceded'. The Foreign Office had no answer to that, but at least it had been quite candid about it. The minute for the Colonial Office, drafted when the islands were transferred to its charge, had summed the matter up as follows: 'The ostensible object in acquiring them was to form a coal depot for steamers between India and Suez; the real object to gain possession for British purposes of the guano supposed to exist on the islands.' That was frank enough, as befitted a communication with colleagues in Whitehall; but what was to be said to Said? The Foreign Office appears to have been sincerely anxious to compensate him for the loss of what was, potentially at any rate, a source of wealth. It wanted, as has been seen, to pay him as much as £10,000; and now also it wanted to share with him such part of the spoil as would fall to Government by way of royalties. But this meant an admission that the guano was there or might be there. The only thing to do, it seemed, was to be frank again and yet not wholly frank: a shred of the old pretence was to be maintained. So Hamerton was instructed, when thanking Said warmly for the cession, to tell him—what he probably doubted —that the islands would be valuable to Britain as a coaling or naval station, but also to admit—what he had always known— that a further reason for the Government's desire to acquire the islands was that there might be guano on them. 'Her Majesty's Government would be unwilling', Clarendon's dispatch continued, 'that the Imam by his generous cession of the islands to the British Crown should be altogether deprived of any advantage in a commercial point of view which he might have derived from a continued possession of them.' It would wish, therefore, to pay the Imam a fixed sum and to render him a share of any profits that might accrue. But Said would have none of it, and all that Clarendon could do to ease his conscience was to send him a snuff-box as a token of the British Government's appreciation of his readiness to comply with its wishes. A year later Clarendon wrote again to inform Hamerton of the licence granted for the removal of the guano, and he took occasion to tell him to repeat the offer of a pecuniary settlement. But

Hamerton could not obey this order. After bidding Said farewell in 1854, he had never seen him again.[1]

The business of exploiting the guano, meantime, had been put on a legal footing. By the end of 1855 a licence had been issued to Ord and two partners, Messrs. Hindon and Hayes, Liverpool men like himself, who had joined him in the enterprise. At the beginning of the affair, two years earlier, Clarendon in an interview with Ord had told him that, while his secret would be kept, there could be no monopoly in the guano, 'no exclusive advantage to any individual'. But this good intention had not lasted. The licence gave the three adventurers the 'sole and exclusive right ... to appropriate and remove the said guano' for a period of five years, provided that the Government were paid a royalty of two shillings a ton for the first two years and four shillings a ton for the last three. The guano was to be shipped to British ports and sold in the open market to British farmers.[2]

It only remained to provide Ord, who was now anxious to get to work on the spot, with some protection. On the need of it Ord was insistent, fearing, it seems, not so much any difficulty with the inhabitants of the islands as attempts by unlicensed merchants, especially Americans, to steal the guano in violation of his rights. He asked the Foreign Office for a warship. He had chartered several vessels, he said, to go and load up with guano. But the Foreign Office had anticipated his wish, though not quite for his reasons. The Admiralty had been asked if the senior naval officer in those seas could take measures, in communication with H.M. Consul at Zanzibar, 'to protect the natives on the islands and to levy the royalty on the guano exported'. So far the Admiralty had done all the Foreign Office wanted, but this was asking too much. Any vessel passing that way, the Lords replied, would be instructed to call at the islands; but it was 'perfectly impossible for the naval officers on the

[1] Merivale for Grey to F.O. 19.xi.54; minute for C.O. 7.x.54; F.O. to C.O. re transfer, 13.x.54; C. to H. 30.xii.54 and 17.v.56; H. to C. 10.ix.55 (F.O. 54. 16). Compensation was offered to Said's successor, Majid, in 1859 and refused: (F.O. 54. 17).

[2] F.O. to Ord, 25.xi.53; Ord to C. 26.xi.53; C.'s minute, 2.xii.53; F.O. to C.O. 18.xii.55; C.O. to F.O. 22.xii.55 and 2.ii.56 (F.O. 54. 16).

station to undertake the general superintendence of the settlers on, or the natives of, the islands, or the collection of dues or royalties'. A little later Clarendon pressed the Admiralty again. Could not a ship be sent from time to time to see what was happening? But the Admiralty was not to be persuaded, and it had found a way of diverting these tiresome requests elsewhere. Such visits by ships on the East African station, it said, would be contrary to custom: those waters were usually patrolled by ships of the East India Company. The Foreign Office took the hint. It appealed to the India Board for one of the Company's ships, and the India Board, more tractable than the Admiralty, sent instructions to the Government of Bombay to send one. Such long-range correspondence was bound to take time, and in the late summer of 1856 Ord sailed for his islands without waiting for the issue of it.[1]

It was not what he had hoped. John Elphinstone, nephew of Mountstuart, was now Governor of Bombay, and he and his advisers had not unnaturally resented the action taken in Whitehall. The whole of the Arabian coast from the Persian Gulf to the Red Sea was primarily their concern. It was their agents who, as Residents in the Gulf and at Aden, conducted British relations with the Arabs. These experienced officers knew the Arabs as no one else could, and the Bombay Government depended on their information and advice. Yet the Foreign Office had not merely invaded this Arab world, but had actually acquired Arab territory for the Crown, without any consultation with Bombay. And this delicate and possibly dangerous step had been taken merely in the hope of enabling British farmers to obtain a cheaper supply of manure with the aid, and presumably to the great pecuniary advantage, of Messrs. Ord & Company. The attitude of the Bombay Government, therefore, had been frankly hostile to the whole enterprise. At an earlier stage it had demolished the 'ostensible reason' for the cession of the islands. They were quite useless, it had reported, as a coaling-

---

[1] Ord's memorial, 30.v.56; Adm. to F.O. 5.ii.56; C. to Adm. 13.iii.56; Adm. to F.O. 15.iii.56; F.O. to India Board, 29.iii.56; I.B. to F.O. 11.iv.56 (F.O. 54. 16).

station in view of the course taken by steamships and the direction of the prevailing winds; and since they possessed no harbours, they would be quite untenable by an enemy in face of British sea-power. And now, when a guard-ship was asked for, the answer was simply that it was impossible to send one.[1]

3

It was not till December 20, 1856, that the Foreign Office learnt that no ship had been or would be sent. Six days later it received from the India Board another piece of information. Ord, it was reported, had been expelled from the islands.[2]

Ord's own account of the incident was forthcoming. 'I deeply regret to state', he wrote, 'that, in consequence of the protection promised me at the Kuria Muria Islands not having been rendered, I have been compelled to abandon the guano project.' At six o'clock on the morning of October 22 the tents which he and his companions had pitched on Haski Island had been surrounded by 150 'armed pirates' from the mainland. These 'savages' had 'demanded to know my business there', and, on being informed through Ord's interpreter that the islands had been ceded by the Imam of Muscat to Great Britain, they declared that they 'never belonged to the Imam'. 'They belonged, they told me, to the Chief of Marbat or some place near there, and insolently demanded that I should quit the place in *one hour* or we should all die.' 'I cautioned them against any act of violence and that, if one English life was taken, the English Government would visit them with fearful retribution.' It took Ord thirty-six hours to get his party and their belongings on board ship. Thus 'narrowly escaping with our lives', they sailed for Bombay. The labourers they had brought with them to excavate the guano were dispatched to Aden in two open boats.[3]

[1] I.B. to F.O. 2.ii.55 and 20.xii.56 (ibid.).
[2] I.B. to F.O. 26.xii.56 (ibid.).
[3] Ord to Political Resident at Aden, 29.x.56: printed in *Sessional Papers*, xxxviii, 1857, Session 2, 308, 1–2.

The comment of the Political Resident at Aden, Colonel W. Coghlan, on Ord's statement was forcible.

'It is only because the Arabs are not the "pirates" and "savages" which Mr. Ord represents them, that the expulsion was not attended by bloodshed. It appears to me that they evinced great moderation in expelling the intruders from their soil. A reasonable time was allowed them to depart, they were permitted to take away their property, and neither insult, violence, nor plunder was attempted. The most civilised nation of Europe could hardly have been more considerate.'

The Arabs, he went on, were bound to regard Ord's party as intruders. The cession of the islands by the Imam of Muscat was 'simply a nullity' in which presumably the Government of Bombay had had no part. The Imam possessed no real authority there. No tribute had ever been paid to him. As to the guano, it was not Ord's 'discovery'. Thousands of tons had been removed in the past by the people of Shihr and Makalla. If it were wanted in England, the Bombay Government could easily have secured the right to export it by negotiation between the Resident at Aden and the people on the spot. As it was, the expulsion of Ord's party would be represented far and wide as a blow to the British and would have a bad effect on their prestige throughout Arabia. No further attempt should be made to form a 'mercantile establishment'. If the islands were needed for public purposes, as a cable-station for instance, they should be occupied by Government. 'To permit private speculators, utterly unacquainted with the Arab language and character, to settle there is highly inadvisable.' It was 'a source of satisfaction' that the protection Ord asked for had not been provided. The dispatch of a warship to the islands might have led to fighting in which Ord and his companions might have lost their lives, while, if the Arabs had been driven out with bloodshed, an amicable settlement for the future would have been made impossible.[1]

The Bombay Government, as was to be expected, shared Coghlan's views. When Ord presented a demand for a ship to

[1] P.R. at Aden to Secret Committee, 19.xi.56 (F.O. 54. 16).

protect him, he received a chilly answer. No ship was available, 'even if it were deemed proper to comply with your request'. His right course was to approach the Chief of the Maharra tribe on the coast opposite the islands, and, with the help of the Resident at Aden, negotiate a friendly bargain with him. Hamerton, when he heard of the trouble, took the same line. There would have been no difficulty, he wrote, if Ord had had a little tact and known anything about Arabs.[1]

In March 1857 Ord's agent obtained an interview with Elphinstone and again asked for a ship. He was closely questioned on the validity of Ord's claim to the guano, and forced to admit that not Arabs only but American traders had taken it from the islands before Ord's 'discovery'. He was given the same advice as Ord—to come to terms with the Arabs. As to a ship, Elphinstone declared he had not got one and could not promise one in the future. 'We should not feel ourselves justified in sending one to enable him to carry off the guano by force until we had ascertained beyond doubt that the Arabs who claimed it had no right to it.'[2]

'The Arabs themselves', said Clarendon when he had perused the papers from Bombay, 'could not show more ill-will about these islands than the Indian authorities.' His petulance was not unnatural; for he was still responsible for the wretched islands in the House of Lords, and he and his colleagues were exposed to more disagreeable pressure than Elphinstone or Coghlan.

On the one hand, Messrs. Hindson and Hayes had promptly made the most of their partner's mishap. 'I consider it a most shameful thing, on the part of the Home Government,' Ord had written to them, 'the way in which they have deceived us.' Given the promised protection, he would by now have had 'upwards of 50,000 tons of first-rate guano ready for shipment next season'. The catastrophe had meant, declared Hindson and Hayes to the Colonial Office, the loss of capital invested in the enterprise to an amount little short of £10,000.

[1] O. to G. of B. 12.xi.56; G. of B. to O. 17.xi.56; H. to. G. of B. 10.iii.57 (ibid.).
[2] Elphinstone's minute, 26.iii.57 (ibid.).

For this they claimed compensation since it had been due to the failure to provide the promised protection. In any case, especially in view of the fact that the guano was now known to be of high value, almost as high as that of Peruvian guano, they proposed to continue its exploitation, and requested first that protection should be definitely guaranteed to the next expedition, and secondly that the term of the lease should be extended.[1]

On the other hand, the conditions of the lease as it stood had become known, and the farmers' representatives in Parliament had persisted in worrying ministers about it for several weeks in the early part of 1857. Questions had been asked and repeated, and the correspondence called for, in the Commons, and a motion for papers had been carried in the Lords. In both Houses the attack was based on the farmers' need of guano at a cheaper rate than that maintained by the Peruvian 'ring'. The monopoly granted to Ord & Co. would mean, it was urged, no lowering of the price, and would Arab opposition, it was asked, be permitted to make it impossible to get the stuff at all? The member for Berwickshire startled the House by asserting that the islands were believed to contain between one and two million tons of guano, worth at the current price about £24,000,000. The Government's defence was made by Clarendon and Labouchere, the new Colonial Secretary. Both of them asserted their lively interest in obtaining more guano for British farmers. Had not the Foreign Office told British consuls in all countries wherein guano was likely to be found to send immediate information of any discovery? Had not the Admiralty given similar instructions to the captains of Her Majesty's ships? As to the monopoly, it was justified by Ord's discovery and the speculative character of the enterprise; and its effect would be tempered not only by the limited term of the lease, but also by the pledge originally given by Ord & Co. to sell the guano by auction in the open market and by their subsequent offer to permit other merchants to export it from the islands if they paid a royalty of £1 a ton. Lastly, the further exploitation of

[1] O. to H. & H. (*Sessional Papers*, xxxviii, 1857, Session 2, 308, 2). H. & H. to C.O. 20.xii.56 (F.O. 54. 16).

the guano would be effectively protected. With these assurances Parliament had seemed satisfied. When a country member asked whether the papers would be available before the dissolution, Palmerston himself, now Prime Minister, had gently banished the subject of the Kuria Muria Islands from the parliamentary stage. Opinions differed, he said, as to the amount of guano to be found there—some thought it was very great, others very little; and the papers asked for were not likely to supply any information that was not already known.... Parliament was dissolved on March 21. The papers were ordered to be printed on August 25. No more questions on the subject were asked.[1]

4

Ord's case against the Government was not a strong one. The Arabs, as a matter of fact, had taken him by surprise. It was not their intrusion but that of rival adventurers he had feared; and, while he had certainly expected a warship to be provided when he left England, he had planned to arrive at the islands himself some weeks before she could be expected at her post. But, whoever might be to blame for the initial mishap, the Government did not mean it to be repeated. Since the guano was wanted in England, Ord and his partners were to get it. The firm on their part gave an assurance, a guarded assurance, that they would try to avoid trouble with the Arabs. 'All that can be done to a reasonable extent to conciliate them shall be done.' The Colonial Office on its part obtained a promise from the Admiralty that this time a ship should be sent to protect the guano-seekers and to help 'in effecting an arrangement with the Arabs'. Early in October, accordingly, H.M. steam-sloop *Cordelia* cast anchor at the islands. Ord and Hayes were there,

[1] Hansard, cxliv (1857), 934, 1031, 1057, 1588, 1951, 2367. The critics in the Lords were the Duke of Montrose, the Earl of Hardwicke, and Lords Berners and Polworth; in the Commons, J. E. Denison (Malton), Lord Naas (Coleraine), and Hon. F. Scott (Berwickshire). The papers appeared as No. 308 of Session 2 in the *Sessional Papers*, xxxviii, 1857. Ord's account of the expulsion was given; the rest was almost wholly concerned with the details of the lease.

reported Commander Vernon, with three ships. The Arabs had not attempted to interfere and showed no signs of doing so. No measures of 'conciliation', therefore, seemed required. The only hitch, in fact, was lack of labour. The Government of Bombay, its antagonism to the whole enterprise stiffened, perhaps, by Coghlan's report of the sufferings endured by the men returned by Ord to Aden in the previous year in open boats, had instructed Coghlan to forbid any further hiring of labourers at Aden for employment on the islands. That was a strong step; for, while an ordinance was in force prohibiting the employment of natives of India anywhere as 'coolies' overseas, there was nothing illegal in hiring non-natives of India for this purpose. And when Ord & Company protested to the Colonial Office, and the Colonial Office passed it on to the India House, the Court of Directors told the Bombay Government that its action had been 'unnecessary and uncalled for' and ordered it to put no obstacle in the way of Ord's recruitment of non-natives of India. Valuable months, meantime, had passed; and, since the work could not be done effectively by the British crews of Ord & Co.'s ships —digging and sifting and carrying sacks of guano over burning rocks soon proved too much for some of them—Ord had gone to Muscat and hired some seventy men there. But, like other white men before and since, seeking to get rich quickly in tropical or subtropical lands, Ord was not too careful how he treated his coloured workers. Reporting again at the end of the year, Vernon described how laggard Arabs had been knocked about by Ord and his subordinates with fists and sticks, and how, when he had informed them that he was expecting shortly to proceed to Australia, they had vigorously protested on the ground *inter alia* that they had to go armed about the work for fear of the labourers attacking them. Vernon had replied with a caustic reference to the way they had been handled.

'I will not take upon myself to characterise such a mode of treatment. You are aware of the feeling of our countrymen on that point. You may also perhaps know that an Arab never forgets, seldom forgives a blow.... If, therefore, you do not feel beyond all doubt perfectly assured of your ability to control these men without recourse to measures happily prosecuted by the laws of our country, and certainly without the necessity of your "wearing arms when directing them", my urgent advice to you is to return them without delay to Muscat. For rely upon it, you will be held responsible for any bloodshed or other catastrophe that may result from such treatment as I have described.'

In his report to the Admiralty Vernon suggested that the retention of the *Cordelia* at the islands—an unpleasant, inactive, tedious business, bad for the health and morale of his men— might be of no advantage to the labourers. Ord and his people might behave better if there were no British seamen there to save them from the worst results of their misconduct.[1]

The Admiralty agreed. 'There does not appear', the Lords informed the Colonial Office, 'to have been an attempt of any kind on the part of the Arabs of the neighbouring coasts to interfere with the proceedings of the guano vessels.' The Colonial Office acquiesced. The *Cordelia* was ordered back to the islands only for the first few months of 1858. In June she was released from her irksome duty and departed for Ceylon and Sydney. When Ord & Co. again demanded protection in the following autumn, they were told that a ship could not be sent every year, and Vernon's warning as to the treatment of the labourers was repeated.[2]

But in the primitive conditions of the Kuria Muria Islands the labourers were exposed to far worse dangers than blows and kicks. The water-supply was limited. There was no effective protection from the weather. No proper medical attention was available, nor adequate medical stores. The result in that climate and under the strain of ceaseless work was virtually inevitable. Towards the close of the season 1858–9 Coghlan reported to Bombay that the death-rate among the labourers was

[1] O., H., & H. to Labouchere, 7.v.57; Adm. to C.O. 7.v.57 (F.O. 54. 16); F.O. memo. 19.i.57; Coghlan to G. of B. 17.iv. and 17.v.57; G. of B. to Secret Committee, 29.vii.57; Court of Directors to G. of B. 10.x.57; C.O. to H. & H. 3 and 13.xi.57; Vernon to Adm. 7.x.57; V. to O. & H. 15.xi.57; V. to Adm. 4.xii.57; Adm. to C.O. 7 and 31.xii.57 (C.O. 143. 1).
[2] Adm. to C.O. 31.xii.57; V. to Adm. 25.ii.58 and 17.v.58; Lytton to O., H., & H. 4.ix.58 (C.O. 143. 1).

terribly high. Of forty-seven men who had left Aden in September only thirty had returned 'enfeebled and useless' in February. The other seventeen were dead. Elphinstone and his colleagues must have reflected that Coghlan's original prohibition of all recruitment had not been so 'unnecessary' or so 'uncalled for' as their superiors in London had asserted. In the existing circumstances they did what they could to protect the 'underdogs' of Aden. They ordered—and the India Board approved—that no further recruitment of labourers should be permitted unless the employers gave security for their welfare on the islands, for proper transport there and back, and for the provision of a competent doctor and sufficient medical stores. But scarcely had this order been made when another dispatch arrived from Coghlan, reporting that heavy mortality continued. Thereupon the Bombay Government resumed its original highhandedness. It told Coghlan to forbid the recruitment of any more 'coolies' for the islands, and then reported its action to the Home authorities. This time there was no criticism: the action was approved; and thenceforward Ord & Co., if they could still obtain their victims from Muscat or Socotra or the Arab coast, at least could not obtain them on British soil.[1]

Meantime a substantial amount of guano had been acquired. If on a closer acquaintance with the two favoured islands the original estimate of their richness seemed too high, yet it was believed by Ord and his associates on the spot that there were at least 500,000 tons on Kiblia and 250,000 on Haski. Little could be done to appropriate this treasure in the summer months, but from October till the following May or June quite a fleet of ships were busy loading up for two successive years. There were as many as seventy there in the spring of 1858. For the season of 1857-8 the total amount of guano taken away was 26,191 tons, for 1858-9, 14,250 tons. Presumably Ord & Co. made some profit out of it, though even that is uncertain in the

[1] Coghlan to G. of B. 6.iv. and 10.v.59; G. of B. to India Board, 25.iv.59; Stanley to G. of B. 14.vi. and 4.viii.59 (I.O., *Political Dispatches*, vol. 117, pp. 88-9, 235-6).

light of the sequel. Quite certainly the Government made none. For against the cost of the *Juno*'s voyage and the *Cordelia*'s detention there was nothing to set off by way of royalties. The royalties due on those first two years were £4,800 and £2,850; but Ord & Co. pleaded to be excused or to be allowed to defer the payment of those sums on various grounds—the original failure of protection, the unauthorized prohibition of labour-recruitment, and finally the 'serious losses' they had suffered. In view of the initial set-back and the Company's claims on that account, the first debt (£4,800) was remitted; and in a new licence, issued in June 1859 on the understanding that all claims against the Government were withdrawn and securities against the ill treatment of labourers undertaken, the period of monopoly was extended up to March 1, 1864, and the lower rate of royalty (2s. a ton) applied throughout. These were not illiberal concessions, and when Ord & Co. asked for delay in the payment of their second debt (£2,850), the Colonial Office and the Treasury stiffened their backs. Postponement was conceded till May 31, 1860, with the warning that payment must be punctual in future years; and when the appointed date came and passed, and application was made for the money, and the only result was yet another plea for delay, a demand for immediate payment was presented. There was no response, and, after prolonged consideration of the legal issues involved, the licence to Ord and his partners was formally terminated on May 18, 1861. Further attempts were made to recover the sum due from the defaulting firm. A prosecution was contemplated but not launched. At the end of 1861 the claim of the Crown was abandoned.[1]

[1] Early optimism: Letters in *The Times*, 2. and 10.xii.57; 3.iii.58. Royalties: Treasury to C.O. 7.viii.58; Lytton to H. & H. 28.x.58 (C.O. 143. 1). Commissioners of Colonial Lands and Emigration to Treasury, 28.xii.60 (C.O. 386. 4). The royalties were dealt with by the above-named Commissioners, and the documents on the default from Jan. 1860 to Nov. 1861 are in C.O. 386. 178. An outline of events is given in the Commissioners' printed *Annual Reports*, 1859, p. 57; 1860, p. 55; 1861, p. 42; 1862, p. 60. The termination of the licence was published in the *London Gazette*, 21.v.61. Messrs. William Dixon were permitted to complete a contract they had undertaken with Ord

5

Twenty-two years later two British officers, Miles and Lang, visited Hellaniya. All signs of European invasion had by then long vanished from the islands. The precious excrement which had once lain thick on Kiblia and Haski was gone. And with it had gone all reason for European interest in those sea-girt mountain-tops: for the cable landed on Hellaniya by the Red Sea and Karachi Telegraph Company in 1861 had broken down in the following year and been abandoned. Only Hellaniya, as of old, was inhabited, and, as of old, the inhabitants were few— 5 men, 20 women, and 11 children. Miles's description of them in 1883 is almost a repetition of Fremantle's in 1854.

'I walked with Lang to the huts which are of the most primitive description, generally oval or round, six feet in diameter and three or four feet high, built of loose stones with a scanty roofing of mats, with barely room to sit upright. In these wretched habitations and in caves at certain seasons these islanders live, subsisting on fish, shell-fish and goats' milk, occasionally exchanging their dried fish for dates and rice with passing dhows. . . . They fish entirely with the hook, and possess neither boats, canoes, nor nets. . . . They were much gratified by being given a little sugar, rice, tobacco and cotton cloth.'[1]

It cannot be said, then, that the islanders profited by becoming subjects of Queen Victoria instead of subjects of Seyyid Said. It would seem, indeed, that they had lost a trifle by the change, since those of them who ventured to Muscat presumably no longer received the little attentions which Said's agent had bestowed on them. British annexation may have meant, at the time it was effected, a greater measure of security against piratic or slave-raiding Arabs, but by 1883 the Arabian Sea had become reasonably safe for peaceful folk whatever their allegiance; and

& Co. for the extraction of 20,000 tons of guano, and paid a few hundred pounds in royalties. Accounts: C.O. 386. 178, p. 415. The Kuria Muria guano was a very small fraction of the total amount landed in England which continued at a fairly stable level from 235,000 tons in 1854 to 233,000 tons in 1863: *The Times*, 19.iii.64.

[1] Miles, 548. For another visit in the following year, 556.

on the positive side the islands were too small and too remote to obtain such benefits as might normally have resulted from British administration. To-day they are formally included in the Colony of Aden, but its Government, 800 miles away, cannot be said to govern them. Since the Persian Gulf is some 300 miles nearer, the British Resident there is entrusted with their administrative control; and they are visited from time to time by the Political Agent at Muscat. Otherwise the islanders are left, as they themselves perhaps would wish, to live their customary stinted life in peace.[1]

Against the wide range of time and events traversed in this book the incidents related in this chapter may seem to shrink to trivial proportions. Yet the story has been deliberately told in detail because it illustrates so forcibly a persistent feature in the contact of Europe with Africa and Asia. European greed or *laissez-faire* has been responsible for many such things as happened in the Kuria Muria Islands, and for far worse things. The Slave Trade was far worse. And, while the doings just recorded were British doings—and that is another reason for telling the tale in full—it is fair to remember that in East Africa and the Arabian Sea in the period under review no other such case of misconduct or negligence can be charged against the people who fought and were finally to kill the Slave Trade.

[1] Hellaniya was visited in 1936 and found to contain about 50 inhabitants.

XVIII
THE END OF AN EPOCH

I

Neither Said nor Hamerton lived to see what happened on the Kuria Muria Islands; and it is time to return from that digression to the two men round whom so much of the later chapters of this book have been written. Their relationship was indeed the dominant factor in East African history for the last fifteen years of Said's reign. On Said's personality a good deal of light has been thrown in the course of the preceding narrative, but what of Hamerton's? What manner of man was he, and what did he really think of Said, and Said of him?

Every one who visited Zanzibar in those days was impressed by Hamerton's unaffected friendliness, his *bonhomie*, his exuberant Irish hospitality. When Speke and Burton came to Zanzibar as the starting-point of their expedition into the interior, the 'two strangers' were received 'like sons'; the Consulate was made their home; and when they set off for the mainland, their 'generous, thoughtful old host' not only stored their ship with 'delicacies of all kinds', but insisted on escorting them himself across the water, though he was suffering from his last painful illness at the time. During their stay, says Speke, the house was 'one continuous scene of pleasure and festivities'.

'The British Consulate was the common rendezvous of all men: Arab, Hindi, German, French or American were all alike received without distinction or any forced restraint. Indeed the old Consul literally studied the mode of making people happy; and Zanzibar, instead of being an outlandish place, such as to make one wonder how men could exile themselves by coming here, was really a place of great enjoyment.'

Krapf makes no reference to pleasure or festivity; and, as has been seen, Hamerton was a little biased against missionaries. On each of his visits to Zanzibar, nevertheless, Krapf's journal records the Consul's unfailing hospitality. And Guillain found that foreigners received the same hearty welcome as Englishmen. He, too, was struck by Hamerton's frank cordiality, his enjoyment of life and society—he sums him up in English idiom as 'a good fellow'—but Guillain, being concerned with politics at Zanzibar, was more interested in the qualities that lay behind the mask of 'merry Irishman'—the diplomatic *finesse* and *savoir faire* which he detected there, the fruits of long training in the East India Company's 'machiavellian' school, and the unwavering devotion to the policy of the Governments he served.[1]

Hamerton's jollity and energy are the more remarkable since in the course of those fifteen years he was often ill and on three or four occasions dangerously ill. Burton has left a portrait of him drawn a few months before his death in 1857.

'I can even now distinctly see my poor friend sitting before me, a tall, broad-shouldered, and powerful figure, with square features, dark, fixed eyes, hair and beard prematurely snow-white, and a complexion once fair and ruddy, but long ago bleached ghastly pale by ennui and sickness. . . . The worst symptom in his case was his unwillingness to quit˅the place which was slowly killing him. At night he would chat merrily about a remove, about a return to Ireland; he loathed the subject in the morning. To escape seemed a physical impossibility.'[2]

Hamerton's amiability did not impair his judgement. He was on the best of terms with Consuls Broquant and Belligny, but he warmly encouraged Said's resistance to French designs. He was courteous and friendly to the Arabs of Zanzibar, but his opinion of them was not flattering. 'A miserable class', he thought them, proud, indolent, vicious, and deceitful. In the last sentence of his official report to the Bombay Government in 1855 he betrays his irritation with them. 'There are no people in the world from whom it is so difficult to get information as from Arabs: they have a religious dislike to talk of the past and they care little for the present and for the future nothing at all.' The more marked, therefore, is the tribute to Said which closed his earlier report of 1844. 'Never will His Highness' dominions be under the rule of so benevolent and considerate a prince or one who has so much

---
[1] Burton, *Lake Regions*, i. 68. Speke, *What led to the Discovery of the Source of the Nile*, 160, 187, 189, 195. Krapf, 121, 282, 430. Guillain, ii. 23–4.
[2] Burton, *Zanzibar*, i. 35.

endeavoured to fulfil the engagements he has entered into with European nations.'[1]

Said for his part had been quick to appreciate Hamerton's qualities and make friends with him. During his first dangerous illness in 1843 Said visited him every day for some weeks and stayed an hour or two at his side, though the sick man was often quite unconscious of his presence.[2] There was only one clouded period in all their years of intercourse—in the course of 1844 and 1845—and then the clouds were fabricated by personal intrigue. It will be remembered that in 1842 Said had complained of Hamerton's attitude towards him and that Cogan had backed the complaint at the Foreign Office.[3] Nothing had been done at that time; but two years later the story was again put about by Cogan that Said resented Hamerton's overbearing manners.[4] Asked to explain the charge, he replied that he was not aware of any discourtesy; and he suggested that the attack on him was due to the annoyance of influential Arabs at his interference with their illegal attempts to extort money from 'banyans' at the coast-ports and with the stoppage of the commissions they had been accustomed to obtain from the Slave Trade.[5] That he was not really unpopular with the Imam was evident, he suggested, from the fact that Said had frankly told him that he was constantly hearing complaints about him. Hamerton significantly added that Captain Cogan professed to be 'in the full confidence of Her Majesty's ministers'.[6] This should have stopped the intrigue, but it persisted. In the autumn of 1846 Hamerton felt impelled to warn the Foreign Office of the influence which self-seeking Europeans at Zanzibar were able to exercise on Said.

'Doubts on many subjects are continually engendered in the mind of the Imam by being told to His Highness' authorities by European adventurers who are constantly arriving at Zanzibar and who are attracted by the instances related of the Imam's munificence and generosity. Such people generally become the *protégés* of one or other

---

[1] Guillain, ii. 22. Hamerton's *Reports* of 1844 and 1855. For Hamerton on the Arabs see also p. 484, above. [2] Crofton, 10.
[3] See p. 511, above. [4] Cogan's memo., F.O. 54. 6.
[5] See pp. 485–6, above. [6] H. to A. 24.iii.45 (F.O. 54. 7).

of the principal people about the Imam to whom they represent themselves as men of influence in their own country and of great wisdom in all. Questions of doubt are referred to their opinions which are told to the Imam, and in this absurd way the most astounding and childish reports are circulated which after a short time pass for truths. There are several such persons about His Highness at present—miners, sugar-makers, men skilled in finding long-concealed treasures, French and English writers. It is truly distressing to see a prince with the endowments the Almighty has given him so easily cajoled and imposed upon.'[1]

This time Hamerton mentions no names; but it was early in 1847 that the agitation conducted by Cogan's associates, Messrs. Peters & Pollock, for commercial advantages on the coast, was quashed by Hamerton's opposition, and it was Cogan's representations or misrepresentations that had induced the Foreign Office to go farther in 1846 than it had been willing to go in 1842. The India Board was persuaded to ask for Hamerton's removal. But the Bombay Government was jealous, and, as events had shown, not unreasonably jealous, of interference from home in its management of British relations with Zanzibar. It informed Hamerton of the charge that he was not *persona grata* with Said and invited his comment thereon. Whether Hamerton was aware of Cogan's machinations or not, he made no reference to him in his reply. He told Bombay as he had previously told Whitehall that, if he was unpopular, it must be because he had exposed the corrupt practices of Said's officials, who had consequently complained about him to their master. That was enough for the Bombay Government. It informed the Secret Committee that it was unable to find a fit successor to Hamerton and proposed to keep him at his post.[2]

So the incident was closed; and the clouds, if clouds they really were, soon rolled away. There are frequent references in Hamerton's dispatches to Said's friendliness. After his serious illness in the spring of 1849, for instance, he writes: 'It is impossible for me to express my sense of gratitude for the extra-

[1] H. to A. 24.ix.46 (F.O. 54. 10).
[2] Cogan's representations: ibid. Secret Committee to G. of B. 10.ii.46; G. of B. to Secret Committee, 26.viii.46 (ibid.).

ordinary kindness I have received during my illness from His Highness the Imam. He almost constantly visited me or sent some of his family to see me.' In the following year, when Hamerton was again very ill, Said 'behaved in the kindest possible way'. When Hamerton had to go to Muscat or to the African coast, Said always put one of his ships, the *Artemeise*, at his disposal: it was known, indeed, as 'the Consul's yacht'. In the winter of 1852–3 he sailed in it from Muscat to Bombay and thence back to Zanzibar. 'His Highness came down to the beach accompanied by all his sons and the principal Arabs of the place and embraced me.' The moving scene in 1854 when Said, on the eve of his departure for Muscat, begged Hamerton to stay in Zanzibar and committed his son—and virtually the government —to his charge has already been described.[1]

In its obituary notice of Hamerton the *Bombay Gazette* referred to his intimate relations with Said.

It is not at all unlikely that to his influence with that prince we may in some degree owe the warm friendship and faithful alliance of the latter.... It is at all events improbable that the noted partiality of the Imam for all things English would have survived an intercourse of many years with an unworthy representative of the nation.[2]

It is remarkable that British interests at Muscat and Zanzibar for nearly a hundred years should have been represented by an almost unbroken series of able and high-minded men—Seton, Hamerton, Rigby, and, not least, John Kirk. And in the light of what has appeared in previous chapters of this book and of what will appear in another volume now in preparation, there can be no question that in serving British interests each of those four was serving also the interests of the Arab ruler to whose court he was attached.[3]

[1] F.O. 54. 14. Crofton, 20, 21, 23. See p. 454, above.
[2] *Bombay Gazette*, 20.viii.57, quoted by Crofton, 36.
[3] Among Hamerton's many duties one of the most delicate, as it happened, was the presentation of the gifts made to Said by British sovereigns. They were not very happily chosen. The *Prince Regent*, presented by William IV by way of return for the *Liverpool* (see p. 479 above), was a handsome steam yacht, but, as Palmerston once minuted, it was 'perfectly useless to the Imam', who passed it on in 1840, with per

The End of an Epoch

2

Said's presence at Muscat in 1854 was overdue, though it is doubtful whether he could have averted the last of the recurrent blows which in the course of his long reign were dealt at his Arabian dominions by the fierce puritans of the desert. In 1853 the Wahabi once more invaded Oman, led by Abdulla, son of the Emir Feisal. Baraimi was reoccupied. The Omani chiefs were summoned to pay allegiance to the Emir. Thwain, Said's regent at Muscat, was bidden to surrender the fortress of Sohar. Faced with his old foe, Thwain turned to his old friends. He besought the intervention of Captain Kemball, Resident in the Persian Gulf, who sailed at once for the Pirate Coast in the cruiser *Clive* and persuaded Abdulla to be content with the raising of the annual tribute to 12,000 dollars together with the payment of arrears to the amount of 6,000 dollars. Thwain perforce acquiesced. By the end of 1853 there was peace again; but a Wahabi garrison remained at Baraimi.[1]

Said arrived in time to deal in person with the next storm, which blew up from the opposite quarter. In the course of 1854 the Persians suddenly expelled the Omani Governor and his garrison from Bunder Abbas. That prosperous port, it will be

mission, to the Governor-General of India (F.O. 54. 11: cf. Burton, *Zanzibar*, i. 268). In 1842 Queen Victoria sent out a state carriage and harness, which Said asked in 1851 to be allowed to give to the Nizam of Hyderabad. 'The Imam has never made any use of it', wrote Hamerton; 'indeed he could not as there are no roads of any description whereon he could use it in this island.' Said had had it taken out to look at once and then had it repacked (F.O. 54. 14). Finally, in 1844, the Queen ordered a silver-gilt tea-service to be sent to Said. Forewarned of its coming, Hamerton assumed that a large case which arrived early in 1845, 'to be taken the greatest care of', contained the precious gift; and he took it to the palace and opened it in Said's presence. Unfortunately it was not the tea-service which emerged, but a tombstone. 'His Highness took this affair in the highest good-humour' (F.O. 54. 6 and 7). When the tea-service did arrive, Said had just been dealing with Wahabi demands for 'tribute' and had pleaded poverty: so, though he 'examined every article minutely and appeared exceedingly well pleased', he asked Hamerton to keep the service at the Consulate till the 'Northern Arabs' had finished their annual visit to Zanzibar and sailed away home (F.O. 54. 10). It is not recorded whether Said ever drank tea.

[1] Miles, 350.

remembered, had been leased to the Imam of Muscat before the end of the eighteenth century; and long occupation had accustomed the Omani to regard it as virtually their own. In the Treaty of 1798, indeed, Seyyid Sultan had granted to the British the right to maintain a 'factory' there and troops for its protection.[1] Prestige and the commercial advantage of retaining so valuable a trading-post alike required vigorous action on Said's part to counter the Persian move. He sent a strong force to Bunder, Abbas under Thwain and himself blockaded it by sea. But these his last military operations were no more fortunate than their predecessors. Persian reinforcements from Shiraz drove Thwain from the town, and the blockade was effectually broken. Once more Said asked for British help, but this time it was refused. British relations with Persia were then acutely strained: and it seemed more important at the moment to prevent or to postpone their actual rupture than to uphold Said's claims. If the British Government, indeed, had wanted to fight, it had a good enough excuse of its own, since the Persians had destroyed the British 'factory'. As it was, it did nothing for Said. It even discouraged the lesser Arab chiefs in the vicinity from helping him. So, in the spring of 1856, Said was forced to accept a humiliating settlement. The lease was renewed, but only for twenty years. The annual rental was doubled. And Said's Governor was not only to hold his office subject to Persian approval but would be required to exclude 'the agents of any foreign government' from the town and to protect the coast from attack by enemies of Persia.[2]

3

The business of Bunder Abbas had taken far more time than Said had expected. When he left Zanzibar in April 1854 it was understood that he intended to return in the following November. A year went by, and he was expected, so Hamerton wrote to Bombay, in mid-winter 1855–6.[3] But it was not till the next

[1] See p. 95, above.
[2] Miles, 351–2. Said-Ruete, 87–9. Text of Treaty, Badger, xciv, footnote. [3] Crofton, 25.

autumn that Said could escape at last from Oman and set sail for the Happy Island which, for many years now, he had regarded as his real home.

On September 15, 1856, he left Muscat in the frigate *Queen Victoria*. He seems to have had a presentiment that this was to be his last voyage and that he might not even live to complete it.

'He took a final leave of his aged mother and said he felt confident he would see her no more, and, what is exceedingly strange, he had a number of planks prepared at Muscat which he took on board with him, and gave orders that in the event of any one dying on board his frigate a coffin should be made and the body of whoever might die on the voyage should be placed therein and conveyed to Zanzibar, but under no circumstances should the burial take place at sea.'[1]

The *Queen Victoria* put in at Sur and then sailed south on a curving course for Zanzibar. She was not far out when on September 18 Said was taken ill. He grew steadily worse as, week after week, the ship ploughed slowly through the hot Arabian Sea. On October 13 dysentery set in. His one desire now was to reach Zanzibar alive, but the voyage was little more than half over when he began to sink. In delirium or semi-consciousness he kept calling again and again for Hamerton. On the morning of October 19, while passing an outlying island of the Seychelles group, he died.[2]

The *Queen Victoria* and her consorts arrived off Zanzibar at dusk on October 25 and anchored some five miles from the town. It was not till the next morning that the people, gathered on the water-front to welcome Said home, observed that the ships were dressed in mourning. Meantime, in the middle of the night, Barghash, who, as has been mentioned, had accompanied his father to Muscat, had secretly brought the coffin ashore and buried it near the palace beside the body of Khalid. There followed both at Muscat and at Zanzibar a period of tension such as often occurs on the death of an Arab ruler whose throne is not inherited by right of primogeniture. At Muscat Thwain

[1] H. to G. of B. 8.xi.56: quoted by Crofton, 26.
[2] Hamerton's account, as cited in previous note. Burton (*Zanzibar*, i. 315) repeats the characteristic story current at Zanzibar, that Said only wanted to tell Hamerton where his wealth was hidden.

forestalled any attempt by either of his two brothers who were then in Oman to set aside Said's dispensation by concealing his death from them till he had warned his officers throughout the country to stand on guard. When the news was published, says the Arab chronicler, 'it caused such a wailing throughout the town that the hills were almost shaken by it'.[1] At Zanzibar the situation was more dangerous: for Barghash, relying on the support of the el-Harthi and the pro-French party, was determined to make a bid for the throne, and it was he, not Majid, who for that one critical night knew the secret of Said's death. After burying the body he tried to get possession of the Fort, the only stronghold in Zanzibar, but the *jemadar* of the Baluchi garrison was suspicious, remembering perhaps what had happened two years before, and refused to admit him. For the rest of the night he was busy buying arms and trying to persuade his supporters to rise on his behalf. But, when morning came and Said's death was known, the mass of the people loyally observed his wish and acclaimed Majid as their ruler. Only the el-Harthi, the one tribe in Zanzibar that had never wholly bowed the knee to Said, were still ready to make trouble. They thought it wise, however, to consult the British Consul before taking action, and their wealthiest chief, Abdalla-bin-Salim, paid a visit to Hamerton and 'asked him what they should do, as the island was without a ruler'. Hamerton's reply was prompt and forcible. He told Abdalla that 'if he attempted to disturb the peace, his head would fall within twenty-four hours', and turned him out of the Consulate. A fortnight later Hamerton was able to report that 'all things here at present are quiet'. That the outbreak he had so firmly discountenanced might have been serious was demonstrated three years afterwards when the el-Harthi did revolt, headed by Barghash, and only the intervention of Hamerton's successor, Consul Rigby, and British naval forces kept Majid on his throne.[2]

[1] Badger, xcvi–xcvii.
[2] *Commission on the disputes between the Rulers of Muscat and Zanzibar*, 94. H. to Clarendon, 10.xi.56 (F.O. 54. 17). C. E. B. Russell, *General Rigby, Zanzibar, and the Slave Trade* (London, 1935), chap. vii.

The End of an Epoch

That was Hamerton's last service to the peace and integrity of Said's realm. For the next few months he was busily engaged in doing all he could to promote the success of Burton's and Speke's expedition. 'I have every reason to believe that I have succeeded in overcoming the old prejudices and fears which the people of this country have long entertained of foreigners penetrating into Africa.'[1] No later letters of Hamerton's have been preserved, and his last recorded act was to accompany the explorers to the coast. He died on July 5, 1857.

The words just quoted from Hamerton's last dispatch to Bombay seem rather startling when it is remembered that in 1841, when Hamerton first came to Zanzibar, he had warned Said of the danger to his realm involved in European contact with the coast, and that in 1847 he had foretold that European trade on the Mrima would mean the end of Said's authority there. If Burton and Speke had not been explorers only, if they had been traders or even, perhaps, missionaries, the old Consul might not have been so anxious to smooth their path into the interior. But, in fact, though he could not know it, those explorers were opening a new chapter in the history of East Africa. In another thirty years—not much more than half the length of Said's reign—the whole situation all along the coast and far inland was to be transformed. And in the process Hamerton's hopes and fears alike were to be realized—his hopes for the success of European exploration in East Africa, his fears for the survival of Said's East African 'dominions'.

Not many years were needed for tearing away the veil which had so long hidden the interior from European knowledge. By 1863 the old myth of one huge inland sea had taken scientific shape as a system of great lakes from Nyasa to Nyanza, and the source and course of the Nile were known. By 1873, when Livingstone died, he had penetrated beyond Lake Nyasa to the fringe of the Katanga plateau and beyond Lake Tanganyika to the upper waters of the Congo. It only remained to follow up other lines of access from the coast, especially the direct

[1] H. to G. of B. 26.xii.56, quoted by Crofton, 32.

route from Mombasa through the Masai country to Kampala, and the map of Mid-East Africa in its essential outline was made.

A few years more, and the new map had been engraved with the frontiers and coloured with the tints of European sovereignty. By 1891 Said's one-time realm had shrunk to the islands of Zanzibar and Pemba and a narrow strip of coast between Vanga and Kismayu, and even this remnant had become a British Protectorate, while all the rest of Said's 'dominions' had been 'partitioned' between Britain, Germany, and Italy.

Thus ended the epoch of Arab domination in East Africa which, broken only by the period of Portuguese conquest and control, had lasted in one form or another for about a thousand years. And thus began a new age of East African history—it might almost be said a new kind of East African history. For now at last it was to concern itself more closely with the East African people. The first European conquest had meant nothing to them except a change of masters; but the second European conquest meant a revolution in their lives far greater than anything that had ever happened in the past. Mixed though the motives were which prompted it, and mixed its good and ill effects on the East Africans, it had this one supreme result— it brought them out of the darkness into the life of the civilized world, a world in which, if indeed it was civilized, they would be treated no longer as a multifarious collection of 'living tools' for stronger and luckier folk to use, but as a people or group of peoples as much entitled as any other people to be given a chance of leading their own lives for their own ends.

INDEX

Abdallah-bin-Salim, chief of the El-Harthi, 554.
Abdul Aziz, Amir, 105.
Abdul Malik, Caliph, 22.
Abdulla, Emir of the Wahabi, 148.
Abdulla, son of Emir Feisal of the Wahabi, 551.
Abdullah, Governor of Zanzibar, 240, 268.
Abdullah, of Johanna Isl., 247.
Abdullah-bin-Ahmed, Sheikh, 220, 222–4.
Abdullah-bin-Salim, Governor of Tabora, 358.
Aberdares, mountains, 7.
Aberdeen, Lord, 413, 447–8, 450, 454, 474, 475, 489, 508, 510–16, 518, 522.
Abou-Zaid-Hassan, 29.
Aboukir, 99, 121.
Abu Zaid Hassan of Siraf, 22.
Abu'l Abbas, ruler of Bagdad, 32.
Abusheher, 96.
Abyssinia, 9, 10, 291, 300, 304, 387, 388, 408, 417, 457, 468; missionaries, 388; slaves from, 501, 516.
Abyssinie, the, 78.
Acre, 90.
Acts for Abolition of Slavery, *see* Slave-trade.
Adams, Newton, 375.
Adams, President, 372, 373.
Aden, 10, 15, 38, 43, 402, 425, 457, 461, 468, 480, 527, 534, 537, 540, 542; Covilhão at, 42; defies Portuguese attack, 47; British military post at, 99; British-Indian soldiers at, 100; annexed by the British (1839), 155, 417, 436, 446, 450, 465–7, 471, 478, 493; Blankett's squadron at (1799), 170; Kraft at, 388, 401; French trade of, 426; made a coal station, 464; British ship plundered at (1837), 465.
Adowa, 388.
Aethiopia, 17, 31.
Afghans, the, 120, 127.
African Association, 156, 387.

Afrika, the, 383.
Ahmed-bin-Said, Omani ruler, 69, 89, 108, 217, 220, 257.
Ahmed-bin-Seif, Governor of Zanzibar, 255.
Al Hassa district, 461.
al-Idrisi, his map, 24, 36.
Al Kabith, Persian adventurer, 32.
Alaska, 362.
Albatross, sloop, 227.
Albuquerque, Affonso d', 31, 43, 45–7, 52, 464.
Albusaid dynasty, 69, 107, 257.
Aleppo, 441.
Alexandria: Napoleon at, 88, 93, 94, 99, 100; British agent appointed at, 92; French service from Marseilles to, 462.
Algiers, French occupation of (1830), 280, 460.
Ali, son of Hassan, 23.
Ali-bin-Nasir, Governor of Mombasa, 391, 392; sent as Said's envoy to London, 332, 339, 389, 447, 448, 480, 508–13, 522.
Ali-bin-Othman, of Mombasa, 217–18.
Aligarh, 105.
Allawah, Sultan of Johanna (1812), 173.
Allen, Captain, 430, 431, 444.
Almeida, de, Governor of Mozambique, 117.
Almeida, Francisco de, in East Africa, 43–5.
Almeida, Pedro de, 66.
Alph, the, 382.
Amani Institute, 395.
Ambergris, 19, 36, 62.
Amboyna Island, 97, 140.
America, Columbus in, 41; trade with E. Africa, 117, 213, 408, 411, 421, 423, 426, 474, 486, 487, 491, 492; and slave-trade, 160, 187, 287, 364, 430, 498; Said's best market, 315; early shipping trade with the East, 362–81; Anglo-American conflict (1812–15), 363; suggested colony in E. Africa, 372–6; emigration to, 384; no desire

558 INDEX

for colonial expansion in East Africa, 456; consul appointed for Zanzibar, 482; traders in guano, 537.
America, South, 365, 382; British commercial exploitation in, 154; African slaves sent to, 172, 364, 494; emigration to, 154, 384; slave-trade, 189.
American Board of Commissioners for Foreign Missions, 374.
American flag, dispute with Said over saluting, 381.
American trade in Indian Ocean, 362, 364, 367, 370, 373, 376.
American War of Independence, 54, 77, 91, 154, 157, 362, 380, 381.
American whaling ships, 364, 375, 376.
Americans: founded a mission in W. Africa, 402; at Delagoa Bay (1835), 472; favoured at Zanzibar, 477, 478.
Anaiza, 461.
Anatolia, 108, 460.
Anaya, Petro d', 44.
Angoche, 27, 226.
Angola, 77, 157.
Anjouam Island, French occupation of, 445.
Ann, the, 365, 366.
Anne, the, 489, 490.
Antananarivo, 281, 282.
Antilles, French, 433.
Antimony mines, 490.
Antioch, 462.
Arabia, Hamites of, 10; slaves in, 31, 500; trade of, 36, 103, 299, 316, 370, 379; Portuguese ejected from, 65; and Napoleonic wars, 71; Owen's policy for, 285; Mahomet Ali in, 461, 463, 470.
Arabia, South-West, Said's authority over, 437.
Arabia Felix, 111.
Arabian Nights, 32.
Arabic language, 23, 31, 78, 234, 245, 328, 336, 389, 424, 507.
Arabs: colonization of, 15–40; importance of their traders (6th–16th cent.), 18–20; and spread of Islam, 22; settlers in E. Africa, 22, 24–30; slave-trade of, 31–6,

203–8, 215, 216, 431–4; revolt against Portuguese, 57–9; immigration of 'Northern Arabs' to Zanzibar, 168; conflict between those of Africa and Oman, 217; disputes over succession to the throne, 292, 553, 554; invasion of interior of Africa by, 305–12; migrant habits of, 297, 311, 319, 322, 335, 343, 357, 358, 360; schools for, 389; attitude of their traders to missionaries, 410, 411; and French traders, 421; Hamerton's opinion of, 484, 547; character of, 485.
Archangel, 382.
Ariadne, H.M.S., 239, 241.
Arland, Captain, 267, 269, 270.
Arnold, ship's surgeon, 55.
Artemeise, the, 550.
Ascension, the, 55.
Assaye, battle of (1803), 105.
Athi, river, 398.
Aubad Isle, bought by Britain, 468.
Augustines, 62, 63.
Ausan, state, 17.
Austerlitz, battle of, 120.
Australia, 154, 157, 526, 540.
Austria, 136, 387, 441.
Azd, tribe, 21, 22.
Aziz, Amir Abdul, assassinated, 105.

Bab-el-Mandeb Straits, 457, 465.
Bagamoyo, 5, 305, 306, 308, 314, 319, 353, 354.
Bagdad, 104, 105, 108, 461, 463; 'Lord of the Blacks', a negro of, 32; Rousseau French consul-general at, 85; Harford Jones consul at, 99; slave-market at, 500.
Bagdad, University of, 39.
Bahrein Isl., 222, 461; and the French, 102; Said's attack on, 276, 278; Said's desire to annex, 276, 470, 475, 476, 509, 510, 512, 516; taken by British, 463.
Baird, General Sir David, 99, 104.
Bakari, Fumo, 338.
Baldwin, George, consul-general in Egypt, 91–2.

INDEX 559

Baltic ports, 382.
Baluchis, Said's troops, 274, 282, 297, 307, 319, 327, 331, 334, 338, 352, 355, 356, 409, 456, 554.
Bambetoke, 79, 164, 170, 364.
Bananas, 181, 394.
Banks, Sir Joseph, 156.
Bantu language, 11.
Bantu tribes, 10–11, 50, 335.
Banyans: position of in Zanzibar, 182–3, 300–3, 315, 351, 359, 378, 477, 548; ill treatment of, 249–50, 302; at Mombasa, 267; missionaries and, 389; number of in E. Africa, 484; under British consul's protection, 485, 486.
Baraimi, Wahabi at, 105, 144–5, 474, 551; Mutlak advances on Muscat from, 148; Egyptians at, 470.
Barawa, 343, 366, 439, 451, 487; foundation of, 23, 25; Portuguese conquest of, 31, 38, 46, 47, 59, 61; mentioned by Linschoten, 54; Mirale Bey at, 58; Blankett's squadron at, 165, 169; mentioned by Prior (1812), 176; and slave-trade, 178, 180; Smee's account of (1811), 179; attacked by Abdullah-bin-Ahmed, 220; acknowledges Said's sovereignty, 221, 336, 337; Owen at, 234, 251, 252; description of, 330.
Baraza, 323, 326.
Barbak Shah, 33.
Barbosa, Duarte, 29, 36, 38, 329.
Barghash, younger son of Said, intrigues against his father, 456; tries to take the throne at Said's death, 553, 554.
Barlow, Sir George, 114, 115, 119, 126.
Barracoons, 227, 496, 498, 520.
Barracouta, H.M.S., British brig, 224, 226, 249–52, 254, 287, 427.
Barreto, Francisco, 50.
Barros, 42.
Barth, H., 387.
Basel Missionary College, 388.
Basra, 22, 85, 87, 461–3; capture of, 32; French consulate at, 53; the

English in, 54, 84; slave-trade at, 517.
Bassain, 67.
Batavia, 97, 101, 141.
Bates, Mr., American agent at Majunga, 365.
Bathurst, Lord, colonial secretary, 213, 216, 229, 240, 243, 245, 256, 261–3, 265, 266; and slave-trade, 190, 196; and Owen's protectorate, 262.
Batineh, the, 105, 145, 277, 474, 475.
Battuta, Ibn, 226, 329.
Bauzan, M., 425.
Baylen, 136.
Beads, 30, 36, 163, 307, 309, 310, 316, 317, 359, 383, 490, 509.
Beauchamp, M., French consul at Muscat, 88, 89.
Beaver, 222, 228; and Bulama expedition, 158; and expedition of the *Nisus* to Johanna, &c., 171–8.
Bedouin, 106.
Bedr-bin-Seif, ruler of Muscat, 108, 110, 274.
Beeswax, 182, 366, 443.
Bega, King, 345.
Beke, C. T., 473.
Belligny, M. de, French consul at Zanzibar, 414, 425, 453, 547; his unfortunate conversation with Krapf, 415–17.
Bengal, 32, 33, 74, 88, 115, 124, 205, 465; and slave-trade, 204, 206, 208.
Beni Bu Ali, tribe, 150–1.
Benia, Wat, 324.
Bérard, M., 425.
Berbera, 467, 510.
Berceau, the, 424.
Berenike, 16.
Berlin Missionary Society, 387.
Bertram, John, and Co., of Salem, 376–8, 381, 487.
Beyrouth, 441.
Bialloblotzky, Dr., 473, 474.
Birmingham, 480.
Bissell, Austin, Lieutenant of the *Daedalus*, 161, 163–70, 228, 421.
Black Warrior, the, 376.
Blankett, John, Commodore, 173, 179, 222; his squadron in E. African waters, 162–7, 342, 343.

INDEX

Blumhardt, missionary, 388.
Boger, Philip, boatswain of the *Leopard*, 166.
Bogle, Surgeon, British resident at Muscat, 97, 98, 103.
Bohora sect, 302.
Bombay, the English in, 54, 74, 91, 99, 127, 142, 147, 148, 149, 222, 225, 260, 277; and Napoleon, 101, 124; Said's request to for protection against French, 112, 113; Smee sails from, 178, 179; and slave-trade, 203, 206, 207, 289, 500; Captain Owen at, 227, 231, 233, 236; Moslems from, at Zanzibar, 302; trade with, 316, 363, 370, 380, 425; resents Whitehall's action regarding Kuria Muria Islands, 534.
Bombay, the, 218.
Bookeen, *see* Nossi-bé.
Boston, early shipping trade with the East, 362, 363, 367, 376.
Botany Bay, 157.
Boteler, Lieutenant T., 220, 224–8, 236, 249, 329, 333, 343.
Boulogne, 125.
Bourbon, 237, 279, 353, 438, 440, 441, 457, 474, 528; occupied by the French, 53; population of, 74; decline of importance of, 75, 436; and slave-trade, 80, 82, 191–4, 199–201, 210, 280, 366, 427; British capture of (1810), 140, 189; restored to the French (1814), 141, 155, 421; cloves first planted in, 314; Said's trade with, 318; and Maizan incident 354; French trade at, 425, 437; and labour problem, 428–33; name changed to Réunion (1848), 434; and Nossi-bé, 443–5.
Bouvet, 140.
Brandy, 80, 163.
Brazil, 70, 73, 189, 364, 495.
Bremen, 382, 385.
Brest, 77, 101.
Britain: first invasion of E. Africa, 52, 54, 56; activities in Indian Ocean, 73–107, 189, 191, 221, 222, 256, 285, 286, 436; French damage to shipping of, 106, 140; and Mozambique, 117, 333; colonies, and slave-trade, 203–8, 291, 361, 381, 430; Said's trade to ports of, 318; her cotton goods superseded by American, 379; value of trade with Zanzibar, 426, 492; and coolie labour, 433; direct trade with Zanzibar, 479, 486–93; *see also* Treaties.
British Guiana, 429, 430.
Brookhouse, R., 378.
Broquant, M., French consul at Zanzibar, 353, 355, 424–6, 547.
Brown, George, acting-Governor of Bombay, 147, 148.
Bruce, British resident at Bushire, 149, 213.
Bruce, James, 90.
Brucks, Captain, 208, 299, 300, 302, 316, 317, 463.
Brydges, Sir Harford Jones, *see* Jones, Harford.
Buga, King, 345.
Buganda, 307.
Bulama, attempted colonization of, 154, 157–8, 171, 175, 287.
Bulwer, Lytton, 444.
Bunce, W. C., British representative at Muscat, 143, 149.
Bunder Abbas (Gombroon), 95, 132, 293; proposed British occupation of, 96; danger of French at, 128, 129; treaty with Seton (1806), 143, 509; Said's request for British help at refused, 531, 551, 552.
Bunyoro, 307.
Buonaparte, Joseph, king of Spain, 136.
Buonaparte, Napoleon: his letter to Sultan-bin-Ahmed, 89; in Egypt, 86, 90, 93–7; designs on India, 100, 120, 162; further designs on the East, 101–4, 106, 116, 120–2, 125–34, 448; and the Peninsular War, 124, 135, 136; end of his dream of oriental conquest, 137–42, 154, 470.
Burckhardt, J. L., 387.
Burgash, Sultan, 23.
Burgenej, 305.
Burka, Wahabi garrison at, 109.
Burke, Edmund, 126, 171.
Burton, R. F., his expedition to E. Africa, 215, 305–11, 332, 333,

INDEX

339, 350, 354, 408, 425, 526, 546, 547, 555.
Bushire, East India Co. at, 54, 84; British resident at, 95, 277, 469, 470, 500; and Malcolm's mission, 131, 132; slave-trade at, 517.
Bussora, 96, 143; slave-market at, 500.
Buxton, T. F., 196, 197, 287-91, 417.
Buyeni, 352.

Cabreira, Francisco de Seixas de, commandant at Mombasa, 65, 66.
Cabul, British mission to, 127.
Cairo, 39, 462, 463, 470; Covilhão at, 42; George Baldwin in, 92-3; as centre of French action against the British, 87-8; British consulate abolished, 92; advance of British force on (1801), 99; slave-supply of, 500.
Calabar, British missionaries at, 156.
Calcutta, the English in, 54, 91; Malcolm's visits to 97; Napoleon's designs on, 101; British ships sold at, 107; and slave-trade, 203, 204, 206, 257; Said's trade with, 315, 370; Salem merchants at, 363; American ship at, 372; and missionaries, 417; steamship service to Suez from, 465.
Calcutta Journal, The, 204.
Caledon, Lord, Governor of the Cape, 192, 317.
Calicut, Arab trading settlement at, 19; Covilhão at, 42; da Gama at, 42.
Cambay, 36, 38, 39, 215, 502.
Cameron, Sir Donald, 350.
Cameroons, the, 10.
Campbell, Rear-Admiral, 374.
Campbell, P., consul-general at Cairo, 463.
Canada, 154.
Canning, George, 445, 464.
Cannstätt, 393.
Canot, Théodore, slave-trader, 193.
Canton, 19, 362, 363.
Cape Colony, 161, 163, 171, 190, 227, 266, 317; captured by British, 155, 373, 438; Moravian Brethren at, 387.

Cape of Good Hope, 52, 140, 188-92, 216, 226, 362, 364, 365, 373-5, 382, 427, 448, 462; British seizure of, 101, 459; Cavaignac at, 103.
'Cape-to-Cairo' railway, 409.
Capetown, 100, 227, 229, 263, 264, 372, 430; and slave-trade, 190, 196; Owen at, 227.
Caroline, the, Omani frigate, 149.
Castlereagh, Lord, 94, 193.
Caucasus, 121, 460.
Cavaignac, M. de, 110, 117, 422, 452; official mission to Muscat (1802), 103-6.
Cayenne, 314.
Ceylon, 18, 53, 73, 97, 99, 100, 370, 541; captured by British (1795), 56, 100, 101, 155, 171; French attack on Muscat ships off, 110, 112; and the slave-trade, 196, 205.
Chagga country, 344, 353, 392, 393, 396, 398, 402.
Chan ju k'ua, 20.
Chandernagore, 53, 154, 436.
Charles et George, the, seized (1858), 435.
Chichester, Lord, 412.
China, 155, 362, 363, 378, 379, 382; first connexions with E. Africa, 18-20, 37; African slaves in, 33-4; Said's trade to, 315, 318.
China, imported, 182.
Chole Island, 383.
Christian, Commodore, 263-9, 427.
Christie, J., 325.
Christopher, Lieutenant, 302, 331, 332, 335, 366, 343, 433, 480, 487.
Chronicles of Kilwa, The, 29.
Chumbi, 346, 348.
Church Missionary Society, 387, 390, 399, 401, 408, 409, 412, 413, 417.
Clapham Sect, 204.
Clarendon, Lord, 414, 416, 525, 527, 530, 531, 532, 533, 534, 537, 538.
Clive, Lord, 54.
Clive, the, 551.
Cloth, 36, 171, 182, 307, 309, 310, 316, 365, 509; *see also* merikani.
Cloves, 313-16, 318, 319, 322, 383, 425, 484, 490.

INDEX

Coaling stations, 464, 527, 528, 532, 534.
Coates, Dandeson, 388.
Cochet, M., French consul at Zanzibar, 425.
Cochin China, 298, 363, 367.
Coconuts, 16, 36, 173, 304, 314, 490.
Coffee, 228, 365, 366, 404, 425.
Coffrees, 203.
Cogan, Captain Robert, 492, 500, 502; sent to negotiate a treaty with Said, 375, 481, 483, 496; accompanies Ali-bin-Nasir to London (1838), 480; his firm at Zanzibar, 488, 489, 491; dislike of Hamerton, 506, 510, 511, 548, 549.
Coghlan, Col. W., resident at Aden, 536, 540–2.
Cole, Sir Lowry, Governor of Mauritius, 227, 238, 240–2, 251, 256, 262–6, 272; and cession of Mombasa, 243–6.
Colombo, 75.
Columbus, Christopher, 41.
Colville, Sir Charles, 428.
Comoro Islands, 26, 163, 191, 439, 445, 446; settlement of, 23, 25; escaped Portuguese conquest, 47; Sir James Lancaster in, 54; Sharpeigh at, 55; and E.I. Co., 79; and slave-trade, 201, 447; Owen at, 227, 228; consul suggested for, 448; all in French hands, 449; free labourers of, 489.
Concan, the, 301.
Congo, river, 6, 306, 556.
Conseil Général des Communes, suppression of, 196.
Constantinople, 89, 92, 108, 121, 148, 460, 503.
Cooley, W. D., 393.
Coolie labour, 429, 430, 433, 540, 542.
Copal, *see* Gum-Copal.
Copper, 20, 383.
Copra, 304.
Cordelia, H.M.S.S., 539, 540, 543.
Cordova, 39.
Cornelis, 141.
Cornwallis, Lord, 114.
Coromandel coast, 124.

Corrientes, Cape, 25.
Corunna, 136.
Cossigny, M. de, 76–84, 161, 437.
Cotton, 20, 36, 316, 228, 365, 379, 380, 486, 490, 509; *see also* merikani.
Cotton factories, 73.
Covilhão, João Pires de, 42, 52.
Cowie, C. G., 525.
Cowley, Lord, 450, 451.
Cowries, 382, 383.
Cradock, Sir John, Governor of Cape Colony, 171, 173.
Crofton, R. H., 324.
Cuba, 189, 365.
Currency, 302, 304, 310, 317, 451.
Cutch, 182, 267, 301, 302, 315, 500, 501, 504.

Da Cunha, Tristão, 31, 46.
Da Cunha, Nuno, 57.
Da Gama, Vasco, 26, 37–9, 42–4, 52, 175, 330.
Da Silveira, Gonzalo, Jesuit missionary, 51.
Daedalus, the, 162–3, 166, 167.
Daendals, Marshal, 101, 141.
Dalhousie, Lord, 413, 417.
Dallons, M., first French consul at Muscat, 118, 119, 422.
Dalrymple, H., 157.
Damji, Ludha, 325.
Darayyah, 148.
Dar-es-Salaam, 5, 6, 305.
Darling, General, 196, 200.
Dates, 168, 182, 316, 366.
de Hill, Admiral, Governor of Bourbon, 438, 440, 457.
de Rosily, 86, 87, 96.
de Seixas, 224.
Decaen, General, Napoleon's Captain-General of the East, 101; at Port Louis, 102, 122, 123, 137, 138; dealings with Said, 110–12, 120; treaties with Said (1807–8), 116–19, 124, 125, 133; lack of substantial achievement in Madagascar, 124; re-establishes French influence in Muscat, 124; defeated at Port Louis (1810), 140.
Decaen, René, 125.
Deccan, the, 33, 501.
Decrès, French minister of Marine, 102, 125, 135, 137.

INDEX

Degelamhora, 354, 356.
Delagoa Bay, 5, 361; Portuguese at, 51, 52; Captain Owen at, 226–9, 240; and Americans, 364, 373, 374, 472.
Deland, T., 378.
Delgado, Cape, 25, 41, 52, 61, 62, 67, 70, 162, 215, 230, 329, 333, 341, 399, 434, 437, 454, 472, 502, 504, 510, 517, 520.
Delhi, 33, 105, 204.
Derendingen, 387.
Dessolles, Marquis, 193.
Diaz, 41, 42, 52.
Diu, 47, 67, 501.
Diu Head, 215, 502.
Diwans, 351, 354.
Dixon, C. W., 205.
Dixon, Messrs. William, 543.
Djibouti, 468.
Dofa, 346.
Dominican missions, 51–2, 62.
Dost Muhammad, Russian alliance with (1839), 460.
Drake, Sir Francis, 52.
Drugs, 309, 377, 479.
Ducombez, merchant of Île de France, 118.
Ducouëdic, the, 355, 451.
Duncan, Jonathan, Governor of Bombay, 111–13, 130, 133, 143, 147, 157.
Dundas, Henry, Visc. Melville, 92, 94.
Dupleix, Joseph François, 74.
Dupont, General, 136.
Durban, 364.
Durbar, held daily in Zanzibar, 323.
Duruma tribe, 490.
Dutch, colonial expansion of, 52–4, 56, 65, 101, 161; and slave-trade, 73, 172; and French rivalry at Kilwa, 77; at Mozambique, 117.

East India Company (British): first establishment of, 52, 73, 84, 127, 256, 462, 534, 547; in Egypt, 92; and Wellesley, 93–6; treaty with Muscat (1798), 95–6; at Muscat, 98, 112, 119, 202; French capture ships of, 140; Jawasmi treaty binding them to respect, 142, 143; protests against monopoly of in the East (1792), 160–1; and slave-trade, 205–6, 214, 215, 515; Americans undersell, 362; hostile attitude to missionaries, 413; and Said, 506.
East India Company (Dutch), 52.
East India Company (French), 73, 76, 79.
East Indies, *see* Indies, East.
Earthenware, 182, 486, 490.
Ebro, river, 136.
Education, native, 409, 419.
Edward Bonaventure, the, 55.
Egypt, 22, 108, 299; slaves sent to, 31, 500; Mamelukes in, 33; cloth exported to, 36; Napoleon's campaign, 71, 86–90; British interest in, 90, 91, 92, 93; Egyptians in Medina, 147; Said's trade with, 315; missionaries to, 388; army of occupation, 441; French interest in, 460–3; independence of secured by Mahomet Ali, 461; *see also* Mahomet Ali.
El-Harthi tribe, 23, 217, 296, 322, 324, 455, 554.
El Hasa, seven brothers of, 22.
Elephants and tusks, 19, 20, 223, 307, 310, 366; *see also* Ivory.
Eliot, Sir Charles, 12.
Elliott, Sir Gilbert, *see* Minto.
Elphinstone, John, Governor of Bombay, 534, 537, 542.
Elphinstone, Mountstuart, and slave-trade, 210, 212, 213; his replies to Mazrui appeals, 223, 224; and Owen's protectorate, 231, 252, 260–1, 266; Cole's note to, on cession of Mombasa, 246.
Emancipation Acts, *see* Slave-trade.
Emancipators' colony, at Sierra Leone, 159.
Emery, Midshipman, 249; commandant at Mombasa, 263, 265, 267–70, 389, 390.
Emigration System, Free Labour, 432–5.
Emmerton, E., 378.
England, *see* Britain.
English Point, 249, 250, 417.

INDEX

Enterprize, the, 462.
Erhardt, J. J., missionary, 352, 399, 401, 406, 407, 414–16; first arrival of, 397; his map, 408.
Erythraean Sea, 16.
Escurial, 86.
Estaing, Comte d', 85.
Eugambo, river, 394.
Euphrates, river, 32, 94, 121, 461, 462.
Eylau, battle of, 120.

Falmouth, 462.
Far East, 154, 155, 315, 367, 376.
Farquhar, Sir Robert, Governor of Mauritius, 141, 239, 428; and slave-trade, 195–8, 202–16; accused of intrigue by the French, 199.
Fars, 132, 146, 503.
Fartak, 464.
Fath Shah, 32, 33.
Favorite, the, slave-ship, 193.
Faza, 58, 62, 65, 68, 252, 338, 339; destroyed by Portuguese, 59; capture of, by Sultan-bin-Seif, 66; Captain Owen at, 253.
Feisal, Emir, 475, 551.
Ferguson, Lieutenant, 320.
Fernando Po, 288.
Fez, 39.
Fezzan, 179.
Fillmore, President of U.S.A., 381.
Finkenstein, Napoleon at, 120, 122, 131.
Fitch, Ralph, 52.
Flints, 199, 383.
Flushing, 125.
Forbes, Captain, 365.
Forbes, Sir Charles, 511.
Fire-arms, 80, 163, 171, 345; *see also* Muskets; Powder.
Firuz, Saif-ud-din-, 33.
Fort Dauphin, 123, 280.
Fort Hall, 404.
Fort Jesus, *see* Mombasa.
Fort William, Presidency of, 206.
Foulpointe, 123.
France: colonial expansion in E. Africa, 53, 56, 160, 161, 381, 415, 436; in the Indian Ocean, 73–107; attitude to slave-trade, 80, 82, 83, 174, 186, 193, 194, 202, 213, 366, 427, 428, 494, 498, 522, 523; Franco-Persian alliance, 87; many agents in the East, 121; Roman Catholic missionaries from, 198; July Revolution (1830), 280, 428; sesamum from Zanzibar exported to, 316; and Queen Ranavolana, 333; cotton trade of, 380; consulate at Zanzibar, 414, 422, 426; Arabs favour traders of, 421, 478; value of trade with Zanzibar, 426, 492; warships guard slave-vessels, 434; interest in Africa confined to trade, 437; occupation of Nossi-bé Island, 438–48; befriends Mahomet Ali, 460–3; activity in India, 462; trade with Zanzibar declines, 491; *see also* French *and* Treaties.
Fraser, J. B., 153, 296, 301, 317, 319.
Fréjus, 90.
Fremantle, Captain, 526–30, 531, 544.
French, the: damage to British shipping by (1793–1804), 106; attacked by the Sakalava at Fort Dauphin, 280; give protection to Nossi-bé island, 334; force Said to take action against P'hazi Mazungere, 354–6; in Northern Africa, 388; and Maizan affair, 391; in W. Africa, 402; account of their settlement in E. Africa, 421–58; *see also* France.
French Islands in Indian Ocean, African slaves sent to, 172.
French ports, Said's trade to, 318.
'Fresh Water River', 168.
Friedland, battle of, 120, 121.
Friedrich Wilhelm, King, 401.
Fugomi, 394.
Fumo Bakari, 338.

Gabon, river, 402.
Galla, tribe, 10, 300, 388, 389–92, 397, 398, 419; character of, 342–4.
Galla-land, 398.

INDEX

Gambia, river, 6, 156, 157, 159, 256.
Gardane, General, 121, 122, 127, 131, 132, 138, 139, 460.
Gaur, 32, 33.
Geisinger, Captain, 298.
Geledi, 336.
George III, King, 173.
George IV, King, 264, 265, 268, 272.
Georgia, 132.
Gerlingen, 390.
German Confederation, North, 386.
German crowns, 299, 304, 318.
Germany: her cotton trade, 380; missionaries in E. Africa, 387-; overseas trade, 381, 411, 421; trade with Zanzibar, 382-6, 408, 426, 474, 486, 491; imperial policy, 384; consulate at Zanzibar, 386; no desire for colonial expansion, 456; value of trade with Zanzibar (1859), 492; *see also* Treaties.
Gholam, Mahomed, 130, 134.
Glass, imported, 17.
Glenelg, Lord, 287-9, 428, 466.
Goa, 47, 290; Covilhão at, 42; Portuguese at, 53, 58, 59, 64-6, 68, 76; Yussuf at, 63; Sultan Hassani invited to, 63; slaves from, 205.
Goats, 36, 366, 395.
Gold, 3, 19, 20, 26, 30, 36, 48, 50, 51, 67.
Gold Coast, the, 156, 159.
Gold-dust, 117, 171, 173, 189, 377, 479.
Gombroon, *see* Bunder Abbas.
Gondokoro, 387.
Good Hope, the, slave-ship, 160.
Goree, 157, 192, 458.
Grahamstown Journal, 375.
Grain, 223, 307, 366.
Grallert, Emil, German consul at Zanzibar, 386.
Granada, capture of, 41.
Grant, Aldin, 375, 408.
Grant, Charles, of the Clapham Sect, 204.
Grant, Sir Robert, Governor of Bombay, 466.
Granville, Lord, ambassador in Paris, 441, 442, 444, 450.

Great Lakes, 28, 300, 305, 307, 309.
Great Rift Valley, 7.
Greece, slaves sent to, 31.
Green, Rufus & Co., 378.
Grenville, Lord, 92, 94.
Grey, Earl, 429.
Grey, Sir George, 531.
Guano: of Latham Island, 488, 489; of Hellaniya Island, 525-45.
Guardafui, Cape, 16, 170, 179, 233, 329, 510.
Guavas, 181.
Guillain, Captain, 318, 320, 339, 340, 437, 449, 450; visit to Zanzibar and coast towns (1846-8), 274, 301, 323, 328, 330, 354-7, 399, 424, 436, 451, 473, 546, 547; at Mogadishu, 335, 337; description of Said's dominion, 342; commander of *La Dordogne*, 353; views on Suez Canal, 457, 464; tribute to English with regard to slave-trade, 522, 523.
Guinea, Gulf of, 155.
Guinea, Portuguese, 157.
Guizot, M., 442, 446, 451.
Gujerat, 19, 33, 301, 370.
Gum, 30, 163, 171, 189, 366, 479, 492.
Gum-copal, 55, 62, 304, 316, 366, 376, 377, 383, 386, 423, 425, 479, 484, 485, 487.
Gunamma, 178.
Gunpowder, 80, 163, 199, 383, 490.
Gurzond Island, 531.

Hadimu, tribe, 317, 319, 321.
Hadramaut coast, 527.
Hagermann, 402.
Haines, Commander, 465-7.
Hall, General, anti-slave-trade measures of, 196.
Hamburg, merchants of, in E. Africa, 382-7, 426, 485.
Hamed, Sultan, 180.
Hamed-bin-Ahmed, 338-40.
Hamed-bin-Azan, chief of Sohar, rebellion against Said, 469.
Hamed-bin-Said, of Muscat, 83, 85, 86.
Hamed-bin-Sulayyim, Sheikh, 311; murder of, 312.

566 INDEX

Hamerton, Atkins, 332, 424, 430, 491, 500, 551–3; appointed consul to Zanzibar (1841), 298, 378, 477, 484, 488; his estimates of Zanzibar trade, 316, 318–20; description of Suliman-bin-Hamed, 323, 357; account of Zanzibar, 325, 326, 340; his reports, 337, 342, 379, 431–3, 449, 450, 475, 476, 499; dealings with Said, 338, 341, 344, 372, 423, 472, 473, 487, 507, 508; warns Maizan, 353; and Krapf, 388, 401, 407, 412–17; views on Nossi-bé, 444, 447; and French activities, 451–6; appointed political agent in Said's dominions (1840), 471; intervention on behalf of banyans 485, 486; Cogan's dislike of, 489, 506, 510, 511, 548, 549; anxious to keep out other white traders from E. Africa, 492, 493; Said's request for his removal refused, 512; and slave-trade, 514–22; and Kuria Muria Islands, 526–9, 532, 537; farewell to Said (1854), 533; friendly relationship with Said, 546–50; character of, 546–50; death of, 555.
Hamil, imprisoned by Said, 277.
Hamites, 9, 10.
Hamud, Seyyid Said's cousin, 277.
Hanover, missionaries from, 387.
Hanoverian Protestant Missionary Society, 414.
Hanseatic League, 382, 386.
Hanseatic Republics, Consulate at Zanzibar, 386.
Hanseatic Treaty with Majid (1859), 385, 386.
Hansing, Messrs., 383.
Hardinge, Lord, Governor-General of India, 413.
Hardware, 171, 486, 490.
Hardy, Lieutenant, his 'voyage of research' (1811) 178–85.
Hart, Captain, H., R.N., 282–5, 298; sent by Admiralty to Zanzibar (1834), 314, 319, 324, 373, 374, 376, 377, 379; estimates of, 316, 317; description of Said, 328.
Hasan, 'Mwenyi Mkuu' of the Hadimu, 319.

Hasan-bin-Ahmed, sultan of Malindi, 62, 63.
Haski Island, 524, 529, 531, 535, 542, 544.
Hassan bin Ali and his seven sons, 23.
Hastings, Warren, Governor-General of India, 54, 91, 126, 203, 256.
Havannah, 365.
Hawkesbury, Lord, 162.
Hawkins, Sir Richard, 160.
Hawthorne, Nathaniel, 377.
Hayes, Mr., 533, 537, 539.
Hedjaz, 148, 461.
Helicon, the, 267, 269, 270.
Hellaniya Island, 524, 525, 529; visited for guano, 1854; granted to Britain by Said, 531; visited in 1883, 544; 1936, 545.
Hembe, Chief, 354.
Hennell, Captain, resident in Persian Gulf, 439–41, 500–3, 506.
Herat, Shah of Persia's attack on (1838), 460.
Hercules, the, 372.
Herz, A. J. & Sons, 382.
Hickey's Gazette, 203.
Hides, 365, 366, 383, 490.
Hilal, Said's eldest son, 274, 322, 324, 439; disinherited and banished by Said, 453, 454; death of, 454.
Hindon, Mr., 533, 537.
Hindus: early traders, 16; sanction slavery, 204; immigration to E. Africa, 300–3.
Hindustan, 126, 138.
Hindustani language, 328.
Hippalus, *see* Monsoon.
Hodges, Consul-General at Cairo, 470.
Hollis, Sir Claud, 290.
Homone, Portuguese leader, 50.
Hong Kong, 25.
Hormuz, 22; occupied by Portuguese, 42, 43, 47; captured by Persia, 53, 65.
Horn, Cape, 362, 367.
Horn, Messrs., 382.
Hornemann, Freidrich, 156, 178–9, 182, 387.
Hosea, 366.
Hottentots, 45.

INDEX 567

Hovas, the, tribe, 198, 333, 441.
Hugh Lindsay, the, 462, 464.
Humboldt, Baron, 401.
Husain-bin-Ali, Jawasmi chief, 144.
Hyderabad, Nizam of, 93, 94, 126, 551.

Ibn Battuta of Tangier, 24, 29, 31, 36–7, 226, 329.
Ibo, 70, 226, 427, 496, 498.
Île de France, 163, 314, 438, 474; obtained by French (1715), 53, 73; and slave-trade, 74, 76, 77, 80, 117, 191–3, 436; population of, 74; French base, 75, 101, decline of importance of, 75–6; commercial relation with Muscat, 81, 82, 84, 85, 94, 96, 103, 106, 118, 421; Napoleon and, 88, 122, 123, 125, 128, 135, 137; Wellesley's proposed attack on, 99; British ships bought at, 107; captured by British (1810), 140, 141, 142, 147, 181, 189; Salem ships trade with, 363.
Imam, title of ruler of Muscat, 21.
Imogene, H.M.S., 373.
India: settlement in, 2–3; African slaves in, 32, 203; and slave-trade, 33, 35, 183, 204, 205, 233; da Gama in, 44; Almeida and, 45; shipping to and from, 46, 85; Portuguese and, 47, 48; Dutch in, 53; Napoleon's designs on, 71, 100, 120 seqq.; British aims in, 93, 94; coolie immigration from, 302, 428, 433, 435; Said obtains coin from, 304; trade with Said, 216, 299, 315, 316, 318; American trade with, 362; hostility of, to missionaries, 413; French activity in, 462; danger from Russia, 468; value of trade with Zanzibar (1859), 486; increase of British trade with, 491; import of slaves, 203, 494; slaves smuggled into, 500, 501, 502.
India Act (1794), 93.
Indiamen, 140.
Indian Ocean: course of western shore of, 15–16; early trade of the, 42, 47, 48; Portuguese dominate, 65, 71, 75; French designs on, 86–90, 127; British protection in, 154; decline of Arab trade in, 175.
Indians in E. Africa in early times, 27–8, 310; *see also* Banyans.
Indies, East, 314, 362, 373, 388; early trade with, 19; Dutch, 122, 139, 141, 155, 315; Portuguese, 52; West, 76, 80, 83, 157, 193, 197, 204, 207, 226, 373, 430, 494, 514.
Indigo factories, 73.
Indil Khan, 33.
Indus, river, 15, 138.
Inhambane, 70, 226.
Iraq, 100, 460; slaves in, 32; Anglo-French conflict in, 94; Mahomet Ali's designs to annex, 461, 462.
Ireland, 125, 547.
Iringa, 8.
Iron, 36, 163, 182, 383.
Isaacs, Nathaniel, 364.
Isenberg, 388.
Islam, 22, 41, 63, 105.
Islington, C.M.S. College in, 390.
Ispahan, 503.
Istakhri, 20.
Italy, 138.
Ivory, trade in, 17, 20, 30, 36, 171, 174, 178, 306, 312, 351, 399, 419, 484; Portuguese, 62, 67; French, 80, 423, 425, 426; Zanzibar, 182, 304, 314, 316, 317, 359, 487, 492; American, 364, 376, 377; British trade in, 377, 479; German trade in, 383, 386; duties on, 352, 353.

Jaca, King of, 65.
Jackson, President of U.S.A., 368, 369.
Jackson, Sir Frederick, 219.
Jacobin Club in Mauritius, 194.
Jagga, *see* Chagga.
Jairam Sewji, customs master at Zanzibar, 324, 414, 485, 486.
Jamaica, 194, 203, 429, 430.
Jannsens, General, 141.
Japan, 298, 367, 457.
Jaunpur, 33.
Java, 83, 101, 123, 137, 370; early trade of, 19; Wellesley's proposed attack on, 99; captured by the British, 140, 208; American trade with, 363.

Java Head, 363.
Jawasmi tribe, 107, 296, 504, 520; and Said, 109, 110, 133, 134, 135, 151, 209, 219; conflict with the British, 142-4, 149, 212; sign British treaty (1820), 150, 502, 505.
Jedda, 64, 91, 99, 100, 151.
Jesuit missions, 51-2, 62.
Jezeer, 252.
João II, Dom, 42.
Johanna Island, 79, 160, 163, 449; Arab settlement of, 23; Blankett's squadron at (1798), 163-5, 170, 178; character of the natives, 164; the *Nisus* at, 171, 173, 174, 200; Bombay Jack of, 171; Captain Owen at, 227, 228, 247; and British protection, 201, 445-7; consuls of, 448, 449; treaties with Britain (1844-50), 447, 448.
Jokha, Hamil's sister, rebellion of, 277.
Joliba, river, 156.
Jones, Harford (afterwards Sir Harford Jones Brydges), consul in Bagdad, 94, 99, 139.
Joshua Carroll, the, 430, 431, 433.
Jowett, C. C., 381.
Juba, river (Nilo, or Rogue's river), 5, 6, 165, 166, 168, 170, 178-80, 335, 342, 487.
Jukes, Dr., 153.
Juno, H.M.S., 526, 528, 543.
Jura mountains, 393.

Kadango, 346.
Kadi, 37, 325, 340, 342.
Kadiaro, Mount, 392, 394, 397, 398.
Kaffraria, 372.
Kalifi, 58, 61.
Kamba, the, Bantu tribe, 11, 300, 344, 349, 350, 398, 404-6, 410, 419.
Kampala, 307, 556.
Kandahar, tribes of, 121.
Kapell, King of Tembe, 228, 229.
Karachi, 16, 204, 207.
Karikal, 436.
Karrack, island of, 132.
Kasembe, 306.
Katanga copper-mines, 306.

Katanga plateau, 556.
Kathiawar, 149, 302, 315, 500, 501, 504, 517.
Katif district, 461.
Kaye, J. W., 95, 97, 98, 132.
Kazenge Island, 306, 311.
Kebrabasa Rapids, 6.
Keir, General Sir W. G., 149.
Kemball, Captain, resident in Persian Gulf, 551.
Kennedy, Commodore, 371.
Kenya, 3, 6, 398; area and population, 11; tribes of, 343-5.
Kenya Highlands, 6-9, 300, 384, 399, 403, 409.
Kerenge valley, 344.
Keswere, 366.
Khalid, Said's second son, 293, 326, 440, 453; inherits Said's African possessions, 454, 455; death of, 456, 553.
Khamis-bin-Osman, 327.
Khan, Mirza Mehdi Ali, Persian agent of E.I.C., 95.
Khoja, sect, 302.
Kibuga, 307.
Kidd, Captain, 163.
Kiblia Island, 524, 529, 531, 542, 544.
Kigoma, 305.
Kikuyu, 300, 398, 403.
Kilema, 394-6.
Kilifi, 25.
Kilimanjaro, 8, 11, 20, 305, 345, 351, 384, 392, 393, 396-9, 401; discovery of, 409.
Kilindini, 218, 236, 398.
Kilwa, 118, 302, 303, 305, 319, 386, 433, 481, 499, 515; *Chronicles of Kilwa* (*Sinet el Kilawia*), 23, 24; early settlement of, 23, 25-7; Ibn Battuta on, 29, 30, 36; Barbosa at, 38; da Gama at, 39, 42-4; population (16th cent.), 45; Portuguese in, 45-8, 54, 84; decline of, 49; Zimba attack on, 61; proposed French colony at, 76-83; and slave-trade, 76, 80, 82, 117, 191, 192, 203, 230, 306, 417, 434, 513, 519; treaty of king of, with the French (1776), 78, 81; French trade with, 83, 103, 421, 449; no British trade with, 161, 487;

INDEX

the *Nisus* at (1812), 174–6; seized by the Omani, 83, 218; description of, 330; Said's garrison at, 331, 332, 336.
Kilwa Kisiwani, 5, 399, 400.
Kilwa Kivinje, 400.
Kima ja Kegnia, 399.
Kimweri, King of Usambara, account of his reign, 345–52; Krapf's visit to, 380, 394–6, 406, 407, 410, 411, 415, 416.
King, Rear-Admiral, 431.
Kionga, 520.
Kirangozi, the, 307.
Kirk, Sir John, 23, 219, 314, 317, 400, 407, 482, 550.
Kisara, 344, 346.
Kishm Island, 98, 150.
Kismayu, 5, 58, 556.
Kissaki (or Zungomoro), 305.
Kiswere, 230, 427, 499.
Kitui, 398, 403.
Kivoi, Kamba chief, 398, 399, 403–5, 410; death of, 404, 405.
Kiwayu Island, 515.
Knoblecher, 387.
Kojah sect, 310.
Koran, the, 32, 207, 273, 325, 336.
Kosseir, 88, 99.
Krapf, Johann Ludwig, 306, 308, 327, 331, 332, 339, 341, 354, 383, 384, 397, 398, 425, 426, 451, 452, 474, 485, 490; his attempt to penetrate into Kenya, 343, 344, 405, 406; visit to Kimweri, 345, 346–52; and slave-trade, 380, 499, 519; account of his missionary work in E. Africa, 387–96; and Kivoi, 398, 403–5, 410; first reaches the Tana river, 398, 404; inspects coast of E. Africa, 399–401; his plan for a chain of missions, 402, 403, 409; forced by health to leave Africa, 407–8; disliked by Swahili, 411; Hamerton's friendly relations with, 412–15, 546; causes Said to change his attitude to missionaries, 414; his unfortunate conversation with de Belligny, 415–17, 473; views on relations with natives, 418–20.
Kubla Khan and Madagascar, 19.
Kuhlmann, Mr., 414.

K'un lun, 20, 34.
Kunguni, Wasin Isl., 290.
Kuria Muria Islands, 329, 465; British annexation of, 524–46; granted to Britain by Said (1854), 531.
Kurshid Pasha, 461.
Kwale, 394.
Kwavi, tribe, 343, 344, 391, 392.

La Bourdonnais, Governor of Île de France, 73–5, 102, 438.
La Dordogne, 353.
La Guène, Admiral, 455.
Labouchere, H., Colonial Secretary, 538.
Labour, free, 427–35, 489.
Lagos, annexed by Britain (1861), 159, 291.
Lahej, Sultan of, treaty with Britain (1802), 99, 464, 465.
Lake, Lord, 105.
Lamu, 5, 180, 282, 283, 313, 339, 366, 383, 415, 425, 438, 451, 454, 513, 515; Arab settlement of, 25; and Portuguese, 46, 48, 58, 59, 61, 66; appeal for help to Said, 219; and Owen's protectorate, 234, 235, 242, 243, 246, 251–4, 257, 258; the Mazrui and, 241; Americans at, 275, 365; description of, 330; Said's garrison at, 331, 334–6, 338.
Lancashire cotton trade, 380.
Lancaster, Sir James, 52, 54–5, 160, 168.
Lang, Mr., 544.
Lannigan, William, capture and rescue of, 166, 168–70.
Latham Island, Cogan's design for trading in guano of, 488, 489.
Le Succès, French slave-ship, 202.
Leavitt, Captain Henry, 275.
Lechmere, Thomas, of Salem, 363.
Ledyard, John, traveller, 156.
Leghorn, 92.
Leopard, the, 162–3, 165–8.
Leven, H.M.S., 227, 231, 234, 235, 239, 240, 249, 250, 254, 263, 328.
Libya, 17.
Libyan desert, 387.
Lily, H.M.S., 430, 477.

Lindi, 5, 230, 240, 329, 331, 333, 366, 427, 499.
Linjah, burnt by the British, 144.
Linschoten, J. H. van, 52, 54.
Lions, 398.
Lisbon, 42, 44, 49, 61, 66, 69, 136, 216.
List, F., German economist, 384.
Liverpool, 160, 161, 193, 382, 489, 490, 525, 533.
Liverpool, Lord, 195, 197.
Liverpool, the, Said's flagship, 273, 297, 298, 480, 550.
Livingstone, David, 6, 7, 155, 160–1, 172, 187, 305–7, 325, 358, 386, 401, 418, 556; at Ujiji, 311; Zambesi expedition, 394, 400, 432, 435.
Livingstone Mountains, 8.
Loanda, 306.
London, slave-trade at port of, 193; Said's clove trade with, 318; Ali-bin-Nasir's visit to, 332, 339, 389, 447, 448, 480, 508–13, 522.
London African Association, 387.
London Missionary Society, 198, 445.
London Society for Colonization of Bulama (1792), 157.
Losewa, 305.
Louis XVI, 85.
Louis-Philippe, King, 423, 446.
Lucknow, 501.
Ludha Damji, 310, 311, 325.
Lübeck, 385.
Luft, seized by the British, 144.
Luzira, king of, 65.
Lynn, Captain, 189.

Maarwal Valley, 147.
Machakos, 398.
Machame, 396, 397, 407.
McLeod, Lyons, consul at Mozambique, 432, 435.
McMullen, American consul at Zanzibar, 378.
Madagascar, 3, 20, 155, 160, 275, 291, 362, 366, 373, 378, 436; early Malayans and Javanese in, 19; Arab settlement of, 25, 49; da Cunha and Albuquerque on, 46; escaped Portuguese conquest, 47; French attempts to colonize, 53; the English in, 54; Napoleon's interest in, 71, 122, 123; and slave-trade, 73, 192, 194, 196, 199, 200–2, 214, 235, 499, 517; Decaen's lack of success in, 124; forts in captured by the British (1811), 140; restorations made to France in (1814), 141, 198, 440, 472; suggested penal settlement in, 162; trade of, 163, 318, 365; attack on Johanna, 164, 170, 171; slave-hunters, 172, 173, 200–1; Prior's account of, 177; Captain Owen at, 227, 246, 255; missionaries in, 280, 417, 445; Said's attempts to get help from, 280–4, 333; French expansion in, 422, 425, 444, 457, 458; first French designs on, 437; all in French hands, 449; free labourers of, 489; few British ships at, 487; *see also* Radama, King of, *and* Treaties.
Madanga, 347.
Madeira, 172, 228.
Madras, 54, 74, 101, 138, 363.
Madrid, 136, 137.
Mafia Island, 5, 18, 39, 176, 218, 293, 314, 383, 513, 515; Arab settlement of, 25; Portuguese conquest of, 47.
Magallon, C., Governor of Port Louis, 88, 102–4.
Maharra tribe, 537.
Mahé, 176, 191, 250.
Mahomed-bin-Othman, Governor of Mombasa, 217.
Mahomet Ali of Egypt, 151, 422; captures Medina and Mecca from the Wahabis, 147, 148; his attempt to create a great Moslem empire, 436, 441, 460–7, 470; befriended by France, 460; and Aden, 467; his designs on Muscat frustrated, 470; and slave-trade, 502.
Mahrattas, the, 94, 126, 128.
Maitland, Sir Thomas, 205.
Maizan, his expedition into the interior, and murder, 353–7, 391, 400, 451, 473, 493.
Maize, 36, 70.

INDEX

Majid, Sultan of Zanzibar, Said's fourth son, 296, 322, 350; audience with Stanley, 325; treaty with Hanseatic Republics (1859), 385; and French slave-vessels, 434; appointed Said's heir, 456; succeeds Said at Zanzibar, 554.
Majid-bin-Khalfan, 115, 147.
Majunga, 364, 365, 425.
Makalanga, tribe, 51.
Makalla, 528, 536.
Makasane, Chief, 229.
Makran coast, 500, 502, 504.
Malabar, 97.
Malacca, 19, 43, 47, 53, 97, 101, 140.
Malambo tribe, 283.
Malartic, M., Governor of Port Louis, 88–9, 102.
Malay Peninsula, 19, 34, 53, 256, 362.
Malcolm, Captain, afterwards Sir John, treaty with Said (1800), 97, 98, 102, 110, 130–1, 142, 498, 507; treaty with Shah of Persia (1800), 99, 104; missions to Persia, 127–8, 131–2, 139.
Maldive Islands, 382, 465.
Malindi, 31, 54, 57, 218, 224, 226, 249, 313; Arab settlement of, 25, 42, 417; feud with Mombasa, 27, 66, 221; iron mines at, 36; Barbosa at, 38; Vasco da Gama at, 38, 43; Portuguese conquest of, 45–8, 58, 63, 68; Mirale Bey at, 59; Zimba attack on, 61; decline of importance, 62; description of, 330.
Malta, 462.
Mamelukes, 33, 87, 92.
Mamkinga, Chief, 396, 397, 410.
Manchester, 480.
Manda, 61, 65, 66, 339.
Manika, 50, 51.
Manila, 425.
Manioc, 36, 70, 73.
Mansour, Sheikh, *see* Maurizi, V.
Manuel, King of Portugal, 42.
Mapharatic chief, 17.
Maratha League, 105.
Marbat tribe, 535.
Maria II of Portugal, 495.
Maria, the, 430, 432.

Maria Theresa dollars, 299, 304, 451.
Marianne, the, 467.
Mariette, M., French agent at Tamatave, 123.
Marseilles, 318, 425, 426, 458, 462.
Martin, Montgomery, surgeon, 287, 288.
Marungu, river, 306.
Masai, tribe, 13, 300, 357, 392, 398, 410, 556; origin, 10; description of, 343, 344.
Masaki, tribe, 394–7.
Masansa (Msene), 311.
Mascarenes, the, 71, 80, 123, 362, 427; escaped Portuguese conquest, 47; colonized by the French, 56, 139, 140, 161; British conquest of, 79, 172, 208, 421; Said's trade with, 168; and slave-trade, 183, 494.
Mashah Islands, bought by Britain, 468.
Masirah island, 370, 371.
Masna'ah, 148.
Mass, Buonaventura, slave-dealer, 425, 434.
Massachussetts, 362, 363, 379.
Masudi of Bagdad, 20, 24, 25, 32.
Masury, Samuel, 378.
Matabele, the, 357.
Mataka's, 305.
Maungu, Mount, 398.
Maurice of Nassau, 53.
Mauritius Island, 97, 128, 191, 239, 216, 237, 270, 441, 447, 528; first visited by Dutch and named after Maurice of Nassau, 53; occupied by the French and named Île de France, 53; captured by British, 56, 141, 155, 171, 459; under La Bourdonnais, 73; Captain Beaver's visit to, 174; and slave-trade, 193–9, 206, 210, 214, 251, 427, 428, 431, 494; export of arms forbidden (1818), 199; Owen at, 227, 228, 240, 245, 246, 252, 255, 263; Mbaruk's embassy to, 258; British at, support King Radama, 280; Said's trade with, 318; coolie labour at, 429, 430–3; sugar industry, 488; *see also* Île de France.

INDEX

Maurizi, V. (Sheikh Mansour), Italian physician, 108, 109, 119, 120.
Mayotta, 433, 435, 445, 446, 451, 457, 458; annexed by French (1843), 449.
Mazrui, the, dominion of Mombasa under, 26, 217–21, 296, 334, 350; appeal to the British, 221–4; envoys at Bombay, 231; and Owen's protectorate, 235–7, 239, 241–7, 255, 257, 259, 262, 264, 268, 269; Moorsom's unfavourable account of, 241; unreliability of, 247; and slave-trade, 249, 250; and Said, 272–4, 233, 328, 332, 341, 390.
Mbaruk, Mazrui leader at Mombasa, struggle against Said, 220–1; and British, 224, 226, 253, 268; and cession of Mombasa, 241–7; his brother, 248; embassy to Mauritius, 258, 262; agreement with Said, 273.
Mbereko, 346, 347, 349, 411, 415.
Mboki, 346, 347.
Mbweni, 485.
Mdoe (Vizier), 346, 347, 349.
Mears, Lieutenant, of the *Leopard*, killed by natives, 165, 166.
Mecca, 36, 88, 97, 147, 465, 521; Mahomet Ali and, 148; Said's pilgrimage to, 151.
Medina, 97, 147; captured by Mahomet Ali, 148.
Mediterranean, 36, 100, 459.
Mekrani, the, 327.
Melbourne, Lord, 288.
Melindi, 163, 176.
Menai, H.M.S., 202.
Mendoza, Governor of Mozambique, 172.
Menouthias Island, 18.
Mentor, the, 382.
Mercury, the, slave-ship, 160.
Merikani, 359, 379, 380, 396, 486.
Merka, 169, 179, 234, 330, 336, 366.
Meru, Mount, 8.
Metal-work, 30.
Metcalfe, Charles, 204.
Methodist Free Churches, United, mission of, 408.
Metzler, 402.
Meyer, Dr. Hans, 393.

Middle Passage, 188, 189.
Mikindani, 230, 427.
Miles, Mr., 89, 106, 107, 110, 143, 145, 274, 339, 544.
Milius, Governor, of Bourbon, 199–200.
Millet, Charles, 365.
Minerva, the, British merchant-ship, 143.
Mines, 36, 490, 549.
Ming ware, 37.
Minto, Lord, governor-general of India: measures against Napoleon, 121, 126 seqq.; and Malcolm's missions, 127, 128, 131, 132, 139, 460; the 'Madras Mutiny', 138; moves against the French, 140; expedition against Jawasmi, 143; Said and, 145.
Mirale Bey, Turkish commander, in E. Africa, 58, 59, 64; capture of, 60–1.
Missionaries, 7, 473, 490; Roman Catholic, 51, 52, 198; British, 155–6, 198, 441; first invaders of E. Africa, 361, 386–420; American, 374; native attitude to, 409–12, 418, 420; in India, 413; native education by, 409, 419.
Missionary Societies: Hanoverian Protestant, 414; London, 198, 445.
Missions, Krapf's plan for chain of, 402, 403, 409.
Mlau, 346.
Mnasi, 520.
Mocha, 89, 99, 100, 111, 113, 115, 425, 464; people of, 17; Maurizi at, 108; Blankett's squadron at, 170; Smee at, 179; American trade with, 362, 363, 365, 366; slaves from, 516.
Mogadishu, 226, 319, 342, 360, 454, 510; founding of, 23; Arab settlement of, 25, 26; Sheikh's Palace at, 31–2; cloth woven at, 36; Chinese records of, 37; Barbosa and da Gama at, 38; Portuguese at, 46; Mirale Bey at, 58, 59; Blankett's squadron at, 169; Smee's account of, 179; and Captain Owen, 234, 250, 252; in league against Said, 234; sack of, 274, 275; description

INDEX 573

of, 329–31, 335, 336; Said appoints a governor of, 337, 450; slave-trade at, 519.
Mohacs, battle of, 41.
Mohammedan faith, 164, 213, 214, 233.
Mohilla Island, 163, 449.
Moluccas, the, 101, 140, 228, 313, 314; British occupation, 140, 141.
Mombasa, 1, 5, 6, 15, 177, 179, 216, 300, 308, 331, 336, 342, 417, 556; Arab settlement of, 23, 25, 26, 57; feud with Malindi, 27, 63, 66; fighting nature of its people, 29, 176; Ibn Battuta on, 36; Barbosa at, 38, 39; da Gama at, 43; Portuguese conquest of, 44, 45, 48, 54, 57, 59, 61, 62, 65–9; population, 45, 320; Mirale Bey at, 58, 59; massacres at, 60, 64; king of Malindi removes to, 62; Cabreira at, 65, 66; capture of, by Sultan-bin-Seif, 66; and French, 76, 103, 427, 450–2; Said opens his attack on (1824), 152; manuscript chronicle of, 161, 217; Blankett's squadron at (1799), 167; Mazrui rule in, 216–23, 264, 268, 270, 275, 276, 351; Owen's protectorate established at, 224, 227, 231–70, 409; Said's conquest of, 219–21, 235, 257–66, 272–4, 277–85, 334, 372; suggested annexation by Britain, 284, 288, 472; proposed purchase of from Said, 288, 289; Said finally captures, 289–94, 329, 338, 412; ill treatment of banyans of, 302; the *Ann* at, 366; Krapf at, 332, 339, 344, 348, 388–90, 391, 392, 395, 397–9, 401–3.
— Fort Jesus: building of, 61, 62; Yussuf at, 64; restored by Cabreira, 65; siege of, 66–9; seized by Ahmed-bin-Said, 217; Ali-bin-Othman's escape from, 218; Captain Owen at, 224, 239; Mazrui and, 241–3, 272; bombarded by Said, 273–5, 279, 283, 284, 291, 344; possession of by Said, 292, 293, 336, 338; Baluchi in, 331; *see also* Treaties.
Mongo Bay (Mongorella), 427.

Monomotapa, 3.
Monsoon, 15, 16, 25, 151, 165, 168, 170, 179, 277, 389.
Moors, 28, 36, 38, 39, 77.
Moorsom, Captain, 239, 241, 247, 262–4.
Moravian Brethren, 387.
Moresby, Adm. Sir Fairfax, investigation of slave-trade, 202; *see also* Treaties.
Moresby, Captain Robert, 467.
Moresby, Commander, 463.
Morice, Captain, French slave-trader, 103, 118, 161, 175, 218, 437; and proposed French colony at Kilwa, 76–83; Treaty with King of Kilwa (1776), 78.
Morice Islet, 174.
Moscow, 137.
Moshi, 396.
Moslems, 41, 98, 232, 281, 310, 336, 407, 412, 426, 460; and slave-trade, 204, 502; immigration from India of, 302; Mahomet Ali's designs for empire of, 461–3; numbers of in East Africa, 484.
Mountstuart, Lord, 534.
Mozambique, 4, 5, 28, 75, 425, 432, 435, 438, 494, 496, 498; Arab settlement of, 25, 37, 57; subject to Sultan of Kilwa, 26–7; da Gama at, 42, 43; Portuguese conquest of, 46–9, 51, 61, 62, 66–8, 70, 329, 333, 360, 361; Linschoten's description of, 54; French attacks on, 56; Zimba raids on, 60; Omani attack on, 66; and slave-trade, 73, 79, 80, 189, 194, 201, 205, 216, 226, 230, 235, 364, 427, 499, 520; trade with, 75, 80, 117, 118, 163; in Talleyrand's report to Napoleon (1802), 102; decline of French influence in, 124; population of 171–2, 320; Captain Owen at, 227, 240, 255.
Mozambique Channel, 439, 449.
Mrima, the, 423, 487, 491, 492, 555.
Mringano, 347.
Msene (Masansa), 311.
Mtangata (Tangate), 64, 351, 386, 481.
Mtotana, 400.
Muitinge, 499, 500.

Mukhadim tribute, 321, 324.
Müller, Messrs., 383.
Murad III, of Turkey, 58.
Murat, in Madrid, 136.
Murphy, Michael, 165–70.
Musa Mzuri, 310, 311.
Muscat, 15, 69, 77, 219, 220, 273–5, 277–9, 286, 297, 338, 339, 366, 390, 414; trade of, 21, 22, 79, 84, 85, 106, 107, 113, 117, 118, 168, 182, 316, 318, 367–71, 375, 421; and Portuguese, 47, 65, 66, 67; Cossigny on, 82; British relations with, 84, 110, 115; de Rosily at, 86; and French, 84–90, 94–5; Malcolm at, 97–9; Napoleon's designs on, 102–6, 128; Wahabi representative at, 105; Bedr-bin-Seif ruler of, 108; the *Vigilant* privateer at, 110; French influence re-established, 124, 125, 127; Malcolm at, 130–1, 139; Bunce, British representative at, 143; British troops at, 144, 145; attacked by Mutlak al-Mutairi, 146–7; governor appointed by Said, 176; slave-trade, 183, 206, 207, 259, 290, 452; Captain Moresby at, 214; Captain Owen at, 227, 232, 356; Americans arrive at, 281; Said transfers his court to Zanzibar from, 295–301, 312, 320, 322, 326; French consul appointed at, 422; in British hands (1839), 436; Hamed-bin-Azan's attempt to seize, 469; Mahomet Ali's designs on frustrated, 470; Said's last journey from, 553.
Muskets, trade in, 199, 316, 317, 364, 365, 368, 380, 383, 486, 490.
Mutlak al-Mutairi, Wahabi general, 144–8.
Mwanza, 305, 307.
'Mwenyi Mkuu', 319, 321.
Myrrh, 366.
Mysore, Typoo-Sahib of, 88, 89, 94, 97.

Nabahani, tribe, 217.
Nails, 365, 380, 383.
Nairobi, 404.
Names, European, adopted by natives, 163, 164, 173, 228, 402.

Nantes, 202.
Napier, Josiah, 448–9.
Napier, Lord, 408.
Napoleon, see Buonaparte, Napoleon.
Napoleon III, 435.
Napoleonic wars, 54, 71, 381, 384, 421, 436, 459, 471, 508.
Nasor-bin-Suliman, Governor of Pemba, 252–5, 275, 276.
Natal, 140, 224, 364, 387; slaves from, 160; American mission-station at, 374; strained relations between blacks and whites at, 375.
Nawanagar, Jam Sahib of, 501.
Negroland, 9, 10, 19.
Nejd, 21, 105, 145, 148.
Nelson, Lord, 84, 90.
Nepean, Sir Evan, 208–10.
Netherlands, 52, 141.
New, Charles, missionary, 393.
New Bedford, 364, 376.
New Brunswick, 287.
New England, 362, 382.
New Hampshire, 367.
New Testament, translation of into Swahili, 391.
New York, 364, 376.
New Zealand, 154, 457.
Ngombo, 305.
Ngura, 345.
Nicolay, Sir William, 428.
Niger Expedition of 1841, 287.
Niger, river, 6, 156, 178.
Nigeria, 3, 5, 387.
Nile, battle of, 90, 95.
Nile, river, 4, 9, 31, 100, 178, 307, 387, 397, 461, 502, 555.
Nile, source of, 35, 408, 473.
Nilo, river, see Juba, river.
Nilotic Tribes, 500.
Nisus, the, frigate, expedition to E. Africa (1812), 162, 170–8, 189, 200.
North, Lord, 91.
Nossi-bé (Bookeen) Island, ruled by the Sakalava tribe, 333, 438; Queen Seneekoo's treaty of surrender to Said (1838), 333; obtained by the French (1841), 334, 337, 355, 438–48, 457, 472, 508; Said's concern about the French at, 441, 442; slave-trade at, 433, 435.

INDEX 575

Nourse, Commodore, 216, 227, 229, 240, 241, 245, 249, 263, 265, 269.
Nubian desert, 387.
Nugniri, 346.
Nupe country, 179.
Nyamwezi, the, Bantu tribe, 11, 307, 308, 353, 396.
Nyanza, Lake Victoria, 305, 307, 408, 555, 556.
Nyasa, Lake, 7, 8, 357, 400, 401, 435, 555; discovery of, 305, 306; chief seat of slave-trade, 519.
Nyika, the, Bantu tribe, 6, 7, 11, 63, 221, 250, 300, 344, 349, 350, 390, 391, 397, 403, 406, 408, 419, 490; and the missionaries, 409, 412.

Oil, 156, 228.
Oja, 46.
Oman, account of, 20–3; and slave-trade, 31, 82, 207, 208, 521; English factories in, 51, 96; Sultan-bin-Seif ejects Portuguese from 65–8; Zanzibar in submission to, 71, 83, 274; and Anglo-French conflict over Muscat, 84–7, 90; British intervention in affairs of, 95; and the Wahabi, 105, 145, 148, 150, 551; effect of Sultan-bin-Ahmed's death on, 107; Said becomes ruler of, 108; British policy in, 113 seqq.; deliverance from Persians, 217; and the Mazrui, 220, 221; Captain Owen in, 231; revolts in, 277, 278, 322, 324; Said moves his capital to Zanzibar from, 279, 281, 295–300, 321, 322; trade of, 421; Egyptian designs on, 470; Said's last visit to, 533.
Omani, growing power of, 67–70; blockade Mombasa, 235; control of Kilwa by, 332; in Said's army, 338, 339; Hamed-bin-Azan's hold over, 469; expelled from Bunder Abbas, 551, 552.
Orange river, 387.
Oranges, 36, 181.
Ord, Captain, his expedition to Kuria Muria Island for guano, 525–7, 533–43, 539.
Order of the Lion and the Sun, 139.

Orestes, the, 162, 164, 167, 168.
Osman, Kimweri's physician, 346, 407.
Ostrich-feathers, 366.
O'Swald, Albrecht, 385, 386.
O'Swald, W. H., burgomaster of Hamburg, 385.
O'Swald, Wilhelm, of Hamburg, 359, 382, 383–6.
Otondo, king of, 65.
Owen, Sir Edward, 226.
Owen, Captain William Fitzwilliam, 176, 217, 224, 225, 273, 328, 332, 336, 343, 382, 389, 409, 420, 507, 530; treaty with Mombasa establishing a protectorate (1824), 78, 81, 235–40, 253, 374; and slave-trade, 189, 226–8, 230, 237–8, 240; his Protectorate, 216–70, 291, 341, 459; after-effects of, 257–70; end of, 270; Said's satisfaction at end of, 271–2; account of, 226; ideas of annexation, 228–9; interview with Said at Muscat, 231–3, 251–3, 355; his survey of the coast, 329, 399: Mogadishu, 234; Lamu, 234, 251, 334; Mozambique, 240; Delagoa Bay, 240; Mauritius, 240, 246; Madagascar, 246, 250; Johanna, 247; Mahé, 250; Barawa, 251; his farewell, 254–5; suggestions for E. Africa, (1834), 284–7, 483; retires to his island off New Brunswick, 287; his map, 365.
Oxford, University of, 39.
Oxus country, 33.
Ozi, 252.

Pacific Isles, South, 362–3.
Palgrave, W. G., 300, 301.
Palmer, Richard, first American consul at Zanzibar, 378.
Palmerston, Lord, 413, 434, 447, 448, 473, 476, 480, 491, 503, 504, 508, 518, 539, 550; and slave-trade, 198, 215, 291, 496, 522; and Owen's policy, 284–9; American settlements, 374, 472; Said's appeal to about the French, 439–44, 447, 482, 483; and Mahomet Ali, 462, 463.
Palm-oil, 17, 36, 304.

576 INDEX

Pamplemousses, Royal Botanical Garden at, 314.
Pangani, 5, 18, 42, 248, 303, 332, 344, 347, 350, 351, 395, 400, 406, 414, 415, 473, 485, 487.
Pangani, river, 5, 6, 10, 45, 218, 236, 248, 345, 346, 352, 395.
Pare Mountains, 8, 345.
Park, Mungo, explorer, 156, 178, 180, 182, 404.
Parker, Captain, 489, 490.
Pasni (Pussem), 502.
Pate Island, 22, 26, 64; *History of Pate*, 24; Arab settlement of, 25; Portuguese at, 48, 61, 62, 65, 66, 67; Mirale Bey at, 58, 59; French trade at, 76, 421; no British trade with (1792), 161; Smee at (1811), 179, 180; Nabahani at, 217; independence of, 218; disputed Sultanate of, 219–20; Said's overlordship of, 219, 221, 334–6, 340, 342; rebels against Said, 234, 337–9, 341, 450; and Owen's protectorate, 235, 241–3, 246, 252–4; 257, 258; description of, 330; Said's Baluchis at, 331; French slave-trade at, 427; Said's second attack on, 476.
Peacock, the, 298, 367, 370, 373, 374.
Pellew, Admiral, 114.
Pemba Island, 5, 18, 20, 57, 79, 293, 320, 452; early settlement of, 23, 25, 26; trade of, 39, 62, 318; Portuguese at, 47, 48, 59, 61, 65, 177; Sharpeigh at, 56; annexed by the Mazrui, 218, 219; under Said's overlordship, 220, 221, 321, 556; and Owen's protectorate, 235, 239, 241–3, 246, 252, 268; clove-plantations of, 314, 315; Krapf at, 389; and slave-trade, 431, 513, 515.
Penal settlements, 157, 162.
Peninsular War, the, 135–8.
Pepper, 20, 363.
Perim, 99, 464, 465.
Periplus of the Erythraean Sea, 16–18, 24.
Perronet, M., 425.
Persia, 22, 53, 65, 69, 100, 105, 217, 233, 297, 475; trade of, 16, 35, 54, 103, 299, 315, 316, 379; early settlers in E. Africa, 23, 24; slave-trade, 31, 500, 503, 504, 520; and Napoleonic wars, 71; Malcolm's mission to, 97, 98, 104, 127, 138, 139; French and Russian missions to, 131, 132; helps Said against Wahabi, 146; Said's trade with, 182, 318; British resident in the Gulf, 372, 439–41, 500–3, 506; relations with Britain, 460, 468, 552; *see also* Treaties.
Peru, guano in, 526, 538.
Peters, Mr., of Cogan & Co., 488, 490–2, 549.
Peyton, Commodore Edward, 74.
Pfefferle, missionary, 402.
P'hazi Mazungere, 354–6.
Philip II of Spain, 52, 58.
Philip, Dr., missionary, 229, 373.
Philippine, La, 85.
Philippines, 19, 53, 122, 137, 382.
Phillips, Midshipman, acting commandant at Mombasa, 247, 249.
Phillips, S. W., of Salem, 363, 378, 379.
Piedmontese, the, 284.
Pineapples, 36, 70, 181.
Pingree, D., 378.
Pioneer, the, 400.
Piracy, 143, 149–50.
Pirate Coast, the, 109, 144, 149, 292, 551.
Pitt, William, 93, 94, 155, 157, 287, 462.
Poivre, Pierre, Intendant of Île de France, 314.
Poland, 120.
Pollock, Mr., 490, 491, 549.
Polo, Marco, 19.
Pomare, Queen of Tahiti, 445, 446.
Pombe, 346.
Pomegranates, 181.
Pondicherry, 53, 74, 91, 92, 101, 103, 154, 237, 436.
Popham, Admiral, his expedition of 1799, 99, 465.
Port Amelia, 5.
Port Durnford, 22.
Port Louis, La Bourdonnais at, 73, 74; Morice's scheme for, 76, 78, 81, 161, 437; *La Philippine* at,

INDEX

85; Tippoo's envoy at, 88; General Decaen at (1802), 102, 122; mission from Muscat to, 103; Muscat agents at, 106; and Said, 112, 142, 439; French traders in, 117–18; base for Napoleon's descent on India, 125; captured by the British, 140, 459; British warships at, 191; attitude to French Revolution, 194; H.M.S. *Menai* sails from, 202; and slave-trade, 207, 427–31; Owen at, 238, 239, 246.
Port Natal, 367.
Porter, Captain, 430, 431.
Portsmouth, 162.
Portugal, and slave-trade, 34, 171, 186, 188–90, 213, 434, 435, 494–6, 499, 500.
Portuguese, the, early conquests in E. Africa, 5, 24, 26, 27, 41–72, 420, 556; decline of influence, 52, 65–72; her rivals in E. Africa, 52–7; and Napoleonic wars, 117, 124, 135–7; bad treatment of natives, 361, 419.
Portuguese E. Africa, 8, 320.
Potatoes, 181.
Powder, trade in, 364, 365, 368, 490.
Preussische Seehandlung, 382.
Prince Regent, the, 173, 550.
Prior, James, surgeon on the *Nisus*: account of her voyage, 77, 171–8, 228, 305, 421; and slave-trade, 192, 194, 522.
Pritchard, George, 445, 446.
Privateers, French, 90, 94, 106–7, 110.
Provence, 425.
Providence Island, 202.
Prussia, 136, 137.
Pussem (Pasni), 502.
Pyrenees, 22.

Queen Victoria, the, 553.
Queribo, and slave-trade, 75, 79, 80.
Quilimane, and slave-trade, 189, 226, 230, 496–9; subject to Sultan of Kilwa, 27; Portuguese at, 70.

Rabai, Great, 345.
Rabai, Sultan Hassani murdered at, 63.
Rabai Mpia (New), missionaries at, 390, 391–2, 395–9, 401–3, 406–10, 418, 419, 490.
Rabaud Frères, 425.
Radama, King of Madagascar, 438, 441, 445; and slave-trade, 198, 199, 200–2, 214, 216; recognized by the British, 280, 281; treaty with Britain, 201, 494.
Raffles, Sir Stamford, 140, 256.
Railways, 392, 395, 398, 409.
Rainier, Admiral, 99.
Rajkot, 501.
Rajput princes, 126.
Ranavolana, becomes queen of Madagascar, 280; Said's appeal for help to, 281; Said's proposal of marriage to, 281–3; anti-European attitude, 280, 333, 437, 438, 441.
Rangoon, 363.
Ranjit Sing, ruler of the Sikhs, 127.
Ras-al-Khyma: captured by British, 144; Mutlak at, 145; Jawasmi restore stronghold at, 149; Jawasmi treaty with British (1820), 150.
Ras Hafun, promontory, 17.
Rashid-bin-Hamed, Mazrui chief, 250, 252; Said takes Fort Jesus from, 292–4.
Ravasco, Ruy Lourenço, 44.
Rebmann, Johann, his missionary journey with Krapf, 344, 358, 384, 387, 390–9, 401, 402, 406–8, 410, 418; forced by health to leave Africa, 408.
Red Sea and Karachi Telegraph Co., 544.
Reduit, 246.
Regent, Prince, the, 173, 550.
Reitz, Lieutenant, commandant at Mombasa, 241, 247–9, 259, 389.
Retief, Piet, 375.
Réunion, Isle of, 432–5; *see also* Bourbon.
Revenant, the, French privateer, 140.
Revue, river, 51.
Rhapta, 18.

Rhenish Society, the, 387.
Rhinoceros-horn, 17.
Rhodes, Cecil, 409.
Rhodesia, 8, 20, 305.
Rice, 36, 163, 173, 182, 223, 307, 316, 366, 372, 394.
Rice, Thomas Spring, Colonial Secretary, 285.
Richelieu, Duc de, 193.
Rigby, C. P., British consul at Zanzibar (1858–61), 208, 296, 300, 302, 316, 318, 319, 322, 325, 326, 339, 340, 426, 433, 434, 484, 550, 554.
Rio de Janeiro, 496; and slave-trade, 189, 226, 496, 498.
Ripon, Lord, 474.
Robert, Count, of Sicily, 24.
Roberts, Captain, American Commissioner, 298, 361, 367–71, 373.
Rodriguez, 75, 140–2.
Rogers, N. L., 378.
Rogue's river, see Juba, river.
Romain-Desfossés, Commandant, 354, 356, 423, 424.
Roman Catholic missionaries, 198, 388, 445.
Rome, slaves sent to, 31.
Rope-makers, 309.
Ross, Captain, 464.
Rousseau, J. F. X., French consul-general at Bagdad, 85, 87.
Roux, Sylvain, French agent at Tamatave, 123, 140, 141.
Rovuma, river, 5, 6, 70, 75, 217, 240, 305, 360, 361, 399, 400, 401, 415.
Royal Geographical Society, 401.
Ruanda, 307.
Rudolph, Lake, 10.
Rüppell, G. P. E., 387.
Ruete, Emily, Said's daughter, memoirs of her father, 274, 318, 319, 328, 453.
Rufigi, river, 5, 6, 16, 18.
Rukn-ud-din Barbak, King of Gaur, 32.
Ruschenberger, W. S. W., 301.
Russegger, J. I., 387.
Russia, 120, 121, 126, 131, 132, 137, 139, 441, 460, 468.

Sabaki, river, 5, 6.
Sadleir, Lieutenant, 149, 150.

Sagara, Bantu tribe, 11.
Sahara desert, 387.
Said, Salim, brother of Seyyid Said, 108.
Said, Seyyid, Sultan of Zanzibar: murders Bedr-bin-Seif and becomes Imam of Muscat (1806–56), 108; relations with the Wahabi, 109, 119, 134, 144–8, 219, 278; conflict with the Jawasmi, 109, 134, 142–4, 219; difficulty of gaining help from the French or British, 109–12; and Duncan, 111–13, 130, 133, 143, 147, 157; gradual development of his friendship with Britain, 112, 114, 120, 121, 128 seqq., 143–53; the treaty of friendship with French (1807), 115–16; his dissatisfaction with it, 124–5; and Malcolm's missions to Muscat, 132, 139, 142; relations with Seton, 133–5; defeated by Mutlak al-Mutairi, 147; Wahabi finally overcome, 148, 470; wounded on the *Caroline*, 149, 153; climax of his power in Muscat, 151; has ideas of overseas expansion, 151–2; cordial relations with the French and British, 152–3; sovereignty over Zanzibar, 168, 175, 181–3, 192; negotiations with, respecting slave-trade, 202–16, 230, 427, 431, 432, 498, 499, 504–23; signs Moresby anti-slavery treaty (1822), 215, 216; account of his dominion and dependencies, 217 seqq., 361, 400, 409; end of his dominion, 555, 556; conquest of Mombasa, 219–21, 235, 242–6, 257–66, 272–84, 334, 372; final surrender, 288, 289, 291–3, 390; and Mogadishu, 234; and Owen's protectorate, 231–3, 251–5, 284–7; after-effects of on, 257–70; satisfaction at abandonment of, 271–2; personal life and character, 272, 327, 328, 546–50; intrigues with Arabs of the 'Pirate Coast', 272; first designs for moving court to Zanzibar, 274; assault on Bahrein, 276, 278; turns to Madagascar for help,

INDEX

279–84; his proposals to Queen Ranavolana, 282–4, 333; his fleet, 297, 298, 318, 319, 336, 338, 339, 370, 376, 473, 518, 550; and the Maizan incident, 354–7; gives help to American ship *Peacock*, 371, 374; and American trade, 278, 377, 380, 381, 383, 384; portrait of, 379; friendliness to Krapf, 388, 389, 391, 395, 406, 411, 412, 413, 414; British sovereigns' gifts to, 401, 550, 551; and Belligny's unfortunate conversation, 415, 416; and free labour, 433, 435; alarmed at French aggrandizement, 422, 439, 446–8, 450–7; disinherits Hilal, 454; British support against his enemies, 468–78; his title changed to Sultan, 480; asks Palmerston to appoint a consul, 482, 483; trade with Europe, 490, 491; fear of white traders' invasion, 492, 493; character of, 528–30; cedes Kuria Muria Islands to Britain (1854), 531, 544; death of, 553, 554; his daughter, *see* Ruete, Emily; *see also* Treaties *and* Zanzibar.
Said, Omani chief of house of Azd, 22.
Said-bin-Salim, Governor of Tabora, 358.
Saif-ud-din-Firuz, 33.
Saigon, 363.
St. Augustine Bay, 54.
St. Domingue, 122, 314, 425.
St. Helena, 73, 205, 364, 462.
St. John's, New Brunswick, 289.
St. Lucia, 428.
Sainte Marie, 227, 457.
St. Michael, the, 364.
Sakalava tribe, 141, 280, 333, 425, 438, 439, 442, 443.
Saleh, the, Omani frigate, 85–7.
Salem, Mass., early shipping trade with E. Africa, 275, 362–6, 377–84, 479; decline of, 376, 380; factories for treating gum-copal at, 377.
Salil-ibn-Razik, 208, 338, 339.
Salim-bin-Ahmed, sheikh of Mombasa, 268, 269, 272, 273, 275–7; death of, 292.

Salim-bin-Rashed Mazrui, 257.
Salla, 395.
Salt, 163.
Saltpetre, 116.
Sambaa, the, Bantu tribe, 11, 348.
Sandal-wood, 19.
Sandwich Islands, 382.
Saüd, Bedr's nephew, 274.
Saud, Emir Ibn, threatens Said, 145, 148; death of (1814), 148.
Scheluge, King, 345.
Schultz, Theodor, German consul at Zanzibar, 386.
Seahorse, the, frigate, 84.
Sebastiani, Colonel, secret mission to Egypt, 101.
Segeju tribe, 61, 62.
Seif-bin-Hamed, Governor of Lamu, 234, 235, 251, 252, 334.
Seif-bin-Sultan, Imam of Muscat, 67, 69, 208, 217, 220, 257.
Sémillante, La, French privateer, 140.
Sena, 30, 50, 60, 70, 309.
Seneekoo, Queen of Nossi-bé Island, 333, 442, 443.
Senegal, river, 4, 6, 192.
Serampore, 413.
Seringapatam, 94.
Sesamum, 313, 316, 425, 426.
Sesquehannah, the, 381.
Seton, Captain, British resident at Muscat, 103, 104, 107, 109, 113, 115, 127–9, 142, 144, 178, 452, 470, 482, 550; recalled to India, 132; relations with Said, 133–5; death of, 135.
Seven Years' War, 54, 86.
Seville, 39.
Sewji, Jairam, 318, 324, 325, 337.
Seychelles, the, French settlements on, 75, 87, 141, 142, 174, 191, 196, 202, 227, 250, 252, 255, 553.
Seyyid Mohammud of Muscat, 255.
Shah Allum, the, 424.
Shambaa, the, 345.
Shangaya (Port Durnford), 22.
Sharp, Granville, 156.
Sharpeigh, Alexander, 55.
Sheep, 36, 223.
Sheepskins, 366.
Shepherd, Michael, 378, 381.
Shepherd, W. A., 328.

Shihr, 536.
Shiites, 22.
Shimba plateau, 394, 418.
Shimoni, 290.
Shinas, 144, 145.
Shiraz, 23, 132, 272, 552.
Shiré Highlands, 418.
Shoa, 388, 397.
Shore, John, Lord Teignmouth, Governor-General of India, 93, 94, 114, 115.
Siam, 19, 298, 367.
Sicily, 41.
Sidi, Badr, 33.
Sierra Leone, home for emancipated slaves, 156, 159, 241, 417, 430.
Simba Island, 400.
Simonstown, 227.
Sind, 103, 127, 132, 149, 182, 500, 502.
Sinet el Kilawia, see Kilwa, *Chronicles of*.
Sing, Ranjit, British mission to (1808), 127.
Singapore, 25, 155, 256, 303, 382.
Siraf, 20, 22.
Sisal plantations, 404.
Siu, 61, 65, 66, 252; failure of Said's expeditions to, 338–40.
Slave-trade: its retarding effect on population and development, 4, 11, 13, 30, 35, 175; early establishment of in E. Africa, 17–20, 28, 30–6; described in the *Periplus*, 17–18; early Chinese reference to, 20; treatment of slaves, 32, 226, 227, 326, 428, 432, 514; Portuguese traders, 34–5, 171, 188–9, 226, 230, 499–500; European, 34–5; mentioned by Linschoten, 54; and India, 62, 204–6, 208, 501; under La Bourdonnais, 73–5; Morice's plan for establishing, 76–83; French, 117, 118, 123, 124, 191–3, 230, 424, 427, 428, 452, 453, 455, 478; Atlantic and American, 160, 187, 287, 364, 430, 498; British Navy's hatred of, 163, 187, 188; flourishing in Mozambique, 163, 171, 172, 201–2, 435; at Kilwa, 174, 400; at Barawa, 180, 251; account of slave-market, 184–5; Britain and the slave-trade, 186–216; British laws against, 186, 190, 195, 204–6, 214, 516, 517; actions by other European countries against, 186; Spanish, 186, 499; British, 159, 160; problem of freed slaves, 156, 159, 241, 249, 250, 265, 266, 417, 430; campaign in England against, 153, 155–6, 163, 203, 204, 411; smuggling, 159, 186–7, 192–9, 215, 216, 287, 364, 449, 515; Abolition Acts against, 190, 193, 205, 214, 428, 494, 496, 516, 517; at Mauritius, 196–8, 206, 428, 431, 447; numbers of slaves, 178, 208, 500, 514; at Zanzibar, 163, 181, 183–5, 192, 207–8, 304, 316, 434, 500, 514; negotiations with Said, 202–16; Bombay Regulations, 206; and Owen's protectorate, 226, 228, 230–3, 235–8, 240, 241, 244, 245, 256, 261, 291; Captain Owen's interview with Said concerning, 231–3; sale of slaves to Christians prohibited by Said, 215, 216; 'King' Abdullah and, 247; in W. Africa, 289, 290; Said's revenue from, 299, 300, 318; Palmerston's plans for suppressing, 288–91; Bourbon menaced by emancipation, 436; raids, 357, 380, 493; and Ali-bin-Nasir's mission to England, 447, 448; Arabs desire to resume, 457; carried on by banyans, 484; measures taken for ending, 501–23; finally abolished, 545; *see also* Treaties.
Smallpox, 190.
Smee, Captain, 222, 303, 317, 319, 320, 324, 327, 421, 522; his 'voyage of research', 178–85; and Zanzibar slave-trade, 161, 184–5, 192, 208.
Smith, General, 151.
Smith, Dr. A., 367.
Smith, Hankey, 139.
Smith, Sir Lionel, Governor of Mauritius, 144, 149, 197, 431, 432.
Snay-bin-Amir, Sheikh of Tabora, 307, 310.

INDEX

Society Islands, 445.
Socotra, 46, 179, 215, 233, 273, 446, 464, 465, 542.
Soda Island, 531.
Sofala, 25, 163, 171, 226, 378; gold mines of, 26, 36, 38, 39, 56; subject to Sultan of Kilwa, 27; iron mines at, 36; Covilhão at, 42; Portuguese conquest of, 44, 47, 48, 51, 70; decline of importance of, 49; Linschoten's description of, 54.
Sohar, 85, 145, 277, 469, 551, 553; prohibits slave-trade, 503.
Somali, the, tribe, 10, 300, 352, 510; description of, 335, 342–3; Said fails to subdue, 336–7; treaty with Britain (1825), 467.
Somaliland, 4, 5, 46, 304, 335, 341, 437, 438, 468, 502, 512.
Somerset, Lord Charles, Governor of the Cape, 190, 229.
Somerset Judgement (1772), 204.
Songo Mnara (Pagoda) Point, 515, 520.
Souillac, de, Governor of Port Louis, 85, 87.
South Sea Islands, 391.
Sowaik, 105.
Spain, annexation of Portugal by, 52; and Napoleonic wars, 126, 136–8; and slave-trade, 186, 191, 494, 499.
Spanish dollars, 304, 317, 425, 451, 496.
Sparrman, Professor, 159.
Speke, J. H., explorations in E. Africa, 35, 305–7, 309–12, 332, 350, 354, 408, 546, 555.
Spice Islands, 43, 313.
Spices, 309, 318.
Stanley, Lord, 431, 432.
Stanley, H. M., 325, 358.
Stanners, Colonel E. G., 259–60.
Steamships, introduction of, 462.
Stein, Prussian commander, 137.
Stephens, Thomas, 52.
Stout, Captain Benjamin, 372–4.
Stuart, Sir Charles, 193.
Sudan, the, 31, 178, 307, 387, 500; Mahomet Ali's conquest of, 461, 463.
Suez, 3, 87, 88, 91, 92, 444, 457, 462–4, 467, 480, 532.

Sugar industry, 73, 181, 182, 228, 394, 428, 488, 549.
Suleem, Sultan of Johanna Island, 445, 447; treaties with England (1844, 1850), 447, 448.
Suleiman, Omani chief, 22.
Suleiman-bin-Hamed, Governor of Zanzibar, 323, 356, 357.
Suliman-bin-Ali, Chief of Mombasa, 220, 224, 226, 239, 243, 245, 248, 264, 265, 268.
Sultan-bin-Ahmed, Imam of Muscat (1792–1804), captures Kilwa, 83; Napoleon and, 89, 93, 94, 102, 119, 128; treaties with Britain (1798, 1800), 95–8; failure of Cavaignac's mission to (1802), 103–6, 110; killed in battle, 107; succeeded by Seyyid Said, 108.
Sultan-bin-Seif, Imam of Muscat, 65–7.
Sultan-bin-Suggur, Jawasmi chief, 143.
Sultaneh, the, 371, 372, 508.
Sulphur, 116.
Sumatra, 363, 370.
Suna, King, 307.
Sunley, William, consul at Johanna, 449.
Sur, 150, 371.
Surat, 54, 79, 80, 97, 82, 112, 181–3, 267, 302, 310, 370.
Surcout, Robert, 140.
Swahili (Wangwana), 59, 64, 292, 344, 348, 355, 380, 391, 409, 426, 490; early beginnings of, 11, 28, 29; language, 11, 28, 218, 328, 353, 390; slave-traders, 350, 496, 499, 517, 519; friendly with Said, 352, 353; schools for, 389; dislike of Krapf, 410, 411, 415, 416.
Swiss explorers, 387.
Swords, 383.
Sydney, 541.
Sykes, Colonel, 320.
Sylph, the, British brig at Surat, 143, 162, 183.
Syria, 22, 90, 121, 461–3.

Table Bay, 45, 53, 56, 101, 157, 362.
Tabora, 11, 305–11, 357, 358; founding of, 309.

Tagus, river, 435.
Tahiti Island, becomes a French protectorate, 445, 446, 448.
Taita, the, Bantu tribe, 11, 300, 392, 398.
Tajura, 467, 468.
Takaungu, 389.
Talavera, battle of, 137, 138.
Talleyrand, 87, 102–3, 106.
Tamatave, 79, 123, 140, 141, 196, 199, 280, 438.
Tambatu, 25.
Tana, river, 5, 6, 10, 398, 403, 404.
Tang emperor, 33.
Tanga, 5, 64, 248, 305, 332, 345, 350–3, 400, 406.
Tanga–Moshi railway, 395.
Tanganyika, 3, 6, 345, 348, 350, 409; area and population, 11.
Tanganyika, Lake, 35, 305–7, 311, 357, 384, 400, 408, 556.
Tangate (Mtangata), 64, 351, 386, 481.
Tarleton, John, 160.
Tarshish, 25.
Tea, Chinese, 362.
Teheran, French missions to, 88, 120–2, 138; Malcolm's mission to, 98, 127, 128, 130–1.
Tembe, ceded to Britain, 228, 229.
Terassin, M., 425.
Ternate, the, 162.
Tete, 6, 50, 60, 70.
Thompson, Captain, Resident on the Persian Gulf, 150.
Thouars, Admiral du Petit, 446.
Thwain, Said's third son, 454, 469, 475, 551, 552; succeeds Said at Muscat, 553, 554.
Tibet, guano in, 526.
Tigris, the, 480.
Tilsit, 121, 131, 135.
Tippoo-Sahib of Mysore, 88, 89, 93, 94, 97, 121.
Tiva, river, 398.
Tobacco, 365, 528.
Toledo, 39, 41.
Tongwé, Mount, 346, 352, 407.
Tools, 380.
Tortoise-shell, 17, 173, 174, 182, 365, 366, 377, 479.
Toulon, 77, 88.
Tozer, Bishop, 389.
Trafalgar, battle of, 120.

Treaties:
 America and Said (1833), 281, 282, 286, 315, 316, 367–72, 375, 381, 384–6, 421, 422, 437, 479, 481, 482, 487.
 Britain and Sultan-bin-Ahmed of Muscat (1798, 1800), 94–7, 115, 116, 129, 552; and Said (1800), 102, 110, 130–1, 142, 498, 507; and Persia (1800, 1809), 99, 104, 130; and Sultan of Lahej (1802), 99, 464, 465; and Sultan-bin-Suggur, Jawasmi (1806), 142, 143; and French and Dutch (1814), 141; and Portuguese (1815, 1817), 189; and King Radama of Madagascar (1817, 1820, 1823), 199, 200, 280, 494; and Jawasmi, 'General Treaty' (1820), 150, 209, 502; and Said (1822, 'Moresby Treaty'), 214–16, 220, 222, 230–3, 259, 261, 284, 329, 341, 400, 427, 447, 449, 459, 463, 482, 494, 499, 517, 522; supplement (1839), 502, 504; and King Kapell of Tembe (1823), 229; and Mombasa (1824), 78, 81; and Somali (1825), 467; and Barawa (1825), 251; and France (1831), 428, 433; and Spain (1835), 494, 495; and Said (1839), 288, 315, 385, 421–3, 448, 481, 487, 493; and Tajura (1840), 467, 468; and Zeila (1840), 468; and Johanna (1844, 1850), 447, 448; and Said (1845), 514–23; and France (1861), 435.
 France and King of Kilwa (1776), 78; and Egypt (1785), 87; and Muscat (1790), 103; and Persia (1807), 120, 139; and Said (1807, 1808), 115–20, 124, 125, 133; and Said (1817), 152; and Said (1822), 421; and Said (1844), 315, 385, 421–4, 437, 450, 487.
 Hanseatic Republics and Majid (1859), 385, 386.
 Other treaties: Said and Bourbon (1817), 152; Said and Mazrui (1828), 273, 274, 276,

INDEX

277; Said and Queen Seneekoo of Sakalava (1838), 333, 442, 443; Treaty of Amiens (1802), 100, 101, 117; of Paris, 199; of Schönbrunn (1809), 136; of Vienna, 154.
Trinidad, 429, 430.
Tsavo, river, 398, 403.
Tshikanga, tribe, 51.
Tübingen, 388.
Tumbatu, tribe, 321.
Tunis, 39.
Turkey, 89, 92, 103, 104, 460; and Mahomet Ali, 441, 463; slave-trade, 31, 500, 503.
Turks in E. Africa, 58–61.
Turner, Captain, 430.
Tyne, H.M.S., 196.
Tyre, 25.

Uganda (Buganda), 13, 307, 383, 409.
Uganda Railway, 392, 398.
Ugogo, 10.
Ujiji, 305–8, 311, 358.
Ukamba, 398, 399, 402, 403, 406, 407.
Uluguru mountain, 8.
Umba, river, 394.
Umzimvubu, river, 372.
United States, *see* America.
Universities' Mission, 389.
Unyamwezi, 353, 396, 400.
Unyanyembe, 305.
Urua, 306, 312.
Usambara, Krapf's missionary project in, 332, 344, 348–50, 353, 394, 395, 402, 406–11, 414, 415; account of, 13, 345–52; *see also* Kimweri, King.
Usambara, mountain, 8, 11, 346, 394.
Usanga, 306.
Usenga, 306.
Utinde, 346.
Uvira, 307.

Vaal, river, 387.
Valentia, Lord, 464.
Vanga, 290, 350, 415, 473, 556.
Veers, Robert, 386.
Venn, secretary of the C.M.S., 401, 417.
Verde, Cape, 3, 4.

Vernon, Commander, 540, 541.
Victoria, the, 339.
Victoria, Queen, 381, 446, 455, 480, 508, 531, 544, 551.
Victoria Falls, 394.
Victoria Nyanza, Lake, 305, 307, 408.
Vidal, Captain, 224–6.
Vidal Frères, 425.
Vienna, 41, 154, 304, 437.
Vigilant, the, French privateer, 110–14.
Vignard, M., 425.
Vimiero, 136.
Virginia, slaves in, 160.
Virginia, the, 274, 275, 366.
Vögel, E., 387.
Voi, 8.
Vuga, 344, 345, 347, 349–52, 394, 395, 406, 407, 411, 415.
Vumba, 25.

Wadstrom, C. B., *Essay on Colonization*, 158–9.
Wagner, Johann, missionary, 397.
Wagram, battle of, 136.
Wahabi, tribe: and Sultan-bin-Ahmed, 103, 105, 106, 108; and Seyyid Said, 109, 119, 129, 133, 134, 144–6, 148, 183, 219, 278, 279, 296, 299; peace with Said (1833), 278, 470; and Mecca and Medina, 147, 148; power of, broken by Mahomet Ali, 148–9, 151, 212, 461; invasion of the Batineh by (1844), 474–6; occupy Baraimi (1853), 551.
Waller, Rev. H., 433.
Wangwana, *see* Swahili.
Ward, C., 378, 381.
Wasin Island, 290, 352.
Wat Benia, 324.
Waters, Captain, 370, 378.
Waters, R. P., American consul at Zanzibar, 378, 388, 389, 486, 506.
Webb, W. G., 378.
Webi Doboi, river, 335, 336.
Wellesley, Marquis of, Governor-General of India, 99, 101, 113, 114, 126.
Wellesley, M., 425.
Wellington, Arthur Wellesley, first duke of, 94–5, 97, 105, 113, 114,

205; proposed attack on Île de France by (1801), 99; in Peninsular War, 136–8.
West, B. H., 378.
West, G., 378.
Whaling industry, 364, 376, 487.
Wilberforce, William, h anti-slavery crusade, 155. 57, 186, 187, 214, 287, 291, 413.
William IV, 550.
Windsor Castle, 401, 480.
Wine, 17, 383.
Wire, 307, 309, 310, 383, 486, 490.
Witt, Johann, 386.
Wizard, ex-slave ship, 246.
Woodbury, Senator, 367.
Württemberg, 408.
Wyvill, Commodore, 520.

Yacout, Governor of Zanzibar (1811), 181–3.
Yao tribe, 305, 306.
Yaqut, Greek freedman, 24.
Yaruba, 217.
Yata, 398, 403, 405, 406.
Yemen, 21, 461.
Yousoufou, Sultan of Kilwa, 175, 176.
Yusuf-bin-Hasan (Dom Jeronimo), 63–5.

Zaidiyah, Arab tribe, 22.
Zambesi, river, 5, 6, 50, 60, 70, 171, 227.
Zambesi Expedition, 400, 432, 435.
Zanzibar, Island, climate, 1, 5; position of, 15, 16, 75; early name for, 18, 20; Arab settlement of, 25, 29, 69; in 14th century, 26; Barbosa in, 38, 39; Portuguese at, 44, 47, 48, 55, 57, 62, 64, 65, 66, 68; Lancaster at, 55, 160, 168; under Imam of Muscat, 71, 79, 218, 221; Dutch at, 77; Morice plans French colony at, 76, 80–3, 103, 118; and slave-trade, 117, 118, 178, 183–5, 191, 192, 201, 203, 205, 207–9, 213, 216, 230, 290, 361; no British trade with (1792), 161; Blankett's squadron at (1799), 167–9; governor appointed by Imam of Muscat, 168; annual northern immigration to, 168; Prior's account of (1812), 177; Smee's account of (1811), 179–85; slave-market, 184; British agent at, to watch slave-trade, 215; El Harthi family of, 217; Captain Owen at, 227, 231, 234, 251, 255, 259, 260; Seyyid Said's first visit to, 274; Said moves his court from Muscat to, 279, 295–300, 471; Captain Hart visits, 285, 298, 373, 376; clove cultivation at, 313–15; population of, 319, 320; American trade at, 366, 377, 379–81, 487; British and American consulates first established at, 378, 460, 479, 482; German trade with, 382–6; Krapf at, 388–91, 395, 401, 407, 412, 413–17; Krapf and Swahili traders of, 411; French trade at, 421, 426; French consuls to, 424, 425; direct British trade almost nil, 486–93; incident of Said's ship being searched for slaves, 506; pleasant atmosphere of British Consulate at, 546, 547; *see also* Said *and* Treaties.
Zeila, 468.
Zigua, tribe, 344, 345, 352.
Zimba, Bantu tribe, 60–1, 175.
Zinj, 19, 20, 29, 32.
Zulu tribe, 60, 357, 375.
Zululand, 60, 374.
Zungomero (Kissaki), 305, 311.